THE
WORLD BOOK COMPLETE
WORD POWER
LIBRARY

Volume Two

A Word Builder Guide

A Word Finder Thesaurus of Selected Words

Published by
World Book–Childcraft International, Inc.
A subsidiary of The Scott & Fetzer Company
Chicago London Paris Sydney Tokyo Toronto

The World Book Complete Word Power Library

Copyright © 1981 by
World Book–Childcraft International, Inc.
Merchandise Mart Plaza, Chicago, Illinois 60654

All rights reserved. This volume may not be reproduced
in whole or in part in any form without written permission
from the publishers.

Printed in the United States of America

ISBN 0–7166–3111–3

Library of Congress Catalog Card No. 80–53648

The World Book Complete Word Power Library

Contributors

Edgar Dale, Ph.D.
Emeritus Professor of Education
The Ohio State University
Columbus, Ohio

Walter D. Glanze
Walter Glanze Word Books, Associates
New York, New York

Joseph O'Rourke, Ph.D.
Research Associate in the College of Education
The Ohio State University
Columbus, Ohio

Contents of Volume Two

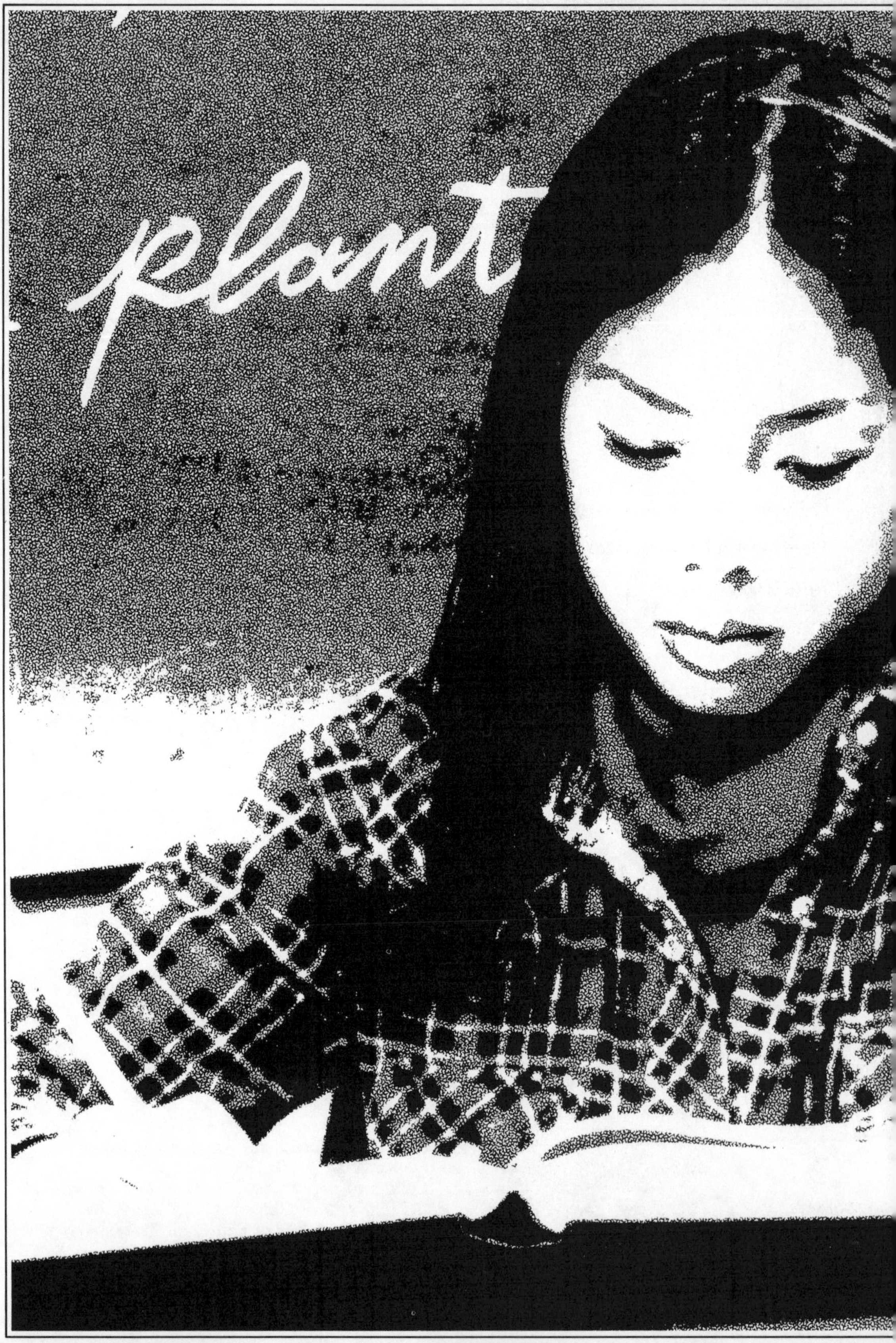
plant

Part 3

A word builder guide

The contributors of the word builder guide are Dr. Joseph O'Rourke, Research Associate in the College of Education, The Ohio State University, Columbus, Ohio; and Dr. Edgar Dale, Emeritus Professor of Education, The Ohio State University, Columbus, Ohio.

Introduction

"A word builder guide" has been designed to present you
with a variety of techniques and strategies that could help you
to achieve two important goals. In the first place, diligent
application of the suggestions given here could help you
significantly increase the number of words you have at your
command for everyday use. In the second place, commitment
to developing a personal pattern of word building could
deepen your understanding of words you already know.

These two goals cannot be separated. We all know people
who, as a matter of course, delight in the use of "big" words
and "fancy" words. We admire people who know many words
and use them well. But there are other people who have a
large number of words at their disposal but a less than
complete understanding of what many of these words really
mean. The result may be mix-ups in communication; misused
words fail to convey the full and exact meaning the writer or
speaker intends you to get.

We all have hundreds, perhaps thousands, of ideas and
emotions we are interested in communicating to others. And
all of these ideas and emotions are laced with many different
shades of meaning. To choose exactly the right word or words
that will express our meaning to others requires both an ample
vocabulary *and* a thorough understanding of the words that
make up that vocabulary. Dedicated use of "A word builder
guide" can help you achieve both of those goals.

Section 1, "Expanding your vocabulary," stresses the
importance of developing a well-rounded vocabulary. Social
interaction depends to a large degree on our ability to
communicate through the written and spoken word.

This first section shows you how to treat each and every

word you encounter according to four levels of word consciousness. Becoming aware of these levels enables you to move a word in gradual stages from the level of "I've never seen the word" all the way to "I know the word well."

The section also includes an inventory of key terms from various fields of knowledge. Reviewing the inventory and completing the activities should help you to identify basic strong and weak points in your current vocabulary.

The second section, "Learning word elements," introduces you to the skills of word analysis. Most words are made up of parts called roots, prefixes, and suffixes. Even if you do not know a word, you may be able to get some idea of its meaning if you know the meaning of a root, prefix, or suffix from which the word is constructed. Tables of important roots, prefixes, and suffixes help you quickly find the meanings of frequently encountered word parts.

"Classifying ideas and words," section 3, develops the technique of expanding vocabulary by learning groups of related words rather than by concentrating upon a word or two in isolation. You are shown how to use context clues to understand unfamiliar words. Inventory lists and activities help you to see the significance of using groups of synonyms and antonyms to expand your overall vocabulary.

Section 4, "Using the dictionary," describes in detail the significance of a publication that virtually everyone has but few use fully. The dictionary contains a wealth of information that makes it the single most important tool in vocabulary development. Section 4 provides you with all the information you need to make a dictionary the cornerstone of your personal vocabulary building program.

"Word games and vocabulary," section 5, is a collection of activities provided for the simple enjoyment of playing with words. At the same time, these word games will reinforce your understanding of the techniques and strategies presented throughout "A word builder guide." The guide is completed by "Words worth knowing"—an extensive list of words that you can practice and eventually learn in order to help expand your vocabulary.

As you move through this vocabulary building material, you will quickly discover that the guiding principle is to *learn by doing.* You will find many "Self-help" exercises and self-tests scattered throughout. An answer key to these activities is provided to help you check your progress. Using the learn-by-doing approach should help you to achieve your goal, namely a more extensive and more well-rounded vocabulary, in the most efficient and effective manner.

1   Expanding your vocabulary

Why should you study words? Words are an important part of your life. You think with words. You also speak, listen, read, and write with words. Words help you communicate your ideas. They also help you understand other people's ideas. Developing your vocabulary is one of the most useful projects you can undertake.

Vocabulary development and success go hand in hand, both in school and in later life. Students with the best vocabularies usually do best in school. Adults with broad vocabularies can deal more effectively in social and business situations. Spending more time developing your vocabulary is a rewarding activity. A rich vocabulary pays rich dividends.

This section asks you to think about words—to become "word conscious." It offers suggestions for getting started toward your goal of building your vocabulary. It includes activities to help you check your present knowledge of words. And it shows how you can build on that knowledge by approaching words actively. It suggests many ways you can learn words in the experiences you have every day.

Vocabulary and life

Vocabulary is a central part of your life. The words you know and use show what your interests are. Your vocabulary tells where you've been, what you've done, and where you're heading. You *are* your words.

If you are interested in cooking, you'll learn words such as *broil, blanch, marinate, baste, sauté,* and *soufflé.* If you know the special meaning of *free throw, pivot, rebound, traveling, press, dunk,* and *stuff,* you have some knowledge of basketball.

You study vocabulary to increase the range of your concepts, or ideas. Words express ideas. They are the names of things. Every area of experience has key terms you need to know. If you don't, you may be at a disadvantage. If you don't know words such as *plaintiff, defendant, writ, indict, acquit, impeach, plea bargaining,* and *habeas corpus,* you don't know a great deal about law or legal matters.

Words show experience

People familiar with words such as *filly, foal, dam, yearling, Clydesdale, Percheron,* and *sorrel* know something about horses. But people who know the special meaning of *hands, withers, cannon, hock, tack, snaffle, curb,* and *pommel* probably know more about horses.

You are your vocabulary. When you change your vocabulary you change your life. When you learn a new word it opens up possibilities for new experiences. One word leads to another and one experience leads to another. Your experiences broaden your vocabulary and your vocabulary broadens your experiences. Words have momentum. They carry you from one experience to another. When your words change, you change.

You may, for example, learn the word *serendipity* (making a pleasant, unexpected discovery by chance). Just knowing the word may influence your attitude, cause you to think about the good, unexpected things that have happened to you. This word may make you a more sensitive, more appreciative person.

Hearing or seeing the word *serendipity* for the first time may arouse your curiosity and cause you to look it up in the dictionary. That can be a good experience, too. Maybe you didn't realize how much information you can find in the dictionary.

In addition to the meaning of *serendipity,* you'll learn that the word was coined (made up) by the English writer Horace Walpole, after the fairy tale "The Three Princes of Serendip." The three princes of Serendip (the old name of Sri Lanka) were always making fortunate, accidental discoveries, hence the new word *serendipity.*

Your curiosity may further lead you to learn more about Horace Walpole, who wrote *The Castle of Otranto,* the first Gothic novel. Many other writers copied the style of this tale of mystery, terror, and the supernatural. The author of *Frankenstein,* Mary Wollstonecraft Shelley, is one of those other writers. Studying the word *serendipity* can lead you to this discovery.

Words show knowledge

The thought may not have occurred to you before, but all knowledge includes vocabulary development. Education is vocabulary development. In and after school you deal with words all the time. You communicate mostly with words. Words stand for your ideas.

You understand a subject if you know the important words of that subject. If you know the words *adjective, adverb, preposition,* and *conjunction,* for example, you know something about the parts of speech. If you know the meaning of *infinitive, participle,* and *gerund,* you probably know something about grammar. If you know the words *axiom, isosceles, subtend,* and *hypotenuse,* you are at least acquainted with geometry.

You need language skills to deal effectively in society. You also need many opportunities to practice language skills that can help you be a better student or a more efficient worker.

There are many ways to develop your vocabulary. Mainly you learn words by having many experiences, doing things: traveling, seeing new objects, playing games, having hobbies, doing jobs, speaking and listening to people. You learn words from radio and television. You learn many words by reading books, magazines, and newspapers. Keep in mind also that the more words you know, the better you can read. Word power is reading power.

Indeed, reading is one of the best ways to learn words. But you have to read actively, not passively. Read with the idea that you are going to use the information you pick up. You have to speak, write, and think about what you read. You can't build an effective vocabulary by reading passively, as if unknown words don't really matter. You have to be on the alert, ready to attack unknown words. To learn words effectively by reading, therefore, you have to read actively— that is, you have to do something.

Using this word builder guide

This guide to word building emphasizes *doing.* To use it successfully you have to react to the suggestions that are offered. You have to do something—sometimes alone, sometimes with a partner or a group. The more you do, the more your vocabulary will grow.

Readers of this guide may have differing points of view regarding the outcome of their efforts to improve vocabulary. Some may see this material as just another obstacle in the study of English, something to be gotten over with that will have little effect. Some, on the other hand, may approach this material with high motivation, thinking there is a kind of magic that can be easily applied to produce a sharp, revolutionary change in their vocabularies.

The change in your vocabulary won't be revolutionary, but it will be lasting and useful. Remember that there is no quick and easy way to increase and sharpen your vocabulary. But the activities here do offer you a regular, systematic approach to vocabulary study.

Some of you may approach the idea of vocabulary development with distaste. In school you might have gone through the fairly typical procedure, two or three times a week, of being assigned a list of words to learn, to look up in a dictionary, and to use in a sentence. This assignment is one of the most disliked among high school students. You won't be asked to do this. But you will be shown many other ways to become more aware of words and add to your vocabulary significantly.

Becoming word conscious

You can learn words in many ways. Effectively using the activities that follow will assure you some gain in vocabulary above what you would ordinarily achieve. What's more, you'll pick up the habit of really looking closely at words. You'll become *word conscious*.

You can gain in word knowledge because we know you already have a knowledge of thousands of words at various stages of learning. Here are your word-knowledge stages:

1. I've never seen the word.
2. I've heard of it, but I don't know it.
3. I would probably recognize it in context—it deals with . . . (We'll say these words are in your "twilight zone.")
4. I know the word well.

Some words you just don't know. You have never heard of them. Examples may be *apocope, wodge, resipiscence.* But there are many other words that are further along on your learning scale and you at least recognize them *(ductile, obtuse, apartheid).* Some words you have heard of and know how to use, but only vaguely *(caucus, quorum, fresco).* These words are in your twilight zone. Some words you know very well *(jury, history, politics).* The purpose of this word builder guide is to move the twilight-zone words you know partly or dimly into the area where you'll know them very well.

Your twilight-zone words

You should try to discover what words you almost know, and then learn to use them. One way is to find out what words you are familiar with in various subjects. Here is a typical example using the category food, or nourishment:

	Word	Familiarity
	food, nourishment	(well known)
	nutrient, nurture	(fairly well known)
twilight zone	sustenance	(less well known)
for most of us	provender	(hardly known)
	aliment	(unknown)

Moving your twilight-zone words into a higher level of understanding means bringing them into sharp focus. Using the words you almost know will sharply increase your active vocabulary. An athlete improves because of practice. The more you practice using words, the better you'll be at it.

Actually, you are developing your vocabulary day by day in the many social or school situations in which you find yourself. The material presented here can help you learn short cuts to a bigger, more effective vocabulary. But first you ought to know how broad your vocabulary is now. Check yourself with the following lists. Then, if you want to test yourself further, turn to the section "Words worth knowing" that appears at the end of the word builder guide.

Self-help

Self-inventory of key words

The following are lists of key words from various fields. Cover the definitions on the right. Then list the words you think you know in a notebook or on a separate piece of paper. When you have finished, look at the definition for each word. Note your score (*9* out of *12,* for example). This activity will give you some idea of your vocabulary strength in each field. You'll know your strong and weak points.

Business words

Word	Definition (Cover this column.)
1. assets	property
2. inflation	increase in prices
3. deficit	shortage
4. mortgage	claim on property
5. compound interest	interest on interest and principal
6. commerce	trade
7. merger	combining of companies
8. liability	total of debts
9. tariff	tax on imports and exports
10. trust	property held for another
11. recession	reduction of business activity
12. usury	high interest rates

Chemistry words

Word	Definition (Cover this column.)
1. acid	sour chemical compound
2. electron	electrically charged atomic particle
3. valence	capacity to unite, react, or interact
4. chromosome	body carrying hereditary traits
5. compound	chemical union
6. dehydration	removal of water
7. dissolve	make liquid
8. distill	condense from vapor
9. element	basic chemical substance
10. formula	recipe for chemicals
11. gas	not liquid or solid (like steam)
12. laboratory	testing room

Geography words

Word	Definition (Cover this column.)
1. isthmus	connecting neck of land
2. plateau	high plain
3. sierra	range of hills
4. belt	broad strip or band
5. cape	point of land
6. international	between or among countries
7. meridian	line of longitude
8. outlet	stream flowing out from a body of water
9. planet	body moving around the sun
10. tropics	earth's hottest climate belt
11. tundra	level, treeless plain in Arctic regions
12. urban	of a city or cities

Health words

Word	Definition (Cover this column.)
1. abscess	collection of pus
2. allergy	body sensitivity
3. anemia	weakness due to lack of red blood cells
4. asthma	disease making breathing difficult
5. antidote	remedy for poison
6. chronic	constant, continuous
7. diabetes	disease of pancreas
8. contagion	spreading of disease
9. convalescent	getting well
10. hemorrhage	bleeding
11. immune	protected from disease
12. inoculate	vaccinate against disease

History words

Word	Definition (Cover this column.)
1. enact	make law
2. bicameral	two-house legislature
3. dynasty	one-family rule
4. emancipation	setting free
5. unicameral	one-house legislature
6. caste	social class
7. epoch	period in history
8. autonomy	self-government
9. franchise	right to vote
10. colony	territory with ties to parent state
11. democracy	majority rule
12. socialism	belief in government ownership

Language words

Word	Definition (Cover this column.)
1. antonym	word with opposite meaning
2. synonym	word with same meaning
3. conjugation	verb formation
4. anthology	collection of writings
5. metaphor	indirect comparison
6. hyperbole	exaggeration
7. etymology	study of word history
8. inflection	voice variation
9. euphemistic	pleasantly expressed
10. accentuation	stress on word parts
11. homily	moral writing
12. simile	direct comparison

Law words

Word	Definition (Cover this column.)
1. acquit	clear of blame
2. convict	find guilty
3. defendant	one who is accused
4. hearing	court review of facts
5. offense	crime
6. plaintiff	one who accuses
7. prosecute	bring to trial
8. testify	talk before the court
9. verdict	legal judgment
10. witness	one who testifies
11. jury	group of persons who decide
12. sentence	punishment

Mathematics words

Word	Definition (Cover this column.)
1. dividend	number to be divided
2. per cent	1 unit in 100
3. product	result of multiplying
4. quotient	result of division
5. square root of 4	2 ($2 \times 2 = 4$)
6. volume	quantity held
7. congruent	coinciding
8. perimeter	distance around the edge
9. decimal	a fraction like .60
10. difference	result of subtraction
11. centimeter	$\frac{1}{100}$ of a meter
12. denominator	number below the line in a fraction ($\frac{1}{4}$)

Music words

Word	Definition (Cover this column.)
1. bass	lowest male voice
2. beat	mark of rhythm
3. chord	many notes in harmony
4. composer	one who writes music
5. lyrics	words for songs
6. melody	tune
7. measure	unit of music
8. note	single musical sound
9. orchestra	group of musicians
10. rhythm	repetition of beats
11. scale	series of tones
12. woodwinds	wind instruments of wood or metal

Physical science words

Word	Definition (Cover this column.)
1. gravity	earth's pull
2. kinetic	resulting from motion
3. dissect	cut apart for examination
4. saturated	filled to maximum concentration
5. solvent	substance that dissolves
6. chain reaction	many effects from a cause
7. mass	quantity of matter
8. nuclear	atomic
9. sound barrier	speed of sound
10. vacuum	empty space
11. acoustic	relating to sound
12. anatomy	animal or plant structure

Religion words

Word	Definition (Cover this column.)
1. revelation	act of making known
2. Hanukkah	Jewish "Feast of Lights"
3. parable	truth shown by tale
4. Eucharist	Holy Communion
5. genesis	creation
6. dogma	religious belief
7. apocalypse	revelation
8. beatitude	blessing
9. messiah	savior
10. theology	study of God
11. creed	set of beliefs
12. vespers	early evening prayers

Building vocabulary

Building a good vocabulary takes a long time. It is an ongoing process related to what you do in life. The richer your experience, the richer your vocabulary. But the decision to build a solid, effective vocabulary must be a long-term commitment. You must be conscious of it every day, not just once in a while. Conscious, regular attention to vocabulary leads to effective language skill. Remember, the more words you know, the better you can think.

Is your vocabulary good?

One way to check your vocabulary knowledge is to see how well you can distinguish between words that look or sound somewhat alike but have quite different meanings. Some people use words they are unsure of and end up using them in the wrong way.

Mrs. Malaprop (a comic character in Sheridan's play *The Rivals*) misused words. From her name we derive the word *malapropism,* or a "word ridiculously misused." Referring to her daughter, for example, Mrs. Malaprop says, "I would have her study *geometry* so she'd know about *contagious* countries." She, of course, meant to say *geography* and *contiguous* (touching boundaries).

People often make mistakes by using words they don't know well. Examples are:

The governor has a lot of *affluence* with this committee. (influence)
The golfer carefully *reproached* the ball. (approached)
He was attracted by the *flagrant* odor of her perfume. (fragrant)
She belongs to two different religious *sex.* (sects)
They looked up the facts in a *reverence* book. (reference)
He suffered only *supercillious* cuts. (superficial)

Your ability to distinguish between words that look or sound alike is a good measure of your vocabulary skills. Following is a self-check on words that look or sound alike. They are often misused or misspelled. See how well you know these words.

Confused word pairs   Self-help

Match the words in each word pair with the definitions *a* and *b* on the right. Record your answers, and then check them in the **Answer Key** that begins on page 137.

Example: their   a. not here   **Answers:** b
            there   b. of them   a

1. acrostic   a. word puzzle
   acronym   b. word made by initials

2. aerie   a. eagle's nest
   eerie   b. fearful

3. alimentary   a. simple
   elementary   b. pertaining to food

4. alterative   a. tending to alter
   alternative b. a choice

5. apiary   a. bird shelter
   aviary   b. beehive

6. assay   a. short piece of writing
   essay   b. analyze ore

7. basilisk   a. tall stone column
   obelisk   b. lizard

8. bouillon   a. mass of gold or silver
   bullion   b. clear soup

9. breech   a. part of a gun
   breach   b. break

10. broach   a. ornamental pin
    brooch   b. bring up a subject

11. burly   a. tobacco
    burley   b. strong, heavy

12. callous   a. insensitive
    callus   b. hard place on skin

13. canter   a. singer leading choir or
                    congregation
    cantor   b. easy gallop

14. contemn   a. scorn
    condemn   b. disapprove strongly

15. cosmology   a. science of the universe
    cosmetology b. study of cosmetics

16. council   a. law-making group
    counsel   b. advise

17. demur   a. take exception
    demure   b. modest

18. discomfit   a. lack of pleasure
    discomfort   b. upset

19. discrete   a. wisely cautious
    discreet   b. separate

20. exceptional a. extraordinary
    exceptionable b. objectionable

21. feign   a. gladly
    fain   b. pretend

22. gamut   a. complete range
    gambit   b. a chess term

23. idol   a. about country life
    idyl   b. worshiped object

24. indict   a. charge with an offense
    indite   b. put down in writing

25. ingenuous   a. innocently sincere
    ingenious   b. good at inventing

26. interment a. burial
  internment b. confinement

27. maize   a. network of paths
  maze   b. corn

28. militate   a. work against or in favor
  mitigate b. lessen

29. urban   a. of the city
  urbane b. suave

30. viol   a. stringed musical instrument
  vial   b. small bottle

How well you did distinguishing the confused word pairs will give you some idea of how closely you look at words, what words confuse you, and what words to watch for.

Earlier you were introduced to the idea of a twilight zone— where words are almost known. You might hesitate to use these words because they could cause you embarrassment. Students have, for example, made the following mistakes:

Avoiding mistakes

The *circulation* system includes veins and *artilleries.* (circulatory, arteries)
The farmer *irked* out a bare existence. (eked)
The interrupted speaker was *decomposed.* (discomposed)
My father had *very close* veins. (varicose)
I had to bear the *blunt* of it. (brunt)
Our old dog's eyes were *bloodshed.* (bloodshot)
They rode *slipshod* over the enemy. (roughshod)
He stayed home with *indolent* fever. (undulant)
He used to be a *jubilant* delinquent. (juvenile)
He was *stork* naked. (stark)

With a little concentration on these almost-known words, these students could bring them into sharp focus and then incorporate them into an active vocabulary.

A good vocabulary does not come about by chance. Words and meanings have to be learned. Some people, of course, grow up in an environment that provides the experiences needed to develop a broad vocabulary. They have rich experiences that they need to name, so these individuals develop a rich stock of words.

Reading for vocabulary

 The majority of people, however, acquire a good vocabulary only by some plan: either a self-plan for word development or the plan of parents and teachers who organize experiences, opportunities, and study techniques for effective vocabulary development. Parents who take their children to a concert or to a zoo, for example, set the stage for learning. They provide experiences that children can label. Going to a concert may make it necessary to use the terms *cymbal* or *kettledrum*. A trip to the zoo may give rise to the words *grizzly* or *bison*.

Reading is one vocabulary-building experience needed at all levels: Mother Goose rhymes, mystery and adventure stories, myths, fiction, magazine and newspaper articles, biography, history, poetry, drama—all literature in these areas helps develop your vocabulary.

Some experiences are not directly available, such as sailing on the ocean or chasing a whale. You have to depend on reading—on literature—for these. You may read *Moby Dick*, for example, and learn about both sailing and whaling. *Moby Dick* and many other classic stories are worthwhile to read and to reread because of their excellent vocabulary and language usage.

Reading widely and developing a vocabulary go hand in hand. Reading books also offers you a chance to relive history, appreciate the beauty or hardships of nature—even roam the woods with Daniel Boone or follow a trail with Davy Crockett. Through biography you may in your imagination accompany the Norwegian explorer Amundsen to the South Pole or trek through the African jungle with Stanley.

Through reading literature you'll discover the origins of pioneer words such as *backwoods, powder horn,* and *latchkey,* which are found in stories about Daniel Boone and Johnny Tremain. Words like *railsplitting* and *lumberjack* crop up in stories about early American pioneers. The more you read, the broader your vocabulary will be. Further discussion of this subject will appear later in this word builder guide.

Words you know

By the time you started school you already knew about 3,000 words. You learned them from your family and from friends. You learned mostly by listening, speaking, and looking. Your parents repeated words until they were sure you had learned them, and you helped yourself by practicing words over and over again.

Up to about the fourth grade you were surrounded primarily by words that deal with ordinary living. You learned words about family, friends, clothing, games, shelter, transportation, food, animals, and plants. You learned these words well because you heard or saw them often.

But you learned them well especially because you used them often; that is, you practiced them. These words became a part of you. Then, by the time you were in the sixth grade, you had to start learning a new set of words.

These new words were not a part of you or your family life. They took you beyond your normal vocabulary of words such as *house, bread, dress, church, classroom, zoo,* and *vacation.* Instead you had to learn specialized words such as *citizen, colony, continent, equator, latitude, longitude,* and *treaty.*

Specialized words

The new words had special uses. They were primarily academic or social terms. If you expected to get along in school, you had to learn them. To master mathematics you learned words such as *numerator, denominator, dividend, fraction, decimal,* and *triangle.* To perfect language you had to understand words such as *noun, verb, adverb, adjective, preposition, tense, clause, paragraph,* and *indent.* To discuss scientific matters you brought into your vocabulary words such as *geology, hydrogen, magnet, energy, artery, radar,* and *photosynthesis.* These were *specialized* words—used for a special purpose and not frequently heard.

Your friends have probably never talked much about photosynthesis or fractions. These are terms that found their way into your active vocabulary only through instruction and probably will remain there only through individual effort. You must have a method of attacking and remembering these specialized words. You have to go back to the method you used as a child—you have to practice.

The activities that follow are filled with special-purpose words related to many areas of experience. Your success in finding the right answers will indicate your areas of vocabulary strength. You will also discover areas where your vocabulary is weak.

Occupational terms

Self-help

Here you are asked to name a given job, sport, or hobby by recognizing terms related to that occupation. The terms are listed from hard to easy, with the hardest on the left (worth 5 points). You receive 5 points when you name the occupation after reading the clue in the first column. If you must go to the second column, you receive 4 points. Your score lessens depending on the number of clue words you must see before you identify the occupation or activity.

Begin by covering all but the first word in the left column. Uncover clue words one by one as you need them. Make sure to note your score as you go along. Check your answers in the **Answer Key.** Then count up your points (total possible, *100*).

5	4	3	2	1

Example: harrow   combine   reaper   plow   haymow
Answer: farming (points earned _____)

	5	4	3	2	1
1.	tympany	overture	finale	baton	strings
2.	palette	pigment	mural	easel	smock
3.	rook	pawn	bishop	knight	checkmate
4.	spectrum	nebula	galaxy	constellation	telescope
5.	rabbet	bevel	dowel	brace	plane
6.	advantage	love	volley	backhand	serve
7.	fricassee	skewer	soufflé	coddle	fritter
8.	blind	mallard	decoy	12-gauge	retriever
9.	compost	mulch	prune	trowel	bulb
10.	yaw	tack	jib	boom	stern
11.	font	slug	pica	proof	galley
12.	distaff	woof	warp	shuttle	loom
13.	ingot	slag	smelt	coke	ore
14.	gandy dancers	shunt	hopper	express	locomotive
15.	clogs	moccasins	oxfords	slippers	boots
16.	jig	reel	minuet	shindig	ballet
17.	euchre	cribbage	bridge	pinochle	poker
18.	roadster	coupé	limousine	convertible	sedan
19.	dinghy	skiff	junk	gondola	kayak
20.	pedagogue	tutor	lecturer	professor	instructor

Self-help   Can you file it?

One way you can remember a word is to have a place for it in your mental filing system. Write down the words *Sports, Cooking,* and *Handicrafts* on a sheet of paper; then classify the words given below under the appropriate category. Check your answers in the **Answer Key.** Then look up any unfamiliar words in the dictionary.

Examples:

Sports	Cooking	Handicrafts
discus	ricer	bobbin
snorkel	microwave	T-pin
goal	strainer	kiln

Words to be filed:

crochet	awl	bogey	aqualung	ceramics
croquet	filet	warp	crawl	paprika
croquette	creel	Olympics	jute	blanch
puck	purl	broil	loom	half hitch
sage	toboggan	fold	screen	
emboss	bobbin	braise	coxswain	
spatula	ladle	woof	braid	
Nimrod	embroider	darn	half gainer	

Sporting words   Self-help

Take your test of sports words a step further with this
exercise. Write on a piece of paper the sport suggested by the
clue word in the left-hand column. Check your answers in the
Answer Key.

Example: racket   t_____   **Answer:** tennis

Clue word	Sport
iron	1. g_____
traveling	2. b_____
trap	3. f_____
trap	4. g_____
screen	5. f_____
touché	6. f_____
reddog	7. f_____
pole vault	8. t_____
shot	9. b_____
shot	10. t_____
shot	11. h_____
rebound	12. b_____
puck	13. h_____
squeeze play	14. b_____
down	15. f_____
Texas leaguer	16. b_____
balk	17. b_____
rack	18. b_____
serve	19. v_____
post	20. h_____

What's your theater I.Q.?   Self-help

Now you will give your theater vocabulary a thorough test by
filling in the missing letters to make theater-related words.
The better your score, the more you probably know about the
theater. Check your answers in the **Answer Key.**

Example: bal__ __ __y   **Answer:** balcony

1. apr__ __   8. cur__ __ __ __
2. burl__ __ __ __ __   9. desi__ __ __r
3. ca__ __   10. dir__ __ __ __r
4. cho__ __ __ __   11. dr__ __ __ __
5. com__ __y   12. foot__ __ __ __ __s
6. comp__ __ __r   13. inter__ __ __ __ __ __ __
7. cost__ __ __   14. mak__ __ __

15. mys_ _ _ _   28. backd_ _ _ _
16. o_ _ _ _a   29. cri_ _ _ _
17. prod_ _ _ _r   30. c_ _ _
18. pr_ _ _s   31. fin_ _ _ _
19. rev_ _ _ _   32. foy_ _ _
20. sc_ _ _ _   33. gre_ _ _ _   pa_ _ _ _
21. scr_ _ _ _   34. log_ _
22. spotl_ _ _ _   35. mezz_ _ _ _ _ _
23. tr_ _ _ _ _y   36. monol_ _ _
24. vil_ _ _ _   37. pl_ _ _
25. pro_ _ _ _ _ _ist   38. prom_ _ _ _r
26. anta_ _ _ _ist   39. sta_ _ _-i_
27. ang_ _   40. wi_ _ _s

Practice and learn

Up to this point you have become acquainted with many ways to improve your vocabulary once you take charge. You have to discipline yourself and work through the exercises. It isn't necessary to spend hours at a time memorizing and learning. You need to spend only about 10 or 15 minutes a day with these exercises.

What you need most of all is regular practice, intelligent practice in vocabulary study. Even Jack Nicklaus has to practice or lose the rhythm of his swing. When he won the U.S. Open and PGA golf championships in 1980, he said he did so because he had practiced harder than he had in some time. If a professional has to practice to keep his golf game in shape, you also have to practice to keep your word game in shape.

You learn what you practice and you practice what you learn. The more familiar you become with words the more you will use them. But you must have a definite goal: the general improvement of language skills.

Remember, vocabulary study isn't merely a matter of memorizing lists of words or looking up the meaning of words in a dictionary. Vocabulary study means becoming familiar with words, feeling at home with them. Some words become good friends. You may have some favorite words either because of their looks or their sounds.

Some people like the sound of words such as *zizz*. Do you know what this word means? It is a short sleep, like the *zzz's* in comic strips that indicate a character is asleep. Some people like short words like *ai*. What does this term mean? An *ai* is one of those lazy-looking animals that hang from tree limbs: a three-toed sloth. One teacher said she had a lot of five-toed sloths in her classroom.

Some people like a word for its sound: *huggermugger* (a great confusion), *sesquipedalian* (a long word, literally a "foot and a half"). Do you know the longest word in the dictionary?

Do you think that it's *antidisestablishmentarianism?* No, it's *pneumonoultramicroscopicsilicovolcanoconiosis,* 45 letters long. It means the black lung disease that afflicts miners.

What you should develop from this vocabulary study is an attitude about learning and caring for words. You should become involved with words, become word conscious. You can't be a good speller unless you develop a spelling consciousness, and you can't develop a good vocabulary unless you become conscious of words.

To become word conscious, notice words. Some people see trees every day on their way past them, but only a few notice them—that is, really observe them. The observant person notices the kind of bark or the shape of the leaves or the fruit.

Most people don't really notice words until someone points them out. After learning to read, they pay more attention to phrases, clauses, sentences, and paragraphs than to words. As a result, they don't look carefully at words and miss a lot. Did you, for example, ever notice the *vapor* in *evaporate?* The *sign* in *signature?* The *heal* in *health?* The *miser* in *miserable?* The *simile* in *facsimile?* The *minus* in *minuscule?*

Important words

Many important words are short and easy to learn. Many simple, ordinary words deal with important aspects of life: *love, kindness, fairness, truth, justice, equality,* and *courage.*

Some courage goes beyond the ordinary. Not long ago, a young man had his leg amputated due to cancer. The cancer continued but so did he. He continued to remain cheerful and hard working. He finished college. He maintained this courageous attitude until he died. Perhaps you or your family know of this kind of courage. It is worth talking about. It is worth having the right words to describe it. How would you describe it? The right words grow out of your experiences. The words you use are the labels you put on your experiences. Through words you let others share your experiences.

Ordinary words can motivate you. When you learn a word like *responsibility,* you learn more than its dictionary definition. You also learn what it means to have responsibility, to see how it affects your life with your family, your friends, your teachers, or your co-workers. Words describe these experiences. That's what successful writers discovered. They also knew that a good stock of words was necessary to express what they discovered about family ties, love of country, equality of opportunity, liberty, and justice.

Terms like *liberty* and *justice* are important words. *Truth* is important, too. One of the best reasons for developing a good vocabulary is to be able to understand what others say about important ideas in the world. You need to be able to distinguish between truth and falsehood in speeches, books, newspapers, and magazines. If you do not understand the words the writers use, you will be unable to judge their accuracy.

Although you might want to learn some hard words for fun, important words for you are not "jawbreakers." The important words are those you know or almost know but ought to know better. You need to know them better so you can use them in the right place at the right time with the right effect.

Words you should know

If you're a student, you should know the key words in the subjects you study in school. People in and out of school need to know important words related to their personal needs and the needs of society.

Knowing the names of important cities and capitals of the states and countries is useful. You should also know other geographic and historical words. You should know key words in mathematics, language, science, government, business, economics, health, safety, and communication. In short, you need to know well the meaning of words related to all your activities within society.

Classify to remember

Now you are aware that when it comes to learning specialized words you're on your own. You have to teach yourself the way you did as a youngster, with practice—but with intelligent practice.

How do you provide yourself with intelligent practice? By working according to a plan. That should be your aim: to extend your present vocabulary by using a planned, systematic approach.

You learn many words incidentally, or by chance. But this incidental approach can also be accidental. Too much may be left to chance.

If you learn words the usual way, through your experiences, your vocabulary will develop to some extent. But if you approach vocabulary study in a planned, organized way, you add another important dimension to your vocabulary development.

One of the best ways to learn new words is to classify them. You learned to classify, or generalize, ideas as a child. At first you probably called all women "Ma" or "Mom." You may have called all men "Dad." Your parents fit into the classifications of "moms" and "dads"; that is, men and women, masculine and feminine.

As a child, you classified and named people by putting them in a broad category. You also classified your thoughts, which you expressed in words. Later (after you had placed people or objects in a general classification), you began to see slight differences. You began to be more specific. Certain females became known to you as grandmothers or aunts. You recognized males as grandfathers or uncles.

In time you began to discriminate, or distinguish, between one person or object and another. But you had already begun by putting the males in one general classification and the females in another. You made what is called a "broad generalization." This helped you remember new ideas and new words by putting them in categories, or classifications. Classifying words (especially the new terms you learn in school or on the job) is a matter of seeing meaningful relationships, seeing likenesses or differences.

Seeing relationships

You will notice that certain words can be classified or grouped because they are alike in some way. Sometimes they have about the same meaning—for example, *wish* and *want*.

Sometimes words deal with the same topic: *backstroke* and *breaststroke*. Sometimes they have a similar construction. Why would you classify *telephone* and *telegraph* together, for example? One reason is that they are both a form of long-distance communication. But there is another reason to put these words into the same group. Look at their construction: Both *telephone* and *telegraph* begin with the root *tele,* meaning "far away" or "distant." On a telephone you can hear a voice from far away, and a telegraph carries a message for a long distance. You can think of other words formed from the root *tele.*

In learning words by the classifying, or grouping, method you must be on the lookout for words formed from the same roots. This approach is especially important in remembering words completely new to you. To be successful in our society, you must learn new technical words often. You will notice if you look closely that these terms are formed from combinations of prefixes, roots, and suffixes that show their relationship to one another.

A hard way to accumulate vocabulary is to learn *gyroscope* one day and *microscope* the following week. A more efficient approach is to learn several *scope* words together: *gyroscope, microscope, periscope, telescope, radarscope,* and *horoscope.* The root *scope* means "see," and all these words have something to do with seeing.

It is easier to learn several *mono-* words together: *monorail* (one rail), *monotonous* (one tone), *monoxide* (one oxygen atom), *monocle* (for one eye). As you can see, classifying, or grouping, words is a useful technique and a short cut to learning and remembering hundreds of words.

Transfer of learning

The big reason for classifying words is to transfer learning. This is an important principle for effective vocabulary study. *Transfer of learning* means "making meaningful associations."

Sometimes, by chance, you will make meaningful associations between words. But much of the time the relationship between words will go unnoticed. Unless someone points the relationship out to you, you will not necessarily see that one exists between *palace* and *palatial.* You will see these as isolated words. Then you will expend more energy than is needed in learning two ideas instead of one. You need to develop the habit of noticing words. The more associations you can make, the easier your learning task will be.

Try to see the connections between words whenever they exist. If the prefix *uni-* means "one," for example, you should be aware of the idea of "oneness" in these words: *unique* (one of its kind), *unite* (become one), *unicorn* (one-horned, mythical animal), *univalve* (one-shelled animal), *unicycle* (having one wheel). You will learn much more about relationships between word parts in 2, "Learning word elements."

Learning word elements

An important skill you should learn is to be able to take words apart to find their meanings. You should have no difficulty splitting the word *bicycle* apart and discovering that *bi-* means "two" and *cycle* means "wheel." You may also be able to break up words like *biennial, bicentennial,* and *bilateral.*

If you already know the word *substance,* you'll find it much easier to learn *substantial, substantive,* and *insubstantial* because these are words that have been built from the same word parts. All of these words belong to the same family. This section will introduce you to numerous words belonging to the same families. Take the word *numerous* itself, for example. The Latin word *numerus* leads to *number, numerable, innumerable, numeral, numerator, enumerate, numerical,* and *numerology.*

This section asks you to look carefully at the elements that are put together to build words—roots, prefixes, and suffixes. It shows how to analyze words so that you are aware of the elements they contain. At the end of this section, there are tables listing the common roots, prefixes, and suffixes that are important in building English words. Refer to those tables whenever you need to find the meaning of a word element.

For every new word part you learn, you will be able to understand the meanings of many new words. Learning word elements will help you expand your vocabulary tremendously.

Your interest in words

Are you interested in learning word parts? How interested are you in meaningful vocabulary building? What about your interest, say, in chess, fishing, needlepoint, or gourmet cooking? If you already know quite a bit about these activities, you are probably enthusiastic about learning more. If you don't know much about them, your interest may be low.

Many persons who don't break *100* in golf stop playing. The same is true in playing bridge: If you succeed at it, you probably like it. If you don't succeed, you lose interest. Success is the best motivator.

Ask yourself these simple questions: How important to you is the mastery of vocabulary? How well have you succeeded at it in the past? Do you have a favorable or unfavorable attitude toward vocabulary development? In short, are you convinced before you start that you can't learn new words effectively or that you can't learn the words you almost know better? Do you approach the study of vocabulary without hope?

Effort leads to interest

You should approach the study of words with high hopes. All you need to put out is effort. If interest is not already there, it will come and it will grow, especially when you see that the more skill you have with words, the richer your life becomes.

You might ask, "Why should I learn words I may never use?" One reason is the unfamiliar words you will find in the wide variety of material you'll read. There are literally thousands of so-called hard words used in every aspect of life. Many of these words aren't really hard at all. They just look hard at first glance.

A look at "hard" words

Tonsillectomy isn't much harder than *tonsil* and *tonsillitis:* words you probably already recognize. Look closely at the parts of the word: *ectomy* means "cut out," from *ec- (ex-)* (out) + *tom* (cut). And you can easily guess what kind of operation a tonsillectomy is because you know the word *tonsil.* The important point, however, is now that you have learned the *ectomy* in *tonsillectomy,* your learning won't stop there. It will go on and on. You'll see *ectomy* in hundreds of words, especially in the sciences, and wherever you see this word you will know it has something to do with "cutting out." In medicine it will always refer to the surgical removal of an organ or part of it. See how many of the medical *ectomy* words you can figure out in the exercise that follows.

Medical meanings   Self-help

Here are words for medical operations. Write the meanings of
the words you know. Look up the others in the dictionary.
Check your answers in the **Answer Key.**

Example: appendectomy   **Answer:** removal of the
                                        appendix

1. adenoidectomy	10. duodenectomy
2. esophagectomy	11. splenectomy
3. pharyngectomy	12. nephrectomy
4. laryngectomy	13. gastrectomy
5. carcinomectomy	14. neurectomy
6. pneumectomy	15. glossectomy
7. hysterectomy	16. hepatectomy
8. ophthalmectomy	17. mastectomy
9. adenectomy	18. thoracectomy

How many of the *-ectomy* words did you figure out? It
doesn't matter so much how many of the words you know.
What does matter is that you know the meaning of a key
word part, *ectomy,* and that you will recognize it when you see
it in other words.

Ectomy contains the root *tom* (cut), which adds many other
medical words to our language. Here are some examples:

Phlebotomy is cutting (opening) a vein (from Greek *phlebos,*
    vein).

Lobotomy is cutting into a lobe of the brain (from Latin *lobus,*
    round and projecting part).

Osteotomy is cutting away or dividing bone (from Greek *osteon,*
    bone).

Bronchotomy is incision into the trachea (from Greek *bronchos,*
    windpipe).

Lithotomy is surgical removal of bladder stones (from Greek
    lithos, stone).

Craniotomy is cutting the skull (from Greek *kranion,* skull).

Entomotomy is insect dissection (from Greek *entoma,* insects).

Anthropotomy is the anatomy (literally, "cutting up") of the
    human body for study (from Greek *anthropos,* man).

Chondrotomy is cutting into the cartilage (from Greek *chondros,*
    cartilage). Note also the word *hypochondria* from *hypo-*
    (under) + *chondros* (cartilage of the breast bone); people
    once thought that the location and source of melancholy
    was under the breast bone.

Sclerotomy is incision into the sclerotic, or hard, white outer
    membrane of the eye (from Greek *skleros,* hard). Note that
    arteriosclerosis is also called "hardening of the arteries."

Roots, prefixes, and suffixes

The idea here is not to burden you with learning a lot of scientific words (although some of you will use them at one time or another). The point is to convince you to look carefully at words, to notice their structure. As you have seen, a single word may be the basic part of many words. If you learn key roots, prefixes, and suffixes, you will more easily learn words using those word parts.

A *root word* is simply a word from which other words are made. Many of these roots are of Greek or Latin origin. A *prefix* is a syllable or syllables put at the beginning of another word to change its meaning—to make another word. A *suffix* is a syllable or syllables put at the end of another word to change its meaning or to make another word. On pages 50–63, you will find lists of important roots, prefixes, and suffixes you should know. Refer to these lists of word parts as you work on this section.

Noticing word parts

You have just learned *ectomy* (cut out) and *tom* (cut). Become actively aware of these same key parts in other words. You already know the word *atom*. But did you see the parts before? They are *a-* (not) + *tom* (cut). Scientists once believed that the atom could not be split (cut). Maybe now you'll look more closely at *atom, atomic, atomize, atomizer.*

Do you know what diatoms are? They're tiny water plants with hard shells. Their cell walls are divided into two equal halves (valves). The word *diatom* comes from Greek *diatomos* (cut in half). The word parts are *dia-* (through) + *tom* (cut). Maybe you didn't know *diatom* before, and the word may never be useful to you. But the point is that you are now even more aware of the important role word parts play.

An entomologist studies insects (from *entoma*, insects). Notice the parts *en-* (in) + *tom* (cut). If you look closely at an ant (an insect), you'll see that its body is "cut into" segments. It's in three parts. Notice the word *insect*, from Latin *in-* (in) + *secare* (cut).

Compound words in English

Early in school you learned that two words could be joined to form a new word: *blue* + *bird*, *butter* + *cup*, *suit* + *case*. You learned that words such as *meanwhile* and *furthermore* are compound words. It is important to realize that the English language grows mainly by the process of compounding. Therefore, most people need to spend more time practicing using meaningful roots, prefixes, and suffixes as compound forms of words.

The word *postscript* is a compound of two meaningful forms, *post-* (after) and *script* (write). The word *predict* is a compound of the meaningful parts *pre-* (before) and *dict* (say). The forms *pre-* and *post-* compound with other parts to create words carrying the ideas of "before" and "after." Here are some examples:

Before: preview, preface, preliminary, preposition,
        prescription, precede, preamble, prelude, preclude,
        precursor
After: postwar, postpone, posterior, posterity, posthumous,
        post meridian, post-mortem, postnasal, postlude

Roots and words

By noticing, learning, and classifying word parts you begin to
see how certain words are related in meaning. Many words
belong to the same family because they are formed from the
same root; thus the origin of their meaning is the same. For
example, many words dealing with writing are formed from
graph (write). Many words having to do with believing and
trusting are formed from *cred* (believe, trust). Here are some
examples:

Writing: paragraph, autograph, biography, stenographer,
        telegraph, graphite
Believing or trusting: credibility, incredible, credo,
        incredulous, credit, creditor

Because these words are not in sentences, you have no
external, or outside, context clues to help you. But if you
know the roots of the words, you can find meaning from the
internal, or inside, context clues in the words themselves.

If you notice and learn the roots *scrib* or *script* (write) in
words such as *scribble, scribe, describe, inscribe, manuscript, prescription,*
and *scripture,* you will be more aware that words formed from
these roots all have something to do with writing. A *postscript*
(P.S.) is, for example, written "after" *(post-)* "writing" *(script)* a
letter.

The more roots you know, the better. As the material you
read becomes harder, you will notice that many of the new
words you learn for each subject are formed from key roots.
The names of inventions, discoveries in medicine, parts of the
body, and technical words in all the sciences are often made
up of roots from Greek or Latin. Here are some examples:

Latin *agr(i)* (field) + Latin *cultus* (cultivate) = *agriculture*
Greek *tele* (distant) + Latin *vis* (see) = *television*
Latin *appendix* (hang on) + Greek *-itis* (inflammation) =
    appendicitis
Greek *thermo* (heat) + Greek *meter* (measure) = *thermometer*
Latin *aqua* (water) + Latin *duct* (lead) = *aqueduct*
Latin *bibl(io)* (book) + Greek *graph* (write) = *bibliography*
Latin *bursa* (pouch, sac) + Greek *-itis* (inflammation) = *bursitis*
Greek *neuro* (nerve) + Greek *osis* (disease) = *neurosis*

Transfer your knowledge

It's obvious, then, that if you don't know the roots of technical words, it is much harder to figure out their meaning. If you know key roots, you can transfer your knowledge from one word to another, no matter what subject you are studying.

If you learn that *phobia* means "fear of," you already know half of the meaning of *acrophobia* (*acro* means "height"). *Acrophobia* means "fear of being up high." If you see *claustrophobia,* you know it means "fear of" something. In this case it is fear of enclosed places, from Latin *claustrum* (closed place). Think of the word *closet.* It comes from the same root. If you've never seen the word *agoraphobia,* you now know it means "fear of" something. In this case, it is fear of being in open places. *Agora* is the Greek word for "market place," also an open assembly place where the public gathered.

Some of those *phobia* words are fairly hard, of course, but many words are made this way, whether they are hard or easy.

Analyzing words

Word analysis (breaking words apart) is a quick way to learn words because it helps you classify them. Notice how the word parts in the following examples help you understand and remember the meaning of the words:

abduct—from *ab-* (away) + *duct* (lead)
   Abduct means to "lead away," to "carry off."
megaphone—from *mega-* (great) + *phone* (sound)
   A *megaphone* increases the loudness of the voice.
Acropolis—from *acro* (highest part) + *polio* (city)
   This is the high, fortified citadel of Athens. (Do you remember the meaning of *acro* in *acrophobia?*)
manicurist—from manus (hand) + *cur* (care) + *-ist* (one who)
   A manicurist is a person who cares for the hands and fingernails.
micrometer—from *micro-* (small) + *meter* (measure)
   This instrument measures very small objects or angles.
apogee—from *apo-* (away from) + *ge* (earth)
   The *apogee* is the point of an orbit farthest from the earth. *Perigee*—from *peri* (around)—is the point in an orbit nearest the earth.
leukemia—from *leukos* (white) + *emia* (blood)
   A person with *leukemia* has an excess of white blood cells.
aristocrat—from *aristo-* (best) + *crat* (rule)
   An *aristocrat* belongs to the aristocracy, the rule of the nobility.
kleptomania—from *kleptes* (thief) + *mania* (madness)
   This person has an irresistible desire to steal certain objects.
intravenous—from *intra-* (within) + *vena* (vein)
   Where does an intravenous injection go?

barometer—from *baros* (weight) + *meter* (measure)
   This instrument measures the weight (atmospheric pressure) of the air.
intersect—from *inter-* (between) + *sect* (cut)
   To *intersect* means to "cut or divide by passing through."
bicameral—from *bi-* (two) + *camera* (chamber)
   This word means having two chambers or houses. The United States Congress is bicameral (made up of the Senate and the House of Representatives). The state of Nebraska has a one-house legislature; it is called a *unicameral,* or "one-house" legislature.
insomnia—from *in-* (not) + *somnus* (sleep)
   An *insomniac* is a person with *insomnia* (the inability to sleep). Do you know what a *somnambulist* does? He walks in his sleep. (*Ambulo* means "walk.") Do you know what a *somniloquist* does? He talks in his sleep. (*Loguor* means "talk.") Where do all these "sleepy" words come from? In Latin mythology, Somnus was the god of sleep.

Keep in mind that classifying roots, prefixes, and suffixes helps you remember them. It also helps you remember words made from these word parts. Classifying gives you a mental filing system. Your memory bank will be only as useful as your filing system. You must deposit your words where they can be easily found and used. Apply your understanding of word parts in the exercise that follows.

Using word parts   Self-help

This exercise breaks up words into roots, prefixes, and suffixes and then gives the meaning of each part. Try to put the definitions of the word parts together to find the meaning of each word. Check your answers in the **Answer Key.**

   Example: If *bi-* means "two" and *ped* means "foot," what are *bipeds?*
   Answer: animals with two feet (humans and birds, for example)

1. If *in-* means "into" and *cis* means "cut," what does *incision* mean?
2. If *in-* means "not" and *clemens* means "gentle" or "mild," what is *inclement* weather?
3. If *biblio* means "book" and *phil* means "love," what is a *bibliophile?*
4. If *vor* means "eat," what is an *insectivor?*
5. Although bats are insectivorous, baby bats are also *lactivorous* (*lactis* means "milk"). What do baby bats' diets consist of?

The "measure" root

The root *meter* (measure) appears in many words ranging from the *speedometer* that measures the speed of a car to the *telemeter* that measures the speed of a space rocket. The following lists contain many *meter* words. Some of the words could be placed under more than one heading, but each is assigned to only one list. How many *meter* words do you know? Check over the lists first, then read the explanation of *meter* words that follows the lists.

Electricity
ammeter
galvanometer
ohmmeter
voltmeter
wavemeter

Mechanics
comptometer
macrometer
micrometer
odometer
speedometer
tachometer

Human body
acoumeter
anthropometry
audiometer
biometrics
calorimeter
cardiotachometer
craniometer
dosimeter
isometric
optometrist
pedometer
pulsimeter
sphygmomanometer
thermometer

Poetry and fine arts
asymmetrical
dimeter
hexameter
metrical
metrician
metrist
metromania
metronome
octameter
pentameter
symmetrical
symmetry
tetrameter

Mathematics
centimeter
diameter
geometry
kilometer
meter
metric
metricate
millimeter
perimeter
telemeter
telemetry
trigonometry

Science
altimeter
anemometer
barometer
bathometer
colorimeter
magnetometer
photometer
spectrometer

The root *meter* (measure) plays a big part in your life. A person comes to the house to read the *meters* that measure the amount of gas, water, and electricity you use. Many homes have *thermometers* that measure the amount of heat in a room. The cars and buses you ride have *speedometers* or *tachometers,* which measure speed. They also have *odometers* to measure distance.

In school you learned in mathematics that the United States uses the English system of measurement and that Europeans use the *metric* system. It's true that 39.37 inches equal a *meter;* $\frac{1}{100}$ of a meter is a *centimeter;* a mile is 1.609 *kilometers;* a *kilometer* is 1,000 *meters;* a *millimeter* is $\frac{1}{1000}$ of a meter. The United States is now in the process of *metricating* (changing to the metric system).

In *geometry* you learned that the *diameter* is the distance across a circle. The study of the relationship between the sides and angles of triangles is *trigonometry.* The outer boundary of a figure is the *perimeter.*

In science you may have learned that an *altimeter* measures altitude and a *bathometer* measures the depth of water. An *anemometer* measures wind speed, and a *barometer* measures air pressure.

Macrometers measure the size of objects very far away or hard to reach. *Micrometers* measure very small distances or objects. Data from stars, planets, and spaceships are obtained by *telemetry.*

Music teachers use *metronomes* to measure tempo, and art teachers speak of *symmetrical* forms. Some forms lack *symmetry* and are said to be *asymmetrical.* An artist or a scientist might measure the shade or intensity of a color with a *colorimeter.* A *spectrometer* measures the wave length of colors in the spectrum. Light intensity is measured with a *photometer,* or light meter.

In the field of electricity, the *wavemeter* measures the length of electromagnetic waves. A *galvanometer* measures the strength of an electric current. The strength of an electric current is also measured in amperes by an *ammeter.* A *voltmeter* measures electric voltage. An *ohmeter* measures electrical resistance.

You can add, subtract, and multiply with a *comptometer.* You can measure the distance you walk with a *pedometer.* Metal objects on airline passengers are detected by a *magnetometer.*

Some poets suffer from *metromania* (a mania for writing verse). Poetry deals with *meter* (rhythm in verse). A person skilled in *metrical* composition, or *meters,* is called a *metrist* or a *metrician.* A poet can write iambic *tetrameter* (4 feet or measures to the line), as Scott did in *The Lady of the Lake;* dactylic *hexameter* (6 feet), as Virgil did in the *Aeneid;* iambic *pentameter* (5 feet), as Shakespeare did in his sonnets; dactylic *dimeter* (2 feet), as in Tennyson's "The Charge of the Light Brigade"; or trochaic *octameter* (8 feet) as in Poe's "The Raven."

Meters also collect information about your physical
characteristics and health. The science of measuring the human
body is *anthropometry*. Skulls are measured with a *craniometer*.
Biometrics is a branch of biology that deals with measuring
statistically how many years the average person will live.

The keenness of your hearing is measured with an *audiometer*
or an *acoumeter*. An *optometrist* measures the power of your
eyesight. A *pulsimeter* measures the strength of your pulse, and
a *sphygmomanometer* measures your blood pressure. A
cardiotachometer measures the rate of your heartbeat.

There is a *dosimeter* to measure the dose or amount of
radiation to which you are exposed, and a *calorimeter* to
measure the heat given off by, or present, in your body. You
can keep in shape by doing *isometric* exercises.

**More words
from roots**

The following short lists of roots are presented in such a way
that you can easily see how one root produces many useful
words. The more familiar you become with the roots in these
lists, the easier it will be to figure out new words. Use the
dictionary to check the meanings of any unfamiliar words.

acro **(highest)**
acrobat
acronym
acropolis
acrophobia

ama, ami **(love)**
amateur
amiable
amicable
amity

calc **(stone, computing)**
calculate
incalculable
calcium
calculator

cend **(set fire to)**
incendiary
incensed
incense
censer

class **(class, group)**
classify
classics
classical
classicist

commun **(common)**
community
communion
communism
communicate

corp **(body)**
corporation
corps
corpuscle
corpse

crat **(rule)**
democratic
aristocrat
bureaucrat
autocratic

crit **(separate, judge)**
critic
criticize
critical
criterion

crypt **(secret)**
cryptic
crypt
cryptogram
cryptography

culp (blame)
culprit
culpable
exculpate
inculpable

cumb (lie, recline)
incumbent
succumb
recumbent
incumbency

deb (owe)
debt
indebted
debtor
debit

derm (skin)
hypodermic
dermatology
dermis
pachyderm

do (give)
donate
donor
donee
antidote

dur (hard)
endure
durable
endurable
duress

dyna (power)
dynamite
dynamic
dynasty
dynamo

esth (feeling)
esthetic
anesthetic
anesthesia
anesthetist

fid (faith)
confide
fidelity
infidel
bona fide

fus (pour)
transfusion
fusion
diffuse
profuse

habit (dwell)
inhabitant
habitat
habitable
habitation

hem (blood)
hemorrhage
hemorrhoid
hemostat
hemoglobin

hom (man)
homage
Homo sapiens
homicide
hombre

homo (same)
homogenized
homogeneous
homonym
homograph

hum (earth, soil)
humble
humiliate
humus
exhume

hydr (water)
hydrant
hydrogen
hydrophobia
dehydrate

ign (fire)
ignite
ignition
igneous
ignescent

ir (anger)
irritable
irritate
irate
ire

mania (mad)
mania
maniac
bibliomania
monomania

mers (sink, dip)
immerse
emersed
submerse
submersion

mim (imitate)
mimic
mimeograph
pantomime
mime

mnem (memory)
amnesia
mnemonic
mnemonics
mnemic

morph (shape)
metamorphosis
morphology
metamorphic
amorphic

umbra (shade)
umbrella
umber
penumbra
umbrage

vari (different)
various
variety
varied
variable

ven (vein)
venous
intravenous
venule
venesection

ventr (belly)
ventriloquist
ventricle
ventral
ventrodorsal

verb (word)
adverb
verbal
proverb
verbatim

via (way)
via
trivial
deviate
viaduct

vor (eat)
devour
carnivorous
herbivorous
omnivorous

vulg (common people)
vulgar
vulgarity
divulge
vulgarism

Prefixes and words

If you know the meaning of roots, prefixes, and suffixes, you have an advantage in vocabulary study. You receive *external* clues about the meaning of new words from the sentences, and you derive meaning from the words themselves (*internal* clues). It's a matter of analysis and synthesis. You *analyze* (break up) the words into meaningful parts and you *synthesize* (put together) the parts again by forming whole words.

When you study and learn words in this way, you are using a systematic approach: you are classifying roots, prefixes, and suffixes according to meaning. The technique becomes a habit. You notice words and the parts of words automatically. This gives your memory a boost.

When you learn that the prefixes *un-*, *in-*, *il-*, and *ir-* mean "not," you begin to see the idea of "not" in words such as *unaware, inappropriate, illegal,* and *irresponsible.* You can classify these prefixes under the idea "negative prefixes." They carry the idea "not." *Active* becomes *inactive, appropriate* becomes *inappropriate, adequate* becomes *inadequate.*

An abridged dictionary is a shortened dictionary. Many words have been left out. What is an *unabridged* dictionary? One that hasn't been shortened. Most words have been included. Notice the prefix *un-* in *unabridged.*

An accented syllable is pronounced with force; for example, *AC cent.* An *un*accented syllable (notice the *un-*) is not pronounced with force. It is *not* accented, as with the last syllable *(-ed)* in *AC cent ed.*

Notice the negative prefix in this statement: "We hold these truths to be self-evident, that all men are created equal, that they are endowed by their Creator with certain *un*alienable Rights. . . ." You should have picked out the word *unalienable* right away (notice the *un-*). Unalienable rights cannot be given away or taken away.

Many prefixes can be classified and remembered by the way they are used. Some prefixes deal with moving forward or being in front: *pre-, pro-, ante-* (as in *precede, proceed, antecedent*). Some prefixes deal with numbers in a general way: *poly-, multi-, extra-* (*polygon, multicolored, extrasensory*).

Other prefixes deal with numbers in a specific way: *bi-, oct-, dec-, kilo-* (*bifocal, octopus, decimal, kilometer*). You will learn more about number prefixes later in this section.

Here are several other prefixes that show the negative side of words: *in-, un-, non-, im-, il-, ir-, a-* (as in *inactive, unemployed, nonaddictive, impractical, illegal, irresponsible, acentric*).

Take another look at the word *acentric.* If you know that the Greek prefix *a-* means "not" or "without," you can apply it to many roots to form words: *a-* (not) + *centric* = *acentric* (not

The negative prefix *a-*

centered). *A-* (not) + *theist* means "one who doesn't believe in God," an *atheist*. *Theos* is Greek for "god."

Before an operation, a physician gives a patient *anesthesia*, from *an-* (not) + *esthesia* (feeling). Anesthesia eliminates feeling. Note that *a-* becomes *an-* in *anesthesia* (*n* is added to *a-* before words beginning with vowels, as when *"a apple"* becomes *"an apple"*). Another example is *anemia: an-* (not) + *emia* (blood), means "without good blood."

If someone told you *chromatic* means "color," what would *achromatic* mean? The answer is *a-* + *chromatic* = *achromatic*, "having no color." A *typical* situation is ordinary. Can you think of a word for extraordinary, or not typical? The word is *atypical*. Follow the construction of some more *a-* (not) words in this list:

pathetic (with pity or feeling)	*apathetic* (without pity or feeling)
septic (having bacteria)	*aseptic* (free from bacteria)
moral (having morals)	*amoral* (without morals)
esthetic (having feeling)	*anesthetic* (loss of feeling)
symmetrical (with proportion)	*asymmetrical* (without proportion)

You can see that *a-* (not) is an important prefix. Here are a few other words for practice with the negative prefix *a- (an-)*. If you are curious about a word, look it up in the dictionary.

atrophy (without nourishment)
aphonic (loss of voice)
aphotic (without light)
abyss (without a bottom)
anonymous (without a name)
adynamic (having no power)
amnesia (without memory)
amnesty (not remembering)

Organize for study

When you classify words you bring a kind of organization, or order, into your study of vocabulary. By classifying words, you anchor them. There are several ways, for example, to classify antonyms, or words of opposite meaning. One is to think about words formed from opposite prefixes, as with *indoors* and *outdoors, inhale* and *exhale*. See how well you can complete the antonym exercise that follows. Your success will be based on your awareness of opposite prefixes.

Working with opposites   **Self-help**

Form antonyms (words of opposite meaning) for the following
words by changing only the italicized prefix. Look up
unfamiliar words in a dictionary when you are through. Check
your answers in the **Answer Key.**

    Example: *in*clude   **Answer:** exclude

1. *in*flate
2. *a*scend
3. *in*ject
4. *under*pass

5. *pre*fix
6. *pre*paid
7. *pro*pel
8. *im*migrate

9. *pre*date
10. *im*plode
11. *pre*test
12. *pro*gress

As you can see, using opposite prefixes is a simple but
efficient way of organizing your study of words. In the next
exercise, you will learn a new technique: discovering new
words by using the prefixes that make things bigger.

"Make it big" prefixes   **Self-help**

This exercise introduces augmentative prefixes (prefixes that
show greatness in size, number, and scope). Form "big" words
by matching each prefix in column A with the appropriate
root word in column B. Look up any unfamiliar words in the
dictionary. Check your answers in the **Answer Key.**

    Examples: mega-   man   **Answers:** superman
               super-   phone   megaphone

A	B
macro-	1. theism
hyper-	2. highway
poly-	3. lopolis
ultra-	4. activity
multi-	5. modern
extra-	6. ordinary
mega-	7. scopic
super-	8. faceted

Learning number prefixes is an important part of your
vocabulary-building program. Perhaps you haven't noticed
how many words are formed from the Greek and Latin
number prefixes.

Number prefixes

    mono- and *uni-* (one), as in *monoplane* and *unicycle*
    bi- and *di-* (two), as in *bicycle* and *diphthong*
    tri- (three), as in *triple*

quad- (four), as in *quadrangle*

pent- and quint- (five), as in *pentagon* and *quintuplets*

sex- and hex (six), as in *sextet* and *hexagon*

sept- (seven), as in *September* (seventh month of Roman calendar)

oct- (eight), as in *October* (eighth Roman month)

novem- (nine), as in *November* (ninth Roman month)

Notice the importance and basic meaning of the prefix in each of these words:

monarch (*one* ruler)

monotone (*one* tone)

unique (*one* of a kind)

unicorn (*one*-horned animal)

bienniel (*twice* a year)

bifocal (having *two* focuses)

bisect (to cut in *two*)

dioxide (*two* oxygen atoms)

duet (*two* singers)

duplicate (*two* copies)

triplicate (*three* copies)

tripod (*three*-legged)

quadrangle (*four* sides)

quartet (group of *four*)

quintet (group of *five*)

sextet (group of *six*)

septet (group of *seven*)

octet (group of *eight*)

decade (*ten* years)

century (*100* years)

Here are some more useful words from number prefixes:

mono- (one)
monastery
monocle
monolog
monopoly
monorail
monotonous

dua-, duo- (two)
dual
duo
duplex
duplication
duplicator
duplicity

uni- (one)
uniform
unify
union
unit
unity
universal

tri- (three)
triangle
triceps
tricycle
trigonometry
trillion
trinity

bi-, di- (two)
bicentennial
billion
bimonthly
binocular
digraph
dilemma

quad-, quart- (four)
quadrant
quadruple
quadruplet
quadruplicate
quart
quarter

penta-, pent- (five)
pentagon
pentameter
pentangular
pentasyllable
pentathlon
pentecost

sex-, hex- (six)
sexennial
sextant
sextuplet
hexagonal
hexameter
hexapod

sept-, hept- (seven)
September
septet
septicentennial
septuplet
heptagon
heptameter

octa-, octo- (eight)
octagon
octane
octave
October
octopus
octuplet

novem-, non- (nine)
nonagenarian
nonagon
nones
noon
November
novena

dec-, deca- (ten)
decagon
decapod
December
decennial
decimal
decimate

cent-, centi- (100)
cent
centenary
centigrade
centigram
centimeter
centurion

How many of the following words would you know without help from the dictionary? Notice they all begin with a number prefix. As you go through the list, notice the root words, which are also important.

Unicameral means a *one*-house legislature (*cameral* = house).
A *unicorn* is a mythical animal with *one* horn (*corn* = horn).
Uniflorous means bearing *one* flower (*florous* = flower).
Unify means to make into *one* (*fy* = make).
A *unipod* is a stool with *one* leg (*pod* = foot).
A *monarchy* is a government ruled by *one* person (*archy* = rule).
A *duarchy* is a government ruled by *two* persons (*archy* = rule).
A *duologue* is a conversation between *two* persons (*log* = speak).
A *diphthong* is *two* vowel sounds pronounced as one syllable—
   the *ou* in *mouse,* for example (*phthong* = sound).
Binocular means using *both* eyes (*ocular* = eyes).
Biped animals, such as gorillas, have *two* feet (*ped* = foot).

A *bipod* is a support with *two* legs (*pod* = foot).

A *biparous* animal has *two* young at birth (*parous* = birth).

A *triangle* is a figure with *three* sides (*angle* = corner).

A *triarchy* is ruled by *three* persons (*archy* = rule).

A *tricorn* hat has *three* hornlike projections (*corn* = horn).

A *bicuspid* is a *two*-pointed tooth (*cuspid* = point).

Neptune, the god of the sea, carries a *trident,* or *three*-pronged spear (*dent* = tooth).

Trifocals are glasses with *three* focuses (*foc* = focus).

Trigamy means having *three* wives or husbands at the same time (*gamy* = marriage).

A *tripod* is a *three*-legged stand for a camera (*pod* = foot).

A *quadrangle* is a space with *four* corners (*angle* = corner).

A *quadrennium* is a period of *four* years (*ennium* = year).

A *quadrilateral* figure has *four* sides (*lateral* = side).

A *quadrarchy* is a government ruled by *four* persons (*archy* = rule).

A *quadrilingual* person speaks *four* languages (*lingual* = tongue).

A *quatrifoil* is a *four*-leaf clover (*foil* = leaf).

A *tetrarchy* is a government ruled by *four* persons (*archy* = rule).

A *quincentennial* celebration occurs every *five* hundred years (*cent* = 100, *ennial* = year).

The *Pentagon* in Washington, D.C., is a *five*-angled, *five*-sided building (*gon* = angle).

Iambic *pentameter* is a line of poetry with *five* feet or measures (*meter* = measure).

When an athlete competes in the *pentathlon,* the event consists of *five* contests (*athlon* = exercise of skill).

A *sexagonal* figure has *six* angles (*gon* = angle).

A *sexcentenary* is a *six* hundred year anniversary (*centenary* = a hundred years).

Sexennial means occurring every *six* years (*ennial* = year).

A *hexagon* is a figure with *six* angles and *six* sides (*angle* = corner).

Hexapod means having *six* feet (*pod* = foot).

Septennial is a double-duty word: it means occurring every *seven* years; it also means lasting *seven* years. (*ennial* = year).

An *octagon* is a figure with *eight* angles (*gon* = angle).

An *octofoil* is an ornamental figure with *eight* leaves (*foil* = leaf).

A *nonagon* is a *nine*-angled figure (*gon* = angle).

A *decagon* has *ten* angles (*gon* = angle).

A *centigrade* thermometer is divided into *100* degrees (*grade* = degree).

A *millennium* is a period of *1,000* years (*ennium* = year).

A *millimeter* is a *thousandth* of a meter (*meter* = measure).

Now see how well you remember what you've learned about number prefixes by completing the following exercise.

Learning number prefixes

The Greek and Latin prefixes from one to ten are (1) *mono-,
uni-;* (2) *bi-, di-;* (3) *tri-;* (4) *quad-, tetra-;* (5) *quint-, penta-, pent-;*
(6) *sex-, hex-;* (7) *sept-, hept-;* (8) *octo-;* (9) *novem-;* (10) *dec-.* If you
have learned these number prefixes, you can easily complete
the prefix problems that follow. Check your answers in the
Answer Key.

  Example: mono + uni = b__   **Answer:** bi
  1. sex + bi = o__ __ __
  2. bi + di = q__ __ __
  3. penta + quad = n__ __ __ __
  4. tri + di = q__ __ __ __
  5. quad + bi = h__ __
  6. quad + uni = p__ __ __ __
  7. quint + mono = s__ __
  8. bi + di = t__ __ __ __
  9. tri + quad = s__ __ __
 10. tetra + hex = d__ __
 11. penta + di = h__ __ __
 12. mono + bi = t__ __
 13. quad + tetra = o__ __ __
 14. bi + tri = p__ __ __ __
 15. octo − quad = t__ __ __ __
 16. tri × tri = n__ __ __ __
 17. bi ÷ di = m__ __ __
 18. octo − di = h__ __
 19. sex ÷ hex = u__ __
 20. dec ÷ penta = b__

Suffixes and words

Some people don't realize the importance of suffixes in
vocabulary development. Most do recognize, however, that *-er*
added to a noun such as *labor* gives us *laborer* (one who labors).
People learn to generalize that *-er* often means "one who." In
addition, the suffix *-er* can be used to compare things *(strong/
stronger)* because *-er* also means "more."

  As a child, you learned that the suffix *-ed* at the end of a
verb such as *claim* forms the past tense, *claimed.* But on the
whole you didn't think about the importance of suffixes in
changing the parts of speech. Through the use of *suffixes,* words
are formed such as *vocal* (adjective), *vocally* (adverb), *vocation*
(noun), and *vocalize* (verb).

There are many suffixes whose meanings and uses are less
well known than *-er* and *-ed.* Notice, for example, that the

**Suffixes have
meaning**

suffix -*fy* in *purify* means "make." This suffix is found in many words: *simplify, beautify, amplify, fortify, satisfy, pacify.*

The suffix -*less* means "without," as in *fearless.* The suffix -*ness* means "condition of" or "state of." Thus *haughtiness* means the "state of being haughty." The suffix -*ment* also means "state of," and so *refinement* means the "state of being refined."

Through experience, you learn which suffix to use. The self-test that follows will give you practice in choosing the appropriate suffix.

Self-help	**Suffix self-test**

Which suffix does your experience tell you to add to the following words? Your choices are -*less*, -*ness*, and -*ment*. Check your answers in the **Answer Key.**

Example: beard   **Answer:** beardless

1. prepared	6. blame
2. induce	7. establish
3. thought	8. commence
4. guilt	9. stain
5. assort	10. accompany

Note that the last word in the suffix self-test required you to change the *y* to *i* before adding the suffix. Additional words with this spelling change are *worthiness, worldliness, craftiness, sturdiness, ugliness, manliness, embodiment, juiciness,* and *weariness.*

Suffixes meaning "like"

Some suffixes mean "like," "somewhat like," or "belonging to" (for example, -*ish* and -*ine*). If a child "wolfs down food" or "eats like a pig," the child may be *wolfish* or *piggish.* Sharp teeth are *canine* (like a dog's teeth). A *serpentine* vine is snakelike.

A person may be *childish, boyish, girlish, sheepish, amateurish,* or *bookish.* You don't hear the words *boorish, knavish, loutish, oafish,* and *churlish* much nowadays, but people are still occasionally *foolish, selfish, snobbish,* and even *freakish.*

Sherlock Holmes is described as having an *aquiline* nose (like an eagle). Ice on a pond may be *crystalline.* Some veterinarians care for *canines* (dogs), *felines* (cats), and *equines* (horses). You can also metaphorize, or compare, people's actions or appearance with those of animals: She gave him a *bovine* stare (like a cow's). A large dog's walk may appear *leonine* (like a lion's). A huge figure may be described as *elephantine.* What does an elephantine figure look like?

Other -*ine* words you might see are *hircine* (like a goat); *lupine* (like a wolf); *sealine* (like a seal); *ermine* (like a weasel—

pronounced differently, *ermine* is the word for the weasel's fur); *piscine* (like a fish—remember Pisces, the sign of the fish in the zodiac?); *ursine* (like a bear—have you heard of *Ursa* Major, the Big *Bear* constellation?).

Scientists form many technical terms from roots and the suffix *-logy* (the study of, or science of). Following is a list of roots with their meanings. These roots, combined with the suffix *-logy*, make up words often used in science. Study these roots. You will be able to use some of them to complete the matching exercise that follows.

The scientific suffix *-logy*

Roots used in science

astro (star)
apio (bees)
anthropo
  (mankind)
archae (beginning)
ethno (race)

ornitho (bird)
pharmaco (drug)
bio (life)
geo (earth)
psycho (soul,
  mind)

entomo (insect)
etymo (true, real)
herpeto (reptile)
theo (god)
zoo (animal)

Words of science

Self-help

Match the *-logy* word with its definition. Check your answers in the **Answer Key.**

Example: biology   **Answer:** k. the study of life

Word

1. geology
2. anthropology
3. psychology
4. archaeology
5. entomology
6. ethnology
7. etymology
8. ornithology
9. herpetology
10. pharmacology

Study of

a. the mind
b. insects
c. birds
d. snakes
e. drugs
f. a word's origin
g. humankind
h. earth's crust
i. early civilization
j. races of people

In addition to combining with roots, the suffix *-logy* or *-ology* also combines with words. You can probably figure out the meaning of these *-logy* words: *oceanology, musicology, mineralogy, fossilology, audiology, Egyptology, embryology, meteorology, mythology.*

The suffix *-itis* is often heard in a doctor's office. A person says, "I think I have *tonsillitis.*" Another says, "I've had *bursitis* for quite a while." You may not know the source of your

The "hurt" suffix *-itis*

health problem, but you can easily learn the meaning of the root word in the name of a disease. The root *arthr*, for example, means "joint." If your joints are swollen or inflamed, you might have *arthritis*, an inflammation of the joints.

The suffix *-itis* (disease or inflammation) is highly useful in medicine. It has been used to create the names of many diseases and health disorders. You've just seen three *-itis* words. Notice the use of *-itis* in these words: *appendicitis, sinusitis, bronchitis, dermatitis, gastritis, laryngitis, meningitis, osteomyelitis, neuritis, phlebitis.*

Here is a quick look at some of the roots in these medical words:

bronchitis, from Greek *bronchos* (windpipe) + *-itis* (inflammation) = inflammation of the bronchial tubes

bursitis, from Latin *bursa* (bag, purse) + *-itis* = inflammation of the sac near the shoulder joints

dermatitis, from Greek *derma* (skin) + *-itis* = inflammation of the skin

gastritis, from Greek *gastros* (stomach) + *-itis* = inflammation of the stomach

Now you can pick out the general meaning of these words:

laryngitis, from Greek *larynx* (upper windpipe)
meningitis, from Greek *meningos* (membrane)
osteomyelitis, from Greek *osteon* (bone) and *myelitis* (marrow)
neuritis, from Greek *neuron* (nerve)
phlebitis, from Greek *phlebos* (vein)

In the autumn many people come down with *footballitis.*

Everyday words with suffixes

Suffixes, then, are useful in forming many medical and other technical terms. But you have also seen that they are important in the development of words you use every day. Now complete the exercises that follow, which deal with suffixes that form (1) familiar antonyms, (2) words showing gender (sex), and (3) words meaning "little."

Self-help

The suffix *-less*

The suffix *-less* is used to form antonyms (words of opposite meaning) for many common words. Examples are: *color* + *-less* = *colorless; worth* + *-less* = *worthless.* See if you can form antonyms for the words below simply by dropping the suffix already there and then adding the suffix *-less.* (For one answer, you will have to alter the end spelling of the root word somewhat.) Check your answers in the **Answer Key.**

Example: bearded   **Answer:** beardless

1. hopeful
2. thoughtful
3. sinful

4. graceful
5. useful
6. sensible

Suffixes and gender   Self-help

Now you will change the *gender* (sex) of a word by adding
female gender suffixes. Your choices are *-ine, -ette,* and *-ess.* (For
some answers, you will have to alter the spellings of root
words somewhat.) Check your answers in the **Answer Key.**

Example: waiter   **Answer:** waitress

1. major
2. lion
3. tiger
4. hero
5. Paul
6. prince
7. emperor

8. host
9. actor
10. heir
11. baron
12. priest
13. usher
14. sorcerer

"Little" suffixes   Self-help

The suffixes that follow are called *diminutive* suffixes—ones that
express the idea "smallness." Match the diminutive suffixes
with the root words listed after them to form words
expressing "small." Check your answers in the **Answer Key.**

Example: dear + -ie   **Answer:** dearie (little dear)

Diminutive suffixes:

-ette	-ule	-ling
-ie	-icle	-cule
-et	-kin	-let

1. flor
2. stream
3. duck
4. kitchen

5. caps
6. tub
7. bird
8. ring

9. part
10. lamb
11. gos
12. statu

13. mani
14. leaf
15. cigar
16. pig

Have you ever noticed that we can say *blacken, whiten,* and
redden, but not *bluen, brownen,* and *greenen?* The colors are
adjectives and, like many adjectives, some can change to verbs
simply with the addition of the suffix *-en.* Here are some more
adjectives that you can change to verbs by adding *-en:*

**Suffixes and
parts of speech**

Adjective	Verb	Adjective	Verb
wide	widen	straight	straighten
deaf	deafen	bright	brighten
length	lengthen	fright	frighten
like	liken	moist	moisten
ripe	ripen	flat	flatten

Some antonym pairs both fit into the -en verb pattern. In other antonym pairs, one word fits into the -en pattern but the other does not.

lighten and *darken*	*fatten* but not *thinnen*
gladden and *sadden*	*broaden* but not *narrowen*
harden and *soften*	*sharpen* but not *dullen*
strengthen and *weaken*	*shorten* but not *longen*
heighten and *deepen*	*stiffen* but not *limpen*
tighten and *loosen*	*sweeten* but not *souren*

Suffixes and spelling

These examples may have made you keenly aware that suffixes change the spellings of words. Knowing the various suffixes (and how they are added to roots to form words) can help you spell words correctly. Notice that you change *swim* to *swimmer* by adding -er. But also notice that you doubled the consonant *(m)* before adding the suffix. Here are some other examples: *spin* to *spinner, stop* to *stopped, drop* to *dropping.*

What's the rule? When a root word has *one vowel* and ends in a *single consonant,* you double the consonant before adding a suffix *beginning with a vowel;* for example, *sin* to *sinner* and *thin* to *thinner.* Words with two vowels *(speak, shoot)* don't double the consonant before adding suffixes beginning with vowels; for example, *speak* to *speaking, shoot* to *shooting, shear* to *shearing, sleep* to *sleeping, school* to *schooling.* Add the suffix -ing to some more root words and see how they're spelled:

cup to cu*pp*ing	spoon to spoo*n*ing
kid to ki*dd*ing	boat to boa*t*ing
put to pu*tt*ing	

Here's another way that a knowledge of suffixes helps spellers: Did you know that the word *tailless* has two *ll*'s? If you can pick out the root word and suffix, you will see why *(tail + -less = tailless).* If you look closely at suffixes such as -*less,* you will be more aware of them in other words such as *soulless* (one *l* for the root word and one *l* for the suffix -*less*). Notice the use of the two consonants in all of these words: *wheelless, sailless, mealless, brownness, meanness, greenness, suddenness, openness.*

Note that adding suffixes is a matter of compounding parts to make words. It is the same form of compounding discussed earlier. Spelling is an important part of compounding. That is why you should learn how to classify and use word parts such as suffixes. It is important, for example, to notice that the words *can* and *not* form *cannot* (with two *n*'s). The same is true of *bookkeeping* and *roommate.* Double-consonant spelling causes trouble for many of us in words such as *underrated* (one *r* for *under-* and one *r* for *rated*), *overreach, overrule, override.*

Notice that *under-* and *over-* are prefixes. You should also consider prefixes in spelling words. The prefixes *mis-* and *dis-,* for example, can cause trouble in spelling. But if you are conscious of the prefixes, you are unlikely to leave out the double consonant.

If you learn that *mis-* means "wrong," you'll remember the prefix in spelling words such as *misspent, misstate, misstep, misshapen* (two *s*'s). Likewise, knowing the prefix *dis-* (not) helps you spell correctly (with two *s*'s) words such as *dissimilar, disservice,* and *dissatisfied.* And don't ever misspell *misspell.*

Sometimes roots appear in a suffix position (at the end). An example is *graph* (write), which may appear in a word at the beginning *(graphite),* in the middle *(stenographer),* or at the end *(photograph).*

Roots in suffix position

The root *cide,* meaning "kill," from *caedo* (slay or kill) is found in the suffix position. Many words are formed from *cide,* as in *pesticide* (kills pests). How many *cide* words do you know?

Killers

Self-help

This exercise tests your knowledge of words formed with the suffix *-cide* (slay or kill). See if you can match the words with their definitions. Check your answers in the **Answer Key.**

Example: tyrannicide   **Answer:** p. kill a tyrant

1. algaecide	a. kill a god
2. deicide	b. kill the environment
3. ecocide	c. kill algae
4. fungicide	d. kill a race
5. genocide	e. kill weeds
6. herbicide	f. kill a man
7. homicide	g. kill a fungus
8. insecticide	h. kill parents
9. mariticide	i. kill a mind (brainwash)
10. matricide	j. kill a father
11. menticide	k. kill an insect
12. parricide	l. kill a spouse
13. patricide	m. kill a mother
14. regicide	n. kill a rat
15. rodenticide	0. kill a king

Important roots to know

Review the following list of roots from time to time. Look at the words and mentally check or write down those you don't know. Next, look at the root and its meaning. Notice how the root helps you understand the *basic* meaning of the sample words. The root *acro,* for example, means "high." The root *phobia* means "fear." So *acrophobia* means a "fear of heights."

Table of roots

Sample words	Root	Meaning
acrophobia, acrobat, acronym, acropolis	*acro*	height, high, tip, end
agriculture, agrarian, agronomy, peregrinator	*agr*	field, land
nostalgia, analgesic, neuralgia, cardialgia	*alg, algos*	pain
alias, alien, unalienable, alienate	*ali*	another
altitude, alto, altimeter, exalt	*alt*	tall, high
alternate, alternative, alter ego, altruism	*alter, altr*	other
amateur, amiable, amicable, amorous	*ama, ami*	love
amble, ambulatory, somnambulist, perambulator	*ambul*	walk
angle, rectangle, quadrangle, triangular	*angle, angul*	corner
anniversary, annual, biannual, annuity	*annus*	year
anthropology, misanthrope, philanthropist, anthropophagi	*anthropo*	man, humankind
aquarium, aquatic, aquamarine, aqueduct	*aqua*	water
architect, monarch, archbishop, hierarchy	*arch*	chief
archaeology, archaic, archive, archetype	*arch, arche*	ancient, first
armor, armory, armistice, armada	*arm*	weapon
asterisk, disaster, astronomy, astronaut	*aster, astro*	star
athlete, athletic, decathlon, pentathlon	*athl, athlon*	prize, contest
auditorium, audience, audition, audible	*aud*	hear
autobiography, autocracy, autonomy, autograph	*auto*	self
aviator, aviary, aviculture, avicide	*avi*	bird
barometer, barograph, baroscope, isobar	*baro*	weight
belligerent, bellicose, post-bellum, ante-bellum	*belli*	war
benediction, benefit, beneficiary	*bene*	good, well
Bible, Biblical, bibliography, bibliophile	*bibl*	book
biology, biography, biopsy, antibiotic	*bio*	life
brevity, breviary, abbreviate, breve	*brev*	short
bronchitis, bronchial, bronchotomy, bronchopneumonia	*bronch*	windpipe
bursar, bursitis, reimburse, disburse	*bursa*	bag, purse
bicameral, camera, unicameral, chamber	*camera*	vault, chamber
candle, candidate, candelabra, incandescent	*cand*	glow, white, pure
canto, incantation, canticle, cantor	*cant*	song
cap, captain, capital (city), decapitate	*cap*	head
capture, captivity, captivate, captor	*capt*	take, receive

Sample words	Root	Meaning
electrocardiogram, cardiac, cardiograph, cardiectomy	*cardi*	heart
chili con carne, incarnation, carnivorous, carnal	*carn*	flesh
cave, cavern, concave, excavate	*cav*	hollow
precede, recede, accede, antecedent	*ced, ceed*	go, yield
censor, censorship, census, censure	*cens*	judge
reception, conception, accept, receptive	*cept*	take, receive, catch
choreography, chorus, chorister, Terpsichore	*choreia, chorus*	dancing
anachronism, chronicle, chronic, chronological	*chron*	time
suicide, fratricide, herbicide, genocide	*cide*	kill
circle, circus, circuitous, circuit	*circ*	ring, around
civilization, civil, civility, civic	*civ*	citizen
acclaim, exclaim, declaim, proclaim	*claim*	shout
exclamation, proclamation, acclamation, clamor	*clam*	shout
clarify, declarative, declaration, clarity	*clar*	clear
classify, classical, classic, declassify	*class*	class, group
declination, decline, recline, incline	*clin*	lean
include, preclude, exclude, seclude	*clud*	shut
conclusive, exclusive, seclusion, inclusion	*clus*	shut
recognize, cognitive, cognizant, incognito	*cogn*	know
colony, agriculture, culture, cultivate	*colo, cult*	cultivate, settle
community, commune, communicate, communicable	*commun*	common
unicorn, cornucopia, bicorn, cornet	*cornu*	horn
corporation, corps, corpuscle, corpulent	*corp*	body
cosmopolitan, microcosm, cosmos, macrocosm	*cosm*	order, universe
aristocracy, democratic, bureaucrat, plutocrat	*cracy, crat*	rule
creditor, credulous, credentials, credibility	*cred*	believe
crime, criminal, incriminate, discriminate	*crim*	judge, accuse
critic, criticize, criterion, critical	*crit*	separate, judge
cryptic, crypt, cryptogram, cryptography	*crypt*	secret
culpable, exculpate, culprit, inculpate	*culp*	fault, blame
accumulate, cumulative, cumulate, cumulus	*cum*	pile up
incubate, incumbent, succumb, incumbency	*cumb, cub*	lie, recline
course, courier, current, excursion	*cur, cour*	run
cure, manicure, accurate, curator	*cur*	care
bicycle, cyclic, cyclone, cyclist	*cycl*	ring, circle
data, postdate, mandate, antedate	*dat*	give
debt, indebted, debtor, debit	*deb*	owe
decoration, decor, indecorous, decorum	*decor*	proper, fitting
deity, deify, deiform, deism	*dei*	god
democracy, epidemic, demography, demagogue	*demos*	people
dentist, dental, dentifrice, trident	*dent*	tooth
hypodermic, dermatology, dermatitis, epidermis	*derm*	skin
diary, per diem, *sine die,* dismal	*dia, die*	day
dictate, predict, verdict, contradict	*dic, dict*	say

Sample words	Root	Meaning
dignity, dignitary, condign, dignify	*dign*	worth
divide, divisor, divisive, dividend	*div*	separate
donate, donor, condone, donee	*do*	give
doctor, doctrine, indoctrinate, documentary	*doc*	teach
dormitory, dormant, dormer, dormancy	*dorm*	sleep
unorthodox, heterodoxy, orthodoxy, paradox	*doxa*	belief, praise
conduct, abduct, aqueduct, seduce	*duc*	lead
durable, endurable, endure, duress	*dur*	hard
dynamite, dynamic, dynasty, dynamo	*dyn*	power
egotistic, ego, egocentric, egomania	*ego*	I
exempt, *caveat emptor,* redemption, preempt	*em, empt*	buy, obtain
anemia, leukemia, hemostat, hemorrhage	*emia, hemia*	blood
biennial, centennial, perennial, bicentennial	*enni*	year
equality, equator, inequity, equation	*equ*	equal, even, just
energy, erg, anergy, synergy	*erg*	work
err, error, erratic, erroneous	*err*	wander
esthetic, anesthetic, esthete, anesthetist	*esth*	feeling
manufacture, factory, benefactor, facsimile	*fac*	make, do
fallacy, infallible, falsify, false	*fall, fals*	deceive
female, feminine, feminist, effeminate	*femina*	woman
transfer, refer, infer, melliferous	*fer*	carry, bear
efficient, beneficial, sufficient, proficient	*fic*	do, make
confide, fidelity, infidel, bona fide	*fid*	faith
filial, affiliate, filicide, affiliation	*fili*	son, daughter
final, finite, infinite, finale	*fin*	end
confirm, infirm, affirm, confirmation	*firm*	steady
suffix, affix, fixture, prefix	*fix*	fasten
flame, inflammable, flammable, flamboyant	*flam*	blaze
reflect, reflector, deflect, inflection	*flect*	bend
reflex, flexible, flex, circumflex	*flex*	bend
flora, floral, efflorescent, florist	*flor*	flower
fluid, fluent, influx, affluent	*flu*	flow
portfolio, foliage, folio, defoliate	*fol*	leaf
uniform, reform, formation, transform	*form*	shape
fort, fortify, fortification, fortitude	*fort*	strong
fraction, fracture, fragment, fragile	*fract, frag*	break
fraternity, fraternal, fraternize, fratricide	*frat*	brother
fruit, fruitful, fructify, fruition	*fru*	enjoy
fugitive, refuge, refugee, centrifugal	*fug*	flee
functional, malfunction, defunct, dysfunction	*funct*	perform
transfusion, fusion, diffuse, profuse	*fus*	pour
monogamy, bigamy, trigamy, polygamy	*gam*	marriage
generation, progeny, genetics, genocide	*gen*	race, birth

Sample words	Root	Meaning
geography, geology, apogee, perigee	*geo*	earth
agnostic, diagnose, diagnostic, prognosticate	*gnos*	know
trigonometry, octagonal, polygon, pentagon	*gon*	angle
degrade, graduation, gradation, retrograde	*grad*	step
monogram, telegram, grammar, epigram	*gram*	letter, written
grain, granary, grange, granulated	*gran*	grain
autograph, paragraph, graphite, biography	*graph*	write
grateful, congratulate, gratis, gratitude	*grat*	please, thank
congregation, gregarious, aggregate, desegregate	*greg*	herd
monogyny, polygyny, gynecologist, misogynist	*gyn*	woman
polyhedron, tetrahedron, cathedral, *ex cathedra*	*hedr*	side, seat
helium, heliotrope, heliocentric, heliograph	*heli*	sun
homage, *Homo sapiens*, homicide, hombre	*hom*	man
homogenized, homonym, homograph, homophone	*homo*	same
humus, humiliate, exhume, inhume	*hum*	earth, soil
hydrant, hydrogen, hydrophobia, dehydrate	*hydr*	water
pediatrician, psychiatric, geriatrics, podiatry	*iatrik, iatro*	healing art
identify, identical, identification, identity	*ident*	same
idiot, idiom, idiomatic, idiosyncrasy	*idio*	peculiar
ignite, ignition, igneous, ignitron	*ign*	fire
imperative, empire, emperor, imperious	*imperi*	command
peninsula, insulate, insularity, insular	*insul*	island
integrity, integrate, integral, integer	*integ*	whole, untouched
irritate, irate, ire, irascible	*ir*	anger
exit, initiate, adit, obit	*it*	go
project, inject, reject, eject	*ject*	throw
joke, jocose, jocular, jocund	*jocus*	joke
journal, journalism, journey, sojourn	*journ*	daily
judge, judicial, judgment, judicious	*ju, jud*	law, right
junction, conjunction, juncture, adjunct	*junct*	join
jury, perjury, jurisdiction, jurisprudence	*jur*	law, right
just, justice, injustice, justification	*jus*	law, right
collaborate, laboratory, elaborate, laborious	*labor*	work
elapse, relapse, lapse, collapse	*laps*	slip
lateral, unilateral, bilateral, quadrilateral	*lat*	side
collect, elect, select, electoral	*lect*	gather, choose
lectern, legend, legible, illegible	*lect, leg*	read
legal, delegate, legitimate, legislate	*leg*	law, contract
elevator, leverage, lever, levee	*lev*	raise, lift
liberty, liberate, libertarian, liberal	*liber*	free
library, librarian, librettist, libretto	*libr*	book
lingual, linguistics, linguist, bilingual	*lingu*	tongue
literature, literary, illiterate, literal	*litera*	letter
monolith, paleolithic, neolithic, lithograph	*lith*	stone

Sample words	Root	Meaning
local, location, dislocate, localize	*loc*	place
locution, elocution, circumlocution, interlocutor	*locu*	speak
dialogue, prologue, epilogue, eulogy	*log, logue, logy*	speech
elope, interloper, elopement, lope	*lop*	run, leap
eloquence, soliloquy, colloquial, loquacious	*loqu*	speak
deluge, antediluvian, ablution, dilute	*lu*	wash
lucid, translucent, elucidate, Lucifer	*luc*	light
interlude, prelude, postlude, ludicrous	*lud*	play
lunar, lunatic, translunar, cislunar	*luna*	moon
magnify, magnitude, magnanimity, magnificent	*magni*	great
malice, malady, malign, malignant	*mal*	bad
manual, manuscript, manipulate, manicure	*man*	hand
command, demand, mandatory, mandate	*mand*	order
marine, submarine, mariner, maritime	*mare*	sea
maternal, maternity, alma mater, matron	*mater, matri*	mother, source
medium, mediate, medieval, mediocre	*med*	middle
commemorate, memorize, memorandum, memorial	*memoria*	memory
mental, demented, mentality, memento	*ment*	mind
merge, submerge, merger, emerge	*merg*	plunge, dip
diameter, barometer, altimeter, perimeter	*meter*	measure
metric, geometric, isometric, symmetrical	*metr*	measure
migrate, emigrate, immigrant, migratory	*migr*	move
militant, military, militia, militate	*mil*	soldier
mimic, mimeograph, pantomime, mime	*mim*	imitate
miserable, miser, misery, commiserate	*miser*	wretched, pity
mission, missionary, missive, missile	*miss*	send, let go
amnesia, mnemonic, amnesty, Mnemosyne	*mnem*	memory
automobile, mobile, immobile, mobility	*mob*	move
admonish, monitor, admonition, premonition	*mon*	advise, warn
moral, morality, morals, mores	*mor*	custom
mortal, immortal, mortality, mortician	*mort*	death
motion, motor, promote, demote	*mot*	move
move, movable, remove, movie	*mov*	move
mutual, commute, mutuality, mutation	*mut*	change, exchange
native, nativity, natal, innate	*nat*	born
nausea, nautical, nautilus, aquanaut	*naus, naut*	ship
navy, navigate, naval, circumnavigate	*nav*	ship
Indonesia, Polynesian, Micronesia, Dodecanese	*nes*	island
astronomy, economy, autonomy, taxonomy	*nom*	law, arrangement
nomenclature, denomination, nominative, nominate	*nomen*	name
novel, novelty, novice, innovate	*nov*	new
numeral, numerator, numerous, enumerate	*numer*	number
ocular, oculist, binoculars, monocular	*ocul*	eye

Sample words	Root	Meaning
antonym, synonym, homonym, acronym	*onym*	name
myopic, optic, optometrist, optical	*op, opt*	sight
oral, oracle, orator, oratory	*orare*	speak, pray
ossify, osteopath, osteomyelitis, osteotomy	*oss, osteo*	bone
oval, ovum, ovary, oviparous	*ov*	egg
encyclopedia, pedantic, pedagogue, pediatrician	*paed, ped*	child, teach
parent, parentage, biparous, viviparous	*par*	give birth
compare, comparable, parable, parity	*par*	equal, compare
pastor, pastoral, pastorale, pasture	*past*	shepherd
paternal, patriarch, patriot, repatriation	*pater, patr*	father
sympathy, empathy, pathos, antipathy	*path*	feel, suffer
pedal, pedestrian, biped, centipede	*ped*	foot
repel, dispel, expel, propel	*pel*	drive
penal, penitentiary, penalize, punitive	*pen, pun*	punishment
pendulum, appendage, suspend, appendix	*pend, pens*	hang
petrify, petroleum, petrification, petrol	*petr*	rock
esophagus, dysphagia, sarcophagous, anthropophagi	*phag*	eat
philharmonic, philosopher, philatelist, Philadelphia	*phil*	love
Phobos, agoraphobia, claustrophobia, acrophobia	*phobos*	fear
phone, symphony, phonics, telephone	*phon*	sound
euphoria, dysphoria, metaphor, semaphore	*phor*	to carry
photocell, photosynthesis, photography, photostatic	*photo*	light
placate, placid, complacent, placebo	*plac*	please
pneumatic, pneumonia, apnea, pneumonoultramicroscopicsilicovolcanoconiosis	*pne*	air, lung, breathe
bipod, tripod, chiropodist, octopus	*pod, pus*	foot
acropolis, metropolis, politics, politician	*poli, polit*	city
transport, import, export, deport	*port*	carry
port, seaport, portal, Puerto [Porto] Rico	*porta*	gate
depose, deposit, preposition, apposition	*pos*	place, set
helicopter, pterodactyl, pterosaur, lepidopterous	*pter*	wing, feather
repulse, expulsion, compulsory, propulsion	*puls*	drive, push
query, questionnaire, inquest, inquire	*quer, quest, quir*	seek, ask
correct, rectify, erect, rectangle	*rect*	straight, right
refer, reference, referendum, referent	*referre*	carry back
regal, regime, regency, interregnum	*reg, regn*	rule
deride, ridiculous, ridicule, derision	*rid, ris*	laugh
rodent, erode, corrode, erosion	*rod, ros*	gnaw
interrogate, interrogative, prerogative, abrogate	*rogare*	ask, request
rotate, rotary, rotunda, rotor	*rota*	wheel, round
rupture, erupt, interrupt, disrupt	*rupt*	to break
sacrifice, sacrament, sacred, sacrilege	*sacr*	holy
sane, sanity, sanitation, sanitarium	*san*	healthy, sound

Sample words	Root	Meaning
sanctuary, sanctity, sanctify, sanctimonious	*sanct*	holy
satiety, saturate, insatiable, satisfy	*sat, satis*	enough
dinosaur, tyrannosaurus, sauropod, brontosaurus	*saur*	lizard
descend, ascend, transcend, ascension	*scend, scens*	climb
school, scholastic, scholarship, scholar	*schole*	leisure, school
science, conscious, scientific, omniscient	*sci*	know
telescope, microscope, periscope, kaleidoscope	*scope*	to watch
describe, inscribe, manuscript, inscription	*scrib, script*	write
dissect, bisect, insect, intersect	*sec, sect*	cut
sedative, sedentary, session, preside	*sed, sess, sid*	sit, settle
seminary, disseminate, seminarian, seminar	*semin*	seed
senator, senior, seniority, senile	*sen*	old
sensitive, sensation, assent, dissent	*sens, sent*	feel
antiseptic, septic, aseptic, septicemia	*seps, sept*	decay
sequence, subsequent, sequel, consequently	*sequ*	follow
reservoir, reservation, preservation, conservation	*servo*	save, keep
service, servitude, subservient, servile	*servus*	slave, server
sex, sexual, sexism, bisexual	*sexus*	division, sex
signify, signal, signature, insignia	*signi*	mark, sign
similarity, simile, simultaneous, simulate	*simil, simul*	like, same
solitude, solitary, desolate, soliloquy	*sol*	alone
solid, solidarity, consolidate, solidify	*solidus*	solid
soluble, dissolve, solvent, absolve	*solu, solv*	loosen, free
insomnia, insomniac, somnambulist, somnolent	*somn*	sleep
unison, sonorous, dissonant, subsonic	*son*	sound
philosopher, sophisticated, sophomoric, sophistry	*soph*	wise
spectator, spectacular, spectacle, prospect	*spec, spect*	look
atmosphere, hemisphere, stratosphere, spherical	*spher*	ball, sphere
conspirator, inspire, respiration, expire	*spir*	breathe, live
respond, respondent, correspondent, responsive	*spond, spons*	answer
stationary, standard, stability, stagnant	*sta*	stand
construct, structure, instruct, structural	*stru*	build
student, studious, study, studio	*studeo*	be eager
surge, resurgence, resurrection, insurrection	*surg, surr*	rise
syllable, syllabus, syllabify, syllabification	*syllaba*	take together
table, tablet, entablature, tabular	*tabl, tabula*	board, tablet
intact, tangent, tangible, intangible	*tact, tang*	touch
attain, retain, detain, tenacious	*tain, ten*	hold
tactics, syntactical, syntax, taxidermist	*tact, tax*	to arrange, order
telephone, telegraph, telescope, television	*tele*	distant
temporary, contemporary, temporal, extemporaneous	*temp*	time, season
extend, tendon, tensile, extent	*tend, tens, tent*	tend, stretch
terrify, terror, terrorist, terrible	*terrere*	to frighten
testify, testimony, testament, intestate	*testare*	to witness

Sample words	Root	Meaning
thanatophobia, thanatopsis, euthanasia, Thanatos	*thanatos*	death
theism, atheist, theology, monotheism	*the*	god
thermos, thermometer, thermal, thermostat	*thermo*	heat
appendectomy, tonsillectomy, neurectomy, anatomy	*tom*	cut
topical, topography, utopia, topology	*topos*	place, spot
distort, extort, retort, torture	*tort*	twist, turn
toxin, antitoxin, toxic, intoxication	*tox*	poison
attract, tractor, distract, extract	*tract*	pull, draw, drag
intrude, protrude, extrude, obtrude	*trud*	thrust
tuition, tutorial, tutelage, tutor	*tuitus*	watch over
turbine, turbid, turbulent, perturb	*turb*	whirling, turmoil
antepenult, ultimate, penult, ultimatum	*ultimus*	last
umbra, umbrella, adumbrate, penumbra	*umber, umbra*	shade, shadow
undulate, inundate, abundant, redundant	*unda*	wave
urban, urbane, suburb, suburban	*urb*	city
vacate, vacant, vacuum, evacuate	*vaca, vacu*	empty, hollow
invade, evade, pervade, evasive	*vad, vas*	go
vagrant, vagrancy, vagabond, extravagant	*vag*	wander
valid, equivalent, invalid, valetudinarian	*val*	strong, worth
vanguard, van, avant-garde, vantage point	*van*	front, forward
vapor, vaporous, vaporizer, evaporate	*vapor*	steam
vary, variant, variety, variegated	*vari*	different, various, spotted
convention, convent, intervention, convene	*ven*	come
vend, vendor, venal, *caveat vendor*	*ven*	sale
vein, venous, intravenous, venule	*ven*	vein
verdict, verify, veracity, verification	*ver*	true
reverence, reverend, revere, irreverent	*ver, verer*	fear, awe
verb, adverb, proverb, verbatim	*verb*	word
reverse, inverse, divert, invert	*vers, vert*	turn
vespers, Vesper, Hesperus, vespertilionid	*vesper*	evening
vest, vestment, divest, investiture	*vest*	clothing
vet, veteran, veterinary, veterinarian	*veter*	old, experienced
viaduct, trivial, trivia, deviate	*via*	way
victory, evict, victorious, victress	*vict*	conquer
video, providence, evident, videotape	*vid*	see
vision, visualize, visible, supervision	*vis*	see
vitamin, vitality, vital, revitalize	*vit*	live
survive, revive, vivid, vivacious	*viv*	live
vocal, vocabulary, avocation, evoke	*voc, voke*	call
volunteer, benevolent, malevolent, involuntary	*vol*	wish, will
revolt, revolve, evolve, revolver	*vol, volv*	roll, turn
devour, voracious, carnivorous, herbivorous	*vor*	eat
zoo, zoologist, protozoan, zodiac	*zo*	animal

Important prefixes to know

Review the following list of prefixes from time to time. Look at the words and mentally check or write down those you don't know. Next, look at the prefix and its meaning. Notice how the prefix affects the meaning of the sample words. The prefix *a-*, for example, means "on" in the word *ashore* (on shore).

Table of prefixes

Sample words	Prefix	Meaning
ashore, aboard, afire, atop	*a-*	on
atom, aseptic, anemia, anergy	*a-, an-*	not, without
absent, abduct, abdicate, abnormal	*ab-*	from
adhere, adjoin, adverb, adjunct	*ad-*	to
ambidextrous, ambiguous, ambivalent, ambient	*ambi-*	both, around
amphibious, amphitheater, amphipod, amphora	*amphi-*	both, around
anteroom, anterior, antecedent, antechamber	*ante-*	before
antifreeze, antidote, antislavery, antiseptic	*anti-*	against
apogee, apostle, apostasy, apocryphal	*apo-*	away from, from
autograph, automobile, automatic, autobiography	*auto-*	self
benefit, beneficial, benediction, benefactor	*bene-*	well, good
bicycle, binocular, bigamy, biceps	*bi-, bin-, bis-*	two, twice
century, centigrade, centimeter, centennial	*cent-*	hundred
circus, circuit, circa, circular	*circu-*	around, about
circumnavigate, circumpolar, circumference, circumlocution	*circum-*	around
co-worker, cooperator, coincident, coalition	*co-*	with, together
collect, collaborate, collate, colleague	*col-*	together, with
companion, compost, compact, compose	*com-*	together, with
connect, concentrate, conference, congress	*con-*	together, with
contrast, contradict, contrary, controversy	*contra-, contro-*	against
counterclockwise, counteract, counterbalance, counterrevolution	*counter-*	against, in return
descend, degrade, depress, dejected	*de-*	down
deflect, deter, detract, dehydrate	*de-*	away
decade, decimal, December, decathlon	*dec-*	ten
decimal, decimate, decibel, decimeter	*deci-*	tenth
demigod, hemidemisemiquaver, hemisphere, semiconscious	*demi-, hemi-, semi-*	half, partly
diphthong, dioxide, digraph, dilemma	*di-*	two
diameter, diagonal, dialogue, diagnosis	*dia-*	through, between
dishonest, distrustful, discontent, disobey	*dis-*	not
dismiss, discard, disarm, dislocate	*dis-*	apart from
disarrange, discomfort, disconnect, disown	*dis-*	opposite
dual, duet, duplex, duplicate	*du-*	two

Sample words	Prefix	Meaning
dyspepsia, dysfunction, dysentery, dystrophy	*dys-*	bad
eject, emit, erupt, elevate	*e-*	out
encircle, enfold, encase, enslave	*en-*	in
endoderm, endocrine, endocarp, endogamy	*endo-*	inside, within
epilogue, epidermis, epitaph, epidemic	*epi-*	upon, in addition
eulogy, euphemism, euphoria, euphonious	*eu-*	well, good
exit, extract, exclude, excerpt	*ex-*	out
extramural, extravagant, extraordinary, extradite	*extra-*	outside, beyond
heptagon, heptarchy, septennial, September	*hept-, sept-*	seven
heteronym, heterogeneous, heterodox, heterosexual	*hetero-*	different
homonym, homogeneous, homogenesis, homologous	*homo-*	same
hypersensitive, hyperbole, hyperacidity, hypertension	*hyper-*	over, beyond
hypoactive, hypochondriac, hypodermic, hypotenuse	*hypo-*	under, too little
illegal, illogical, illegible, illiterate	*il-*	not
immerse, immigrate, implant, impale	*im-*	into
immovable, immobile, immaculate, impartial	*im-*	not
intake, inhale, include, incision	*in-*	into
inactive, incorrect, indecent, informal	*in-*	not
infrared, infrahuman, infraglacial, infrastructure	*infra-*	below
international, interurban, intermission, interjection	*inter-*	between, among
intramural, introduce, introvert, introspective	*intra-, intro-*	within
irregular, irreverent, irrational, irrelevant	*ir-*	not
isobar, isometric, isotope, isosceles	*iso-*	equal, same
kilocycle, kilogram, kilometer, kilowatt	*kilo-*	1,000
macron, macroscopic, macrometer, macrocosm	*macro-*	large, long
megalomania, megaphone, megalith, megaton	*mega-*	large
metaphor, metamorphic, metabolism, metastasis	*meta-*	change
metaphysics, metapsychosis, metabiological, metachrome	*meta-*	beyond
microscopic, microphone, micrometer, microfilm	*micro-*	small
millimeter, milligram, millisecond, milliwatt	*milli-*	$\frac{1}{1,000}$
misspell, misdeed, misinterpret, misbehave	*mis-*	wrong
monarch, monocle, monorail, monotone	*mono-*	one
multitude, multimillionaire, multicolored, multilateral	*multi-*	many
neologism, neophyte, neolithic, neonate	*neo-*	new, modern
nonstop, nonsense, nonentity, nonpolitical	*non-*	not
nonagon, November, novena, novennial	*non-, novem-*	nine
objection, obstacle, obstruct, obverse	*ob-*	against, opposite
octagon, octopus, October, octogenarian	*octa-, octo-*	eight
oligarchy, oligopoly, oligochrome, oligocarpous	*olig-*	few
omnipotent, omnivorous, omniscient, omnibus	*omni-*	all
pandemonium, Pan-American, pandemic, panorama	*pan-*	all
paragraph, parallel, parasite, paraphrase	*para-*	beside

Sample words	Prefix	Meaning
peninsula, penannular, penultimate, peneplain	*pen-, pene-*	almost
pentagon, Pentecost, pentameter, pentad	*penta-*	five
pervade, perpetual, permanent, perforate	*per-*	throughout, thoroughly
periscope, perimeter, periphery, perigee	*peri-*	around, near, about
polygon, polysyllable, polygamy, polytheism	*poly-*	many
postscript, postpone, postdate, posterity	*post-*	after
predict, presume, precede, premeditate	*pre-*	before
prognosis, program, progenitor, prophesy	*pro-*	before
pronoun, pronominal, proconsul, proconsulate	*pro-*	in place of
project, propel, progress, promenade	*pro-*	forward
proslavery, pro-American, pro-liberal, proponent	*pro-*	in favor of
prologue, proboscis, program, proseminar	*pro-*	in front
protozoa, prototype, protoplasm, protocol	*proto-*	first
pseudonym, pseudopod, pseudo-event, pseudoscience	*pseudo-*	false
quadruplet, quadruped, quarter, quatrain	*quad-, quart-, quatr-*	four
quasi-humorous, quasi-historical, quasi-judicial, quasi-legislative	*quasi-*	seemingly, partly, as if
quintet, quintuplet, quintuple, quintessence	*quin-*	five
refund, retract, repay, remit	*re-*	back
reread, rearrange, rediscover, reabsorb	*re-*	again
retrorocket, retroactive, retrograde, retrospection	*retro-*	back
semicircle, semiannual, semiconscious, semifinals	*semi-*	half
September, septennial, septet, septuagenarian	*sept-*	seven
sesquilateral, sesquicentennial, sesquioxide, sesquipedalian	*sesqui-*	one and a half
sextet, sextuplet, hexagonal, hexameter	*sex-, hex-*	six
submarine, subsoil, submerge, subterranean	*sub-*	under, below
supersede, supernatural, superheat, supercilious	*super-*	over
sympathy, symphony, symmetry, symposium	*sym-*	together, with
synonym, synthesis, synopsis, synchronous	*syn-*	together, with
tetragonal, tetrameter, tetrarchy, tetrachloride	*tetra-*	four
transfer, transmit, transit, transcontinental	*trans-*	across, over
triangle, tricycle, trigonometry, triad	*tri-*	three
ultraviolet, ultramodern, ultranationalism, ultrasonic	*ultra-*	beyond
unsafe, unsure, unreliable, unmanned	*un-*	not
unit, unicycle, unify, unique	*uni-*	one
vice-president, vice-principal, vice-admiral, viceroy	*vice-*	in place of

Important suffixes to know

Review the following list of suffixes from time to time. Look at the words and mentally check or write down those you don't know. Next, look at the suffix and its meaning. Notice how the suffix affects the meaning of the sample words. The suffix *-able,* for example, means "can be done" in the word *eatable* (can be eaten).

Table of suffixes

Sample words	Suffix	Meaning
eatable, lovable, readable, credible	*-able, -ble, -ible*	can be done
peaceable, perishable, affordable, durable	*-able, -ble, -ible*	inclined to
candidacy, privacy, infancy, agency	*-acy, -cy*	office, rank of, state of
orangeade, lemonade, limeade, marmalade	*-ade*	result, product, substance made
parade, blockade, escapade, promenade	*-ade*	process, action
alumnae, formulae, algae, larvae	*-ae*	Latin feminine plural
orphanage, parsonage, anchorage, frontage	*-age*	place of
ravage, pillage, marriage, pilgrimage	*-age*	action, process
filial, natural, ornamental, royal	*-al*	relating to
veteran, American, Anglican, European	*-an*	relating to
resistance, avoidance, importance, exuberance	*-ance*	state of
vacancy, truancy, occupancy, ascendancy	*-ancy*	state of
multiplicand, addend, dividend, subtrahend	*-and, -end*	to be done
defiant, radiant, vacant, buoyant	*-ant*	state of, condition of
immigrant, emigrant, assistant, resident	*-ant, -ent*	person who
grammarian, librarian, humanitarian, libertarian	*-arian*	person who, place where, object which
secretary, sanctuary, dictionary, infirmary	*-ary*	person who, place where, object which
literary, military, reactionary, secondary	*-ary*	characterized by, relating to
annihilate, liberate, radiate, venerate	*-ate*	to make, cause to be
narration, continuation, visitation, computation	*-ation*	process, action
occupation, moderation, decoration, refrigeration	*-ation*	state of, quality of, result of
oratory, reformatory, laboratory, conservatory	*-atory*	process, action, place where
miniscule, molecule, animalcule, pedicule	*-cule*	small
freedom, martyrdom, wisdom, boredom	*-dom*	state of
tonsillectomy, gastrectomy, appendectomy, hysterectomy	*-ectomy*	surgical removal
lengthen, shorten, weaken, strengthen	*-en*	to make

Sample words	Suffix	Meaning
dependence, confidence, competence, absence	-ence	state, quality, condition of
potency, despondency, clemency, frequency	-ency	quality of, state of
faster, lighter, clearer, tighter	-er	comparative degree
carpenter, barber, actor, orator	-er, -or	person connected with
bakery, rookery, bindery, laundry	-ery, -ry	place where
Japanese, Maltese, Chinese, Nepalese	-ese	derivation, language
picturesque, burlesque, Romanesque, statuesque	-esque	in the manner, style of, like
poetess, actress, shepherdess, countess	-ess	feminine ending
islet, dinette, kitchenette, statuette	-et, -ette	small
amateur, chauffeur, masseur, saboteur	-eur	agent
cupful, spoonful, mouthful, handful	-ful	enough to fill
satisfy, amplify, deify, qualify	-fy	make of, form into
knighthood, manhood, falsehood, womanhood	-hood	state of, quality of, condition of
connubial, industrial, commercial, remedial	-ial	characterized by, related to
Christian, physician, Parisian, barbarian	-ian	characterized by, related to
angelic, iambic, volcanic, quixotic	-ic	of the nature of, characterized by
magic, classic, public, rhetoric	-ic	to form nouns
critical, fantastical, comical, political	-ical	of the nature of, characterized by
canticle, particle, article, icicle	-icle	little
cashier, gondolier, chiffonier, lawyer	-ier, -yer	person who, place where
canine, feline, asinine, feminine	-ine	like, characterized by, pertaining to
heroine, Caroline, Josephine, Clementine	-ine	feminine suffix
sleeping, walking, writing, acting	-ing	present participle
roofing, bedding, siding, quilting	-ing	material
earnings, shavings, furnishings, filings	-ings	noun associated with the verb form
construction, rebellion, revolution, electrocution	-ion	act, process
ambition, dominion, subjection, suspicion	-ion	state of
gracious, ambitious, infectious, dubious	-ious	characterized by
exorcise, baptize, sterilize, civilize	-ise, -ize	subject to, make, carry on
Scottish, Turkish, clownish, whitish	-ish	like, pertaining to
baptism, plagiarism, despotism, heroism	-ism	action, process
hypnotism, barbarism, racism, pacifism	-ism	state of, condition of
stoicism, Quakerism, Americanism, realism	-ism	doctrine, system
biologist, monopolist, botanist, socialist	-ist	person who
appendicitis, bronchitis, arthritis, meningitis	-itis	inflammatory disease

Sample words	Suffix	Meaning
calamity, felicity, necessity, acidity	*-ity*	state of
witless, fruitless, doubtless, careless	*-less*	without
streamlet, ringlet, leaflet, bracelet	*-let*	small
homelike, lifelike, apelike, ghostlike	*-like*	like
duckling, gosling, hireling, nestling	*-ling*	small
anthropology, biology, zoology, psychology	*-logy*	science of
fatherly, motherly, regally, timely	*-ly*	characteristic of, in the manner of
development, abridgment, government, embezzlement	*-ment*	action, process
amazement, adornment, arrangement, refinement	*-ment*	state of
greatness, kindness, wilderness, dimness	*-ness*	state of, quality of, condition of
adenoid, asteroid, spheroid, planetoid	*-oid*	like, resembling
auditor, donor, creditor, executor	*-or*	person who
auditorium, natatorium, emporium, conservatorium	*-orium*	place for, object used for
laboratory, conservatory, consistory, purgatory	*-ory*	place where
hypnosis, psychosis, neurosis, otiosis	*-osis*	abnormal condition, state of
poisonous, riotous, joyous, polygamous	*-ous*	possessing the qualities of
jewelry, revelry, masonry, citizenry	*-ry*	collection of
hardship, friendship, censorship, ownership	*-ship*	state of
clerkship, lordship, authorship, partnership	*-ship*	office, profession
stewardship, scholarship, readership, ownership	*-ship*	art, skill
mobster, gangster, huckster, youngster	*-ster*	one belonging to, characterized by
capsule, molecule, plumule, tubule	*-ule*	little, small
clockwise, counterclockwise, lengthwise, slantwise	*-wise*	way, manner, respect

3   Classifying ideas and words

Classifying words helps you understand how many words are related in meaning, idea, and form. The formation, or construction, of words is often neglected by those who rely mostly on memory to learn each word separately. Rather than learning new words one at a time, you can learn new words in groups. Classifying ideas and words into groups is a good way to expand your vocabulary.

This section shows you how to learn new words you encounter by using context clues. It gives suggestions for learning words that are related in meaning, or synonyms. It explains how to use a thesaurus to find synonyms—and gives advice about choosing the word you need from a group of synonyms. It also explains how studying words of opposite meaning, or antonyms, can help you build your vocabulary.

Recognizing context clues

There are of course many ways to learn words. One is by paying close attention to context clues in the sentences you read. Often you can guess the meaning of a word from its context—from the sentence or paragraph in which the word appears. Sometimes the way the word is used gives you a clue to its meaning. Other times the context may actually define the word for you—either directly or indirectly. Or the word itself may contain word parts you recognize, which give you an idea of its meaning. All of these kinds of clues to the meaning of a word may be called *context clues*.

Let's look first at the kind of context clue that provides a definition of a word within the sentence or paragraph. Here are some ways that a word can be defined within its context:

Definitions in context

Formal definition. This clue is usually a direct statement that defines the word for you.

An oyster is a *sea animal with a soft body inside a hard, two-piece shell.*

Definition by example. The clue is an example included to help you.

Erosion wears away the earth. *Running water, for example, carries loose soil, sand, gravel, and boulders and then deposits them in new places.*

Definition by description. Here, the description of a word helps you visualize that word.

The saber-toothed tiger was a *catlike prehistoric animal with long, pointed teeth near the front of its mouth. The teeth were shaped like sabers.*

Definition by simile. *Simile* is a Latin word meaning "like" or "similar." In a phrase beginning with *like* or *as*, the simile gives you a context clue by comparing a word with something else.

Badminton is a game somewhat *like tennis.*

Definition by comparison and contrast. This context clue goes a step farther than the simile, comparing and contrasting a word in greater detail.

Badminton is a game somewhat like tennis. *But the shuttlecock (made of feather and cork) must be hit back and forth over the net without hitting the ground.*

Definition by appositive. An appositive explains or identifies a noun in the sentence. Commas usually set off this clue.

Schussing, *skiing straight down a slope without turning or stopping,* is the fastest form of skiing.

Definition by origin. This explanation of a new word consists of information about the language in which the word originated.

Do you know the drink of the gods? It's an *ancient Greek word we still use today: nectar.*

Parenthetical definition. This clue is in parentheses.

Amphetamine drugs may cause people to hallucinate *(see, hear, or feel stimuli that are not present).*

Indirect definition. Writers often define words indirectly. You may even be unaware that they are doing so. Look for signal words such as *called, also called, or, known as, referred to,* and *that is.* This type of clue is sometimes italicized.

Cameras control the amount of light passing through the lens with changeable openings *called stops.*

External context clues

The context clues just discussed are called *external (external* means "out of"). The context clues you hear about most are external; that is, they are outside the key words being defined or explained. Notice the external clues for the word *divert* in this sentence:

The farmers dug ditches to *divert* the water flow in the stream through the dry field.

You receive a few clues about the meaning of *divert* from the other words in this sentence. Clearly, the ditches are changing, or turning aside, the direction of the water's flow. So, without looking up the word, you can guess in this case that *divert* means "turn aside" or "change."

Internal context clues

If you learn the meaning of key word parts, you can also use *internal* clues (*internal* means "within") to explain the meaning of *divert.* You would note the root *vert* (which means "turn") and the prefix *di- (dis-)* (which means "aside"). *Divert* literally means to "turn aside." These context clues are internal; that is, they are within the word itself.

With this new understanding of the importance of internal clues in vocabulary mastery, now is a good time to review the material presented in 2, "Learning word elements." You will recognize that the root words, prefixes, and suffixes you have learned will provide you with important internal clues whenever you come across these word parts.

Using synonyms

Classifying words according to their general meaning and relationship to one another is essential to effective vocabulary study. You won't sharpen your vocabulary much if you don't learn to notice the similarities and dissimilarities, the likenesses and differences in words.

Look at the similarities first. A *synonym* is a word that means about the same as another word. A keen blade, for example, is a sharp blade. *Keen* and *sharp* are synonyms. They are synonymous. They can therefore be classified, or grouped, together because of their similarity in meaning.

Synonyms are *substitute words.* They permit you to express the same idea in different ways. Sometimes one synonym will be more appropriate than another. The context of the sentence, the setting, or the mood of the writer or speaker suggests which synonym to pick. A sergeant would not wake up his men, for example, by saying, "It's time to arise." He'd say, "Get up!" *Arise* and *get up* are synonyms that can be classified together, but you must decide when to use which word. How will you learn which synonym to use? You'll learn only through experience and practice.

If a show you saw was "really good," if your lunch was "really good," if your team has a "really good" pitcher and "really good" coach, what is happening to your vocabulary? Nothing. It's in a rut. Neither your vocabulary nor you are getting anywhere.

Remember, synonyms are substitute words. When a player is tired or isn't playing well, the coach puts in a substitute. Maybe some of your adjectives (descriptive words) and adverbs (words that tell how, when, why, where, and to what extent) are worn out. Why continue to overuse them? Here, for example, are several synonyms you could use instead of the word *really: very, quite, particularly, surprisingly, exceptionally, considerably, extremely, relatively, exceedingly, uncommonly.*

Perhaps some of these words would be inappropriate for everyday use. There's no need to dress up your language simply for effect. But you are now aware that you have many choices in your selection of words to express your ideas.

The word *synonym* is from Greek *syn-* ("together, like") + *onym* ("name"). Synonyms are words "like" other words. They are grouped together in the same semantic, or meaning, classification. Here's a group of synonyms for the meaning "walk": *hike, stroll, stride, tramp, march, roam, lope, ramble, amble, meander, saunter,* and *promenade.*

Classifying synonyms

Although these words all describe walking, have you noticed that they are not identical? They express subtle differences, known as *nuances,* in meaning. A stroll is a walk, and a lope is a walk. But a stroll is not a lope.

Once you learn to classify synonyms according to their general meaning, you can then concentrate on the nuances among the meanings of words. Through experience and practice you learn that there are fine distinctions, or differences, in the meanings of *under, below,* and *beneath.* Even though these three words stand for a general idea "downward," you wouldn't say that you live *below* a democratic form of government. You would say you live *under* a democratic form of government. You wouldn't say that misconduct was *under* someone. You would say it was *beneath* that person.

So while synonyms are useful as a tool for classifying words in general terms, they also help you make fine discriminations, or distinctions.

The mental filing system

If you don't classify ideas you may lose them. Your mind can't receive and register every word separately. Attacking each new word as a separate task is too much work. Classify the word first in general terms, then make fine choices about the specific meaning as the need arises. Your aim should be to see the broad relationships existing among words and to classify them in broad categories. Learn to group words for study. It's an important part of your mental filing system in vocabulary development.

When you use your mental filing system, you make learning words easier. You form the habit of classifying words and ideas under general topics. You can classify and learn several synonyms dealing with the idea "leading," for example: *rule, reign, direct, guide, manage, control, conduct, administer, govern, regulate, supervise, oversee, legislate,* and *take charge.*

When you become fluent (when you speak or write easily) with synonyms, you have words at your fingertips. You can make choices about which word to use. When your store of synonyms is low, you have difficulty finding the right word to express your ideas.

Putting a word in a neat category or group may seem to hinder, or restrain, its use. But that is not the case. The effect is just the opposite. Classifying extends the word's usefulness and makes the word more flexible. It causes more ideas to become attached to the word.

When you classify the word *mind* as having something to do with thinking or intellect, for example, you then see the word in a variety of contexts. Notice these uses of the word *mind:* *mind* reader, change your *mind,* never *mind,* bear in *mind,* on my *mind,* peace of *mind,* give someone a piece of my *mind,* bring to *mind,* be of one *mind,* put me in *mind* of, *mind* your manners.

In short, classifying synonyms broadens their use, and it encourages creativity in the use of words. It leads to the use of metaphor in language.

A *metaphor* is a word taken from one context and used in another. When you say, "He's muleheaded," you suggest that someone is as stubborn as a mule. You are giving the name and characteristics of an animal to a person. Metaphors like this example are another way to extend your vocabulary. When you metaphorize a word you extend its meaning, make it more useful.

Look at the big difference between the meanings of *headache* in the following sentences:

She has a *headache* (pain in the head).
Her son is a *headache* (source of anxiety).

The second *headache* has been metaphorized. In this context it has taken on the characteristics of an *idiom* (a phrase that cannot be understood from the specific meaning of the words alone). Another example is "He's in *hot water*" (in trouble). Your knowledge of this idiom tells you that this person is not literally in a hot tub. You will learn more about the use of metaphor and idioms later in the word builder guide.

An important point to remember in vocabulary study is that classifying words is not a matter of filing them away but of filing them for use. Classifying ideas is not like putting them in a closet. It is more like hanging them on a peg where they're within easy reach. You create a web of relationships among words that becomes an important part of effective vocabulary development and use.

Specific and suggested meanings

The study of synonyms is more than merely lumping words of like meaning together. It also involves seeing the subtle likenesses and differences in words and ideas. The study of words is the study of ideas. Words are not isolated ideas; they are surrounded by and attract other ideas.

The literal, or specific, meaning of a word is called its *denotation*. But the denotative meaning of a word is often stretched to include other ideas. The idea of *dense* (thick) in "a dense forest" can be applied to a person's intelligence. Instead of saying, "He's not very smart," you can say, "He's dense" (thick headed). When you add ideas and associations to the word *dense*, you are using connotation. The *connotation* of a word is the circle of ideas and emotions that the word carries.

The more you study synonyms, the more you will become aware not only of their denotative, or literal, meaning but also of the connotative, or suggested, ideas that surround the words. Connotative meanings come from a variety of experiences. Note that the following words used to describe the meaning "stupidity" connote, or suggest, a variety of ideas: *birdbrain, blockhead, bonehead, boob, cabbagehead, chowderhead, cluck, deadhead, dimwit, dingbat, dope, dumbbell, dumb bunny, dummy, fathead, gnatbrain, goof, jughead, knothead, lamebrain, muttonhead, nitwit, numbskull, puddinghead, sap, schlemiel, schnook.*

**Using a
thesaurus**

You've learned that one of the best ways to learn words is to develop a mental filing system: a way to classify words. An important tool to help you group words is a thesaurus (a Latin word that means "treasure" or "storehouse"). A *thesaurus* is a treasury of words. It classifies words according to ideas and helps you see the relationship between one word and another. It helps you connect ideas.

Part 4 of this publication consists of a thesaurus. A typical entry looks like this:

> **giant** *n.* MONSTER, colossus, muscleman,
>   powerhouse, CELEBRITY.
>   —*adj.* HUGE, LARGE, ENORMOUS, colossal,
>   IMMENSE, VAST, GIGANTIC.

From this thesaurus entry, you learn that the word *giant* can be either a noun or an adjective. You also learn five synonyms for *giant* when used as a noun and seven that will replace the word when it is used as an adjective.

Each thesaurus has a special style of presentation. The words that appear capitalized in the above entry, for example, are words that have their own alphabetical listings. If you look under *monster,* for example, you will find *giant* and more synonyms for *monster.* Always read the instructions at the beginning of a thesaurus before trying to use it. That way, you will know how the various devices in the entries are used.

A thesaurus helps you learn and remember words that are related by their ideas. In fact, a thesaurus is useful because it deals with ideas *and* words, not just words. When you are writing, sometimes you already have the idea of what you want to say, but you cannot find the right word to express your idea. This is where a thesaurus helps. It is a treasure house of ideas.

**Apply the
thesaurus
approach**

By applying the thesaurus approach to learning words, you learn to classify words generally and master specific meanings later. The general idea "little," for example, may be expressed by the words *small, tiny, puny, slight, minute, undersized, paltry, miniature, diminutive, smidgen, microscopic, iota,* and *Lilliputian.* You could add other "small" words to this general list yourself.

Once you have developed a solid list of "small" words, you will begin to notice their specific meanings. The words *little* and *small,* for example, are similar and are often used interchangeably. But while you might say, "He had *little* financial help," you would not say, "He had *small* financial help." Keep in mind that knowing the general classification of a word is only the first step in learning it. You must also learn the different *shades of meaning,* or connotations, the word carries with it.

Now you will check your ability to recognize groups of similar words. When you are through with the following exercise, consult the thesaurus for even more synonyms to place in the meaning groups featured.

Recognizing synonyms   **Self-help**

Choose the word that does *not* belong with the synonyms in each of the meaning groups below. Then look up any unfamiliar words in a dictionary. Check your answers in the **Answer Key.**

    Example: *Sad or glad*
           pleasant   smiling   sorrowful   cheerful
    Answer: sorrowful

1. *Sad or glad*
   a. grouchy   cranky   joyous   grim
   b. amiable   jocose   morose   blithe
   c. rollicking   splenetic   cantankerous   disconsolate

2. *Wise or foolish*
   a. wisdom   knowledge   sense   folly
   b. nonsense   reasoning   stupidity   idiocy
   c. erudition   acumen   astuteness   absurdity

3. *Fortunate or unfortunate*
   a. lonesome   merry   joyful   delighted
   b. miserable   comfortless   happy   deserted
   c. destitute   buoyant   vivacious   exhilarated

4. *Restricted or unrestricted*
   a. untied   chained   unbound   freed
   b. barred   enslaved   confined   released
   c. exempt   fettered   unconstrained unencumbered

5. *Friend or enemy*
   a. pal   rival   companion   chum
   b. ally   opponent   foe   competitor
   c. adherent   confidant   accomplice   antagonist

6. *Calm or disturbed*
   a. angry   mild   peaceful   quiet
   b. furious   wild   crazy   meek
   c. vehement   benign   placid   serene

7. *Harsh or gentle*
   a. serene   mild   kindly   rough
   b. severe   cross   pleasant   stern
   c. moderate   congenial   benevolent   acrimonious

8. *Top or bottom*
a. head   foot   cap   peak
b. floor   ground   foundation   summit
c. superstructure substratum   pinnacle   apex

9. *Honest or dishonest*
a. crooked   fair   sincere   truthful
b. tricky   fair   unjust   false
c. reputable   equitable   treacherous creditable

10. *Important or unimportant*
a. chief   significant   urgent   slight
b. critical   trivial   light   nonessential
c. paramount   foremost   grave   frivolous

Choose the right synonym

Now you will learn more about choosing the right word. As you have seen, two words may be *almost* alike, but only one will say exactly what you want. Mark Twain said that the difference between the right word and the almost right word is the difference between lightning and the lightning bug.

There are many words you may use to mean "large": *huge, enormous, massive, immense, monstrous, gigantic, monumental, titanic, macroscopic.* But you must decide which word fits your meaning best. The word *titanic,* for example, comes from mythology. The Titans were the offspring of the Gigantes, or giants, said to have been the first creatures on earth. (One famous offspring of the Gigantes was Atlas, who held up the heavens on his shoulders.)

The British ocean liner *Titanic* was so named because at the time of its construction it was the largest ship ever built. From the history of the word *Titanic* you can see that the ship's name was appropriate. Calling it the *Enormous* or the *Monstrous* would have been inappropriate because these names would not have carried the same meaning and emotion as the name *Titanic.*

Look carefully at synonyms to see what meaning or meanings they carry. The words *leave* and *abandon* are synonyms, but they aren't always interchangeable. There is quite a difference in meaning between "He *left* the child at the bus station" and "He *abandoned* the child at the bus station."

Notice the difference between the connotative (suggested) meanings surrounding these words:

1. I'm a *humanitarian.*
   You're a *do-gooder.*
2. Sarah is *youthful.*
   Jane is *childish.*
3. My proposals are *bold.*
   Your proposals are *ambitious.*
4. The battalion *withdrew.*
   The army *retreated.*
5. John is *frugal.*
   Jack is *stingy.*

The first sentence in each of these examples is more or less complimentary; that is, the italicized word carries a *good connotation*. The second sentence in each example suggests a lack of success or character; that is, the italicized word carries a *bad connotation*. In the following exercise, you will check your understanding of good and bad connotations.

Words for the good and bad   Self-help

In each word pair, select the word that carries a bad connotation. Check your answers in the **Answer Key**.

Example: flatter/praise   **Answer:** flatter

1. arty/artistic
2. short/squat
3. prisoner/jailbird
4. jailer/guard
5. error/blunder
6. clever/shy
7. cheap/inexpensive
8. inquisitive/nosy
9. gullible/credulous
10. slender/skinny
11. plan/scheme
12. plump/fat
13. young/green
14. elderly/old
15. frisk/search

When you are writing, the skillful use of synonyms eliminates repetition. One of the best places to find appropriate synonyms is the thesaurus because it classifies words according to ideas.

The thesaurus and writing

A quick check in a thesaurus would help you to avoid the repetition in the writing sample that follows. Notice that possible substitutes appear on the right.

The history of the English language is *different from* most European languages. In 500 A.D. *different* tribes lived in Britain. (various)
Their language was *different from* present-day English. (dissimilar to)

(unlike that of)

Different Roman emperors had ruled the (A number of)
tribes for 400 years. Some of the natives
had to learn a *different* language: Latin. But (strange)
most of the people continued to speak
their native tongue, a language *not much* (akin to)
different from Welsh.

About the year 400 many *different* tribes (foreign)
invaded the islands. Their language (the
tongue of the Angles, Saxons, and Jutes)
was *not much different from* the Dutch (somewhat like)
language. The new tongue spread into

different parts of Britain. But the tribes in   (other)
Wales and Scotland continued to speak
their *different* languages: Welsh and Gaelic.   (individual)

From the 700's to 1014, the Danes and
Norwegians attacked and began invasions
of the islands. *Different* Scandinavian kings   (A series of)
ruled Britain from 1014 to 1029. During
the invasion and ruling periods, many
Scandinavian words were introduced into
English. English also continued to borrow
different words from Latin due to Rome's   (a variety of)
efforts to Christianize the world during
the Middle Ages.

In 1066 William the Conqueror brought
over *a different* language: French. Thus from   (an additional)
1066 to the 13th century, two *different*   (separate)
languages were spoken in England:
English by most of the common people,
and French by the courtiers and other
aristocrats.

The idea behind this sample is not to show that you should
avoid the word *different* altogether. You should, however, be
alert to the fact that there are many ways to express your
ideas without repetition. You should not avoid repeating a
word such as *different* if that word is appropriate and the
repetition does not distract the reader.

The responsibility for choice of words (often called *diction*)
rests with you as a speaker or writer trying to communicate.
In choosing words, the main goal is clear communication.
Choose the synonyms that make things clear and always use a
thesaurus with care and thought.

Although a great many synonyms are listed for your choice
in a thesaurus, you must still consider both the denotation and
connotation of the word you choose. You must also keep in
mind *semantic shift;* that is, the change in meaning that words
undergo. Words in a thesaurus are not always exact synonyms
for given words; they are often only related—sometimes
faintly.

The following exercise will give you some practice in
recognizing synonymous relationships between words. Notice
the variety and discrimination that the word choices add to
each sentence.

Synonym recall   Self-help

This exercise tests your recognition of synonyms. Add letters
to complete each synonym for the word underlined in the
sentence. Check your answers in the **Answer Key.**

Example: The old man <u>walked</u> down the street.
shu_ _ _ _ _
st_ _ _ _ _ _ _
am_ _ _ _ _
str_ _ _ _ _ _
Answers: shuffled, stumbled, ambled, strolled

1. The children were wary of the <u>strange</u> old woman.
o_ _
ecc_ _ _ _ _ _ _
biz_ _ _ _ _
pec_ _ _ _ _ _

2. Everyone likes John because he is a <u>friendly</u> person.
soc_ _ _ _ _ _
cor_ _ _ _ _
ami_ _ _ _ _
nei_ _ _ _ _ _ _ _

3. Tom <u>ate</u> all of the candy.
con_ _ _ _ _ _
gob_ _ _ _ _
dev_ _ _ _ _ _
gor_ _ _

4. Mrs. Jones is known for her <u>frugal</u> ways.
thr_ _ _ _ _
eco_ _ _ _ _ _ _ _
sav_ _ _
pars_ _ _ _ _ _ _ _

5. An illness left her in a <u>weak</u> condition.
fee_ _ _
fr_ _ _ _ _e
fr_ _ _ _
del_ _ _ _ _

6. Do you think she will <u>pardon</u> his tardiness?
ex_ _ _ _ _
fo_ _ _ _ _e
ov_ _ _ _ _ _k
di_ _ _ _ _

7. The teacher does not tolerate <u>mistakes</u> in spelling.
   er_ _ _ _
   sli_ _
   blu_ _ _ _ _
   fau_ _ _

8. The little girl was <u>crying</u>.
   so_ _ _ _g
   ba_ _ _ _g
   whi_ _ _ _ _ _g
   blu_ _ _ _ _ _g

9. She <u>puzzled</u> Sam with her actions.
   con_ _ _ _ _
   per_ _ _ _ _ _
   bew_ _ _ _ _ _ _
   mys_ _ _ _ _ _

10. The boys were engaged in a noisy <u>quarrel</u>.
    squ_ _ _ _ _
    dis_ _ _ _
    arg_ _ _ _ _
    br_ _ l

11. The principal was known for acting <u>prudently</u>.
    wi_ _ _ _
    cau_ _ _ _ _ _ _
    dis_ _ _ _ _ _ _
    jud_ _ _ _ _ _ _ _

12. The children's <u>behavior</u> embarrassed their mother.
    man_ _ _ _
    con_ _ _ _
    comp_ _ _ _ _ _ _
    dep_ _ _ _ _ _ _ _

13. The flowers began to <u>fade</u> after we picked them.
    dr_ _ _
    wi_ _ _ _r
    sh_ _ _ _l
    wi_ _

14. The man paid for his <u>rash</u> actions.
    rec_ _ _ _ _
    foo_ _ _ _ _ _
    tho_ _ _ _ _ _ _s
    ha_ _ _

15. He <u>admires</u> his grandfather.
    ado_ _ _
    ido_ _ _ _ _
    wor_ _ _ _ _
    rev_ _ _ _

16. Mary's father <u>advised</u> her to save money.
    ur__ __ __
    inst__ __ __ __ __
    cou__ __ __ __ __
    adm__ __ __ __ __ __ __

17. Will there be a <u>large</u> supply of apples this year?
    amp__ __
    abu__ __ __ __ __
    pl__ __ __ __f__ __
    cop__ __ __ __

18. The teacher <u>reprimanded</u> Tom for his habitual tardiness.
    cri__ __ __ __ __ __d
    reb__ __ __ __
    repr__ __ __ __ __
    chi__ __ __

19. The new girl <u>charmed</u> all the boys.
    enc__ __ __ __ __ __
    fas__ __ __ __ __ __ __
    cap__ __ __ __ __ __ __
    all__ __ __ __ __

20. The old woman was <u>cheated</u> out of her savings.
    tri__ __ __ __
    swi__ __ __ __ __
    du__ __ __
    fle__ __ __ __

Using antonyms

You have been looking at how you can conveniently classify words by the similarity of their general meaning. These words are synonyms. Another way to group words is to think about their differences. Word pairs of opposite meaning include examples such as *wet* and *dry, hot* and *cold, forward* and *backward, praise* and *blame, blunt* and *sharp*. Words of opposite meaning are antonyms, from *anti-* ("opposite, against") + *onym* ("name").

Studying and using antonyms helps you realize the importance of the idea of opposites in your language. You develop another technique for classifying. The best time to learn the word *female*, for example, is when you learn the word *male*. It's easier to learn *gander* when you learn *goose*. (Do you know which one is feminine?)

Classifying antonyms

You should learn *pessimism* when you learn *optimism*. You might as well learn *substructure* while you're learning *superstructure*. The words *alpha* ("beginning") and *omega* ("ending") are easily learned together. This approach will save

time and energy. You will master two ideas at a time instead
of one.

What is the great importance of opposites, or antonyms, in
language? Their importance comes from *opposition,* which shows
relationship. There is a connection of ideas between words of
opposite meaning. You understand *big* objects because you've
seen *small* ones. You recognize *death* because you know *life.*

**Hidden
relationships**

There are hidden relationships between words of opposite
meaning such as *left* and *right, motion* and *rest, good* and *evil.* You
understand *darkness* because you've experienced *light.* Without
heat there is no idea of *cold.* One word is understood through a
knowledge of the other.

You deal with opposites in all areas of life. Examples are
emotion (*love* and *hate*), direction (*north* and *south*), mathematics
(*positive* and *negative*), shape (*convex* and *concave*). The study of
opposite ideas is an important part of vocabulary building and
language development. Think hard about word opposites and
underlying relationships between them. Understand that words
don't stand by themselves like statues. They are mobile and
dynamic. They mingle with other words. Remember, one word
leads to another.

Think of masculine and feminine words that can be learned
in pairs: *nannygoat* and *billygoat, mare* and *stallion, doe* and *buck,
peahen* and *peacock.* Did you know that a female whale is a *cow*
and a male is a *bull?* Here are some other female/male pairs:

	Female	Male
bear	sow	boar
fox	vixen	dog
donkey	jenny	jackass
rabbit	doe	buck
rat	doe	buck

In learning opposite word pairs, you learn two words at once,
you learn two ideas at once, and you have them classified.
They're in your mental filing system. See how solid your
knowledge of antonyms can become with the following
exercises.

Self-help

Opposites worth learning

This exercise deals with antonym pairs. It has two parts, the
second built upon the first. In part 1, you add letters to
complete the clue given to the right of each word to form
antonyms. Part 2 lists all the answers, but the exercise is
reversed. You add letters to the clue to the right again, this

time remembering the words that were listed for you in part
1. When you have finished, look up any unfamiliar words in
the dictionary. The two parts serve as each other's answer keys.

Examples: Part 1: alpha and om_ _ _   **Answers:** omega

Part 2: omega and al_ _ _   alpha

Part 1

1. zenith   na_ _ _
2. prologue   ep_ _ _ _ _ _
3. progress   re_ _ _ _ _ _
4. propel   re_ _ _
5. immigrate   em_ _ _ _ _ _
6. prone   su_ _ _ _
7. microcosm   ma_ _ _ _ _ _ _
8. centrifugal   ce_ _ _ _ _ _ _ _
9. ante meridiem   po_ _ _ _ _ _ _ _ _ _
10. plethora   de_ _ _ _ _
11. explode   im_ _ _ _ _ _
12. homogeneous   he_ _ _ _ _ _ _ _ _
13. hypersensitive hy_ _ _ _ _ _ _ _ _ _
14. megaphone   mi_ _ _ _ _ _ _
15. multilateral   un_ _ _ _ _ _ _
16. polygamy   mo_ _ _ _ _ _
17. post-bellum   an_ _ _-_ _ _ _ _ _
18. extramural   in_ _ _ _ _ _ _ _
19. benefactor   ma_ _ _ _ _ _
20. overpass   un_ _ _ _ _ _ _
21. neolithic   pa_ _ _ _ _ _ _ _ _
22. import   ex_ _ _ _
23. excise   in_ _ _ _
24. accord   di_ _ _ _ _
25. anterior   po_ _ _ _ _ _ _
26. superior   in_ _ _ _ _ _
27. interior   ex_ _ _ _ _
28. claustrophobia ag_ _ _ _ _ _ _ _ _
29. hibernate   es_ _ _ _ _ _
30. ameliorative   pe_ _ _ _ _ _ _ _ _

Part 2

1. nadir   ze_ _ _ _ _
2. epilogue   pr_ _ _ _ _ _
3. regress   pr_ _ _ _ _ _
4. repel   pr_ _ _ _
5. emigrate   im_ _ _ _ _ _ _
6. supine   pr_ _ _
7. macrocosm   mi_ _ _ _ _ _ _
8. centripetal   ce_ _ _ _ _ _ _ _ _
9. post meridiem   an_ _ _ _ _ _ _ _ _ _ _

10. dearth   pl__ __ __ __ __ __
11. implode   ex__ __ __ __ __ __
12. heterogeneous   ho__ __ __ __ __ __ __ __ __
13. hyposensitive   hy__ __ __ __ __ __ __ __ __ __ __
14. microphone   me__ __ __ __ __ __ __
15. unilateral   mu__ __ __ __ __ __ __ __ __
16. monogamy   po__ __ __ __ __ __ __
17. ante-bellum   po__ __-__ __ __ __ __ __ __
18. intramural   ex__ __ __ __ __ __ __ __
19. malefactor   be__ __ __ __ __ __ __ __
20. underpass   ov__ __ __ __ __ __ __
21. paleolithic   ne__ __ __ __ __ __ __
22. export   im__ __ __ __ __
23. incise   ex__ __ __ __ __
24. discord   ac__ __ __ __ __
25. posterior   an__ __ __ __ __ __ __
26. inferior   su__ __ __ __ __ __ __
27. interior   ex__ __ __ __ __ __ __
28. agoraphobia   cl__ __ __ __ __ __ __ __ __ __ __
29. estivate   hi__ __ __ __ __ __ __
30. pejorative   am__ __ __ __ __ __ __ __ __ __

Self-help   Recognizing antonyms

Now remove antonyms from meaning groups in which they do not belong. Pick the antonyms out of each meaning group given. When you are done, look up any unfamiliar words in the dictionary. Check your answers in the **Answer Key.**

> **Example:** *Heavy:* fat, thin, rotund, obese, lean, overweight, emaciated
>
> **Answer:** The antonyms are *thin, lean,* and *emaciated.* They do not belong in the meaning group "heavy."

1. *Sadness:* somber, blithe, convivial, inconsolable, pensive, pathetic, saturnine, dispirited, melancholy, despondent, calamitous, rapturous, dejected, doleful, grave, jovial

2. *Like or same:* corresponding, reconstructing, discrepant, unique, resembling, homogeneous, simulating, monotonous, antonymous, analogous, synonymous, homogenized, homonymous, homographic, congruent

3. *Changing:* transposed, convertible, commuting, transient, fluctuating, deviating, stable, inverted, reformed, veering, variable, transferred, migrating, mutating, intransigent, modified

4. *Rough:* gnarled, prickly, crinkled, unctuous, furrowed, knurled, suave, abrasive, corrugated, craggy, angular, scabrous, scraggly, gruff, serrated, lubricated

5. *Short:* concise, curt, pruned, contracted, abridged, expanded, condensed, terse, succinct, curtailed, precise, cropped, abbreviated, gangling, protracted, clipped

6. *Weak:* decrepit, debilitated, stalwart, languid, infirm, pungent, irresolute, potent, effete, enervated, impotent, hamstrung, anemic, flaccid, feckless, feeble

7. *Beginning:* debut, origin, expiration, prelude, commencement, genesis, outset, nativity, awakening, prologue, overture, ultimatum, primeval, epilogue, inception, consummation

8. *Important:* prominent, paltry, eminent, esteemed, weighty, paramount, cardinal, imposing, consequential, momentous, overriding, imperative, salient, trifling, material, inane

Completing the preceding exercises should have increased your awareness of antonyms, reinforced your understanding of synonyms, and sharpened your vocabulary through the study of each. Your final practice in this section involves word files of likes and opposites. This time decide whether pairs of words are made up of two synonyms or two antonyms.

Word files of likes and opposites   Self-help

The word files that follow are classified under headings that contain antonym pairs (like "Success or Failure"). Following the headings are more word pairs that you will file. Some are synonym pairs and some are antonym pairs.

File each word in the pair by assigning it the first letter of the appropriate synonym in the heading. Then indicate if the pair is a synonym pair or antonym pair. When you have completed all the pairs under a heading, go back to see how many synonym pairs and how many antonym pairs you have under the heading. Check your answers in the **Answer Key.**

   Examples: *Success or Failure*
                   a. setback   rout
                   b. succumbed   ascended
   Answers: a. F, F—synonyms [*Setback* and *rout* are both
                               synonyms for *failure* (F). They
                               form a synonym pair.]
                   b. F, S—antonyms [*Succumbed* is a synonym for
                               failure (F); *ascended* is a synonym
                               for *success* (S). They form an
                               antonym pair.]

Word files

1. *Success or Failure*
   a. progress   blunder
   b. conquer   muff
   c. advance   stymie
   d. slip   hold
   e. achieve   stumble
   f. profit   win
   g. prosper   decline
   h. botch   triumph
   i. wrest   fumble
   j. bungle   accomplish

2. *Wealth or Poverty*
   a. riches   destitution
   b. fortune   want
   c. capital   privation
   d. need   indigence
   e. lack   surplus
   f. treasure   impoverishment
   g. bonanza   pay dirt
   h. pauper   starveling
   i. opulence   beggarliness
   j. affluence   penury

3. *Proud or Humble*
   a. boast   brag
   b. meek   submissive
   c. swagger   demure
   d. strut   flaunt
   e. lowly   lordly
   f. arrogant   humiliated
   g. bragging   overbearing
   h. servility   shame
   i. haughty   stiff
   j. unassuming   modest

4. *Equal or Unequal*
   a. evenness   inferiority
   b. balance   harmony
   c. inequality   disparity
   d. matched   lopsided
   e. level   convoluted
   f. uneven   equitable
   g. equalize   overmatch
   h. superior   equilateral
   i. tie   standoff
   j. dead heat   shutout

5. *Sure or Unsure*

a. certain	doubtful
b. unreliable	uncertain
c. hazy	hesitating
d. uncontested	foggy
e. secure	guaranteed
f. assured	ascertained
g. positive	manifest
h. dubious	insecure
i. unerring	inviolate
j. confident	determined

6. *Life or Death*

a. vitality	liveliness
b. fatality	mortality
c. alive	vibrant
d. manslaughter	homicide
e. nourishment	nurturing
f. perished	lifeless
g. suicide	killing
h. resuscitate	revive
i. expire	depart
j. nascence	nativity

7. *Ruly or Unruly*

a. disciplined	wild
b. mild	violent
c. reckless	barbarian
d. undisciplined	savage
e. trained	meek
f. restrained	fierce
g. domesticated	vandalistic
h. primitive	cultured
i. subdued	muted
j. docile	submissive

8. *Accuse or Excuse*

a. case	lawsuit
b. sentence	acquittal
c. justify	challenge
d. citation	summons
e. acquit	condemn
f. clear	whitewash
g. sue	settle
h. indict	dismiss
i. pardon	impeach
j. incriminate	vindicate

Many people never become familiar with one of the most useful books they can own: the dictionary. Unfortunately, many high school and college students sell their dictionaries when they finish the courses for which a dictionary is required.

Some people consider the dictionary merely a book containing a list of words and meanings, nothing more. They use the dictionary to define or spell a word, and that's the end of their interest. But in addition to defining words, a dictionary provides a great deal of other useful information about words.

This section shows how to make the maximum use of a dictionary. It explains all the different kinds of information about words that you can find in a dictionary. And it gives you ways of using that information to improve your use of words.

The dictionary: a wealth of knowledge

The Greeks and Romans made the first dictionaries. The word *dictionary* is from Latin *dictionarium,* related to *dicere* (say). The word *diction* means "speech" or "word." A dictionary explains the many words of a language. It helps you extend and sharpen your vocabulary because it broadens the number of words you meet and the number of ways you can use them.

But the dictionary is not only a record of words and their meanings; it is also a kind of depository for people's experiences through the ages. Words are the labels of experiences. The dictionary helps you learn more *about* words, and the more you know about words the better you use them.

Make up your mind to use the dictionary intelligently, and both your vocabulary and your understanding of words will grow quickly. You can benefit most from a dictionary by learning what its abbreviations and symbols represent. This section will explain how to understand and use dictionary entries. The sample dictionary entries shown on page 86 come from *The World Book Dictionary.*

Learning from the dictionary

Look carefully at the sample dictionary entries. See what a collection of useful information the dictionary is? It gives you information on spelling, syllables, accents, pronunciation, parts of speech, definitions, inflections (changes in a word, such as stead*y* and stead*ier*), cross-references, common and proper nouns, abbreviations, symbols, illustrations, punctuation, synonyms, antonyms, homonyms (words that sound the same), and heteronyms (words usually spelled alike but having a different sound or meaning).

The dictionary also includes information on word usage; idioms (phrases peculiar to a language—for example, *give in* means "yield"); foreign terms and phrases; word origins (for example, the word *volt* is named after the Italian physicist Alessandro Volta); coined, or made-up, words; slang; etymology (word derivation); neologisms (new words or new meanings for old words); and archaisms (out-of-date words such as *methinks*). The dictionary also includes figures of speech (expressions in which words are used out of their literal meaning or in striking combinations to add beauty or force).

A good dictionary also contains helpful historical and literary allusions, or references. If you look up words in the *A* section of the dictionary you will find, for example, *armada* (a fleet of warships), but you will also find a reference to the famous Armada, the Spanish fleet England defeated in 1588.

Authors often refer to a final great conflict as an *Armageddon.* The dictionary tells you that Armageddon (in the Bible) is the scene of the final battle between good and evil.

Sample dictionary entries

Word Entries begin in bold black type. Only proper nouns are capitalized. The first letter of the entry extends into the margin for easy location. This dictionary uses an asterisk to indicate that the entry is accompanied by an illustration.

Illustrations clarify the definitions. Labels show which meaning of the word is illustrated.

Pronunciations are given in phonetic symbols. This dictionary has a key to its phonetic symbols at the bottom of each right-hand page, with more detailed information at the front of the book.

Parts of Speech Labels show the word's grammatical use. Any word used as more than one part of speech is defined accordingly. The parts of speech are abbreviated, as in adj. for adjective and n. for noun. Verbs are shown as transitive (v.t.) or intransitive (v.i.).

Phrases that include the key word but have special meanings of their own are explained separately.

Synonyms that have the same or nearly the same meaning as the defined words appear immediately after the definition.

Synonym Studies explain in detail the various shades of meaning of some synonyms. All these studies include examples.

Usage Notes explain points of spelling or grammar and advise how to use the word in speaking or writing.

---

*ab|do|men (ab′də mən, ab dō′-), *n.* **1a** the part of the body containing the stomach and the intestines; belly. In man and other mammals the abdomen is a large cavity between the chest (thorax) and the pelvis, and also contains the liver, pancreas, kidneys, and spleen. **b** a corresponding region in vertebrates below mammals. **2** the last of the three parts of the body of insects and many other arthropods, including spiders and crustaceans. [< Latin *abdōmen*]

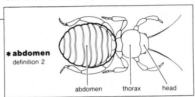

*abdomen
definition 2

abdomen   thorax   head

ab|dom|i|nal (ab dom′ə nəl), *adj.* of the abdomen; in the abdomen; for the abdomen: *Bending the body exercises the abdominal muscles.* SYN: ventral, visceral. — **ab|dom′i|nal|ly,** *adv.*
abdominal brain, = solar plexus.
ab|dom|i|nous (ab dom′ə nəs), *adj.* = potbellied.

a|bide¹ (ə bīd′), *v.,* **a|bode** or **a|bid|ed, a|bid|ing.**
— *v.t.* **1** to put up with; endure; tolerate: *A good housekeeper can't abide dust. She can't abide him.* SYN: bear, stand. **2** to await submissively; submit to; sustain: *He must abide his fatal doom* (Joanna Baillie). **3** to await defiantly; withstand: *He soon learned to abide … terrors which most of my bolder companions shrank from encountering* (Hugh Miller). **4** *Archaic.* to wait for; await: *I will abide the coming of my lord* (Tennyson).
— *v.i.* **1** to stay; remain; wait: *Abide with me for a time. I'll call upon you straight: abide within* (Shakespeare). *He within his ships abode the while* (William Cowper). **2** to continue to live (in a place); reside; dwell: *No martin there in winter shall abide* (John Dryden). **3** to continue (in some state or action): *… ye shall abide in my love* (John 15:10). **4** to continue in existence; endure: *Thou hast established the earth, and it abideth* (Psalms 119:90). SYN: last. **5** *Archaic.* to be left. **6** *Obsolete.* to stay behind.
abide by, a to accept and follow out; be bound by: *Both teams will abide by the umpire's decision.* **b** to remain faithful to; stand firm by; be true to; fulfill: *Abide by your promise.*

a|bil|i|ty (ə bil′ə tē), *n., pl.* **-ties. 1** the power to do or act: *the ability to think clearly. The old horse still has the ability to work.* SYN: capability, capacity. **2** skill: *Washington had great ability as a general.* **3** power to do some special thing; natural gift; talent: *Musical ability often shows itself early in life.* [< Middle French *habilité,* learned borrowing from Latin *habilitās* aptness < *habilis* able]
— **Syn. 2, 3 Ability, talent** mean special power to do or for doing something. **Ability** applies to a demonstrated physical or mental power to do a certain thing well: *She has developed unusual ability as a dancer.* **Talent** applies to an inborn capacity for doing a special thing: *a child with a remarkable talent for painting.*
▶ After **ability** the infinitive of a verb preceded by *to* is used, rather than the gerund preceded by *of: A lawyer needs the ability to think clearly,* not *of thinking clearly.* The preposition used after *ability* and before a noun is *in: in ability in music.*

A|bim|e|lech (ə bim′ə lek), *n.* a son of Gideon who was set up as king of Israel by the people of Shechem (in the Bible, Judges 9).
ab init., ab initio.
ab in|i|ti|o (ab′ i nish′ē ō), *Latin.* from the beginning: *The decree was not a nullity in the sense of being void ab initio* (London Times).

Definitions give the precise meanings of words. If a word has more than one meaning, the definitions are numbered. This dictionary lists the most common meanings first. Some dictionaries present definitions in historical order, with the earliest meanings first.

Examples point out how the word is used in phrases or sentences.

Cross-References show that the form consulted is less widely used than some other form, which has its own main entry.

Other Forms of the word include the principal parts of verbs, unusual plural forms, and comparative forms for adjectives.

Quotations from well-known authors or publications illustrate the meaning of the word. The sources of quotations are identified.

Levels of Usage Labels, such as *Slang, Informal, Archaic,* and *Obsolete,* indicate when and where the word is acceptable in current English usage. Each label is defined in a list at the front of the dictionary.

Derivations tell what language or languages a word comes from, usually with its meaning in the original language. The symbol < means comes from.

Foreign Words and Phrases in common use in English have entries that give their pronunciation and translation, often with examples or illustrative quotations.

If you look up the word *arachnid* (spider), nearby you will also find a mythological character, *Arachne,* who challenged the goddess Athena to a spinning contest. The goddess changed the challenger into a spider. *Arachne* literally means "spider."

As you can see, the historical and literary information that the dictionary provides is important to your vocabulary development. This dictionary use will be discussed in more detail later in this section.

How to use the dictionary

If you open the dictionary to find a word and you flip through the pages hoping to find it by chance, you're going about dictionary use the wrong way. The dictionary is organized to help you find words quickly. You have to become familiar with this organization to use the dictionary effectively.

Dictionaries have a guide word at the top of each page. Notice that term again: A *guide word* is meant to guide you, help you find a word quickly and efficiently. If you ignore guide words (and many people do), you are wasting valuable time running your eyes up and down the pages looking for your word.

Let guide words be your guide

If the guide words on facing pages are *symbolic* and *sympathy,* you won't find *symphonic* between them. These guide words show the first and last entries on the two pages. You know you have to turn to the next page to find *symphonic.* If the guide words are *sack* and *saddlesore,* would you find *saddletree* somewhere on the two pages? No, you would not. But you would find *sacrament.*

The dictionary contains *word entries.* These are listed alphabetically and appear in boldface type. Entries may be single words, compound words, or phrases. Compound words are listed alphabetically according to the first word *(sweat suit).*

Word entries

Some words have more then one spelling. *Vise* (a holding tool), for example, is also listed as *vice. Homographs* (words spelled alike but different in meaning) are assigned numbers: for example, *vice*[1] (evil habit); *vice*[2] (a vise); and *vice*[3] (in place of).

Although a small dictionary is useful at times, it is often inadequate for significant word study. Be wary of a dictionary that gives only one or two definitions for each word, as may be the case with smaller editions.

Dictionary definitions

Good dictionaries include all known definitions of a word and often include appropriate sentences to illustrate the word's meaning(s). The word *pot* in a good dictionary, for example, will have several illustrative sentences:

pot: He ate a *pot* of soup. (a dish or vessel)

The Englishman drank a *pot* of ale. (container for liquid)

His business partner got the bigger share of the *pot.* (money)

The best poker player won the *pot.* (all the money bet)

The old ballplayer developed a *pot.* (belly)

He lost his job and went to *pot.* (an idiom meaning "ruin")

Golfers in Scotland try to stay out of *pot* bunkers. (deep sand traps)

Parts of speech

Some people don't realize that the dictionary indicates the parts of speech of words. Here are the eight parts of speech, along with an example of each.

noun—jury	*adjective*—intense
pronoun—they	*preposition*—with
verb—admonish	*conjunction*—but
adverb—solemnly	*interjection*—hurrah!

Sometimes a word can be used as more than one part of speech. In this case, abbreviations of the parts of speech that apply to that word will appear alphabetically. If the entry word is *second,* for example, *adj.* (adjective), *adv.* (adverb), *n.* (noun), and *v.* (verb) will appear after the word. Sample sentences will also appear for each part of speech:

second: *adj.,* the next after the first

He won *second* prize.

adv., in the second group

She speaks *second* on the program.

n., an assistant

The *second* gave the boxer the advice.

v., to support

I *second* the motion.

Synonyms in the dictionary

One of the useful features of a good dictionary is the presence of adequate synonyms. A good dictionary might, for example, include the word *steal* and useful synonyms like *pilfer* and *filch.* It will also illustrate the shades, or nuances, of meaning for each synonym:

Steal is a general word for taking from another. (Thieves tried to *steal* the crown jewels.)

Pilfer means to "steal in small amounts." (The number of bolts *pilfered* from the factory is small.)

Filch means "stealthy pilfering of insignificant items." (The boys *filched* the matches from the mantel.)

Looking carefully at synonyms in a good dictionary will help you learn more about the *denotation* (literal meaning) and *connotation* (emotional or suggested meaning) of words. You'll begin to see the differences in meaning between the words *color, tinge, tint,* and *hue.* You'll begin to notice the slight differences between the meanings of words in color families: *brown, brunette, tan, olive, khaki, fawn, auburn, umber, henna, puce.*

A good dictionary includes antonyms as well as synonyms. Under a given entry you may learn, for example, that the word *clean* has the antonym *dirty.* Other antonyms for *clean* may also appear: *filthy, soiled, vile, sordid,* and *squalid.* Seeing these antonyms at a glance helps you develop greater fluency in your choice of adjectives. It increases your awareness of the great variety of words available to express an idea.

Antonyms in the dictionary

An interesting feature of a good dictionary is the presence of commonly used phrases such as "hammer and tongs" or "hammer and sickle." Some of these phrases are called clichés, or overly used expressions. Sometimes we use phrases such as these without analyzing them. Their meaning arises from the associations surrounding the word pair, not from the words themselves. Would you know what *fro* means, for example, if you didn't see it in "to and *fro* (back)"? What's *tucker* in "bib and *tucker?"* Look in the dictionary to find out. Then complete the following exercise, which introduces you to many phrases found in the dictionary.

Phrases and clichés

Analyzing phrases   Self-help

Complete the following phrases by finding the word that fits the blanks. Check your answers in the **Answer Key.**

    Example: back and f_ _ _ _   **Answer:** forth

1. bride and g_ _ _ _ _
2. law and o_ _ _ _ _
3. fine and d_ _ _ _ _
4. safe and s_ _ _ _ _
5. wear and t_ _ _ _
6. ball and c_ _ _ _ _
7. assault and b_ _ _ _ _ _ _
8. trial and e_ _ _ _ _
9. stress and s_ _ _ _ _ _
10. breaking and e_ _ _ _ _ _ _ _ _
11. cap and g_ _ _ _
12. leaps and b_ _ _ _ _ _
13. life and l_ _ _ _
14. null and v_ _ _

15. nook and c_ _ _ _ _
16. beck and c_ _ _ _
17. cloak and d_ _ _ _ _ _
18. cease and d_ _ _ _ _ _
19. fair and s_ _ _ _ _ _
20. input and o_ _ _ _ _ _
21. length and b_ _ _ _ _ _ _
22. nip and t_ _ _ _
23. means and e_ _ _ _
24. meek and m_ _ _ _
25. rant and r_ _ _ _
26. rack and r_ _ _ _
27. straight and n_ _ _ _ _ _
28. rank and f_ _ _ _
29. rough and r_ _ _ _ _
30. flotsam and j_ _ _ _ _ _
31. frankincense and m_ _ _ _ _
32. overt and c_ _ _ _ _ _
33. passive and a_ _ _ _ _ _
34. shield and b_ _ _ _ _ _ _
35. kith and k_ _
36. spit and p_ _ _ _ _
37. sum and s_ _ _ _ _ _ _ _
38. time and t_ _ _ _
39. vim and v_ _ _ _ _
40. wax and w_ _ _ _
41. ways and m_ _ _ _ _
42. lo and b_ _ _ _ _

Dictionary use improves word use

You can see that a good dictionary helps you build a good
vocabulary. The dictionary is especially useful in learning about
metaphor.

**Metaphor and
the dictionary**

A good dictionary contains many metaphors that will extend
and refine your vocabulary. A metaphor is a figure of speech
that suggests likeness.

When you say someone is "level-headed," you are using
metaphor. Your meaning is not literal. You are saying that the
person is well balanced, has good sense or good judgment.
You are comparing the person's mind with the balance of a
level. You do not mean that the person's head looks level. In
other words, you are creating a mental picture outside the
specific words you have used. You are creating a metaphor.

A good dictionary explains that the word *metaphor* means to
"carry over or across," to "transfer." *Metaphora* is Greek for
"transfer," from *meta-* (across) + *pherein* (to carry). When you

use a metaphor, you transfer the characteristics of one word or idea to another. In doing so, you add zest to a sentence and make ideas clearer and sharper.

The use of metaphor in speech is a natural thing. People *metaphorize* in their speech every day. If people are angry, they may say they're "burned up." If something is clear, they might say "it's plain as day." If someone is clever or shrewd, he or she may be called a "sly fox."

Vocabulary grows by the use of metaphors. They deal with ordinary life. Here are some metaphors made up from words for parts of the body: This street is a main "artery." That street is a traffic "bottleneck." Make a "left-hand" turn. A highway sign reads "soft shoulders."

People use phrases such as won by a "hair," the "tongue" of a shoe, the "leg" of a chair, and "foot" the bill. They speak of a "head" of cabbage, a "heel" of bread, "lady fingers," and "navel" oranges. People also discuss the long "arm" of the law, "intestinal" fortitude, buildings "gutted" by fire, the last man on the "face" of the earth, "digital" computers, and electronic "brains."

People say: I can't "stomach" him. She made no "bones" about it. The worker is the "backbone" of the country. How can we "head" off growing inflation? Aren't you just splitting "hairs"? Don't try to "palm" it off on me. It's an affair of the "heart." She'll make them "toe" the mark. That was a real "rib" tickler.

Body metaphors are used in all areas of living. A plumber uses "elbow" joints. He puts a pipe in the "jaws" of a vise. There's talk about the "mouth" of a river, the "eye" of a hurricane, the "teeth" of a storm. Miners speak of a "vein" of ore or coal. Cape Canaveral is called the "nerve-center" of the space program. A space rocket has a "nose" cone and an "umbilical" cord. In short, metaphor is the substance of life.

H. W. Fowler in *A Dictionary of Modern English Usage* remarks that ". . . our vocabulary is largely built on metaphors, even though we are not always aware that we are using them." You should be aware of the metaphors you use. Practice finding metaphors in the exercise that follows.

Recognizing metaphors   **Self-help**

Find the metaphor in each of the following sentences. Check your answers in the **Answer Key.**

> **Example:** Winter's icy fingers have arrived.
> **Answer:** icy fingers

1. Many loyal hearts followed the king into battle.
2. The dog's fur felt soft and feathery.
3. The Reds slaughtered the Pirates.
4. The fifth hole on this golf course doglegs to the right.
5. Moonlight sifted through the shutters.
6. There was only a handful of fans left.
7. Her luggage weighs a ton.
8. The explorers feasted their eyes on the bay.
9. We need to uproot crime in the cities.
10. His happiness made his heart dance.

Clichés

Some metaphors are used so often that they become *clichés*—overused and worn-out phrases. Many metaphors using body parts have become clichés: She's a "highbrow." He's "nosy." He's looking for a "hand-out." They "wink" at her faults. They see "eye" to "eye." He kept them under his "thumb." You'll have to "face" the music. He's a pain in the "neck."

Colors also become metaphorized into clichés. People can be described as being "green" with envy and "purple" with rage. Someone may be called a "yellow-bellied" coward. An inexperienced worker is "green." A sad person is "blue." Your credit may be as good as "gold." If you owe money, you're in the "red."

Many similes are also overused. (A *simile* is a phrase that uses *like* or *as* to make a direct comparison.) You hear these simile clichés quite often: "right as rain," "quick as a wink," "slow as molasses," "ugly as sin," "pretty as a picture."

Clichés, though fun at times, should be avoided in formal writing. Sometimes they are necessary for social purposes, however, or for informal writing.

People often make mistakes when they write clichés, as in "pretty as a *pitcher*" instead of *picture.* In the following exercise, see if you can spot the spelling mistakes.

Self-help   Spelling clichés

Find the misspelled word(s) in each of the following clichés; then rewrite the word correctly. Check your answers in the **Answer Key.**

Example: a marshall tread   **Answer:** martial

1. the ilk of human kindness
2. overhelping odds
3. pails into insignificance
4. the paramount tissue

5. boor but honest
6. goes without staying
7. leave no scone unburned
8. led to the halter
9. wore a jeerful aspect
10. flagrant flowers
11. generous to a vault
12. great minds running in the same canal
13. preen with envy
14. hail and hardy
15. the curse of true love
16. mourned the deer departed
17. an enemy in our mist
18. sent a florid tribute
19. a lavishing beauty
20. wait with baited breath

The dictionary includes and explains the use of homonyms. Many people pay little attention to these, but homonyms are worth looking at for various reasons. Let's find out why.

Homonyms and vocabulary

Words that sound the same are *homonyms* (from *homo-*, "same," + *onym*, "name"). Homonyms sound alike but they may or may not be spelled alike. When homonyms are spelled alike, they are *homographs* (from *homo-*, "same," + *graph*, "write"). The words *hail* (a greeting) and *hail* (balls of ice) are homo*graphs*. They are spelled the same and they sound the same. *Fair* (average) and *fair* (weather) are also homographs.

When homonyms are not spelled alike, but are still pronounced the same way, they are called *homophones*. The word *homophone* comes from *homo-* (same) + *phone* (sound). Examples include *air* and *heir; bear* and *bare;* and *sight, cite,* and *site.* Notice again that these homophones are spelled differently but they are pronounced identically.

Homonyms fit into the classifying approach to vocabulary study. To acquaint yourself with these words, use the following table.

Homonyms

Term	Example	Same pronunciation?	Same spelling?	Same meaning?	Same derivation?
Homophones	write, right all, awl lead (metal) led (past tense of *lead*)	yes	no	no	no
Homographs	mail (letter) mail (armor)	yes	yes	no	no

Homonyms for fun

How can you change *manslaughter* to something funny? Add an apostrophe: *man's laughter*. Indeed, one of the best ways to improve your vocabulary is to have fun with words. You work with words, but you should also play with words. You can do so by creating riddles and puns with homonyms. Have you heard this riddle?

Why wasn't the symphony director hit by lightning?
He was a non-conductor.

Have you noticed that riddles involve the use of *puns,* or plays on words that sound alike? Have you ever thought of why puns exist? Creating puns is possible because some words have identical sounds. They are homonyms. Homonyms are the bases for puns. The context in which homonyms appear generally indicates their meaning, but puns put words into contexts in which the meanings can become confused. This librarian's remark had a double meaning:

"No talking *aloud (allowed)."*

The remark is a pun, a play on words.

When you use puns you take advantage of the ambiguity, or double meaning, of their sense. You also take advantage of their similar sound (remember, puns are homonyms). You can make statements like these:

The *buck* went into the bank to get a little *doe.*
The *baker* went to the bank because he needed *dough.*
The *baker* was not well *bred.*
They *told* the sexton, and the sexton *tolled* the bell.

Homonyms and spelling

Puns encourage you to look closely at words. You notice the difference in the meaning and spelling of often confused words. The study of homonyms (puns) is like the study of synonyms and antonyms. It is another useful way to practice word discrimination (choosing the right word according to the meaning you wish to express). Remember, spelling is word formation. Where you place the letters in a word makes a big difference.

Although they sound alike, there is a difference between *there* and *their*. The spelling is different and so is the meaning. This caution applies to other homonyms: *whose* and *who's, minor* and *miner, isle* and *aisle, principle* and *principal, steps* and *steppes.*

Some homonyms are a triple threat: *air, ere, heir; flew, flue, flu; frees, freeze, frieze; holy, wholly, holey; need, kneed, knead; oar, ore, o'er; rain, rein, reign; sear, sere, seer; sent, cent, scent; vein, vain, vane.* If you look closely at these homonyms together and practice spelling them, you'll soon learn to distinguish between them and you'll make fewer spelling errors. The following table lists homonyms for you. By looking at the homonyms grouped together, you are more likely to notice the differences in their spelling. Use the dictionary to find the meaning of the words you don't know.

Homonym list

air	ball	blue	bridal
heir	bawl	blew	bridle
ere			
e'er	band	bole	broach
	banned	boll	brooch
ale		bowl	
ail	bard		brows
	barred	bore	browse
all		boar	
awl	baron		burro
	barren	bored	burrow
aloud		board	borough
allowed	bass		
	base	born	bury
altar		borne	berry
alter	bate		
	bait	bow	but
ant		beau	butt
aunt	bazaar		
	bizarre	bow	by
arc		bough	buy
ark	be		bye
	bee	bowled	
assent		bold	cannon
ascent	bear		canon
	bare	boy	
ate		buoy	canvas
eight	beet		canvass
	beat	brake	
auger		break	carrot
augur	bell		carat
	belle	braze	caret
aught		braise	karat
ought	berth		
	birth	breach	cask
aye		breech	casque
eye	bier		
	beer	bred	cast
bad		bread	caste
bade	bin		
	been	brews	ceiling
bail		bruise	sealing
bale			

cellar	desert	feign	gauge
seller	dessert	fain	gage
chews	dew	feint	gild
choose	due	faint	guild
choir	die	ferule	gilt
quire	dye	ferrule	guilt
clause	discreet	find	gnu
claws	discrete	fined	knew
			new
clime	doe	fir	
climb	dough	fur	great
			grate
close	dun	flee	
clothes	done	flea	grown
			groan
colonel	dying	flew	
kernel	dyeing	flue	guessed
		flu	guest
core	earn		
corps	urn	flour	hail
		flower	hale
course	ewe		
coarse	yew	fold	hare
	you	foaled	hair
coward			
cowered	eyelet	fore	haul
	islet	four	hall
creek			
creak	faint	foul	heart
	feint	fowl	hart
crews			
cruise	fair	fourth	heel
cruse	fare	forth	heal
			he'll
cue	faker	frieze	
queue	fakir	frees	herd
		freeze	heard
current	fate		
currant	fete	gamble	here
		gambol	hear
dam	faun		
damn	fawn	gate	him
		gait	hymn
dear	feet		
deer	feat		

hoard
horde

hoarse
horse

hoes
hose

holy
wholly
holey

hour
our

hue
hew

idle
idol

I'll
isle
aisle

indict
indite

knows
nose

lane
lain

leaf
lief

leak
leek

least
leased

led
lead

lee
lea

lei
lay

lesson
lessen

liar
lyre

liken
lichen

lo
low

load
lode

lone
loan

loot
lute

lye
lie

maid
made

male
mail

mane
main

manner
manor

marry
merry

marshal
martial

maul
mall

maze
maize

mead
mede

meet
meat
mete

metal
mettle

mien
mean

might
mite

mind
mined

minor
miner

moan
mown

moat
mote

morn
mourn

muse
mews

mussel
muscle

mustered
mustard

nave
knave

nay
neigh

need
knead
kneed

night
knight

no
know

noes
nose
knows

none
nun

not
knot

oar
ore
o'er

ode
owed

one
won

oral
aural

our
hour

pair
pear
pare

palate
pallet

pale
pail

pane	praise	rest	sale
pain	prays	wrest	sail
	preys		
passed		right	seam
past	pray	write	seem
	prey	rite	
patients		wright	sear
patience	principal		seer
	principle	rime	sere
paws		rhyme	
pause	quartz		see
	quarts	ring	sea
peak		wring	
pique	rabbit		seed
	rabbet	rock	cede
pearl		roc	
purl	rack		seen
	wrack	rode	scene
peddle		road	
pedal	racket	rowed	sees
petal	racquet		seize
		roe	
peel	rain	row	sell
peal	rein		cell
	reign	roll	
piece		role	sense
peace	raise		cense
	raze	root	cents
pier	rays	route	
peer			sent
	rap	rows	cent
plane	wrap	rose	scent
plain			
	rapt	rude	serial
plate	rapped	rood	cereal
plait	wrapped		
		ruff	session
please	read	rough	cession
pleas	reed		
		rung	shoe
plum	real	wrung	shoo
plumb	reel		
		rye	sight
pole	reck	wry	site
poll	wreck		cite
		sac	
	red	sack	sign
	read		sine

skull	steal	team	vein
scull	steel	teem	vain
			vane
slay	step	tear	
sleigh	steppe	tare	vice
			vise
slight	stoup	tear	
sleight	stoop	tier	wade
			weighed
so	strait	the	
sow	straight	thee	wait
sew			weight
	style	there	
soar	stile	their	waste
sore		they're	waist
	succor		
soared	sucker	threw	wave
sword		through	waive
	suite		
sold	sweet	throws	way
soled		throes	weigh
	sunny		
some	sonny	time	we
sum		thyme	wee
	surf		
son	serf	toe	wear
sun		tow	ware
	surge		
soul	serge	told	week
sole		tolled	weak
	tale		
staid	tail	two	whole
stayed		to	hole
	taught	too	
stare	taut		wood
stair		use	would
	tax	yews	
stationery	tacks	ewes	wreak
stationary			reek
	tea	vale	
steak	tee	veil	
stake			

A homonym exercise follows. Your success will indicate how much you have learned about homonyms.

Self-help	Spelling homonyms

Select the correct homonym(s). Check your answers in the **Answer Key.**

> **Example:** Some modern cars have disk (breaks, brakes).
> **Answer:** brakes

1. Shaw's play *Pygmalion* was made into the play *My (Fare, Fair) Lady.*
2. Stainless (steal, steel) resists corrosion, or rust.
3. The (capital, capitol) of Brazil is Brasília.
4. The (Piece, Peace) Treaty of Versailles ended World War I.
5. Achilles' (heal, heel) was his only vulnerable spot.
6. In mythology, Orpheus enchanted wild beasts with his (liar, lyre).
7. In the Middle Ages, (knights, nights) often wore a (cote, coat) of (mail, male) in battle.
8. A feudal lord lived in a (manor, manner) with many servants.
9. John Philip Sousa composed popular (martial, marshall) music.
10. In Britain corn is called (maze, maize).
11. Oysters, clams, and (muscles, mussels) are species of mollusks.
12. After the war the troops were (mustard, mustered) out of the army.
13. John Keats wrote "(Owed, Ode) on a Grecian Urn."
14. The miner (mind, mined) a (vein, vain, vane) of iron (oar, ore, o'er).
15. (Beach, Beech) trees lined the (beech, beach).
16. Wedding (bells, belles) often ring for (bells, belles).
17. The (coward, cowered) (coward, cowered) behind the tree.
18. The captain changed (cruise, crews) for the (cruise, crews).
19. Do horses shed the (hare, hair) of the (main, mane) or the (tale, tail)?
20. A comma indicates a (paws, pause) after a (claws, clause).

Literature and the dictionary	The dictionary also contains literary and historical information. You may recall that in reading literature, you've seen expressions such as "It's like carrying coals to Newcastle" or "He met his Waterloo." You must fully recognize the meanings of these expressions in order to understand what an author is trying to say. Authors allude (indirectly refer) to Biblical, historical, or literary characters because they know that the allusion (reference) carries with it rich associations. The allusion will have a dramatic effect for those who understand it. It will clarify or emphasize a point. And writers

assume that the reader will already have made the acquaintance of the allusions used.

To understand the expression "carrying coals to Newcastle," you must know that Newcastle, England, mines coal. It is a coal center. Taking coals to Newcastle would therefore be like taking water to the ocean: a fruitless act. "Met his Waterloo" is a reference to Napoleon, who in 1815 lost a decisive battle at the site of this town in Belgium. To "meet one's Waterloo" means to take a tremendous loss.

Acquaintance with literary, historical, and Biblical allusions such as the "Gordian knot," "Pandora's box," "crossing the Rubicon," "the prodigal son," and "the patience of Job" increases your enjoyment and understanding of literature and extends your stock of words, meanings, and concepts. Many of these allusions are included in the dictionary. See how many Biblical allusions you know by completing the exercise that follows.

Biblical allusions   Self-help

Complete the following sentences by defining the italicized Biblical expressions. (All these expressions appear in the dictionary.) Check your answers in the **Answer Key.**

Example: He's in the *Land of Nod* means _____.
Answer: he is asleep

1. The *prodigal son* was a person who _____.
2. The *Promised Land* is _____.
3. If a person *raises Cain,* he or she _____.
4. He's like a *Samson* means _____.
5. A *shibboleth* is a _____.
6. The reporter called the judge another *Solomon,* meaning _____.
7. They were *good Samaritans* means _____.
8. It was a *behemoth* means _____.

A good dictionary also includes references to mythological characters. Vulcan, for example, is the Roman god of fire and the blacksmith for the gods. From Vulcan's name come the words *volcano* and *vulcanize.* From Fortuna, the Roman goddess of fortune or luck, comes the word *fortune.* Now test your knowledge of "mythological" nouns.

Self-help   Words from mythology

Write down as many words as you can think of that might come from the names of the gods and goddesses listed. To aid you, the duties or realms of the gods and goddesses appear with their names. You may be able to think of more than one word for each. It is also possible that some of your answers will not appear in the **Answer Key.** When you are through, check your answers in the **Answer Key** and in the dictionary.

Examples: a. Mars   (war)
             b. Somnus   (sleep)
Answers: a. *martial*   (suited for war or a warrior)
              Martian   (related to the planet Mars or its fictional inhabitants)
           b. *somnambulist*   (sleepwalker)

1. Uranus   (sky)
2. Pluto   (underworld, wealth)
3. Atlas   (Titan who held up the sky)
4. Helios   (sun)
5. Flora   (plants)
6. Luna   (moon)
7. Pan   (all nature)
8. Hygeia   (health)
9. Oceanus   (ocean)
10. Nox   (night)
11. Terra   (earth)
12. Ge   (earth)
13. Phobos   (fear)
14. Hypnos   (sleep)
15. Furies   (avengers)
16. Ceres   (agriculture)
17. Gratiae   (graces)
18. Fata   (fates)
19. Janus   (beginnings, doors)
20. Mnemosyne   (memory)
21. Musae   (arts)
22. Libertas   (freedom)
23. Iris   (rainbow)
24. Terpsichore   (dance)
25. Phosphor   (Venus, morning star)
26. Lucifer   (Venus, morning star)
27. Concordia   (agreement)
28. Fides   (loyalty)
29. Fornax   (baking)
30. Salus   (good health)

You need to pay close attention to pronunciation in vocabulary study. Here the dictionary can help you again. All good dictionaries have pronunciation keys that appear at the front of the volume. Then the dictionary provides a formula for pronouncing each word. Here's an example:

Pronunciation and the dictionary

clan│like (klan′ līk′), *adj.* having the qualities of a clan; clannish

The formula (klan′ līk′) will correspond to the dictionary's pronunciation key.

Pronunciation involves discriminations, or differences, between sounds that combine to form words. You must make distinctions between words such as *whether* and *weather, where* and *wear, our* and *are, for* and *fur.* Mispronouncing some words is socially unacceptable and can lead to misunderstanding and poor communication. Some examples are *liberry (library), athalete (athlete), ast (asked), excape (escape), goverment (government), quanity (quantity),* and *probly (probably).*

Pronouncing heteronyms

Earlier in this section you learned about *heteronyms* (from *hetero-,* "different," + *onym,* "name"). These words are spelled alike but pronounced differently. (Don't confuse heteronyms with homonyms, which always sound alike.)

Depending on how you pronounce *sewer,* for example, it is either a person who sews or a big, underground drain. Other heteronyms are *bass* (a fish) and *bass* (a male singer).

In the following exercises, notice the differences in pronunciation as you select the right heteronym to agree with each definition.

Choosing the right heteronym   Self-help

Write the heteronyms to complete each pair of definitions. Since the heteronyms will be spelled alike, read each completed definition pair aloud, noticing how the heteronyms' pronunciations change. Check your answers in the **Answer Key.**

Example: The third-person singular of the verb *do*
  is _____ .
  A group of female deer are called _____ .
Answer: does (pronounced "duzz")
  does (pronounced "doze")

1. Liquid from the eyes is called a _____ .
   To rip is to _____ .
2. The front part of a ship is the _____ .
   A _____ is used to shoot an arrow.

3. A heavy metal is _____ .
   To conduct an orchestra is to _____ it.
4. A pile of hay is a _____ .
   To cut down grass is to _____ .
5. A big argument is a _____ .
   To move with oars is to _____ .
6. Moving air is called _____ .
   To twist around is to _____ .

Self-help	## Quick review of heteronyms

In these sentences, point out the heteronyms you have just learned.

Example: What does the zoo do with the does?
Answer: does, does

1. A tear came to her eye when she saw the tear in her coat.
2. A Viking aimed the arrow in his bow from the bow of the ship.
3. Lead pipes lead water into buildings.
4. You have to mow the hay before you can make a hay mow.
5. They had a row over who would row the boat.
6. The swirling wind made the clothesline wind around the tree trunk.

Back formations   Would you like to trace the development of certain words? Look in the dictionary. Of special interest are the back formations you'll find there.

Back formation refers to the process of forming a new word from another by *inference,* or by one's assumption that the word already exists. In time the new word is thought to be the source of the old word.

Burgle is a back formation (not a source of) *burglar.* English had the noun *burglar,* so logic said it must have come from a verb *burgle.* Since the verb *burgle* didn't exist at the time, someone invented it.

Back formations eventually gain the status of bona fide words. In time, people forget where back formations came from. This way of creating words results in terms such as *diagnose* (from *diagnosis*) and *resurrect* (from *resurrection*).

Here are some more back formations:

escalate from *escalator*	*donate* from *donation*
greed from *greedy*	*difficult* from *difficulty*
grovel from *groveling*	*ellipse* from *ellipsis*

peeve from *peevish*   *reminisce* from *reminiscence*
orate from *oration*   *democrat* from *democracy*
edit from *editor*   *peddle* from *peddler*

When they first come into use, some back formations are
thought to be substandard and many people avoid them.
Enthuse, for example, is a back formation from *enthusiasm.* Most
people still avoid using the word *enthuse* in formal speaking
and writing, though its informal use has been acceptable for
some time.

Back formations can also be humorous, and many form a
part of our slang *(buttle* from *butler, plumb* from *plumber).* As your
final exercise in this section, you will create back formations
on your own. You may find that some of them are bona fide
words you didn't know about.

Fun with back formations   Self-help

Create back formations from the nouns given to make
complete sentences. Try to decide which back formations you
create are bona fide words (formal or informal). Check your
answers in the **Answer Key.** The dictionary used as reference
for the answers given in the key is *The World Book Dictionary.*

Example: A broker _____ .
Answer: brokes (a bona fide word)

1. A bounder _____ .
2. A grocer _____ .
3. A swindler _____ .
4. A dentist _____ .
5. A doctor _____ .
6. A television _____ .
7. A tinker _____ .
8. A hawker _____ .
9. A butcher _____ .
10. A jelly _____ .

5   Word games and vocabulary

How can word games aid your vocabulary growth? They help
you develop and maintain an interest in words. Working with
spelling recall, anagrams, palindromes, words within words,
puns, word camouflage, and word progressions is no chore.
There's an element of fun in these mental activities. In fact,
they're word play.

This section consists almost exclusively of word games of all
sorts. The purpose of these games can be expressed with one
short word: *enjoy!*

Word games are word builders

In addition to the element of fun in word games, when you are doing them, you are still dealing with useful aspects of language development. First, you come to realize that to play word games successfully, you must use word skills; that is, you have a chance to practice with words.

Second, word games are mental exercises requiring discipline. Word games make you notice words. Both construction and spelling of words are important. Word games make you more aware of word similarities and differences. They require you to notice nuances in word meaning.

Third, in using word games, you develop fluency. The more often you must select and use words, the more skillful you become. Your stock of words increases and so do the skill, ease, and discrimination with which you use them.

Fourth, word games help you become aware of the relationship between words and meaning in language. When you manipulate letters, you manipulate words. When you manipulate words, you manipulate meanings. Finally, word games also point up the presence and importance of wit and humor in language. Word games help you develop not only an interest in but an appreciation for the fun in language.

Spelling recall games

These games require you to spell correctly words you come across every day. Some are common nouns and some are geographic terms you may think you have already mastered. Find out whether you have done so by completing the spelling recall games.

Self-help   **Animal antics**

Complete the names of the animals described. Each name contains one or more *o*'s. Check your answers in the **Answer Key.**

> **Example:** It's lazy. __ __o__ __   **Answer:** sloth

1. It barks.   __o__
2. It's sly.   __o__
3. It croaks.   __ __o__
4. It's related to the frog.   __o__ __
5. It eats hay.   __o__ __ __
6. It howls.   __o__ __
7. It butts.   __o__ __
8. It slides.   o__ __ __ __
9. It howls.   __o__ __ __ __
10. It washes its food.   __ __ __ __oo__

Self-help   **Bird watch**

Following the example in the preceding word game, complete the names of the birds described here. Each bird name has one or more *a*'s. Check your answers in the **Answer Key.**

1. symbol of the United
   States   __a__ __ __
2. swoops down on its prey   __a__ __
3. trained to hunt other
   birds   __a__ __ __ __
4. also called "bobwhite"   __ __a__ __
5. talking bird   __a__ __ __ __
6. another talker   __ __ __ __a
7. often stands on one leg   __ __a__ __
8. has a long, curved neck   __ __a__
9. large sea bird   a__ __a__ __ __ __
10. has a bill with a pouch   __ __ __ __ __a__

Hidden cities   Self-help

This game checks your spelling recall of key cities in the
United States. Sometimes, but not always, context clues
appear. In each item, rearrange the underlined letters to
reconstruct the name of a U.S. city. You must include in the
city name *all* underlined letters given in that item. Check your
answers in the **Answer Key.**

> **Example:** If the Angels have to play a double-header, they
>   may lose one game.
> **Answer:** Los Angeles

1. Phil heard about the oracle of Delphi in a Latin class a
   year ago.
2. Clothes stylish five years ago are not so chic now.
3. Ted was in a riot in this city.
4. A night snow fell on this historic city.
5. Sheila read about a city in Ohio that was looted.
6. The Russians work for rubles, but the Japanese work for
   yen.
7. The lame, frightened lion either bit or scratched the
   trainer.
8. From the back of the classroom, I heard the boy shout,
   "No, Alaska is the largest state now!"
9. In the novel, the old Frenchman lit a candle to search for
   his sous.
10. The sportswriter said, "I predict the Cowboys will
    probably maul the Colts next week."
11. If you scan the newspapers, you generally find there is
    some reference to Franco-American relationships.
12. To him she seemed a snob.
13. The girls were all sad because she was leaving.
14. When the road gets dark he puts on the car's bright lights.
15. In a town in Texas, she saw some ants eating an onion.

Self-help More hidden cities

Using the same example as in the previous game, test your
spelling recall of key cities of the world. Remember, you must
account for every underlined letter as you reconstruct the
name of a city. Check your answers in the **Answer Key.**

1. This toy is OK.
2. That pin holds the tap in the keg.
3. The twins, Don and Lon, are inseparable.
4. The police managed to keep the mob at bay.
5. Someone said the mice in the city eat enough each day to
   feed an ox for weeks.
6. Because the patient's bile duct was inflamed, an R.N.
   stayed in the room through the night.
7. In the model's closet there are over 20 pairs of shoes.
8. There were more people at the game than the Colosseum
   would hold.
9. The farmer had to get rid of the beaver dam, which
   caused flooding of his garden.
10. I've got an idea that Ann will be a waltz fan when she
    returns from Europe.

Anagrams

Sometimes you can form words simply by rearranging the
letters of other words. The word games that follow deal with
anagrams (words formed by the letters in other words). See
how successful you are at unscrambling the anagrams to find
new words.

Self-help Scrambled spellings

Rearrange these simple words to find anagrams. Check your
answers in the **Answer Key.**

Example: lemon   **Answer:** melon

1. horse
2. clasp
3. blame
4. groan

5. north
6. risen
7. forest
8. therein

Anagrams in context   Self-help

Rearrange the letters of each italicized word to find the
anagram that is appropriate in the sentence. Check your
answers in the **Answer Key.**

Example: He gave the money back to *slave* his conscience.
Answer: salve

1. Many young men *listen* in the army.
2. The poet wrote about the *fringe* of fate.
3. Sailors are sometimes called *rats.*
4. The meanings "star" and *"stare"* are related.
5. She seemed to *blister* at the remark.
6. He fired the *flier* into the air.
7. The *steel* came down and made the streets slippery.
8. She pressed the *plates* in her dress.
9. The bear destroyed the beehive with his *wasp.*
10. The thief carried the *bruise* across the border.
11. The actress *marched* the audience from her entrance to her
    exit.
12. Because the artist lived near the beach, he enjoyed
    painting pictures of the *seahorse.*
13. The coach complained about his *mate.*
14. The members of the aviation board participated in a *plane*
    discussion.
15. Roman soldiers defended the Roman *dialect* from the
    invading Gauls.

Backward and forward: palindromes

What did Adam say to Eve when he met her?

MADAM, I'M ADAM

Now read these words backward. They become

MADAM, I'M ADAM

You just read a *palindrome*, from Greek *palindromos* (running back again). The root *palin* means "back again" and *dromos* means "running." A palindrome reads the same backward and forward. Here's another situation that gives rise to a palindrome:

When Napoleon was exiled to the island of Elba, what is he said to have written?

ABLE WAS I ERE I SAW ELBA

Read this sentence backward. You will see it's another palindrome. Here are some more palindromes:

NIAGARA, O ROAR AGAIN

A MAN, A PLAN, A CANAL—PANAMA

WAS IT A BAR OR A BAT I SAW?

PAT AND EDNA TAP

Some palindromes are made up of only three words: EVIL MADAM, LIVE; GOLDENROD ADORNED LOG. Some are two-word palindromes: STOPS SPOTS, GOLD LOG. Some are one-word palindromes: ROTOR, RADAR, KAYAK, MA'AM.

Some girls' names are palindromes: ANNA, HANNAH, EVE, NAN. Some boys' names are palindromes, too: BOB, OTTO. Mothers and fathers also have palindromes for names: MOM, DAD.

Now work through the palindrome game that follows.

Find the palindrome   Self-help

Write the palindrome that completes each sentence that
follows. Check your answers in the **Answer Key.**

Example: Another word for *looks* is s_ _ _.
Answer: sees

1. If you want to use a palindrome, don't say *peek* or *peer,* say
   p_ _ _.
2. I don't like this wallpaper; let's r_ _ _ _ _ _ the wall.
3. Until recently the leaders of Iran have been called
   s_ _ _ _.
4. To keep the bricks even, bricklayers use a l_ _ _ _.
5. When eating, a baby wears a b_ _.
6. The sun is overhead at n_ _ _.
7. Public officials are highly interested in c_ _ _ _ affairs.
8. Two other slang words for *dope* or *nut* are b_ _ _ and
   k_ _ _.
9. The Boy Scout did a good d_ _ _.
10. My apple's red, but yours is r_ _ _ _ _.
11. He was always nervous when he sang his s_ _ _ _.
12. They can spot enemy airplanes with r_ _ _ _ _.
13. Zane Grey wrote many Western s_ _ _ _.
14. Eskimos paddle in a k_ _ _ _.
15. A girl's name beginning with *a* is A_ _ _.

Words within words

Sometimes you can discriminate (pick out) words within larger words, as you are asked to do in the games that follow. These games will help prepare you for the pun games to follow because finding "hidden" words makes you distinguish like sounds and spellings within words.

These games are not an attempt to formally analyze word parts (roots, prefixes, and suffixes). You are merely to find words that incidentally appear within other words.

Self-help   ## Long-lost pets

Find the "pet" word that answers each question. Check your answers in the **Answer Key.**

Example: What *pet* is part of a flower?   **Answer:** petal

1. What *pet* is turned to stone?
2. What *pet* is an oily liquid?
3. What *pet* is British gasoline?
4. What *pet* is an underskirt?
5. What *pet* is a funnel-shaped flower?

Self-help   ## Rats in hiding

Following the example for "Long-lost pets," find the "rat" words that answer these questions. Check your answers in the **Answer Key.**

1. What *rat* is a giddy person?
2. What *rat* makes a noise with its tail?
3. What *rat* is an old car?
4. What *rat* is on a wrench?
5. What *rat* approves or confirms?

Self-help   ## Your thinking cap

Following the example for "long-lost pets," find the "cap" words that answer these questions. Check your answers in the **Answer Key.**

1. What *cap* is an economic system?
2. What *cap* is the tenth sign of the zodiac?
3. What *cap* is to overturn?
4. What *cap* is used in space travel?
5. What *cap* explains a picture?

Recognizing nations   Self-help

Complete each blank with an appropriate word containing the
word *nation*. Check your answers in the **Answer Key.**

Example: Her favorite flower is the c_ _ _ _ _ _ _ _ _ _ .
Answer: carnation

1. Making a gift is called a do_ _ _ _ _ _ _ .
2. Anger is ind_ _ _ _ _ _ _ _ _ _ .
3. When you take a test you take an
   ex_ _ _ _ _ _ _ _ _ _ .
4. Extreme patriotism is na_ _ _ _ _ _ _ _ _ _ .
5. A person who puts off until tomorrow what he can do
   today is guilty of pro_ _ _ _ _ _ _ _ _ _ _ _ _ .
6. A nation whose people decide what kind of government
   they want has self-de_ _ _ _ _ _ _ _ _ _ _ _ _ .
7. The Treaty of Versailles was an
   in_ _ _ _ _ _ _ _ _ _ _ _ agreement.
8. A person who imagines he sees things has
   hal_ _ _ _ _ _ _ _ _ _ _ _ _ .
9. State control of industry is
   na_ _ _ _ _ _ _ _ _ _ _ _ _ _ .
10. Heads of state are sometimes the victims of
    as_ _ _ _ _ _ _ _ _ _ _ _ _ .

Name the state   Self-help

Find the state that contains the italicized word in each
question. Check your answers in the **Answer Key.**

Example: What state has an *ask* in it?   **Answer:** Alaska

1. What state has a *lab* in it?
2. What state has *for* in it?
3. What state has *color* in it?
4. What state has *connect* in it?
5. What state has a *law* in it?
6. What state has *set* in it?
7. What state has *sis* in it?
8. What state has *sour* in it?
9. What state has a *tan?*
10. What state has a *ham* in it?
11. What state contains *ore?*
12. What state has a *hod* in it?
13. What state has a *shin* in it?
14. What state has *sin* in it?
15. What state has an *ark* in it?

Pun games

Now you are ready to work with riddles whose answers are based on puns (plays on words). See how many of these riddles you can solve.

Self-help

"Punny" word endings

Solve the following riddles by finding the appropriate pun. Check your answers in the **Answer Key.**

Example: What is taller than a short ant?
Answer: a tolerant

1. What relatives are red?
2. What's the opposite of "love red"?
3. What ship carries equestrians?
4. What ship carries students along?
5. What ant is a big show?
6. What do you call a ring in a cow's nose?
7. Why did the Scotsman feel guilty?
8. How does a flower scare off insects?
9. If you rub lard on your head and get taller, why can't you use Crisco?
10. Why is a broken horn indifferent?
11. Why was the engineer so polite?
12. If Mr. Hood dies what is the state of Mrs. Hood?

Self-help

Guess the tree

Complete the pun this time by finding the tree that completes the sentence. Check your answers in the **Answer Key.**

Example: Before a big date, Bill likes to _____up.
Answer: spruce

1. A weight on the end of a line is a _____.
2. After the forest fire the ranger found an _____.
3. What tree stays close to the ocean?
4. What tree covers a bear?
5. What tree do you stick in a bottle?
6. What tree is found on a calendar?
7. What tree is hidden when your hand is closed?
8. What tree is an ill-fated car?
9. What tree is a crybaby?
10. What tree belongs to the canine family?

What do they eat or drink?   Self-help

Match the appropriate food or drink in column **B** with the
persons described in column **A**. Your answers may be puns.
Check your answers in the **Answer Key.**

Examples: 1. bank teller   a. roe
              2. oarsman   b. bread
Answers: 1. b
             2. a

A	B
1. boxer	a. ham
2. diamond expert	b. steaks
3. army officer	c. plum
4. golfer	d. jam
5. traffic police officer	e. yolk
6. walking police officer	f. corn
7. electrician	g. leeks
8. foot doctor	h. carrots
9. actor	i. rabbit
10. mathematician	j. beet
11. calendar maker	k. sole
12. sick person	l. currants
13. oxen driver	m. pear
14. carpenter	n. punch
15. dry humorist	o. ale
16. building constructor	p. pie
17. a gambler	q. kernel
18. twins	r. rye
19. plumber	s. tea
20. shoemaker	t. dates

Self-help   International puns

Find the country that answers each question. Check your answers in the **Answer Key.**

Example: Where do germs go? _ _ _ _ _ _ _
Answer: Germany

1. Where should warm persons go to cool off? _ _ _ _ _ _
2. Where should a lap dog go? _ _ _ _ _ _ _
3. Where should a squeaking wheel go? _ _ _ _ _ _ _
4. Where's a good place to be for Thanksgiving?
   _ _ _ _ _ _
5. What country breaks when you drop it? _ _ _ _ _ _
6. Where do fish go? _ _ _ _ _ _ _
7. What country is worth 21 shillings (money)?
   _ _ _ _ _ _
8. When a man doesn't eat he gets _ _ _ _ _ _ _ _ _.
9. Where would a pole vaulter go? _ _ _ _ _ _ _
10. Where can you buy ties? _ _ _ _ _ _ _ _ _
11. What island would you visit for a cup of coffee?
    _ _ _ _
12. The angry man came from _ _ _ _ _ _ _ _.
13. In what other island would an Irishman settle?
    _ _ _ _ _ _ _ _ _
14. Why did the gambler come to Monte Carlo? _ _ _ _ _ _

Alphabet puns   Self-help

Find the alphabet letter that each sentence suggests. Then
make up the riddle that goes with the sentence. Check your
answers in the **Answer Key.**

> **Example:** This bird is blue.
> **Answer:** j (jay)
> **Riddle:** What letter is a blue bird? A j.

1. This letter buzzes.
2. You can sail on this letter.
3. You can drink this letter.
4. TV performers use these cards.
5. If you borrow, you __.
6. You see with this letter.
7. You can eat this letter (vegetable).
8. What letter is a tree?
9. What letter is two *u*'s?
10. What two letters describe a vacant house?
11. What two letters are an antonym of *difficult?*
12. What two letters crawl up the walls?
13. What two letters tell where some Indians live?
14. A synonym for *jealousy* is __ __ .
15. What three letters mean "you are seen by me"?

Word camouflage

See how alert to words your eyes have become by finding the words camouflaged in the games that follow. You will locate birds, flora, "cold" words, and then "small" words in these four games. Check your answers in the **Answer Key.**

Self-help   ## Hidden birds

```
B  L  U  E  B  I  R  D  P  E  N  G  U  I  N
L  O  V  E  B  I  R  D  A  S  W  A  N  B  F
A  R  U  A  C  K  H  U  R  O  B  I  N  L  L
C  I  L  G  O  I  A  C  R  A  N  E  I  U  A
K  O  T  L  C  W  W  K  O  G  O  O  S  E  M
B  L  U  E  K  I  K  S  T  O  R  K  W  J  I
I  E  R  O  A  D  R  U  N  N  E  R  A  A  N
R  S  E  T  T  U  R  K  E  Y  E  L  L  Y  G
D  Q  W  O  O  D  P  E  C  K  E  R  L  O  O
C  U  C  K  O  O  T  I  C  I  G  D  O  V  E
R  A  V  E  N  E  L  L  R  T  U  O  W  L  E
O  S  W  I  F  T  O  A  O  E  L  W  R  E  N
W  H  I  P  P  O  O  R  W  I  L  L  A  R  K
```

Hidden flora   Self-help

```
M   A   R   I   G   O   L   D   E   N   R   O   D

U   V   A   R   T   I   C   H   O   K   E   D   O

S   O   B   A   L   S   A   M   A   N   E   E   G

H   C   A   C   T   U   S   K   K   U   D   W   W

R   A   T   K   U   M   Q   U   A   T   Y   B   O

O   D   P   L   L   A   U   R   E   L   C   E   O

O   O   E   O   G   C   A   C   T   I   O   R   D

M   Y   R   T   R   A   S   P   B   E   R   R   Y

E   E   S   U   A   S   H   P   E   O   N   Y   T

S   W   I   S   S   C   H   A   R   D   A   S   H

Q   I   M   K   S   A   S   P   R   U   C   E   I

U   N   M   A   N   G   O   A   Y   I   O   F   S

I   G   O   U   R   D   S   Y   A   R   R   I   T

T   N   N   B   A   O   B   A   B   I   K   G   L

E   U   C   A   L   Y   P   T   U   S   L   O   E
```

Self-help   "Cold" words

```
F  R  O  S  T  B  I  T  E  T  U  N  D  R  A
R  N  U  M  B  L  C  O  L  D  N  E  S  S  R
I  Z  E  R  O  I  E  A  T  H  E  R  M  I  C
G  A  S  U  B  Z  E  R  O  W  I  N  D  N  T
I  F  R  E  E  Z  E  R  B  A  C  K  S  K  I
D  R  B  C  R  A  G  A  L  P  I  N  E  S  C
F  E  O  O  E  R  E  T  E  I  C  E  A  G  E
R  O  R  N  F  D  L  H  A  C  L  A  M  A  C
I  N  E  E  R  C  A  A  K  O  E  T  A  S  A
G  L  A  C  I  A  T  I  O  N  M  A  I  N  P
O  C  L  O  G  P  I  L  A  G  I  G  L  O  O
R  A  C  O  E  H  O  C  K  E  Y  E  P  W  B
I  R  E  L  R  A  N  D  E  A  F  L  O  E  E
F  I  T  A  A  L  G  I  D  L  I  I  L  I  R
I  M  E  N  T  H  O  L  A  T  E  D  A  C  G
C  E  S  T  E  T  H  A  W  I  N  T  R  Y  S
```

"Small" words   Self-help

```
M  E  A  G  E  R  M  I  N  I  A  T  U  R  E
I  O  T  A  L  L  I  E  P  I  T  O  M  E  G
C  J  O  T  I  S  C  A  N  T  D  W  A  R  F
R  S  M  A  L  L  R  M  O  L  E  C  U  L  E
O  U  T  I  N  Y  O  P  O  I  N  T  W  R  X
C  N  H  O  M  U  N  C  U  L  U  S  A  U  I
O  D  U  R  C  H  I  N  T  L  T  E  E  N  G
S  E  M  I  C  R  O  B  E  I  E  S  S  T  U
M  R  B  S  W  E  E  M  R  P  Y  G  M  Y  I
I  S  A  T  D  I  M  I  N  U  T  I  O  N  T
N  I  N  U  U  M  I  N  U  T  E  L  F  O  Y
I  Z  T  N  M  A  R  U  D  I  M  E  N  T  M
M  E  A  T  P  C  E  T  O  A  T  H  I  N  I
U  A  M  E  Y  R  L  I  O  N  F  I  N  E  T
M  L  O  D  E  O  P  A  R  T  I  C  L  E  E
```

Word progressions

The word games you've just completed took concentration and a sharp eye. The word progressions to follow may be an even greater challenge. This final word game should keep you busy for quite some time.

Self-help   ## One word at a time

Move from one key word to another by changing only one letter at a time. Check your answers in the **Answer Key.** If your answers vary from those in the key, recheck them. There probably is more than one way to solve some of these progressions.

Example with answers: MICE

m i t e
m a t e
m a t s
CATS

1. MARE	4. FIT	7. RISE
— — — —	— — — —	— — — —
— — — —	— — — —	— — — —
— — — —	— — — —	— — — —
COLT	— — — —	— — — —
	ILL	FALL
2. CAME		
— — — —	5. DULL	8. HOPE
— — — —	— — — —	— — — —
— — — —	— — — —	— — — —
WENT	— — — —	— — — —
	— — — —	— — — —
3. FORE	KEEN	WISH
— — — —		
— — — —	6. CORE	9. WILD
— — — —	— — — —	— — — —
BACK	— — — —	— — — —
	— — — —	— — — —
	— — — —	— — — —
	PULP	TAME

In review

As you reflect on the ideas discussed in this word builder guide, you might consider these points:

1. Words are the names you give your experiences. Rich experiences make a rich vocabulary. You are your words.
2. The incidental approach to vocabulary study is often accidental. You must use a regular, systematic approach to develop word power.
3. Learn to classify your words. At the same time you'll be classifying your ideas and your experiences.
4. Find out what words you know and how well you know them. Move your almost-known words into sharper focus.
5. Use the principle of transfer. Apply your knowledge of words to other words. Study key roots, prefixes, and suffixes. They are an important part of the process of compounding in language.
6. Use context clues, both external and internal.
7. Read widely. Reading broadens your experiences and your vocabulary.
8. Use every method of communication to learn words: reading and writing, speaking and listening, visualizing and observing.
9. Use the dictionary. It is a treasure house of language information.
10. Enjoy words! Don't forget the element of fun in language.

Words worth knowing

The lists that follow feature words that you are likely to encounter in various specialized areas such as business, health care, and the law. Whatever your particular interest or your need to know, familiarity with these words can increase your overall ability to use words.

Review these words periodically. Determine how many of these words you know well enough to use in your writing and speaking. Look up in a dictionary the words you do not know. Use the lists as a foundation upon which you will build greater word power.

Business

account	deposit	indemnity	preemption
accredit	depreciate	inflation	premium
affiliate	depression	insolvency	prepayment
agency	disburse	intangible	price
allot	discount	interest	principal amount
amalgamation	diversification	inventory	production
amend	dividend	investment	profit
applicant	double entry	invoice	promissory note
appraisal	down payment	joint account	proprietor
appreciate	draft	layoff	provision
assessment	drawee	lease	realty
assets	dun	legal tender	recession
auditor	duty	lessee	refund
backing	economics	lessor	remit
balance	elapse	liquidate	remuneration
bear market	embezzle	loan	rent
bidding	encumbrance	lottery	resources
bill of sale	endorse	Ltd.	retail
bond	endowment	management	retirement
boycott	enterprise	margin	return
broker	entrepreneur	market	revenue
budget	equity	maximum	risk
bull market	estate	merchandise	salary
capital	ex-dividend	merger	sale
cartel	executor	middleman	sell
census	expenditure	minimum	sell short
charter	expiration	minority	shareholder
checkbook	export	monopoly	simple interest
claim	extension	mortgage	speculate
clause	face value	negligence	stock exchange
client	Federal Reserve Bank	negotiable	sublet
COD	finance	net	supply
code	fiscal year	notary	surplus
collateral	FOB	note	tangible
common stock	forecast	obligation	tariff
compound interest	foreclosure	organization	technology
consolidation	franchise	outgo	tenant
consumption	free trade	outlay	trade
contract	fund	overdraft	trade union
copyright	guarantor	ownership	treasurer
corporation	gross	parity	turnover
cost	gross income	partnership	undersigned
credit	heir	par value	usury
currency	holding	passbook	utility
dealer	hypothecate	patent	value
decrease	immune	penalty	warranty
deduction	import	pension	wholesale
default	incorporate	per capita	withdrawal
deficit	increment	personnel	write-off
deflation	indebtedness	petty cash	yield

Chemistry

absorption
acetylene
acid
agent
alcohol
aldehyde
alkaline
alloy
alpha ray
alum
aluminum
analyze
antacid
antifreeze
antihistamine
antimatter
antimony
apparatus
argon
arsenic
atom
atomic energy
atomic number
atomic weight
balanced
barbiturate
barium
base
beaker
beta rays
biochemistry
bismuth
bond
boron
bromine
bronze
Bunsen burner
burette
butane
calcium
californium
carbohydrate
carbon
carbonation
carbon dioxide
carbon monoxide
carcinogen
catalyst
caustic
cell

cellulose
centrifuge
chlorine
chloroform
chlorophyll
chromium
cobalt
compound
concentration
condense
corrosion
cosmetology
covalence
crucible
DDT
decay
decomposition
dehydration
density
dextrose
diffusion
dilution
direct current
dissolve
distill
DNA
drug
ecology
einsteinium
electrolysis
electrolyte
electron
element
enzyme
ethylene
fermentation
fertilizer
filtration
fluid
formaldehyde
formula
gas
germicide
glucose
glycerine
gold
gram
helium
homogenize
hydrates

hydrocarbon
hydrogen
inorganic
iodine
ion
iron
isotope
krypton
lead
liquefy
litmus
lodestone
magnesium
manganese
mass
matter
mercury
methane
methanol
mixture
molecular weight
molecule
mortar
neon
neutron
nickel
nicotine
nitric acid
nitrogen
nucleus
nylon
octane
organic
osmosis
oxidation
oxygen
pasteurize
periodic table
pestle
petrification
phases
phosphorus
photosynthesis
pipette
plastic
platinum
plutonium
potassium
precipitate
propane

properties
proton
radical
radioactive
radium
radon
rayon
reactant
reagent
receptacle
resin
respiration
RNA
rust
saccharin
salt
saturation
secretion
sedative
silicon
sodium
solidify
soluble
solution
solvent
specific gravity
starch
steroid
strontium
substance
substitution
sucrose
sulfur
suspension
synthesis
synthetic
tannic acid
test tube
tin
titanium
TNT
toxicology
uranium
vacuum
valence
vapor
vinyl
viscosity
xenon
zinc

Geography

agrarian	distribution	importation	rainfall
agribusiness	district	inhabitant	rain forest
agriculture	divide	inland	ranch
agronomy	doldrums	inlet	range
altitude	domestic	insular	rapids
annual	drainage	international	raw material
Antarctic	drought	irrigation	reef
Arctic	earth	island	region
area	earthquake	isobar	reservoir
arid	east	isotherm	revolution
axis	eclipse	isthmus	ridge
barren	ecology	jungle	rotation
basin	equator	latitude	rural
bay	erosion	lava	sand bar
beach	eruption	levee	sea level
belt	evergreen	location	seaport
blizzard	exportation	lock	seismology
border	extinct	longitude	settlement
boundary	fallow	lowland	shoreline
canal	farmland	mainland	sierra
canyon	fertile	map	soil
cape	firth	meridian	sound
cartographer	fisheries	migrate	south
channel	fjord	monsoon	South Pole
circumference	flood plain	mountain chain	sphere
climate	forage	mouth	steppe
climatology	foreign	nation	strait
coast	forest	natural resources	swamp
colony	fossil	nomad	Temperate Zone
compass	frontier	north	temperature
conservation	geyser	North Pole	territory
consumption	glacier	oasis	tornado
continent	globe	oceanography	Torrid Zone
continental shelf	government	ore	Tropic of Cancer
coral	grassland	outlet	Tropic of Capricorn
country	grid	pasture	tropics
county	growing season	peak	tundra
crater	gulf	peninsula	typhoon
crop	Gulf Stream	petroleum	urban
cultivate	harbor	plain	valley
current	harvest	plateau	village
cyclone	headland	pogonip	volcano
dam	hemisphere	polar	waterfall
deciduous	highland	population	watershed
degrees	hinterland	prairie	waterway
delta	horizon	precipitation	weather
demography	humidity	primitive	west
dense	hurricane	production	westerlies
desert	hybrid	province	wilderness
dike	iceberg	race	zone

Health

abscess
addiction
adrenalin
allergy
amnesia
analgesic
angina
antibiotic
antidote
antiseptic
artery
artificial respiration
aseptic
asthma
astigmatism
atrophy
auditory
bacteria
benign
botulism
bronchitis
bursitis
caffeine
calorie
cancer
carbohydrate
carcinogen
cardiac
cardiogram
caries
cataract
cerebral
cervix
chemotherapy
cholesterol
chromosome
chronic
circulatory
cirrhosis
coagulate
colon
coma
communicable
compress
concussion
contagious
convalesce
convulsion
cornea
coronary

corpuscle
cranium
cyst
dehydration
dermatitis
diabetes
diagnosis
diaphragm
diarrhea
diastolic
diet
dietetic
digitalis
dilate
diphtheria
diuretic
donor
dysentery
dystrophy
embryo
emotion
emphysema
enzyme
epidemic
epidermis
epileptic
esophagus
fester
fibrillation
gallstone
gangrene
gastric
gene
germicide
glandular
glaucoma
halitosis
hepatitis
hernia
histamine
hygiene
hypochondria
immunization
impetigo
incisor
infectious
influenza
inoculation
insomnia
insulin

intoxication
intravenous
iris
larynx
leukemia
ligament
lymph
malaria
malignant
malnutrition
marrow
maturation
measles
medication
membrane
meningitis
metastasis
migraine
minerals
molar
mononucleosis
mucus
mumps
myelitis
myopia
narcotic
neuralgia
neuritis
neurotic
nicotine
nutrient
obese
optic
orthodontic
orthopedic
ovary
ovum
pancreas
pasteurization
pelvis
penicillin
peritonitis
phlebitis
phobia
physique
pituitary
placebo
plaque
plasma
pleurisy

pneumonia
polio
psoriasis
psychiatric
psychosis
ptomaine
pyorrhea
quarantine
rabies
respiratory
retina
rheumatism
Rh factor
rickets
sanitarium
sanitation
sclerosis
sedative
septic
serum
shingles
sinew
sinusitis
smallpox
spastic
spleen
sterile
strep throat
stress
sulfa
symptom
syndrome
systolic
tetanus
therapy
thyroid
tourniquet
toxic
trachea
tuberculosis
tumor
typhoid
ulcer
umbilical cord
uterus
vaccination
vein
venereal
vertigo
vitamin

History

abdication
absolutism
administration
alien
amend
amnesty
anarchy
ancestor
antiquity
apartheid
appoint
aristocracy
armament
Armistice Day
barbarian
bicameral
bill
Bill of Rights
blockade
border
bourgeois
bureaucracy
cabinet
campaign
capitalism
century
charter
circumnavigate
citizen
civil
civilization
Civil War
coalition
coexistence
Cold War
colonist
commerce
committee
communism
Confederacy
Congress
congressional
conquer
conscription
conservatism
conservative
constituency
constitution
constitutional
consul

contemporary
coronation
council
coup
creed
crown
crusade
culture
custom
czar
deflation
delegate
democracy
Democrat
depose
depression
despot
détente
dictator
diplomat
disarmament
document
dominion
draft
duty
dynasty
economy
election
electoral college
electorate
Emancipation
    Proclamation
embargo
emigrate
emperor
empire
enlist
enslave
era
establishment
executive
exploration
fascism
federal
federation
feminist
feudalism
fiscal
forebear
foreign policy

found
franchise
freedom
free trade
frontier
government
governor
guerrilla
hearing
historical
homeland
immigrate
imperialism
inauguration
industrialization
inflation
internationalism
invasion
judiciary
jurisdiction
king
labor union
law
leftist
legislature
levy
liberalism
loyalist
Magna Carta
majority
Mayflower
medieval
migration
military
minority
minuteman
monarch
monopoly
nationalism
nationalization
neutrality
nobility
office
official
oligarchy
pacifist
parliamentary
party
patrician
Pentagon

per capita
pilgrim
plebeian
plebiscite
politician
politics
polls
power
President
primary
prime minister
proletarian
queen
racial
rebellion
realm
reign
representative
republic
Republican
resign
revolution
rightist
right wing
rule
secede
secretary
serf
settler
slavery
socialism
society
statecraft
states' rights
strategy
Supreme Court
taxation
Tory
totalitarian
trade
tradition
treason
tribe
truce
unicameral
United States
USA
USSR
vice-president
vote

Language

abbreviation	diagram	intransitive	prose
ablative	dialect	irony	proverb
abstract	diction	jargon	pun
accusative	didactic	linking verb	punctuation
active	diminutive	literature	quotation
adjective	direct object	litotes	redundancy
adverb	double negative	lyric	referent
affix	doublet	main clause	reflexive
agreement	drama	masculine	rhyme
allegory	elegy	metaphor	rhythm
alliteration	elliptical clause	meter	root word
allusion	emphasis	metonymy	run-on sentence
ameliorative	encyclopedia	modify	sarcasm
antecedent	epic	mood	satire
antonym	epigram	narration	scansion
apostrophe	eponym	neologism	semantics
appositive	essay	neuter	semicolon
archaism	etymology	nominative	sentence
augmentative	euphemism	nonfiction	short story
auxiliary	euphony	noun	simile
bibliography	exclamatory	novelette	slang
biography	exposition	number	solecism
blank verse	fable	ode	soliloquy
case	feminine	onomatopoeia	sonnet
clause	fiction	oxymoron	split infinitive
cliché	figure of speech	parable	stanza
coherence	free verse	paragraph	subject
collective noun	future	paraphrase	subjunctive
colloquial	gender	parody	subordinate clause
colon	genitive	participle	suffix
comedy	gerund	passive	superlative degree
common noun	glossary	pejorative	syllabification
comparative degree	grammar	pentameter	synecdoche
complement	homily	perfect	synonym
complex sentence	homonym	person	synopsis
compound sentence	hyperbole	phrase	syntax
concrete	hyphen	pitch	tense
conjugation	iambic	plagiarism	theme
conjunction	idiomatic	plot	thesaurus
connotation	imperative	plural	topic sentence
contraction	independent clause	poetry	tragedy
correlative	index	positive degree	transitive
dative	indicative	possessive	trite
declarative	indirect object	predicate	trochaic
declension	infinitive	preface	unity
demonstrative pronoun	inflection	prefix	usage
denotation	intensive	preposition	verb
dependent clause	interjection	pronoun	vernacular
derivation	interrogative	pronunciation	verse
diacritical mark	intonation	proper noun	vocabulary

Law

abduction	counterfeit	judgment	plea bargaining
accessory	court	judicial	police
accomplice	court-martial	juror	prison
accusation	courtroom	jury	probation
accuse	crime	justice	prosecute
acquit	criminal	juvenile court	prosecutor
adult	culprit	kangaroo court	public defender
affidavit	damages	kidnap	quorum
alias	decision	kleptomania	ransom
alimony	deed	larceny	rape
amend	defendant	law	repeal
amendment	defense	lawful	resist
annul	delinquent	lawsuit	right
appeal	deposition	lawyer	robbery
appearance	detention	legal	ruling
apprehension	district attorney	legitimate	search warrant
arbitration	divorce	libel	self-defense
arrest	embezzle	license	sentence
arson	enact	lie detector	sheriff
assassination	enforcement	line-up	slander
assault	eviction	magistrate	smuggle
assault and battery	evidence	malice	solitary confinement
attorney	execution	malpractice	sue
autopsy	eyewitness	manslaughter	suit
bail	felony	martial law	summons
ban	fine	minor	Supreme Court
bankruptcy	fingerprint	Miranda card	suspect
battery	forgery	misdemeanor	swear
bench	frame	mistrial	swear in
bigamy	fraud	motion	tax dodging
birthright	grand jury	murder	testify
blackmail	grand larceny	negligence	testimony
break-in	guilt	negotiate	theft
bribery	habeas corpus	nonsupport	traffic ticket
burglary	hearing	notary public	treason
capital punishment	heir	null and void	trespass
case	hijack	oath	trial
citizenship	homicide	offense	trust
civil liberties	hung jury	officer	try
civil rights	immunity	outlaw	unconstitutional
commissioner	impeach	pardon	valid
commute	imprison	parole	vandalism
complaint	incompetent	patent	verdict
confession	indict	patrol	violate
conspiracy	informer	penal	warden
constable	innocent	perjury	warrant
constitution	inquiry	petition	will
contract	interrogation	petty larceny	wiretapping
convict	jail	plaintiff	witness
counselor	judge	plea	workhouse

Mathematics

abscissa
absolute
accurate
acute
addition
adjacent
algebra
amount
analysis
angle
apex
arabic numerals
arc
area
arithmetic
array
average
axiom
axis
base
binomial
bisect
bushel
calculation
calculus
cancellation
Celsius temperature
centimeter
circle
circumference
component
composite
computation
computer
congruent
conversion
convex
cube
curve
data
decagon
decibel
decimal
deduction
deficit
degree
denominator
denotation
depth
derivation

deviation
diagonal
diagram
diameter
difference
digit
dimension
direction
distance
distribution
divide
dividend
divisor
domain
double
dozen
element
eliminate
ellipse
empty set
equal
equal sets
equation
equilateral
equivalent
even numbers
exponent
extract
face value
factor
Fahrenheit
figure
finite
focus
formula
fraction
frequency
function
geometry
heptagon
hexagon
hypotenuse
hypothesis
inch
increase
inequality
infinite
integer
intersect
interval

invariable
inverse
invert
isosceles
kilometer
length
line
linear
logarithm
logic
mathematics
maximum
mean
measure
median
meter
mile
minimum
minus
multiple
multiply
negative
nonagon
number
number line
numeral
numerator
obtuse
octagon
odd numbers
operation
order
ordinate
origin
ounce
parabola
parallel
pentagon
per cent
perimeter
perpendicular
pi
plane
plus
point
polygon
positive
pound
power
probability

product
proportion
pyramid
quadrangle
quadratic
quantities
quotient
radian
radical
radius
range
rate
ratio
real numbers
reciprocal
rectangle
remainder
right angle
roman numerals
root
rotation
round off
secant
segment
semicircle
set
simplify
slide rule
solid
solution
space
sphere
square
square root
statistics
substitute
subtract
sum
symbol
symmetry
system
tangent
term
tetrahedron
theorem
trapezoid
triangle
trigonometry
volume
width

Physical science

absolute zero	dynamo	meteorology	rotation
acoustics	E = mc²	metric	seismograph
activate	electric	microfilm	short circuit
aerodynamics	electrode	microscope	simulation
aerosol	electromagnet	microwave	slide rule
aerospace	electron	modulation	smelter
alloy	element	molten	solar
alternator	energy	momentum	solar cell
ampere	equilibrium	motion	sonar
amplifier	erg	motor	sonic boom
anemometer	Fahrenheit	move	sound barrier
anode	fission	negative	specific gravity
armature	frequency	neutron	spectrum
asteroid	fulcrum	nova	stabilizer
atom	fusion	nuclear	static
ballast	generator	nucleus	static electricity
barometer	gram	odometer	stress
battery	gravity	orbit	subsonic
calibrate	humidistat	ore	substance
calipers	hydraulic	oxidation	suction
cam	hydroelectric	ozone	sunspot
catalytic converter	hydrometer	parameter	supersonic
cathode	incandescent	penumbra	symmetrical
centigrade	inclination	photoelectric	tachometer
centrifugal	inertia	photon	tension
centripetal	infrared	physics	terminal
chain reaction	insulation	physiology	thermal
charge	intensity	plastic	thermodynamics
circuit	internal combustion	polaroid	thermonuclear
compound	ion	pole	thermostat
concave	ionosphere	polygon	thrust
conductor	isotope	positive	torque
convert	kilogram	power pack	transformer
convex	kilowatt	pressure	transistor
cosmic ray	laboratory	prism	transmission
current	laser	propellant	transmute
damper	lathe	proton	turbine
data	launch	pulsar	ultrasonic
decibel	lens	quasar	ultraviolet
declination	lever	radar	uranium
deduce	light-year	radiation	vacuum
dehumidifier	linear	radioactive	vector
dehydrate	magnetic field	radiometer	vertex
differential	magnify	radiotelescope	volt
diffraction	maser	ray	volume
dimension	matrix	reflect	watt
direct current	matter	refract	wavelength
discharge	mechanics	relativity	weight density
distillation	megahertz	resistor	wet cell
dry cell	megaton	retrorocket	worm gear

Religion

abbey
absolution
Advent
agnostic
Allah
almighty
altar
amen
angel
apostle
archangel
atheist
atonement
baptism
Baptist
bar mitzvah
bas mitzvah
beatitude
belief
Bible
bishop
blaspheme
blessing
breviary
Buddhism
canonize
canticle
cantor
cardinal
Catholic
celibacy
chalice
chapel
charity
choir
Christ
christen
Christian
church
clergy
commandment
communion
confession
confirmation
Confucius
congregation
convent
creed
cross
crucifix

cult
damnation
devil
devout
disciple
divine
dogma
doomsday
Easter
ecumenical
ethics
Eucharist
evangelism
evil
exalt
excommunicate
Exodus
faith
feast
forgiveness
free will
friar
fundamentalist
genesis
gentile
genuflect
God
golden rule
gospel
grace
Grail
hallow
Hanukkah
heaven
Hebrew
Hegira
hell
heresy
heterodoxy
high priest
holy
Holy Ghost
hope
hymn
idol
Immaculate Conception
immortal
incarnation
Islam
Jehovah

Jesus
Jew
Koran
laity
Lent
Lord
Lutheran
Madonna
Magi
martyr
mass
Messiah
Methodist
minister
miracle
missionary
Mohammed
monastery
monk
mortal
nave
nun
offertory
ordain
orthodox
papacy
parable
parochial
parson
pastor
penance
Pentecost
piety
pilgrimage
pious
Pope
pray
preach
Presbyterian
priest
prophet
Protestant
psalm
pulpit
purgatory
purification
Puritan
Quaker
rabbi
redemption

reincarnation
religion
repent
resurrect
revelation
rite
rosary
Sabbath
sacrament
sacred
sacrilege
sacristy
saint
salvation
sanctify
Satan
Savior
scripture
sect
seminary
sermon
Shinto
sin
soul
spiritual
Star of David
synagogue
tabernacle
Taoism
temple
Ten Commandments
Tenebrae
Testament
theology
tithe
Torah
transept
trespass
Trinity
Vatican
verse
vespers
vestibule
vicar
Virgin Mary
vow
worship
Yom Kippur
zealot
Zionism

Answer key

1   Expanding your vocabulary

Self-inventory of key words
Page 8

Answers (definitions of words) are included
within the exercise

Confused word pairs
Page 13

1. a, b	16. a, b
2. a, b	17. a, b
3. b, a	18. b, a
4. a, b	19. b, a
5. b, a	20. a, b
6. b, a	21. b, a
7. b, a	22. a, b
8. b, a	23. b, a
9. a, b	24. a, b
10. b, a	25. a, b
11. b, a	26. a, b
12. a, b	27. b, a
13. b, a	28. a, b
14. a, b	29. a, b
15. a, b	30. a, b

Occupational terms
Page 17

1. music
2. painting
3. chess
4. astronomy
5. carpentry
6. tennis
7. cooking
8. hunting
9. gardening
10. sailing
11. printing
12. weaving
13. metal industry
14. railroad
15. shoe industry
16. dancing
17. cards
18. car industry
19. boating
20. teaching

Can you file it?
Page 18

Sports	Cooking	Handicrafts
croquet	croquette	crochet
puck	sage	emboss
Nimrod	spatula	ceramics
creel	filet	awl
toboggan	ladle	purl
bogey	paprika	bobbin
Olympics	broil	embroider
aqualung	fold	warp
crawl	braise	woof
coxswain	blanch	darn
half gainer		jute
screen		loom
		screen
		braid
		half hitch

Sporting words
Page 19

1. golf
2. basketball
3. football
4. golf
5. football
6. fencing
7. football
8. track
9. basketball
10. tennis, track
11. hockey, hunting
12. basketball
13. hockey
14. baseball
15. football
16. baseball
17. baseball
18. billiards, pool
19. volleyball
20. horse racing

What's your theater I.Q.?
Page 19

1. apron
2. burlesque
3. cast
4. chorus
5. comedy
6. composer
7. costume
8. curtain
9. designer
10. director
11. drama
12. footlights
13. intermission
14. makeup
15. mystery
16. opera
17. producer
18. props
19. review
20. scene
21. screen, script
22. spotlight
23. tragedy
24. villain
25. protagonist
26. antagonist
27. angel
28. backdrop
29. critic
30. cue
31. finale
32. foyer
33. grease paint
34. loge
35. mezzanine
36. monolog
37. play, plot
38. promoter, prompter
39. stand-in
40. wings

2   Learning word elements

Medical meanings
Page 27

Removal of:

1. adenoids
2. esophagus
3. pharynx
4. larynx
5. cancer
6. lung
7. uterus
8. eye
9. gland
10. duodenum
11. spleen
12. kidney
13. stomach
14. nerve
15. tongue
16. liver
17. breast
18. thorax

Using word parts
Page 31

1. cut into
2. not mild, bad
3. a lover of books
4. eats insects
5. milk

Working with opposites
Page 39

1. deflate
2. descend
3. eject
4. overpass
5. suffix
6. postpaid
7. repel
8. emigrate
9. postdate
10. explode
11. posttest
12. regress

"Make it big" prefixes
Page 39

1. polytheism
2. superhighway
3. megalopolis
4. hyperactivity
5. ultramodern
6. extraordinary
7. macroscopic
8. multifaceted

Learning number prefixes
Page 43

1. octo
2. quad
3. novem
4. quint
5. hex
6. penta
7. sex
8. tetra
9. sept
10. dec
11. hept
12. tri
13. octo
14. penta
15. tetra
16. novem
17. mono
18. hex
19. uno
20. bi

Suffix self-test
Page 44

1. preparedness
2. inducement
3. thoughtless
4. guiltless
5. assortment
6. blameless
7. establishment
8. commencement
9. stainless
10. accompaniment

Words of science
Page 45

1. h	6. j
2. g	7. f
3. a	8. c
4. i	9. d
5. b	10. e

The suffix *-less*
Page 46

1. hopeless	4. graceless
2. thoughtless	5. useless
3. sinless	6. senseless

Suffixes and gender
Page 47

1. majorette	8. hostess
2. lioness	9. actress
3. tigress	10. heiress
4. heroine	11. baroness
5. Pauline	12. priestess
6. princess	13. usherette
7. empress	14. sorceress

"Little" suffixes
Page 47

1. floret	9. particle
2. streamlet	10. lambkin
3. duckling	11. gosling
4. kitchenette	12. statuette
5. capsule	13. manikin
6. tubule	14. leaflet
7. birdie	15. cigarette
8. ringlet	16. piglet

Killers
Page 49

1. c	9. l
2. a	10. m
3. b	11. i
4. g	12. h
5. d	13. j
6. e	14. o
7. f	15. n
8. k	

3   Classifying ideas and words

Recognizing synonyms
Page 71

1a. joyous
 b. morose
 c. rollicking
2a. folly
 b. reasoning
 c. absurdity
3a. lonesome
 b. happy
 c. destitute
4a. chained
 b. released
 c. fettered

5a. rival
 b. ally
 c. antagonist
6a. angry
 b. meek
 c. vehement
7a. rough
 b. pleasant
 c. acrimonious
8a. foot
 b. summit
 c. substratum

9a. crooked
 b. fair
 c. treacherous
10a. slight
 b. critical
 c. frivolous

Words for the good and bad
Page 73

1. arty
2. squat
3. jailbird
4. jailer

5. blunder
6. sly
7. cheap
8. nosy

9. gullible
10. skinny
11. scheme
12. fat

13. green
14. old
15. frisk

Synonym recall
Page 75

1. odd, eccentric, bizarre, peculiar
2. sociable, cordial, amicable, neighborly
3. consumed, gobbled, devoured, gorged
4. thrifty, economical, saving, parsimonious
5. feeble, fragile, frail, delicate
6. excuse, forgive, overlook, dismiss
7. errors, slips, blunders, faults
8. sobbing, bawling, whimpering, blubbering
9. confused, perplexed, bewildered, mystified
10. squabble, dispute, argument, brawl
11. wisely, cautiously, discreetly, judiciously
12. manners, conduct, comportment, deportment
13. droop, wither, shrivel, wilt
14. reckless, foolhardy, thoughtless, hasty
15. adores, idolizes, worships, reveres
16. urged, instructed, counseled, admonished
17. ample, abundant, plentiful, copious
18. criticized, rebuked, reproved, chided
19. enchanted, fascinated, captivated, allured
20. tricked, swindled, duped, fleeced

Opposites worth learning
Page 78

Answers are included within the exercise. Parts
1 and 2 serve as each other's answer keys.

Recognizing antonyms
Page 80

1. blithe, convivial, rapturous, jovial
2. discrepant, unique, antonymous
3. stable, intransigent
4. unctuous, suave, lubricated
5. expanded, gangling, protracted
6. stalwart, pungent, potent
7. expiration, ultimatum, epilogue, consummation
8. paltry, trifling, inane

Word files of likes and opposites
Page 81

1a. S, F—antonyms
 b. S, F—antonyms
 c. S, S—synonyms
 d. F, S—antonyms
 e. S, F—antonyms
 f. S, S—synonyms
 g. S, F—antonyms
 h. F, S—antonyms
 i. S, F—antonyms
 j. F, S—antonyms
8 antonym pairs, 2 synonym pairs

2a. W, P—antonyms
 b. W, P—antonyms
 c. W, P—antonyms
 d. P, P—synonyms
 e. P, W—antonyms
 f. W, P—antonyms
 g. W, W—synonyms
 h. P, P—synonyms
 i. W, P—antonyms
 j. W, P—antonyms
7 antonym pairs, 3 synonym pairs

3a. P, P—synonyms
 b. H, H—synonyms
 c. P, H—antonyms
 d. P, P—synonyms
 e. H, P—antonyms
 f. P, H—antonyms

g. P, P—synonyms
h. H, H—synonyms
i. P, P—synonyms
j. H, H—synonyms
3 antonym pairs, 7 synonym pairs

4a. E, U—antonyms
b. E, E—synonyms
c. U, U—synonyms
d. E, U—antonyms
e. E, U—antonyms
f. U, E—antonyms
g. E, U—antonyms
h. U, E—antonyms
i. E, E—synonyms
j. E, U—antonyms
7 antonym pairs, 3 synonym pairs

5a. S, U—antonyms
b. U, U—synonyms
c. U, U—synonyms
d. S, U—antonyms
e. S, S—synonyms
f. S, S—synonyms
g. S, S—synonyms
h. U, U—synonyms
i. S, S—synonyms
j. S, S—synonyms
2 antonym pairs, 8 synonym pairs

6a. L, L—synonyms
b. D, D—synonyms
c. L, L—synonyms
d. D, D—synonyms
e. L, L—synonyms
f. D, D—synonyms
g. D, D—synonyms
h. L, L—synonyms
i. D, D—synonyms
j. L, L—synonyms
10 synonym pairs

7a. R, U—antonyms
b. R, U—antonyms
c. U, U—synonyms
d. U, U—synonyms
e. R, R—synonyms
f. R, U—antonyms
g. R, U—antonyms
h. U, R—antonyms
i. R, R—synonyms

j. R, R—synonyms
5 antonym pairs, 5 synonym pairs

8a. A, A—synonyms
 b. A, E—antonyms
 c. E, A—antonyms
 d. A, A—synonyms
 e. E, A—antonyms
 f. E, E—synonyms
 g. A, E—antonyms
 h. A, E—antonyms
 i. E, A—antonyms
 j. A, E—antonyms
7 antonym pairs, 3 synonym pairs

4   Using the dictionary

Analyzing phrases
Page 89

1. groom
2. order
3. dandy
4. sound
5. tear
6. chain
7. battery
8. error
9. strain
10. entering
11. gown
12. bounds
13. limb
14. void
15. cranny
16. call
17. dagger
18. desist
19. square
20. output
21. breadth
22. tuck
23. ends
24. mild
25. rave
26. ruin
27. narrow
28. file
29. ready
30. jetsam
31. myrrh
32. covert
33. active
34. buckler
35. kin
36. polish
37. substance
38. tide
39. vigor
40. wane
41. means
42. behold

Recognizing metaphors
Page 91

1. loyal hearts
2. feathery
3. slaughtered
4. doglegs
5. sifted
6. handful
7. a ton
8. feasted
9. uproot
10. heart dance

Spelling clichés
Page 92

1. milk
2. overwhelming
3. pales
4. issue
5. poor
6. saying
7. stone unturned
8. altar
9. cheerful
10. fragrant
11. fault
12. channel(s)
13. green
14. hale
15. course
16. dear
17. midst
18. floral
19. ravishing
20. bated

Spelling homonyms
Page 100

1. *Fair*
2. steel
3. capital
4. Peace
5. heel
6. lyre
7. knights, coat, mail
8. manor
9. martial
10. maize
11. mussels
12. mustered
13. Ode
14. mined, vein, ore
15. Beech, beach
16. bells, belles
17. coward, cowered
18. crews, cruise
19. hair, mane, tail
20. pause, clause

Biblical allusions
Page 101

1. is wasteful
2. perfect land, place of joy
3. causes a great disturbance
4. he's strong
5. password, watchword
6. the judge was wise, made a wise decision
7. they helped those in need
8. it was a huge and powerful animal

Words from mythology
Page 102

1. uranium
2. plutocrat, plutonium
3. Atlantic, atlas
4. helium, heliotrope
5. florist, flower, flora
6. lunar, lunatic
7. pandemonium, panic
8. hygiene

9. ocean, oceanic
10. nocturne, equinox
11. terrestrial, territory, territorial, terrain
12. geography, geology
13. phobia, claustrophobia, acrophobia, agoraphobia
14. hypnotism, hypnosis
15. furious, fury, furor
16. cereal
17. grace
18. fate, fatality, fatalism
19. January, janitor
20. amnesty, amnesia
21. music, musical, museum
22. liberty
23. iris, iridescent
24. chorus, choreography
25. phosphorous, phosphorescent
26. lucid, translucent
27. concord, accord
28. fidelity, bona fide
29. furnace
30. salutation, salute

Choosing the right heteronym
Page 103

1. tear, tear
2. bow, bow
3. lead, lead
4. mow, mow
5. row, row
6. wind, wind

Quick review of heteronyms
Page 104

Answers exactly as for "Choosing the right heteronym."

Fun with back formations
Page 105

1. bounds (not a bona fide word)
2. groces (not a bona fide word)
3. swindles (a bona fide word)
4. dents (not a bona fide word)
5. doctors (a bona fide word)
6. televises (a bona fide word)
7. tinkers (a bona fide word)
8. hawks (a bona fide word)
9. butches (not a bona fide word)
10. jells (a bona fide word)

5 Word games and vocabulary

Animal antics
Page 108

1. dog
2. fox
3. frog
4. toad
5. horse
6. wolf
7. goat
8. otter
9. coyote
10. raccoon

Bird watch
Page 108

1. eagle
2. hawk
3. falcon
4. quail
5. parrot
6. myna
7. crane
8. swan
9. albatross
10. pelican

Hidden cities
Page 109

1. Philadelphia
2. Chicago
3. Detroit
4. Washington
5. Toledo
6. New York
7. Baltimore
8. Houston
9. St. Louis
10. Milwaukee
11. San Francisco
12. Boston
13. Dallas
14. Pittsburgh
15. San Antonio

More hidden cities
Page 110

1. Tokyo
2. Peking
3. London
4. Bombay
5. Mexico City
6. Berlin
7. Paris
8. Rome
9. Madrid
10. Vienna

Scrambled spellings
Page 110

1. shore
2. scalp
3. amble
4. organ
5. thorn
6. siren
7. softer
8. neither

Anagrams in context
Page 111

1. enlist
2. finger
3. tars
4. aster
5. bristle
6. rifle
7. sleet
8. pleats
9. paws
10. rubies
11. charmed
12. seashore
13. team
14. panel
15. citadel

Find the palindrome
Page 113

1. peep
2. repaper
3. shahs
4. level
5. bib
6. noon
7. civic
8. boob, kook
9. deed
10. redder
11. solos
12. radar
13. sagas
14. kayak
15. Anna

Long-lost pets
Page 114

1. petrify
2. petroleum
3. petrol
4. petticoat
5. petunia

Rats in hiding
Page 114

1. rattlebrain
2. rattler, rattlesnake
3. rattletrap
4. ratchet
5. ratify

Your thinking cap
Page 114

1. capitalism
2. Capricorn
3. capsize
4. capsule
5. caption

Recognizing nations
Page 115

1. donation
2. indignation
3. examination
4. nationalism
5. procrastination
6. determination
7. international
8. hallucinations
9. nationalization
10. assassination

Name the state
Page 115

1. Alabama
2. California
3. Colorado
4. Connecticut
5. Delaware
6. Massachusetts
7. Mississippi
8. Missouri
9. Montana
10. New Hampshire
11. Oregon
12. Rhode Island
13. Washington
14. Wisconsin
15. Arkansas

"Punny" word endings
Page 116

1. kindred
2. hatred
3. horsemanship, horsewomanship
4. scholarship
5. pageant
6. mooring
7. He had a kilt complex.
8. with its pistil
9. It's shortening.
10. It doesn't give a hoot.
11. He was a civil engineer.
12. widowhood

Guess the tree
Page 116

1. plum (plumb)
2. ash
3. beech (beach)
4. fir (fur)
5. cork
6. date
7. palm
8. lemon
9. weeping willow
10. dogwood

What do they eat or drink?
Page 117

1. n	11. t
2. h	12. o
3. q	13. e
4. s	14. i
5. d	15. r
6. j	16. c
7. l	17. b
8. f	18. m
9. a	19. g
10. p	20. k

International puns
Page 118

1. Chili	8. Hungary
2. Lapland	9. Poland
3. Greece	10. Thailand
4. Turkey	11. Java
5. China	12. Ireland
6. Finland	13. Greenland
7. Guinea	14. Tibet

Alphabet puns
Page 119

1. b	9. w
2. c	10. mt
3. t	11. ez
4. q	12. iv
5. o	13. tp
6. i	14. nv
7. p	15. icu
8. u	

Hidden birds
Page 120

bluebird, penguin, lovebird, swan, robin, crane, goose, stork, roadrunner, turkey, woodpecker, cuckoo, dove, raven, owl, swift, wren, whippoorwill, lark, blackbird, crow, oriole, vulture, eagle, cockatoo, kiwi, hawk, duck, parrot, crow, kite, gull, owl, swallow, bluejay, flamingo

Hidden flora
Page 121

marigold, goldenrod, artichoke, balsam, cactus, kumquat, laurel, cacti, raspberry, ash, peony, Swiss chard, spruce, mango, gourd, baobab, eucalyptus, sloe, mushroom, mesquite, avocado, yew, persimmon, grass, sumac, papaya, berry, iris, reed, corn, cork, dewberry, fig, dogwood, thistle

"Cold" words
Page 122

frost, frostbite, tundra, numb, cold, coldness, zero, thermic, athermic, subzero, freeze, freezer, ski, alpine, ice, ice age, glaciation, igloo, hockey, floe, algid, mentholated, thaw, wintry, frigid, frigorific, freon, rime, boreal, cone, cool, coolant, refrigerate, blizzard, ice, gelation, hail, bleak, congeal, icicle, gelid, polar, snow, icy, arctic, ice cap, bergs

"Small" words
Page 123

meager, germ, miniature, iota, epitome, jot, scant, dwarf, small, molecule, tiny, point, homunculus, urchin, microbe, wee, pygmy, diminution, minute, elf, rudiment, thin, fine, particle, microcosm, minimum, undersize, atom, Tom Thumb, bantam, stunted, dumpy, micron, minutia, Lilliputian, ant, runt, runty, exiguity, mite.

One word at a time
Page 124

1. male, mole, molt
2. cane, cant, cent
3. bore, bare, bark
4. fir, air, ail, all
5. duel, fuel, feel, keel
6. pore, pole, poll, pull
7. wise, wile, file, fill
8. rope, ripe, rise, wise
9. mild, mile, male, tale

Part 4

A word finder thesaurus of selected words

The contributor of the word finder thesaurus is Walter D. Glanze, Walter Glanze Word Books, Associates.

Introduction

This "Word finder thesaurus of selected words" gives you 14,000 of the most common and therefore most powerful words of our time. They are grouped as synonyms, that is, by closely related meanings.

This arrangement *suggests* a word, it does not *describe* it, as the dictionary does. In this sense, the "Word finder" is the opposite of the dictionary. You turn to the dictionary if you have the word but not the meaning; you turn to the "Word finder" if you have the meaning but not the word.

Use the "Word finder" when you have an idea but don't know how to put it in words; or when you have thought of a word but it is not the one that fits; or when you do have a word that fits, but you don't want to use it over and over again and need a fresh word just for variety. Whether the right word is on the tip of your tongue or still far beyond the horizon, open the "Word finder" and begin with a word you *do* think of, and see where it leads you. You may find the proper word in the first entry you look up. Or the first entry may refer you to a second entry or a third entry, and you find the word you need there.

One way that the "Word finder" refers you from one entry to another is through the synonyms that appear in small capital letters. The synonyms printed in small capital letters are themselves *lead words;* that is, they in turn appear as the headwords of other entries with their own lists of synonyms. If you are not satisfied with the words you find in an entry, take any one of these small-capital synonyms as a point of departure. Let those words carry you to fresh groups of synonyms in other entries, until you find the words that express clearly what you want to say.

Before actually using your "Word finder," spend an hour with it just browsing for the sheer pleasure of adventure. A book of synonyms is often called a *thesaurus,* which, along with our word *treasure,* comes from a Greek word meaning just that—a treasure, a treasury, a storehouse. Let this "Word finder" show you again the richness and the beauty of our language. Let it stimulate your thinking.

While you probably don't need further special instructions to use this "Word finder," you will work with it more effectively, and you may enjoy it more, if you are familiar with the tightly efficient way it is organized.

There are two kinds of entries—lead entries and reference entries. (See the "Key to entries and abbreviations" on page 159.) A *lead entry* consists of one of the 5,100 lead words and its synonyms. The synonyms are grouped by part of speech and often by different meanings within a part of speech. All synonyms that in turn are also lead words at their own alphabetical place (and in the same meaning) are printed in small capital letters; all other synonyms are printed in lower-case letters and are listed as headwords of the 9,000 reference entries. A *reference entry* consists of a reference word (followed by a colon and "see") and the lead word or lead words under which the reference word is given as a synonym. (Note that the lead words listed in a reference entry are not necessarily synonymous with each other.)

In this manner, all words that appear as synonyms are listed also as headwords in one alphabetical order. Through repetition of these 14,000 different words as synonyms, this "Word finder" contains a total of about 100,000 words in synonymous relationship.

Many words are given with more than one basic *meaning.* Consider the difference between *acute appendicitis* and *acute eyesight* or the even greater difference between *a new pupil* and *the pupil of the eye.* Such separate meanings are numbered and introduced by example phrases if the separate meanings occur within the same part of speech.

These *example phrases,* of which there are thousands in this "Word finder," are meant to be a handy way of showing how one basic meaning, with one group of synonyms, differs from another basic meaning, with another group of synonyms. But these phrases are not meant to contain a "slot" into which all synonyms of a group have to fit. For example, in the entry **act** in the "Key to entries and abbreviations," the phrase *an act of mercy* is followed by the synonyms "deed, action, feat, exploit." While we would hardly say "an exploit of mercy," the sample phrase leaves no doubt that these four synonyms are entirely different from the synonyms that follow the other sample phrases: *to vote for the act* (bill, law, etc.); *to put on an act* (pretense, fakery, etc.); and *the audience applauded her act* (performance, routine, etc.).

Compiled by Walter D. Glanze, a noted word expert, this "Word finder" is the first collection of synonyms with a controlled vocabulary. The 14,000 entries are based on *The Living Word Vocabulary,* a study conducted by Edgar Dale and Joseph O'Rourke, which was published in 1976 and 1979. The 5,100 lead words of this "Word finder" were chosen among words that are understood by 4th- to 10th-graders. All other synonyms, about 9,000, were chosen among words that are understood by 4th- to 12th-graders, except for certain carefully selected words on the college level. Besides the Dale-O'Rourke grading for word *recognition,* word *usage* was taken into account in choosing the 5,100 lead words. All are among the most commonly used words according to major word frequency studies, from the Thorndike-Lorge count of 1943 to the American Heritage count of 1971.

This "Word finder" may also be the first one to emphasize that the common words are the most expressive ones—that the basic stock of the English language, if effectively used, is more beautiful, more alive, and, yes, richer than a vast but vaguely managed vocabulary. Most books of synonyms go in the opposite direction, dipping at random into the 200,000- or 400,000-word range of the language, reaching for rarer and rarer synonyms. There is, no doubt, a place and a need for such books. But there is also a place and a need for the new kind of "Word finder" you have before you.

While you should *know* many words—hundreds of thousands if you can—it does not matter how many words you *use* as long as you say what you want to say. Shakespeare's vocabulary is often considered huge, and yet he used not more than about 20,000 different words in all his works. The Bible makes do with 6,000. In most situations, you are better off using few words. But choose them well, use them wisely, and let your language be simple, clear, sincere.

Be *comfortable* with the words you use. Use only words that you know. If you are not sure what a word means, look it up in the dictionary. Make it your own.

Always keep your "Word finder" close by. Even when you don't need a word at the moment, browse in it. See how rich and flexible the English language can be. It is living and breathing, like you.

Key to entries and abbreviations

Lead words (with part-of-speech label): entry words followed by synonyms

act *n.* **1** *(an act of mercy)* DEED, ACTION, feat, exploit; **2** *(to vote for the act)* bill, LAW, measure, statute; **3** *(to put on an act)* pretense, fakery, deception; **4** *(the audience applauded her act)* PERFORMANCE, ROUTINE, PART, DIVISION.

Words in small capital letters: synonyms that are lead words at their own alphabetical place (see **action** below)

Additional parts of speech of a lead word placed in separate paragraphs (see list of abbreviations below)

— *v.* **1** *(to act constructively)* FUNCTION, OPERATE, WORK, officiate; **2** *(to act in a show)* PERFORM, PLAY, impersonate.

Words in lower-case letters: synonyms that do not occur as lead words and are therefore listed as reference words (see **feat** below)

Basically different meanings within a part of speech are numbered

action *n.* **1** *(a man of action)* movement, ACT, ACHIEVEMENT, OPERATION; **2** *(he died in action)* BATTLE, COMBAT, fighting; **3** *(to bring an action against the company)* lawsuit, SUIT.

Example phrases identify the basically different meanings

bill *n.* **1** *(an overdue bill)* ACCOUNT, STATEMENT, invoice; **2** *(a five-dollar bill)* dollar, bank note, greenback, BUCK, MONEY; **3** *(a duck's bill)* BEAK, neb; **4** *(a bill of goods)* LIST, STATEMENT, tally. See also ACT.

"See also": reference to additional meanings of the same part of speech

Reference words (with a colon and "see"): entry words followed by reference to the lead word(s) under which they appear (see **act** above)

fakery: see ACT.

feat: see ACHIEVEMENT; ACT; DEED; PERFORMANCE; STROKE; STUNT.

fleet *n.* NAVY, armada, GROUP, FORMATION.
— *adj.:* see QUICK; RAPID; SWIFT.

Parts of speech with "see": additional reference entries

Words that are spelled alike and pronounced alike (words that are homographs and homophones) are listed as one entry

lie *v.* **1** *(he lied about his age)* DECEIVE, misinform, falsify, FIB, perjure, fabricate; **2** *(Mexico City lies on a plateau)* BE, LOCATE, repose, recline, STRETCH, REMAIN.
— *n.* falsehood, untruth, deception, libel, perjury, MYTH, fabrication.

Words that are spelled alike but pronounced differently (words that are homographs but not homophones) are listed as one entry

tear *v.* RIP, SPLIT, SHRED, INJURE, SPEED.
— *n.* **1** *(wear and tear)* SPLIT, rip, OPENING, RENT, ABUSE; **2** *(to shed tears)* teardrop, droplet, WATER.

Abbreviations

adj. adjective	*n.* noun
adv. adverb	*pl.n.* plural noun
art. article	*prep.* preposition
conj. conjunction	*pron.* pronoun
interj. interjection	*v.* verb

A

a *adj., art.* ONE, SINGLE, EACH, EVERY, ANY, SOME, SAME, an.

abandon *v.* give up, SURRENDER, cede, YIELD, relinquish, LEAVE, DESERT, QUIT.
— *n.* FREEDOM, DASH, ENTHUSIASM, immorality.

abandoned: see AGROUND; DESOLATE; FORGOTTEN; LEFT.

abandonment: see SURRENDER.

abash: see EMBARRASS.

abashed: see ASHAMED.

abate: see DECREASE; DIMINISH; LESSEN; SLACKEN.

abbey: see CONVENT.

abbot: see MONK.

abbreviate *v.* CUT, SHORTEN, abridge, CONDENSE, cut down, REDUCE.

abbreviation *n.* REDUCTION, CONTRACTION, shortening, condensation.

A.B.C., ABC's: see ALPHABET.

abdicate: see RESIGN; RETIRE.

abdomen: see BELLY.

abhor: see DESPISE; HATE.

abhorrence: see DISGUST; HATRED.

abhorrent: see HATEFUL.

abide by *v.* conform to, tolerate, stomach, keep, FULFILL.

ability *n.* TALENT, CAPACITY, GENIUS, dexterity, SKILL, competency, aptitude, knack, flair, GIFT, POWER, FORCE, ENERGY, faculty.

able *adj.* CAPABLE, qualified, talented, apt, COMPETENT, proficient, masterly, skillful, CLEVER, INGENIOUS, ADEQUATE.

abnormal *adj.* UNNATURAL, DEFORMED, PECULIAR, STRANGE, QUEER, perverted, IRREGULAR, UNUSUAL, SINGULAR, EXCEPTIONAL.

abnormality: see FREAK; ODDITY.

aboard *adj., prep.* IN, ON, into, INSIDE.

abode: see HEARTH; HOME; HOUSE; MANSION.

abolish *v.* CANCEL, END, ELIMINATE, ERASE, obliterate, DESTROY.

abolition: see ELIMINATION.

abomination: see DISGUST.

abortion: see GOOF.

abortive: see UNSUCCESSFUL.

abound: see SWARM.

abounding: see ABUNDANT.

about *prep.* AROUND, surrounding, CONCERNING, OVER, THROUGHOUT, THROUGH, NEAR, round.
— *adv.* AROUND, APPROXIMATELY, ALMOST, CLOSE, NEARBY.
— *adj.* ready.

above *prep.* OVER, BEYOND.
— *adv.* overhead, UPWARD, aloft, BEFORE, earlier.
— *adj.*: see SUPERIOR.

aboveboard: see OPEN.

abreast: see EQUAL.

abridge: see ABBREVIATE; SHORTEN.

abridgment: see DIGEST; SUMMARY.

abroad *adv.* overseas, AWAY, expansively, widely, extensively, publicly.

abrupt *adj.* **1** (*an abrupt manner*) SUDDEN, BLUNT, HASTY, curt, SHORT, RUDE, UNEXPECTED; **2** (*an abrupt cliff*) STEEP, sheer, SHARP, RUGGED.

abruptly: see UNAWARES.

abscess: see BLISTER; BOIL.

absence *n.* **1** (*two absences*) nonattendance, LEAVE, furlough; **2** (*absence of proof*) LACK, deficiency, NEED, want, emptiness.

absent *adj.* AWAY, gone, MISSING, lacking, LOST, ABSENT-MINDED.

absent-minded *adj.* FORGETFUL, inattentive, distracted, musing, dreaming, day-dreaming, preoccupied, lost.

absent-mindedness: see FORGETFULNESS.

absolute *adj.* COMPLETE, PERFECT, POSITIVE, CERTAIN, unquestionable, INDEPENDENT, PURE, GENUINE, unqualified, TOTAL, unlimited, despotic, authoritarian.

absolutely *adv.* COMPLETELY, unconditionally, unquestionably, DEFINITELY, POSITIVELY, REALLY, TRULY, INDEED, ACTUALLY.

absolution: see EXCUSE; FORGIVENESS.

absolve: see EXCUSE.

absorb *v.* **1** (*a sponge absorbs water*) take in, imbibe, DEVOUR, CONSUME, assimilate; **2** (*to be absorbed in a book*) engross, immerse, OCCUPY, FILL, CONSUME.

absorbed: see DEEP.

absorbing: see INTERESTING.

abstain: see DIET; FAST.

abstract: see DIGEST; INVISIBLE.

abstruse: see DIFFICULT.

absurd *adj.* FOOLISH, SILLY, NONSENSICAL, UNREASONABLE, irrational, SENSELESS, wild, preposterous, RIDICULOUS, inconsistent.

absurdity: see FOLLY; NONSENSE; STUPIDITY.

abundance *n.* PLENTY, profusion, ampleness, FLOOD, extravagance, accumulation, EXCESS, oodles.

abundant *adj.* PLENTIFUL, AMPLE, abounding, bountiful, RICH, lavish, EXCESSIVE.

abuse *v.* 1 (*to abuse one's privileges*) misuse, misapply, DECEIVE, BETRAY; 2 (*to abuse a child*) MISTREAT, maltreat, HARM, SCOLD, berate, vilify, reproach, INSULT, libel, slander, VIOLATE, ravish.
— *n.* misuse, mistreatment, SCORN, reproach, oppression, TORTURE, libel, slander, vituperation.

abut: see ADJOIN; JOIN.

abyss: see DEEP; GULF; PIT.

academician: see INTELLECTUAL; PROFESSOR.

academy *n.* SCHOOL, COLLEGE, seminary, institute, SOCIETY.

accede: see BEND; CONSENT.

accelerate *v.* HASTEN, SPEED, quicken, spur, expedite, STIMULATE.

accelerated: see FAST, HURRIED.

accent *n.* STRESS, emphasis, BEAT, METER, drawl, PRONUNCIATION, MARK.
— *v.* STRESS, emphasize, MARK.

accentuate: see STRESS.

accept *v.* RECEIVE, TAKE, RECOGNIZE, APPROVE, ALLOW, ADMIT, BEAR, tolerate, SUPPOSE.

acceptable: see AGREEABLE; PASSABLE; REASONABLE; RESPECTABLE; TOLERABLE.

acceptance: see ADOPTION; APPROVAL; BELIEF; MEMBERSHIP; RECEIPT; RECEPTION; RECOGNITION.

accepted: see IN; SUPPOSED.

accepter: see RECEIVER.

access: see ADMISSION; ADMITTANCE; DOOR; ENTRANCE; ENTRY; MOUTH.

accessible: see AVAILABLE; CENTRAL; CONVENIENT; OPEN; READY.

accessory *n.* 1 (*a car equipped with all the accessories*) EQUIPMENT, ARTICLE, PART, AID; 2 (*an accessory to the crime*) auxiliary, helper, crutch, accomplice, CONFEDERATE.

accident *n.* CHANCE, HAZARD, LUCK, FORTUNE, MISFORTUNE, mishap, casualty, DISASTER.

accidental: see CASUAL; RANDOM.

accidentally: see INCIDENTALLY; UNAWARES.

acclaim: see APPLAUD; PRAISE.

acclamation: see APPLAUSE.

accommodate *v.* 1 (*a room accommodating three persons*) HOUSE, LODGE, quarter, HOLD; 2 (*to accommodate differences*) ADAPT, ARRANGE, conform, SUIT, AID, COMPOSE, HELP, FURNISH.

accommodating: see ADJUSTABLE; COOPERATIVE.

accommodation *n.* SEAT, PLACE, ROOM, lodging, CONVENIENCE, ADVANTAGE.

accompany *v.* go with, ATTEND, ESCORT, chaperon, convoy, FOLLOW.

accompanying: see WITH.

accomplice: see ACCESSORY; AID; CONFEDERATE.

accomplish *v.* ACHIEVE, PERFORM, carry out, DO, REALIZE, FULFILL, EXECUTE, COMPLETE, FINISH.

accomplished *adj.* 1 (*mission accomplished*) done, completed, OVER, EXISTENT; 2 (*an accomplished pianist*) proficient, SKILLED, polished.

accomplishment *n.* ACHIEVEMENT, attainment, SKILL, SUCCESS, TRIUMPH.

accord: see AGREE; AGREEMENT; CORRESPONDENCE; HARMONIZE.

accordance: see HARMONY.

accordingly: see THUS.

according to *prep.* depending on, BY.

accost: see ADDRESS; APPROACH.

account *v.* COUNT, CONSIDER, JUDGE, BELIEVE, ESTEEM, THINK.
— *n.* 1 (*a bank account*) DEPOSIT, MONEY, SAVINGS, RECORD, ledger; 2 (*of no account*) IMPORTANCE, VALUE; 3 (*on this account*) BASIS, REASON, CONSIDERATION; 4 (*to give an account of it*) EXPLANATION, REPORT, recital.

accountability: see RESPONSIBILITY.

accountable *adj.* RESPONSIBLE, answerable, LIABLE, GUILTY.

account for *v.* EXPLAIN, JUSTIFY, INTERPRET, SOLVE, CAUSE, amount to.

accredit: see TRUST.

accrue: see ACCUMULATE.

accumulate *v.* PILE, pile up, COLLECT, GATHER, STORE, hoard, GROW, accrue, INCREASE.

accumulation: see ABUNDANCE; HEAP; MASS; PILE.

accuracy: see AIM; CLOSENESS; EXACTNESS; JUSTICE; PRECISION; TRUTH.

accurate *adj.* CORRECT, EXACT, TRUE, PRECISE, FAITHFUL, STRICT, CLOSE, unerring.

accurately: see EXACTLY; PROPERLY.

accusation: see CHARGE; COMPLAINT.

accuse *v.* BLAME, CHARGE, indict, arraign, impeach, censure.

accused: see SUSPECT.

accustom *v.* familiarize, habituate, TRAIN, drill, season.

accustomed *adj.* USUAL, REGULAR, HABITUAL, routine, TRADITIONAL.

ace: see ONE.

ache *v.* **1** (*my leg aches*) HURT, pain; **2** (*he's aching to get even*) YEARN, long, CRAVE, pine, aspire. — *n.* PAIN, discomfort, longing.

achievable: see PRACTICAL.

achieve *v.* GAIN, ATTAIN, OBTAIN, WIN, GET, ACCOMPLISH, PERFORM, COMPLETE, EARN, DO.

achievement *n.* ACCOMPLISHMENT, feat, DEED, attainment, PERFORMANCE, exploit, completion, fulfillment.

aching: see PAINFUL; SORE; SUFFERING.

acid *adj.* SHARP, biting, stinging, SOUR, tart. — *n.* COMPOUND, vinegar, LSD.

acidity: see BITTERNESS.

acknowledge *v.* **1** (*to acknowledge a favor*) THANK, APPRECIATE, ACCEPT; **2** (*to acknowledge a fact*) ADMIT, GRANT, CONFESS, concede, ALLOW, ACCEPT, RECOGNIZE.

acknowledgment: see ADMISSION; APPRECIATION; CONFESSION; CREDIT; RECEIPT; RECOGNITION; REPLY; RESPONSE; THANKS.

acme: see CROWN; TOP.

acquaint *v.* familiarize, TELL, INFORM, NOTIFY, apprise, MENTION.

acquaintance *n.* **1** (*an old acquaintance*) FRIEND, ASSOCIATE, colleague; **2** (*to make one's acquaintance*) KNOWLEDGE, familiarity.

acquiesce: see AGREE; CONSENT.

acquiescence: see CONSENT.

acquire *v.* GET, GAIN, OBTAIN, secure.

acquired: see LEARNED.

acquirer: see RECEIVER.

acquisition: see CATCH; PURCHASE.

acquit: see CLEAR; FORGIVE; PARDON; RELEASE.

acquittal: see DISCHARGE; FORGIVENESS; PARDON.

acreage: see AREA; ESTATE; PROPERTY; TRACT.

acrid: see BITTER.

acrimony: see BITTERNESS.

acrobatic: see ATHLETIC.

across *prep.* OVER, facing, opposite to. — *adv.* crosswise, cross, crisscross, aslant, transversely, OPPOSITE.

act *n.* **1** (*an act of mercy*) DEED, ACTION, feat, exploit; **2** (*to vote for the act*) bill, LAW, measure, statute; **3** (*to put on an act*) pretense, fakery, deception; **4** (*the audience applauded her act*) PERFORMANCE, ROUTINE, PART, DIVISION. — *v.* **1** (*to act constructively*) FUNCTION, OPERATE, WORK, officiate; **2** (*to act in a show*) PERFORM, PLAY, impersonate.

action *n.* **1** (*a man of action*) movement, ACT, ACHIEVEMENT, OPERATION; **2** (*he died in action*) BATTLE, COMBAT, fighting; **3** (*to bring an action against the company*) lawsuit, SUIT.

activate: see FUEL; STIMULATE.

activation: see APPLICATION.

active *adj.* LIVELY, sprightly, ALERT, BRISK, nimble, agile, ENERGETIC, INDUSTRIOUS, BUSY, diligent, unexpired.

activity *n.* movement, liveliness, ACTION, ENERGY, OCCUPATION, FUNCTION.

actor *n.* doer, participant, PERFORMER, PLAYER.

actors: see CAST.

actress: see PERFORMER.

actual *adj.* REAL, EXISTENT, SURE, GENUINE, TRUE, CERTAIN, POSITIVE, factual, PRESENT, latest.

actuality: see BEING; REALITY; TRUTH.

actually *adv.* REALLY, TRULY, SURELY, CERTAINLY.

actuated: see MECHANICAL.

acute *adj.* **1** *(acute appendicitis)* SEVERE, SHARP, SUDDEN, crucial, CRITICAL, SHRILL, POINTED; **2** *(acute eyesight)* KEEN, SHARP, QUICK, shrewd, FINE, discerning, INTELLIGENT, ALERT.

acutely: see SHARPLY.

acuteness: see SMARTNESS.

ad: see ADVERTISEMENT; COMMERCIAL.

adage: see PROVERB.

adapt *v.* ACCOMMODATE, ADJUST, FIT, MODIFY, SUIT, *reconcile, conform.*

adaptability: see FLEXIBILITY.

adaptable: see ADJUSTABLE; HARMONIOUS.

adaptation: see APPLICATION.

add *v.* JOIN, ATTACH, INCREASE, SUPPLEMENT, augment, total, sum up, UNITE.

added: see ADDITIONAL; ANOTHER.

added to: see PLUS.

addenda: see SUPPLEMENT.

addendum: see APPENDIX.

addiction: see HABIT.

adding: see ADDITION.

adding machine: see COUNTER.

addition *n.* INCREASE, ENLARGEMENT, SUPPLEMENT, ATTACHMENT, adding, TOTAL, SUM.

additional *adj.* added, EXTRA, SUPPLEMENTARY, auxiliary, MORE.

additionally: see ALSO; BESIDES; INCREASINGLY; MORE.

additive: see SUPPLEMENT.

address *n.* **1** *(their address in New York)* HOME, RESIDENCE, LOCATION, STREET; **2** *(an address lasting one hour)* SPEECH, TALK, oration, LECTURE, PAPER.
— *v.* GREET, HAIL, accost, SALUTE, direct, speak to.

add up: see AMOUNT; SUM; SUMMARIZE.

adept: see EXPERT; MECHANICAL; PRACTICED; SKILLED; VETERAN.

adequate *adj.* ENOUGH, SUFFICIENT, AMPLE, ABLE, EQUAL, SUITABLE.

adequately: see SOMEWHAT; WELL.

adhere: see BIND; CLING; GLUE; STICK.

adherent: see CLIENT; PUPIL.

adhere to: see HOLD.

adhesive *adj.* sticky, gluey, tacky, gooey, glutinous.
— *n.* PASTE, GLUE, mucilage, GUM, CEMENT.

adieu: see FAREWELL; GOOD-BYE.

adios: see GOOD-BYE.

adjacent: see HEAR; NEXT.

adjacent to: see BESIDE; NEAR.

adjoin *v.* border, TOUCH, MEET, neighbor, abut.

adjoining: see BESIDE; NEAR; NEXT.

adjourn *v.* SUSPEND, DISSOLVE, CLOSE, END, POSTPONE, defer, put off, terminate.

adjournment: see SUSPENSION.

adjust *v.* CORRECT, rectify, reconcile, ADAPT, ARRANGE, SETTLE, FIT, SUIT, REGULATE, attune, AMEND, ACCOMMODATE, orientate.

adjustable *adj.* adaptable, FLEXIBLE, VARIABLE, accommodating, elastic, versatile, movable.

adjustment: see COMPROMISE; JUSTIFICATION.

administer: see CARRY ON; ENFORCE; GOVERN; MANAGE; PRESIDE; PROVIDE.

administering: see ADMINISTRATION.

administration *n.* **1** *(the administration in Washington)* GOVERNMENT, executive, officials, bureaucracy; **2** *(the administration of a school)* MANAGEMENT, DIRECTION, REGULATION, CONDUCT, CONTROL, SUPERVISION; **3** *(the administration of a medicine)* administering, giving, dispensing, DISTRIBUTION.

administrative: see OFFICIAL; POLITICAL.

administrator: see EXECUTIVE; MANAGER; OFFICER; OFFICIAL; PRESIDENT; SUPERINTENDENT; SUPERVISOR.

admirable *adj.* praiseworthy, commendable, meritorious, EXCELLENT, FINE.

admiration *n.* ESTEEM, RESPECT, APPROVAL, delight, WONDER, adoration.

admire *v.* ESTEEM, RESPECT, ADORE, APPROVE.

admired: see POPULAR.

admirer: see FOLLOWER; LOVER.

admissible: see PASSABLE; PERMISSIBLE.

admission *n.* **1** *(his admission of guilt)* CONFESSION, acknowledgment; **2** *(the admission*

of immigrants) ADMITTANCE, ENTRANCE, access;
3 *(admission: $4)* PRICE, TICKET, FEE, PASS.

admit *v.* **1** *(admitted to the bar)* let in, RECEIVE,
ACCEPT, take in; **2** *(admitting his guilt)* CONFESS,
ACKNOWLEDGE, concede, own.

admittance *n.* ADMISSION, ENTRANCE, access.

admonish: see CAUTION; FOREWARN.

admonition: see SERMON.

adolescence: see YOUTH.

adolescent: see MINOR; YOUNG; YOUNGSTER.

adopt *v.* APPROPRIATE, TAKE, USE, EMPLOY.

adoption *n.* SELECTION, CHOICE, acceptance,
enactment, espousal, affiliation, SUPPORT.

adorable *adj.* LOVABLE, LOVELY, PRECIOUS, DEAR,
DARLING, CUTE, SWEET, DELIGHTFUL.

adoration: see ADMIRATION; LOVE; WORSHIP.

adore *v.* WORSHIP, ADMIRE, ESTEEM, HONOR,
RESPECT, LOVE, FAVOR, IDOLIZE.

adored: see BELOVED; DARLING; DEAR; FAVORITE.

adorn *v.* DECORATE, ORNAMENT, bedeck, array.

adorned: see FANCY.

adorning: see DECORATIVE.

adornment: see ORNAMENT.

adrift *adj.* afloat, LOOSE, aimless, drifting,
uncontrolled, derelict.

adulate: see FLATTER.

adult *n.* GROWN-UP, WOMAN, MAN.
— *adj.* GROWN-UP, GROWN, MATURE, full-grown.

adulthood: see AGE; MATURITY.

advance *v.* **1** *(the boss advanced him fifty dollars)*
GIVE, LEND, LOAN; **2** *(to advance one's interests)*
PROMOTE, FURTHER, go on, MOVE, PROCEED,
PROGRESS, IMPROVE, INCREASE.
See also SUBMIT; SUGGEST.
— *n.*: see LOAN; OFFER.

advanced *adj.* foremost, improved, MATURE,
upper, ELABORATE, complicated, PROGRESSIVE.

advancement *n.* PROGRESS, headway,
IMPROVEMENT, ELEVATION, PROMOTION,
PROPOSAL.

advancing: see ONWARD.

advantage *n.* SUPERIORITY, EDGE, vantage, POWER,
BENEFIT, PROFIT, GAIN.

advantageous: see FAVORABLE; HELPFUL;
PROFITABLE; USEFUL; WORTHY.

advantageously: see PAT, PRACTICALLY.

advent: see ARRIVAL.

adventure *n.* VENTURE, UNDERTAKING, enterprise,
escapade, lark, EXPERIENCE.

adventurer: see EXPLORER; PIONEER; SOLDIER.

adventurous *adj.* DARING, BOLD, BRAVE,
COURAGEOUS, enterprising, audacious, RASH.

adventurousness: see DARING.

adversary: see COMPETITION; COMPETITOR; FOE;
OPPONENT; OPPOSITION; RIVAL; SIDE.

adverse: see UNFORTUNATE.

adversity: see HARDSHIP; REVERSE.

advertise *v.* PUBLISH, BROADCAST, DISPLAY,
FEATURE, INFORM, ANNOUNCE, ballyhoo.

advertisement *n.* advertising, PUBLICITY,
COMMERCIAL, ANNOUNCEMENT, NOTICE, ad,
DISPLAY, ballyhoo, blurb, broadcast, POSTER,
billboard, handbill.

advertising: see ADVERTISEMENT.

advice *n.* counsel, SUGGESTION, INSTRUCTION,
OPINION, RECOMMENDATION, CAUTION,
WARNING.

advise *v.* INFORM, NOTIFY, INSTRUCT, counsel,
RECOMMEND, SUGGEST, CAUTION, WARN.

advisedly: see PURPOSELY.

adviser: see ATTORNEY; COUNSELOR; GUIDE.

advisers: see CABINET; PANEL.

advisory: see INFORMATIVE.

advocate: see ATTORNEY; COUNSELOR; LAWYER;
SUPPORT; SUPPORTER.

aeronautics: see FLIGHT.

afar *adv.* faraway, AWAY, OFF, FAR, far off,
ELSEWHERE, ABROAD, REMOTE, remotely.

affability: see FLEXIBILITY.

affable: see SOCIABLE.

affair *n.* **1** *(affairs of state)* CONCERN, MATTER,
INTEREST, FUNCTION, BUSINESS, WORK, PROJECT;
2 *(a love affair)* ROMANCE, ENGAGEMENT, CASE,
INCIDENT, OCCASION, EVENT.

affect *v.* **1** *(it affected us all)* INFLUENCE, MOVE,
TOUCH, IMPRESS, CONCERN, CHANGE, MODIFY,
UPSET, SICKEN; **2** *(to affect ignorance)* PRETEND,
feign, fake, simulate, IMITATE.

affected: see ARTIFICIAL.

affecting: see EXCITABLE.

affection *n.* fondness, LOVE, TENDERNESS, ATTACHMENT, WARMTH, friendliness.

affectionate *adj.* loving, WARM, TENDER, FOND, EMOTIONAL, KIND, attached.

affidavit: see CERTIFICATION.

affiliate: see BELONG; CHAPTER; MEMBER.

affiliated: see ALLIED; RELATED.

affiliation: see ADOPTION; ALLIANCE; CONNECTION; MEMBERSHIP.

affirm: see ASSURE; CLAIM; CONFIRM; STATE; SWEAR; VERIFY; VOW.

affirmation: see DECLARATION; STATEMENT; VERIFICATION; VOW; WORD; YES.

affirmative: see INSISTENT.

affix: see APPLY; POST.

afflict: see AIL; DISTRESS; GRIEVE; INFECT; SICKEN; TORTURE.

afflicted: see CURSED; MISERABLE; STRICKEN.

affliction: see AILMENT; CURSE; CONTRACTION; DISEASE; GRIEF; INFECTION; MISFORTUNE; PAIN; TROUBLE; WOE.

affluence: see LUXURY; PROSPERITY; RICHNESS; WEALTH.

affluent: see PROSPEROUS; RICH.

afford *v.* PAY, BEAR, SUPPORT, MANAGE, GIVE, GRANT, SPARE, YIELD, SUPPLY, FURNISH.

affront: see INJURE; INJURY.

afield: see AWAY.

afloat: see ADRIFT.

aforementioned: see PREVIOUS.

aforesaid: see FOREGOING; PRECEDING.

aforethought: see INTENTIONAL.

aforetime: see ONCE.

afraid *adj.* frightened, FEARFUL, TIMID, scared, alarmed, RELUCTANT, regretful.

after *prep.* chasing, following, behind, later than, subsequent to, CONCERNING.
— *adv.* BEHIND, subsequently, later, AFTERWARDS.
— *adj.*: see NEXT; REAR.

aftereffect: see CONSEQUENCE.

aftermath: see OUTCOME.

afterthought: see FOOTNOTE.

afterwards *adv.* subsequently, later, AFTER, BEHIND.

again *adv.* repeatedly, anew, MOREOVER, BESIDES, FURTHER.

against *prep.* facing, opposite to, contrary to.
— *adv.*: see OFF.

age *n.* **1** *(the iron age)* PERIOD, TIME, ERA, epoch; **2** *(of age)* years, MATURITY, adulthood.
— *v.* RIPEN, MATURE, MELLOW.

aged *adj.* OLD, elderly, ADVANCED, MATURE, RIPE, STALE, MELLOW, ANCIENT, FEEBLE, decrepit, dilapidated.

agency *n.* **1** *(a welfare agency)* OFFICE, BUREAU, ORGANIZATION, COMPANY, BUSINESS; **2** *(nominated by the agency of friends)* FORCE, MEANS, METHOD, ACTION, OPERATION, FUNCTION.

agenda: see CALENDAR; CARD; SCHEDULE.

agent *n.* **1** *(an FBI agent)* representative, go-between, proxy, DEPUTY, OFFICIAL, MANAGER, CONDUCTOR; **2** *(a cleansing agent)* CAUSE, FACTOR, MEANS, INSTRUMENT, SUBSTANCE.

agents: see REPRESENTATION.

age-old: see TRADITIONAL.

aggravate: see INFURIATE; PESTER.

aggregation: see COLLECTION; HEAP; TOTAL.

aggression: see INVASION.

aggressive *adj.* FORCEFUL, ENERGETIC, VIGOROUS, enterprising, combative, pugnacious, warlike, belligerent, HOSTILE.

aggressiveness: see HOSTILITY.

aggressor: see FIGHTER; INVADER.

agile: see ACTIVE.

agility: see BRISKNESS.

aging: see MATURITY; OLD; OLD-FASHIONED.

agitate: see SHAKE; STARTLE; STIR; FAN.

agitated: see FEVERISH; IMPATIENT; RESTLESS; SHAKEN.

agitation: see DISTRACTION; EXCITEMENT; HURRY; IMPATIENCE; SHUDDER.

aglow: see RADIANT.

ago *adj.* PAST, gone, gone by, bygone.
— *adv.* PAST, heretofore, SINCE, FORMERLY, ONCE.

agonize: see FRET; SUFFER; WORRY.

agonizing: see PAINFUL; SORROWFUL.

agony *n.* MISERY, TORMENT, TORTURE, DISTRESS, PAIN, SUFFERING.

agree *v.* CONSENT, concur, accord, acquiesce, comply, ACCEPT, YIELD, HARMONIZE, coincide, MATCH, SETTLE, UNITE.

agreeable *adj.* amiable, FRIENDLY, good-natured, PLEASANT, PLEASING, acceptable, inclined.

agreed: see CERTAIN; YES.

agreeing: see UNANIMOUS.

agreement *n.* **1** *(to sign an agreement)* accord, pact, CONTRACT, COVENANT, BARGAIN, DEAL, TREATY; **2** *(to come to an agreement)* UNDERSTANDING, unanimity, conformity, HARMONY, SETTLEMENT.

agricultural: see RURAL.

agriculture *n.* farming, husbandry, cultivation, culture, horticulture.

aground *adj.* grounded, beached, stranded, ASHORE, shipwrecked, abandoned.

ahead *adv.* FORWARD, ONWARD, BEFORE.

aid *n.* **1** *(foreign aid)* HELP, ASSISTANCE, AID, RELIEF, SUPPORT, subsidy; **2** *(to volunteer as an aid)* helper, aide, ASSISTANT, auxiliary, CONFEDERATE, ally, backer, accomplice, aide-de-camp.
— *v.* HELP, ASSIST, SUPPORT, RELIEVE, BACK, subsidize, facilitate, PROMOTE, BENEFIT.

aide: see AID, ASSISTANT; ATTENDANT; DEPUTY; HELP.

aide-de-camp: see AID.

ail *v.* TROUBLE, pain, ACHE, DISTRESS, afflict, SUFFER.

ailing: see UNHEALTHY.

ailment *n.* SICKNESS, ILLNESS, COMPLAINT, DISEASE, disorder, affliction.

aim *n.* **1** *(within the cannon's aim)* DIRECTION, sighting, aiming, pointing, accuracy; **2** *(her aim in life)* GOAL, TARGET, PURPOSE, DESIGN, END, MARK, INTENTION, PLAN, objective.
— *v.* DIRECT, LEVEL, POINT, TRY, ENDEAVOR, STRIVE, INTEND, purpose.

aiming: see AIM.

aimless: see ADRIFT; POINTLESS.

air *n.* **1** *(high in the air)* SPACE, airwaves, atmosphere, GAS, WIND, BREEZE, DRAFT; **2** *(an air of mystery)* ATTITUDE, bearing, MANNER, APPEARANCE, BEHAVIOR, look, CHARACTER. See also SONG.
— *v.* ventilate, purify, deodorize, DRY, BROADCAST, televise, publicize, EXPOSE, REVEAL, REPORT, PUBLISH, DISPLAY.

air-condition: see CHILL; REFRIGERATE.

aircraft: see PLANE.

air force: see MILITARY; SERVICE.

airily: see LIGHTLY.

airiness: see CHEERFULNESS.

airliner: see PLANE.

airplane: see JET; PLANE; SHIP.

air rifle: see GUN; RIFLE.

airship: see SHIP.

airtight *adj.* sealed, TIGHT, impregnable, impervious.

airwaves: see AIR.

airy: see BREEZY; LIGHT.

aisle *n.* passageway, walkway, pathway, ALLEY.

akin: see ALIKE; KIN.

alarm *n.* **1** *(to experience much alarm)* FRIGHT, TERROR, PANIC, DISMAY, FEAR; **2** *(the fire alarm)* siren, ALERT, WARNING, BELL, gong.
— *v.* FRIGHTEN, TERRIFY, PANIC, STARTLE.

alarmed: see AFRAID; PANICKY.

alarming *adj.* FRIGHTFUL, startling, SCARY, threatening, disturbing, upsetting.

albeit: see ALTHOUGH.

album: see RECORD.

alcazar: see CASTLE.

alchemical: see CHEMICAL.

alcohol: see LIQUOR.

alcoholic: see DRUNK; HARD.

alcove: see CHAMBER.

alert *adj.* wide-awake, WATCHFUL, ATTENTIVE, LIVELY, PROMPT, ACTIVE, QUICK, spirited, INTELLIGENT, ACUTE, SHARP.
— *n.* ALARM, WARNING, SIREN, watch.
— *v.* WARN, ALARM, CAUTION, tip off.

alertness *n.* sharpness, vigilance, readiness, watchfulness, diligence, keenness.

alias: see NAME.

alien *n.* STRANGER, FOREIGNER, IMMIGRANT, noncitizen.
—*adj.*: see FOREIGN; REMOTE; STRANGE.

alight: see LAND.

align: see FILE; JUSTIFY; RANK.

alignment: see JUSTIFICATION.

alike *adj.* SIMILAR, IDENTICAL, SAME, synonymous, resembling, RELATED, akin.

alikeness: see SAMENESS.

alive *adj.* **1** (*it's good to be alive*) LIVING, existing, LIVE, breathing; **2** (*a picture alive with color*) LIVELY, QUICK, BRISK, ACTIVE, vivacious, sprightly, AWARE, KEEN, responsive, SENSITIVE, joyous, CHEERFUL.

all *adj.* WHOLE, ENTIRE, TOTAL, COMPLETE, ANY, EVERY, MUCH.
—*pron.* everybody, EVERYTHING, EVERYONE, EACH.
—*n.* WHOLE, TOTAL, entirety, totality, EVERYTHING, WORLD, UNIVERSE.
—*adv.* wholly, ENTIRELY, COMPLETELY, QUITE.

Allah: see GOD.

allegation: see CHARGE; COMPLAINT.

allege: see CHARGE; STATE.

allegiance *n.* LOYALTY, faithfulness, homage, OBEDIENCE, DUTY, OBLIGATION, fidelity.

allegory: see FABLE.

all-embracing: see UNIVERSAL.

alleviate: see EASE; REDUCE; RELIEVE.

alleviation: see RELIEF.

alley *n.* WALK, PASSAGE, LANE, STREET, PATH, passageway, AISLE, byway, FOOTPATH, strip.

alleyway: see STREET.

alliance *n.* ASSOCIATION, UNION, confederation, LEAGUE, coalition, affiliation, COMBINATION, MARRIAGE, RELATIONSHIP, CONNECTION, TREATY, pact, COMPACT, AGREEMENT, COOPERATION.

allied *adj.* RELATED, joined, associated, united, affiliated, connected, amalgamated, combined, federated.

allocation: see DONATION.

allot: see ASSIGN; DEAL; PART; PORTION; RATION; SHARE.

allotment: see ALLOWANCE; DISTRIBUTION; PENSION; PORTION; RATION; SHARE.

allow *v.* PERMIT, tolerate, LET, GRANT, authorize, ENTITLE.

allowable *adj.* PERMISSIBLE, PROPER, RIGHT, JUST, LAWFUL, LICIT.

allowance *n.* PAYMENT, subsidy, GRANT, BONUS, allotment, PORTION, PERCENTAGE, discount.

alloy: see BLEND; COMPOUND; STEEL.

all right: see SATISFACTORY.

allude: see REFER.

allure: see ATTRACT; CHARM; GLAMOUR.

allurement: see ATTRACTION; CHARM.

alluring: see APPETIZING; ATTRACTIVE; INTERESTING; PERSUASIVE.

allusion: see MENTION; RECORD; REFERENCE.

ally: see AID; ASSOCIATE; COMRADE; CONFEDERATE; FRIEND; PARTNER; SUPPORTER.

almanac: see CALENDAR.

almost *adv.* NEARLY, APPROXIMATELY, somewhat, ABOUT, TOWARD, well-nigh.

aloft: see ABOVE; UPWARD.

alone *adj.* SINGLE, SOLE, UNIQUE, SEPARATE, APART, ONLY, SOLITARY, isolated, LONELY, LONESOME, deserted, DESOLATE, forsaken, forlorn, unattended.
—*adv.* singly, solely, ONLY, exclusively, solitarily.

aloneness: see LONELINESS.

along *prep.* alongside, LIKE, BY, OVER, THROUGH.
—*adv.* lengthwise, longitudinally, TOGETHER, simultaneously.

alongside: see ALONG; BESIDE; BY.

aloof: see APART; CALM; CHILLY; COOL; COLD; UNFRIENDLY.

aloofness: see DISTANCE; FROST.

aloud *adv.* loudly, audibly, vocally, noisily.

alphabet *n.* ABC's, A.B.C., letters, characters, INDEX, FILE, INTRODUCTION, BEGINNING, basics, fundamentals.

already *adv.* NOW, previously, beforehand, presently, YET.

also *adv.* TOO, BESIDES, LIKEWISE, MOREOVER, FURTHERMORE, additionally.

altar *n.* SHRINE, sanctuary, TABLE.

alter *v.* CHANGE, ADJUST, MODIFY, REVISE, VARY, TRANSFORM, CONVERT, SHIFT.

alteration: see AMENDMENT; CHANGE; CORRECTION; VARIATION.

alternate *v.* CHANGE, ROTATE, interchange, REVERSE, reciprocate, VARY.
— *n.*: see SUBSTITUTE.

alternately: see INSTEAD.

alternation: see TURN.

alternative: see CHOICE.

alternatively: see INSTEAD.

alternator: see GENERATOR.

although *conj.* THOUGH, notwithstanding, DESPITE, whereas, albeit, even if.

altitude *n.* HEIGHT, ELEVATION, eminence, stature, perpendicular.

altogether *adv.* wholly, COMPLETELY, TOTALLY, outright, utterly, ENTIRELY, QUITE.

alumna: see GRADUATE.

alumnus: see GRADUATE.

always *adv.* CONTINUALLY, habitually, EVERMORE, EVER, FOREVER, eternally, everlastingly.

A.M.: see MORNING.

amalgamate: see BLEND; UNITE.

amalgamated: see ALLIED.

amalgamation: see BLEND.

amass: see BUNCH; COLLECT; CONCENTRATE; GATHER; PILE.

amateur *n.* hobbyist, dabbler, blunderer, BEGINNER, novice, nonprofessional, layman.

amaze *v.* astound, ASTONISH, STUN, dumfound, SURPRISE, stupefy, perplex.

amazement *n.* ASTONISHMENT, SURPRISE, WONDER, awe, ADMIRATION, confusion, perplexity.

amazing *adj.* astonishing, SURPRISING, awesome, breathtaking, STUNNING.

ambassador *n.* representative, emissary, AGENT, envoy, diplomat.

ambiguous: see DOUBTFUL.

ambition *n.* GOAL, AIM, PURPOSE, TARGET, OBJECT, DESIRE, aspiration, zeal, longing, eagerness, yearning.

ambitious *adj.* EAGER, aspiring, zealous, showy, grandiose, vast, impressive.

amble: see STRCLL; WALK.

ambush: see ATTACK; TRAP.

amend *v.* REVISE, REFORM, ADJUST, rectify, IMPROVE, BETTER, MEND, REMEDY.

amendment *n.* REVISION, alteration, CHANGE, IMPROVEMENT, RESOLUTION, LAW, REGULATION.

amends: see APOLOGY.

amiable: see AGREEABLE; FRIENDLY; HOSPITABLE; LOVABLE; PLEASANT.

amicable: see HARMONIOUS; PEACEFUL.

amid: see AMIDST; AMONG; BETWEEN.

amidst *prep.* amid, amongst, surrounded by, AMONG.

amiss: see WRONG.

amity: see PEACE.

ammunition: see EXPLOSIVE.

amnesia: see FORGETFULNESS.

amnesty: see PARDON.

among *prep.* amongst, amid, AMIDST, BETWEEN, surrounded by, IN.

amongst: see AMIDST; AMONG.

amorous: see PASSIONATE.

amorphous: see FLUID; SHAPELESS.

amount *n.* WHOLE, SUM, NUMBER, MASS, QUANTITY, MEASURE, VALUE, MONEY.
— *v.* add up, reach, equal, total.

amount to: see ACCOUNT FOR.

amour: see INTRIGUE.

amperage: see OUTPUT.

amphitheater: see ARENA; THEATER.

ample *adj.* PLENTY, plenteous, PLENTIFUL, RICH, LIBERAL, GENEROUS, WIDE, SPACIOUS, ROOMY, LARGE, GREAT, bountiful, ADEQUATE, ENOUGH, SUFFICIENT, substantial.

ampleness: see ABUNDANCE.

amplification: see CLARIFICATION; ENLARGEMENT; EXAGGERATION.

amplify: see BROADEN; ENLARGE; EXAGGERATE; MAGNIFY; MULTIPLY.

amplitude: see WIDTH.

amply: see MUCH.

amputate: see OPERATE.

amulet: see CHARM.

amuse *v.* ENTERTAIN, divert, CHARM, PLEASE, interest, enliven.

amusement *n.* ENTERTAINMENT, pastime, SPORT, PLEASURE, INTEREST, RELAXATION, recreation, ENJOYMENT.

amusing: see COMICAL; DELIGHTFUL.

an: see A.

analogy: see SIMILARITY.

analysis *n.* EXAMINATION, TEST, INVESTIGATION, SEPARATION, DIVISION, resolution, psychoanalysis.

analyst: see CRITIC.

analyze *v.* EXAMINE, TEST, INVESTIGATE, take apart, SEPARATE, DIVIDE, EXPLAIN, REASON.

anarchy: see REVOLUTION.

anatomy *n.* **1** *(the anatomy of an organ)* ANALYSIS, DIVISION, SEPARATION, autopsy, vivisection; **2** *(the anatomy of reptiles)* STRUCTURE, BODY, FORM, nature, makeup.

ancestor *n.* forebear, forefather, FATHER, PARENT, predecessor, sire, forerunner.

ancestors: see FOREFATHERS.

ancestry: see BLOOD; CRADLE; FAMILY; FOREFATHERS; PARENTAGE.

anchor *n.* HOOK, anchorage, SUPPORT, PILE.
— *v.* **1** *(to anchor at Norfolk)* STOP, VISIT, SETTLE CALL; **2** *(a post is anchored in the cement)* lodge, embed, FIX, FASTEN, PIN, HOLD.

anchorage: see ANCHOR; BAY; PORT.

ancient *adj.* OLD, ANTIQUE, olden, PRIMITIVE, antiquated, OLD-FASHIONED, time-honored.

and: see INCLUDING; PLUS.

anecdotal: see FICTIONAL; STORY.

anecdote: see TALE; YARN.

anesthetic: see DRUG.

anesthetize: see DRUG.

anew: see AGAIN; NEWLY; OVER.

angel *n.* MESSENGER, herald, saint, GUARDIAN, SPIRIT, INFLUENCE, benefactor, backer.

angelic: see HEAVENLY.

anger *n.* wrath, RAGE, FURY, RESENTMENT, choler, dander, indignation, exasperation, TEMPER, displeasure, IRRITATION, PASSION, tantrum.
— *v.* ENRAGE, INFURIATE, madden, AROUSE, OFFEND, inflame, exasperate, nettle, PROVOKE.

angle *n.* intersection, point, CORNER, EDGE, projection, branching, FORK, ASPECT, VIEW, SIDE, PHASE.
— *v.*: see FISH.

angry *adj.* FURIOUS, MAD, offended, wrathful, enraged, indignant, RESENTFUL, bad-tempered, SORE, threatening, inflamed, irate.

anguish: see ANXIETY; DISTRESS; PAIN; STING.

animal *n.* **1** *(the animals in the zoo)* BEAST, BRUTE, CREATURE, critter, varmint, mammal; **2** *(she married an animal)* barbarian, SAVAGE, fiend, MONSTER, DEMON, BEAST, BRUTE.

animate: see AWAKEN; INSPIRE; THRILL.

animated: see LIVE; LIVELY; VIVID.

animation: see GO; LIFE; VITALITY.

animosity: see FEUD; RESENTMENT.

anklet: see STOCKING.

anklets: see HOSE.

annals: see HISTORY; PAST; REGISTER.

annex *n.* ADDITION, EXTENSION, wing, BUILDING, ATTACHMENT, SUPPLEMENT, SECTION.
— *v.* ATTACH, ADD, EXTEND, JOIN, APPEND.

annihilate: see DESTROY.

anniversary *n.* commemoration, FESTIVAL, DATE, FEAST, CELEBRATION, REMEMBRANCE.
— *adj.*: see ANNUAL.

announce *v.* proclaim, REVEAL, PUBLISH, DECLARE, disclose, divulge, REPORT.

announcement *n.* NOTICE, REPORT, PROCLAMATION, DECLARATION, manifesto, MESSAGE, COMMERCIAL, POSTER, handbill, placard, LETTER.

annoy *v.* IRRITATE, BOTHER, PROVOKE, harass, weary, exasperate, displease, TROUBLE, DISTURB.

annoyance *n.* IRRITATION, bother, provocation, harassment, exasperation, TROUBLE, NUISANCE.

annoyed: see MAD; SORE; WOUNDED.

annoying: see BOTHERSOME; TROUBLESOME; TRYING; UNPLEASANT.

annual *adj.* yearly, yearlong, twelve month, anniversary, perennial.

annuity: see PENSION.

annul: see CANCEL; DISSOLVE.

anoint: see OIL.

another *adj., pron.* ADDITIONAL, added, FURTHER, OTHER, ELSE, DIFFERENT, DISTINCT.

answer *n.* **1** *(an answer to a question)* REPLY, RESPONSE, retort; **2** *(an answer to a problem)* SOLUTION, EXPLANATION, KEY, RESOLUTION, REACTION.
— *v.* RESPOND, REPLY, retaliate, SOLVE, RESOLVE.

answerable: see ACCOUNTABLE; LIABLE; RESPONSIBLE.

antagonism: see DIFFERENCE; HOSTILITY; OPPOSITION; RESISTANCE.

antagonist: see COMPETITOR; ENEMY; FOE; OPPONENT; OPPOSITION; RIVAL.

antagonistic: see HOSTILE; OPPOSING.

antagonize: see OFFEND.

anteroom: see PARLOR.

anthem *n.* HYMN, SONG, CHANT, CAROL.

antiaircraft: see ARTILLERY.

antibiotic: see MEDICINE.

antic: see STUNT.

anticipate *v.* EXPECT, FORESEE, AWAIT, SUPPOSE, PREPARE, prevent.

anticipated: see ONCOMING.

anticipating: see EXPECTANT; HOPEFUL.

anticipation: see EXPECTATION; foresight; FORETHOUGHT; HOPE; PRECAUTION; PREDICTION; SUSPENSE.

anticommunism: see RIGHT.

antidote: see CURE.

antiquated: see ANCIENT; OLD; OLD-FASHIONED.

antique *adj.* ANCIENT, AGED, archaic, obsolete.
— *n.* relic, TREASURE, rarity, heirloom, vestige.

antiquity: see PAST.

antonym: see OPPOSITE; WORD.

anxiety *n.* WORRY, anguish, CONCERN, misgiving, FEAR.

anxious *adj.* **1** *(anxious to leave)* EAGER, ENTHUSIASTIC, desirous; **2** *(anxious about the news)* FEARFUL, troubled, UNEASY, neurotic.

anxiously: see COWARDLY.

any *adj., pron.* SOME, EVERY, SINGLE, ONE, INDIVIDUAL, unspecified, indefinite.
— *adv.* ever, YET, SOMEWHAT.

anybody: see ANYONE; SOMEBODY; SOMEONE.

anyhow *adv.* ANYWAY, MOREOVER, NEVERTHELESS, anywise, haphazardly, randomly.

anyone *pron.* anybody, EVERYONE, SOMEONE, ONE, PEOPLE.

anyplace: see SOMEWHERE.

anything *pron., n.* EVERYTHING, WHATEVER, SOMETHING.

anyway *adv.* ANYHOW, NEVERTHELESS, HOWEVER, anywise.

anywhere *adv.* EVERYWHERE, wherever, vaguely, APPROXIMATELY.

anywise: see ANYHOW; ANYWAY.

apart *adv.* **1** *(they spoke apart)* ASIDE, aloof, remotely, separately, ALONE, singly; **2** *(to break apart)* asunder, separately.
— *adj.* asunder, disassembled, LOOSE, undone, BROKEN, DISTANT.

apart from: see BESIDES.

apartment *n.* FLAT, quarters, LODGINGS, ROOM, RESIDENCE.

apartness: see PRIVACY.

apathy: see DULLNESS.

ape: see IMITATE; MONKEY.

apex: see CROWN; PEAK; PRIME.

apiece *adv.* EACH, respectively, separately, severally.

apologetic *adj.* SORRY, repentant, remorseful, regretful, defensive.

apologize *v.* EXCUSE, JUSTIFY, REGRET, atone, CONFESS, recant.

apology *n.* EXCUSE, REGRET, PLEA, amends, atonement, retraction, DEFENSE.

appall: see DISMAY; TERRIFY.

appalling: see FRIGHTFUL.

apparatus: see APPLIANCE; ASSEMBLY; DEVICE; EQUIPMENT; INSTRUMENT; TACKLE; UNIT; UTENSIL.

apparel: see COSTUME; DRESS; TOILET; WARDROBE.

apparent *adj.* VISIBLE, CLEAR, manifest, EVIDENT, OBVIOUS, seeming, POSSIBLE, ostensible.

apparently *adv.* EVIDENTLY, seemingly, CLEARLY, obviously.

apparition: see GHOST; PHANTOM.

appeal *v.* **1** *(to appeal for mercy)* REQUEST, URGE, beseech, petition; **2** *(he appeals to her)* ATTRACT, INTEREST, TEMPT, INTRIGUE.

— *n*. **1** *(to reject an appeal)* REQUEST, petition, SUIT; **2** *(a person of great appeal)* interest, attractiveness, CHARM.

appealing: see APPETIZING; DELIGHTFUL; INVITING; LOVELY; PLEASING; PRETTY.

appear *v*. **1** *(to appear at the window)* EMERGE, loom, come out, materialize; **2** *(to appear interested)* SEEM, LOOK, RESEMBLE.

appearance *n*. **1** *(of odd appearance)* looks, ASPECT, demeanor, AIR; **2** *(to make an appearance)* emergence, ARRIVAL, entrance, PRESENTATION, coming, EXHIBITION.

appease: see CONTENT; QUENCH; SATISFY.

appendix *n*. ADDITION, ATTACHMENT, INDEX, SUPPLEMENT, addendum.

appertain: see BELONG; CONCERN.

appetite *n*. DESIRE, HUNGER, craving, NEED, longing.

appetizer: see RELISH.

appetizing *adj*. INVITING, delectable, savory, alluring, TEMPTING, palatable, stimulating, appealing.

applaud *v*. cheer, acclaim, PRAISE, CLAP, exalt, RECOGNIZE.

applause *n*. acclamation, PRAISE, cheers, ovation, HAND.

appliance *n*. MACHINE, apparatus, DEVICE, tool, IMPLEMENT.

appliances: see TACKLE.

applicant: see CANDIDATE.

application *n*. **1** *(the application of force)* USE, utilization, activation, adaptation, employment; **2** *(to submit an application)* REQUEST, solicitation, requisition.

apply *v*. **1** *(to apply makeup)* USE, utilize, EMPLOY, ADOPT, affix; **2** *(to apply for a position)* SEEK, solicit, REQUEST, BEG, ADDRESS.

appoint *v*. designate, SELECT, ASSIGN. See also FURNISH.

appointee: see DELEGATE.

appointment *n*. **1** *(the appointment of the director)* SELECTION, CHOICE; **2** *(a ten-o'clock appointment)* DATE, ENGAGEMENT, MEETING.

apportion: see DEAL; DEDICATE; DISTRIBUTE; PARCEL; PART; RATION; SLICE.

apportionment: see DISTRIBUTION; SHARE.

appraisal: see ESTIMATE; ESTIMATION; MEASUREMENT.

appraise: see CRITICIZE; ESTIMATE; GAUGE; PRICE.

appreciate *v*. ESTEEM, evaluate, RISE, INCREASE.

appreciated: see WELCOME; WELL-KNOWN.

appreciation *n*. ESTEEM, valuation, INCREASE, acknowledgment, RECOGNITION.

appreciative *adj*. GRATEFUL, THANKFUL, mindful, conscious, beholden, indebted.

apprehend: see ARREST; CAPTURE.

apprehension: see DISMAY; DREAD; UNDERSTANDING.

apprehensively: see COWARDLY.

apprentice *n*. BEGINNER, novice, STUDENT, AMATEUR.

apprise: see ACQUAINT; BRIEF; INFORM; WARN.

apprised: see AWARE.

approach *v*. NEAR, converge, accost, ADDRESS, APPROXIMATE.
— *n*.: see STRATEGY; TACTICS; TREATMENT.

approaching: see NEAR; ONCOMING.

appropriate *adj*. FITTING, LIKELY, RIGHT, PROPER, SUITABLE, CONVENIENT, opportune.
— *v*.: see ASSUME; SEIZE.

appropriateness: see FITNESS.

approval *n*. acceptance, ESTEEM, FAVOR, ratification, endorsement.

approve *v*. FAVOR, SUPPORT, endorse, ACCEPT, RECOMMEND, ratify.

approved: see FAVORED; OFFICIAL.

approximate *v*. NEAR, APPROACH, RESEMBLE.

approximately *adv*. NEARLY, ALMOST, AROUND, ABOUT, roughly, circa.

approximation: see RESEMBLANCE.

apt *adj*. LIKELY, SUITABLE, inclined, LIABLE, APPROPRIATE. See also ABLE.

aptitude: see ABILITY; FITNESS; GENIUS; GIFT; INSTINCT; QUALIFICATION; TALENT; TURN.

aptly: see LIKELY.

aquamarine: see GREEN.

aqueduct: see CHANNEL.

arbitrate: see BARGAIN; TRY.

arbitration: see COMPROMISE.

arbitrator: see JUDGE.

arc: see ARCH; BOW.

arcade: see ARCH.

arch *n.* archway, arc, arcade, vault, CURVE.
— *v.* curve, BEND, overarch, SPAN, flex, bridge.

archaic: see ANTIQUE.

arched *adj.* vaulted, curved, BENT, ROUND, overarched, concave, convex.

archenemy: see ENEMY.

archfiend: see DEVIL.

architect *n.* designer, planner, draftsman, engineer, ARTIST, builder, originator.

architecture *n.* **1** *(to commision the architecture)* DESIGN, PLAN, blueprint; **2** *(baroque architecture)* STYLE, TYPE, FASHION; **3** *(of solid architecture)* QUALITY, CONSTRUCTION, workmanship, engineering, planning.

archive: see FILE.

archives: see HISTORY; REGISTER.

archway: see ARCH.

arctic: see ICY.

ardent: see BREATHLESS; FIERY.

ardently: see HEARTILY.

ardor: see HEAT.

arduous: see DIFFICULT.

arduousness: see DIFFICULTY.

area *n.* **1** *(the coastal area)* REGION, DISTRICT, domain, PART, ZONE, FIELD, SPHERE; **2** *(an acre in area)* SPACE, EXTENT, expanse, SURFACE, MEASUREMENT, acreage, footage, ROOM, scope.

arena *n.* amphitheater, THEATER, RING, FIELD, stadium, battlefield, STAGE.

argue *v.* **1** *(to argue its merits)* DISCUSS, DEBATE, ANALYZE, CONSIDER; **2** *(I argued with them)* DISPUTE, QUARREL, DISAGREE, DIFFER, feud.

argument *n.* **1** *(a moot argument)* SUBJECT, ISSUE, MATTER, DISCUSSION, CASE, QUESTION; **2** *(to have a loud argument)* QUARREL, DISPUTE, FIGHT, ROW, DISAGREEMENT.

arguments: see GROUNDS.

aria: see SONG.

arid: see BARREN; DRY.

arise *v.* **1** *(I arise at six)* RISE, get up, STAND, MOUNT, ASCEND, CLIMB, LIFT; **2** *(this arises every year)* spring up, APPEAR, RISE, ISSUE, ORIGINATE, BEGIN.

aristocrat *n.* nobleman, peer, gentleman, LADY, patrician.

aristocratic: see NOBLE; ROYAL.

arithmetical: see MATHEMATICAL.

arm *n.* **1** *(my right arm)* forearm, LIMB, extremity, MEMBER; **2** *(the arm of a chair)* wing, HANDLE, handhold, rest; **3** *(an arm of the company)* BRANCH, wing, UNIT, CORPS, EXTENSION; **4** *(arms and ammunition)* WEAPON, armament, GUN, FIREARM, hardware.
— *v.* SUPPLY, EQUIP, OUTFIT, fortify, COCK.

armada: see FLEET; NAVY.

armament: see ARM; ARMS; WEAPON.

armchair: see CHAIR.

armed forces: see ARMY; MILITARY; SERVICE.

armistice *n.* TRUCE, cease-fire, cessation, DELAY, PEACE.

armor *n.* SHIELD, PROTECTION, mail, coat of mail, helmet, breastplate.

armored: see PROTECTIVE.

arms *pl. n.* armament, weaponry, guns, munitions, ARTILLERY.

army *n.* TROOPS, armed forces, militia, reserves, infantry, MULTITUDE.

aroma: see FRAGRANCE; ODOR; SCENT.

aromatic: see FRAGRANT; SPICE.

around *adv.* NEAR, ABOUT, NEARBY, nigh, APPROXIMATELY, randomly.
— *prep.* ABOUT, THROUGH, via, round, encircling, nigh.

arousal: see EXCITEMENT.

arouse *v.* AWAKEN, ROUSE, STIR, CAUSE, STIMULATE, incite, instigate.

arousing: see EXCITABLE.

arraign: see ACCUSE.

arrange *v.* **1** *(to arrange a banquet)* PREPARE, PLAN, ORGANIZE, set up; **2** *(to arrange one's affairs)* ORDER, ORGANIZE, REGULATE, systematize, tidy; **3** *(to arrange a medley)* score, PREPARE, ADAPT, orchestrate.

arranged: see FIXED.

arrangement *n.* **1** *(a colorful arrangement)* layout, ORDER, DISPOSITION, array, FORM; **2** *(an* *arrangement to share expenses)* pact, AGREEMENT, UNDERSTANDING, COMPROMISE, ACCOMMODATION, orchestration.

array: see ADORN; ARRANGEMENT; ASSORTMENT; COLLECTION; DISPLAY; EQUIP; ROBE.

arrears: see DEBT.

arrest *v.* **1** *(the drug arrested his fever)* stop, detain, restrain, CHECK, HALT; **2** *(the police arrest wrongdoers)* SEIZE, CAPTURE, detain, apprehend, imprison.
— *n.* seizure, capture, detention.

arrival *n.* coming, APPEARANCE, advent, homecoming.

arrive *v.* COME, REACH, APPEAR, report, show up, HAPPEN.

arrogance: see PRIDE.

arrogant: see LOFTY; VAIN.

arrow *n.* dart, SHAFT, SPEAR, MISSILE, projectile, pointer, indicator.

art *n.* **1** *(an art student)* fine arts, beaux-arts, masterpiece, REPRESENTATION, paintings, MUSIC, SCULPTURE, LITERATURE, dance; **2** *(done with art)* SKILL, creativity, ingenuity, GRACE, CRAFT, handicraft, artfulness.

artfulness: see ART.

article *n.* **1** *(an article of clothing)* OBJECT, ITEM, THING, ELEMENT, PIECE; **2** *(a magazine article)* ESSAY, REPORT, PIECE, COMPOSITION, FEATURE, clause.

articulate: see PRONOUNCE; SOUND; SPEAK.

articulated: see ORAL.

articulation: see PRONUNCIATION; SPEECH.

artifact: see PRODUCT.

artificial *adj.* FALSE, synthetic, COUNTERFEIT, UNNATURAL, affected, ersatz.

artillery *n.* cannon, gunnery, weaponry, battery, antiaircraft, howitzer, mortar.

artisan: see WORKMAN.

artist *n.* MASTER, creator, craftsman, painter, composer, PERFORMER, sculptor, musician, ACTOR, SINGER, dancer, virtuoso, PROFESSIONAL.

artistic *adj.* esthetic, DECORATIVE, STUDIED, skillful, GRACEFUL, tasteful, HARMONIOUS, SENSITIVE, ELEGANT, BEAUTIFUL, EXQUISITE, cultured.

artless: see NATURAL.

as *adv., conj.* WHILE, SINCE, BECAUSE, equally, similarly, comparatively, WHEN, qua, LIKE.

ascend *v.* RISE, CLIMB, MOUNT, SCALE, SOAR, take off, skyrocket.

ascending: see UPWARD.

ascent: see RISE.

ascertain: see CALCULATE; DETECT; DISCOVER; FIND; FIND OUT; LEARN; TRACE.

ascertained: see KNOWN.

ascribe: see ATTRIBUTE.

ascription: see REFERENCE.

ash: see DUST.

ashamed *adj.* shamed, embarrassed, regretful, abashed, sheepish, remorseful, humiliated, discomforted.

ashen: see GRAY; PALE.

ashes *pl. n.* cinders, REMAINS, residue, RUIN, DUST.

ashore *adv.* AGROUND, beached, grounded, stranded.

aside *adv.* APART, AWAY, OUTSIDE, ALONE, NEARBY, sidewise, laterally.

asinine: see FOOLISH; IDIOTIC; SENSELESS.

ask *v.* INQUIRE, query, QUESTION, interrogate, REQUEST, petition, SEEK, BEG, PLEAD, beseech, EXAMINE.

asking: see PLEA; REQUEST.

aslant: see ACROSS.

asleep *adj.* **1** *(the child is asleep)* sleeping, slumbering, UNCONSCIOUS, dormant, latent, dozing, napping, hibernating; **2** *(my foot is asleep)* NUMB, inert, torpid, insensible, unfeeling.

aspect *n.* APPEARANCE, image, LOOK, AIR, REGARD, perspective, LIGHT, PHASE, viewpoint, OUTLOOK.

asphalt: see CEMENT.

asphyxiate: see DROWN; SMOTHER.

aspirant: see CANDIDATE.

aspiration: see AMBITION; DESIRE; DREAM; SUMMIT; WISH.

aspire: see ACHE; INTEND; SCHEME; WISH.

aspiring: see AMBITIOUS.

ass *n.* DONKEY, burro, jackass, FOOL, blockhead, nincompoop.

assail: see ASSAULT; ATTACK; CHARGE.

assailant: see INVADER.

assassin *n.* KILLER, MURDERER, executioner, hangman, cutthroat, gunman, BUTCHER.

assassinate *v.* SLAY, KILL, MURDER, EXECUTE, liquidate.

assassination *n.* MURDER, killing, slaying EXECUTION, homicide, manslaughter, genocide, ELIMINATION.

assault *v.* ATTACK, assail, STRIKE, storm, mug, ravish, VIOLATE, rape.
— *n.* ATTACK, onset, CHARGE, onslaught, violation, rape.

assemblage: see GROUP; MASS.

assemble *v.* **1** *(we assemble in the hall)* MEET, convene, GATHER, muster, RALLY, CONGREGATE; **2** *(to assemble a kit)* ERECT, CONSTRUCT, set up, MOUNT, compile, collate.

assembling: see MANUFACTURE.

assembly *n.* **1** *(the assembly honored the dead)* CONGREGATION, MEETING, GATHERING, REUNION, RALLY, COLLECTION; **2** *(a television chassis assembly)* OUTFIT, STRUCTURE, apparatus, gear, MECHANISM, contraption, contrivance.

assent: see CONSENT; YES.

assert: see CLAIM; COMMENT; DECLARE; EXCLAIM; EXPRESS; MAINTAIN; STATE; SWEAR; TESTIFY.

assertion: see CLAIM; MOUTHFUL; STATEMENT; UTTERANCE.

assertive: see INSISTENT.

assess: see CONSIDER; ESTIMATE; GAUGE; PRICE; TAX.

assessment: see TAX.

assets: see CAPITAL; PROPERTY; RICHES; WEALTH.

assign *v.* DELEGATE, COMMISSION, allot, entrust, PRESCRIBE, RESERVE.

assigning: see DISTRIBUTION.

assignment *n.* TASK, JOB, DUTY, APPOINTMENT, RESPONSIBILITY, homework.

assimilate: see ABSORB; DIGEST.

assist *v.* AID, SUPPORT, HELP, BENEFIT, SERVE, PROMOTE.

assistance *n.* HELP, AID, SUPPORT, backing, compensation, RELIEF.

assistant *n.* aide, helper, DEPUTY, subordinate, CLERK, flunky.

assistants: see STAFF.

associate *v.* **1** *(I associate them with crime)* LINK, RELATE, CONNECT, GROUP, JOIN, merge; **2** *(we will associate nationally)* UNITE, ally, incorporate, fraternize, collectivize.
— *n.* PARTNER, colleague, co-worker, COMRADE, BUDDY, CONFEDERATE, ally.

associated: see ALLIED; RELATED.

associates: SEE FIRM; PARTNERSHIP.

association *n.* **1** *(his association with good causes)* RELATIONSHIP, CONNECTION, CONTACT, COMMUNICATION, fraternization, intercourse; **2** *(a national association)* UNION, BODY, SOCIETY, federation, congress, consortium.

assort: see CLASSIFY.

assorted *adj.* varied, MISCELLANEOUS, diverse, mixed, sundry.

assortment *n.* array, SELECTION, COLLECTION, VARIETY, miscellany, SET, SERIES.

assuage: see CALM.

assumable: see THINKABLE.

assume *v.* **1** *(I assume it is true)* presume, SUPPOSE, BELIEVE, GRANT, ACCEPT, theorize; **2** *(to assume control)* take over, undertake, appropriate, SEIZE; **3** *(to assume an appearance)* PRETEND, simulate, AFFECT.

assumed: see SUPPOSED.

assumption: see THEORY.

assurance: see CERTIFICATION; EXPECTATION; INSURANCE; OPTIMISM; POISE; PROMISE; GUARANTEE; SEAL; SECURITY; TRUST; VOW.

assure *v.* GUARANTEE, vouch for, attest, PROVE, affirm, PLEDGE, reassure.

assured *adj.* **1** *(an assured manner)* CONFIDENT, poised, BOLD; **2** *(an assured outcome)* SURE, CERTAIN, DEFINITE, guaranteed, proven.

assuredly: see SURELY.

asterisk: see STAR.

astern: see BEHIND.

asteroid: see SATELLITE.

astonish *v.* AMAZE, astound, SURPRISE, SHOCK, DAZZLE.

astonishing: see AMAZING; EXTRAORDINARY; MARVELOUS; STUNNING; SURPRISING; UNEXPECTED; WONDERFUL.

astonishment *n.* AMAZEMENT, WONDER, DISMAY, awe, wonderment.

astound: see AMAZE; ASTONISH; OVERWHELM; STUN; SURPRISE.

astounding: see MARVELOUS; STUNNING; WONDERFUL.

astray: see MISSING.

astringency: see BITTERNESS.

astringent: see BITTER.

astute: see KEEN; SHARP; WISE.

asunder: see APART.

asylum: see HOME; INSTITUTION; REFUGE.

at: see BY; ON.

atelier: see STUDIO.

athlete *n.* sport, sportsman, PLAYER, gymnast, combatant, CHAMPION.

athletic *adj.* **1** (*an athletic figure*) MUSCULAR, robust, LIMBER, wiry, HARDY, STRONG, VIGOROUS; **2** (*athletic activities*) PHYSICAL, recreational, gymnastic, acrobatic.

athletics: see SPORT.

atmosphere: see AIR; MEDIUM; SKY; TONE.

atoll: see ISLAND.

atom *n.* PARTICLE, MOLECULE, FRAGMENT, jot, BIT, nucleus.

atomizer: see SPRAY.

atone: see APOLOGIZE.

atonement: see APOLOGY.

attach *v.* FASTEN, SECURE, STICK, JOIN, BIND, CONNECT, ADD, ASSOCIATE.

attached: see AFFECTIONATE; BOUND; FOND; ON.

attachment *n.* **1** (*attachment of the water line*) CONNECTION, TIE, BOND, LINK; **2** (*a lifelong attachment*) AFFECTION, fondness, LOVE; **3** (*appliance with attachments*) ACCESSORY, ANNEX, enclosure.

attack *v.* **1** (*to attack in force*) assail, STRIKE, ASSAULT, besiege, CHARGE, RAID, ambush, mug; **2** (*to attack a task*) BEGIN, TACKLE, initiate, START, COMMENCE.
— *n.* **1** (*a sneak attack*) ASSAULT, STRIKE, CHARGE, ambush, SIEGE; **2** (*an asthma attack*) bout, seizure, onslaught, onset.

attacker: see FIGHTER.

attain *v.* OBTAIN, REACH, GET, ACHIEVE, WIN, ACQUIRE.

attainable: see PRACTICAL.

attainment: see ACCOMPLISHMENT; ACHIEVEMENT; SUCCESS.

attempt *v.* TRY, ENDEAVOR, STRIVE, AIM, undertake.
— *n.* TRIAL, EFFORT, ENDEAVOR, VENTURE, shot, ATTACK.

attend *v.* **1** (*to attend the theater*) VISIT, FREQUENT, show up, ARRIVE; **2** (*to attend a royal personage*) ACCOMPANY, ESCORT, SERVE, wait on, WATCH.

attendance *n.* PRESENCE, participation, APPEARANCE, AUDIENCE, clientele.

attendant *n.* SERVANT, aide, steward, ORDERLY, WAITER, MONITOR, lackey, custodian, cicerone.

attending: see WITH.

attention *n.* **1** (*to pay attention*) OBSERVATION, HEED, NOTICE, CONSIDERATION, REGARD, vigilance; **2** (*I appreciate your attentions*) INTEREST, COURTESY, FAVOR, KINDNESS, POLITENESS; **3** (*to the attention of the manager*) CONCERN, CARE, CONSIDERATION.

attentive *adj.* OBSERVANT, heedful, considerate, THOUGHTFUL, ALERT.

attest: see ASSURE; CERTIFY; DECLARE; SEAL; SIGN.

attic *n.* loft, GALLERY, balcony, hayloft, rafters, TOP.

attire: see CLOTHES; COSTUME; DRESS; ROBE; TOILET.

attitude *n.* MOOD, OPINION, TEMPERAMENT, POSITION, standpoint, morale.

attorney *n.* LAWYER, advocate, counsel, COUNSELOR, adviser, defender, mouthpiece, DEPUTY, AGENT.

attorney at law: see LAWYER.

attract *v.* LURE, entice, allure, TEMPT, CHARM, fascinate, DRAW, PULL.

attraction *n.* LURE, PULL, DRAW, allurement, fascination, TEMPTATION, CHARM, seduction, ENTERTAINMENT.

attractive *adj.* good-looking, alluring, TEMPTING, INVITING, seductive, engaging, magnetic.

attractiveness: see APPEAL; BEAUTY; CHARM.

attribute *v.* ascribe, credit, REFER, impute, ATTACH, ACCUSE, BLAME.
— *n.* QUALITY, TRAIT, CHARACTERISTIC, MARK, PECULIARITY, PROPERTY.

attune: see ADJUST.

audacious: see ADVENTUROUS; SHAMELESS.

audacity: see BOLDNESS; COURAGE; DARING.

audible: see CLEAR; SHARP.

audibly: see ALOUD.

audience *n.* **1** *(the radio audience)* hearers, viewers, playgoers, ASSEMBLY, CONGREGATION, PUBLIC; **2** *(an audience with the Pope)* INTERVIEW, CONFERENCE, hearing.

audit: see CHECK; CHECKUP.

auditorium: see HALL; THEATER.

auger: see DRILL.

augment: see ADD; EXTEND; MAGNIFY.

augmentation: see EXPANSION; EXTENSION.

augur: see PREDICT; PROMISE.

austere: see THRIFTY.

austerity: see SERIOUSNESS; SIMPLICITY; THRIFT.

authentic *adj.* GENUINE, TRUE, ACTUAL, PURE, unadulterated, trustworthy.

authenticate: see CONFIRM; ESTABLISH; VERIFY.

authentication: see PASSPORT.

author *n.* **1** *(an author of novels)* WRITER, composer, scribe, journalist, scribbler, hack; **2** *(the author of his own ruin)* INVENTOR, creator, originator, initiator, FATHER.
 — *v.*: see WRITE.

authoritarian: see ABSOLUTE; STRICT.

authoritarianism: see RIGHT.

authoritative: see FIRSTHAND; OFFICIAL; STANDARD.

authority *n.* jurisdiction, RIGHT, POWER, prestige, renown, EXPERT.

authorization: see CERTIFICATION; CHARTER; LICENSE; PASSPORT; RIGHT; SEAL.

authorize: see ALLOW; COMMISSION; DELEGATE; ENTITLE; LEGALIZE; LICENSE; PERMIT.

authorized: see LEGAL; OFFICIAL.

autocrat: see MONARCH.

autograph: see PEN; SIGNATURE.

automatic *adj.* **1** *(an automatic lens adjustment)* mechanized, MECHANICAL, labor-saving; **2** *(an automatic response)* HABITUAL, involuntary, spontaneous, instinctive, autonomous.
 — *n.*: see PISTOL; REVOLVER.

automobile *n.* motorcar, CAR, VEHICLE, taxicab, limousine, convertible, sedan, jeep, jalopy.

autonomous: see AUTOMATIC; INDEPENDENT.

autopsy: see ANATOMY.

autumn *n.* fall, HARVEST, DECLINE.

auxiliary: see ACCESSORY; ADDITIONAL; AID; SUPPLEMENTARY.

avail: see BENEFIT.

available *adj.* accessible, usable, READY, HANDY, CONVENIENT, obtainable.

avalanche: see SLIDE.

avenge *v.* retaliate, PUNISH, REVENGE, get even, repay.

avenue *n.* STREET, boulevard, ROAD, PATH, COURSE, ROUTE.

average *adj.* TYPICAL, ORDINARY, normal, mean, FAIR, mediocre.
 — *n.* midpoint, norm, mean, STANDARD, median, par.
 — *v.* equalize, BALANCE, pair off, even, REDUCE.

averse: see RELUCTANT.

aversion: see DISGUST; HORROR; HOSTILITY; REVOLT.

avert *v.* PREVENT, thwart, ward off, forestall, sidetrack.

aviation: see FLIGHT.

aviator: see PILOT.

avoid *v.* elude, DODGE, shun, refrain.

avoidance: see PREVENTION.

await *v.* WAIT, ANTICIPATE, EXPECT, forecast.

awaiting: see EXPECTANT.

awake *adj.* ALERT, CONSCIOUS, OBSERVANT, vigilant, WAKEFUL, wakened, risen, roused, wide-awake.
 — *v.*: see ROUSE.

awaken *v.* WAKE, wake up, ROUSE, STIR, STIMULATE, animate, AROUSE.

award *v.* GRANT, PRESENT, confer, bestow, REWARD.
 — *n.* PRIZE, REWARD, HONOR, decoration.

aware *adj.* cognizant, mindful, knowing, CONSCIOUS, enlightened, apprised.

awareness: see LIGHT; MIND; OBSERVATION; REALIZATION.

aware of: see ONTO.

away *adv., adj.* ABSENT, APART, OFF, DISTANT, AFAR, afield, ELSEWHERE, MISSING, FOREVER, endlessly.

away from: see OFF.

awe: see AMAZEMENT; ASTONISHMENT; DREAD; WONDER.

awesome: see AMAZING; FEARFUL; SURPRISING; TERRIBLE.

awful *adj.* DREADFUL, dire, repulsive, offensive, HORRIBLE.

awfully: see TERRIBLY.

awhile *adv.* briefly, temporarily, momentarily, SHORTLY, right away.

awkward *adj.* CLUMSY, unskillful, unwieldy, BULKY, inept, RUDE, ROUGH.

awkwardness *n.* inaptitude, clumsiness, RUDENESS, COARSENESS, inconvenience.

awl: see BIT.

axis *n.* CENTER, AXLE, pivot, swivel.

axle *n.* AXIS, spindle, SHAFT, PIN.

aye: see YES.

B

babble *v.* prattle, jabber, GAB, blab, gurgle, coo.
— *n*: see CHATTER.

babe: see BABY; CHILD; INFANT; LAMB.

baboon: see MONKEY.

babushka: see SCARF.

baby *n.* INFANT, babe, newborn, CHILD, tot, crybaby.
— *v.* coddle, pamper, SPOIL, indulge, overindulge.

baby carriage: see CARRIAGE.

babyhood: see CHILDHOOD.

babyish: see CHILDISH.

baby-sit: see CARE; MIND.

bacillus: see GERM.

back *n.* REAR, stern, posterior, backside.
— *adv.* **1** (*don't look back*) BACKWARD; **2** (*some years back*) AGO, BEHIND.
— *adj.* REAR, posterior, HIND. See also BEHIND.
— *v.* SUPPORT, AID.

backbone *n.* **1** (*a deformed backbone*) SPINE, vertebrae, sacroiliac; **2** (*to show backbone*) COURAGE, DETERMINATION, spunk, guts, CHARACTER.

backer: see AID; ANGEL; CHAMPION; PATRON; SUPPORTER.

background: see EDUCATION; ENVIRONMENT; EXPERIENCE; GROUNDWORK; SCENE.

backing: see ASSISTANCE.

backlog: see RESERVE; STOCK; SUPPLY.

backpack: see HIKE; PACK.

backside: see BACK; REAR.

backward ADV. **1** (*to draw the arrow backward*) rearward, BACK; **2** (*he wrote it backward*) inverted, WRONG, oddly; **3** (*his policy leads backward*) downhill, worse, BACK.
— *adj.* DULL, SLOW, RETARDED, underdeveloped, BEHIND.

backwardness: see RESERVE.

backwoods: see COUNTRY; RURAL.

bacterium: see GERM.

bad *adj.* **1** (*a bad influence*) WICKED, EVIL; **2** (*bad merchandise*) defective, INFERIOR, spoiled; **3** (*what a bad boy*) NAUGHTY, DISOBEDIENT; **4** (*he gave us a bad time*) DISAGREEABLE, UNPLEASANT, unwholesome.

badge *n.* shield, identification, marker, EMBLEM, MEDAL, SYMBOL.

badger: see PESTER.

badlands: see DESERT.

badly: see ILL; POORLY; TERRIBLY.

bad-natured: see UGLY.

badness: see EVIL.

bad-tempered: see ANGRY; SOUR.

baffle *v.* CONFUSE, perplex, AMAZE, PUZZLE, BEWILDER, FOIL, HINDER.

bag *n.* **1** (*a paper bag*) SACK, POUCH, poke; **2** (*her new bag*) PURSE, pocketbook; **3** (*pack your bag*) suitcase, valise, grip; **4** (*the sour old bag*) biddy, hag, WITCH.
— *v.* DROOP, sag, WILT, flag. See also CAPTURE; CATCH; TRAP.

baggage *n.* LUGGAGE, bags, EQUIPMENT, gear, suitcases.

baggy: see LOOSE; SLACK.

bagpipe: see PIPE.

bags: see BAGGAGE; LUGGAGE.

bail: see SCOOP.

bait *n.* LURE, enticement, come-on, inducement,
TEMPTATION.
— *v.*: see TEMPT.

bake *v.* **1** *(to bake a cake)* COOK, TOAST, ROAST.
2 *(to bake clay pottery)* fire, HARDEN, DRY.

baker: see COOK.

bakery: see OVEN.

baksheesh: see TIP.

balance *n.* equilibrium, EQUALITY, symmetry,
SCALE. See also REMAINDER; SURPLUS.
— *v.* **1** *(to balance the books)* reconcile, equate,
JUSTIFY; **2** *(to balance opposing forces)* offset,
counterpoise, counteract, stabilize.

balanced: see EVEN; SANE.

balcony: see ATTIC; GALLERY.

bald: see NAKED.

bale *n.* PARCEL, BUNDLE, BUNCH, SHOCK, packet,
CASE.
— *v.*: see BUNDLE.

ball *n.* **1** *(a ball of string)* GLOBE, SPHERE; **2** *(to play
ball)* GAME, ball game; **3** *(a masked ball)* dance,
RECEPTION; **4** *(a cannon ball)* bullet, projectile,
MISSILE; **5** *(the ball of the foot)* sole, BASE; **6** *(to
have a ball)* PLEASURE, FUN, AMUSEMENT.

ballad: see CAROL; POEM; SONG.

ball game: see BALL.

balloon: see BUBBLE.

ballot *n.* VOTE, TICKET, tally.

ballpoint: see PEN.

ballroom: see CASINO.

ball up: see COMPLICATE.

ballyhoo: see ADVERTISE; ADVERTISEMENT;
PROMOTION; PUBLICITY.

balm: see LOTION; OINTMENT.

baloney: see BUNK.

bamboozle: see TRICK.

ban: see DAMN; EXCEPT; FORBID; PROHIBIT;
PROHIBITION.

band *n.* **1** *(a rubber band)* STRIP, TAPE, STRAP,
thong, TIE, BELT; **2** *(decorated with a red band)*
STRIPE, ribbon, RING; **3** *(a wedding band)* RING;
4 *(a dance band)* orchestra, troupe, combo; **5** *(a
band of pirates)* PARTY, GROUP, ASSEMBLY,
COLLECTION.
— *v.* UNITE, MEET, ASSEMBLE.

bandage *n.* dressing, gauze, binding, compress.
— *v.* DRESS, WRAP, BIND.

bandanna: see HANDKERCHIEF; SCARF.

bandit: see OUTLAW; ROBBER.

bang *n.* **1** *(a loud bang)* REPORT, NOISE, CLAP,
CRACK, whack; **2** *(to get a bang)* kick, THRILL,
ENJOYMENT, EXCITEMENT.
— *v*: see SNAP; SNARL.

banish *v.* EXILE, ostracize, EXPEL, expatriate,
DISMISS.

banishment: see EXILE.

banister: see RAIL; RAILING.

bank *n.* **1** *(a savings bank)* repository, treasury,
coffer; **2** *(a river bank)* EDGE, SHORE, levee,
embankment; **3** *(to break the bank)* kitty, pot,
POOL, FUND.
— *v.* **1** *(to bank a paycheck)* DEPOSIT, SAVE; **2** *(to
bank soil)* HEAP, PILE.

banking: see FINANCE.

bank note: see BILL; NOTE.

bank notes: see PAPER.

bankrupt *adj.* ruined, failed, insolvent,
penniless, broke, strapped, impoverished,
destitute.

bankruptcy: see FAILURE.

banned: see CURSED; FORBIDDEN.

banner *n.* pennant, flag, standard, colors,
ensign.

banquet *n.* DINNER, FEAST, MEAL,
ENTERTAINMENT, repast.
— *v.*: see CELEBRATION; DINE; EAT.

bantam: see MINIATURE.

banter: see CHIT-CHAT; RIDICULE.

bar *n.* **1** *(a handle bar)* SHAFT, crosspiece, STICK;
2 *(a sand bar)* BARRIER, impediment, obstruction;
3 *(a refreshment bar)* COUNTER, TABLE, canteen;
4 *(a bar of gold)* slab, BLOCK, LUMP, STRIP; **5** *(his
favorite bar)* saloon, TAVERN, cabaret; **6** *(to play
the first bar)* measure. See also COURT.
— *v.* BLOCK, impede, HINDER.

barb: see THORN.

barbarian: see ANIMAL; BEAST; BRUTE; SAVAGE;
VANDAL.

barbaric: see BRUTAL.

barbarous: see INHUMAN; SAVAGE.

barbecue: see FEAST; ROAST; SPIT.

bare *adj.* **1** *(a bare cupboard)* EMPTY, unfurnished; **2** *(her bare shoulders)* NAKED, unclothed, uncovered; **3** *(the bare minimum)* MERE, scant, meager.
— *v.* REVEAL, disclose, STRIP, EXPOSE.

barely *adv.* **1** *(barely two years old)* HARDLY, scarcely, JUST; **2** *(barely able to see)* meagerly, POORLY, scantily.

barfly: see DRUNK.

bargain *n.* **1** *(to strike a bargain)* AGREEMENT, CONTRACT; **2** *(every item a bargain)* DEAL, steal, discount.
— *v.* **1** *(to bargain with a vendor)* haggle, barter, wrangle; **2** *(to bargain collectively)* negotiate, arbitrate.

barge: see FERRY; RAFT.

bark *n.* **1** *(Fido's bark)* yelp, yap, bay, HOWL; **2** *(a coarse bark)* husk, HIDE, SKIN, rind, CRUST. See also COUGH.
— *v.*: see COUGH; GROWL; HOWL; SNAP.

barrel: see CHAMBER.

barren *adj.* unproductive, infertile, sterile, devoid, arid, BARE.

barricade *n.* BARRIER, FENCE, WALL, BAR, RAILING, roadblock.
— *v.* obstruct, BLOCK, ENCLOSE, fortify.

barrier *n.* obstruction, BARRICADE, hurdle, FENCE, BAR, ENCLOSURE.

barring: see BUT; EXCEPT.

barroom: see CAFE.

barrow: see TRUCK.

barter: see BARGAIN; DEAL; EXCHANGE; SELL; TRADE.

base *n.* **1** *(the base of the tower)* BOTTOM, FOOT, FOUNDATION, BASIS; **2** *(a naval base)* STATION, CAMP, encampment, CENTER; **3** *(their base of operations)* headquarters, CENTER, depot; **4** *(to steal third base)* marker, plate, home plate.
— *v.* ESTABLISH, FOUND, DETERMINE.
— *adj.*: see FEARFUL; VILLAINOUS.

basement *n.* CELLAR, FOUNDATION, footing, VAULT, ground floor.

baseness: see INFERIORITY.

bash: see KNOCK.

bashful *adj.* SHY, MODEST, TIMID, sheepish, coy, reserved.

bashfulness *n.* shyness, MODESTY, TIMIDITY, RESERVE, HESITATION, EMBARRASSMENT.

basic *adj.* FUNDAMENTAL, ESSENTIAL, PRIMARY, ELEMENTARY, indispensable, underlying.

basically: see PRACTICALLY.

basics: see ALPHABET; MEAT; SKELETON; STAPLE.

basin *n.* **1** *(a wash basin)* PAN, BOWL, tub; **2** *(a river basin)* watershed, VALLEY, DEPRESSION.

basis *n.* FOUNDATION, PRINCIPLE, REASON, GROUND, premise.

basket *n.* **1** *(bread basket)* bushel, pannier, hamper, CONTAINER, wicker; **2** *(to score a basket)* SCORE, point.

bassinet: see CRADLE; CRIB.

baste: see SEW.

bat *n.* **1** *(a baseball bat)* CLUB, STICK, POLE, cudgel; **2** *(blind as a bat)* vampire.
— *v.*: see BLINK; KNOCK.

batch *n.* LOT, AMOUNT, QUANTITY, BUNCH, SET, COLLECTION.

bath *n.* WASH, shower, soak, bathing, douche.

bathe *v.* WASH, shower, SCRUB, SOAK, SWIM, immerse.

bathing: see BATH; SWIM; WASH; WASHING.

bathroom: see TOILET.

baton *n.* STICK, STAFF, ROD, wand.

batsman: see BATTER.

batter *v.* BEAT, PUNISH, MISTREAT, pummel, pelt, POUND.
— *n.* **1** *(a mix batter)* dough, mix, PASTE, preparation; **2** *(the batter is out)* hitter, batsman, slugger.

battery: see ARTILLERY.

battle *n.* FIGHT, fray, WAR, ENGAGEMENT, strife, STRUGGLE, COMBAT.
— *v.*: see COMBAT; CONFLICT; FIGHT.

battlefield: see ARENA; FRONT.

battleground: see FRONT; THEATER.

battler: see WARRIOR.

battleship: see SHIP.

bauxite: see MINERAL.

bawl *v.* CRY, WEEP, BELLOW, SHOUT, YELL.
— *n.*: see CRY; HOWL.

bawling: see TEARFUL.

bay *n.* GULF, bayou, inlet, lagoon, cove, anchorage, HARBOR. See also BARK.

bayonet: see STAB.

bayou: see BAY.

bazaar: see FAIR; MARKET.

BB gun: see GUN; RIFLE.

be *v.* EXIST, LIVE, ENDURE, subsist, rest, consist, OCCUR, constitute.

beach *n.* SHORE, seaside, waterfront, strand, COAST, shoreline.
— *v.*: see GROUND.

beached: see AGROUND; ASHORE.

beacon: see SIGNAL; TORCH.

bead *n.* **1** *(a string of beads)* pellet, GRAIN, PARTICLE, STONE, PEARL; **2** *(beads of sweat)* DROP, droplet, DEW, perspiration.

beads: see JEWELRY.

beak *n.* BILL, nose, prow, snout, nib.

beaker: see JAR.

beam *n.* **1** *(a roof beam)* joist, TIMBER, rafter, girder; **2** *(a moonbeam)* RAY, SHAFT, GLARE, emission, STREAM; **3** *(a radio beam)* transmission, SIGNAL, emission; **4** *(on the beam)* COURSE, SIGNAL, TRACK, PATH.
— *v.* SMILE, GRIN, GLOW.

beaming: see RADIANT; SUNNY.

bear *v.* CARRY, SUSTAIN, SUPPORT, convey, ENDURE, PRODUCE, spawn.

bearable: see TOLERABLE.

beard *n.* whiskers, brush, goatee, stubble, bristles.

bearer: see PORTER.

bearing: see AIR; BEHAVIOR; CARRIAGE; CONDUCT; DIRECTION; JEWEL; MANNERS; POSITION; PRESENCE.

bear upon: see CONCERN.

beast *n.* **1** *(a wild beast)* ANIMAL, BRUTE, CREATURE; **2** *(a sadistic beast)* SAVAGE, BRUTE, barbarian, MONSTER, sadist, pervert.

beat *v.* **1** *(to beat mercilessly)* BATTER, MAUL, WHIP, pummel, THRASH; **2** *(to beat time)* CONDUCT, drum, measure; **3** *(to beat batter)* MIX, churn, WHIP; **4** *(to beat the champion)* DEFEAT, CONQUER, vanquish; **5** *(the heart beats)* pulsate, drum, THROB, VIBRATE, oscillate, FLUTTER.
— *n.* **1** *(to mark the beat)* rhythm, cadence,

STRESS, MEASURE; **2** *(to walk the beat)* PATROL, rounds, CIRCUIT, COURSE.
— *adj.* WEARY, TIRED, fatigued, worn out.

beaten *adj.* **1** *(beaten by a worthy opponent)* defeated, conquered, humbled, overthrown; **2** *(a leaf of beaten gold)* hammered, forged, worked, pounded.

beautiful *adj.* LOVELY, HANDSOME, comely, PRETTY, GRACEFUL, ATTRACTIVE, GORGEOUS, charming, good-looking, DELIGHTFUL, STUNNING, ravishing.

beautify *v.* ADORN, dress up, spruce up, primp, preen, bedeck, DECORATE, embellish.

beautifying: see DECORATIVE.

beauty *n.* attractiveness, GRACE, CHARM, comeliness, ELEGANCE, symmetry.

beaux-arts: see ART.

because *conj.* whereas, SINCE, FOR, inasmuch as, AS, considering, owing to, due to.

because of: see BY.

beckon *v.* GESTURE, WAVE, SIGNAL, gesticulate, CALL, LURE, ATTRACT.

becloud: see CLOUD.

become *v.* DEVELOP, evolve, turn out, CHANGE, GROW, result.

becoming: see PRETTY; SUITABLE.

bed *n.* **1** *(to go to bed)* COUCH, BUNK, mattress, COT, berth; **2** *(a flower bed)* GARDEN, PATCH, AREA, GROUND, CHANNEL.

bedclothes: see SHEET.

bedeck: see ADORN, BEAUTIFY.

bedpad: see PAD.

bedroom: see CHAMBER.

bedspread: see SPREAD.

beer: see REFRESHMENTS.

beetle: see INSECT.

befall: see HAPPEN; OCCUR.

befit: see BELONG.

befog: see BLUR.

before *prep.* PRECEDING, facing, UNTIL.
— *adv.* earlier, previously, beforehand, AHEAD, sooner, FORMERLY.
— *conj.*: see TILL; UNTIL.

beforehand: see ALREADY; BEFORE; EARLY.

befriend *v.* AID, FAVOR, patronize, WELCOME, fraternize, EMBRACE.

beg *v.* entreat, solicit, beseech, REQUEST, APPEAL, PLEAD, PRAY, ASK, panhandle.

beget: see BREED; REPRODUCE.

beggar *n.* supplicant, petitioner, moocher, pauper, panhandler, TRAMP.

begin *v.* START, COMMENCE, initiate, ORIGINATE, OPEN.

beginner *n.* starter, novice, APPRENTICE, freshman, learner, AMATEUR, newcomer, initiator.

beginning *n.* START, commencement, outset, ORIGIN, OPENING, DAWN, genesis, SOURCE, BIRTH.
— *adj.*: see FIRST; INITIAL; OPENING; ORIGINAL; PRELIMINARY.

be good: see FAREWELL.

begrudge: see GRUDGE; RESENT.

beguile: see TRICK.

behave *v.* ACT, PERFORM, FUNCTION, OBEY, cope, MANAGE.

behavior *n.* CONDUCT, ACTION, comportment, self-control, MANNERS, bearing, demeanor, CARRIAGE, PERFORMANCE, OPERATION.

behead: see EXECUTE.

beheading: see EXECUTION.

behind *adv.* AFTER, later, subsequently, BACKWARD, astern.
— *adj.* LATE, overdue, back, TARDY, SLOW.
— *prep.*: see AFTER.

behindhand: see TARDY.

beholden: see APPRECIATIVE; THANKFUL.

being *n.* **1** (*a human being*) CREATURE, PERSON, MORTAL, INDIVIDUAL, entity, THING; **2** (*being and nothingness*) EXISTENCE, actuality, LIFE, NATURE, essence.
— *adj.*: see EXISTENT.

belated: see SLOW.

belie: see DISAPPOINT.

belief *n.* **1** (*his belief in God*) FAITH, CREED, dogma, tenet, PERSUASION; **2** (*to test one's belief*) OPINION, credence, CREDIT, TRUST, acceptance.

believable: see LIKELY; RELIABLE; THINKABLE.

believe *v.* ACCEPT, HOLD, MAINTAIN, TRUST, CONSIDER, RELY ON, swear by.

believed: see SUPPOSED.

believe in: see RELY ON.

believer: see DISCIPLE.

believing: see RELIGIOUS; TRUSTFUL.

belittle: see DEGRADE; HUMILIATE; SCOFF.

bell *n.* chime, gong, SIGNAL, ALARM, doorbell, buzzer.

bellboy: see BOY; PAGE.

belligerence: see HOSTILITY.

belligerent: see AGGRESSIVE.

bellow *v.* SHOUT, CRY, ROAR, HOWL, BAWL, clamor, blare.
— *n.*: see ROAR.

belly *n.* stomach, gut, abdomen, paunch, tummy, bowels, swelling, BULGE.

bellyache: see COMPLAIN.

belong *v.* **1** (*it belongs to me*) pertain, RELATE, appertain, befit, CORRESPOND; **2** (*to belong to a society*) ASSOCIATE, affiliate, CORRESPOND.

belonging: see RELATED.

belongings: see PROPERTY.

beloved *adj.* DEAR, esteemed, adored, cherished, valued, FAVORITE.
— *n.* DARLING, SWEETHEART, fiance, fiancee, love, PET, favorite.

below *prep., adv.* BENEATH, UNDER, UNDERNEATH.

belt *n.* BAND, waistband, STRAP, GIRDLE, sash, ribbon, RING, ZONE, REGION.
— *v.* **1** (*a road belts the city*) gird, EMBRACE, ENCLOSE, SURROUND, BAND; **2** (*to belt on the jaw*) STRIKE, PUNCH, wallop, SMASH, clobber.

beltway: see HIGHWAY.

bemoan: see GROAN; MOAN; SADDEN; WEEP.

bemoaning: see MOURNFUL.

bench *n.* **1** (*the players' bench*) SEAT, pew, settee, STOOL, bleacher; **2** (*to work at a bench*) workbench, trestle, COUNTER, BOARD. See also COURT.

bend *v.* curve, TWIST, WARP, BUCKLE, flex, WILT, accede, YIELD.
— *n.*: see BOW; CORNER; CURVE; ELBOW; FOLD; KNOT; LOOP; TURN; TWIST.

bending: see LIMBER.

beneath *prep.* BELOW, UNDER, UNDERNEATH.
— *adv.*: BELOW, UNDERNEATH, downstairs.

benediction: see BLESSING.

benefactor: see ANGEL.

beneficial: see HELPFUL; PRODUCTIVE; PROFITABLE; USEFUL.

beneficiary: see HEIR.

benefit *v.* SERVE, PROFIT, ADVANCE, enhance, avail, FAVOR.
  — *n.* PROFIT, GAIN, ADVANTAGE, good, FAVOR.

benevolence: see CHARITY; GOODNESS; HUMANITY; PITY.

benevolent: see CHARITABLE; FATHERLY; GOOD; KINDLY.

bent *adj.* curved, warped, twisted, CROOKED, MISSHAPEN, inclined, bowed, stooped.
  — *n.*: see INCLINATION; TACK; TURN.

benumb: see DRUG; STUN.

benumbed: see STUPID.

bequeath: see DONATE; GIVE; LEAVE; WILL.

bequest: see WILL.

berate: see ABUSE; SCOLD.

bereavement: see LOSS.

beret: see CAP.

berry: see FRUIT.

berth: see BED; BUNK; COT; SLIP.

beseech: see APPEAL; ASK; BEG.

beside *prep.* adjacent to, next to, PARALLEL, adjoining, alongside, WITH.
  — *adv.*: see NEARBY.

besides *adv.* ALSO, TOO, MOREOVER, OTHERWISE, FURTHERMORE, additionally.
  — *prep.* BEYOND, apart from, EXCEPT.

besiege: see ATTACK; BLOCKADE; BOMBARD.

besmear: see SOIL.

bespattered: see MUDDY.

best *adj.* prime, choicest, SUPREME, peerless, paramount, tops.
  — *v.*: see OUTWIT; TOP.

bestial: see MONSTROUS.

bestow: see AWARD; BLESS; DONATE; GIVE; GRANT; INVEST.

bet *n.* wager, GAMBLE, VENTURE, HAZARD, RISK, speculate.
  — *v.* wager, PLAY, GAMBLE, stake.

betray *v.* DECEIVE, delude, double-cross, sell out, two-time, let down.

betrayal: see TREASON.

betrayer: see TRAITOR.

betroth: see MARRY.

betrothal: see ENGAGEMENT.

better *adj.* SUPERIOR, PREFERABLE, choicer, finer.
  — *v.* IMPROVE, CORRECT, emend, OUTDO.

betterment: see IMPROVEMENT; REFORM.

between *prep.* amid, AMONG, WITHIN.
  — *adv.* midway, halfway, MEANWHILE.

beverage *n.* DRINK, potion, refreshment, sip, nip, swig, LIQUID.

beverages: see REFRESHMENTS.

bewail: see REGRET.

beware *v.* OBSERVE, HEED, MIND, WATCH, GUARD, look out.

bewilder *v.* CONFUSE, perplex, daze, DAZZLE, BAFFLE, mystify, EMBARRASS.

bewildered: see FOGGY.

bewilderment: see DISTRACTION; FOG; SURPRISE.

bewitch *v.* CHARM, enchant, entrance, fascinate, captivate.

bewitching: see INVITING; MAGICAL.

beyond *prep.* AFTER, OUTSIDE, exceeding, PAST.
  — *n.*: see HEAVEN; UNKNOWN.

bias: see INCLINATION; TENDENCY; TILT.

biased: see PARTIAL.

bicker: see DISAGREE.

bicuspid: see TOOTH.

bid *n.* OFFER, PROPOSAL, PROPOSITION, tender, TRY, EFFORT, REQUEST.
  — *v.*: see COMMAND; INVITE; SUMMON; WISH.

biddy: see BAG.

biform: see TWIN.

big *adj.* LARGE, GREAT, HUGE, MASSIVE, expansive, CONSIDERABLE, EXTENSIVE, SIZABLE, GROWN, monumental.

biggish: see SIZABLE.

bigness: see SIZE.

bigoted: see NARROW; NARROW-MINDED.

big shot: see CELEBRITY.

bigwig: see CELEBRITY.

bill *n.* **1** *(an overdue bill)* ACCOUNT, STATEMENT, invoice; **2** *(a five-dollar bill)* dollar, bank note, greenback, BUCK, MONEY; **3** *(a duck's bill)* BEAK, nib; **4** *(a bill of goods)* LIST, STATEMENT, tally. See also ACT.

billboard: see ADVERTISEMENT; POSTER.

billfold *n.* wallet, portfolio, handbag, PURSE, pocketbook.

billow: see RIPPLE; SURGE.

bills: see CASH; CURRENCY; PAPER.

billy: see CLUB.

bin *n.* hopper, CONTAINER, CAN, locker, CRIB, receptacle.

binary: see DOUBLE; TWIN; TWO.

bind *v.* **1** *(to bind with cord)* TIE, truss, restrain; **2** *(I bind books)* WRAP, encase, BANDAGE, DRESS; **3** *(bind them with glue)* JOIN, ATTACH, SECURE, adhere, UNITE; **4** *(the contract is binding)* obligate, REQUIRE, COMPEL.

binder: see FOLDER; STAPLE.

binding *adj.* obligatory, compulsory, required, imperative, ESSENTIAL, unconditional.
— *n.*: see BANDAGE; BOND; PLASTER.

biographical: see HISTORICAL.

biological: see BODILY.

biotic: see ORGANIC.

bipartite: see PART.

birch: see SWITCH.

bird *n.* FOWL, flier, birdie, poultry.

bird call: see PIPE.

birdhouse: see NEST.

birdie: see BIRD.

bird shot: see SHOT.

birth *n.* ORIGIN, BEGINNING, START, genesis, CREATION, outset, DELIVERY, childbearing.

birthplace: see HOME.

birthright: see INHERITANCE.

bis: see TWICE.

biscuit: see COOKIE, ROLL.

bit *n.* **1** *(taste a bit)* jot, TRIFLE, morsel, PARTICLE; **2** *(the horse refused the bit)* BRIDLE, mouthpiece, CHECK, CURB; **3** *(the bit overheated)* DRILL, borer, cutter, gimlet, awl.

bitch: see COMPLAIN.

bite *v.* **1** *(some dogs bite)* nip, GNAW, CUT, CHOP, SEIZE; **2** *(pepper bites the tongue)* STING, burn, SMART, IRRITATE, pain.
— *n.* morsel, MOUTHFUL, nip, SNACK.

biting: see ACID; BITTER; POINTED; RAW; SHARP.

bitter *adj.* tart, biting, acrid, SOUR, astringent.

bitterness *n.* tartness, acidity, astringency, acrimony, spite.

bivouac: see CAMP.

bizarre: see CRAZY; SICK; STRANGE; UNFAMILIAR.

blab: see BABBLE; CACKLE; SQUEAL.

blabbermouth: see TELLTALE.

black *adj.* DARK, ebony, inky, pitch-black, sable.

blackjack: see CLUB.

blackmail: see BLEED.

blacktop: see CEMENT.

blade *n.* **1** *(double-edge blade)* KNIFE, SWORD, vane, cutter, EDGE, razor; **2** *(blade of grass)* LEAF, shoot, frond.

blame *v.* ACCUSE, CHARGE, indict, CONDEMN, fault, CRITICIZE, censure.
— *n.*: see CHARGE; GUILT; FAULT; RAP; RESPONSIBILITY; WRONG.

blameless *adj.* faultless, GUILTLESS, INNOCENT, CLEAN.

blameworthy: see GUILTY; RESPONSIBLE.

blanch: see WHITEN.

blanched: see WHITE.

bland: see MILD; SMOOTH.

blank *adj.* CLEAR, WHITE, FRESH, unused, VACANT, unspotted, expressionless.
— *n.* **1** *(fill out a blank)* questionnaire, FORM, APPLICATION; **2** *(shoot blanks)* dud, phony, fake. See also SPACE.

blanket: see CARPET; COATING; COVER; COVERING.

blare: see BELLOW.

blasé: see VETERAN.

blaspheme: see CURSE; SWEAR.

blast *n.* **1** *(a dynamite blast)* EXPLOSION, BURST, detonation, discharge, ERUPTION; **2** *(a blast of wind)* GUST, GALE, DRAFT, squall.
— *v.* blow up, dynamite, bomb, SHATTER.

blaze *v.* BURN, flare up, FLASH, FLAME.
— *n.*: see FLAME; GLARE.

blazing: see HOT.

bleach: see FADE; WHITEN.

bleached: see WHITE.

bleacher: see BENCH.

bleak: see CHEERLESS; RAW.

bleed *v.* **1** *(he bleeds easily)* hemorrhage, exudate, ooze, DRIP, FLOW; **2** *(they used to bleed the sick)* phlebotomize, EXTRACT, lance, extort, ROB, STEAL, blackmail.

blemish *n.* flaw, DEFECT, STAIN, FAULT, mole, pockmark, dishonor.
— *v.* STAIN, mar, SPOIL, SOIL, tarnish.

blemished: see DEFORMED.

blend *v.* COMBINE, MIX, MINGLE, COMPOUND, fuse, amalgamate, meld, commingle.
— *n.* COMPOUND, alloy, MIXTURE, amalgamation, fusion.

blended: see COMPOSITE.

blending: see HARMONIOUS.

bless *v.* consecrate, glorify, commend, sanctify, bestow.

blessed *adj.* consecrated, sanctified, HOLY, SACRED, FAVORED, JOYFUL, blissful.

blessing *n.* benediction, consecration, godsend, APPROVAL, commendation, FAVOR.

blight: see INFECT; WITHER.

blind *adj.* sightless, eyeless, purblind, impaired, heedless, UNAWARE, blocked.
— *v.* darken, SHADE, DAZZLE, hoodwink.
— *n.*: see CAMOUFLAGE; CONCEALMENT.

blinding: see DAZZLING.

blindness: see DARK; IGNORANCE.

blink *v.* WINK, bat, TWINKLE, FLICKER.
— *n.*: see WINK.

bliss: see HEAVEN; JOY.

blissful: see BLESSED; HAPPY; HEAVENLY.

blister *n.* sac, BUBBLE, BOIL, pimple, sore, ERUPTION, abscess, swelling.

blizzard: see STORM.

bloat: see INFLATE.

blob: see BUBBLE.

block *n.* **1** *(building blocks)* cube, cake, brick, slab;
2 *(a block from here)* SQUARE, LOT; **3** *(a roadblock)* BARRIER, BAR, OBSTACLE, BLOCKADE. See also STAMP.
— *v.* BAR, impede, obstruct, CLOSE, SEAL, HINDER.

blockade *v.* SURROUND, ENCIRCLE, ENCLOSE, besiege, ISOLATE.
— *n.* SIEGE, BARRICADE, BARRIER, roadblock, OBSTACLE, embargo.

blocked: see BLIND.

blockhead: see ASS; DONKEY; HALF-WIT; MORON.

blockhouse: see FORTRESS.

blond: see FAIR.

blood *n.* plasma, serum, gore, SAP, JUICE, stock, extraction, ancestry.

bloodless: see PALE.

bloodshed: see BUTCHERY; FORCE; SLAUGHTER.

bloodthirsty: see MURDEROUS.

bloody: see MURDEROUS; RED.

bloom *v.* FLOWER, BLOSSOM, PROSPER, THRIVE, FLOURISH.
— *n.*: see BLOSSOM; BUD; FLOWER; FRESHNESS; YOUTH.

blooming: see GREEN.

blossom *n.* FLOWER, BUD, bloom.
— *v.* BLOOM, FLOWER, bud, PROSPER.

blot *n.* STAIN, smudge, SPOT, BLEMISH, flaw, stigma, slur.
— *v.* **1** *(don't blot your honor)* STAIN, SOIL, SMEAR, smirch; **2** *(to blot the wet ink)* DRY, ABSORB, CLEANSE, expunge.

blotch *n.* STAIN, SPOT, smear, smudge, stigma, DISGRACE.

blotted: see OUT.

blow *v.* PUFF, EXHALE, FAN, FLOW, SWEEP.
— *n.* **1** *(to forecast a heavy blow)* WIND, BLAST, GALE, GUST, hurricane; **2** *(a blow on the head)* RAP, whack, cuff, PUNCH, clout; **3** *(to suffer a cruel blow)* MISFORTUNE, setback, calamity.

blower: see FAN.

blowout: see BURST; FLAT.

blow up: see BLAST; BURST; INFLATE.

blowup: see EXPLOSION.

blowy: see WINDY.

blubber: see WEEP.

blubbering: see TEARFUL.

blue *adj.* SAD, glum, down, depressed, dejected, despondent.

blue-blooded: see NOBLE.

bluegrass: see GRASS.

blueprint: see ARCHITECTURE; DESIGN; MAP.

blues *pl.n.* **1** *(to have the blues)* melancholy, DEPRESSION, SADNESS, dejection; **2** *(to sing the blues)* lament, WAIL.

bluff *v.* DECEIVE, TRICK, delude, PRETEND, simulate.
— *n.*: see CLIFF.

blunder *n.* error, MISTAKE, lapse, SLIP, boner, fiasco, oversight.
— *v.*: see MISTAKE; TRIP.

blunderbuss: see GUN; RIFLE.

blunderer: see AMATEUR.

blunt *adj.* **1** *(a blunt knife)* DULL, THICK, obtuse; **2** *(a blunt answer)* RUDE, unfeeling, brusque, insensitive, straightforward.
— *v.* SOFTEN, deaden, temper, subdue, COOL, lighten.

blunted: see DULL.

bluntness: see DULLNESS.

blur *v.* SMEAR, smudge, DIM, FADE, obscure, befog.
— *n.* smudge, smear, CONFUSION, DIMNESS, haze, FOG, CLOUD.

blurb: see ADVERTISEMENT.

blurred: see FUZZY; VAGUE.

blurry: see FOGGY.

blush *v.* flush, redden, COLOR, GLOW.
— *n.*: see FLUSH.

blushing: see RED.

bluster: see BOAST; RAGE; ROAR; STORM.

blustery: see WINDY.

boar: see HOG; PIG.

board *n.* **1** *(building board)* PLANK, LUMBER, lath, PANEL, slab, tile, slate; **2** *(the school board)* COUNCIL, COMMITTEE, CABINET; **3** *(room and board)* meals, FOOD, keep, provisions.
— *v.* ENTER, embark, MOUNT. See also LODGE.

boarder: see LODGER.

boards: see LUMBER.

boast *v.* BRAG, gloat, swagger, crow, bluster, flaunt.

boat *n.* SHIP, VESSEL, CRAFT, LAUNCH, steamer, liner.

boatman: see SAILOR.

bob *v.* **1** *(to bob and weave)* BOUNCE, dance, nod, wobble; **2** *(to bob hair)* CUT, SHORTEN, CROP.

bobbin: see REEL; SPOOL.

bodily *adj.* PHYSICAL, carnal, FLESHLY, biological, BASIC, HUMAN, concrete.

body *n.* **1** *(the human body)* FRAME, FORM, BUILD, torso, carcass, cadaver; **2** *(an automobile body)* chassis, FRAME, ASSEMBLY, WHOLE, MASS, ANATOMY, MATERIAL; **3** *(a governing body)* GROUP, SOCIETY, COUNCIL, BOARD, CORPORATION.

bodyguard: see ESCORT; GUARD; PROTECTOR.

bog: see MARSH; SWAMP.

boil *v.* seethe, COOK, percolate, ferment, STEW, fume, RAGE.
— *n.* SORE, carbuncle, tumor, pimple, abscess.

boiler: see FURNACE; KETTLE.

boiling: see HOT.

boisterous: see NOISY; ROWDY.

bold *adj.* **1** *(bold explorers)* DARING, FEARLESS, BRAVE, dauntless, intrepid; **2** *(a bold scamp)* impertinent, brazen, presumptuous, cheeky.

boldness *n.* COURAGE, spunk, audacity, NERVE, guts, brass.

bolster: see BRACE; CUSHION; PILLOW.

bolt *n.* **1** *(nut and bolt)* SCREW, PIN, dowel, rivet, spike; **2** *(a bolt of lightening)* thunderbolt, lightning, STREAK, FLASH.
— *v.*: see CLOSE; FLEE; LOCK.

bolted: see SHUT.

bomb: see BLAST; MINE; SHELL.

bombard *v.* ATTACK, SHELL, pepper, BATTER, pelt, besiege.

bombshell: see SURPRISE.

bond *n.* **1** *(held in bonds)* binding, shackle, TIE, ATTACHMENT; **2** *(savings bonds)* SECURITY, debenture, WARRANTY, PLEDGE, CONTRACT.

bondage: see SLAVERY.

bonded: see BOUND.

bondman: see SLAVE.

bone *n.* SKELETON, cartilage, core, FRAME, rib, horn.

boner: see BLUNDER; FOLLY.

boneyard: see CEMETERY.

bonnet: see HAT.

bonus *n.* extra, TIP, GIFT, REWARD, dividend, bounty.

boo: see HISS.

booby trap: see MINE.

boogie-woogie: see SWING.

book *n.* VOLUME, PUBLICATION, WORK, STUDY, compendium, manual.
 — *v.*: see RESERVE; TICKET.

bookcase: see CABINET.

booking: see RESERVATION.

bookish: see LITERARY.

booklet: see CATALOG; MAGAZINE; PAMPHLET.

books: see LITERATURE.

bookworm: see STUDENT.

boom *n.* ROAR, BLAST, THUNDER, detonation. See also INFLATION.
 — *v.*: see ROAR.

boomerang: see BOUNCE; MISSILE.

boon: see GRANT.

boondocks: see COUNTRYSIDE; FRONTIER.

boorish: see COARSE.

boost: see ELEVATION; LIFT.

boot *n.* 1 *(hiking boots)* SHOE, footware, rubber, overshoe, galosh; 2 *(he gave him a boot)* kick, BLOW, JOLT, punt, ejection, rejection.
 — *v.*: see KICK.

booth: see BOX.

booty: see HAUL; LOOT.

boozy: see DRUNK.

bop: see SWING.

border *n.* 1 *(a guarded border)* BOUNDARY, COAST, FRONTIER, threshold; 2 *(an ornate border)* EDGE, MARGIN, RIM, FRINGE, HEM.
 — *v.*: see ADJOIN; EDGE; HEM.

bordering: see MARGINAL.

borderland: see FRONTIER.

bore *v.* 1 *(novels bore her)* TIRE, weary, irk, vex;

2 *(to bore a hole)* DRILL, PIERCE, perforate, PENETRATE.
 — *n.* PEST, NUISANCE, bother. See also DIAMETER; PUNCH.

bored: see WEARY.

boredom *n.* WEARINESS, tedium, MONOTONY, DULLNESS.

borer: see BIT; DRILL.

boring: see DRY; DULL; LONG-WINDED; MONOTONOUS; TAME.

borrow *v.* LOAN, RECEIVE, PLEDGE, PAWN.

bosom *n.* CHEST, BREAST, bust, CONSCIENCE, SOUL, CENTER.

boss *n.* CHIEF, SUPERVISOR, taskmaster, FOREMAN, EMPLOYER.
 — *v.* DIRECT, SUPERVISE, oversee, superintend.

botch: see GOOF; MESS.

both: see EITHER.

bother *v.* 1 *(noise bothers me)* inconvenience, vex, DISTURB, DISTRACT; 2 *(don't bother to knock)* TROUBLE, CONCERN, WORRY, DISTURB.
 — *n.*: see ANNOYANCE; BORE; DRAG; FUSS; NUISANCE.

bothered: see CROSS.

bothersome *adj.* annoying, vexing, TROUBLESOME, irksome, distracting.

bottle *n.* CONTAINER, flask, decanter, JUG, thermos.

bottom *n.* BASE, underside, FOOT, FOUNDATION, FLOOR, SEAT, buttocks, nadir.

bottomless: see DEEP.

bough *n.* BRANCH, LIMB, offshoot, ARM.

boulder: see ROCK; STONE.

boulevard: see AVENUE; ROAD; STREET.

bounce *v.* 1 *(balls bounce)* SPRING, BOB, ricochet, jounce, recoil, boomerang; 2 *(she bounced in)* SPRING, LEAP, HOP, bound, dance.
 — *n.*: see SPRING.

bouncy: see JERKY.

bound *adj.* 1 *(bound with twine)* tied, trussed, shackled, tethered, confined, bonded, attached, fastened; 2 *(bound to succeed)* BENT, intent, FIRM, compelled, determined.
 — *v.*: see BOUNCE; JUMP; LEAP; LIMIT; SPRING.
 — *n.*: see JUMP; LEAP; RUN; SPRING.

boundary *n.* LIMIT, EDGE, MARGIN, FRONTIER, FENCE, BORDER, circumference, confines.

boundless: see IMMEASURABLE; INFINITE; VAST.

boundlessness: see ETERNITY.

bounds: see OUTSIDE.

bounteous: see LIBERAL.

bountiful: see ABUNDANT; AMPLE; PLENTIFUL.

bounty: see BONUS.

bouquet: see CLUSTER; ODOR; SPRAY; WREATH.

bout: see ATTACK; COMPETITION; SIEGE; SPELL.

boutique: see SHOP; STORE.

bow *v.* BEND, STOOP, incline, curtsy, salaam, SUBMIT, SURRENDER.
— *n.* **1** *(bow and arrow)* longbow, arc, CURVE, bend, fiddlestick; **2** *(to tie a bow)* ribbon, LACE, BAND, spangle, TIE, KNOT. See also SALUTATION; SALUTE; STEM.

bowed: see BENT.

bowels: see BELLY; INSIDE.

bowl *n.* BASIN, tureen, VESSEL, saucer, receptacle, crater, DEPRESSION.

box *n.* **1** *(cardboard box)* CONTAINER, crate, BIN, carton, CASE, receptacle; **2** *(box on the ear)* cuff, BLOW, PUNCH, slap; **3** *(box at the theater)* PEN, COMPARTMENT, booth, ENCLOSURE.

boxer: see FIGHTER.

box in: see PEN.

box up: see CAGE.

boy *n.* CHILD, LAD, YOUNGSTER, FELLOW, YOUTH, bellboy, KID.

boycott: see PICKET.

boyfriend: see ESCORT.

brace *n.* PROP, STAY, SUPPORT, truss, buttress. See also PAIR; TWO.
— *v.* HOLD, SUPPORT, bolster, STRENGTHEN, reinforce.

bracelet: see CHARM.

bracelets: see JEWELRY.

bracer: see REFRESHMENTS.

bracing *adj.* REFRESHING, invigorating, BRISK, FRESH, stimulating.

bracket: see CLASS; COUPLE; LEDGE; LINK; SHELF.

brag *v.* BOAST, crow, gloat, swagger.

braid: see CORD; LACE; LOCK; STRIPE; TWIST; WEAVE.

brain: see GENIUS; MIND.

brainless: see NONSENSICAL; STUPID.

brains: see WIT.

brainstorm: see INSPIRATION.

brainwash: see PERSUADE.

brainwashing: see PERSUASION.

brainy: see INTELLECTUAL; INTELLIGENT.

braise: see FRY.

brake *n.* CHECK, damper, governor, CURB, BLOCK, constraint.

bramble: see BUSH; SHRUB.

bran: see MEAL.

branch *n.* **1** *(perched on a branch)* BOUGH, LIMB, offshoot, ARM; **2** *(the administrative branch)* DIVISION, subsidiary, wing, EXTENSION; **3** *(a river branch)* FORK, tributary.
— *v.*: see DIVIDE; SPROUT.

branching: see ANGLE.

brand *n.* **1** *(the ranch's brand)* MARK, SCAR, STAMP, EMBLEM, earmark; **2** *(a famous brand)* VARIETY, KIND, trademark, MAKE, line.
— *v.*: see BURN; MARK.

brandish: see FLOURISH.

brand-new: see FRESH.

brass: see BOLDNESS; NERVE; TRUMPET.

brassy: see SHAMELESS.

brat *n.* urchin, snip, imp, RASCAL, scamp, guttersnipe.

brave *adj.* COURAGEOUS, DARING, valiant, intrepid, unafraid, undaunted.
— *v.* RISK, CHALLENGE, DARE, DEFY, confront, WITHSTAND.

bravery *n.* COURAGE, valor, DARING, BOLDNESS, spunk, BACKBONE, guts.

brawl: see FIGHT; SCRAP.

brawny: see MUSCUALR; STRONG.

brazen: see BOLD; SHAMELESS.

breach: see DISRUPT; GAP; RENT; VEIN.

bread *n.* FOOD, ROLL, cake, bun, toast, loaf, NOURISHMENT, MONEY.

breadth: see THICKNESS; WIDTH.

breadwinner: see HUSBAND; SUPPORTER.

break *v.* **1** *(to break bread)* TEAR, PART, sever, SHATTER, DASH, fracture; **2** *(to break and run)* ESCAPE, RUN, FLEE, SCATTER; **3** *(to break a horse)* TAME, domesticate, TRAIN.
— *n.* REST, PAUSE, interim, INTERRUPTION, RECESS.

breakable: see BRITTLE; CRISP.

break down: see DISSOLVE.

breakdown *n.* **1** *(to suffer a breakdown)* mishap, malfunction, DISORDER, COLLAPSE, FAILURE, stoppage; **2** *(a detailed breakdown)* ANALYSIS, EXAMINATION, REVIEW, SURVEY.

breaker: see WAVE.

breakfast: see EAT; MEAL.

break in: see RAID.

break-in: see BURGLARY.

breaking: see PARTING; VIOLATION.

break off: see CHIP.

breakout: see ESCAPE; FLIGHT.

breakthrough: see DISCOVERY.

breakup: see DIVORCE.

breast *n.* CHEST, bust, BOSOM, thorax, HEART, CONSCIENCE.

breastplate: see ARMOR.

breath *n.* respiration, exhalation, INSPIRATION, breathing, whiff, LIFE.

breathe *v.* respire, INHALE, draw, emit, instill, LIVE, EXIST.

breathing: see ALIVE; BREATH; LIVING.

breathless *adj.* **1** *(we arrived breathless)* winded, gasping, panting, LIFELESS; **2** *(breathless with excitement)* EAGER, TENSE, ardent, frightened.

breathtaking: see AMAZING; SURPRISING.

breeches: see TROUSERS.

breed *v.* RAISE, bring forth, beget, CAUSE, PRODUCE.
— *n.* VARIETY, RACE, STRAIN, lineage, STOCK, FAMILY.

breeder: see RANCHER.

breeding: see COURTESY; CULTURE; GENERATION; MANNERS.

breeze *n.* WIND, zephyr, flurry, PUFF, CURRENT, DRAFT.

breezy *adj.* gusty, WINDY, airy, REFRESHING, BRIGHT, sprightly.

brethren: see CONGREGATION.

brevity: see SHORTNESS.

brew *v.* concoct, COOK, BOIL, percolate, DEVISE, DEVELOP, PREPARE.

bribe *v.* BUY, SWAY, INFLUENCE, corrupt, entice, seduce, fix, soap, TIP.
— *n.*: see TIP.

brick: see BLOCK.

bridal *adj.* nuptial, marital, wifely.
— *n.* WEDDING, MARRIAGE, matrimony.

bridegroom: see GROOM; HUSBAND.

bridge *n.* SPAN, overpass, trestle, viaduct, transit, catwalk, causeway.
— *v.*: see ARCH; LINK; SPAN; STRETCH.

bridle *n.* leash, curb, CHECK, CONTROL, reins, restraint.

brief *adj.* SHORT, concise, terse, curt.
— *v.* apprise, orient, ADVISE, SUMMARIZE, INFORM.

briefly: see AWHILE; LITTLE.

brigade: see CORPS.

bright *adj.* **1** *(bright colors)* SHINY, gleaming, sparkling, lighted, CHEERFUL, vivacious, GAY; **2** *(a bright child)* INTELLIGENT, ALERT, CLEVER.

brighten *v.* **1** *(the day brightened)* CLEAR, dawn, ILLUMINATE, illumine, WAKE; **2** *(the sun brightened the room)* SHINE, POLISH, cheer, GLADDEN.

brightness: see GLOW; LIGHT; LUSTER.

brilliance *n.* **1** *(a diamond's brilliance)* SHINE, LUSTER, radiance, GLARE; **2** *(the brilliance of Einstein)* ingenuity, GENIUS, WISDOM, TALENT, INTELLIGENCE.

brilliant *adj.* gleaming, sparkling, RADIANT, BRIGHT, KEEN, INGENIOUS, INTELLIGENT.
— *n.*: see DIAMOND.

brim *n.* EDGE, BORDER, RIM, brink, BANK, SHORE, verge.

brimful: see CHOCK-FULL.

brine: see OCEAN; SALT.

bring *v.* CARRY, convey, BEAR, TRANSPORT, LEAD, EFFECT, induce.

bring about: see EFFECT; PROVOKE.

bring forth: see BREED; PRODUCE.

bring in: see YIELD.

bring out: see ISSUE.

brink: see BRIM; COAST; EDGE; MARGIN; RIM.

brisk *adj.* ACTIVE, LIVELY, peppy, PERKY, stimulating, BRACING.

briskness *n.* pep, SPIRIT, lightness, ENERGY, EASE, agility.

bristle *n.* HAIR, quill, whisker, stubble.

bristles: see BEARD.

britches: see TROUSERS.

brittle *adj.* fragile, breakable, WEAK, CRISP, STIFF, RIGID, inflexible.

broad *adj.* WIDE, SPACIOUS, AMPLE, EXTENSIVE, expansive.

broadcast *v.* TRANSMIT, SEND, emit, televise, ANNOUNCE, SPREAD, disperse, disseminate.
— *n.*: see ADVERTISEMENT; PUBLICATION.

broaden *v.* widen, EXPAND, amplify, ENLARGE, INCREASE.

broad-minded: see LIBERAL.

broadness: see DIAMETER.

broadsword: see SWORD.

brochure: see CIRCULAR; PAMPHLET.

broil: see COOK; ROAST; SWEAT.

broke: see BANKRUPT; FLAT.

broken *adj.* **1** (*a broken heart*) shattered, smashed, fractured, crippled; **2** (*a broken man*) defeated, demoralized, spent, weakened.

broken-down: see OLD.

brokenhearted *adj.* dejected, SAD, heartsick, grief-stricken, despondent.

broker *n.* AGENT, salesman, DEALER, middleman, intermediary.

brooch: see CLASP; PIN.

brooches: see JEWELRY.

brood: see LITTER.

brooding: see SULLEN.

brook *n.* STREAM, CREEK, rill, rivulet.

broom: see BRUSH.

brother *n.* sibling, FELLOW, COMPANION, confrere, NEIGHBOR.

brotherhood *n.* **1** (*their lasting brotherhood*) FRIENDSHIP, fellowship, ESTEEM, CLOSENESS, INTIMACY; **2** (*to join a brotherhood*) fraternity, SOCIETY, UNION, ORGANIZATION.

brotherly *adj.* fraternal, FRIENDLY, CHARITABLE, neighborly.

brow *n.* forehead, eyebrow, FRONT.

brown: see FRY; TOAST.

bruise *v.* INJURE, HURT, WOUND.
— *n.* contusion, INJURY, hurt, lesion, sore, MARK.

bruised: see SORE; WOUNDED.

brunch: see MEAL.

brush *n.* **1** (*a paint brush*) broom, MOP, whisk, tuft, TAIL; **2** (*hidden in the brush*) bushes, underbrush, scrub, shrubbery. See also BEARD.
— *v.* PAINT, COAT, daub, SCRUB, GRAZE, TOUCH, CLEAN.

brusque: see BLUNT.

brutal *adj.* CRUEL, HARSH, PITILESS, barbaric, unmerciful, CRUDE, COARSE.

brutality: see CRUELTY; HARSHNESS.

brute *n.* BEAST, ANIMAL, SAVAGE, barbarian, BULLY, SCOUNDREL.

bubble *n.* sac, balloon, globule, blob, BEAD.
— *v.*: see FOAM; SIMMER; SPARKLE.

bubbling: see FOAMY.

buccaneer: see PIRATE.

buck *n.* **1** (*bucks and does*) deer, stag, roebuck, bull; **2** (*it costs a buck*) dollar, BILL, greenback.
— *v.* LEAP, PITCH, FIGHT, OPPOSE.

bucket *n.* PAIL, canister, scuttle, scoop.

buckle *n.* fastener, CLASP, CATCH, turnbuckle, hasp.
— *v.* **1** (*to buckle a belt*) FASTEN, SECURE, CLOSE, HOOK; **2** (*to buckle from strain*) sag, COLLAPSE, CRUMPLE, WARP.

buckler: see SHIELD.

bud *n.* shoot, FLOWER, bloom, SPROUT, embryo.
— *v.*: see BLOSSOM; GROW; SPROUT.

buddy *n.* PAL, CHUM, crony, COMRADE, COMPANION, PARTNER, sidekick.

budge *v.* STIR, SHIFT, dislodge, inch, MOVE, CREEP.

budget *n.* PLAN, ESTIMATE, funds, AMOUNT.

buff: see POLISH; SHINE.

buffer: see CUSHION; SHIELD.

buffet: see REFRESHMENTS; SPREAD.

bug: see INSECT; PEST.

buggy: see CARRIAGE; CART; STAGE.

bugle: see TRUMPET.

build *v.* ERECT, CONSTRUCT, ASSEMBLE, fabricate, reinforce.
— *n.* physique, SHAPE, FIGURE, FORM.

builder: see ARCHITECT; MANUFACTURER.

building *n.* HOUSE, STRUCTURE, edifice, CONSTRUCTION.

buildings: see DEVELOPMENT.

build-up: see INFLATION.

bulb *n.* **1** (*a tulip bulb*) knob, BUD, onion, tulip; **2** (*a light bulb*) LAMP, GLOBE, TUBE, filament.

bulge *n.* LUMP, BUMP, swelling, hump, cam, protrusion, projection, BELLY, BLISTER.
— *v.* SWELL, sag, protrude, jut.

bulk: see MAGNITUDE: MAJORITY; MASS; MOST; VOLUME; WHOLE.

bulky *adj.* LARGE, MASSIVE, HUGE, AWKWARD, CLUMSY, unwieldy.

bull: see BUCK; BUNK.

bullet: see BALL; LEAD; MISSILE; SHELL; SHOT.

bulletin *n.* NEWS, REPORT, ITEM, communique, ANNOUNCEMENT, JOURNAL, quarterly.

bullion: see METAL.

bull's-eye: see CENTER; EYE; MARK; MIDDLE; TARGET.

bully *n.* ROWDY, ruffian, tough, harasser, tormentor.

bulwark: see GUARD.

bum *n.* TRAMP, hobo, LOAFER, vagrant, vagabond.
— *adj.* defective, BROKEN, SORE, WORTHLESS, FALSE.
— *v.* BORROW, BEG, mooch, panhandle, LOAF, DRIFT.

bumbling: see CLUMSY.

bump *v.* STRIKE, KNOCK, jounce.
— *n.* LUMP, knob, BULGE, swelling, welt, tumor. See also KNOCK.

bumpkin: see CLOWN.

bumpy: see COARSE; ROUGH; UNEVEN.

bun: see BREAD; ROLL.

bunch *n.* clump, BATCH, BUNDLE, GROUP, FLOCK, ASSORTMENT.
— *v.* GATHER, amass, BUNDLE, CLUSTER.

bundle *n.* PACKAGE, PARCEL, BATCH, BUNCH.
— *v.* PACK, WRAP, bale, DRESS.

bungalow: see COTTAGE; LODGE.

bungle: see GOOF; TRIP.

bunk *n.* **1** (*a lower bunk*) berth, BED, COT, RACK; **2** (*that's bunk!*) NONSENSE, baloney, bull, hokum, hooey, falsehood.

bunkhouse: see HUT.

buoyancy: see CHEERFULNESS; OPTIMISM.

buoyant: see LIGHT; YOUTHFUL.

burbling: see FOAMY.

burden *n.* LOAD, CARGO, WEIGHT, CHARGE, RESPONSIBILITY, worry.
— *v.*: see DRAG; FREIGHT; IMPOSE.

burdened: see LOADED.

burdensome: see TROUBLESOME.

bureau *n.* **1** (*the travel bureau*) OFFICE, AGENCY, DEPARTMENT, BOARD, COMMISSION, ORGANIZATION, DIVISION, UNIT; **2** (*the bureau near the bed*) dresser, CHEST, chest of drawers, DESK.

bureaucracy: see ADMINISTRATION.

bureaucrat: see OFFICIAL.

bureaucratic: see POLITICAL.

burglar *n.* ROBBER, THIEF, housebreaker, yegg, CROOK.

burglarize: see LOOT; ROB.

burglary *n.* THEFT, ROBBERY, larceny, thievery, break-in.

burial *n.* FUNERAL, entombing, rites, SERVICE. See also CEMETERY.

buried: see DEEP.

burlap: see CANVAS.

burly: see HEFTY.

burn *v.* FLAME, BLAZE, FLARE, GLOW, CONSUME, ignite, char, singe, SCORCH, incinerate, cremate, scald, brand. See also BITE.
— *n.*: see IRRITATION.

burning: see FIERY; HOT; INFLAMMATION.

burro: see ASS; DONKEY.

burrow v. DIG, TUNNEL, MINE, SCOOP, NESTLE, SNUGGLE.
— n.: see DEN.

burst v. EXPLODE, CRACK, blow up, SPLIT, BREAK, SHATTER, ERUPT, POP.
— n. EXPLOSION, ERUPTION, CRACK, BLAST, shattering, SPLIT, blowout, PUFF, spurt.

bursting: see CHOCK-FULL.

bury v. entomb, CONCEAL, HIDE, COVER, PLUNGE, ENCLOSE.

bush n. **1** (an azalea bush) SHRUB, shrubbery, BRUSH, HEDGE, bramble, thicket; **2** (far out in the bush) hinterland, FRONTIER, FOREST, JUNGLE, woods.

bushed adj. TIRED, worn out, fagged, BEAT, WEARY, tuckered, exhausted, spent.

bushel: see BASKET.

bushes: see BRUSH; HEDGE.

business n. **1** (what business is it of yours?) CONCERN, INTEREST, AFFAIR, MATTER; **2** (his business is poultry farming) calling, TRADE, OCCUPATION, CRAFT, PROFESSION, CAREER, LINE, field, SPECIALTY, vocation, livelihood, COMMERCE, INDUSTRY, PURSUIT, EMPLOYMENT, VENTURE, TRAFFIC, UNDERTAKING; **3** (a business located on Main Street) COMPANY, PARTNERSHIP, CORPORATION, enterprise, FIRM, CONCERN, ORGANIZATION, HOUSE, ESTABLISHMENT.
— adj.: see INDUSTRIAL.

businesslike: see COMMERCIAL.

businessman: see DEALER; EXECUTIVE; MERCHANT; TRADER.

bust: see BOSOM; BREAST; CHEST; STATUE; WRECK.

bustle: see RUSTLE.

bustling: see FUSSY.

busy adj. occupied, ACTIVE, INDUSTRIOUS, diligent, engaged, employed, hard-working.
— v.: see OCCUPY.

but prep. EXCEPT, excepting, save, barring.
— conj. still, HOWEVER, YET, contrariwise, EXCEPT, except that, UNLESS, THOUGH, ALTHOUGH, NEVERTHELESS, notwithstanding.
— adv. ONLY, JUST, MERELY, solely, SIMPLY.

butcher n. meatcutter, meatman, MURDERER, ASSASSIN, cutthroat.
— v.: see MASSACRE; SLAUGHTER.

butchery n. SLAUGHTER, killing, MASSACRE, MURDER, extermination, mutilation, mayhem, bloodshed, gore, havoc.

butler: see SERVANT.

butt: see RAM; STOCK; STUB; TARGET.

butter up: see FLATTER.

buttery: see GREASY.

butt in v. meddle, TAMPER, INTRUDE, INTERFERE, encroach.

buttocks: see BOTTOM.

button: see SWITCH.

buttress: see BRACE; PROP; STRENGHTHEN.

buy v. PURCHASE, SHOP, MARKET, OBTAIN, GET, BARGAIN.
— n. PURCHASE, BARGAIN, steal, OPPORTUNITY.

buy back: see REDEEM.

buyer: see CONSUMER; CUSTOMER; DEALER; PATRON; TRADER.

buzz n. HUM, humming, drone, gossip, RUMOR, MURMUR.
— v.: see HUM; RING.

buzzer: see BELL; SIGNAL.

buzzing: see HUM.

by prep. PAST, NEAR, at, BESIDE, alongside, BEFORE, OVER, THROUGH, because of, following, ACCORDING TO, IN, DURING, ON, FROM, PER.
— adv. PAST, AWAY, NEAR, BESIDE, ASIDE, alongside, OVER.

bygone: see AGO; PAST.

by-pass: see NEGLECT; OMIT; SKIP; SWITCH.

bystander: see WITNESS.

byway: see ALLEY.

byword: see MOTTO; PROVERB.

C

cab: see CABIN.

cabaret: see BAR; CAFE; TAVERN.

cabin n. **1** (a cabin in the woods) HUT, SHACK, shanty, COTTAGE, log cabin; **2** (the cabins of an ocean liner) stateroom, ROOM; **3** (the pilot's cabin) COMPARTMENT, controls, cab, cockpit.

cabinet n. **1** (the cups in the cabinet) CLOSET, cupboard, bookcase, pantry; **2** (the President's Cabinet) COUNCIL, BOARD, COMMITTEE, ministry, advisers.

cable *n.* CHAIN, ROPE, wire, CORD, cablegram.
— *v.* wire, telegraph, COMMUNICATE, radio.

cablegram: see CABLE.

caboose: see CAR.

cache: see SAFE; STORE.

cachet: see STAMP.

cackle *v.* gabble, jabber, LAUGH, HOWL, crow.
— *n.* cluck, LAUGHTER, blab, CHATTER, gabbing, gobble, peal.

cad: see VILLAIN.

cadaver: see BODY; CORPSE; REMAINS.

cadence: see BEAT.

cadet: see STUDENT.

cadre: see STAFF.

caesar: see EMPEROR.

cafe *n.* cafeteria, diner, restaurant, lunchroom, TAVERN, cabaret, night club, barroom.

cafeteria: see CAFE.

cage *n.* coop, CELL, pound, FOLD, BOX, PRISON, ENCLOSURE.
— *v.* coop up, box up, imprison, shut in, PEN, CONFINE, fence in, ENCLOSE, incarcerate, corral.

cagey: see CAUTIOUS; CLEVER; SLY.

cake: see BLOCK; BREAD; COOKIE; TABLET.

calamitous: see UNFORTUNATE.

calamity: see BLOW; DISASTER; TRAGEDY.

calcified: see ROCKY.

calculate *v.* compute, RECKON, FIGURE, tally, ESTIMATE, DETERMINE, NUMBER, rate, MEASURE, JUDGE, ADD, SUBTRACT, MULTIPLY, DIVIDE, ascertain.

calculated: see DELIBERATE; STUDIED.

calculating: see CAREFUL.

calculation: see ESTIMATION.

calculator: see COUNTER.

caldron: see KETTLE.

calendar *n.* almanac, chronology, year, TABLE, timetable, SCHEDULE, agenda, PROGRAM, DIARY, BULLETIN, LIST, events.

caliber: see QUALITY.

call *v.* **1** *(to call a meeting)* INVITE, SUMMON, convene, ASSEMBLE, COLLECT, BECKON, AROUSE, AWAKEN, telephone, RING, ring up, PHONE;

2 *(everyone calls him Bob)* NAME, designate, title, nickname, LABEL, ADDRESS; **3** *(to call at the top of one's lungs)* SHOUT, CRY, cry out, EXCLAIM, call out; **4** *(to call at a friend's house)* VISIT, drop in, SEE, APPEAR, ENTER, come in, moor, disembark.
— *n.* **1** *(to issue a call)* INVITATION, SUMMONS, COMMAND, calling; **2** *(on call)* DEMAND, NEED, OCCASION, CLAIM; **3** *(to hear a call)* SHOUT, CRY, YELL, OUTCRY; **4** *(to make a call)* VISIT, MEETING, INTERVIEW, CONFERENCE, APPOINTMENT.

caller: see COMPANY; GUEST; VISITOR.

call for: see INVITE; REQUIRE.

call forth: see SUMMON.

calling: see BUSINESS; CALL; CAREER; LINE; OCCUPATION.

call off: see CANCEL.

call out: see CALL.

callow: see CHILDISH.

calm *n.* QUIET, CALMNESS, stillness, REST, lull, PEACE, serenity, doldrums, TRANQUILLITY.
— *adj.* QUIET, STILL, restful, PEACEFUL, serene, TRANQUIL, SMOOTH, windless, STEADY, staid, soothing, COOL, MILD, unruffled, composed, collected, placid, poised, aloof, unexcited, level-headed, even-tempered.
— *v.* quiet, STILL, lull, pacify, SOOTHE, tranquilize, DRUG, QUENCH, sober, assuage, COMPOSE.

calming: see REFRESHING.

calmly: see EVENLY.

calmness *n.* **1** *(the calmness of snowfall)* PEACE, quietness, TRANQUILLITY, quietude, stillness, CALM; **2** *(to act with calmness)* composure, self-control, self-possession, equanimity.

cam: see BULGE.

cameo: see RELIEF.

camouflage *v.* CONCEAL, DISGUISE, cloak, mask, SCREEN, falsify, feign.
— *n.* DISGUISE, mask, VEIL, blind, deception, masquerade, subterfuge, CONCEALMENT, pretense.

camouflaged: see HIDDEN.

camp *n.* encampment, bivouac, campground, TENT, HUT, FORT, ARMY.
— *v.* encamp, bivouac, tent, STAY, INHABIT, vacation.

campaign *n.* crusade, operations, EXPEDITION, BATTLE, CONFLICT, propaganda, TOUR, speeches, STRATEGY.

— *v.* crusade, STRUGGLE, FIGHT, COMBAT, tour, SPEAK.

campfire: see FIRE.

campground: see CAMP.

campstool: see STOOL.

can *n.* canister, tin, BOX, CONTAINER, receptacle, drum, toilet, PAIL.
— *v.* PRESERVE, KEEP, put up. See also JUNK; DISCARD.

canal *n.* **1** (*the Erie Canal*) CHANNEL, RIVER, inlet, waterway; **2** (*the dentist did canal work*) TUBE, duct, PASSAGE, CAVITY.

canalize: see DIRECT.

cancel *v.* call off, ELIMINATE, ERASE, REMOVE, revoke, annul, invalidate, scratch, equalize, COMPENSATE, counterbalance, neutralize.

cancer: see GROWTH.

candid: see FRANK; FREE; OPEN.

candidate *n.* nominee, contestant, COMPETITOR, aspirant, ENTRY, applicant, protagonist.

candidly: see OPENLY.

candle *n.* taper, LIGHT, FLAME, TORCH, tallow, wax.

candy: see SWEETEN.

cane: see SPANK; STAFF; STICK; WHIP.

canine: see FOX.

canister: see BUCKET; CAN; CONTAINER.

cannon: see ARTILLERY; GUN.

canny: see SLY.

canon: see COMMANDMENT.

canopy: see HOOD; PAVILION; TENT.

cantankerous: see CONTRARY; CRANKY.

canteen: see BAR.

canticle: see HYMN.

canvas *n.* CLOTH, tarpaulin, gunny, burlap, COVERING, PICTURE, PAINTING, sailcloth, denim.

canvass: see PEDDLE; POLL.

canyon *n.* VALLEY, ravine, chasm, GAP, gorge, divide, OPENING.

cap *n.* headcover, COVER, TOP, beret, nightcap, skullcap, tam.
— *v.* COVER, CLOSE, SURPASS, COMPLETE, MATCH, CROWN.

capability: see CAPACITY; EFFICIENCY; FITNESS; POTENTIAL.

capable *adj.* ABLE, EFFICIENT, competent, FIT, skillful, GIFTED, susceptible, SKILLED, proficient, dexterous.

capacity *n.* **1** (*the capacity of the room*) ROOM, VOLUME, ACCOMMODATION, CONTENTS, SPACE, MEASURE, POWER; **2** (*in what capacity shall he serve?*) POSITION, APPOINTMENT, FUNCTION, JOB; **3** (*the capacity for hard work*) ABILITY, SKILL, TALENT, competency, capability, FITNESS.

cape: see CLOAK; ROBE.

caper: see LEAP; STUNT.

capital *n.* **1** (*the need for capital*) WEALTH, MONEY, PROPERTY, resources, assets, principal, INVESTMENT; **2** (*Dover is the capital of Delaware*) metropolis, city, CENTER, capitol.
— *adj.*: see LEADING; PRINCIPAL.

capitalism: see RIGHT.

capital punishment: see EXECUTION.

capitol: see CAPITAL.

capsize: see UPSET.

capsule *n.* **1** (*a time capsule*) CONTAINER, CAN, flask, VESSEL; **2** (*one capsule a day*) TABLET, PILL, dosage; **3** (*a three-man capsule*) SATELLITE, spacecraft, space probe.

captain *n.* OFFICER, COMMANDER, HEAD, LEADER, CHIEF, LORD, DIRECTOR, MASTER, skipper, commandant.

caption: see HEADING; HEADLINE; TITLE.

captivate: see BEWITCH; CHARM; TEMPT; WITCH.

captivating: see GLAMOROUS; LOVABLE.

captivation: see MAGNET.

captive *n.* hostage, PRISONER, CONVICT, inmate, shut-in, SLAVE, ENEMY.

captivity: see SLAVERY.

capture *v.* TAKE, SEIZE, CATCH, ARREST, GRAB, nab, apprehend, TRAP, bag, NET, GAIN, collar, PINCH.
— *n.*: see ARREST; CATCH; occupation.

car *n.* AUTOMOBILE, coach, VEHICLE, trolley, TRAIN, diner, caboose, tender, gondola, CABIN, CAGE.

caravan: see TRAIN.

carbine: see RIFLE.

carbuncle: see BOIL.

carcass: see BODY; CORPSE.

card *n.* pasteboard, BADGE, TICKET, identification, agenda, SCHEDULE, LIST, roster.

cards: see HAND; MAIL; PACK.

care *n.* **1** *(to take care)* ATTENTION, CAUTION, HEED, FORETHOUGHT, watchfulness, diligence; **2** *(in their care)* keeping, custody, CONCERN, INTEREST, CHARGE, PROTECTION, SUPERVISION, MANAGEMENT, guardianship; **3** *(the cares of the day)* ANXIETY, WORRY, CONCERN, TROUBLE.
— *v.* **1** *(not to care)* MIND, NOTICE, THINK, CONSIDER, WISH, DESIRE; **2** *(to care for a child)* KEEP, PROTECT, WATCH, SUPERVISE, MIND, baby-sit.

career *n.* OCCUPATION, PROFESSION, FIELD, specialty, ACTIVITY, WORK, vocation, calling, BUSINESS.

care for: see MIND; NURSE; REAR; TEND.

carefree: see CASUAL.

careful *adj.* CAUTIOUS, prudent, WATCHFUL, wary, heedful, vigilant, guarded, foreseeing, THOROUGH, calculating, meticulous, considered, CONCERNED.

carefully: see EXACTLY; LIGHTLY; PRECISELY.

careless *adj.* inattentive, unthoughtful, RASH, THOUGHTLESS, RECKLESS, unconcerned, SLOPPY, indifferent, uncaring, MESSY, negligent, lax, slipshod.

carelessness: see FORGETFULNESS.

caress *v.* KISS, EMBRACE, fondle, STROKE, PET, PAT, TOUCH, cuddle.
— *n.*: see HUG; KISS.

caretaker: see JANITOR; KEEPER; SUPERINTENDENT.

cargo *n.* LOAD, freightload, FREIGHT, GOODS, MERCHANDISE, shipment.

caring: see PARENTAL.

carnal: see BODILY; EARTHLY; SEXUAL.

carnival: see FESTIVAL.

carol *n.* SONG, HYMN, noël, madrigal, ballad, CHANT, ditty.
— *v.* SING, CHANT, intone, chirrup.

carouse: see RIOT.

carpet *n.* RUG, MAT, runner, COVER, blanket, LAYER.

carriage *n.* **1** *(the horses hitched to the carriage)* buggy, shay, coach, stagecoach, rig, surrey, chariot, CART, go-cart, pram, stroller, baby

carriage; **2** *(the carriage of a soldier as he marches)* bearing, POSTURE, AIR, ATTITUDE, MANNER, STYLE, BEHAVIOR, demeanor.

carrier: see MESSENGER; PORTER.

carry *v.* TRANSPORT, convey, MOVE, TRANSFER, DELIVER, TAKE, BRING, CART, truck, LOAD, CONDUCT, HAUL, lug, tote, BEAR, shoulder, LIFT, FREIGHT, taxi, FERRY, SHIP, SUSTAIN. See also STOCK.

carrying: see TRANSPORT; TRANSPORTATION.

carry on *v.* **1** *(to carry on bravely)* CONTINUE, RESUME, PROCEED; **2** *(to carry on a business)* CONDUCT, OPERATE, administer; **3** *(the kids are carrying on)* misbehave, RAGE, storm, fulminate.

carry out: see ACCOMPLISH; DISCHARGE; DO; EXECUTE; FULFILL; PERFORM; PROSECUTE; REALIZE.

cart *n.* wagon, buggy, chariot, dogcart, pushcart, handcart, wheelbarrow, TRUCK.
— *v.* CARRY, TRANSPORT, lug, tote, HAUL, truck, FREIGHT.

cartilage: see BONE.

carton: see BOX; CASE; PACK.

cartridge: see MISSILE; SHELL; SHOT.

carve *v.* MOLD, SHAPE, fashion, MODEL, chisel, SCULPTURE, whittle, CUT, CHOP, SLICE, tool, dismember, DIVIDE.

carving: see SCULPTURE.

cascade: see TORRENT.

case *n.* **1** *(a serious case of measles)* EVENT, OCCURRENCE, HAPPENING, instance, SITUATION, ILLUSTRATION, EXAMPLE, SAMPLE, plight, ILLNESS, CONDITION, circumstances; **2** *(a case of soda)* CONTAINER, carton, crate, BOX, BIN, CHEST, receptacle, CAPSULE, sheath; **3** *(to win his case in court)* lawsuit, ARGUMENT, SUIT, ACTION, CLAIM, CAUSE.

cash *n.* MONEY, CURRENCY, bills, coins, CHANGE, roll, wad.
— *v.* RECEIVE, GET, pocket, liquidate, EXCHANGE.

casing: see JACKET.

casino *n.* clubhouse, CLUB, LODGE, DEN, HALL, ballroom, discothèque.

casket: see CHEST; COFFIN.

cast *v.* **1** *(to cast the first stone)* HURL, THROW, FLING, SLING, HEAVE, PITCH, TOSS; **2** *(to cast a glance)* direct, TURN; **3** *(to cast a shadow)* SHED, impart, diffuse; **4** *(to cast a ballot)* VOTE, DEPOSIT; **5** *(to cast a statue)* MOLD, FORM, SCULPTURE, pour; **6** *(to cast its skin)* SHED, throw off, DISCARD, REJECT. See also FISH.

−*n.* **1** (*in a plaster cast*) MOLD, FORM, casting, PLASTER, COVERING; **2** (*the cast for the play*) COMPANY, TROUPE, actors, roles; **3** (*a cast of dice*) ROLL, THROW; **4** (*a slight cast of yellowish hue*) tinge, TINT, SHADE, TOUCH; **5** (*to take on a different cast*) look, APPEARANCE, FORM, STRUCTURE, SHAPE, EXPRESSION, REPRESENTATION.

caste: see CLASS; ESTATE; NUMBER.

caster: see WHEEL.

castigation: see DISCIPLINE.

casting: see CAST.

castle *n.* PALACE, FORTRESS, FORT, citadel, stronghold, MANSION, chateau, alcazar, chalet, TOWER.

cast off: see SHED.

casual *adj.* OFFHAND, accidental, nonchalant, unplanned, unintentional, HASTY, OCCASIONAL, superficial, easygoing, INFORMAL, sporty, indifferent, carefree.

casually: see INCIDENTALLY; OFFHAND.

casualty: see ACCIDENT.

cataclysm: see DISASTER.

catafalque: see COFFIN.

catalog *n.* LIST, INDEX, listing, directory, FILE, inventory, RECORD, ROLL, titles, tabulation, TABLE, SCHEDULE, booklet, REGISTER.
−*v.* LIST, inventory, RECORD, FILE, index, tabulate, SCHEDULE.

catapult: see LAUNCH; SLING.

catastrophe: see DISASTER.

catch *v.* SEIZE, collar, CAPTURE, overtake, nab, GRAB, GRASP, entrap, snare, HOOK, NET, lasso, corral, bag, TACKLE, SURPRISE, snag, ENTANGLE, DETECT, UNDERSTAND, HEAR, GET, contract.
−*n.* **1** (*the shortstop made the catch*) seizure, capture, ARREST, taking, acquisition; **2** (*the catch on the door*) BOLT, latch, HOOK, fastener, PIN, CLASP; **3** (*a good catch of fish*) TAKE, HAUL, AMOUNT; **4** (*there must be a catch somewhere*) trick, drawback, DISADVANTAGE, TROUBLE; **5** (*she thought he was a good catch*) PRIZE, TREASURE, BARGAIN.

catching *adj.* contagious, INFECTIOUS, communicable.
−*n.*: see CONTRACTION.

catchword: see LABEL.

category: see CLASS; CLASSIFICATION; COMPARTMENT; DIGNITY.

cater: see PROVIDE.

cathedral: see CHURCH.

catholic: see UNIVERSAL.

cat nap: see NAP; SLEEP.

cat-o'-nine-tails: see WHIP.

cattle: see STOCK.

cattleman: see RANCHER.

catwalk: see BRIDGE.

caucus: see DISCUSSION.

caught: see ENTANGLED.

cauldron: see KETTLE; POT.

cause *n.* **1** (*the cause of the accident*) REASON, ORIGIN, SOURCE, ground, CONDITION, CREATION, MOTIVE, FORCE, CIRCUMSTANCE; **2** (*to work for the cause of women's liberation*) SUBJECT, OBJECT, PROJECT, AIM, MISSION, PURPOSE.
−*v.* ORIGINATE, BEGIN, MAKE, PRODUCE, PROVOKE, CREATE, occasion, EFFECT, trigger, GENERATE.

causeway: see BRIDGE.

caustic: see POINTED.

caution *n.* **1** (*to use caution*) CARE, vigilance, watchfulness, heedfulness, HEED, wariness; **2** (*a word of caution*) WARNING, ADVICE, counsel, NOTICE.
−*v.* WARN, counsel, dissuade, admonish.

cautious *adj.* CAREFUL, WATCHFUL, vigilant, heedful, prudent, discreet, chary, wary, SHY, cagey.

cavalcade: see PROCESSION.

cavalierly: see OFFHAND.

cave *n.* cavern, DEN, grotto, hollow, HOLE, RECESS, CAVITY.

cavern: see CAVE; DEN.

cavity *n.* hollow, excavation, HOLE, OPENING, GAP, DENT, PIT, CAVE, RECESS, GULF, DEPRESSION, void, CHAMBER, POCKET, sinus, crater.

cease *v.* STOP, QUIT, END, HALT, terminate, refrain, PAUSE, DIE.

cease-fire: see ARMISTICE.

ceaseless: see CONTINUAL; ETERNAL; UNENDING.

cede: see ABANDON.

ceiling *n.* covering, ROOF, TOP, LIMIT, MAXIMUM, record, ALTITUDE.

celebrate *v.* OBSERVE, commemorate, HONOR, KEEP, solemnize, REJOICE, banquet, party.

celebrated *adj.* DISTINGUISHED, renowned, FAMOUS, NOTED, WELL-KNOWN, PROMINENT, eminent, POPULAR, GLORIOUS, illustrious, CONSPICUOUS, OUTSTANDING, FAMED.

celebration *n.* PARTY, FEAST, FESTIVAL, commemoration, CEREMONY, jubilee, HOLIDAY, ANNIVERSARY, centennial.

celebrity *n.* STAR, HERO, NAME, personage, dignitary, OFFICIAL, somebody, lion, bigwig, big shot, NOTABLE.

celestial: see DIVINE.

cell *n.* UNIT, protoplasm, SPACE, CAVITY, ROOM, JAIL.

cellar *n.* BASEMENT, storeroom, VAULT, dugout, CAVE, crypt, winery.

cement *n.* **1** (*glue these things with cement*) GLUE, mucilage, PASTE, plastic, ADHESIVE, epoxy; **2** (*a cement road*) concrete, mortar, asphalt, blacktop, paving.
— *v.*: see GLUE; PASTE; PLASTER.

cemetery *n.* graveyard, churchyard, GRAVE, TOMB, burial ground, tombstones, potter's field, boneyard.

censor: see CRITIC.

censure: see ACCUSE; BLAME; CHARGE; CONDEMN; CONVICT; CONVICTION; DISAPPROVAL; JUDGMENT; LECTURE; SCOLD; SENTENCE.

centennial: see CELEBRATION.

center *n.* MIDDLE, MIDST, midpoint, focus, hub, pivot, navel, bull's-eye, HEART, core.
— *v.* centralize, CONCENTRATE, DIRECT, focus, BALANCE.
— *adj.*: see CENTRAL.

central *adj.* halfway, middle, mid, INNER, KEY, MAIN, pivotal, CHIEF, PRINCIPAL, BASIC, FUNDAMENTAL, accessible, CONVENIENT, center, nuclear.

centralize: see CENTER.

cerebral: see INTELLECTUAL; MENTAL.

cerebration: see THINKING.

ceremonial *n.* SERVICE, ritual, FUNCTION, CELEBRATION, observance, CEREMONY.
— *adj.* FORMAL, SOLEMN, stately, DIGNIFIED, TRADITIONAL, OFFICIAL, STIFF.

ceremony *n.* rite, ritual, FORMALITY, etiquette, CEREMONIAL, form, observance, SERVICE, protocol.

certain *adj.* **1** (*certain cities*) PARTICULAR, SPECIAL, SOME, SEVERAL, unnamed, unspecified; **2** (*the witness was certain*) SURE, CONFIDENT, SECURE, ASSURED, agreed, DEFINITE, settled, POSITIVE, RELIABLE, trustworthy, UNFAILING, INEVITABLE, indisputable, FIXED, established, unquestionable, undeniable, AUTHENTIC.

certainly *adv.* SURELY, indisputably, PRECISELY, DEFINITELY, ABSOLUTELY, inevitably, GLADLY, undoubtedly, DOUBTLESS, of course, YES, true.

certainty: see EVIDENCE; FACT; REALITY.

certificate *n.* DOCUMENT, STATEMENT, affidavit, credentials, CERTIFICATION, RECOMMENDATION, PERMIT, PAPER, diploma.

certification *n.* PROOF, authorization, PLEDGE, guaranty, assurance, affidavit, EVIDENCE, DOCUMENT, CERTIFICATE.

certified: see PROFESSIONAL.

certify *v.* CONFIRM, GUARANTEE, attest, notarize, PROVE, TESTIFY, vouch for.

cessation: see ARMISTICE.

cesspool: see SINK.

chafe: see CHAP; ENRAGE.

chagrin: see DISAPPOINTMENT.

chain *n.* **1** (*in chains*) links, CABLE, ROPE, TIE, CORD, tether, leash, BOND; **2** (*a chain of restaurants*) SERIES, RANGE, ASSOCIATION, GROUP, BUSINESS, franchise, monopoly, SEQUENCE.
— *v.* LINK, CONNECT, BIND, TIE, JOIN, UNITE, restrain, imprison.

chair *n.* SEAT, BENCH, armchair, STOOL, CHAIRMAN, OFFICE, POSITION, DIGNITY, AUTHORITY, endowment, fellowship, professorship.

chairman *n.* CHAIR, chairwoman, chairperson, HEAD, CHIEF, DIRECTOR, OFFICER, PRESIDENT, LEADER, moderator, toastmaster, master of ceremonies, emcee.

chairperson: see CHAIRMAN.

chairwoman: see CHAIRMAN.

chalet: see CASTLE; LODGE.

chalk *n.* lime, limestone, crayon, white, marker.

chalky: see WHITE.

challenge *n.* DEMAND, CALL, SUMMONS, DIFFICULTY, dare, THREAT.
— *v.* DEMAND, SUMMON, CALL, DARE, THREATEN, DEFY, BRAVE.

chamber *n.* **1** (*"in my lady's chamber"*) bedroom, ROOM, HALL, alcove; **2** (*a chamber of the heart*) COMPARTMENT, SPACE, hollow, CAVITY, CELL, socket, POCKET, barrel, receptacle; **3** (*the Chamber of Commerce*) BOARD, COUNCIL, COMMISSION, legislature, ASSEMBLY.

champion *n.* **1** (*an Olympic champion*) winner, VICTOR, HERO, medalist, LEADER, FIGHTER, WARRIOR; **2** (*a champion of the underdog*) defender, partisan, PROTECTOR, backer, SUPPORTER, ATTORNEY.

championship: see TITLE.

chance *n.* **1** (*by chance*) HAZARD, coincidence, RISK, ACCIDENT, FATE, toss-up, odds, GAMBLE, wager, BET, STAKE, TICKET, coupon; **2** (*the chance of a lifetime*) OPPORTUNITY, FORTUNE, LUCK, OCCASION, PROSPECT, POSSIBILITY, OPENING.
— *v.*: see GAMBLE; HAPPEN; VENTURE.
— *adj.*: see RANDOM.

chancy *adj.* RISKY, dicey, iffy, erratic, UNCERTAIN, UNRELIABLE, precarious, TRICKY, TICKLISH.

chandelier: see LIGHT.

change *n.* alteration, VARIATION, variableness, VARIETY, TRADE, SUBSTITUTION, CLOTHES, coins, MONEY.
— *v.* ALTER, MODIFY, VARY, TRADE, EXCHANGE, TRANSFORM, SUBSTITUTE, REPLACE, CONVERT, REMOVE.

changeable *adj.* **1** (*changeable weather*) VARIABLE, unsettled, mutable, movable, PORTABLE; **2** (*a changeable personality*) inconsistent, fickle, IMPULSIVE, MOODY, flighty, mercurial.

changed: see NEW.

changeless: see UNBROKEN.

changeover: see TRANSFORMATION.

channel *n.* **1** (*to tow the ship through the channel*) CANAL, STREAM, RIVER, PASSAGE, BED, GROOVE, furrow, DITCH, gully, aqueduct, duct, TROUGH, WAY, runway; **2** (*to go through channels*) ROUTE, MEDIUM, MEANS, agent, COMMUNICATION, STATION, frequency.

chant *n.* MELODY, SONG, singing, HYMN, CAROL, slogan, refrain.
— *v.* intone, CAROL, RECITE.

chaos: see CONFUSION.

chap *v.* roughen, CRACK, OPEN, IRRITATE, dry out, chafe.
— *n.* FELLOW, GUY, YOUTH, BOY.

chaparral: see JUNGLE.

chapeau: see HAT.

chapel: see CHURCH; MISSION.

chaperon: see ACCOMPANY; ESCORT.

chapter *n.* **1** (*the opening chapter*) PART, SECTION, LESSON, subdivision, episode, PHASE; **2** (*the society's local chapter*) BRANCH, UNIT, affiliate, LODGE, POST, CELL, GROUP.

char: see BURN; SCORCH.

character *n.* **1** (*a man of character*) HONESTY, morality, ethics, integrity, HONOR, COURAGE, REPUTATION; **2** (*a character difficult to understand*) PERSONALITY, NATURE, TEMPER, QUALITY, TRAIT, KIND, SORT, makeup, FEATURE, DISPOSITION, constitution, mannerism, CHARACTERISTIC, ATTITUDE, OUTLOOK, viewpoint; **3** (*a funny character*) eccentric, oddball, PERSON, INDIVIDUAL, impersonation, ROLE; **4** (*the characters on the keyboard*) LETTER, TYPE, MARK, SYMBOL, STAMP, FIGURE, NUMBER, insignia.

characteristic *n.* TRAIT, FEATURE, CHARACTER, PROPERTY, PECULIARITY, DISTINCTION, QUALITY.
— *adj.* TYPICAL, representative, distinctive, UNIQUE.

characteristics: see PERSONALITY.

characterization: see DESCRIPTION.

characterize: see TERM.

characters: see ALPHABET.

charge *v.* **1** (*to charge $5*) ASK, DEMAND, levy, IMPOSE, TAX; **2** (*to charge one's purchase*) put off, defer, CREDIT; **3** (*to charge the battery*) LOAD, FILL, electrify; **4** (*to charge the enemy*) ATTACK, ASSAULT, assail; **5** (*to charge the jury*) INSTRUCT, COMMAND; **6** (*to charge someone with murder*) ACCUSE, INDICT, impute, censure, BLAME, subpoena, allege.
— *n.* **1** (*what is the charge for your work?*) PRICE, COST; **2** (*to take charge*) custody, RESPONSIBILITY, CARE, MANAGEMENT, TRUST, safekeeping, OFFICE; **3** (*a low charge in the battery*) LOAD, AMOUNT; **4** (*the charge of the Light Brigade*) ATTACK, RUSH, ASSAULT; **5** (*the charge to the jury*) COMMAND, INSTRUCTION, ORDER, DIRECTION; **6** (*the charge of murder*) accusation, indictment, blame, allegation; **7** (*I got a charge out of riding the roller coaster*) THRILL, kick, EXCITEMENT.

charged: see LOADED; PREGNANT.

charges: see FEE.

chariot: see CARRIAGE; CART.

charitable *adj.* benevolent, GENEROUS, KINDLY, humanitarian, considerate, tolerant, magnanimous.

charity *n.* SERVICE, handout, CONTRIBUTION, GIFT, LOVE, GENEROSITY, leniency, TOLERANCE, KINDNESS, GRACE, MERCY, benevolence, liberality.

charlatan: see CHEAT.

charm *n.* **1** (*she has charm*) fascination, allure, allurement, ATTRACTION, attractiveness, enchantment; **2** (*the sorcerer used a charm*) MAGIC, sorcery, enchantment, SPELL, hex, words, amulet, bracelet.
— *v.* enchant, fascinate, ATTRACT, PLEASE, DELIGHT, LURE, BEWITCH, allure, captivate, entice.

charming: see CUTE; BEAUTIFUL; DELIGHTFUL; GLAMOROUS; GRACEFUL; INTERESTING; LOVELY; PLEASING; WINNING.

chart *n.* MAP, diagram, TABLE, PLAN, SKETCH, plat.
— *v.* PLAN, MAP, diagram, tabulate, SKETCH, delineate.

charter *n.* **1** (*the U. N. charter*) constitution, DOCUMENT, ORGANIZATION; **2** (*William Penn's charter*) authorization, PATENT, PERMISSION, PERMIT, LICENSE, franchise.
— *v.* HIRE, ENGAGE, RENT, lease, ESTABLISH, GRANT.

charter member: see MEMBER.

chary: see CAUTIOUS.

chase *v.* EXPEL, HUNT, PURSUE, FOLLOW, drive out.
— *n.*: see HUNT; PURSUIT; SEARCH.

chaser: see HUNTER.

chasing: see AFTER.

chasm: see CANYON; GAP; GULF.

chassis: see BODY.

chaste: see MODEST; NICE; PURE; VIRGIN; VIRTUOUS.

chasten: see SOFTEN.

chastise: see PUNISH.

chastity: see GOODNESS; VIRGINITY.

chat *v.* TALK, VISIT, CONVERSE, gossip, SPEAK, CHATTER, prattle.
— *n.* TALK, VISIT, CONVERSATION, gossip, VISITING, CHATTER, prattle.

chateau: see CASTLE; ESTATE; PALACE.

chatter *v.* BABBLE, prattle, CHAT, gossip, gibber, maunder.
— *n.* chattering, babble, prattle, gossip, gibberish, NONSENSE.

chattering: see CHATTER; TALKATIVE.

chatty *adj.* TALKATIVE, gabby, SOCIABLE, wordy, windy, verbose, garrulous.

chauffeur: see DRIVE; DRIVER.

cheap *adj.* **1** (*a cheap price*) low-priced, low-cost, cut-rate, inexpensive, nominal; **2** (*that guy is cheap*) stingy, miserly, COMMON, VULGAR, contemptible.

cheat *n.* SWINDLER, FRAUD, CROOK, phony, cheater, deceiver, trickster, charlatan, chiseler.
— *v.* SWINDLE, defraud, DECEIVE, TRICK, dupe, hoax, gull, victimize, hoodwink.

cheater: see CHEAT; SWINDLER.

cheating: see TRICKERY.

check *n.* **1** (*to write a check*) draft, ORDER, BILL, tab, TICKET, TOKEN, STUB, RECEIPT; **2** (*to run a check on the performance*) PROOF, VERIFICATION, INQUIRY, SEARCH, EXAMINATION, STANDARD; **3** (*an effective check on crime*) CONTROL, curb, RESTRICTION, OBSTACLE, LIMIT, BARRIER, restraint, hindrance, BAR.
— *v.* **1** (*to check one's coat*) LEAVE, DEPOSIT, REGISTER; **2** (*to check up on the performance*) INVESTIGATE, VERIFY, TEST, EXAMINE, SEARCH, COMPARE, audit, REVIEW, INSPECT, ANALYZE, PROVE, tally; **3** (*to check the leakage of oil*) STOP, BLOCK, CURB, HALT, restrain, ARREST, CHOKE, stunt, retard, rebuke.

checked: see LIMITED.

checker: see COUNTER.

checking: see PREVENTIVE.

checkup *n.* EXAMINATION, TEST, INSPECTION, REVIEW, scrutiny, audit.

cheek: see NERVE.

cheeky: see BOLD.

cheep: see CHIRP; PEEP.

cheer *n.* JOY, glee, CHEERFULNESS, GLADNESS, gaiety, HAPPINESS, APPROVAL, APPLAUSE, ENCOURAGEMENT, ENTERTAINMENT.
— *v.*: see APPLAUD; BRIGHTEN; COMFORT; ELEVATE; ENCOURAGE; GLADDEN; REFRESH; YELL.

cheerful *adj.* cheering, cheery, MERRY, GAY, sprightly, gleeful, JOYFUL, HAPPY, JOLLY, joyous, HILARIOUS, GLAD, SUNNY, BRIGHT, smiling, HOPEFUL.

cheerfully *adv.* GLADLY, joyfully, cheerily, happily, gaily, merrily.

cheerfulness *n.* JOY, gaiety, merriment, SPIRIT, airiness, buoyancy, zest, DASH, zip.

cheerily: see CHEERFULLY.

cheering: see CHEERFUL.

cheerless *adj.* **1** *(a cheerless face)* glum, SAD, JOYLESS, GLOOMY, SORROWFUL, depressed; **2** *(a cheerless room)* dismal, depressing, bleak, dreary, MISERABLE, COLD.

cheerlessness: see DARKNESS.

cheers: see APPLAUSE.

cheery: see CHEERFUL; HEARTY.

cheesehead: see MORON.

chef: see COOK.

chemical *adj.* synthetic, ARTIFICIAL, ersatz, man-made, UNNATURAL, unauthentic, plastic, alchemical.

cherish *v.* NURSE, NOURISH, nurture, FOSTER, SUPPORT, CULTIVATE, ENTERTAIN, COMFORT, HARBOR, value, PRIZE, IMAGINE, treasure, LOVE.

cherished: see BELOVED; CHOICE; DARLING; DEAR; FAVORITE; PET; PRECIOUS; WELCOME.

cherry: see RED.

chest *n.* **1** *(a chest of drawers)* BOX, CONTAINER, BIN, TRUNK, drawers, coffer, CASE, casket; **2** *(the athlete's muscular chest)* BREAST, bust, BOSOM, thorax.

chest of drawers: see BUREAU.

chesty: see PROUD.

chew *v.* BITE, MUNCH, GNAW, nibble, EAT, crunch, GRIND, CRUSH.

chiaroscuro: see SHADE.

chic: see FASHIONABLE.

chicanery: see TRICKERY.

chicken: see FOWL.

chide: see SCOLD.

chief *n.* chieftain, CAPTAIN, RULER, COMMANDER, DIRECTOR, MANAGER, LEADER, HEAD, BOSS, warlord.
— *adj.* LEADING, PRINCIPAL, FOREMOST, MAIN, HEAD, paramount.

chiefly *adv.* MAINLY, PRINCIPALLY, MOSTLY, PARTICULARLY, ESPECIALLY.

chieftain: see CHIEF; PRINCIPAL.

child *n.* INFANT, BABY, babe, OFFSPRING, HEIR, descendant, YOUNGSTER, KID, BOY, GIRL, SON, daughter, sibling, BROTHER, sister, moppet.

childbearing: see BIRTH.

childbirth: see DELIVERY; LABOR.

childhood *n.* infancy, babyhood, YOUTH, minority, school days.

childish *adj.* IMMATURE, inexperienced, FOOLISH, babyish, CHILDLIKE, infantile, juvenile, callow.

childlike *adj.* INNOCENT, juvenile, infantile, unaffected, NATURAL, IMMATURE, THOUGHTLESS, irresponsible, unthinking, short-sighted, gullible.

children: see FAMILY; ISSUE; OFFSPRING; SEED.

chill *n.* COLD, coldness, coolness, DISMAY, discouragement.
— *v.* refrigerate, ice, COOL, air-condition, FREEZE.

chilled: see FROZEN.

chilly *adj.* **1** *(a chilly night)* COOL, COLD, BRISK, CRISP, BRACING; **2** *(a chilly reception)* aloof, UNFRIENDLY, COLD, DISTANT, haughty.

chime: see BELL; RESOUND; RING; STRIKE; STROKE.

chimney: see STACK.

chimpanzee: see MONKEY.

chip *n.* **1** *(the chip in the dish)* splinter, FRAGMENT, shard, sliver, BREAK, PARTICLE, SLICE, PIECE; **2** *(the chips in a game)* disk, counter, TOKEN, ivory.
— *v.* splinter, BREAK, CRACK, break off, whittle.

chirp *v.* cheep, PEEP, chirrup, TWITTER, SING, pipe, interject, EXCLAIM.
— *n.*: see PEEP.

chirrup: see CAROL; CHIRP.

chisel: see CARVE; ENGRAVE; NOTCH; SCULPTURE.

chiseler: see CHEAT.

chit-chat *n.* CONVERSATION, TALK, banter, CHATTER, CACKLE, gab.
— *v.* CHAT, GAB, CONVERSE, jaw.

chivalrous: see GALLANT.

chock-full *adj.* jam-packed, packed, filled, crammed, cramped, brimful, laden, stuffed, bursting.

choice *n.* SELECTION, PICK, PREFERENCE, option, DECISION, alternative, VARIETY.
— *adj.* SELECT, CHOSEN, preferred, cherished, POPULAR, EXQUISITE, FINE, RARE, VALUABLE, PRECIOUS, COSTLY, DAINTY, EXPENSIVE, SUPERIOR.

choicer: see BETTER.

choicest: see BEST; PREFERABLE.

choke *v.* throttle, STRANGLE, stifle, SMOTHER, clog, congest, CLOSE, CHECK, stunt, retard, STUFF, gag, COUGH.

choler: see ANGER.

choose *v.* SELECT, PICK, PREFER, DECIDE, ELECT.

choosy *adj.* SELECTIVE, picky, PARTICULAR, FUSSY, finicky, fastidious.

chop *v.* CUT, cleave, SPLIT, splinter, SLICE, hack, MINCE.

choppy: see ROUGH.

chorale: see HYMN.

chord: see KEY.

chore *n.* **1** *(to do the chores)* JOB, TASK, WORK, ERRAND, DUTY; **2** *(it became quite a chore)* BURDEN, GRIND, TOIL, LABOR, STRUGGLE, SLAVERY, overwork, travail.

chortle: see GIGGLE.

chosen *adj.* select, selected, preferred, ELECT, hand-picked.

chow: see FOOD.

christen: see NAME.

chromium: see METAL.

chronicle: see DIARY; HISTORY; RECORD.

chronicled: see HISTORICAL.

chronology: see CALENDAR.

chronometer: see CLOCK.

chubby *adj.* FAT, PLUMP, rounded, buxom, fatty, fattish, chunky, dumpy, tubby, STOUT, paunchy.

chuck: see HURL.

chuckle *v.* LAUGH, GIGGLE, CACKLE, titter.
— *n.* chuckling, LAUGH, GIGGLE, CACKLE, titter.

chuckling: see CHUCKLE.

chum *n.* PAL, BUDDY, crony, COMPANION, COMRADE, sidekick.

chummy *adj.* FRIENDLY, intimate, thick, CLOSE, BROTHERLY, fraternal, palsy walsy.

chunk: see LUMP.

chunky: see CHUBBY; STUBBY.

church *n.* sanctuary, SHRINE, TEMPLE, pantheon, chapel, cathedral, synagogue, mosque, parish, tabernacle, RELIGION, GROUP, SOCIETY.

churchman: see PASTOR; PRIEST.

churchyard: see CEMETERY.

churn: see BEAT.

cicerone: see ATTENDANT.

cinders: see ASHES.

cinema: see FILM, SCREEN; THEATER.

cipher: see CODE; COUNT; FIGURE; ZERO.

circa: see APPROXIMATELY.

circle *n.* **1** *(to sit in a circle)* RING, disk, cycle, ORBIT, CIRCUIT, BAND, GLOBE, ZONE, AREA, scope, INFLUENCE, FIELD; **2** *(a meeting of the sewing circle)* GROUP, SOCIETY, CLUB, CLASS, ORGANIZATION, SET, clique, coterie.
— *v.* ENCIRCLE, SURROUND, ROUND, ENCLOSE, REVOLVE, gyrate, WHIRL.

circuit *n.* CIRCLE, REVOLUTION, ORBIT, ROUND, ROUTE, COURSE, TOUR, PATH, JOURNEY, ZONE, hookup, CONNECTION, NETWORK.

circuit breaker: see SWITCH.

circular *adj.* ROUND, spherical, spheroid, rounded, roundabout, indirect.
— *n.* handbill, LETTER, NOTICE, leaflet, brochure, ADVERTISEMENT.

circularly: see ROUND.

circulate *v.* FLOW, CIRCLE, REVOLVE, TRAVEL, DISTRIBUTE, disseminate, BROADCAST, PUBLISH, SCATTER.

circulation *n.* DISTRIBUTION, SPREAD, movement, CIRCUIT, PASSAGE, PUBLICATION, readers, diffusion.

circumference: see BOUNDARY.

circumscribe: see CONFINE; LIMIT.

circumstance *n.* CONDITION, OCCASION, DETAIL, HAPPENING, INCIDENT, FACT, EVENT, OCCURRENCE, episode, SITUATION.

circumstances: see CASE; SURROUNDINGS.

circumstantial: see RELATIVE.

cistern: see TANK.

citadel: see CASTLE; FORT.

citation: see MEDAL; MENTION; QUOTATION; SUMMONS.

cite: see MENTION; QUOTE; SPECIFY; SUMMON.

citizen *n.* NATIVE, RESIDENT, INHABITANT, SUBJECT, NATIONAL.

citizenry: see PUBLIC; POPULATION.

citizenship: see NATIONALITY.

city: see CAPITAL; PLACE.

civic: see CIVIL; NATIONAL; POLITICAL.

civil *adj.* **1** *(civil rights)* PUBLIC, civic, POLITICAL, civilian, municipal; **2** *(be civil)* POLITE, courteous, civilized, obliging, well-bred, well-mannered, gracious, polished.

civilian: see CIVIL.

civility: see COURTESY; POLITENESS.

civilization *n.* CULTURE, SOCIETY, cultivation, refinement.

civilized: see CIVIL; HUMAN.

clack: see CLICK; RATTLE.

claim *n.* DEMAND, assertion, counterclaim, REQUEST, RIGHT, DUE, INTEREST, TITLE, PRIVILEGE, REQUIREMENT.
— *v.* DEMAND, assert, REQUEST, MAINTAIN, affirm, DECLARE, INSIST, REQUIRE.

clamber: see CLIMB; CRAWL; CREEP.

clammy: see MOIST; SLIMY.

clamor *n.* NOISE, tumult, UPROAR, OUTCRY, din, hubbub, RACKET, shouting.
— *v.*: see BELLOW.

clamorous: see NOISY.

clamp: see FASTEN; LOCK.

clan: see FOLK; RELATIONSHIP; TRIBE.

clang: see CLATTER.

clank: see CLATTER.

clap *v.* SLAP, STRIKE, CRASH, APPLAUD.
— *n.* slap, BLOW, clapping, thunderclap, APPLAUSE.

clapping: see CLAP; HAND.

claptrap: see NONSENSE.

clarification *n.* EXPLANATION, definition, INTERPRETATION, amplification, BREAKDOWN, illumination, refinement, filtration, disclosure.

clarify *v.* EXPLAIN, clear up, elaborate, straighten out, DEFINE, REFINE.

clarion: see TRUMPET.

clarity: see LIGHT; SIMPLICITY.

clash *n.* COLLISION, CRASH, DISAGREEMENT, discord, CONFLICT, BATTLE, FIGHT, CONTRAST, run-in.
— *v.* COLLIDE, CRASH, DISAGREE, FIGHT, grate, JAR, GRIND.

clasp *n.* GRASP, embrace, CATCH, fastener, HOOK, BUCKLE, PIN, brooch.
— *v.* GRASP, EMBRACE, GRIP, HOLD, CLUTCH, HUG, CATCH, BUCKLE, HOOK, PIN, FASTEN, SEIZE.

class *n.* **1** *(to attend class)* COURSE, SCHOOL, GROUP, students, GRADE, year, SECTION; **2** *(the upper classes of society)* RANK, caste, GRADE, ORDER, category, bracket, KIND, STRIPE, SET, DIVISION, CLASSIFICATION, subdivision, family, genus, SPECIES, NATURE, MOLD.

classic *adj.* classical, representative, BASIC, TRADITIONAL, STANDARD, SUPERIOR, highest, FIRST-RATE, masterly, PURE, ELEGANT, refined, polished.

classical: see CLASSIC; DIGNIFIED.

classification *n.* **1** *(classification and labeling)* ARRANGEMENT, ASSORTMENT, ANALYSIS, ASSIGNMENT, DISPOSITION; **2** *(a modern classification)* GROUP, SPECIES, genus, family, CLASS, category, KIND.

classify *v.* ARRANGE, GROUP, assort, ANALYZE, DISPOSE, CATALOG.

classy *adj.* STYLISH, FASHIONABLE, ELEGANT, SMART, swanky, nifty, posh, SWELL, LUXURIOUS.

clatter *n.* rattle, clank, CLASH, clang, din, hubbub.
— *v.*: see RATTLE.

clause: see ARTICLE; TERM.

claw *n.* talon, HOOK, NAIL, pincer.
— *v.* TEAR, SCRATCH, RIP, scrabble, SCRAPE, grapple.

clean *adj.* PURE, SPOTLESS, uncontaminated, unsoiled, unstained, immaculate, NEAT, spick-and-span.
— *v.* purify, CLEANSE, WASH, MOP, SCRUB, WIPE, vacuum, DUST, SWEEP.

cleaner's: see LAUNDRY.

cleanliness *n.* NEATNESS, tidiness, SANITATION, decency, purity.

cleanly *adj.* fastidious, TIDY, NEAT, CLEAN, SPOTLESS, immaculate.

cleanse *v.* WASH, CLEAN, SCRUB, purge, FLUSH, purify, expurgate.

cleansing: see WASH.

clear *adj.* TRANSPARENT, unclouded, PLAIN, DISTINCT, APPARENT, OBVIOUS, VISIBLE, understandable, audible, BRIGHT, LIGHT, FAIR, SUNNY, untroubled, serene, unblocked, unobstructed, FREE.
— *v.* **1** *(to clear the room)* empty, STRIP; **2** *(to clear the table of dishes)* RID, REMOVE, FREE; **3** *(to clear one's name)* FREE, acquit, exonerate; **4** *(to clear up a misunderstanding)* EXPLAIN, SOLVE; **5** *(to clear the hurdle)* vault, hurdle. See also EARN; NET; REALIZE.

clearance *n.* **1** *(to have enough clearance)* GAP, SPACE, elbowroom, MARGIN, RANGE, FIELD; **2** *(clearance to take off)* APPROVAL, CONSENT, PERMISSION, LICENSE, go-ahead.

clear-cut: see SPECIFIC.

clearing: see FIELD; OPEN.

clearly *adv.* plainly, EVIDENTLY, APPARENTLY, patently, DISTINCTLY, SURELY.

clearmindedness: see SANITY.

clearness: see SIMPLICITY; VISIBILITY.

clear up: see CLARIFY; RESOLVE; SOLVE.

cleave: see CHOP; CUT; KNIFE.

cleaver: see KNIFE.

clef: see KEY.

cleft: see GAP.

clemency: see FORGIVENESS; KINDNESS; MERCY.

clement: see MERCIFUL.

clench: see CLUTCH.

clergyman: see MINISTER; PASTOR; PRIEST.

cleric: see MINISTER.

clerk *n.* salesclerk, EMPLOYEE, registrar, recorder, OFFICIAL.

clever *adj.* shrewd, cagey, CUNNING, SMART, witty, KEEN, QUICK, INTELLIGENT, talented, EXPERT, skillful, SKILLED.

cleverness *n.* ingenuity, INTELLIGENCE, insight, perception, SKILL, keenness, ABILITY, TALENT, WIT, HUMOR.

cliché: see FORMULA.

click *n.* clack, snap, TICK, CLINK.
— *v.* clink, SNAP, TICK, clack.

client *n.* CUSTOMER, PATRON, dependent, ward, protégé, FOLLOWER, adherent.

clientele: see ATTENDANCE; TRADE.

cliff *n.* precipice, bluff, crag, palisade, BANK, HEIGHT, DROP.

climactic: see DRAMATIC.

climate *n.* weather, meteorology, precipitation, TEMPERATURE, humidity.

climb *v.* go up, clamber, SCALE, MOUNT, RISE, SLOPE, ASCEND.
— *n.*: see SCRAMBLE.

cling *v.* hold on, adhere, STICK, LINGER, CHERISH.

clinging: see DEPENDENT.

clinic: see HOSPITAL.

clink: see CLICK; PRISON.

clip *v.* TRIM, CROP, SHEAR, SNIP, prune, CUT, mow, SWINDLE, CHEAT.
— *n.* **1** *(at a fast clip)* PACE, RATE; **2** *(a fast clip on the jaw)* PUNCH, BLOW, STROKE; **3** *(fastened with a clip)* paper clip, CLASP, fastener.

clique: see CIRCLE; GANG; RING.

cloak *n.* COAT, cape, wrap, mantle, shawl, poncho.
— *v.*: see CAMOUFLAGE; DISGUISE; ROBE; VEIL.

cloaked: see HIDDEN.

clobber: see BELT; THUMP.

clock *n.* timepiece, timekeeper, watch, timer, chronometer, stop watch.
— *v.*: see TIME.

clocklike: see PERIODIC.

clod: see JERK.

clog: see CHOKE; PLUG; SHOE; SHUT.

clonk: see HIT.

close *adj.* **1** *(a town close to us)* NEAR, NEARBY; **2** *(a close race)* EQUAL, NARROW, like, DENSE, COMPACT, intimate, ACCURATE, PRECISE; **3** *(a close room)* stuffy, HUMID; **4** *(close with his money)* stingy, TIGHT, miserly.
— *adv.* NEAR, closely, tightly, TOGETHER.
— *v.* **1** *(to close the door)* SHUT, LOCK, bolt; **2** *(to close the circuit)* JOIN, CONNECT, FILL; **3** *(to close the program)* CONCLUDE, END, STOP, FINISH, COMPLETE, EXPIRE.
— *n.* CONCLUSION, END.

close by: see NEAR.

closed: see SHUT.

closely: see CLOSE; NEAR; NEARBY; NEARLY.

closeness *n.* nearness, DISTANCE, accuracy, SIMILARITY, RESEMBLANCE, RELATIONSHIP, AFFECTION, fondness.

closet *n.* WARDROBE, storeroom, CHAMBER, locker, pantry, CABINET, cupboard.

close to: see NEAR.

clot *n.* scab, thrombus, embolism, curd, gob, LUMP, clump, MASS, BUNCH.

cloth *n.* FABRIC, TEXTILE, MATERIAL, GOODS, tablecloth, washcloth.

clothe *v.* DRESS, attire, drape, don, ADORN, COVER.

clothes *pl. n.* clothing, apparel, attire, DRESS, COSTUME, GARMENT.

clothing: see CLOTHES; GARMENT; GOWN; WARDROBE.

cloud *n.* **1** *(a storm cloud)* VAPOR, haze, FOG, MIST, FILM, SMOKE; **2** *(a cloud of suspicion)* SHADOW, taint, shroud, pall, STAIN.
— *v.* darken, becloud, obscure, CONFUSE, overshadow.

cloudburst: see RAIN.

clouded: see DUSTY; SULLEN.

cloudless: see CRISP; FAIR.

cloudy *adj.* unclear, overcast, FOGGY, MISTY, HAZY, DIM, murky, FUZZY, VAGUE, confused, nebulous.

clout: see BLOW; HIT; PULL.

clown *n.* joker, JESTER, mummer, comic, FOOL, COMEDIAN, goof-off, bumpkin.
— *v.*: see FOOL.

club *n.* **1** *(to beat with a club)* STICK, BAT, billy, nightstick, blackjack; **2** *(a social club)* fellowship, fraternity, ASSOCIATION, ORDER, SOCIETY.
— *v.* BEAT, BATTER, whack, pommel.

clubhouse: see CASINO.

cluck: see CACKLE.

clue *n.* SIGN, HINT, inkling, tipoff, TRACE, EVIDENCE, SUGGESTION, cue.

clump: see BUNCH; CLOT; CLUSTER.

clumsiness: see AWKWARDNESS.

clumsy *adj.* AWKWARD, cumbersome, gawky, CRUDE, bumbling, inept, tactless.

clunk: see THUMP.

clunkhead: see MORON.

cluster *n.* GROUP, BUNCH, clump, BATCH, bouquet.
— *v.* GATHER, COLLECT, ASSEMBLE, GROUP, ACCUMULATE.

clutch *v.* SEIZE, HOLD, GRIP, GRAB, CLASP, clench.
— *n.* coupling, CLASP, GRASP, GRIP, seizure.

clutter: see JUMBLE; LITTER; MUSS.

coach: see CAR; CARRIAGE; EDUCATOR; INSTRUCTOR; STAGE; TEACH; TEACHER; TRAIN; TUTOR; WAGON.

coachman: see DRIVER.

coal: see FUEL; JET; MINERAL.

coalition: see ALLIANCE; FRONT; LEAGUE; UNION.

coarse *adj.* **1** *(coarse sandpaper)* ROUGH, gritty, mealy, scratchy, bumpy, mediocre; **2** *(coarse and ill-mannered)* unrefined, CRUDE, VULGAR, indelicate, gross, boorish.

coarseness *n.* RUDENESS, roughness, grossness, vulgarity, filthiness.

coast *n.* SHORE, shoreline, BEACH, seaside, brink.
— *v.* GLIDE, SLIDE, SAIL, skim, idle, SLACKEN.

coat *n.* **1** *(the dog's coat)* fleece, pelt, HIDE, SKIN; **2** *(a coat and hat)* overcoat, JACKET, CLOAK, tunic, mackinaw, slicker; **3** *(two coats of paint)* LAYER, COATING, glaze.
— *v.* PAINT, COVER, glaze, STAIN, laminate, VARNISH, shellac, lacquer.

coating *n.* COVERING, LAYER, overlay, glaze, PAINT, FILM, POLISH, veneer, SURFACE, blanket.

coat of mail: see ARMOR.

coax *v.* PERSUADE, URGE, wheedle, importune, induce, LURE, entice.

cobble: see ROCK.

cobblestone: see STONE.

cobweb *n.* gossamer, VEIL, gauze, filament, NETWORK, entanglement, conspiracy, PLOT.

cock *n.* rooster, cockerel, peacock, MALE.
— *v.* CHARGE, LOAD, ready, PREPARE.

cockerel: see COCK.

cockpit: see CABIN.

cockscomb: see COMB.

cocktail: see DRINK; PUNCH.

cocktails: see REFRESHMENTS.

coddle: see BABY.

code *n.* **1** *(to send in code)* cipher, WRITING, SECRET, SYMBOL; **2** *(the building code)* LAW, CHARTER, METHOD, TRADITION, morality, regulation.

coed: see STUDENT.

coeducational: see EDUCATIONAL.

coequal: see EQUIVALENT.

coercion: see PRESSURE.

coffer: see BANK; CHEST; SAFE; VAULT.

coffin *n.* casket, sarcophagus, CHEST, CASE, TOMB, catafalque.

cog: see TOOTH.

cogent: see PERSUASIVE.

cogitation: see THINKING.

cognizant: see AWARE.

cohere: see UNITE.

coherent: see LOGICAL.

cohort: see CONFEDERATE.

coiffure: see HAIR.

coil *v.* spiral, WIND, TWIST, entwine, snake.
— *n.* ROLL, spiral, RING, corkscrew, curl.

coiled: see WOUND.

coin *n.* MONEY, CASH, silver, CURRENCY, CHANGE, dollar, penny, nickel, dime, quarter, two bits, shilling, doubloon.
— *v.* MINT, ISSUE, stamp, STRIKE, ORIGINATE, DEVISE.

coincide: see AGREE; CORRESPOND.

coincidence: see CHANCE; CONJUNCTION; CORRESPONDENCE; SIMILARITY.

coincident: see CONTEMPORARY.

coins: see CASH; CHANGE; CURRENCY; GOLD.

coitus: see SEX; UNION.

cold *adj.* **1** *(a cold day)* COOL, frigid, ICY, frosty, wintry, FROZEN; **2** *(a cold stare)* UNFRIENDLY, aloof, indifferent, DISTANT.
— *n.* **1** *(a bone-chilling cold)* CHILL, FROST, frigidity; **2** *(don't catch a cold)* COUGH, congestion, sniffles, grip, flu, rhinitis.

coldness: see CHILL; RESERVE.

collaborate: see COOPERATE.

collaboration: see COOPERATION.

collapse *v.* FALL, FAINT, DROP, give way, topple, CRUMBLE, FAIL.
— *n.* FAILURE, downfall, BREAKDOWN, RUIN.

collar *n.* neckband, neckpiece, RIM, RING, BAND, restraint, HARNESS.
— *v.*: see CATCH; CAPTURE; TAKE.

collate: see ASSEMBLE.

collation: see MEAL.

colleague: see ACQUAINTANCE; ASSOCIATE; COMRADE; CONFEDERATE; PARTNER; PEER.

colleagues: see GENERATION.

collect *v.* **1** *(a crowd collected)* GATHER, MEET, CONGREGATE, convene, amass, ACCUMULATE; **2** *(to collect money)* OBTAIN, solicit, secure, RAISE, amass, compile.

collected: see CALM.

collection *n.* CONCENTRATION, aggregation, MASS, array, ASSORTMENT, STORE.

collective: see COMMUNITY; JOINT.

collectively: see TOGETHER.

collectivize: see ASSOCIATE.

collector: see RECEIVER.

college *n.* SCHOOL, ACADEMY, institute, seminary, faculty, COUNCIL, BODY.

collide *v.* CRASH, CLASH, CONFLICT, BUMP, HIT, STRIKE.

collision *n.* CRASH, smash-up, ACCIDENT, WRECK, SHOCK, JOLT, CONFLICT, CLASH.

colloquial: see SLANG.

cologne *n.* PERFUME, SCENT, FRAGRANCE, essence, LOTION.

colonist *n.* SETTLER, PIONEER, frontiersman, PILGRIM, IMMIGRANT, squatter.

colonization: see IMMIGRATION.

colonize: see IMMIGRATE; PIONEER; SETTLE.

colony *n.* SETTLEMENT, outpost, COMMUNITY, TOWN, protectorate, dependency, POSSESSION, GATHERING, FLOCK.

color *n.* TINT, SHADE, hue, tinge, coloration, COMPLEXION, coloring, pigment, DYE.
— *v.* **1** *(to color Easter eggs)* DYE, PAINT, tinge, SHADE; **2** *(it caused her to color)* BLUSH, flush, redden.

coloration: see COLOR; COMPLEXION.

colorful: see INTERESTING.

coloring: see COLOR; PAINTING.

colorless: see NEUTRAL; PALE.

colossal: see ENORMOUS; GIANT; GIGANTIC; LARGE; TREMENDOUS.

column n. **1** (the columns of the capitol) POST, PILLAR, SHAFT, obelisk, TOWER; **2** (a column of soldiers) LINE, ROW, FILE, PROCESSION, SERIES; **3** (a newspaper column) ARTICLE, ESSAY, REPORT, EDITORIAL, commentary.

comb n. RAKE, currycomb, cockscomb, CREST, honeycomb.
— v. **1** (comb your hair) GROOM, DRESS, untangle, ARRANGE, STRAIGHTEN; **2** (to comb the records) SEARCH, pore, SIFT, PROBE, INVESTIGATE.

combat v. battle, FIGHT, duel, CHALLENGE, RESIST, OPPOSE.
— n. strife, WAR, CONFLICT, BATTLE, skirmish.

combatant: see ATHLETE; FIGHTER; SIDE; WARRIOR.

combative: see AGRESSIVE; MILITARY.

combination n. UNION, MIXTURE, junction, BLEND, UNIFICATION, COMPOUND.

combine v. UNITE, merge, wed, CONNECT, COUPLE, MIX, BLEND.
— n.: see POOL.

combined: see ALLIED; COMPOUND; CONFEDERATE; JOINT; MISCELLANEOUS.

combustible: see FUEL.

come v. near, APPROACH, ADVANCE, ARRIVE, REACH, APPEAR, show up.

comedian n. comic, JESTER, ENTERTAINER, joker, humorist, storyteller, CLOWN, wiseacre, wag.

comedown: see DESCENT.

comedy: see HILARITY; PLAY.

come forth: see EMERGE.

comely: see BEAUTIFUL; HANDSOME; PRETTY; SHAPELY.

come in: see CALL; ENTER.

come-on: see BAIT; TEMPTATION; WINK.

come out: see APPEAR; EMERGE; ISSUE.

come together: see GATHER.

comfort v. console, cheer, SOOTHE, hearten, RELIEVE, reassure, SUSTAIN, ENCOURAGE.
— n. EASE, well-being, CHEER, PEACE, consolation, RELIEF, ENCOURAGEMENT.

comfortable adj. satisfied, restful, CALM, PLEASANT, relaxed, WELL, SNUG, cozy, EASY.

comic: see CLOWN; COMEDIAN; FUNNY; LIGHT; WIT.

comical adj. amusing, entertaining, humorous, FUNNY, RIDICULOUS, farcical, SILLY.

coming: see APPEARANCE; ARRIVAL.

comity: see POLITENESS.

command v. ORDER, DIRECT, CHARGE, DICTATE, bid, DOMINATE, CONTROL.
— n. **1** (to give a command) ORDER, mandate, decree, edict, PROCLAMATION; **2** (under the major's command) AUTHORITY, POWER, CONTROL, jurisdiction; **3** (a command of languages) KNOWLEDGE, mastery, CONTROL, GIFT.

commandant: see COMMANDER; CAPTAIN.

commander n. LEADER, OFFICER, commandant, CAPTAIN, HEAD, CHIEF, DIRECTOR.

commander in chief: see GENERAL.

commanding: see LOFTY; MASTERFUL.

commandment n. ORDER, COMMAND, decree, RULE, mandate, canon, REGULATION, LAW, precept.

commemorate: see CELEBRATE.

commemoration: see ANNIVERSARY; CELEBRATION.

commence v. BEGIN, initiate, undertake, LAUNCH, set out, set off.

commencement: see BEGINNING; DAWN; GRADUATION; ORIGIN; START.

commend: see BLESS; COMPLIMENT; PRAISE; RECOMMEND.

commendable: see ADMIRABLE.

commendation: see BLESSING; COMPLIMENT; PRAISE; RECOGNITION; RECOMMENDATION.

comment n. REMARK, STATEMENT, commentary, OPINION, CRITICISM, OBSERVATION, REPORT.
— v. OBSERVE, REMARK, NOTE, assert, MENTION.

commentary: see COLUMN; COMMENT; CRITICISM; FOOTNOTE; GLOSSARY; NOTE; REVIEW.

commentator: see CRITIC; OBSERVER.

commerce n. BUSINESS, TRADE, marketing, merchandizing, economics, TRAFFIC, COMMUNICATION, intercourse.

commercial adj. businesslike, economic, retail, mercantile, monetary.

— n. MESSAGE, ADVERTISEMENT, ad, plug, pitch, propaganda.

commingle: see BLEND.

commission *n.* **1** *(salary plus commission)* FEE, PAYMENT, ALLOWANCE, stipend; **2** *(an officer's commission)* APPOINTMENT, ASSIGNMENT, LICENSE, PERMISSION, TASK, COUNCIL, BOARD. *— v.* APPOINT, ASSIGN, authorize, CHARTER.

commissioner *n.* DIRECTOR, GOVERNOR, OFFICIAL, MANAGER, DELEGATE.

commit *v.* **1** *(to commit a crime)* DO, PERFORM, perpetrate, EFFECT; **2** *(to commit to an asylum)* CONFINE, intern, hospitalize; **3** *(to commit oneself to a task)* PLEDGE, PROMISE, DEDICATE, ENGAGE.

commitment: see ENGAGEMENT; PLEDGE.

committed: see CONCERNED.

committee *n.* BOARD, COUNCIL, BUREAU, PANEL, COMMISSION, JURY.

commode: see TOILET.

commodious: see ROOMY.

commodity: see SOMETHING, STAPLE.

common *adj.* **1** *(a common occurrence)* EVERYDAY, FREQUENT, FAMILIAR, NORMAL, CUSTOMARY; **2** *(a common thief)* LOW, CHEAP, mediocre, INFERIOR, second-rate, VULGAR, unrefined.

commoner: see PEASANT; SUBJECT.

commonly *adv.* OFTEN, FREQUENTLY, USUALLY, REGULARLY, CUSTOMARILY.

commonplace: see OBVIOUS; ORDINARY; TAME; TYPICAL; USUAL.

common sense: see REASON; WISDOM.

commonwealth: see GOVERNMENT; NATION; NATIONALITY; REPUBLIC.

commotion *n.* DISTURBANCE, to-do, CLAMOR, FUSS, UPROAR, tumult, turmoil, rumpus.

communal: see PUBLIC.

communicable: see INFECTIOUS.

communicate *v.* SPEAK, CORRESPOND, CONTACT, STATE, TRANSMIT, SEND.

communication *n.* CONTACT, intercourse, NEWS, MESSAGE, EXCHANGE, CORRESPONDENCE, TRANSFER.

communicative: see EXPRESSIVE.

communicator: see CORRESPONDENT.

communiqué: see BULLETIN; MESSAGE.

community *n.* **1** *(the professional community)* PUBLIC, SOCIETY, POPULATION, segment; **2** *(a civic-minded community)* NEIGHBORHOOD, BLOCK, VICINITY, suburb, LOCALITY, collective.

commute: see TRAVEL.

commuter: see TRAVELER.

compact *adj.* compressed, DENSE, THICK, SOLID, BRIEF, terse, SHORT.
— n. **1** *(an international compact)* TREATY, pact, AGREEMENT, CONTRACT, ALLIANCE; **2** *(lipstick and compact)* CASE, vanity case, makeup, cosmetics, POWDER, rouge.
— v.: see COMPRESS.

compacting: see COMPRESSION.

compactness: see FIRMNESS.

companion *n.* PARTNER, COMRADE, BUDDY, MATE, TWIN, ASSOCIATE, ATTENDANT, ESCORT.

companionable: see SOCIAL.

companionless: see LONESOME.

companionship *n.* COMPANY, fellowship, FRIENDSHIP, BROTHERHOOD, comradeship, CONTACT, ASSOCIATION, familiarity.

companionway: see LADDER.

company *n.* **1** *(a two-man company)* BUSINESS, FIRM, CORPORATION, ASSOCIATION; **2** *(my company has arrived)* GUEST, PARTY, COMPANION, caller, VISITOR, FRIEND; **3** *(an artillery company)* detachment, CREW, squadron, GANG, BAND.

comparable: see EQUIVALENT; RELATIVE; SIMILAR.

comparative: see RELATIVE.

comparatively: see AS; RELATIVELY.

compare *v.* MATCH, CONTRAST, equate, liken, TEST, ANALYZE.

comparison *n.* CONTRAST, equation, SIMILARITY, likeness, MEASUREMENT, ANALYSIS.

compartment *n.* DIVISION, SECTION, CHAMBER, category, CABIN, roomette, CELL, stall, BIN, cubbyhole, pigeonhole.

compass *n.* **1** *(a ship's compass)* GUIDE, NEEDLE, pointer, polestar; **2** *(a drawing compass)* scriber, dividers.

compassion: see HUMANITY; MERCY; MILDNESS; PITY; SYMPATHY.

compassionate: see EMOTIONAL; KIND; MERCIFUL; SYMPATHETIC.

compatibility: see HARMONY.

compatible: see HARMONIOUS; SUITABLE.

compel *v.* OBLIGE, FORCE, constrain, REQUIRE, DRIVE, necessitate.

compelled: see BOUND.

compelling: see IRRESISTIBLE; PERSUASIVE; STRONG.

compellingly: see FORCIBLY.

compendium: see BOOK; SUMMARY.

compensate *v.* PAY, repay, reimburse, REWARD, offset, counterbalance, neutralize.

compensation: see ASSISTANCE; FEE; INSURANCE; PAY; PAYMENT; RANSOM; SALARY; SETTLEMENT; WAGES.

compete *v.* vie, RIVAL, STRIVE, BATTLE, RACE, cope, RUN.

competency: see ABILITY; CAPACITY; EFFICIENCY.

competent: see CAPABLE; EFFICIENT; GOOD.

competition *n.* **1** (*a talent competition*) CONTEST, rivalry, RACE, MATCH, bout, COMBAT; **2** (*to meet fierce competition*) OPPOSITION, rivalry, OPPONENT, COMPETITOR, adversary, RIVAL, ENEMY.

competitor *n.* RIVAL, OPPONENT, COMPETITION, antagonist, contestant, adversary, ENEMY, FOE.

compile: see ASSEMBLE; COLLECT.

compiler: see EDITOR.

complain *v.* PROTEST, lament, GRUMBLE, GROAN, bellyache, WHINE, squawk, bitch.

complaint *n.* CRITICISM, PROTEST, gripe, grievance, allegation, CHARGE, accusation, AILMENT.

complete *adj.* TOTAL, WHOLE, ENTIRE, FULL, ABSOLUTE, finished, undivided, unabridged, uncut, intact, PERFECT.
— *v.* FINISH, CONCLUDE, END, CLOSE, ACHIEVE.

completed: see ACCOMPLISHED.

completely *adv.* TOTALLY, FULLY, ENTIRELY, wholly, solidly, ABSOLUTELY, ALTOGETHER, perfectly.

completeness: see FULLNESS; PERFECTION.

completing: see OFF.

completion: see ACHIEVEMENT; CONCLUSION; END; EXECUTION; REALIZATION.

complex *adj.* complicated, intricate, involved, multiple, COMPOSITE.
— *n.* mania, BLOCK, phobia, obsession, preoccupation.

complexing: see COMPLICATION; MYSTERY.

complexion *n.* ASPECT, APPEARANCE, makeup, SKIN, TONE, SHADE, COLOR, coloration.

compliance: see COOPERATION; FLEXIBILITY; OBEDIENCE.

compliant: see FLEXIBLE.

complicate *v.* CONFUSE, muddle, INVOLVE, TANGLE, SNARL, ball up.

complicated: see ADVANCED; COMPLEX; ELABORATE; SERIOUS.

complication *n.* CONFUSION, PROBLEM, DIFFICULTY, TANGLE, entanglement, complexity.

compliment *n.* praise, TRIBUTE, commendation, TOAST, APPLAUSE, flattery.
— *v.* commend, PRAISE, CONGRATULATE, HONOR.

complimentary: see FREE.

compliments: see GREETINGS.

comply: see AGREE; COOPERATE; OBEY.

component: see ELEMENT; INGREDIENT; MATERIAL; PART.

comportment: see BEHAVIOR.

compose *v.* make up, WRITE, formulate, score, DESIGN, fashion.

composed: see CALM.

composer: see ARTIST; AUTHOR.

composite *adj.* COMPOUND, blended, mixed, COMPLEX, mingled, MISCELLANEOUS, synthetic.

composition *n.* **1** (*a ten-page composition*) WORK, ESSAY, REPORT, PIECE, THEME; **2** (*the play's composition*) FORMATION, formulation, WRITING, CREATION, ARRANGEMENT, makeup, NATURE.

composure: see CALMNESS; POISE.

compound *n.* MIXTURE, COMBINATION, BLEND, alloy.
— *adj.* combined, COMPLEX, COMPOSITE, mixed.
— *v.*: see MULTIPLY.

comprehend: see CONTAIN; DIG; KNOW; READ; REALIZE; UNDERSTAND.

comprehensible *adj.* intelligible, PLAIN, CLEAR, EVIDENT, REASONABLE, LOGICAL.

comprehension: see INTELLECT; KNOWLEDGE; LIGHT; MENTALITY; REALIZATION; UNDERSTANDING.

comprehensive: see OVERALL.

compress *v.* SQUEEZE, compact, CONDENSE, PRESS, CROWD, CONCENTRATE.
— *n.*: see BANDAGE.

compressed: see COMPACT; DENSE.

compression *n.* REDUCTION, CONCENTRATION, compacting, squeezing, density, PRESSURE, GRAVITY.

comprise: see CONSIST; ENCIRCLE; INVOLVE.

compromise *n.* AGREEMENT, adjustment, reconciliation, arbitration, SETTLEMENT.
— *v.* SETTLE, AGREE, BALANCE, BARGAIN.

comptroller: see MANAGER.

compulsion: see FORCE; HABIT; NECESSITY; NEED; STRESS.

compulsorily: see FORCIBLY.

compulsory: see BINDING; NECESSARY.

computation: see COUNT; ESTIMATE; ESTIMATION.

compute: see CALCULATE; COUNT; ESTIMATE; NUMBER; RECKON.

computer: see COUNTER.

comrade *n.* BUDDY, PAL, CHUM, COMPANION, ally, co-worker, ASSOCIATE, colleague.

comradeship: see COMPANIONSHIP.

con: see PRISONER.

concatenation: see SERIES.

concave: see ARCHED; HOLLOW.

concavity: see DEPRESSION.

conceal *v.* HIDE, COVER, COVER UP, mask, CAMOUFLAGE, DISGUISE, suppress, obscure, secrete.

concealed: see HIDDEN; SECRET; UNKNOWN; UNSEEN.

concealment *n.* **1** (*concealment of a crime*) hiding, DISGUISE, CAMOUFLAGE, sheltering; **2** (*to wait in concealment*) SHELTER, hideout, blind, REFUGE.

concede: see ACKNOWLEDGE; ADMIT; CONFESS; GRANT; SURRENDER; YIELD.

conceit: see PRIDE.

conceited: see LOFTY; VAIN.

conceivable: see POSSIBLE; POTENTIAL, THINKABLE.

conceivably: see EVENTUALLY; MAYBE; PERHAPS; POSSIBLY; PROBABLY.

conceive: see CREATE; DEVISE; PLAN; PRODUCE; THINK.

conceived: see IMAGINARY.

concentrate *v.* **1** (*lenses concentrate light*) intensify, focus, consolidate, COLLECT, amass, GATHER; **2** (*you must concentrate*) THINK, meditate, contemplate, ponder, STUDY.

concentrated: see STRONG.

concentration *n.* **1** (*a concentration of forces*) consolidation, focus, COMPRESSION, MASS; **2** (*concentration is required*) ATTENTION, THOUGHT, deliberation, APPLICATION.

concept: see IDEA; THEME; THOUGHT.

conception: see GENERATION; NOTION.

concern *v.* pertain, interest, appertain, DEAL, bear upon, WORRY, TROUBLE.
— *n.* **1** (*it is not your concern*) MATTER, AFFAIR, BUSINESS, **2** (*his concern is sincere*) worry, INTEREST, ANXIETY, FEAR.

concerned *adj.* preoccupied, worried, ANXIOUS, interested, involved, committed, ATTENTIVE.

concerning *prep.* ABOUT, ON, regarding, respecting, touching.

concert *n.* recital, musicale, PERFORMANCE, PRESENTATION, solo, SHOW.

concession: see CONFESSION.

concise: see BRIEF; LITTLE; SHORT.

concisely: see LITTLE.

conciseness: see SHORTNESS.

conclude *v.* **1** (*we conclude at six*) END, FINISH, terminate, COMPLETE, CLOSE; **2** (*I conclude that you failed*) presume, GATHER, infer.

concluded: see OVER; SILENT.

concluding: see LAST.

conclusion *n.* **1** (*the conclusion was sad*) END, ENDING, CLOSE, termination, completion; **2** (*your conclusion is hasty*) DETERMINATION, DECISION, inference, presumption.

conclusive *adj.* decisive, FINAL, DEFINITE, terminal, unconditional, OBVIOUS.

conclusively: see FINALLY.

concoct: see BREW; CREATE; DEVISE; HATCH; PLAN; PREPARE.

concocted: see FICTITIOUS; MADE-UP.

concrete: see BODILY; CEMENT; POSITIVE.

concur: see AGREE.

concurrence: see COOPERATION; CORRESPONDENCE.

concurrent: see CONTEMPORARY.

concussion: see JAR.

condemn *v.* **1** *(to condemn to death)* CONVICT, SENTENCE, DOOM, DAMN; **2** *(to condemn one's actions)* censure, DISAPPROVE, BLAME, denounce.

condemnation *n.* damnation, CONVICTION, DISAPPROVAL, JUDGMENT, SENTENCE, CURSE, denunciation.

condemning: see CRITICAL.

condensation: see ABREVIATION; CONTRACTION; DEW; DIGEST; VAPOR.

condense *v.* **1** *(condense your report)* SHORTEN, EDIT, CUT; **2** *(this process condenses the volume)* REDUCE, STRENGTHEN, intensify, COMPRESS, thicken; **3** *(water condenses on cold objects)* liquefy, distill, COLLECT.

condiment: see SAUCE.

condition *n.* **1** *(the physical condition)* STATE, SITUATION, status, POSITION, HEALTH; **2** *(to attach a condition)* requisite, stipulation, REQUIREMENT, RESTRICTION, QUALIFICATION.

conditional: see DEPENDENT.

conditions: see ENVIRONMENT; SURROUNDINGS.

condole: see SYMPATHIZE.

condone: see EXCUSE; PARDON.

conducive: see FAVORABLE.

conduct *n.* BEHAVIOR, ACTION, bearing, CONTROL.
— *v.* GUIDE, LEAD, DIRECT, MANAGE, ESCORT.

conducting: see ONWARD.

conductor *n.* **1** *(a railroad conductor)* trainman; **2** *(a symphony conductor)* DIRECTOR, LEADER, GUIDE; **3** *(copper is a conductor)* transmitter, conveyor, CHANNEL, PIPE, duct.

conduit: see DRAIN; PIPE.

confab: see TALK.

confederate *adj.* united, ALLIED, federated, combined, incorporated.
— *n.* ally, colleague, PARTNER, cohort, ACCESSORY, accomplice.

confederation: see ALLIANCE; LEAGUE; UNION.

confer *v.* TALK, CONVERSE, DISCUSS, CONSULT. See also AWARD; GRANT.

conference *n.* DISCUSSION, CONVERSATION, parley, consultation, MEETING, congress.

confess *v.* ADMIT, ACKNOWLEDGE, own up, concede, REVEAL, disclose.

confession *n.* ADMISSION, revelation, disclosure, acknowledgment, concession.

confidant: see FRIEND.

confidante: see FRIEND.

confide in: see RELY ON.

confidence *n.* **1** *(to have confidence)* TRUST, FAITH, BELIEF, ESTEEM, self-confidence; **2** *(to reveal a confidence)* SECRET, TRUST.

confidence game: see RACKET.

confidence man: see FOX.

confident *adj.* ASSURED, CERTAIN, SURE, POSITIVE, FEARLESS, BOLD.

confidential *adj.* PRIVATE, SECRET, reserved, intimate.

configuration: see FORM; FORMATION.

confine *v.* LIMIT, ENCLOSE, circumscribe, repress, restrain, intern, imprison.
— *n.*: see LIMIT.

confined: see BOUND; LIMITED.

confinement: see LIMITATION.

confines: see BOUNDARY.

confirm *v.* **1** *(to confirm a date)* VERIFY, affirm, ratify, authenticate; **2** *(to confirm a victory)* STRENGTHEN, fortify, INCREASE, invigorate.

confirmation: see SEAL; VERIFICATION.

confirmed: see HABITUAL.

confiscate: see DEPRIVE; FINE.

conflagration: see FIRE.

conflict *v.* CLASH, CONTRAST, COLLIDE, FIGHT, OPPOSE, battle.
— *n.* BATTLE, WAR, strife, CLASH, DISPUTE.

conflicting: see OPPOSING.

conform: see ACCOMMODATE; ADAPT; CORRESPOND; FOLLOW; HARMONIZE; SUIT.

conformable: see HARMONIOUS.

conformity: see AGREEMENT; PARALLEL.

conform to: see ABIDE BY.

confound: see CONFUSE.

confrere: see BROTHER.

confront: see BRAVE; FACE; FRONT.

confuse *v.* muddle, COMPLICATE, confound, SNARL, mess up, MISTAKE, misinterpret, misunderstand.

confused: see CLOUDY; FOGGY; MUDDY.

confusing: see TRICKY.

confusion *n.* mix-up, DISORDER, MISTAKE, MESS, welter, madhouse, foul-up, chaos. See also AMAZEMENT.

congenial: see HARMONIOUS; HEARTY; PLEASANT; SYMPATHETIC.

congeniality: see WARMTH.

congest: see CHOKE; STUFF.

congestion: see COLD.

congratulate *v.* APPLAUD, PRAISE, TOAST, COMPLIMENT.

congregate *v.* GATHER, ASSEMBLE, MEET, convene, muster, flock, throng.

congregation *n.* ASSEMBLY, GATHERING, MEETING, CROWD, MULTITUDE, MEMBERSHIP, brethren, COLLECTION.

congress: see ASSOCIATION; CONFERENCE; CONVENTION.

congruent: see FITTING.

congruous: see HARMONIOUS.

conjecture: see GUESS.

conjoin: see UNITE.

conjunction *n.* coincidence, UNION, CONNECTION, joint, junction, juncture.

conjure: see IMAGINE.

connect *v.* **1** *(to connect a hose to a faucet)* ATTACH, JOIN, TIE, COMBINE, UNITE, ADJOIN; **2** *(to connect names with events)* ASSOCIATE, TIE, RELATE, equate.

connected: see ALLIED; RELATED; RUNNING.

connection *n.* RELATION, TIE, junction, BOND, ASSOCIATION, affiliation, CONTACT, KNOWLEDGE.

connections: see KIN.

connector: see GROUND; STAPLE.

connoisseur: see PROFESSIONAL; SPECIALIST.

connotation: see MEANING.

connote: see IMPLY.

conquer *v.* vanquish, DEFEAT, OVERCOME, BEAT, MASTER, TRIUMPH.

conquered: see BEATEN.

conquering: see VICTORIOUS.

conqueror *n.* VICTOR, winner, MASTER, CHAMPION.

conquest *n.* TRIUMPH, win, VICTORY, domination, rout, subjection.

conscience *n.* morality, morals, ethics, superego.

conscious *adj.* AWAKE, AWARE, knowing, ALERT, OBSERVANT, SENSITIVE, vigilant. See also APPRECIATIVE.

consciously: see DELIBERATELY.

consciousness *n.* CONCERN, CARE, REGARD, FEELING, INTELLIGENCE, perception, SENSATION, REALIZATION, KNOWLEDGE.

conscription: see DRAFT.

consecrate: see BLESS; DEVOTE.

consecrated: see BLESSED.

consecration: see BLESSING.

consecutive: see PROGRESSIVE; SUCCESSIVE.

consensus: see CONSENT; POLL; SENSE.

consent *n.* APPROVAL, assent, PERMISSION, LEAVE, AGREEMENT, acquiescence, consensus, willingness.
− *v.* accede, acquiesce, assent, AGREE.

consenting: see WILLING.

consequence *n.* **1** *(a grim consequence)* RESULT, END, OUTCOME, EFFECT, aftereffect, upshot; **2** *(a person of consequence)* SUBSTANCE, NOTE, IMPORTANCE.

consequently: see HENCE; THEN; THEREFORE.

conservation: see SALVATION.

conservatism: see RIGHT.

conservative *adj.* **1** *(a conservative nature)* moderate, CAUTIOUS, TRADITIONAL, SOBER; **2** *(conservative politics)* rightist, reactionary, mossback.

conserve: see PRESERVE.

conserver: see PROTECTOR.

conserves: see JAM.

consider *v.* **1** *(to consider a proposal)* WEIGH, contemplate, ponder, evaluate, assess, STUDY; **2** *(I consider him my friend)* REGARD, THINK, JUDGE, HOLD, VIEW, BELIEVE.

considerable *adj.* SIZABLE, NOTABLE, marked, meaningful, SIGNIFICANT, goodly, MAJOR.

considerably: see GREATLY; QUITE; RATHER.

considerate: see ATTENTIVE; CHARITABLE; COOPERATIVE; SYMPATHETIC; THOUGHTFUL.

consideration *n.* **1** *(to deserve consideration)* evaluation, ATTENTION, STUDY; **2** *(an urgent consideration)* ELEMENT, THING, FACTOR; **3** *(to esteem one's consideration)* REGARD, CONCERN, ATTENTION, FAVOR, COURTESY, KINDNESS.

considerations: see GROUNDS.

considered: see CAREFUL.

considering: see BECAUSE.

consign: see DEVOTE.

consigned: see DEVOTE.

consignment: see DELIVERY.

consist *v.* comprise, INCLUDE, INVOLVE, CONTAIN. See also BE.

consistency: see SAMENESS.

consistent: see EVEN; LOGICAL.

consistently: see EVENLY.

consist of: see INVOLVE.

consolation: see COMFORT.

console: see COMFORT; PITY; SOOTHE.

consolidate: see CONCENTRATE; JOIN, UNIFY; UNITE.

consolidation: see CONCENTRATION; UNION.

consort: see GROOM; HUSBAND; WIFE.

consortium: see ASSOCIATION.

conspicuous *adj.* OBVIOUS, NOTABLE, PROMINENT, glaring, flagrant, striking.

conspicuously: see EVIDENTLY.

conspiracy: see COBWEB; INTRIGUE; PLOT.

conspire: see PLOT; SCHEME.

constancy: see DEVOTION; LOYALTY; STEADINESS.

constant *adj.* STEADY, CONTINUAL, nonstop, everlasting, DEPENDABLE, LOYAL, DEVOTED.

constantly *adv.* STEADILY, uniformly, ALWAYS, continuously, invariably, EVER, FOREVER.

constituent: see ELEMENT; FACTOR; INGREDIENT.

constitute: see BE; ESTABLISH; ORGANIZE.

constitution: see CHARACTER; CHARTER; ORGANIZATION.

constitutional: see ORGANIC.

constrain: see COMPEL; FORCE; OBLIGE; PRESS.

constrained: see UNEASY.

constraint: see BRAKE.

construct *v.* BUILD, ERECT, fabricate, put up, formulate, CREATE.

construction *n.* BUILDING, erection, ASSEMBLY, FORMATION, COMPOSITION.

consul: see MINISTER.

consult *v.* **1** *(to consult with one another)* CONFER, counsel, DISCUSS, negotiate; **2** *(to consult an authority)* INQUIRE, INTERVIEW.

consultant: see PHYSICIAN.

consultation: see CONFERENCE.

consume *v.* utilize, EMPLOY, ABSORB, EAT, DEVOUR, SPEND, expend, EXHAUST, deplete.

consumed: see USED.

consumer *n.* buyer, user, CUSTOMER, shopper.

consummate: see CROWN.

consumption: see EXHAUSTION; EXPENDITURE.

contact *n.* TOUCH, CONNECTION, junction, COMMUNICATION, CORRESPONDENCE, ASSOCIATION.
— *v.* TOUCH, CONNECT, BRUSH, CALL, REACH.

contagion: see DISEASE; INFECTION.

contagious: see CATCHING; INFECTIOUS.

contain *v.* HOLD, EMBRACE, INCLUDE, comprehend, ACCOMMODATE, STORE.

container *n.* holder, receptacle, VESSEL, TANK, CASE, crate, CAN, canister, BOX, wrapper, BAG, BOTTLE, JAR, JUG, CAPSULE.

containing: see OF.

contaminate: see INFECT; POLLUTE; SOIL.

contaminated: see IMPURE.

contamination: see INFECTION; POLLUTION.

contemplate: see CONCENTRATE; CONSIDER; INTEND, REFLECT; REGARD; THINK; WEIGH.

contemplating: see EXPECTANT.

contemplation: see MEDITATION; REFLECTION; STUDY; THINKING.

contemplative: see THOUGHTFUL.

contemporaneous: see CONTEMPORARY.

contemporaries: see GENERATION.

contemporary *adj.* **1** *(contemporary past events)* simultaneous, coincident, contemporaneous; concurrent, **2** *(contemporary political thought)* MODERN, CURRENT, PRESENT, RECENT.
— *n.*: see PEER.

contempt: see HATRED; SCORN.

contemptible: see CHEAP.

contend: see DEBATE; MAINTAIN; QUARREL.

contender: see FIGHTER.

content *v.* SATISFY, PLEASE, GRATIFY, appease.
— *n.*: see SUBJECT; VOLUME.

contented *adj.* pleased, satisfied, HAPPY, COMFORTABLE, relaxed, serene, TRANQUIL.

contentment *n.* SATISFACTION, PLEASURE, COMFORT, HAPPINESS, gratification, serenity.

contents *pl. n.* table of contents, subject, matter, essence, THEME, CARGO, enclosure.

contest *n.* rivalry, COMPETITION, RACE, MATCH, ARGUMENT, BATTLE, FIGHT.
— *v.* DISPUTE, QUESTION, OBJECT, vie, FIGHT.

contestant: see CANDIDATE; COMPETITOR; ENTRY; OPPONENT; OPPOSITION; RIVAL.

contingent: see DEPENDENT.

continual *adj.* ETERNAL, perpetual, UNENDING, ENDLESS, incessant, CONSTANT, STEADY, recurrent, CONTINUOUS, ceaseless, uninterrupted, repeated, REGULAR, FREQUENT.

continually *adv.* CONSTANTLY, STEADILY, continuously, EVER, FOREVER, ALWAYS.

continuance: see CONTINUATION; LENGTH.

continuation *n.* **1** *(continuation of the drought)* persistence, continuity, MAINTENANCE, continuance, SUCCESSION, sequel, follow-up; **2** *(continuation after the interruption)* RESUMPTION, recurrence, renewal, REPETITION.

continue *v.* **1** *(to continue without a break)* PERSIST, KEEP, keep on, REMAIN, persevere; **2** *(we will continue after the rain)* RESUME, CARRY ON, RENEW, follow up.

continuing: see LASTING.

continuity: see CONTINUATION.

continuous *adj.* uninterrupted, UNBROKEN, unceasing, CONSTANT, incessant, ENDLESS, ETERNAL, perpetual, CONTINUAL.

continuously: see CONSTANTLY; CONTINUALLY; EVER; FOREVER; ON; TOGETHER.

continuum: see INFINITY.

contort: see SPRAIN; WARP.

contorted: see CROOKED.

contour: see FORM; LANDSCAPE; OUTLINE; SHAPE.

contract *n.* pact, AGREEMENT, UNDERSTANDING, COMPACT, PLEDGE, OBLIGATION.
— *v.* **1** *(to contract to build)* AGREE, PLEDGE, stipulate, draw up, HIRE; **2** *(the scar contracted slowly)* DIMINISH, recede, ebb. See also CATCH.

contraction *n.* **1** *(this word is a contraction)* REDUCTION, ABBREVIATION, condensation. shortening, shrinkage, COMBINATION, BLEND; **2** *(the contraction of disease)* catching, affliction, INFECTION.

contradict: see DENY; DIFFER; DISPUTE; OVERRULE.

contradicting: see OPPOSING.

contradiction: see DISAGREEMENT; REVERSE.

contradictory: see OPPOSITE.

contraption: see ASSEMBLY; THING.

contrariwise: see BUT; INSTEAD.

contrary *adj.* OPPOSITE, opposed, counter, unfavorable, untimely, cantankerous.
— *n.*: see OPPOSITE.

contrary to: see AGAINST.

contrast *v.* DISTINGUISH, discriminate, COMPARE, CONFLICT, DIFFER, OPPOSE.
— *n.* DIFFERENCE, DISTINCTION, VARIATION.

contrasting: see DIFFERENT.

contribute *v.* DONATE, GIVE, endow, ADD, LEND.

contribution *n.* DONATION, PRESENT, GIFT, GRANT.

contrition: see REGRET.

contrivance: see ASSEMBLY; DEVICE; INSTRUMENT; INVENTION; RESOURCE; TOOL.

contrive: see DEVISE; HATCH; INVENT; PLOT; SCHEME.

contrived: see FICTITIOUS; MADE-UP; MECHANICAL.

control *v.* REGULATE, GOVERN, DISCIPLINE, curb.
— *n.* **1** *(the control of shipping)* REGULATION, AUTHORITY, jurisdiction, POWER; **2** *(temperature control)* regulator, CHECK, REIN.

controlled: see COOL.

controlling: see MASTERFUL; POSSESSIVE.

controls: see CABIN.

controversy: see DEBATE; DISPUTE; FEUD; ISSUE.

controvert: see DISPUTE.

contusion: see BRUISE.

convalesce: see RECOVER.

convalescence: see RECOVERY.

convene: see ASSEMBLE; CALL; COLLECT; CONGREGATE; RALLY; SIT.

convenience *n.* **1** (*at your convenience*) COMFORT, EASE, LIBERTY, FITNESS, suitability; **2** (*modern conveniences*) BENEFIT, DEVICE, TOOL.

convenient *adj.* SUITABLE, accessible, fitted, READY, COMFORTABLE.

conveniently: see PAT.

convent *n.* nunnery, abbey, monastery, RESIDENCE.

convention *n.* **1** (*a sales convention*) MEETING, congress, CONFERENCE, GATHERING; **2** (*a matter of convention*) CUSTOM, TRADITION, PRACTICE.

converge: see APPROACH; MEET.

conversant: see FAMILIAR.

conversation *n.* TALK, parley, DISCUSSION, CHAT.

converse *v.* TALK, DISCUSS, SPEAK, CONFER.
— *adj.* OPPOSITE, CONTRARY, REVERSE, counter.
— *n.*: see OPPOSITE.

conversely: see INSTEAD.

conversion: see EXCHANGE, REVISION; TRANSFORMATION.

convert *v.* CHANGE, TRANSFORM, ALTER, ADAPT, PERSUADE, indoctrinate.
— *n.* DISCIPLE, turncoat, deserter, defector.

convertible: see AUTOMOBILE.

convex: see ARCHED.

convey: see BEAR; BRING; CARRY; SEND; TRANSMIT; TRANSPORT.

conveyance: see VEHICLE.

conveyor: see CONDUCTOR.

convict *v.* CONDEMN, SENTENCE, DOOM, censure.
— *n.* CRIMINAL, felon, jailbird, PRISONER.

convicted: see GUILTY.

conviction *n.* **1** (*conviction on all charges*) CONDEMNATION, damnation, censure, SENTENCE;

2 (*a man of conviction*) PRINCIPLE, BELIEF, CREED, FAITH, PERSUASION.

convince *v.* PERSUADE, WIN, induce, CONVERT.

convinced: see SURE.

convincing *adj.* PERSUASIVE, moving, impressive, credible, REASONABLE, trustworthy, SOUND.
— *n.*: see PERSUASION.

convincingly: see FORCIBLY.

convocation: see COUNCIL.

convoy: see ACCOMPANY; ESCORT.

convulsion: see COUGH; STROKE.

coo: see BABBLE.

cook *v.* PREPARE, ready, WARM, HEAT, STEW, BOIL, broil, ROAST, FRY, BAKE, process, DRY, AGE.
— *n.* chef, baker, SERVANT, dietitian.

cooker: see RANGE.

cookie *n.* biscuit, cake, wafer, tart, PASTRY.

cookstove: see STOVE.

cool *adj.* **1** (*a cool evening*) CHILLY, COLD, nippy; **2** (*a cool manner*) relaxed, controlled, dispassionate, aloof, UNFRIENDLY.
— *v.* CHILL, REFRIGERATE, ice, moderate.

cooler: see JUG; PRISON.

cool-headed: see LEVEL.

cooling: see REFRESHING.

coolness: see CHILL; FROST.

coop: see CAGE; PEN.

cooperate *v.* collaborate, comply, ASSIST, ACCOMMODATE, PARTICIPATE, pool, COMBINE.

cooperation *n.* teamwork, collaboration, COMBINATION, UNION, ALLIANCE, AGREEMENT, concurrence, compliance, participation.

cooperative *adj.* obliging, HELPFUL, FAVORABLE, accommodating, considerate, USEFUL.

coop up: see CAGE; PEN.

coordinate: see ORGANIZE.

coowner: see PARTNER.

cop: see OFFICER.

cope: see BEHAVE; COMPETE.

copied: see DUPLICATE.

copper: see METAL.

cops: see POLICE.

copulation: see SEX.

copy *n.* photostat, reproduction, DUPLICATE, facsimile, replica, IMITATION, counterfeit. See also NUMBER.
— *v.* IMITATE, DUPLICATE, reprint, REPRODUCE, TRACE, counterfeit, FORGE.

copyright: see PATENT.

cord *n.* STRING, TWINE, LINE, ROPE, braid.

cordial *adj.* FRIENDLY, genial, WARM, HEARTY, EARNEST, SINCERE, AFFECTIONATE.

cordiality: see HOSPITALITY; WARMTH.

cordially: see HEARTILY; SINCERELY.

core: see BONE; CENTER; HEART; INSIDE; INTERIOR; MIDDLE; MIDST.

cork: see PLUG; STOP; STOPPER.

corkscrew: see COIL.

corncob: see PIPE.

corner *n.* **1** *(to sit in a corner)* nook, niche, RECESS; **2** *(watch out for the sharp corners)* ANGLE, RIM, EDGE, RIDGE, bend.
— *v.* TRAP, TRICK, snare, FOOL, DECEIVE.

cornered: see ENTANGLED.

cornet: see TRUMPET.

coronet: see CROWN.

corporation *n.* ASSOCIATION, COMPANY, FIRM, SOCIETY, ORGANIZATION, BUSINESS, enterprise.

corps *n.* DIVISION, regiment, brigade, TROOPS.

corpse *n.* cadaver, BODY, REMAINS, carcass, stiff.

corpsman: see NURSE.

corral: see CAGE; CATCH; ENCLOSURE; FOLD; PEN.

correct *adj.* ACCURATE, TRUE, PRECISE, PROPER, rightful, legitimate.
— *v.* rectify, REMEDY, ADJUST, AMEND, REFORM, EDIT, REVISE.

correction *n.* **1** *(a house of correction)* PUNISHMENT, penalization, DISCIPLINE; **2** *(the typist's corrections)* rectification, IMPROVEMENT, modification, AMENDMENT, alteration, CHANGE.

corrective *adj.* remedial, CONTRARY, therapeutic, rehabilitating, disciplinary, penal.

correctly: see EXACTLY; PRECISELY; PROPERLY; RIGHT.

correctness: see EXACTNESS; PRECISION; TRUTH.

correlate: see RELATE.

correlation: see CORRESPONDENCE.

correspond *v.* **1** *(these two situations correspond)* FIT, MATCH, HARMONIZE, AGREE, conform, coincide, square; **2** *(they corresponded as pen pals)* WRITE, COMMUNICATE.

correspondence *n.* concurrence, coincidence, accord, correlation, AGREEMENT, intercourse, letters, MAIL.

correspondent *n.* WRITER, communicator, journalist, reporter, pen pal.

corresponding: see PARALLEL.

corridor *n.* HALL, hallway, entranceway, passageway, GALLERY.

corroborate: see DOCUMENT.

corrode: see EAT; GNAW; MOLD.

corroded: see RUSTY.

corrosion: see RUST.

corrugation: see RIDGE.

corrupt : see BRIBE; EVIL; IMPURE; INFECT; POISON; POLLUTE; ROTTEN; SHAMEFUL; SPOIL; VICIOUS; VILLAINOUS.

corruption: see EVIL; FILTH; POLLUTION; RACKET.

corsair: see PIRATE.

corset: see GIRDLE.

cortege: see FUNERAL; TRAIN.

coruscate: see GLITTER.

coruscation: see GLITTER.

cosmetic: see PAINT.

cosmetics: see COMPACT.

cosmic: see UNIVERSAL.

cosmopolitan: see INTERNATIONAL.

cosmos: see CREATION; UNIVERSE.

cost *n.* **1** *(what is the cost of the article?)* PRICE, CHARGE, AMOUNT, EXPENSE, RATE; **2** *(the earthquake involved heavy costs)* LOSS, DAMAGE, SUFFERING, SACRIFICE, PENALTY.

costly *adj.* EXPENSIVE, DEAR, HIGH, exorbitant, VALUABLE.

costume *n.* OUTFIT, attire, DRESS, SUIT, apparel, CLOTHES, get-up.

cot *n.* BED, berth, BUNK.

coterie: see CIRCLE.

cottage *n.* bungalow, CABIN, LODGE.

cottony: see SOFT.

couch *n.* divan, SOFA, davenport, settee, day bed.

cough *v.* hack, hem, hawk, bark.
— *n.* hack, hem, hawk, bark, convulsion.

council *n.* ASSEMBLY, MEETING, convocation, CONFERENCE, CONVENTION, COMMITTEE, BOARD.

counsel: see ADVICE; ADVISE; ATTORNEY; CAUTION; CONSULT; COUNSELOR; GUIDE; SUGGEST.

counselor *n.* adviser, TEACHER, TUTOR, mentor, LAWYER, ATTORNEY, advocate, counsel.

count *v.* **1** *(to count figures)* ADD, TOTAL, NUMBER, cipher, enumerate, tally, compute; **2** *(can you count on him?)* RELY ON, DEPEND, BANK, LEAN, TRUST.
— *n.* tally, NUMBER, TOLL, computation, TOTAL, tabulation, SUM.

countenance: see FACE.

counter *n.* **1** *(he used a counter to get his total)* calculator, adding machine, computer, tabulator, checker; **2** *(a display counter)* showcase, SHELF, BOARD, LEDGE, BAR, TABLE. See also CHIP; PIECE.
— *adj.*: see CONTRARY; CONVERSE.

counteract: see BALANCE.

counteracting: see OPPOSING.

counteraction: see OPPOSITION.

counterbalance: see CANCEL; COMPENSATE.

counterclaim: see CLAIM.

counterfeit: see COPY; DUPLICATE; FORGE; IMITATE; IMITATION; MOCK; PRETEND.

counterman: see WAITER.

counterpane: see SPREAD.

counterpart: see DOUBLE; PARALLEL.

counterpoise: see BALANCE.

countersign: see WITNESS.

countless: see NUMEROUS.

count on: see RELY ON.

country *n.* **1** *(what country is she from?)* NATION, homeland, fatherland, motherland; **2** *(a trip to the country)* farmland, BUSH, backwoods, woodlands, meadows.
— *adj.*: see RURAL.

countryman: see NATIVE.

countryside *n.* COUNTRY, boondocks, provinces, scenery, LANDSCAPE.

county: see PROVINCE.

coup d' état: see REBELLION.

couple *n.* PAIR, TWO, TEAM, SET, BRACE, newlyweds.
— *v.* PAIR, TEAM, LINK, YOKE, JOIN, UNITE, CONNECT, bracket.

coupled: see MARRIED; TWIN.

couplet: see TWO.

coupling: see CLUTCH.

coupon: see CHANCE.

courage *n.* BRAVERY, valor, DARING, gallantry, HEROISM, audacity, guts, grit, moxie.

courageous *adj.* FEARLESS, BOLD, valiant, BRAVE, dauntless, HEROIC, resolute.

courier: see MESSENGER; RUNNER.

course *n.* **1** *(the course of time)* PASSAGE, RUN, SEQUENCE, PROGRESS, DRIFT; **2** *(an English course)* curriculum, study, SUBJECT, CLASS; **3** *(a running course)* TRACK, PATH, ROUTE, ROAD, CIRCUIT, GROUND. See also DISH.

court *n.* **1** *(the house is in a court)* YARD, LANE, ENCLOSURE, quadrangle, SQUARE, patio; **2** *(they were tried at court)* bench, tribunal, bar, magistrate; **3** *(the king lives at court)* PALACE, CASTLE, HALL.
— *v.* WOO, SUIT, CHASE, PURSUE, PLEASE, FLATTER, solicit.

courteous: see CIVIL; GALLANT; HUMBLE; MANNERLY; NICE; POLITE; SOFT.

courtesy *n.* breeding, MANNERS, POLITENESS, civility, KINDNESS, GOODNESS, CONSIDERATION.

courtly: see DIGNIFIED.

courts: see LAW.

courtyard: see YARD.

cousin: see RELATION; RELATIVE.

cove: see BAY.

covenant: see AGREEMENT.

cover *v.* **1** *(cover the baby)* CLOTHE, WRAP, PROTECT, SHIELD, SHELTER; **2** *(cover your tracks)* CONCEAL, HIDE, SCREEN, mask, CAMOUFLAGE; **3** *(the insurance does not cover wind damage)* INCLUDE, INVOLVE, EMBRACE, embody, CONTAIN.
— *n.* **1** *(bed covers)* blanket, CLOTH, SHEET, TOP, CAP, LID, STOPPER; **2** *(they had to take cover)* SHELTER, PROTECTION, CONCEALMENT.

coveralls: see OVERALLS.

covered: see HIDDEN.

covering *n.* veneer, LAYER, COAT, glaze, POLISH, blanket, wrapper, CONTAINER, LID, CAP. See also CEILING.
—*adj.*: see EXTERNAL.
—*prep.*: see ON; OVER.

coverlet: see SPREAD.

cover up *v.* CONCEAL, HIDE, CAMOUFLAGE, mask, DISGUISE, LIE, SHELTER, DEFEND, whitewash.

covet: see ENVY; GRUDGE; THIRST.

coward *n.* weakling, sneak, deserter, dastard, milksop.

cowardice: see TIMIDITY.

cowardly *adj.* frightened, cowering, AFRAID, TIMID, FEARFUL, faint-hearted, dastardly, nerveless.
—*adv.* weakly, timidly, FEARFULLY, faint-heartedly, apprehensively, nervously, anxiously.

cower: see FEAR; SHRINK; SQUAT.

cowering: see COWARDLY.

co-worker: see ASSOCIATE; COMRADE; MATE; PARTNER.

coy: see BASHFUL.

coyness: see RESERVE.

cozy: see COMFORTABLE; SNUG.

crab: see CRANK; FUSS.

crabby: see CROSS.

crack *v.* **1** (*the gun cracked*) POP, SNAP, BANG, EXPLODE, detonate; **2** (*the glass cracked from the heat*) BREAK, BURST, SPLIT, splinter, fracture.
—*n.* **1** (*a crack of thunder*) CLAP, EXPLOSION, BLOW, snap, POP, detonation; **2** (*a crack in the wall*) SPLIT, fracture, HOLD, OPENING, break; **3** (*his cracks are not funny*) JOKE, JEST, COMMENT, WITTICISM.

crackpot: see CRANK.

cradle *n.* **1** (*a baby's cradle*) CRIB, bassinet, rocker, BED; **2** (*the cradle of civilization*) ORIGIN, SOURCE, BEGINNING, ancestry.
—*v.* HOLD, SUPPORT, CARRY, ENVELOPE, SHELTER.

craft *n.* **1** (*arts and crafts*) SKILL, TALENT, ABILITY, dexterity, CLEVERNESS; **2** (*small craft warnings*) VESSEL, BOAT, SHIP, PLANE.

craftsman: see ARTIST; SCIENTIST; WORKER; WORKMAN.

craftsmanship: see HANDIWORK, SCIENCE.

crafty: see CUNNING; TRICKY.

crag: see CLIFF; ROCK.

craggy: see ROCKY.

cram: see CROWD; FATTEN; FILL; LOAD; PACK; RAM; STUDY; STUFF.

crammed: see CHOCK-FULL.

cramped: see CHOCK-FULL; THICK.

crane: see HOIST.

crank *v.* TURN, ROTATE, SPIN, WIND, START.
—*n.* **1** (*to turn a crank*) HANDLE, ARM, lever, BAR, KEY; **2** (*what a crank!*) grouch, crab, faultfinder, eccentric, crackpot.

cranky *adj.* grouchy, cantankerous, peevish, DISAGREEABLE, CROSS, IRRITABLE.

crash *n.* **1** (*the crash of the orchestra*) din, CLATTER, UPROAR, CLASH, THUNDER; **2** (*a car crash*) ACCIDENT, COLLISION, WRECK, smashup.
—*v.* **1** (*it crashed to the ground*) SMASH, splinter, SHATTER, BREAK, COLLAPSE; **2** (*the two planes crashed*) COLLIDE, HIT, SMASH.

crass: see CRUDE.

crate: see BOX; CASE; CONTAINER.

crater: see BOWL; CAVITY; PIT.

crave *v.* DESIRE, hanker, ENVY, LUST, WANT, NEED.

craving: see APPETITE; DESIRE; HUNGER; HUNGRY; LUST; THIRST; WISH.

crawl *v.* CREEP, SCRAMBLE, clamber.

crayon: see CHALK; PENCIL.

craze: see PASSION; RAGE.

craziness: see MADNESS.

crazy *adj.* INSANE, MAD, lunatic, touched, daffy, ODD, bizarre.

creak: see GROAN; MOAN.

creaky: see NOISY.

cream *n.* CHOICE, PRIME, BEST, PICK, elite. See also LOTION.
—*v.*: see LUBRICATE.

creamy: see FOAMY; SMOOTH.

crease: see FOLD; LOOP; WRINKLE.

create *v.* MAKE, PRODUCE, FORM, concoct, ORIGINATE, DEVELOP, GENERATE, conceive.

creation *n.* **1** (*God's creation*) UNIVERSE, COSMOS,

WORLD, NATURE; **2** (*the creation of a new formula*) INVENTION, origination, DEVELOPMENT, PRODUCTION, BIRTH.

creative: see FERTILE; INGENIOUS; INVENTIVE; ORIGINAL; PREGNANT; PRODUCTIVE.

creativeness: see ORIGINALITY.

creativity: see ART; FERTILITY.

creator: see ARTIST; AUTHOR; FOUNDER; GENERATOR; GOD; INVENTOR; MAKER; MANUFACTURER; PARENT.

creature *n.* **1** (*a living creature*) BEING, ANIMAL, PERSON, MAN, WOMAN, MORTAL, INDIVIDUAL; **2** (*creatures of the night*) MONSTER, THING, BEAST.

credence: see BELIEF; CREDIT; TRUST.

credentials: see CERTIFICATE; PASS; PASSPORT.

credible: see CONVINCING; LIKELY.

credit *n.* **1** (*to buy on credit*) installment, LOAN, TIME, TRUST; **2** (*he gets no credit for what he does*) acknowledgment, DISTINCTION, HONOR, REGARD, MERIT; **3** (*they don't place any credit on his story*) BELIEF, credence, TRUTH, CONFIDENCE, TRUST, FAITH.
— *v.* TRUST, BELIEVE, ACCEPT, LOAN. See also ATTRIBUTE.

credo: see PROFESSION.

creed *n.* BELIEF, CONVICTION, FAITH.

creek *n.* BROOK, run, SPRING, STREAM.

creep *v.* CRAWL, SCRAMBLE, clamber.

cremate: see BURN.

crest *n.* TOP, PEAK, SUMMIT, CROWN, RIDGE.

cretin: see IDIOT; MORON.

crevice: see GAP; SEAM; SLIT; VEIN.

crew *n.* FORCE, TEAM, GANG, STAFF, COMPANY, PARTY.

crib *n.* **1** (*the child's crib*) CRADLE, bassinet, BED; **2** (*a corn crib*) BIN, manger, stall, TROUGH. See also KEY.

crime *n.* wrongdoing, misdeed, offense, malfeasance, misdemeanor, felony, vice, SIN, VIOLATION.

criminal *n.* FELON, CONVICT, offender, malefactor, culprit.
— *adj.* ILLEGAL, unlawful, immoral, sinful, DELINQUENT, VICIOUS.

crimp: see RESTRICT.

crimson: see RED.

cringe: see CROUCH; DREAD

cringing: see FEARFUL.

crinkle: see WRINKLE.

cripple *n.* LAME, handicapped, disabled, injured.
— *v.* INJURE, disable, WEAKEN, DAMAGE, incapacitate, PARALYZE.

crippled: see BROKEN; DEFORMED; HALT; LAME

crisis: see EMERGENCY; INFLATION; URGENCY.

crisp *adj.* **1** (*a crisp morning*) FRESH, CLEAR, cloudless, invigorating, stimulating, vivacious; **2** (*crisp French bread*) crusty, HARD, BRITTLE, breakable, fragile.

crisscross: see ACROSS; WEAVE.

criterion: see GAUGE; STANDARD.

critic *n.* censor, reviewer, JUDGE, faultfinder, commentator, analyst, EDITOR.

critical *adj.* **1** (*a critical mother*) faultfinding, disapproving, nagging, condemning; **2** (*the critical list*) SERIOUS, GRAVE, crucial, ACUTE, DANGEROUS, precarious, HAZARDOUS.

criticism *n.* REVIEW, critique, evaluation, ANALYSIS, commentary.

criticize *v.* STUDY, PROBE, EXAMINE, evaluate, ANALYZE, REVIEW, appraise, EDIT, JUDGE, denounce.

critique: see CRITICISM.

critter: see ANIMAL.

croak: see DIE.

crochet: see KNIT.

crock: see JUG; POT.

crone: see WITCH.

crony: see BUDDY; CHUM; FRIEND; PAL.

crook *n.* **1** (*a shepherd's crook*) HOOK, STAFF, crosier, BEND, CURVE; **2** (*a notorious crook*) THIEF, SWINDLER, pilferer, CRIMINAL, GANGSTER.

crooked *adj.* **1** (*a crooked tree*) BENT, DEFORMED, twisted, gnarled, curved, contorted; **2** (*a crooked politician*) dishonest, deceitful, fraudulent, devious, insidious, CRIMINAL, underhanded.

crooks: see GANG.

croon: see SING.

crooner: see SINGER.

crop *n.* YIELD, PRODUCE, HARVEST, GROWTH.
— *v.* TRIM, CUT, CLIP, SHORTEN, prune, PICK, lop.

crops: see HARVEST.

crosier: see CROOK.

cross *v.* **1** *(to cross the street)* traverse, PASS, SPAN, ford, intersect; **2** *(don't cross him)* OPPOSE, HINDER, obstruct, thwart, frustrate. See also MIX.
— *n.* hybrid, intermixture, half-breed.
— *adj.* crabby, IRRITABLE, CRANKY, touchy, bothered.
— *adv.*: see ACROSS.

crossing: see VOYAGE.

cross out *v.* delete, CANCEL, ERASE, obliterate, REMOVE.

crosspiece: see BAR.

crossroads: see FORK.

cross section: see DIAMETER; SPECIMEN.

crossways: see FORK.

crosswise: see ACROSS.

crossword: see PUZZLE.

crouch *v.* SQUAT, STOOP, DUCK, BEND, cringe, hunch.

crow: see BOAST; BRAG; CACKLE.

crowd *n.* horde, MOB, FLOCK, GROUP, MASS, throng, MULTITUDE.
— *v.* CRUSH, cram, SWARM, HERD, PACK, SQUEEZE, JAM, STUFF.

crowded: see DENSE.

crown *n.* **1** *(the king's crown)* diadem, tiara, coronet; **2** *(the crown of the volcano)* PEAK, TOP, SUMMIT, CREST, RIDGE, HEAD: **3** *(the crown of his achievement)* acme, apex, zenith, culmination.
— *v.* **1** *(they crowned him emperor)* enthrone, INVEST, INSTALL, proclaim; **2** *(they crowned him for his exploits)* GLORIFY, DECORATE, HONOR, REWARD, DIGNIFY; **3** *(he crowned his works with a masterpiece)* PERFECT, CONSUMMATE, FINISH, COMPLETE, culminate.

crow's-nest: see TOWER.

crucial: see ACUTE; CRITICAL; KEY.

crude *adj.* **1** *(a crude finish)* ROUGH, RAW, rustic, COARSE, unrefined; **2** *(a crude joke)* VULGAR, uncouth, indelicate, crass, foul-mouthed.

cruel *adj.* BRUTAL, MEAN, malevolent, ruthless, INHUMAN, WICKED.

cruelty *n.* brutality, savagery, ruthlessness, ferocity, inhumanity, sadism.

cruise: see NAVIGATE; SAIL; TRAVEL; TRIP; VOYAGE.

cruiser: see SHIP.

crumb *n.* PARTICLE, GRAIN, pinch, SCRAP, BIT, DAB, DASH.

crumble *v.* disintegrate, CRUSH, fragmentate, pulverize, deteriorate, DECAY.

crumple: see WRINKLE.

crunch: see CHEW; CRUSH; GNAW; MASH; MUNCH; TRAMPLE.

crusade: see CAMPAIGN; EXPEDITION.

crusader: see PILGRIM.

crush *v.* crunch, squash, SQUEEZE, PRESS, CRUMBLE, MASH, SHATTER.

crust *n.* COATING, shell, hull, rind, SKIN, LAYER.

crusty: see CRISP.

crutch *n.* SUPPORT, PROP, BRACE. See also ACCESSORY.

crux: see URGENCY.

cry *v.* **1** *(the baby is crying)* WEEP, SOB, WAIL, wimper, BAWL; **2** *(he cried out from the hole)* SCREAM, SHOUT, YELL, SCREECH.
— *n.* SCREAM, SCREECH, YELL, HOWL, ROAR, bawl.

crybaby: see BABY.

crying: see TEARFUL.

cry out: see CALL; GASP.

crypt: see CELLAR; TOMB; VAULT.

cryptogram: see PUZZLE; RIDDLE.

crystal: see GLASS; MINERAL; TRANSPARENT.

cub: see INFANT.

cubbyhole: see COMPARTMENT.

cube: see BLOCK; MINCE; MULTIPLY.

cuddle: see CARESS; HUG; NESTLE; SQUEEZE.

cudgel: see BAT.

cue: see DUE; REMIND; SIGNAL.

cuff: see BLOW; BOX; KNOCK.

cull: see PICK; PLUCK.

culminate: see CROWN.

culmination: see CROWN.

culprit: see CRIMINAL; SUSPECT.

cultivate v. DEVELOP, PREPARE, IMPROVE, BETTER, REFINE, nurture, RAISE.

cultivated: see ELEGANT; GROWN; MATURE.

cultivation: see AGRICULTURE; CIVILIZATION; GROWTH; MATURITY.

cultivator: see FARMER.

culture n. refinement, CIVILIZATION, LEARNING, EDUCATION, breeding, MANNERS. See also AGRICULTURE.

cultured: see ARTISTIC; LEARNED; MATURE.

cumbersome: see CLUMSY.

cunning adj. SLY, crafty, shrewd, CLEVER, skillful, SHARP.
— n. ART, CRAFT, deceit, deception, INTRIGUE, subtlety, CLEVERNESS.

cup n. MUG, stein, VESSEL, BOWL, goblet, tumbler.

cupboard: see CABINET; CLOSET.

cupola: see DOME.

curb n. EDGE, RIM, BORDER, LEDGE, lip, pavement. See also BRIDLE; CHECK; CONTROL.
— v. restrain, retard, STOP, impede, CONTROL, CHECK.

curd: see CLOT.

curdle: see SOUR.

cure n. REMEDY, medication, antidote, restoration.
— v. RESTORE, HEAL, remedy, TREAT, rehabilitate. See also SALT.

curing: see MEDICINE.

curiosity n. 1 (a burning curiosity) inquisitiveness, inquiringness, questioning, interrogation, REGARD, CONCERN; 2 (the antique was a real curiosity) PECULIARITY, ODDITY, rarity, phenomenon.

curious adj. 1 (a curious mind) inquisitive, questioning, examining, inquiring, investigating, scrutinizing; 2 (a curious hat) PECULIAR, STRANGE, ODD, QUEER, UNUSUAL, weird.

curiousness: see PECULIARITY.

curl v. TWIST, curve, BEND, COIL, WIND, loop, spiral.
— n.: see COIL; WREATH.

curlicue: see TWIST.

currency n. MONEY, CASH, coins, bills, denomination. See also FRESHNESS.

current adj. POPULAR, COMMON, prevailing, prevalent, PRESENT, MODERN, CONTEMPORARY.
— n. 1 (a swift current) STREAM, FLOW, COURSE, undertow, TIDE; 2 (the old house has direct current) electricity, juice, POWER.

currently adv. presently, NOW, popularly, COMMONLY, GENERALLY.

curriculum: see COURSE.

curry: see GROOM.

currycomb: see COMB.

curse n. PLAGUE, affliction, denunciation, damnation.
— v. 1 (the drunk cursed the bouncer) SWEAR, blaspheme, INSULT, ABUSE, BLAST; 2 (the witch cursed her tormenter) DAMN, denounce, DOOM, CONDEMN, hex.

cursed adj. damned, banned, SWORN, HATEFUL, detestable, tormenting, troubled, afflicted, ill-fated.

curseword: see OATH.

curt: see ABRUPT; BRIEF; SHORT.

curtail: see DECREASE; REDUCE; SHORTEN; TRIM.

curtailed: see LESSER.

curtain n. drapery, drape, SHADE, SCREEN, hanging.

curtsy: see BOW.

curve n. bend, TWIST, ARCH, CROOK, WIND, HOOK.
— v.: see ARCH; BEND; CURL; ROUND; TURN; TWIST; WARP.

curved: see ARCHED; BENT; CROOKED; ROUND.

cushion n. PILLOW, bolster, PAD, MAT, quilt, buffer.

custodian: see ATTENDANT; GUARDIAN; JANITOR; KEEPER; MONITOR; SUPERINTENDENT; WARDEN.

custody: see CARE; CHARGE; TRUST.

custom n. MANNER, TRADITION, PRACTICE, HABIT, USAGE, FASHION.
— adj. SPECIAL, PERSONAL, UNIQUE, exclusive, PARTICULAR.

customarily: see COMMONLY; GENERALLY; REGULARLY; USUALLY.

customary *adj.* HABITUAL, NORMAL, COMMON, REGULAR, USUAL, routine.

customer *n.* buyer, purchaser, PATRON, CLIENT, shopper.

customs: see DUTY; TAX.

cut *v.* **1** *(he cut his finger)* SLICE, SLIT, SPLIT, sever, cleave, DIVIDE, gash; **2** *(the girls were reluctant to cut her)* IGNORE, slight, snub.
— *n.* incision, gash, SLASH, SLICE, WOUND.
— *adj.*: see WOUNDED.

cut down: see ABBREVIATE.

cute *adj.* PRETTY, PLEASING, DAINTY, charming, SWEET, WINNING, CLEVER, shrewd, CUNNING.

cutie: see DOLL; HONEY.

cut in: see INTRUDE.

cutlass: see SWORD.

cut off: see KILL.

cut open: see OPERATE.

cut out: see OPERATE.

cut-rate: see CHEAP.

cutter: see BIT; BLADE; KNIFE.

cutthroat: see ASSASSIN; BUTCHER; DESTRUCTIVE; KILLER.

cutting: see KEEN; REDUCTION; SHARP.

cycle: see CIRCLE; ORBIT; PERIOD; REGULARITY; REVOLUTION.

cyclic: see PERIODIC.

cyclone: see STORM; WIND.

cylinder: see ROUND; SPOOL; TUBE.

cylindrical: see ROUND.

cylindrically: see ROUND.

czar: see EMPEROR; MONARCH.

czarina: see QUEEN.

D

dab *n.* BIT, SPOT, STROKE, PAT, smear, LUMP.
— *v.* PAT, SMEAR, COAT.

dabble *v.* TRIFLE, putter, tinker, fiddle, toy, twiddle, dally.

dabbler: see AMATEUR.

dad: see FATHER.

daddy *n.* FATHER, papa, DAD, PARENT, sire.

daffy: see CRAZY.

daft: see INSANE.

daily *adj.* EVERYDAY, per diem, REGULARLY.
— *n.*: see NEWSPAPER.

dainty *adj.* fragile, DELICATE, TRIM, NEAT, FINE, ELEGANT, PRECIOUS.

dais: see STAGE.

dale *n.* VALLEY, vale, glen, dell.

dally: see DABBLE; DELAY; LOAF; PLAY; TRIFLE; WAIT.

dam *n.* dike, obstruction, embankment, levee.

damage *v.* HARM, RUIN, DESTROY, INJURE, mar, impair, sabotage.
— *n.* HARM, INJURY, LOSS, EVIL, hurt, WRONG, vandalism.

damaged: see FAULTY.

damages: see FINE.

damaging: see DESTRUCTIVE; HARMFUL.

dame: see LADY.

damn *v.* DOOM, denounce, CURSE, ban, put down.

damnation: see CONDEMNATION; CONVICTION; CURSE.

damned: see CURSED.

damp *adj.* HUMID, MOIST, WET, MUGGY.

dampen: see SPONGE; WET.

damper: see BRAKE.

dampness; see MOISTURE; WETNESS.

damsel: see GIRL; VIRGIN.

dance: see ART; BALL; BOB; BOUNCE; ENTERTAINMENT; PARTY; PROMENADE; TWIST.

dancer: see ARTIST; ENTERTAINER; PARTNER.

dander: see ANGER.

dandy *adj.* FINE, GOOD, EXCELLENT, FIRST-RATE, TERRIFIC, ADMIRABLE, SUPERB.

danger *n.* RISK, HAZARD, peril, jeopardy, MENACE.

dangerous *adj.* RISKY, HAZARDOUS, TREACHEROUS, precarious, perilous, threatening, UNSAFE.

dangle *v.* HANG, SUSPEND sag, DROOP, SWING.
— *n.:* see SWING.

dank: see MUGGY.

dapple: see SPOT.

dare *v.* **1** (*he dared enter the haunted house*) RISK,
ATTEMPT, ENDEAVOR, VENTURE, UNDERTAKE;
2 (*he dared his friend to go first*) DEFY,
CHALLENGE, BRAVE.
— *n.:* see CHALLENGE.

daring *adj.* BRAVE, BOLD, FEARLESS, foolhardy,
valiant, COURAGEOUS, GALLANT, venturesome,
venturous.
— *n.* BRAVERY, BOLDNESS, valor, COURAGE,
audacity, impudence, adventurousness, NERVE.

dark *adj.* **1** (*a dark room*) unilluminated, shadowy,
somber, CLOUDY; **2** (*a dark secret*) MYSTERIOUS,
sinister, murky; **3** (*the dark side of life*) GLOOMY,
SAD, UNHAPPY, dreary, SOLEMN, CHEERLESS.
— *n.* murkiness, obscurity, IGNORANCE,
blindness.

darken: see BLIND; CLOUD; SHADE.

darkness *n.* DIMNESS, obscurity, SHADOW,
murkiness, cheerlessness, GLOOM, nighttime.

darling *n.* SWEETHEART, DEAR, BELOVED, LOVE,
favorite, PET, precious.
— *adj.* LOVELY, FAVORITE, cherished, adored,
BELOVED, DEAR.

darn: see PATCH.

dart: see ARROW; FLY; MISSILE; SCRAMBLE; SHOOT;
SPEED.

dash *n.* **1** (*a dash of salt*) TOUCH, tinge, TRACE,
sprinkling, BIT, pinch, HINT; **2** (*forty-yard dash*)
RUN, sprint, RUSH, hurtle, CHARGE; **3** (*a man
greeted her with a lot of dash*) splash, FLASH,
verve, panache, SPIRIT, ENERGY, VIGOR; **4** (*there
is a dash between those two words*) LINE, hyphen,
STROKE.
— *v.* RUN, SCATTER, HURRY, RUSH, HASTEN.

dastard: see COWARD.

dastardly: see COWARDLY; FEARFUL.

data: see INFORMATION; INTELLIGENCE.

date *n.* **1** (*an important date*) APPOINTMENT,
ENGAGEMENT, rendezvous; **2** (*what is today's
date?*) TIME, DAY, MOMENT, PERIOD, epoch, ERA,
AGE.
— *v.* **1** (*how can you date that antique?*) REGISTER,
RECORD, MARK, MEASURE; **2** (*she is dating a law
student*) ESCORT, COURT.

datum: see FOOTNOTE.

daub: see BRUSH; PAINT; SMEAR; SOIL.

daughter: see CHILD.

dauntless: see BOLD; COURAGEOUS; FEARLESS.

davenport: see COUCH; SOFA.

dawdle: see DRAG; LAG; LINGER; LOAF; TRIFLE.

dawdling: see DELAY.

dawn *n.* **1** (*dawn comes early in summer*) sunrise,
daybreak, daylight; **2** (*the dawn of man*)
BEGINNING, ORIGIN, commencement, START,
outset.
— *v.:* see BRIGHTEN.

day *n.* **1** (*a day dreamer*) daytime, daylight; **2** (*in
the olden days*) TIME, AGE, epoch, ERA, DATE.

day bed: see COUCH.

day book: see DIARY; JOURNAL.

daybreak: see DAWN; MORNING.

daydreaming: see ABSENT-MINDED.

daylight: see DAWN; DAY; MORNING.

day off: see HOLIDAY.

daytime: see DAY.

daze: see BEWILDER; DAZZLE; SHOCK; STUN.

dazed: see FOGGY.

dazzle *v.* daze, BLIND, GLARE, ASTONISH,
SURPRISE, BEWILDER.
— *n.:* see GLARE.

dazzling *adj.* BRIGHT, STUNNING, BRILLIANT,
blinding, shining, glaring, flashing,
overpowering, sparkling.

dead *adj.* **1** (*a dead body*) deceased, LIFELESS,
departed, extinct, gone; **2** (*what a dead color!*)
FLAT, LIFELESS, DULL, dreary, lusterless.
— *pl.n.* deceased, departed, defunct.

deaden: see BLUNT; DROWN; DRUG; KILL; NUMB;
PARALYZE.

deadened: see NUMB.

deadfall: see TRAP.

deadly *adj.* MORTAL, FATAL, lethal, DESTRUCTIVE,
MURDEROUS.

deaf *adj.* unhearing, unheeding, STUBBORN,
inattentive.

deafening: see LOUD.

deal *v.* **2** (*to deal the cards*) DISTRIBUTE,

apportion, allot, GIVE, GRANT, SHARE; **2** *(they deal in plastics)* TRADE, SELL, BUY, BARGAIN, barter.
— *n.* COMPROMISE, AGREEMENT, ARRANGEMENT, PLEDGE, pact, BARGAIN.

dealer *n.* trafficker, TRADER, seller, buyer, MERCHANT, businessman, monger.

dealing: see EXCHANGE.

dean: see VETERAN.

dear *adj.* **1** *(beef is very dear nowadays)* COSTLY, EXPENSIVE, high-priced; **2** *(he is mourning over his dear wife)* BELOVED, adored, cherished, DARLING.
— *n.* SWEETHEART, LOVE, DARLING.

dearth: see FAMINE.

death *n.* decease, dying, passing, LOSS, DEPARTURE, extinction, ENDING, END, expiration, EXIT.

deathless: see ETERNAL; IMMORTAL.

debased: see LOW.

debatable: see QUESTIONABLE.

debate *v.* REASON, ARGUE, contend, DISCUSS, DISPUTE, WRANGLE.
— *n.* ARGUMENT, controversy, DISCUSSION, DISPUTE, reasoning.

debenture: see BOND.

debris: see GARBAGE; JUNK; RUBBISH; SCRAP; TRASH.

debt *n.* **obligation,** dues, liability, arrears, NOTE, I.O.U.

debut: see OPENING.

decanter: see BOTTLE.

decay *v.* ROT, decompose, SPOIL, disintegrate, deteriorate, DECLINE.
— *n.:* see DECLINE; MOLD; RUIN; RUST; TWILIGHT; WEAR.

decayed: see ROTTEN.

decaying: see PERISHABLE.

decease: see DEATH; DEPART; DIE.

deceased: see DEAD; LATE.

deceit: see CUNNING; TREACHERY.

deceitful: see CROOKED; HOLLOW; TREACHEROUS; VAIN.

deceive *v.* FOOL, CHEAT, LIE, MISLEAD, delude, SWINDLE, hoodwink.

deceiver: see CHEAT; IMPOSTOR; TRAITOR.

deceiving: see TREACHEROUS.

decency: see CLEANLINESS; MODESTY; VIRTUE.

decent *adj.* CORRECT, seemly, PROPER, RIGHT, SUITABLE, RESPECTABLE, VIRTUOUS.

deception: see ACT; CAMOUFLAGE; CUNNING; FRAUD; LIE; SWINDLE; TRAP; TREACHERY; TRICK; TRICKERY.

deceptive: see FALSE; MISLEADING.

decide *v.* SETTLE, CONCLUDE, RESOLVE, CHOOSE, DETERMINE, JUDGE.

decided: see FOREGONE.

decidedly: see DEFINITELY; POSITIVELY.

decipher: see EXPLAIN; FIND OUT; READ; TRANSLATE; UNFOLD.

decision *n.* JUDGMENT, CONCLUSION, RESOLUTION, DETERMINATION, SETTLEMENT, pronouncement, VERDICT.

decisive: see CONCLUSIVE; FINAL; IMPORTANT.

decisively: see FIRMLY.

decisiveness: see DETERMINATION.

deck: see DECORATE; FLOOR; PACK; PORCH.

declaim: see PRONOUNCE.

declaration *n.* STATEMENT, ANNOUNCEMENT, EXPLANATION, affirmation, PROCLAMATION, PUBLICATION.

declare *v.* STATE, proclaim, attest, assert, EXPOUND, EXPLAIN, ANNOUNCE, INDICATE, PUBLISH.

declination: see DEPTH.

decline *v.* **1** *(the road declines sharply)* SLOPE, SLANT, LEAN, incline, BEND, BOW; **2** *(his health declined)* deteriorate, FAIL, DECAY, DROOP, flag, degenerate, deteriorate, DIMINISH, DECREASE, LESSON, FADE, wane; **3** *(they declined our offer)* REJECT, REFUSE.
— *n.* wane, diminution, deterioration, decay, decrease, FAILURE.

declining: see FEEBLE; PARTING.

declivity: see DESCENT.

decode: see TRANSLATE.

decompose: see DECAY; ROT; SPOIL.

decomposed: see ROTTEN.

decorate *v.* deck, ADORN, BEAUTIFY, TRIM, ORNAMENT.

decorated: see ELABORATE.

decoration: see AWARD; MEDAL; ORNAMENT, TRIM.

decorative *adj.* ornamental, ornate, FANCY, adorning, embellishing, beautifying.

decrease *v.* SHORTEN, DIMINISH, abate, LESSEN, LOWER, curtail, subside, *decline.*
— *n.*: see DECLINE; REDUCTION.

decree: see COMMAND; COMMANDMENT; JUDGMENT; LEGISLATE; PROCLAMATION; SENTENCE; VERDICT.

decrepit: see AGED; OLD.

dedicate *v.* OFFER, DEVOTE, ASSIGN, GIVE, DONATE, apportion.

dedicated: see DEVOTED.

deduce: see PROVE; REASON.

deduct: see SUBTRACT.

deduction: see LOGIC.

deed *n.* **1** (*words and deeds*) ACTION, ACT, feat, PERFORMANCE, doing, ACHIEVEMENT, ACCOMPLISHMENT; **2** (*the deed for a house*) TITLE, CONTRACT, RECORD, DOCUMENT, CHARTER.

deep *adj.* **1** (*a deep well*) LOW, BENEATH, buried, bottomless, subterranean; **2** (*deep thoughts*) profound, absorbed, engrossed, penetrating, ACUTE. See also RICH.
— *n.* OCEAN, SEA, abyss, DEPTH, BOTTOM, vastness.

deepen *v.* intensify, STRENGTHEN, INCREASE, EXTEND, EXPAND.

deepness: see DEPTH.

deer: see BUCK.

deface: see SCAR.

defaced: see DEFORMED.

defamation: see SCANDAL.

defame: see SMEAR.

default: see FOLD.

defeat *v.* OVERTHROW, CONQUER, WIN, BEAT, subdue, rout, outplay, overmaster.
— *n.* OVERTHROW, CONQUEST, rout.

defeated: see BEATEN; BROKEN; FALLEN.

defect *n.* LACK, deficiency, FAULT, flaw, imperfection, drawback, WEAKNESS.
— *v.* DESERT, BETRAY, FLEE.

defective: see BAD; BUM; FAULTY; FEEBLE MINDED; INFERIOR; RETARDED; WANTING.

defector: see CONVERT.

defend *v.* GUARD, PROTECT, SAVE, INSURE, SHIELD, SHELTER, SUPPORT.

defendant: see PARTY; SUSPECT.

defended: see SECURE.

defender: see ATTORNEY; CHAMPION; DISCIPLES; ESCORT; GUARD; GUARDIAN; PROTECTOR.

defense *n.* GUARD, SHELTER, PROTECTION, SUPPORT, JUSTIFICATION, EXCUSE.

defenseless *adj.* HELPLESS, WEAK, unprotected, UNGUARDED, unarmed.

defensible: see EXCUSABLE.

defensive: see APOLOGETIC; PROTECTIVE.

defer: see ADJOURN; CHARGE; POSTPONE; SUSPEND; TABLE.

deference: see RESPECT.

defiance: see DISOBEDIENCE; REBELLION; RESISTANCE.

defiant: see RESISTANT.

deficiency: see ABSENCE; DEFECT; FAILURE; INFERIORITY; MINUS; LACK; SCARCITY; SHORTNESS.

deficient: see FAULTY; INCOMPLETE; MINUS; SCARCE; SHY; WANTING.

defile: see DISGRACE; PASS.

define *v.* **1** (*to define a word*) CLARIFY, EXPLAIN, DESCRIBE, INTERPRET; **2** (*this agreement defines the frontier*) LIMIT, FIX, ESTABLISH, SET, SETTLE, DETERMINE.

defined: see DEFINITE.

definite *adj.* EXACT, defined, DISTINCT, FIXED, PRECISE, ACCURATE.

definitely *adv.* EXACTLY, CLEARLY, PRECISELY, unmistakenly, undoubtedly, SURELY, decidedly, obviously.

definition: see CLARIFICATION; RELIEF.

deformation: see FREAK.

deformed *adj.* distorted, MISSHAPEN, crippled, defaced, disfigured, marred, blemished, UNNATURAL.

deformity: see UGLINESS.

defraud: see CHEAT; MISLEAD; SWINDLE; THIEVE; TRICK.

defray: see PAY.

defrayment: see PAYMENT.

defunct: see DEAD; LIFELESS.

defy *v*. DARE, CHALLENGE, BRAVE, flout, OPPOSE, RESIST, IGNORE.

degenerate: see DECLINE.

degeneration: see LOSS.

degradation: see DISGRACE; HUMILIATION.

degrade *v*. demote, LOWER, SINK, REDUCE, HUMBLE, belittle, downgrade.

degree *n*. **1** *(a high degree of humidity)* MEASUREMENT, GAUGE, RATIO, LEVEL; **2** *(a high degree of intelligence)* AMOUNT, PROPORTION, EXTENT, RATE, RANGE. See also RANK.

dehumidify: see DRY.

dehydrate: see DRY.

deify: see IDOLIZE.

deity: see GOD.

dejected: see BLUE; BROKENHEARTED; DOWNHEARTED; WRETCHED.

dejection: see BLUES; MISERY.

delay *v*. POSTPONE, detain, procrastinate, tarry, LINGER, STALL, dally.
— *n*. postponement, procrastination, lag, wait, dawdling.

delayed: see LATE.

delaying: see WAITING.

delectable: see APPETIZING; DELICIOUS.

delegate *n*. representative, appointee, envoy, DEPUTY, COMMISSIONER, AGENT.
— *v*. ASSIGN, COMMISSION, authorize, empower, APPOINT, entrust.

delegation: see MISSION; REPRESENTATION.

delete: see CROSS OUT; ELIMINATE; ERASE.

deletion: see ELIMINATION.

deliberate *adj*. purposeful, STUDIED, planned, calculated, predetermined, reasoned.
— *v*.: see WEIGH.

deliberately *adv*. determinedly, PURPOSELY, intentionally, willfully, consciously, knowingly.

deliberation: see CONCENTRATION; DISCUSSION; MEDITATION.

delicacies: see DESSERT.

delicacy: see SENTIMENT; STYLE; TACT.

delicate *adj*. FINE, DAINTY, fragile, FRAIL, ELEGANT, refined, PURE.

delicately: see LIGHTLY.

delicious *adj*. savory, luscious, APPETIZING, delectable, TASTY, scrumptious.

delight *n*. SATISFACTION, JOY, PLEASURE, gratification, GLADNESS. See also ADMIRATION.
— *v*. SATISFY, PLEASE, GRATIFY, AMUSE, ENTERTAIN.

delighted: see GLAD; HAPPY; RADIANT.

delightful *adj*. LOVELY, PLEASANT, charming, ENJOYABLE, PLEASURABLE, appealing, amusing, joyous, WELCOME.

delight in: see ENJOY.

delimit: see DETERMINE.

delineate: see CHART; DESCRIBE; MAP.

delineation: see DESCRIPTION.

delinquent *n*. offender, wrongdoer, sinner, malefactor, derelict, felon, CRIMINAL.
— *adj*. negligent, offending, FAULTY, derelict, GUILTY, LATE, TARDY.

delirious: see FEVERISH; FRANTIC; MAD.

delirium: see FEVER; INSANITY; MADNESS.

deliver *v*. **1** *(they deliver pizzas)* BRING, CARRY, TAKE, pass, SHIP, TRANSFER; **2** *(will they deliver the hostages?)* FREE, LIBERATE, RELEASE, SURRENDER, relinquish; **3** *(to deliver a speech)* PRONOUNCE, EXPRESS, UTTER, RECITE, RELATE.

deliverance: see RESCUE; SALVATION.

delivery *n*. **1** *(a quick delivery)* consignment, shipment, DISPATCH, mailing; **2** *(the delivery of prisoners)* SURRENDER, DISCHARGE, liberation, RESCUE; **3** *(the mother had an easy delivery)* BIRTH, childbirth, LABOR, parturition.

dell: see DALE.

delta: see MOUTH.

delude: see BETRAY; BLUFF; DECEIVE; JUGGLE; MISLEAD; PRETEND.

deluding: see MISLEADING.

deluge: see FLOOD; OVERFLOW; RAIN; SWAMP.

delusion: see ILLUSION.

delve: see DIG.

demand v. REQUEST, ASK, WANT, BEG, necessitate.
  — n. REQUEST, REQUIREMENT, CLAIM, petition, stipulation, APPLICATION.

demanding: see DIFFICULT; URGENT.

demeanor: see APPEARANCE; BEHAVIOR; CARRIAGE.

demented: see INSANE.

dementia praecox: see INSANITY.

demerit: see MINUS.

democracy: see EQUALITY; REPUBLIC.

demolish v. DESTROY, SHATTER, SMASH, WRECK, RUIN, dismantle, LEVEL, obliterate.

demolition: see DESTRUCTION.

demon n. DEVIL, fiend, MONSTER.

demoniac: see SUPERSTITIOUS.

demonstrate v. 1. (to demonstrate an experiment) SHOW, PRESENT, DISPLAY, EXPLAIN, EXHIBIT; 2 (they demonstrated their ignorance) PROVE, CERTIFY, TESTIFY, CONFIRM.

demonstrated: see EVIDENT.

demonstration n. 1 (a demonstration of new techniques) EXHIBITION, SHOW, ILLUSTRATION, PRESENTATION, DISPLAY; 2 (an anti-draft demonstration) protestation, RALLY, sit-in, MARCH.

demonstrative: see EMOTIONAL; EXCITABLE; PASSIONATE.

demoralized: see BROKEN.

demote: see DEGRADE.

den n. 1 (a lion's den) lair, cavern, CAVE, burrow, HAUNT, NEST; 2 (a private den) STUDY, RETREAT, hideaway.

denial: see VETO.

denim: see CANVAS.

denomination: see CURRENCY; NAME.

denotation: see MEANING.

denote: see MEAN; SIGNIFY.

denounce: see CONDEMN; CRITICIZE; CURSE; DAMN; FINGER.

dense adj. COMPACT, THICK, SOLID, TIGHT, crowded, compressed.

density: see COMPRESSION; THICKNESS.

dent n. NOTCH, NICK, PIT, DIP, IMPRESSION, hollow, indentation.
  — v. INDENT, depress, gouge, NOTCH, SCRATCH, imprint, MARK.

denude: see UNDRESS.

denunciation: see CONDEMNATION; CURSE.

deny v. REJECT, VETO, contradict, negate, disclaim, repudiate.

deodorize: see AIR.

depart v. LEAVE, WITHDRAW, set out, exit, QUIT, DECEASE.

departed: see DEAD.

departing: see PARTING.

department n. DIVISION, BUREAU, STATION, FUNCTION, PROVINCE, jurisdiction.

departure n. leaving, EXIT, embarkation, leave-taking, FAREWELL, FLIGHT, deviation, exodus, DEATH.

depend v. REST, COUNT, RELY ON, TRUST, REQUIRE.

dependable adj. HONEST, RELIABLE, STEADY, trustworthy, SURE, staunch, steadfast, UNFAILING, STRONG, FIRM.

dependence n. ATTACHMENT, TRUST, CONFIDENCE, reliance, SUPPORT, subservience, submission, RELATIONSHIP.

dependency: see COLONY.

dependent adj. contingent, conditional, subordinate, WEAK, HELPLESS, clinging.
  — n.: see CLIENT; SUBJECT.

depending on: see ACCORDING TO.

depend on: see RELY ON.

depict: see DESCRIBE; DRAW; PAINT; PENCIL; PICTURE; REPRESENT.

deplete: see CONSUME; DRAIN; EXHAUST; WASTE.

depletion: see EXHAUSTION.

deplorable: see UNFORTUNATE.

deplore: see MOAN; REGRET.

deport v. EXILE, EXPEL, BANISH, REMOVE, exclude.

deportation: see EXILE.

deposit *v.* DROP, INSTALL, BANK, INVEST, STORE.
— *n.* **1** *(to pay a deposit)* PLEDGE, HOLD; **2** *(mineral deposits)* sediment, silt, VEIN, lode. See also STORE.

depository: see VAULT; WAREHOUSE.

depot: see BASE; STATION; WAREHOUSE.

depraved: see VILLAINOUS; WICKED.

depreciate: see DROP.

depress: see DENT; DISCOURAGE; LOWER.

depressed: see BLUE; CHEERLESS; SAD.

depressing: see CHEERLESS; DULL; GLOOMY; SULLEN.

depression *n.* **1** *(a depression in the landscape)* DENT, hollow, concavity, DIP, BASIN; **2** *(mental depression)* discouragement, DESPAIR, BLUES; **3** *(the great depression)* stagnation, recession.

deprivation: see LOSS.

deprive *v.* dispossess, STRIP, confiscate, APPROPRIATE, ROB.

depth *n.* deepness, profundity, lowness, declination, profoundness, EXTENT, detailedness, WISDOM.

deputation: see REPRESENTATION.

deputy *n.* aide, lieutenant, subordinate, legislator, DELEGATE.

derange: see LITTER; UPSET.

deranged: see INSANE; MAD; UNBALANCED.

derangement: see MADNESS.

derby: see RACE.

derelict: see ADRIFT; DELINQUENT.

deride: see MOCK; RIDICULE; SCOFF.

derision: see RIDICULE.

derivation: see ORIGIN; SOURCE; WELL.

derive *v.* ACQUIRE, OBTAIN, RECEIVE, DRAW.

derrick: see HOIST.

descend *v.* FALL, DROP, SINK, SET, SETTLE, gravitate, PLUNGE.

descendant: see CHILD; HEIR; SON.

descendants: see GENERATION; OFFSPRING; SEED.

descending: see DOWNWARD.

descent *n.* FALL, downfall, DECLINE, declivity, comedown, slump, COLLAPSE.

describe *v.* depict, portray, EXPLAIN, PICTURE, delineate.

description *n.* PICTURE, portrayal, delineation, characterization, RELATION.

descriptive: see EXPRESSIVE.

desert *n.* wasteland, WILD, WASTE, badlands, solitude.
— *v.* ABANDON, forsake, QUIT, DEFECT, run off.

deserted: see ALONE; DESOLATE; LONE; LONELY; SOLITARY.

deserter: see CONVERT; COWARD; TRAITOR.

desertion: see ESCAPE; TREASON.

deserve *v.* MERIT, EARN, WARRANT, rate.

deserved: see JUST.

deserving: see RESPECTABLE; WORTHY.

design *v.* formulate, CREATE, DRAW, COMPOSE.
— *n.* PLAN, plans, PATTERN, ARCHITECTURE, DRAFT, blueprint, SCHEME, STRATEGY. See also GOAL; PURPOSE.

designate: see APPOINT; CALL; ENTITLE; NOMINATE; NUMBER; SELECT; SPECIFY.

designation: see NAME; SELECTION; TERM; TITLE.

designed: see STUDIED.

designedly: see PURPOSELY.

designer: see ARCHITECT; INVENTOR.

desirable *adj.* PLEASING, PREFERABLE, VALUABLE, GOOD, APPETIZING.

desire *v.* WANT, wish for, CRAVE, long for.
— *n.* PREFERENCE, WISH, aspiration, craving, APPETITE, FANCY, fondness, yen.

desiring: see EAGER.

desirous: see ANXIOUS.

desist: see QUIT.

desk *n.* TABLE, secretary, BUREAU, COUNTER, lectern.

desolate *adj.* deserted, forsaken, abandoned, SOLITARY, isolated, GLOOMY.

desolation: see LONELINESS.

despair *n.* hopelessness, discouragement, desperation, DEPRESSION.
— *v.* despond, give in, give up.

despairing: see DESPERATE; HOPELESS; JOYLESS.

desperado: see PIRATE; ROBBER.

desperate *adj.* HOPELESS, despairing, RECKLESS, RASH, frenzied.

desperation: see DESPAIR.

despicable: see SHAMEFUL.

despise *v.* SCORN, loathe, disdain, abhor, HATE, DISLIKE.

despite *prep.* regardless of, notwithstanding.

despond: see DESPAIR.

despondent: see BLUE; BROKENHEARTED.

despot: see MONARCH.

despotic: see ABSOLUTE.

dessert *n.* sweets, delicacies, sweetmeats.

destination *n.* END, GOAL, objective, terminus, DESTINY, FATE.

destine: see DEVOTE.

destiny *n.* FATE, END, CONCLUSION, FORTUNE, predestination, LOT.

destitute: see BANKRUPT; NEEDY; POOR.

destroy *v.* RUIN, DEMOLISH, raze, annihilate, OVERTHROW, ravage, eradicate, KILL.

destroyed: see LOST.

destroyer: see SHIP; VANDAL.

destructible: see PERISHABLE.

destruction *n.* RUIN, demolition, WRECK, devastation, downfall, toppling, DEATH, MASSACRE, eradication.

destructive *adj.* HARMFUL, hurtful, ruinous, injurious, FATAL, TROUBLESOME, cutthroat, damaging.

detach *v.* SEPARATE, unhitch, unsnap, unfix, unfasten, DISCONNECT, disengage.

detachment: see COMPANY; ISOLATION; UNIT.

detail *n.* PARTICULAR, PART, ITEM, FACT, POINT, FEATURE, SPECIFICATION, PECULIARITY.
— *v.* elaborate, SPECIFY, particularize, ITEMIZE, EXPLAIN.

detailed: see ELABORATE; TECHNICAL.

detailedness: see DEPTH.

detain: see ARREST; DELAY; KEEP.

detect *v.* DISCOVER, DISTINGUISH, ascertain, IDENTIFY, HIT, EXPOSE.

detection: see DISCOVERY.

detective: see INSPECTOR; SPY.

detector: see MONITOR.

detention: see ARREST.

deter: see REIN.

deteriorate: see CRUMBLE; DECAY; DECLINE.

deterioration: see DECLINE; WEAKNESS; WEAR.

determinant: see FACTOR.

determination *n.* decisiveness, FIRMNESS, RESOLUTION, dogmatism, tenacity.

determine *v.* DEFINE, DECIDE, delimit, FIND OUT, IDENTIFY, SHOW, PROVE, RESOLVE.

determined: see BOUND; EARNEST; FIRM; SINGLE-MINDED.

determinedly: see DELIBERATELY.

deterrent: see REIN.

detest: see DISLIKE; HATE.

detestable: see CURSED; HATEFUL.

detonate: see CRACK; DISCHARGE; EXPLODE; POP.

detonation: see BOOM; BLAST; CRACK; EXPLOSION.

detract: see DISTRACT.

detriment: see LOSS.

deuce: see TWO.

devastate: see RUIN.

devastated: see LOST.

devastation: see DESTRUCTION; RUIN.

develop *v.* evolve, REFINE, ELABORATE, FINISH, UNFOLD, GROW, mature.

developed: see GROWN; RIPE.

developer: see INVENTOR.

development *n.* **1** (*the development of new products*) evolution, GROWTH, unfolding, maturation, PROGRESS, elaboration; **2** (*a housing development*) buildings, housing, real estate.

deviate: see DIFFER; VARY.

deviating: see VARIABLE.

deviation: see DEPARTURE; VARIATION.

device *n.* apparatus, INSTRUMENT, contrivance, MECHANISM, TECHNIQUE, METHOD.

devil *n.* **1** *(angels and devils)* DEMON, tempter, fiend, archfiend, Lucifer, Satan; *(poor devil)* WRETCH, RASCAL, VILLAIN.

devilish: see MISCHIEVOUS.

devilment: see MISCHIEF.

deviltry: see SUPERSTITION.

devious: see CROOKED; FOXY.

devise *v.* contrive, INVENT, think up, conceive, DESIGN, concoct, HATCH.

devoid: see BARREN.

devote *v.* DEDICATE, APPLY, consecrate, destine, consign.

devoted *adj.* dedicated, LOYAL, FAITHFUL, CONSTANT, consigned, reserved.

devotee: see FAN; SUPPORTER.

devotion *n.* AFFECTION, LOYALTY, constancy, ALLEGIANCE, SERVICE, FIRMNESS.

devour *v.* CONSUME, EAT, gulp, SWALLOW, wolf, WASTE, SPEND.

devout: see HOLY; RELIGIOUS.

devoutness: see HOLINESS.

dew *n.* MOISTURE, precipitation, condensation, humidity.

dexter: see RIGHT.

dexterity: see ABILITY; CRAFT.

dexterous: see CAPABLE.

diabolical: see MAGICAL.

diadem: see CROWN.

diagram: see CHART; GRAPH; MAP; OUTLINE.

dial: see METER.

dialect: see LANGUAGE; SPEECH; TONGUE.

dialogue: see INTERVIEW; TALK.

diameter *n.* cross section, broadness, WIDTH, bore.

diamond *n.* **1** *(a diamond ring)* solitaire, brilliant, GEM; **2** *(a baseball diamond)* FIELD, infield; *(shaped like a diamond)* rhombus, lozenge, parallelogram.

diary *n.* JOURNAL, chronicle, LOG, memo, REGISTER, RECORD, daybook.

dice: see MINCE.

dicey: see CHANCY.

dictate *v.* **1** *(to dictate a letter)* RECITE, PRONOUNCE, RECORD; **2** *(to dictate new rules)* DIRECT, ORDER, promulgate, IMPOSE.

dictation *n.* MESSAGE, transcription, TRANSCRIPT, stenography.

dictator: see TYRANT.

diction: see PRONUNCIATION; SPEECH.

dictionary *n.* word list, wordbook, lexicon, thesaurus, GLOSSARY, VOCABULARY, word finder.

die *v.* decease, EXPIRE, PERISH, succumb, pass on, pass away, VANISH, croak.
  — *n.*: see MOLD; STAMP.

diet *n.* sustenance, NOURISHMENT, regimen, nutrition, FARE, intake.
  — *v.* REDUCE, FAST, abstain, lose.

dietitian: see COOK.

differ *v.* **1** *(twins often differ)* VARY, diverge, deviate, CONTRAST; **2** *(I beg to differ)* DISAGREE, DISPUTE, dissent, OPPOSE, CLASH, contradict.

difference *n.* **1** *(what's the difference?)* DISTINCTION, disparity, variance, CONTRAST; **2** *(to have a difference)* DISPUTE, DISAGREEMENT, OPPOSITION, antagonism; **3** *(to pay the difference)* BALANCE, inequality, discrepancy, dues.

different *adj.* UNLIKE, dissimilar, disparate, contrasting, varying, diverse, heterogeneous.

differentiation: see SELECTION.

differently: see ELSE; OTHER; OTHERWISE; VARIOUSLY.

difficult *adj.* arduous, demanding, laborious, intricate, elusive, perplexing, abstruse, obscure, fastidious, unaccommodating, strenuous, ROUGH.

difficulty *n.* OBSTACLE, COMPLICATION, rigor, arduousness, entanglement, perplexity, ANNOYANCE.

diffuse: see CAST; EVAPORATE; RADIATE; UNIVERSAL.

diffusion: see CIRCULATION.

dig *v.* **1** *(to dig a trench)* excavate, SCOOP, spade, MINE, unearth, delve; **2** *(I dig you)* UNDERSTAND, comprehend, APPRECIATE, LIKE, ENJOY.

digest *v.* ABSORB, assimilate, CONDENSE, LEARN, MASTER.
— *n.* SUMMARY, epitome, condensation, abridgment, abstract.

digit: see CIPHER; FINGER; NUMBER.

dignified *adj.* stately, classical, majestic, reserved, GRAVE, courtly.

dignify *v.* ELEVATE, HONOR, glorify, ennoble, RAISE, LIFT.

dignitary: see CELEBRITY; OFFICER; OFFICIAL.

dignity *n.* **1** *(to act with dignity)* nobility, self-respect, DISTINCTION, WORTH; **2** *(to confer dignity)* HONOR, RANK, category, TITLE, OFFICE.

dike: see DAM; TRENCH.

dilapidated: see AGED.

dilate: see INFLATE; SWELL.

dilemma: see RIDDLE; PROBLEM; UNCERTAINTY.

diligence: see ALERTNESS; CARE; INDUSTRY.

diligent: see ACTIVE, BUSY; INDUSTRIOUS; THOROUGH.

diligently: see HARD.

dilly-dally: see LAG.

dim *adj.* FAINT, DULL, DARK, tarnished, shadowy, indefinite, unenthusiastic.
— *v.*: see FADE.

dime: see COIN.

dimension: see MAGNITUDE; MEASURE; SIZE; VOLUME.

diminish *v.* REDUCE, LESSEN, abate, SHRINK, CONTRACT.

diminished: see LESSER.

diminishing: see REDUCTION.

diminution: see DECLINE; WEAR.

diminutive: see LITTLE; MINIATURE; SMALL; TINY.

dimness *n.* faintness, obscurity, vagueness, DARKNESS, DULLNESS, mysteriousness, duskiness.

dimwitted: see DULL.

din: see CLAMOR; CLATTER; CRASH; LOUDNESS; NOISE; RACKET; SOUND; UPROAR.

dine *v.* sup, FEAST, banquet, lunch, EAT, FEED.

diner: see CAFE; CAR.

dinner *n.* FEAST, BANQUET, MEAL, supper, repast.

dip *v.* immerse, DUCK, BATHE, douse, LOWER, SCOOP.
— *n.* **1** *(to take a dip)* SWIM, BATH, PLUNGE, immersion; **2** *(a dip in the road)* DEPRESSION, hollow, SLOPE.

diploma: see CERTIFICATE.

diplomacy: see TACT.

diplomat: see AMBASSADOR.

diplomatic: see PEACEABLE; POLITICAL; TACTFUL.

dire: see AWFUL; DREADFUL; SERIOUS.

direct *v.* GUIDE, CONDUCT, ORDER, REGULATE, canalize, INSTRUCT, orient. See also ADDRESS; CAST.
— *adj.* STRAIGHT, undeviating, unswerving, straightforward, unambiguous, PROMPT, IMMEDIATE.

directing: see LEADING.

direction *n.* **1** *(the wrong direction)* COURSE, bearing, objective, ROUTE, viewpoint; **2** *(verbal directions)* CONTROL, guidance, INSTRUCTION, MANAGEMENT.

directions: see RECIPE.

directive: see INSTRUCTION; ORDER; REGULATION.

directly *adv.* straight, RIGHT, expressly, INSTANTLY, PROMPTLY.

directness: see SINCERITY.

director *n.* GUIDE, SUPERVISOR, overseer, CONDUCTOR, COUNSELOR, mentor.

directory: see CATALOG; GUIDE; INDEX.

dirt *n.* SOIL, EARTH, MUD, DUST, FILTH, vileness, smut.

dirty *adj.* soiled, FILTHY, polluted, FOUL, MEAN, vile, INDECENT, MESSY, unwashed.
— *v.* see POLLUTE; SOIL; SPOT.

disability: see SICKNESS.

disable: see CRIPPLE; PARALYZE.

disabled: see CRIPPLE; HALT; HELPLESS; GAME; LAME.

disadvantage *n.* HANDICAP, liability, drawback, unfavorableness, inconvenience, OBSTACLE, hindrance.

disagree *v.* DIFFER, VARY, diverge, DISPUTE, CONFLICT, QUARREL, BICKER, WRANGLE, CLASH, OPPOSE.

disagreeable *adj.* NASTY, quarrelsome, RUDE, UNPLEASANT, offensive, HOSTILE, obnoxious, gross.

disagreement *n.* dissension, QUARREL, DISPUTE, CONFLICT, DIFFERENCE, misunderstanding, contradiction.

disallow: see DISAPPROVE; FORBID; REFUSE.

disappear *v.* VANISH, ESCAPE, dissipate, EVAPORATE, vaporize, CEASE.

disappearance: see FLIGHT.

disappoint *v.* FAIL, dissatisfy, let down, belie, disillusion, frustrate.

disappointing: see UNSATISFACTORY.

disappointment *n.* REGRET, chagrin, DISTRESS, dissatisfaction, FAILURE, setback, BLOW, letdown.

disapproval. *n.* displeasure, CONDEMNATION, censure, OBJECTION, rebuke, scolding, dislike.

disapprove *v.* OBJECT, disfavor, OPPOSE, CONDEMN, disallow, REJECT, reprimand, go against.

disapproving: see CRITICAL.

disarray: see MUSS.

disassembled: see APART.

disaster *n.* calamity, MISFORTUNE, cataclysm, DAMAGE, DEFEAT, LOSS, catastrophe.

disastrous: see EVIL; TRAGIC; UNFORTUNATE; UNLUCKY.

disbelief: see DISTRUST; SUSPICION.

disbelieve: see MISTRUST; REJECT; SUSPECT; WONDER.

disburse: see SPEND.

disbursement: see EXPENDITURE.

discard *v.* SCRAP, REJECT, throw out, can, ABANDON, ELIMINATE, OUST.

discern: see DISTINGUISH; PENETRATE; UNDERSTAND.

discernible: see DISTINCT.

discernibly: see VISIBLY.

discerning: see ACUTE; SENSIBLE; UNDERSTANDING.

discernment: see JUDGMENT.

discharge *v.* **1** *(to discharge a worker)* RELEASE, DISMISS, unload, detonate, FIRE; **2** *(to discharge one's duties)* carry out, PERFORM, EXECUTE, SETTLE.
— *n.* release, liberation, acquittal, PERFORMANCE, EXECUTION. See also BLAST.

disciple *n.* PUPIL, STUDENT, learner, SCHOLAR, FOLLOWER, believer, CONVERT, SUPPORTER, defender.

disciplinary: see CORRECTIVE.

discipline *n.* **1** *(to practice discipline)* self-control, DEPORTMENT, BEHAVIOR, PRACTICE, STUDY; **2** *(to suffer discipline)* PUNISHMENT, castigation, CORRECTION, guidance.
— *v.* TRAIN, DRILL, PUNISH, CORRECT.

disciplined: see ORDERLY; VETERAN.

disclaim: see DENY.

disclose: see ANNOUNCE; BARE; CONFESS; EXPOSE; REPORT; REVEAL; SPRING; UNCOVER; UNFOLD.

disclosed: see OUT.

disclosure: see CLARIFICATION; CONFESSION; EXPOSURE; WHISPER.

discombobulate: see STUN.

discomfort: see ACHE; PINCH.

discomforted: see ASHAMED.

disconcert: see RATTLE.

disconnect *v.* sever, SEPARATE, disunite, DIVIDE, DETACH, unhook, unplug.

disconnected: see OFF.

discontent *n.* dissatisfaction, displeasure, ANNOYANCE, restlessness.

discontented *adj.* dissatisfied, displeased, UNHAPPY, disgruntled.

discontinue *v.* STOP, CEASE, END, QUIT, SUSPEND, FINISH, CLOSE, BREAK, INTERRUPT.

discontinued: see OFF.

discord: see CLASH; JAR.

discordant: see HARSH.

discothèque: see CASINO.

discount: see ALLOWANCE; BARGAIN.

discourage *v.* **1** *(to discourage a person)* depress, dishearten, DISMAY, dissuade; **2** *(to discourage plans)* thwart, impede, PREVENT, CURB.

discouraged: see DOWNHEARTED.

discouragement: see CHILL; DEPRESSION; DESPAIR; DISMAY.

discourse: see SPEECH.

discourteous: see IMPOLITE; UNGRACIOUS; UNREASONABLE.

discourtesy: see RUDENESS.

discover *v.* FIND, LOCATE, ascertain, FIND OUT, DETECT, EXPOSE, IDENTIFY.

discovery *n.* finding, detection, location, FIND, breakthrough, innovation, INVENTION, REALIZATION.

discredit: see DISGRACE; REFLECT; REJECT; SHAME; SMEAR.

discreet: see CAUTIOUS; TACTFUL; WISE.

discrepancy: see DIFFERENCE.

discretion: see JUDGMENT; PRECAUTION; TACT.

discriminate: see CONTRAST; DISTINGUISH.

discriminating: see SELECTIVE.

discrimination: see TASTE.

discuss *v.* CONSIDER, ANALYZE, ARGUE, DEBATE, TALK.

discussion *n.* TALK, CONVERSATION, EXCHANGE, DEBATE, CONSIDERATION, deliberation, evaluation, REVIEW, ARGUMENT, caucus, powwow.

disdain: see DESPISE; REJECT; SNEER.

disease *n.* SICKNESS, malady, DISORDER, INFECTION, contagion, affliction, pox, pestilence.

diseased: see ILL; SICK.

disembark: see CALL; LAND.

disengage: see DETACH.

disengaged: see NEUTRAL.

disentangle: see UNWIND.

disfavor: see DISAPPROVE; DISLIKE; RESENT.

disfigure: see MAUL; SCAR; SPOIL.

disfigured: see DEFORMED; MISSHAPEN; SHAPELESS.

disfigurement: see SCAR.

disgrace *n.* dishonor, SHAME, discredit, HUMILIATION, degradation, disrepute, infamy.
   − *v.* SHAME, DEGRADE, dishonor, defile.

disgraceful *adj.* SHAMEFUL, humiliating, embarrassing, scandalous, dishonorable, disreputable, outrageous.

disgruntled: see DISCONTENTED.

disguise *v.* CONCEAL, feign, mask, cloak.
   − *n.* CLOAK, CAMOUFLAGE, VEIL, COVER, veneer, incognito.

disguised: see HIDDEN.

disgust *n.* loathing, abhorrence, aversion, revulsion, nausea, abomination, distaste.
   − *v:* see REVOLT; SICKEN.

disgusted: see SICK.

disgusting: see FOUL; HORRIBLE.

dish *n.* plate, VESSEL, BOWL, platter, TRAY, course, FOOD, PREFERENCE, liking.

dishcloth: see RAG.

dishearten: see DISCOURAGE; DISMAY; SADDEN.

disheartened: see JOYLESS.

dishonest: see CROOKED; FALSE; ROTTEN; TREACHEROUS; UNFAIR; UNFAITHFUL.

dishonesty: see TREACHERY.

dishonor: see BLEMISH; DISGRACE; HUMILIATION; SCANDAL; SHAME; VIOLATION.

dishonorable: see DISGRACEFUL.

dishrag: see RAG.

disillusion: see DISAPPOINT.

disinclination: see RELUCTANCE.

disinfected: see SANITARY.

disintegrate: see CRUMBLE; DECAY; DISSOLVE; MELT.

disintegration: see SEPARATION.

disjoin: see PART.

disk: see CHIP; CIRCLE; RECORD; WHEEL.

dislike *v.* disfavor, RESENT, AVOID, shun, detest.

— n.: see DISAPPROVAL; GRUDGE; OBJECTION; RELUCTANCE.

dislodge: see BUDGE.

disloyal: see FALSE; TREACHEROUS; UNFAITHFUL.

disloyalty: see TREACHERY; TREASON.

dismal: see CHEERLESS; GLOOMY; SAD; SULLEN.

dismantle: see DEMOLISH; WRECK.

dismay *v.* TROUBLE, UPSET, dishearten, FRIGHTEN, appall.
— n. discouragement, DISTRESS, FEAR, ALARM, apprehension.

dismember: see CARVE.

dismiss *v.* RELEASE, DISCARD, REJECT, DISCHARGE, lay off.

dismissal: see ELIMINATION; REMOVAL.

disobedience *n.* mutiny, REVOLT, defiance, insubordination, disregard, VIOLATION, noncompliance.

disobedient *adj.* insubordinate, revolutionary, malcontent, CONTRARY, uncompliant, RESISTANT, disorderly.

disobey: see VIOLATE.

disorder *n.* malfunction, FAULT, irregularity, jumble, MESS. See also AILMENT.
— v.: see DISTURB; MESS.

disordered: see IRREGULAR.

disorderly: see DISOBEDIENT; IRREGULAR; MESSY; MUDDY; ROWDY.

disorganize: see MUSS.

disown: see SHED.

disparagement: see SCANDAL.

disparate: see DIFFERENT; UNEVEN.

disparity: see DIFFERENCE.

dispassionate: see COOL.

dispatch *v.* send away, dispose of, TRANSMIT, MAIL, SHIP, FORWARD.
— n. COMMUNICATION, MESSAGE, BULLETIN, NEWS.

dispel: see RESOLVE.

dispensary: see HOSPITAL.

dispensing: see ADMINISTRATION.

disperse: see BROADCAST; RADIATE; SCATTER; SPREAD.

displace: see MISLAY; REMOVE; TRANSPLANT.

displacement: see SUBSTITUTION.

display *v.* EXHIBIT, PRESENT, SHOW, EXPOSE, flaunt, show off.
— n. exhibit, SHOW, exposition, array, PRESENTATION, ADVERTISEMENT.

displease: see ANNOY; IRRITATE; OFFEND.

displeased: see DISCONTENTED; UNSATISFIED.

displeasing: see UGLY.

displeasure: see ANGER; DISAPPROVAL; DISCONTENT; IRRITATION.

disposal: see DISTRIBUTION.

dispose *v.* ARRANGE, LOCATE, USE, REMOVE, SELL, DISCARD.

disposed: see PARTIAL.

dispose of: see DISPATCH.

disposition *n.* ARRANGEMENT, makeup, INCLINATION, HUMOR, TEMPER.

dispossess: see DEPRIVE.

disproportioned: see MISSHAPEN; UNEQUAL.

disputable: see QUESTIONABLE.

dispute *v.* ARGUE, DEBATE, QUARREL, contradict, controvert.
— n. controversy, ARGUMENT, DIFFERENCE, FEUD, COMMOTION.

disquiet: see UPSET; WORRY.

disquisition: see SPEECH.

disregard: see DISOBEDIENCE; FORGET; NEGLECT; OMISSION; OMIT; OVERLOOK; VIOLATE; VIOLATION.

disremember: see FORGET.

disreputable: see DISGRACEFUL; NOTORIOUS.

disrepute: see DISGRACE.

disrespect: see RUDENESS.

disrespectful: see FRESH; IMPOLITE.

disrobe: see STRIP; UNDRESS.

disrupt *v.* UPSET, DISTURB, breach, INTERFERE, INTRUDE.

dissatisfaction: see DISAPPOINTMENT; DISCONTENT.

dissatisfied: see DISCONTENTED; UNSATISFIED.

dissatisfy: see DISAPPOINT; SHAME.

dissect: see SLICE.

disseminate: see BROADCAST; CIRCULATE; SCATTER; SEED; SOW; SPREAD.

dissension: see DISAGREEMENT.

dissent: see DIFFER; NO; PROTEST.

dissenter: see REBEL.

dissertation: see PAPER.

dissimilar: see DIFFERENT; UNLIKE; VARIOUS.

dissipate: see DISAPPEAR; WASTE.

dissolution: see DIVORCE.

dissolve v. 1 (the solution dissolved) liquefy, disintegrate, break down, EVAPORATE, FADE; 2 (to dissolve a committee) annul, DISCONTINUE, ELIMINATE, eradicate.

dissuade: see CAUTION; DISCOURAGE.

distance n. SEPARATION, MEASURE, remoteness, SPACE, DIFFERENCE, horizon, aloofness, RESERVE.

distant a. REMOTE, separated, FAR, faraway, far-off.

distaste: see DISGUST; REVOLT.

distasteful: see UNPLEASANT.

distill: see CONDENSE; EVAPORATE; EXTRACT.

distillation: see EXTRACT.

distinct adj. 1 (two distinct theories) UNLIKE, DIFFERENT, SEPARATE; 2 (a distinct advantage) CLEAR, discernible, VISIBLE, DEFINITE, CERTAIN.

distinction n. DIFFERENCE, PECULIARITY, QUALITY, uniqueness, prominence. See also ELEGANCE.

distinctive: see CHARACTERISTIC; EXCELLENT; NOTABLE; SPECIAL.

distinctively: see ORIGINALLY.

distinctly adv. PRECISELY, CLEARLY, DEFINITELY, SHARPLY, noticeably.

distinctness: see RELIEF.

distinguish v. discriminate, discern, DETECT, IDENTIFY.

distinguished adj. NOTED, illustrious, esteemed, CELEBRATED, DISTINCT, CONSPICUOUS, UNIQUE.

distort: see SLANT; STRETCH; TORTURE; TWIST; WARP; WRENCH.

distorted: see DEFORMED.

distortion: see TWIST; WRENCH.

distract v. OCCUPY, divert, detract, CONFUSE, MISLEAD, perplex, DISTURB.

distracted: see ABSENT-MINDED.

distracting: see BOTHERSOME.

distraction n. CONFUSION, COMPLICATION, bewilderment, DISORDER, DIVISION, COMMOTION, agitation.

distress v. afflict, DISTURB, UPSET, GRIEVE, TROUBLE.
— n. ANXIETY, anguish, SUFFERING, PAIN, WOE, worry.

distressed: see SORE; SUFFERING; UNHAPPY; UPSET.

distressing: see PAINFUL; PITIFUL; TROUBLESOME.

distribute v. apportion, ISSUE, DIVIDE, RATION, dole, sow.

distribution n. allotment, dividing, apportionment, rationing, ALLOWANCE, assigning, disposal.

district n. VICINITY, LOCALITY, AREA, precinct, SECTION, sector, NEIGHBORHOOD, DEPARTMENT, COMMUNITY.

distrust v. DOUBT, MISTRUST, SUSPECT.
— n. SUSPICION, disbelief, DOUBT, misgiving, UNCERTAINTY.

distrusting: see SUSPICIOUS.

disturb v. UPSET, disorder, inconvenience, TROUBLE, ANNOY, INTERRUPT.

disturbance n. INTERRUPTION, molestation, DISORDER, COMMOTION, DISPUTE, QUARREL, uprising.

disturbed: see SHAKEN; UNEASY; UPSET.

disturbing: see ALARMING; TROUBLESOME.

disunite: see DISCONNECT; DIVORCE.

ditch n. TRENCH, excavation, gully, DRAIN, CANAL, moat.
— v. ABANDON, DESERT, LEAVE, jilt.

dither: see FLAP.

ditty: see CAROL.

diva: see SINGER.

divan: see COUCH; SOFA.

dive *v.* PLUNGE, SUBMERGE, fathom, SOUND.
— *n.:* see PLUNGE.

diverge: see DIFFER; DISAGREE; VARY.

diverse: see ASSORTED; DIFFERENT; MANY;
MISCELLANEOUS; SEVERAL; UNLIKE; VARIOUS.

diversely: see VARIOUSLY.

diversification: see VARIETY.

diversified: see MISCELLANEOUS.

diversion: see FUN; HOBBY; RELAXATION; SPORT.

diversity: see VARIETY.

divert: see AMUSE; DISTRACT; ENTERTAIN; SWITCH.

divide *v.* PART, SPLIT, halve, CUT, branch,
PARCEL, dole, divvy up.
— *n.:* see CANYON.

dividend: see BONUS; INTEREST; MORE.

divider: see PANEL.

dividers: see COMPASS.

dividing: see DISTRIBUTION; PARTING.

divination: see PREDICTION.

divine *adj.* godlike, celestial, sublime,
superhuman, EXCELLENT, superlative.
— *v.:* see PREDICT.

divinity: see GOD.

division *n.* **1** *(division and multiplication)*
SEPARATION, DISTRIBUTION, partition; **2** *(a
company division)* SECTION, SHARE, UNIT,
FRACTION, COMPANY.

divorce *n.* SEPARATION, breakup, dissolution.
— *v.* disunite, sever, SPLIT, DISSOLVE.

divulge: see ANNOUNCE; REVEAL; SPREAD;
UNFOLD.

divvy up: see DIVIDE.

dizzy *adj.* light-headed, giddy, unsteady, flighty,
harebrained, woozy.

do *v.* ACT, FUNCTION, PERFORM, EFFECT, carry out,
FULFILL, SERVE, suffice.

dobbin: see HORSE.

docility: see OBEDIENCE.

dock *n.* pier, landing, WHARF, platform.

doctor *n.* PHYSICIAN, practitioner, healer,

SPECIALIST, surgeon, veterinarian, SCHOLAR,
PROFESSOR.
— *v.* TREAT, ATTEND, PRESCRIBE, CURE, medicate,
MEND, REPAIR, OPERATE. See also JUGGLE;
REVISE.

doctoring: see TREATMENT.

doctrine: see GOSPEL; POLICY; PRINCIPLE.

document *n.* STATEMENT, EVIDENCE, CERTIFICATE,
INSTRUMENT, DEED, RECORD, CHARTER,
MANUSCRIPT.
— *v.* corroborate, SUPPORT, PROVE, SHOW.

dodge *v.* evade, elude, AVOID, DUCK, shirk, skirt.

doer: see ACTOR; MAKER; WORKER.

dogcart: see CART.

dogma: see BELIEF.

dogmatic: see NARROW; NARROW-MINDED.

dogmatism: see DETERMINATION.

doing: see DEED.

doldrums: see CALM; SADNESS.

dole: see DISTRIBUTE; DIVIDE.

doleful: see MOURNFUL.

doll *n.* **1** *(a child's doll)* mannequin, puppet,
figurine, marionette, plaything; **2** *(guys and
dolls)* GIRL, cutie, BEAUTY, peach, DARLING.

dollar: see BILL; BUCK; COIN.

domain: see AREA; EMPIRE; KINGDOM; PROVINCE;
SPHERE; SUBJECT; TERRITORY; WORLD.

dome *n.* cupola, VAULT, hemisphere, TOP, HEAD,
rotunda.

domestic *adj.* LOCAL, indigenous, NATIVE,
HOMELY, homey, FAMILIAR, INTERNAL.
— *n.:* see MAID; SERVANT.

domesticate: see BREAK; TAME.

domesticated: see TAME.

domicile: see HOME; HOUSE; RESIDENCE.

dominant: see INFLUENTIAL; MAIN; MAJOR;
PRIMARY; SUPERIOR; SUPREME.

dominate *v.* RULE, REIGN, DICTATE, domineer,
predominate.

dominating: see POSSESSIVE.

domination: see CONQUEST; LEADERSHIP; MIGHT;
POWER; YOKE.

domineer: see DOMINATE.

domineering: see MASTERFUL.

dominion: see EMPIRE; KINGDOM; REIGN; YOKE.

don: see CLOTHE; WEAR.

donate *v.* GIVE, bestow, CONTRIBUTE, GRANT, VOLUNTEER, OFFER, bequeath.

donation *n.* CONTRIBUTION, GIFT, GRANT, AWARD, offering, PRESENT, allocation.

done: see ACCOMPLISHED; OFF; PAST.

donkey *n.* ASS, burro, jackass, FOOL, blockhead.

donor: see PATRON.

doodle: see WRITE.

doom *n.* FATE, predestination, RUIN, CONDEMNATION.
 — *v.* CONDEMN, SENTENCE, CURSE.

door *n.* portal, EXIT, ENTRY, hatch, access, PASSAGE, ENTRANCE.

doorbell: see BELL.

doorkeeper: see JANITOR; USHER.

door key: see KEY.

doorman: see PORTER.

dope: see DRUG; POT; SAP.

dopey: see DRUNK.

dormant: see ASLEEP; POTENTIAL

dosage: see CAPSULE.

dose: see DRINK; SHOT.

dot *n.* PERIOD, POINT, SPECK, tittle.
 — *v.* punctuate, SPOT, stipple, spatter, freckle.

double *adj.* TWIN, twofold, DUPLICATE, dual, binary.
 — *n.* TWIN, counterpart, facsimile, DUPLICATE, MATCH, SUBSTITUTE, stand-in.
 — *v.* DUPLICATE, MATCH, MULTIPLY, REPEAT, SUBSTITUTE.

double-cross: see BETRAY; SING.

doubling: see DUPLICATION.

doubly: see TWICE.

doubt *v.* MISTRUST, SUSPECT, WONDER, query, PUZZLE.
 — *n.* indecision, HESITATION, UNCERTAINTY, SUSPICION, misgiving, DISTRUST, unbelief, question.

doubtful *adj.* UNCERTAIN, unsure, puzzling, dubious, ambiguous, QUESTIONABLE.

doubting: see SUSPICIOUS; UNCERTAIN.

doubtless *adv.* undoubtedly, PROBABLY, SURELY, CERTAINLY, unquestionably, POSITIVELY, indisputably.

douche: see BATH.

dough: see BATTER; MONEY.

douse: see QUENCH; DIP; SOAK.

dove: see LAMB.

dowel: see BOLT.

down *adv., prep.* earthward, DOWNWARD, downhill, BELOW, UNDER.
 — *adj.:* see BLUE.
 — *v.:* see FLOOR; TACKLE.
 — *n.:* see HAIR.

downcast: see DOWNHEARTED; MOURNFUL.

downfall: see COLLAPSE; DESCENT; DESTRUCTION.

downgrade: see DEGRADE; DOWNWARD; HUMBLE.

downhearted *adj.* dejected, SAD, discouraged, downcast.

downhill: see BACKWARD; DOWN.

downpour: see TORRENT.

downstairs: see BENEATH.

downward *adv., adj.* earthward, downgrade, descending.

downy: see FUZZY; SOFT.

doze: see NAP; SLEEP; SLUMBER.

dozing: see ASLEEP.

drab: see GRAY; NEUTRAL.

draft *n.* **1** (*a preliminary draft*) OUTLINE, SKETCH, PROPOSAL, prospectus, money order; **2** (*a cold draft*) CURRENT, BREEZE, FLOW; **3** (*the military draft*) conscription, induction, SELECTION. See also CHECK.
 — *v.* **1** (*to draft a plan*) OUTLINE, SKETCH, DRAW; **2** (*they draft young men*) recruit, SELECT, induct.

draftsman: see ARCHITECT.

drafty: see WINDY.

drag *v.* **1** (*he dragged the sack*) HAUL, PULL, TOW, DRAW; **2** (*time drags on*) dawdle, DELAY, LAG,

MOPE; **3** (*the leash dragged*) TRAIL, CURB, HINDER, burden, DELAY.
— *n.* **1** (*the drag of the anchor*) restraint, impediment, hindrance; **2** (*the party was a drag*) BORE, bother, BOREDOM. See also PUFF.

dragnet: see NET.

drain *v.* DRAW, TAP, empty, CONSUME, EXHAUST, deplete.
— *n.* outflow, effluent, WASTE, OUTLET, conduit, sewer.

drama *n.* PLAY, dramatization, TRAGEDY, THEATER, SHOW, PRODUCTION.

dramatic *adj.* moving, climactic, exciting, theatric.

dramatics: see THEATER.

dramatization: see DRAMA.

drape: see CLOTHE; CURTAIN; HANG.

drapery: see CURTAIN.

drastic: see EXTREME.

drastically: see EXTREMELY.

draw *v.* **1** (*filth draws vermin*) ATTRACT, PULL, DRAG, EXTRACT, WITHDRAW; **2** (*he draws with skill*) SKETCH, depict, DESCRIBE, DRAFT. See also BREATHE.
— *n.* PULL, magnetism, SELECTION, LOT, tie, stalemate.

draw back: see RETREAT.

drawback: see CATCH; DEFECT; DISADVANTAGE.

drawers: see CHEST.

drawing *n.* SKETCH, OUTLINE, PICTURE, DESIGN, ILLUSTRATION, REPRESENTATION.

drawl: see ACCENT; TALK.

drawn: see EVEN.

drawn-out: see LENGTHY; LONG.

draw out: see STRETCH.

draw up: see CONTRACT.

dread *v.* FEAR, FRET, cringe, ANTICIPATE, TREMBLE.
— *n.* awe, FEAR, HORROR, ALARM, FRIGHT, apprehension.

dreadful *adj.* AWFUL, FRIGHTFUL, formidable, FEARFUL, dire.

dreadfully: see TERRIBLY.

dream *n.* ILLUSIÓN, VISION, fantasy, FANCY, hallucination, aspiration.

— *v.* FANCY, hallucinate, visualize.

dreaming: see ABSENT-MINDED.

dreamy: see IMAGINARY.

dreary: see CHEERLESS; DARK; DEAD; MONOTONOUS.

dredge: see POWDER.

drench: see DROWN; POUR; SOAK; SWAMP; WATER; WET.

drenched: see WET.

dress *v.* CLOTHE, garb, attire, ROBE, OUTFIT, GROOM, BANDAGE.
— *n.* CLOTHES, GARMENT, apparel, SUIT, COSTUME, WARDROBE.

dresser: see BUREAU.

dressing: see BANDAGE; TOILET.

dress up: see BEAUTIFY.

dressy: see PERKY.

dribble *v.* LEAK, DRIP, TRICKLE, drizzle, DROP, SPOUT, squirt.

dried: see DRY.

drier: see TOWEL.

drift *v.* FLOAT, WANDER, gravitate, TEND.
— *n.* DIRECTION, TENDENCY, INCLINATION, snowdrift.

drifter *n.* vagrant, hobo, bum, transient, wanderer, rambler, roamer, floater, LOAFER.

drifting: see ADRIFT.

drill *n.* **1** (*an electric drill*) borer, auger, gimlet; **2** (*a marching drill*) EXERCISE, TRAINING, DISCIPLINE, REPETITION.
— *v.* **1** (*to drill a hole*) BORE, PIERCE, PENETRATE, perforate; **2** (*to drill students*) TRAIN, DISCIPLINE, EXERCISE. See also ACCUSTOM.

drilled: see PRACTICED.

drink *v.* SIP, imbibe, ABSORB, guzzle.
— *n.* BEVERAGE, sip, dose, potion, LIQUOR, GLASS, SHOT, cocktail, highball.

drinker: see DRUNK.

drinks: see REFRESHMENTS.

drip *v.* DRIBBLE, TRICKLE, LEAK, WEEP, SHED.
— *n.*: see DROP; LEAK.

dripping: see LEAK; RUNNING; WET.

drive *v.* **1** (*to drive a car*) STEER, RUN, RIDE, chauffeur, HANDLE, CONDUCT, LEAD; **2** (*to drive*

the ball) FORCE, propel, PUSH, COMPEL, prod.
— *n.* **1** *(to take a drive)* TRIP, RIDE, TOUR, outing,
SPIN, RUN, driveway, ROAD; **2** *(that person has
lots of drive)* ENERGY, VIGOR, PUSH, initiative,
PRESSURE, CAMPAIGN.

drive out: see CHASE.

driver *n.* chauffeur, CONDUCTOR, coachman,
engineer, motorman, drover.

driveway: see DRIVE.

drizzle: see DRIBBLE; MIST; MOISTURE; RAIN;
SPRINKLE.

drone: see BUZZ; HUM; MURMUR.

droning: see WHINE.

drool: see SLOBBER.

droop *v.* SINK, sag, DANGLE, SETTLE, WEAKEN,
WILT, WITHER.

droopy: see SLACK; TIRED.

drop *n.* **1** *(put in just a drop)* droplet, drip,
BUBBLE, BIT, DASH; **2** *(a fifty-foot drop)* FALL,
HEIGHT, DESCENT, DECLINE, slump.
— *v.* DRIBBLE, DRIP, TRICKLE, FALL, TUMBLE,
SINK, DIP, depreciate. See also FLOOR.

drop in: see CALL.

droplet: see BEAD; DROP; TEAR.

dropout: see MISFIT.

drove: see HERD; PACK.

drover: see DRIVER.

drown *v.* suffocate, asphyxiate, stifle, muffle,
deaden, OVERWHELM, SWAMP, OVERPOWER,
drench, extinguish.

drowse: see NOD.

drowsy: see SLEEPY; TIRED.

drub: see THUMP.

drudge: see TOIL.

drudgery: see GRIND; LABOR; SLAVERY; TOIL;
WORK.

drug *n.* narcotic, anesthetic, MEDICINE, painkiller,
REMEDY, dope.
— *v.* anesthetize, benumb, deaden, stupefy,
dope, knock out.

drum: see BEAT; CAN; FLUTTER; HAMMER; TAP.

drunk *adj.* drunken, alcoholic, inebriated,
intoxicated, soused, LOADED, boozy, tipsy,
tippled, groggy, dopey.

— *n.* drunkard, drinker, alcoholic, lush, rummy,
barfly, toper.

drunkard: see DRUNK.

drunken: see DRUNK.

dry *adj.* **1** *(a dry towel)* dried, waterless,
moistureless, dehydrated, arid, parched,
shriveled, sear, STALE, watertight, waterproof,
thirsty; **2** *(a dry lecture)* DULL, boring, tedious,
tiresome, uninteresting.
— *v.* dehydrate, EVAPORATE, dehumidify, swab,
towel, DRAIN, sear, BAKE, parch, SPONGE.

dry ice: see ICE.

dryness: see DULLNESS; THIRST.

dry out: see CHAP.

dry run: see TEST.

dry up: see WITHER.

dual: see DOUBLE.

dub: see TERM.

dubious: see DOUBTFUL; FISHY; SUSPICIOUS;
UNCERTAIN.

dubloon: see COIN.

duck *v.* STOOP, DODGE, lurch, PLUNGE.

duct: see CANAL; CHANNEL; CONDUCTOR; PIPE;
TUBE.

ductile: see SOFT.

dud: see BLANK.

due *adj.* owed, OWING, unpaid, payable, JUST,
FAIR, merited, expected, scheduled.
— *n.* CLAIM, PRIVILEGE, RIGHT.

duel: see COMBAT; FENCE; TOURNAMENT.

dues: see DEBT; DIFFERENCE; FEE.

due to: see BECAUSE; FOR; FROM.

duffle: see SACK.

dugout: see CELLAR.

dull *adj.* BLUNT, dulled, blunted, obtuse, STUPID,
dimwitted, murky, DIM, DARK, boring,
uninteresting, tedious, LIFELESS, DEAD,
depressing, SLEEPY, uninspired, vapid, mousy.

dulled: see DULL.

dullness *n.* bluntness, STUPIDITY, obscurity,
apathy, dryness, BOREDOM.

dumb: see SPEECHLESS; SOUNDLESS; STUPID.

dumbfound: see AMAZE; SURPRISE.

dumbness: see STUPIDITY.

dummy: see FORM.

dump *v.* unload, DISMISS, DROP, EXPEL, empty.
  – *n.* GARBAGE, RUBBISH, junkyard.

dumpy: see CHUBBY.

dunce: see FOOL; HALF-WIT; IDIOT; MORON.

dungarees: see OVERALLS.

dupe: see CHEAT; FOOL; OUTWIT; TRICK.

duplicate *n.* COPY, DOUBLE, facsimile, repeat,
  reproduction, IMITATION, replica.
  – *v.* DOUBLE, COPY, counterfeit, REPRODUCE,
  REPEAT, IMITATE, mimic.
  – *adj.* IDENTICAL, SAME, DOUBLE, twofold,
  copied, reproduced.

duplication *n.* doubling, IMITATION,
  reproduction, REPETITION, transcription,
  TRANSCRIPT, replication, REPRESENTATION.

durability: see IMMORTALITY; STRENGTH.

durable: see LASTING; PERMANENT; STRONG.

duration: see ETERNITY; LENGTH; PERIOD; TIME.

during *prep.* WHILE, UNTIL, pending,
  THROUGHOUT, WITHIN.

dusk *n.* EVENING, TWILIGHT, sundown, sunset,
  gloaming, nightfall, DARKNESS, DIMNESS,
  shadiness.

duskiness: see DIMNESS.

dust *n.* POWDER, DIRT, SAND, GRIME, smut, soot,
  SOIL, EARTH, GROUND, GRIT, ash, particles.
  – *v.* POWDER, SPRINKLE, CLEAN, WIPE.

duster: see MOP.

dusty *adj.* powdery, clouded, GRAY, grimy, DIRTY.

dutiful: see OBEDIENT.

dutifulness: see OBEDIENCE.

duty *n.* **1** *(to do one's duty)* OBLIGATION, PART,
  TASK, ASSIGNMENT, SERVICE, RESPONSIBILITY,
  REQUIREMENT, FUNCTION, COMMISSION, TRUST,
  CHARGE, OFFICE; **2** *(a duty on imports)* TAX, FEE,
  levy, TOLL, customs, excise.

dwarf *n.* midget, runt, pygmy, gnome, elf.
  – *v.* overshadow, SURPASS, stunt, minimize.

dwell *v.* LIVE, RESIDE, INHABIT, OCCUPY, STAY,
  LODGE. See also NAG.

dweller: see INHABITANT; RESIDENT.

dwelling *n.* HOUSE, HOME, RESIDENCE, BUILDING,
  ADDRESS, APARTMENT.

dwindle: see LESSEN; SINK.

dye *n.* COLOR, STAIN, pigment, TINT.
  – *v.* COLOR, STAIN, TINT.

dying: see DEATH; PERISHABLE.

dynamic: see EFFICIENT.

dynamite: see BLAST; EXPLOSIVE.

dynamo: see ENGINE; GENERATOR; MOTOR.

E

each *adj.* EVERY, SINGLE, RESPECTIVE, PARTICULAR,
  exclusive.
  – *pron.* each one, EVERYONE, ALL.
  – *adv.* APIECE, each one.

each one: see EACH.

eager *adj.* EARNEST, fervent, spirited, ZEALOUS,
  AMBITIOUS, PROMPT, KEEN, ENTHUSIASTIC,
  desiring.

eagerness: see AMBITION; ENTHUSIASM; HUNGER;
  IMPATIENCE.

earlier: see ABOVE; BEFORE; EARLY; ELDER;
  FOREGONE; PAST; PRECEDING; PREVIOUS; PRIOR.

early *adj.* beforehand, ADVANCED, PREMATURE,
  untimely, PREVIOUS, earlier, FORMER, RECENT.
  – *adv.* IMMEDIATELY, presently, DIRECTLY,
  PROMPTLY, SOON, SHORTLY.

earmark: see BRAND.

earn *v.* GAIN, clear, REALIZE, PROFIT, NET,
  COLLECT, MERIT, DESERVE, ACHIEVE.

earnest *adj.* SINCERE, EAGER, SERIOUS, fervent,
  intent, HEARTY, determined.

earnestly: see HEARTILY.

earnestness: see ENTHUSIASM.

earnings *pl. n.* PROFIT, WAGES, receipts, gains,
  REVENUE, INCOME, SALARY, pay.

earrings: see JEWELRY.

earth *n.* **1** *(the planet Earth)* WORLD, planet, GLOBE,
  SPHERE, SURFACE; **2** *(earth mixed with rock and
  sand)* SOIL, GROUND, DIRT, DUST, LAND.

earthly *adj.* WORLDLY, EVERYDAY, temporal,
  carnal, global, planetary.

earthward: see DOWN; DOWNWARD.

ease *n.* QUIET, PEACE, CALM, RELAXATION, REST,
  COMFORT, CONTENTMENT, ENJOYMENT,
  CONVENIENCE, readiness, expertness, facility,
  naturalness, nonchalance.

— v. COMFORT, LESSEN, RELEASE, SOOTHE, REDUCE, RELIEVE, lighten, alleviate, facilitate, expedite, simplify.

easily: see FREE; READILY; SIMPLY; SMOOTHLY.

easy *adj.* SIMPLE, ELEMENTARY, uncomplicated, CONVENIENT, HANDY, SMOOTH, untroubled, MILD, COMFORTABLE, manageable.

easygoing: see CASUAL; FREE; OFFHAND.

eat *v.* CONSUME, CHEW, SWALLOW, DEVOUR, TAKE, DINE, banquet, FEAST, lunch, breakfast, rust, corrode.

eatable: see EDIBLE.

eats: see FOOD.

eavesdrop: see LISTEN; TAP.

ebb: see CONTRACT; RETREAT.

ebony: see BLACK.

eccentric: see CHARACTER; CRANK; GUY; IRREGULAR; ODD; PECULIAR; STRANGE.

eccentricity: see ODDITY; PECULIARITY.

ecclesiastic: see PASTOR; PRIEST.

echo *n.* REPETITION, rebound, repeat, REPLY, REACTION, REFLECTION, repercussion, IMITATION.
— v. RESOUND, RING, reverberate, VIBRATE, rebound, REFLECT, REPEAT, REPLY, RESPOND, IMITATE.

economic: see COMMERCIAL; ECONOMICAL.

economical *adj.* economic, INEXPENSIVE, CHEAP, THRIFTY, moderate, LOW, SPARING, saving.

economically: see PRACTICALLY.

economics: see COMMERCE; FINANCE.

economize: see HUSBAND; SAVE; STRETCH.

economy *n.* **1** *(the national economy)* SYSTEM, ORDER, MANAGEMENT, ADMINISTRATION; **2** *(economy in gas mileage)* saving, THRIFT, CARE.

ecstasy: see HEAVEN; JOY.

ecstatic: see HAPPY; HEAVENLY.

edge *n.* **1** *(the edge of the woods)* BORDER, BRIM, MARGIN, BOUNDARY, TIP, extremity, brink, sharpness; **2** *(to gain an edge on your opponent)* ADVANTAGE, POSITION, upper hand.
— v. **1** *(to edge a skirt)* TRIM, border; **2** *(to edge through a crowd)* inch, CRAWL, PUSH.

edging: see HEM; MARGINAL; TRIM.

edible *adj.* eatable, nourishing, unspoiled.

edict: see COMMAND.

edifice: see BUILDING; STRUCTURE.

edit *v.* REVISE, CORRECT, rectify, IMPROVE, SELECT, ADAPT, rewrite.

edition: see ISSUE; PRINTING; PUBLICATION; REVISION; SPECIAL.

editor *n.* journalist, WRITER, compiler, publisher, reader, SUPERVISOR, proofreader, reviser.

editorial *n.* ARTICLE, STATEMENT, COMMENT, manifesto.

educate *v.* TEACH, TRAIN, INSTRUCT, school, enlighten.

educated: see LEARNED; LITERARY.

education *n.* LEARNING, INSTRUCTION, schooling, TRAINING, KNOWLEDGE, INFORMATION, background, CULTURE, BREEDING.

educational *adj.* instructive, instructional, INFORMATIVE, coeducational, scholastic, ACADEMIC, vocational, PRACTICAL.

educator *n.* TEACHER, trainer, INSTRUCTOR, coach, informant, mentor, GUIDE.

effect *n.* RESULT, CONSEQUENCE, IMPRESSION, PRODUCT, PERFORMANCE, OUTCOME, IMPORTANCE.
— v. EXECUTE, PERFORM, ACCOMPLISH, CAUSE, MAKE, bring about, DISCHARGE, ACHIEVE.

effective *adj.* EFFICIENT, PRACTICAL, telling, impressive, effectual, operative, PRODUCTIVE, functioning.

effectiveness: see EFFICIENCY.

effects: see FURNITURE.

effectual: see EFFECTIVE.

effervesce: see FOAM; SPARKLE.

efficiency *n.* competency, capability, POWER, ABILITY, FITNESS, usefulness, effectiveness, readiness.

efficient *adj.* competent, CAPABLE, APT, FIT, ABLE, talented, skillful, CLEVER, EFFECTIVE, operative, USEFUL, serviceable, proficient, ORDERLY, SYSTEMATIC, saving, THRIFTY, dynamic.

efficiently: see SYSTEMATICALLY.

effluent: see DRAIN.

effort *n.* EXERTION, TOIL, ATTEMPT, ENDEAVOR, STRUGGLE, TRIAL.

effortless: see SIMPLE.

ego: see SELF.

egoism: see GREED; SELF.

egoistic: see GREEDY.

egotism: see PRIDE.

egotistic: see PROUD; SELFISH; VAIN.

either *adj., pron.* ONE, OTHER, EACH, BOTH.
— *adv.* ALSO, TOO.

eject: see FIRE.

ejection: see BOOT.

el: see TRAIN.

elaborate *adj.* COMPLEX, complicated, detailed, intricate, ELEGANT, LUXURIOUS, ornate, ornamented, decorated, DECORATIVE.
— *v.*: see CLARIFY; DETAIL.

elaboration: see DEVELOPMENT.

elapse: see GO.

elastic: see ADJUSTABLE; FLEXIBLE; LIMBER; SOFT.

elasticity: see SPRING; STRETCH.

elated: see JOYFUL.

elation: see HAPPINESS; PLEASURE.

elbow *v.* PUSH, jostle, SHOVE.
— *n.* joint, bend, HOOK.

elbowroom: see CLEARANCE.

elder *adj.* older, SENIOR, ranking, earlier.
— *n.* SENIOR, SUPERIOR, VETERAN, predecessor, OFFICER.

elderly: see AGED; OLD.

elect *v.* SELECT, CHOOSE, VOTE, PICK, PREFER.
— *adj.* SELECT, CHOSEN, elected, CHOICE, privileged, saved.

elected: see ELECT.

election *n.* VOTE, SELECTION, referendum, POLL, ADOPTION, CHOICE.

electorate: see PUBLIC.

electric *adj.* electrical, power-driven, electrifying, stirring.

electrical: see ELECTRIC.

electricity: see CURRENT; JUICE.

electrify: see CHARGE; STIR.

electrifying: see ELECTRIC.

electrocute: see EXECUTE.

electrocution: see EXECUTION.

electron: see MOLECULE.

elegance *n.* refinement, GRACE, POLISH, TASTE, distinction, LUXURY, EXCELLENCE.

elegant *adj.* refined, GRACEFUL, polished, tasteful, LUXURIOUS, DAINTY, EXCELLENT, FINE, cultivated, CHOICE, nobby.

element *n.* component, constituent, MATERIAL, MATTER, SUBSTANCE, TRACE, BIT.

elemental: see ELEMENTARY; FUNDAMENTAL.

elementary *adj.* BASIC, elemental, SIMPLE, EASY, introductory, simplified, uncomplicated, FUNDAMENTAL, PRIMARY, PRIMITIVE.

elevate *v.* RAISE, LIFT, ERECT, HOIST, exalt, DIGNIFY, PROMOTE, upgrade, heighten, CHEER, escalate.

elevated: see HIGH; HILLY; LOFTY.

elevation *n.* HEIGHT, ALTITUDE, loftiness, boost, UPLIFT.

elevator: see HOIST.

elf: see DWARF; FAIRY; SPIRIT.

eliminate *v.* ABOLISH, REMOVE, ERASE, exterminate, eradicate, delete, exclude, DISCARD, leave out, OMIT, EXPEL, excrete, liquidate.

elimination *n.* abolition, REMOVAL, riddance, extermination, eradication, exclusion, dismissal, rejection, erasure, deletion, OMISSION.

elite: see CREAM.

elongate: see EXTEND; LENGTHEN; STRETCH.

elongated: see LONG.

eloquent: see EXPRESSIVE.

else *adj.* OTHER, DIFFERENT.
— *adv.* OTHERWISE, differently, BESIDES.

elsewhere *adj.* SOMEWHERE, NOWHERE, AWAY.

elude: see AVOID; DODGE; ESCAPE.

elusive: see DIFFICULT; SLIPPERY.

emancipate: see LIBERATE.

emancipation: see INDEPENDENCE; LIBERTY; SALVATION.

embankment: see BANK; DAM.

embargo: see BLOCKADE; PROHIBITION.

embark: see BOARD.

embarkation: see DEPARTURE.

embarrass *v.* abash, CONFUSE, SHAME, mortify, HINDER, TROUBLE, ENTANGLE.

embarrassed: see ASHAMED.

embarrassing: see DISGRACEFUL.

embarrassment *n.* CONFUSION, self-consciousness, SHAME, mortification, TROUBLE, uneasiness, AWKWARDNESS.

embed: see ANCHOR.

embellish: see BEAUTIFY.

embellishing: see DECORATIVE.

embezzle: see STEAL; SWINDLE; THIEVE.

embezzler: see SWINDLER.

emblazon: see INSCRIBE.

emblem *n.* insignia, SIGN, SYMBOL, TOKEN, BADGE, MARK, MEDAL.

embody: see COVER.

embolism: see CLOT.

emboss: see IMPRESS.

embrace *v.* HUG, CLASP, HOLD, SQUEEZE, CARESS, KISS, CONTAIN, INCLUDE, COVER, ENCOMPASS, ADOPT, ACCEPT.
— *n.*: see CLASP; GRASP; HUG; KISS.

embryo: see BUD; GERM.

emcee: see CHAIRMAN.

emend: see BETTER; REVISE.

emendation: see REVISION.

emerald: see GREEN.

emerge *v.* come out, exit, STREAM, gush, RISE, come forth, loom, APPEAR, surface.

emergence: see APPEARANCE.

emergency *n.* crisis, NECESSITY, URGENCY, ACCIDENT, DIFFICULTY, JAM, MESS.

emigrate: see MIGRATE.

emigration: see EXILE.

eminence: see ALTITUDE; EXCELLENCE; FAME; GLORY; SUPERIORITY.

eminent: see CELEBRATED; EXCELLENT; FAMOUS; GRAND; GREAT; HIGH; IMMORTAL; IMPORTANT; NOTABLE; REMARKABLE.

emissaries: see REPRESENTATION.

emissary: see AMBASSADOR; MESSENGER.

emission: see BEAM; ERUPTION; SIGNAL.

emit: see BREATHE; BROADCAST; ERUPT; ISSUE; PROJECT.

emotion *n.* FEELING, PASSION, SENTIMENT, SENSATION.

emotional *adj.* PASSIONATE, SENTIMENTAL, moving, stirring, demonstrative, ENTHUSIASTIC, TEMPERAMENTAL, hysterical, SENSITIVE, compassionate.

emotions: see PERSONALITY.

empathize: see UNDERLINE.

empathy: see SYMPATHY.

emperor *n.* RULER, KING, sovereign, caesar, czar, kaiser, shah.

emphasis: see ACCENT; INTENSITY; STRESS.

emphasize: see ACCENT; INSIST; PRESS; STRESS.

emphatic: see INSISTENT.

empire *n.* KINGDOM, dominion, GOVERNMENT, RULE, sway, domain, holdings.

employ *n.* hire, EMPLOYMENT, SERVICE.
— *v.* USE, utilize, ADOPT, HIRE, ENGAGE, COMMISSION.

employed: see BUSY.

employee *n.* WORKER, wage earner, LABORER, staffer, helper.

employees: see STAFF.

employer *n.* BOSS, PROPRIETOR, MANAGER.

employment *n.* WORK, OCCUPATION, TRADE, JOB, SERVICE, POSITION, BUSINESS. See also APPLICATION.

emporium: see STORE.

empower: see DELEGATE; ENABLE; ENTITLE; PERMIT; WARRANT.

empress: see MONARCH; QUEEN.

emptiness: see ABSENCE; VACANCY; VACUUM; WILDERNESS.

empty *adj.* VACANT, unoccupied, BLANK, unfilled, void, HOLLOW, insincere, BARREN, vacuous.
— *v.*: see CLEAR; DRAIN; DUMP; EVACUATE; EXHAUST; STRIP.

empty-headed: see FEEBLE-MINDED; IGNORANT.

enable *v.* FURNISH, empower, implement, QUALIFY.

enact: see LEGISLATE; PASS.

enactment: see ADOPTION; LEGISLATION; PASSAGE.

enamel: see PAINT; VARNISH.

encamp: see CAMP.

encampment: see BASE; CAMP; SETTLEMENT.

encase: see BIND.

enchant: see BEWITCH; CHARM; WITCH.

enchanter: see MAGICIAN; WIZARD.

enchanting: see INTERESTING; MAGICAL; TEMPTING.

enchantment: see CHARM; GLAMOUR; MAGIC; ROMANCE.

encircle *v.* SURROUND, RING, ENCLOSE, ENVELOP, FENCE, encompass, comprise.

encircling: see AROUND.

enclose *v.* SURROUND, ENCIRCLE, encompass, COVER, insert, INCLUDE.

enclosure *n.* COMPOUND, YARD, PEN, corral, CAGE, stockade, sty. See also ATTACHMENT; CONTENTS.

encompass: see ENCIRCLE; ENCLOSE; ENVELOP; RANGE; SURROUND.

encore: see TWICE.

encounter *v.* MEET, DISCOVER, EXPERIENCE.
— *n.* MEETING, DISCOVERY, CLASH, COMBAT, skirmish.

encourage *v.* URGE, PROMOTE, INVITE, SUPPORT, INSPIRE, cheer, hearten.

encouragement *n.* urging, PROMOTION, SUPPORT, INVITATION, INSPIRATION.

encouraging: see HOPEFUL; INVITING.

encroach: see BUTT IN; INVADE; TRESPASS.

encumbrance: see JAM; MORTGAGE.

end *n.* **1** *(at the end of the day)* FINISH, CLOSE, termination, completion, CONCLUSION; **2** *(at the end of the road)* TIP, EDGE, LIMIT, BOUNDARY; **3** *(the end justifying the means)* AIM, GOAL, PURPOSE, DESIGN, CONSEQUENCE.
— *v.* CLOSE, HALT, FINISH, ABOLISH, COMPLETE, terminate, CONCLUDE, CEASE, STOP, EXPIRE.

endanger *v.* imperil, jeopardize, EXPOSE, RISK, HAZARD, COMPROMISE.

endeavor *v.* TRY, ATTEMPT, AIM, undertake, STRIVE.
— *n.* UNDERTAKING, ATTEMPT, EFFORT, STRUGGLE, VENTURE, enterprise, TASK, WORK, PROJECT, AFFAIR, PURSUIT.

ended: see OUT.

ending *n.* CONCLUSION, termination, RESULT, CONSEQUENCE, SETTLEMENT, FINISH.

endless *adj.* limitless, CONTINUOUS, perpetual, ETERNAL, UNENDING, INFINITE.

endlessly: see AWAY.

endorse: see APPROVE; LICENSE; SECOND; SIGN; SUBSCRIBE; UPHOLD.

endorsement: see APPROVAL; SEAL; SIGNATURE; YES.

endow: see CONTRIBUTE; ENRICH.

endowment: see CHAIR; FOUNDATION; FUND; INHERITANCE.

endurable: see TOLERABLE.

endurance: see GO; PATIENCE.

endure *v.* **1** *(to endure forever)* LAST, outlast, SURVIVE, REMAIN, STAND, CONTINUE, PERSIST; **2** *(to endure pain)* tolerate, BEAR, undergo, EXPERIENCE, ABIDE BY, SUFFER, STAND.

enduring: see LASTING; LIVING; PERMANENT.

enemy *n.* FOE, archenemy, OPPONENT, antagonist, RIVAL, COMPETITOR.

energetic *adj.* ACTIVE, VIGOROUS, VITAL, LIVELY, QUICK, spirited.

energetically: see FORCIBLY; HARD.

energize: see FUEL.

energy *n.* FORCE, POWER, STRENGTH, MIGHT, VIGOR, SPIRIT, DASH, vim, enterprise, initiative, DRIVE.

enfeeble: see WEAKEN.

enfold: see HUG; WRAP.

enforce *v.* EXECUTE, implement, administer, COMPEL, FORCE.

engage *v.* **1** *(to engage the gears)* interlock, mesh, FASTEN, ATTACH; **2** *(to engage one's attention)* OCCUPY, ATTRACT, HOLD; **3** *(to engage a workman)* HIRE, EMPLOY, RENT, PROMISE, GUARANTEE, AGREE, BIND. See also PLAY.

engaged: see BUSY.

engagement *n.* DATE, APPOINTMENT, ENCOUNTER, CONTEST, BATTLE, CONTRACT, commitment, PROMISE, betrothal, EMPLOYMENT, hire, meshing.

engaging: see ATTRACTIVE; INTERESTING; PLEASING; READABLE; WINNING.

engine *n.* MOTOR, MACHINE, GENERATOR, turbine, transformer, dynamo, locomotive.

engineer: see ARCHITECT; DRIVER.

engineered: see MECHANICAL.

engineering: see ARCHITECTURE.

engrave *v.* PRINT, imprint, INSCRIBE, etch, CUT, CARVE, chisel.

engraving *n.* PRINT, STAMP, reprint, inscription, etching, IMPRESSION.

engross: see ABSORB.

engrossed: see DEEP.

engulf: see ENVELOP.

enhance: see BENEFIT; ENRICH.

enhancement: see PREMIUM.

enigma: see PUZZLE; RIDDLE.

enjoy *v.* LIKE, delight in, RELISH, USE, APPRECIATE.

enjoyable *adj.* PLEASANT, DELIGHTFUL, likeable, satisfying.

enjoyment *n.* **1** *(reading is their greatest enjoyment)* PLEASURE, THRILL, gratification, DELIGHT; **2** *(the enjoyment of a large income)* POSSESSION, USE, occupancy, RIGHT.

enlarge *v.* INCREASE, amplify, EXPAND, EXTEND, BROADEN, MAGNIFY.

enlarged: see GROWN.

enlargement *n.* INCREASE, EXPANSION, EXTENSION, amplification, magnification, ADDITION, EXTENSION.

enlighten: see EDUCATE; ILLUMINATE.

enlightened: see AWARE.

enlightenment: see KNOWLEDGE; SCIENCE.

enlist *v.* VOLUNTEER, ENROLL, sign up, REGISTER, RECORD, LIST, HIRE, procure.

enlistee: see VOLUNTEER.

enlistment: see TOUR.

enliven: see AMUSE; FRESHEN; PERK; REFRESH.

enmesh: see ENTANGLE.

enmity: see HATRED.

ennoble: see DIGNIFY.

enormous *adj.* HUGE, IMMENSE, VAST, TREMENDOUS, colossal, GIGANTIC, stupendous, prodigious, EXCESSIVE.

enough *adj.* SUFFICIENT, ADEQUATE, AMPLE. — *adv.* sufficiently, QUITE.

enrage *v.* ANGER, INFURIATE, madden, inflame, PROVOKE, EXCITE, chafe.

enraged: see ANGRY; FURIOUS; MAD.

enrich *v.* endow, ADORN, DECORATE, BETTER, IMPROVE, enhance, UPLIFT.

enrichment: see ORNAMENT; REFORM.

enroll *v.* VOLUNTEER, REGISTER, ENLIST, sign up, RECORD, SUBSCRIBE.

ensemble: see WARDROBE; WHOLE.

ensign: see BANNER.

ensnare: see ENTANGLE; NET; TAKE; TANGLE; TRAP.

ensnared: see ENTANGLED.

ensue: see FOLLOW; ISSUE.

ensuing: see FOLLOWING.

ensure: see INSURE.

entail: see REQUIRE.

entangle *v.* TRAP, entrap, ensnare, intertwine, interweave, enmesh, INVOLVE.

entangled *adj.* trapped, ensnared, snarled, caught, cornered, implicated, involved.

entanglement: see COBWEB; COMPLICATION; DIFFICULTY; KNOT; TANGLE.

enter *v.* **1** *(to enter a profession)* go in, come in, BEGIN, PENETRATE; **2** *(to enter a name on a list)* REGISTER, INSCRIBE, RECORD.

entering: see ENTRY.

enterprise: see ADVENTURE; BUSINESS; CORPORATION; ENDEAVOR; ENERGY; FIRM; PROJECT; UNDERTAKING; VENTURE.

enterprising: see ADVENTUROUS; AGGRESSIVE.

entertain *v.* **1** *(to entertain guests)* PLEASE, AMUSE, divert, LODGE, interest; **2** *(to entertain thoughts of revenge)* IMAGINE, HARBOR, CHERISH, CONSIDER.

entertainer *n.* PERFORMER, PLAYER, COMEDIAN, ARTIST, SINGER, dancer, instrumentalist, speaker.

entertaining: see COMICAL; MERRY.

entertainment *n.* AMUSEMENT, recreation, SPORT, FUN, SHOW, games, PARTY, FEAST, DINNER, dance.

enthrone: see CROWN.

enthusiasm *n.* earnestness, eagerness, DESIRE, DEVOTION, heartiness, FIRE, zeal.

enthusiast: see NUT.

enthusiastic *adj.* EARNEST, EAGER, HEARTY, wholehearted, AMBITIOUS, fervent, zealous, PASSIONATE.

enthusiastically: see HEARTILY.

entice: see ATTRACT; BRIBE; CHARM; COAX; LURE; PERSUADE; TEMPT.

enticement: see BAIT; GLAMOUR; LURE.

enticing: see GLAMOROUS; TEMPTING.

entire *adj.* WHOLE, COMPLETE, PERFECT, unmixed, undivided, INTACT, unabridged.

entirely *adv.* FULLY, COMPLETELY, ALTOGETHER, wholly, utterly, QUITE, TOTALLY.

entirety: see ALL; EVERYTHING; FULLNESS; TOTAL; WHOLE.

entitle *v.* **1** *(entitled to a free trip)* GRANT, authorize, empower, WARRANT, ALLOW; **2** *(a song entitled "America")* title, designate, style, CALL, TERM, subtitle.

entity: see BEING; LIFE; SOMETHING.

entomb: see BURY.

entombing: see BURIAL.

entourage: see FOLLOWING; TRAIN.

entrance *n.* ENTRY, OPENING, access, ADMISSION, ADMITTANCE, entree, INTRODUCTION, portal, GATE, DOOR, AVENUE, foothold, INVASION. See also APPEARANCE.
— *v.*: see BEWITCH.

entranceway: see CORRIDOR; GATE.

entrancing: see GLAMOROUS.

entrant: see ENTRY.

entrap: see CATCH; ENTANGLE; HOOK; NET; TRAP.

entrapment: see LURE.

entreat: see BEG; PLEAD; PRAY.

entree: see ENTRANCE; ENTRY.

entrust: see ASSIGN; DELEGATE; INVEST; RECOMMEND; TRUST.

entry *n.* **1** *(entry into the hall)* entering, access, entree, ADMITTANCE, ADMISSION, INTRUSION, INVASION, foothold, ENTRANCE, DOOR,

entryway, OPENING, PASSAGE, vestibule, lobby; **2** *(send in your entry)* LETTER, FORM, EFFORT, ATTEMPT, BID, ENDEAVOR, entrant, contestant, COMPETITOR, RIVAL.

entryway: see ENTRY.

entwine: see COIL; TWINE; TWIST; WIND.

entwist: see TWIST.

enumerate: see COUNT; SPECIFY.

enumeration: see LIST.

enunciate: see EXPRESS; PRONOUNCE.

enunciation: see PRONUNCIATION; SPEECH; VOICE.

envelop *v.* SURROUND, encompass, ENCIRCLE, ENCLOSE, COVER, overspread, WRAP, engulf, EMBRACE.

envelope *n.* COVERING, wrapper, POCKET, JACKET, wrapping, membrane.

envenom: see POISON.

envious: see JEALOUS; RESENTFUL.

environment *n.* SURROUNDINGS, environs, milieu, VICINITY, NEIGHBORHOOD, terrain, habitat, background, setting, conditions.

environs: see ENVIRONMENT; LOCALITY; NEIGHBORHOOD; SURROUNDINGS; VICINITY.

envision: see PREDICT.

envoy: see AMBASSADOR; DELEGATE.

envy *n.* JEALOUSY, RESENTMENT, grudging, heartburn, GREED.
— *v.* covet, WANT, DESIRE, EYE.

ephemeral: see TEMPORARY.

epic: see POETRY.

epidemic: see INFECTION; PLAGUE; RASH.

epidermis: see SKIN.

episode: see CHAPTER; CIRCUMSTANCE; EVENT; EXPERIENCE; OCCASION.

epistle: see LETTER.

epitome: see DIGEST.

epitomize: see SUMMARIZE.

epoch: see AGE; DATE; DAY; ERA; GENERATION.

epoxy: see CEMENT; GLUE.

equal *adj.* EQUIVALENT, ALIKE, matching, SAME, IDENTICAL, uniform, EVEN, abreast, REGULAR, FAIR, impartial, equitable.

— *n.*: see EQUIVALENT; MATCH; PEER.
— *v.*: see AMOUNT; TIE.

equality *n.* equivalence, uniformity, IDENTITY, impartiality, fairness, democracy.

equalize: see AVERAGE; CANCEL; LEVEL; MATE.

equally: see AS; EVENLY.

equanimity: see CALMNESS.

equate: see BALANCE; COMPARE; CONNECT; MATCH.

equation: see COMPARISON.

equidistant: see PARALLEL; REGULAR.

equilibrium: see BALANCE.

equip *v.* FURNISH, PROVIDE, OUTFIT, SUPPLY, PREPARE, DRESS, ADORN, array.

equipment *n.* furnishings, materials, tools, OUTFIT, utensils, apparatus, preparations, supplies, provisions, MATERIAL, materiel.

equitable: see EQUAL; FAIR; JUST.

equity: see JUSTICE.

equivalence: see EQUALITY; SAMENESS.

equivalent *adj.* EQUAL, SAME, ALIKE, PARALLEL, comparable, EVEN, matching, coequal.
— *n.* equal, MATCH, parallel, coequal, SUBSTITUTE.

era *n.* PERIOD, TIME, epoch, AGE, GENERATION, INTERVAL.

eradicate: see DESTROY; DISSOLVE; ELIMINATE; WEED.

eradication: see DESTRUCTION; ELIMINATION.

erase *v.* obliterate, CANCEL, REMOVE, ELIMINATE, delete, rub out.

erasure: see ELIMINATION.

erect *adj.* standing, UPRIGHT, perpendicular, VERTICAL, STRAIGHT, RIGID.
— *v.* BUILD, CONSTRUCT, ELEVATE, RAISE, LIFT, put up, STAND.

erection: see CONSTRUCTION.

erotic: see SEXUAL; SULTRY.

err: see GOOF; MISTAKE; SIN; STRAY; TRESPASS; TRIP.

errand *n.* BUSINESS, TRIP, MISSION, TASK, ASSIGNMENT, COMMISSION, MESSAGE.

errand boy: see PAGE.

errata: see SUPPLEMENT.

erratic: see CHANCY; IRREGULAR; ODD.

erroneous: see FALSE; MISTAKEN; WRONG.

erroneously: see WRONG.

error: see BLUNDER; MISTAKE; SIN; SLIP; WRONG.

ersatz: see ARTIFICIAL; CHEMICAL.

erupt *v.* BURST, BELCH, EJECT, emit, EXPLODE, rupture, DISCHARGE, vomit.

eruption *n.* EXPLOSION, emission, rupture, DISCHARGE, OUTBREAK, outburst, BLAST.

escalate: see ELEVATE; INCREASE; LIFT.

escalation: see LIFT.

escapade: see ADVENTURE.

escape *v.* FLEE, SKIP, evade, elude, AVOID, DESERT, ISSUE, LEAK.
— *n.* FLIGHT, DEPARTURE, desertion, breakout, exodus, release, loophole, OPENING, OUTLET, LEAK.

escort *n.* GUARD, bodyguard, convoy, defender, watchdog, shepherd, CONDUCTOR, chaperon, USHER, COMPANION, PARTNER, boyfriend.
— *v.* GUARD, PROTECT, convoy, PATROL, SCREEN, ATTEND, shepherd, USHER, CONDUCT, ACCOMPANY, chaperon, DATE.

especial: see SPECIAL.

especially *adv.* specially, unusually, notably, PRINCIPALLY, PARTICULARLY, exceptionally, outstandingly.

espousal: see ADOPTION.

essay *n.* COMPOSITION, THEME, thesis, EDITORIAL.
— *v.*: see TRY.

essayist: see WRITER.

essence: see BEING; COLOGNE; CONTENTS; EXTRACT; FLAVOR; FRAGRANCE; HEART; INCENSE; JUICE; LIFE; MEAT; PERFUME; POINT; SCENT; TEXTURE.

essential *adj.* NECESSARY, needed, needful, indispensable, BASIC, requisite, FUNDAMENTAL, required, KEY, VITAL, material, IMPORTANT.
— *n.*: see NECESSITY; QUALIFICATION.

essentially: see MAINLY; NECESSARILY; PRIMARILY; PRINCIPALLY.

essentials: see MEAT; STAPLE.

establish *v.* **1** (*to establish a university*) FOUND, set up, ORGANIZE, BEGIN, LOCATE, constitute, SETTLE; **2** (*to establish his whereabouts*) DETERMINE, PROVE, VERIFY, FIX, authenticate, substantiate.

established: see CERTAIN; PERMANENT.

establishment *n.* **1** (*the establishment of a scholarship*) CREATION, BEGINNING, founding, ORGANIZATION, LOCATION; **2** (*the Establishment*) CLASS, AUTHORITY, INSTITUTION, COMPANY, CONCERN, FIRM, BUSINESS.

estate *n.* **1** (*of low estate*) CONDITION, RANK, standing, POSITION, caste, STATION; **2** (*a large estate*) manor, chateau, FARM, PROPERTY, GROUNDS, acreage, WEALTH, possessions, legacy, INHERITANCE.

esteem *v.* HONOR, RESPECT, FAVOR, APPRECIATE, REGARD, CONSIDER, ADMIRE, value, treasure.
— *n.* HONOR, RESPECT, homage, ADMIRATION, REGARD, reverence, AFFECTION, FAVOR, CARE, ATTENTION, CONSIDERATION.

esteemed: see BELOVED; DISTINGUISHED; FAMOUS; FAVORED; HIGH; IMPORTANT; WELCOME; WELL-KNOWN.

esthetic: see ARTISTIC.

estimate *v.* GUESS, rate, GAUGE, CALCULATE, appraise, APPRECIATE, JUDGE, FIGURE, assess, compute, evaluate.
— *n.* appraisal, GUESS, valuation, VALUE, evaluation, computation.

estimation *n.* appraisal, REVIEW, OPINION, JUDGMENT, evaluation, computation, calculation, ESTIMATE, RESPECT, ESTEEM, GUESS.

etch: see ENGRAVE; PRINT.

etching: see ENGRAVING; PRINT.

eternal *adj.* ENDLESS, INFINITE, deathless, IMMORTAL, perpetual, ceaseless, everlasting, undying.

eternally: see ALWAYS; EVERMORE.

eternity *n.* INFINITY, permanence, timelessness, everlastingness, IMMORTALITY, boundlessness, duration.

ether: see SKY.

ethical: see JUST; MORAL; PROPER; UPRIGHT; VIRTUOUS.

ethics: see CHARACTER; CONSCIENCE.

etiquette: see CEREMONY; FORMALITY.

evacuate *v.* QUIT, DEPART, LEAVE, WITHDRAW, ABANDON, VACATE, empty, DEPORT.

evade: see DODGE; ESCAPE; HEDGE.

evaluate: see APPRECIATE; CONSIDER; CRITICIZE; ESTIMATE.

evaluation: see CONSIDERATION; CRITICISM; DISCUSSION; ESTIMATE; ESTIMATION.

evangel: see GOSPEL.

evangelist: see PREACHER.

evaporate *v.* DISAPPEAR, VANISH, vaporize, distill, FADE, DISSOLVE, steam, diffuse.

evasive: see SHIFTY.

eve: see EVENING.

even *adj.* EQUAL, tied, drawn, matching, EXACT, PARALLEL, plane, FLAT, LEVEL, SMOOTH, STEADY, REGULAR, STILL, CONSTANT, CALM, unruffled, even-tempered, level-headed, uniform, consistent, flush, horizontal, STRAIGHT, DIRECT, TRUE, FAIR, impartial, balanced.
— *adv.* EVENLY, EXACTLY, JUST, STILL, TRULY, verily, LIKEWISE, improbably.
— *v.*: see AVERAGE; LEVEL; SMOOTH; STRAIGHTEN; TIE.

even if: see ALTHOUGH; IF; THOUGH.

evening *n.* eve, sunset, sundown, TWILIGHT, DUSK, gloaming, nightfall, nighttime, NIGHT.

evenly *adv.* EVEN, equally, uniformly, EXACTLY, consistently, STEADILY, REGULARLY, SMOOTHLY, CONSTANTLY, DIRECTLY, horizontally, calmly, impartially, FAIRLY.

evenness: see STEADINESS.

event *n.* OCCURRENCE, INCIDENT, HAPPENING, ACCIDENT, ADVENTURE, milestone, episode, OCCASION.

eventempered: see CALM; EVEN.

events: see CALENDAR.

eventual: see EXPECTANT; FUTURE; POSSIBLE.

eventuality: see POSSIBILITY.

eventually *adv.* FINALLY, ultimately, lastly, POSSIBLY, conceivably.

ever *adv.* ALWAYS, FOREVER, EVERMORE, CONSTANTLY, continuously, EXCEEDINGLY. See also ANY.

everlasting: see CONSTANT; ETERNAL; IMMORTAL; UNENDING.

everlastingly: see ALWAYS.

everlastingness: see ETERNITY.

evermore *adv.* EVER, FOREVER, ALWAYS, perpetually, CONSTANTLY, CONTINUALLY, eternally.

every *adj.* EACH, ALL, TOTAL, COMPLETE, SOME, ANY, BY.

everybody: see ALL; EVERYONE.

everyday *adj.* DAILY, routine, COMMON, USUAL, CUSTOMARY, NORMAL, FREQUENT.

everyone *pron.* everybody, ALL, PEOPLE, persons, SOME, ANY.

everything *n.* ALL, WHOLE, SUM, TOTAL, WORLD, UNIVERSE, entirety.

everywhere *adv.* THROUGHOUT, universally, COMMONLY, extensively, spaciously.

evidence *n.* PROOF, DOCUMENT, CLUE, SIGN, INDICATION, GROUNDS, DEMONSTRATION, TESTIMONY, certainty.

evident *adj.* proven, demonstrated, CERTAIN, APPARENT, CLEAR, PLAIN, indicated, OBVIOUS, VISIBLE, CONCLUSIVE, CONSPICUOUS.

evidently *adv.* obviously, APPARENTLY, CLEARLY, plainly, conspicuously, DISTINCTLY.

evil *n.* SIN, WICKEDNESS, vice, MISERY, WOE, badness, corruption, MISCHIEF, VICIOUSNESS, WRONG, INJURY, HARM, MISFORTUNE, DISASTER. — *adj.* sinful, WICKED, VICIOUS, corrupt, BAD, MISCHIEVOUS, WRONG, injurious, HARMFUL, DESTRUCTIVE, immoral, hurtful, UNHAPPY, UNFORTUNATE, disastrous.

evildoer: see VILLAIN.

evolution: see DEVELOPMENT; GENERATION; GROWTH.

evolve: see BECOME; DEVELOP; RIPEN.

ewe: see SHEEP.

exact *adj.* PRECISE, CORRECT, ACCURATE, STRICT, rigorous, punctual, PARTICULAR, faultless, SPECIFIC, DEFINITE, verbatim, literal. — *v.*: see SQUEEZE; TAX.

exacting: see PARTICULAR; SEVERE.

exactly *adv.* PRECISELY, correctly, accurately, STRICTLY, literally, faultlessly, carefully, faithfully.

exactness *n.* PRECISION, correctness, DETAIL, accuracy, fidelity, faithfulness.

exaggerate *v.* MAGNIFY, overstate, OVERDO, overestimate, STRETCH, EXPAND, amplify, ELABORATE.

exaggerated: see TALL.

exaggeration *n.* overestimation, overstatement, amplification, EXPANSION, magnification, INFLATION.

exalt: see APPLAUD; ELEVATE; RAVE.

exalted: see LOFTY.

exam: see QUIZ.

examination *n.* INVESTIGATION, CHECK, scrutiny, INSPECTION, OBSERVATION, STUDY, ANALYSIS, TEST, POLL.

examine *v.* CHECK, scrutinize, STUDY, QUESTION, INSPECT, INVESTIGATE, REVIEW.

examiner: see INSPECTOR.

examining: see CURIOUS.

example *n.* **1** *(an example of her skill)* SAMPLE, CASE, ILLUSTRATION, REPRESENTATION, SYMBOL, INCIDENT, PIECE, ITEM, FACT; **2** *(an example of courage)* MODEL, STANDARD, PATTERN, COPY; **3** *(let this be an example to you)* WARNING, LESSON, ADVICE, NOTICE.

exasperate: see ANGER; ANNOY; IRRITATE.

exasperated: see MAD.

exasperation: see ANGER; ANNOYANCE; IRRITATION.

excavate: see DIG; MINE; SCOOP.

excavation: see CAVITY; DITCH; MINE; PIT.

exceed *v.* SURPASS, PASS, excel, OUTDO, outstrip, outrank, BEAT, TOP, BETTER, OVERDO.

exceeding: see BEYOND; PAST.

exceedingly *adv.* EXTREMELY, GREATLY, vastly, remarkably, excessively.

excel: see EXCEED; LEAD; MASTER; OUTDO; SHINE; SURPASS; TOWER.

excellence *n.* eminence, SUPERIORITY, MERIT, WORTH, DISTINCTION, PERFECTION, QUALITY, GREATNESS.

excellent *adj.* OUTSTANDING, SUPERIOR, eminent, meritorious, WORTHY, ADMIRABLE, distinctive, NOTED, select, EXQUISITE, EXCEPTIONAL, FINE, WONDERFUL, GREAT, TREMENDOUS.

except *prep.* BUT, saving, excluding, omitting, barring, BESIDES. — *v.* OMIT, exclude, BAR, ban, exempt, EXCUSE, ELIMINATE, REMOVE, REJECT. — *conj.*: see UNLESS.

except if: see UNLESS.

excepting: see BUT; OUTSIDE.

exception *n.* **1** *(an exception to the rule)* irregularity, exclusion, RESERVATION, exemption, LIMITATION; **2** *(to take exception)* OBJECTION, DISAGREEMENT, protestation, offense.

exceptional *adj.* SPECIAL, RARE, UNUSUAL, UNCOMMON, SUPERIOR, REMARKABLE, exclusive, EXTRAORDINARY.

exceptionally: see ESPECIALLY.

except that: see BUT.

excerpt: see QUOTATION; QUOTE; READING.

excess *n.* **1** *(an excess of merchandise)* SURPLUS, overabundance, REMAINDER, glut, overage, overflow; **2** *(his excesses ruined his health)* overdoing, extravagance, immoderation, intemperance.
— *adj.*: see SPARE; UNNECESSARY.

excessive *adj.* SURPLUS, overabundant, EXTRA, superfluous, immoderate.

excessively: see EXCEEDINGLY.

exchange *v.* SUBSTITUTE, CONVERT, barter, SWAP, BARGAIN, TRADE, RETURN, REPLACE, TRANSFER, CHANGE.
— *n.* SUBSTITUTION, conversion, REPLACEMENT, CHANGE, transferal, TRADE, dealing, MARKET, brokerage.

excise: see DUTY; TAX.

excitable *adj.* moving, stirring, stimulating, provoking, arousing, affecting, PASSIONATE, demonstrative.

excite *v.* PROVOKE, inflame, AROUSE, STIR, STIMULATE, instigate, THRILL.

excited: see FEVERISH; FRANTIC; HOT; NERVOUS.

excitement *n.* **1** *(the excitement of the moment)* COMMOTION, agitation, ACTIVITY, DISTURBANCE, IRRITATION, TENSION, SENSATION, arousal, stimulation, THRILL, PASSION, WARMTH; **2** *(the excitement of this possibility)* stimulation, provocation, incitement, IMPULSE, stimulus, MOTIVE, motivation.

exciting: see DRAMATIC; GLAMOROUS; LIVELY; SENSATIONAL.

exclaim *v.* SAY, STATE, UTTER, assert, CRY, SHOUT, CALL, YELL.

exclamation *n.* SHOUT, OUTCRY, CLAMOR, YELL, HOWL.

exclude: see DEPORT; ELIMINATE; EXCEPT; OMIT; PROHIBIT.

excluding: see EXCEPT.

exclusion: see ELIMINATION; EXCEPTION; OMISSION.

exclusive: see CUSTOM; EACH; EXCEPTIONAL; PARTICULAR; PERSONAL; UNIQUE.

exclusively: see ALONE; ONE.

excrete: see ELIMINATE.

excursion: see EXPEDITION; JOURNEY; SAIL; TOUR; TRAVEL; TRIP; VOYAGE.

excusable *adj.* forgivable, pardonable, defensible, ALLOWABLE, justifiable.

excuse *v.* FORGIVE, PARDON, absolve, ACQUIT, FREE, exonerate, APOLOGIZE, condone, JUSTIFY, OVERLOOK.
— *n.* APOLOGY, PARDON, absolution, DEFENSE, PLEA, APPEAL, EXPLANATION, JUSTIFICATION, DISGUISE.

execute *v.* **1** *(the regime executed all opponents)* KILL, MURDER, HANG, electrocute, guillotine, behead; **2** *(they executed the colonel's orders)* PERFORM, DO, carry out, ACCOMPLISH, COMPLETE, ACHIEVE.

executer: see MAKER.

execution *n.* **1** *(the execution took place in the square)* killing, capital punishment, electrocution, hanging, beheading; **2** *(the plan's execution was thwarted)* completion, ACCOMPLISHMENT, ACHIEVEMENT, PERFORMANCE, ADMINISTRATION, OPERATION.

executioner: see ASSASSIN; KILLER; MURDERER.

executive *n.* businessman, administrator, HEAD, SUPERVISOR, DIRECTOR, MANAGER, LEADER, BOSS, CHIEF, PRESIDENT. See also ADMINISTRATION.

exemplar: see MODEL.

exemplary: see IDEAL.

exemplify: see ILLUSTRATE.

exempt: see EXCEPT; RELEASE.

exemption: see EXCEPTION; LIBERTY; PRIVILEGE.

exercise *n.* USE, PRACTICE, ACTIVITY, PERFORMANCE, PURSUIT, APPLICATION, DRILL.
— *v.* USE, PRACTICE, PERFORM, DRILL, TRAIN, DISPLAY.

exert *v.* USE, EXERCISE, EMPLOY, utilize, APPLY, ENDEAVOR.

exertion *n.* LABOR, ATTEMPT, STRAIN, EFFORT, ENDEAVOR, STRUGGLE.

exhalation: see BREATH.

exhale *v.* BREATHE, EXPIRE, EXPEL, PUFF, BLOW, EXHAUST.

exhaust *v.* **1** *(the test exhausted the students)* TIRE, DRAIN, empty, fatigue, wear out, weaken; **2** *(they exhausted all possibilities)* deplete, USE, CONSUME, DISCUSS, CONSIDER.

exhausted: see BUSHED; TIRED; WEARY.

exhaustingly: see HARD.

exhaustion *n.* FATIGUE, WEARINESS, tiredness, depletion, consumption, EXPENDITURE.

exhibit *v.* SHOW, DEMONSTRATE, EXPOSE, PRESENT, ILLUSTRATE, INDICATE, DISPLAY.
— *n.*: see DISPLAY.

exhibition *n.* SHOW, DEMONSTRATION, DISPLAY, PRESENTATION, exposition, FAIR, SPECTACLE, PERFORMANCE.

exhortation: see SERMON.

exile *v.* BANISH, DEPORT, EXPEL, outlaw.
— *n.* banishment, deportation, expulsion, emigration, ostracism.

exist *v.* BE, subsist, SURVIVE, LIVE, BREATHE, ENDURE, REMAIN.

existence *n.* subsistence, BEING, LIFE, survival, PRESENCE.

existent *adj.* being, subsistent, LIVING, surviving, CURRENT, prevalent, REMAINING.

existing: see ALIVE; LIVE; LIVING; PRESENT.

exit *n.* DEPARTURE, withdrawal, leaving, OUTLET, DOOR, AVENUE, SOLUTION.
— *v.*: see DEPART; EMERGE.

exodus: see DEPARTURE; ESCAPE.

exonerate: see CLEAR; EXCUSE; FORGIVE; JUSTIFY; PARDON.

exoneration: see PARDON.

exorbitant: see COSTLY; EXPENSIVE.

exotic: see FOREIGN; STRANGE.

expand *v.* EXTEND, STRETCH, ENLARGE, INFLATE, SWELL, INCREASE, SPREAD, GROW.

expanded: see GROWN; LONG.

expanse: see AREA; FLAT; INFINITY; OCEAN; ROOM; SHEET; SPACE; SPAN; WIDTH.

expansion *n.* EXTENSION, augmentation, swelling, INFLATION, ENLARGEMENT, DEVELOPMENT, GROWTH.

expansive: see BIG; BROAD; ROOMY; SPACIOUS; WIDE.

expansively: see ABROAD.

expansiveness: see FULLNESS.

expatriate: see BANISH.

expect *v.* HOPE, ANTICIPATE, AWAIT, WAIT, ASSUME, presume, SUPPOSE.

expectancy: see PROSPECT; SUSPENSE.

expectant *adj.* anticipating, contemplating, hoping, awaiting, EAGER, expecting, PREGNANT, eventual.

expectation *n.* PROSPECT, anticipation, HOPE, assurance, BELIEF.

expected: see DUE; FUTURE; ONCOMING; USUAL.

expecting: see EXPECTANT; PREGNANT.

expedient: see RESOURCE; SUBSTITUTE; TACTICS.

expedite: see ACCELERATE; EASE; HASTEN; SPARK.

expedition *n.* TRIP, JOURNEY, excursion, VOYAGE, outing, quest, CAMPAIGN, safari, crusade.

expel *v.* DISMISS, DISCHARGE, REMOVE, ELIMINATE, BANISH, DEPORT, oust.

expend: see CONSUME; SPEND; USE.

expendable: see UNNECESSARY.

expenditure *n.* outlay, disbursement, consumption, INVESTMENT, EXPENSE, CHARGE, remuneration.

expense *n.* PAYMENT, COST, CHARGE, RATE, PRICE, EXPENDITURE.

expensive *adj.* COSTLY, DEAR, high-priced, extravagant, VALUABLE, PRECIOUS, RARE, exorbitant.

experience *n.* **1** *(a dangerous experience)* ordeal, ADVENTURE, INCIDENT, episode, OCCURRENCE; **2** *(work experience)* background, SKILL, PRACTICE, KNOWLEDGE, OBSERVATION.
v. FEEL, undergo, MEET, ENCOUNTER, ENDURE.

experienced: see VETERAN.

experiences: see PAST.

experiment *n.* TRIAL, TEST, CHECK, ANALYSIS, EXAMINATION, SEARCH, RESEARCH.
— *v.* INVESTIGATE, ANALYZE, TEST, CHECK, EXAMINE, EXPLORE, PROVE.

expert *n.* SPECIALIST, AUTHORITY, MASTER, whiz.
— *adj.* adept, skillful, MASTERFUL, proficient, APT, CLEVER.

expertness: see EASE.

expiation: see RANSOM.

expiration: see DEATH; PASSAGE.

expire *v.* **1** *(to expire air)* BREATHE, EXHALE, EXPEL; **2** *(he expired after a long illness)* DIE, pass on, END, terminate, PERISH, CEASE.

explain *v.* expound, ILLUSTRATE, INTERPRET, DEMONSTRATE, simplify, CLARIFY, SOLVE, decipher.

explanation *n.* INTERPRETATION, ILLUSTRATION, DEMONSTRATION, explication, DESCRIPTION, TRANSLATION.

explication: see EXPLANATION.

explicit: see SPECIFIC.

explode *v.* BURST, ERUPT, detonate, BLAST, CRACK, POP, SHATTER.

exploit: see ACHIEVEMENT; ACT; STUNT; USE.

exploitation: see SLAVERY; USE.

exploration *n.* INVESTIGATION, RESEARCH, EXAMINATION, INQUIRY, probe, SEARCH, INSPECTION.

explore *v.* INVESTIGATE, EXAMINE, RESEARCH, INQUIRE, PROBE, HUNT, SEARCH.

explorer *n.* PIONEER, TRAVELER, adventurer, wayfarer, COLONIST, PILGRIM.

explosion *n.* BURST, detonation, BLAST, CRACK, blowup, DISCHARGE, ERUPTION.

explosive *n.* dynamite, gunpowder, TNT, ammunition, CHARGE.
 — *adj.* VIOLENT, volatile, stormy, tempestuous, raging.

export *v.* SHIP, TRADE, FREIGHT, TRANSPORT.

expose *v.* BARE, REVEAL, UNCOVER, unmask, disclose, unearth, EXHIBIT.

exposed: see NAKED; NUDE; OPEN; RAW.

exposition: see DISPLAY; EXHIBITION; FAIR; SHOW.

exposure *n.* uncovering, unmasking, disclosure, revelation, CONFESSION, EXHIBITION, showing, PUBLICATION.

expound: see EXPLAIN.

express *v.* **1** *(he expresses himself well)* SPEAK, UTTER, enunciate, STATE, assert, DECLARE; **2** *(what does the music express?)* MEAN, SIGNIFY, INDICATE, REPRESENT, symbolize.
 — *adj.* PRECISE, SPECIAL, EXACT, SPECIFIC, PARTICULAR, DELIBERATE.
 — *n.*: see TRAIN.

expressed: see VERBAL.

expression *n.* DECLARATION, INDICATION, DESCRIPTION, DEMONSTRATION, STATEMENT, COMMUNICATION.

expressionless: see BLANK.

expressive *adj.* meaningful, indicative, SIGNIFICANT, IMPORTANT, communicative, eloquent, descriptive.

expressly: see DIRECTLY.

expressway: see HIGHWAY.

expulsion: see EXILE.

expunge: see BLOT.

expurgate: see CLEANSE.

exquisite *adj.* MAGNIFICENT, BEAUTIFUL, LOVELY, ELEGANT, SUPERB, PERFECT, MARVELOUS, FINE, OUTSTANDING.

extemporaneous: see OFFHAND.

extempore: see OFFHAND.

extend *v.* **1** *(his property extends to the water)* STRETCH, REACH, CONTINUE, SPREAD; **2** *(extend your tape measure)* LENGTHEN, elongate, PROLONG, widen, INCREASE, augment; **3** *(extend her my best wishes)* OFFER, GIVE, GRANT, impart, DONATE, PRESENT.

extended: see LONG; OUT.

extending: see RUNNING.

extension *n.* augmentation, ENLARGEMENT, EXPANSION, INCREASE, ADDITION, delay, postponement, respite.

extensive *adj.* VAST, SPACIOUS, LARGE, BROAD, widespread.

extensively: see ABROAD; EVERYWHERE.

extent *n.* scope, REACH, RANGE, SIZE, DEGREE, MAGNITUDE, MEASUREMENT, PROPORTION.

exterior: see OUTER; OUTSIDE; SKIN; SURFACE.

exterminate: see ELIMINATE; MASSACRE.

extermination: see BUTCHERY; ELIMINATION; MASSACRE.

external *adj.* OUTER, outermost, covering, SURFACE, superficial, APPARENT.

externally: see OUTSIDE.

extinct: see DEAD; LIFELESS.

extinction: see DEATH.

extinguished: see DROWN; OUT.

extol: see RAVE.

extort: see BLEED; SQUEEZE.

extortion: see PROTECTION; RACKET.

extra *adj.* surplus, SPARE, MORE, reserve,
SUPPLEMENTARY, ADDITIONAL.
— *n.*: see BONUS; SURPLUS.
— *adv.*: see INCREASINGLY.

extract *v.* REMOVE, PULL, WITHDRAW, PRY, PLUCK,
distill.
— *n.* essence, JUICE, distillation.

extraction: see BLOOD; PARENTAGE.

extraordinary *adj.* REMARKABLE, UNCOMMON,
UNUSUAL, SPECIAL, INCREDIBLE, EXCEPTIONAL,
astonishing.

extravagance: see ABUNDANCE; EXCESS.

extravagant: see EXPENSIVE; LUXURIOUS;
UNREASONABLE; WASTEFUL.

extravaganza: see PRODUCTION.

extreme *adj.* drastic, SEVERE, EXCESSIVE, radical,
INTENSE, immoderate, flagrant, ultra.
— *n.* LIMIT, END, TOP, CONCLUSION, ultimate,
MAXIMUM.

extremely *adv.* GREATLY, vastly, drastically,
intensely, remarkably, EXCEEDINGLY, utterly,
uncommonly.

extremity: see ARM; EDGE; FOOT; HAND; LEG; LIMB;
TIP.

exuberant: see HEARTY.

exudate: see BLEED.

exult: see REJOICE.

exultation: see TRIUMPH.

eye *v.* GLANCE, STARE, LOOK, PEER, WATCH, VIEW.
— *n.* SIGHT, VISION, JUDGMENT, vigilance,
peephole, CENTER, bull's-eye.

eyeball: see PUPIL.

eyebrow: see BROW.

eyeful: see SIGHT.

eyeglasses: see GLASSES.

eyelash: see LASH.

eyeless: see BLIND.

eyes: see SIGHT.

eye shadow: see SHADOW.

eyesight: see SIGHT; VISION.

eyesore: see UGLINESS.

eyewitness: see WITNESS.

F

fable *n.* STORY, MYTH, TALE, allegory, parable,
FICTION.

fabric *n.* CLOTH, GOODS, STUFF, TEXTILE,
MATERIAL, SUBSTANCE, STRUCTURE.

fabricate: see BUILD; CONSTRUCT; FORGE; INVENT;
LIE; PRODUCE.

fabricated: see MADE-UP.

fabrication: see FICTION; GENERATION; LIE.

fabricator: see MAKER.

fabrics: see GOODS.

fabulous *adj.* NOTABLE, MARVELOUS, unbelievable,
REMARKABLE, AMAZING, IMAGINARY, FANTASTIC,
FICTITIOUS.

facade: see FRONT.

face *n.* countenance, features, visage, FRONT,
LOOK, semblance, APPEARANCE.
— *v.* MEET, confront, BRAVE, STAND, SUBMIT,
ENDURE.

facet: see PHASE; SIDE.

facial *adj.* frontal, SURFACE, superficial.

facile: see SIMPLE.

facilitate: see AID; EASE.

facility: see EASE; SKILL; TALENT.

facing: see ACROSS; AGAINST; BEFORE; OFF;
OPPOSITE.

facsimile: see COPY; DOUBLE; DUPLICATE;
IMITATION.

fact *n.* ACT, EVENT, OCCURRENCE, INCIDENT,
certainty, REALITY, TRUTH.

faction: see PARTY.

factor *n.* determinant, CAUSE, BASIS, PART,
INGREDIENT, constituent.

factory *n.* PLANT, SHOP, works, MILL, foundry,
INDUSTRY.

facts: see TRUTH.

factual: see ACTUAL; HISTORICAL; REAL.

faculty: see ABILITY; COLLEGE; HAND; HEAD; STAFF.

fad: see PASSION; RAGE.

fade *v.* pale, bleach, dim, DIMINISH, DECLINE, DIE.

faded: see OLD.

fagged: see BUSHED.

fail *v.* **1** *(he failed the course)* SLIP, flounder, FALL, falter, MISS, flunk; **2** *(his failing health)* DECLINE, FADE, WEAKEN, worsen, SINK.

failed: see BANKRUPT.

failing: see MINUS.

failure *n.* deficiency, LOSS, DECLINE, DEFEAT, COLLAPSE, negligence, OMISSION, bankruptcy, washout.

faint *adj.* WEAK, FRAIL, DIM, PALE, subtle, VAGUE, indistinct.
— *v.* swoon, FAIL, languish, FADE, DECLINE.

fainthearted: see COWARDLY; FEARFUL.

faintness: see DIMNESS.

fair *adj.* **1** *(a fair trial)* JUST, equitable, impartial, HONEST; **2** *(a fair complexion)* PALE, LIGHT, blond; **3** *(a fair day)* cloudless, CLEAR, SUNNY, PLEASANT, rainless; **4** *(a fair performance)* AVERAGE, MEDIUM, DECENT, mediocre, ORDINARY.
— *n.* exposition, EXHIBITION, MARKET, bazaar, FESTIVAL.

fairly *adv.* honestly, justly, impartially, moderately, SOMEWHAT.

fairness: see EQUALITY; HONESTY; JUSTICE.

fairy *n.* elf, goblin, pixy, genie.

fairy tale: see MYTH.

faith *n.* TRUST, CONFIDENCE, fidelity, LOYALTY, BELIEF, CREED, RELIGION.

faithful *adj.* **1** *(a faithful friend)* LOYAL, trustworthy, steadfast, DEVOTED; **2** *(a faithful copy)* TRUE, RELIABLE, ACCURATE, EXACT, CLOSE.

faithfully: see EXACTLY.

faithfulness: see ALLEGIANCE; EXACTNESS; TRUTH.

faithless: see FALSE; HOLLOW.

faithlessness: see TREACHERY.

fake: see AFFECT; BLANK; MOCK; PRETEND.

faker: see IMPOSTOR.

fakery: see ACT.

fall *v.* **1** *(the bridge falls)* DESCEND, DROP, TUMBLE, COLLAPSE, SINK, TRIP; **2** *(the Dow-Jones average falls)* LOWER, DECLINE, DECREASE.

— *n.* DESTRUCTION, RUIN, OVERTHROW, DEFEAT, COLLAPSE, DROP, DESCENT. See also AUTUMN.

fallacious: see MISLEADING; MISTAKEN.

fallacy: see ILLUSION.

fallen *adj.* **1** *(a fallen tycoon)* SHAMELESS, sinful, ruined; **2** *(the fallen enemy)* defeated, overthrown, surrendered.

fall short: see MISS.

false *adj.* **1** *(a false friend)* disloyal, faithless, dishonest, two-faced; **2** *(a false impression)* untruthful, incorrect, deceptive, erroneous.

falsehood: see BUNK; FIB; INVENTION; LIE; TALE.

falsely: see WRONG.

falsify: see CAMOUFLAGE; FORGE; INVENT; LIE.

falsity: see FRAUD; WRONG.

falter: see FAIL; HESITATE; LIMP; STAGGER; STAMMER; STUMBLE.

fame *n.* renown, REPUTATION, eminence, ESTEEM, prominence, prestige.

famed *adj.* DISTINGUISHED, illustrious, POPULAR, NOTABLE, respected, CELEBRATED.

familiar *adj.* WELL-KNOWN, POPULAR, COMMON, FREQUENT, knowledgeable, conversant.

familiarity: see ACQUAINTANCE; COMPANIONSHIP; KNOWLEDGE.

familiarize: see ACCUSTOM; ACQUAINT.

family *n.* KIN, relatives, folks, children, PARENTAGE, HOUSEHOLD, ancestry, forebears. See also CLASS; CLASSIFICATION.

famine *n.* HUNGER, starvation, want, SCARCITY, dearth.

famish: see FAST; STARVE.

famished: see HUNGRY.

famous *adj.* eminent, esteemed, renowned, reputable, illustrious, NOTABLE, PROMINENT.

fan *n.* **1** *(an electric fan)* blower, ventilator; **2** *(a baseball fan)* SUPPORTER, FOLLOWER, devotee.
— *v.* agitate, BLOW, REFRESH, EXCITE.

fanatic: see NUT.

fanciful: see FICTIONAL; IMAGINARY; QUAINT; ROMANTIC.

fancy *adj.* RICH, ELEGANT, ELABORATE, adorned, intricate.
— *n.* **1** *(to suit one's fancy)* IMAGINATION, MOOD,

TASTE; **2** (*she has taken a fancy to him*) INTEREST, liking, INCLINATION, LOVE.
— *v.* PREFER, FAVOR, LIKE, LOVE, DREAM, IMAGINE.

fang: see TOOTH.

fantastic *adj.* INCREDIBLE, UNUSUAL, STRANGE, ODD, WILD, IMAGINARY, FABULOUS.

fantasy: see DREAM; ILLUSION; IMAGINATION; MYTH; PHANTOM.

far *adv.* GREATLY, remotely, widely, ALMOST.
— *adj.* REMOTE, DISTANT, LONG.

faraway: see AFAR; DISTANT.

farcical: see COMICAL.

fare *n.* **1** (*what is the bus fare?*) TOLL, PRICE, COST, PASSAGE, CHARGE; **2** (*how is the fare at that restaurant?*) menu, FOOD, victuals, provisions, rations.

farewell *interj.* GOOD-BYE, so long, adieu, be good.
— *n.* leave-taking, DEPARTURE, adieu, valediction.

far-fetched: see INCREDIBLE; SUSPICIOUS.

farm *n.* homestead, RANCH, plantation, ESTATE.
— *v.* CULTIVATE, TILL.

farmer *n.* planter, cultivator, RANCHER, homesteader, producer.

farm hand: see HAND.

farming: see AGRICULTURE.

farmland: see COUNTRY.

far off: see AFAR.

far-off: see DISTANT.

far-sighted: see WISE.

farther *adv.* FURTHER, BEYOND, BESIDES, MOREOVER.
— *adj.* FURTHER, ADDITIONAL.

farthest: see UTMOST.

fascinate: see ATTRACT; BEWITCH; CHARM; IMPRESS.

fascinating: see GLAMOROUS.

fascination: see ATTRACTION; CHARM; GLAMOUR; MAGNET; SPELL; TEMPTATION.

fascism: see RIGHT.

fashion *n.* STYLE, vogue, CUSTOM, CONVENTION, MANNER, WAY, TENDENCY. See also CARVE; COMPOSE; FORGE; MINT; PATTERN; SCULPTURE; SHAPE; WORK.

fashionable *adj.* STYLISH, chic, SMART, modish, prevailing, CURRENT, CUSTOMARY.

fast *adj.* RAPID, QUICK, SWIFT, SPEEDY, BRISK, LIVELY, accelerated. See also FROZEN; TIGHT.
— *v.* starve, famish, DIET, abstain.
— *adv.*: see FIRMLY.

fasten *v.* LOCK, TIE, ATTACH, FIX, JOIN, CONNECT, clamp, CLASP.

fastened: see BOUND; SHUT.

fastener: see BUCKLE; CATCH; CLASP; CLIP; HINGE; HOOK; LOCK; PIN; SCREW; SEAL; STAPLE.

fastening: see KNOT.

fastidious: see CHOOSY; CLEANLY; DIFFICULT; FUSSY; NICE; PARTICULAR.

fat *n.* lard, OIL, GREASE.
— *adj.* **1** (*a fat person*) PLUMP, STOUT, obese, CHUBBY, pudgy, fleshy, THICK, BROAD, PROSPEROUS, WEALTHY, INFLUENTIAL; **2** (*a fat soup*) GREASY, OILY, fatty.

fatal *adj.* DEADLY, MORTAL, lethal, DANGEROUS, HARMFUL, injurious.

fate *n.* **1** (*a cruel fate*) DESTINY, inevitability, LUCK; **2** (*a tragic fate*) DOOM, LOT, END, DEATH.

fated: see INEVITABLE.

father *n.* **1** (*her father pays the bills*) dad, DADDY, papa, sire; **2** (*speak to the father after mass*) PRIEST, PASTOR, PREACHER, MINISTER.
— *v.*: see ORIGINATE.

fathering: see GENERATION.

fatherland: see COUNTRY.

fatherly *adj.* paternal, PARENTAL, PROTECTIVE, benevolent.

fathom: see DIVE; GUESS.

fatigue *n.* tiredness, WEARINESS, languor, EXHAUSTION.
— *v.*: see EXHAUST; TIRE.

fatigued: see BEAT; TIRED; WEARY; WORN.

fatten *v.* FEED, FILL, STUFF, cram.

fattish: see CHUBBY.

fatty: see CHUBBY; FAT; GREASY.

faucet: see TAP.

fault *n.* **1** (*it was his own fault*) MISTAKE, RESPONSIBILITY, blame, negligence, BLUNDER;

2 *(his main fault is selfishness)* DEFECT, WEAKNESS, shortcoming, imperfection.
— *v*.: see BLAME.

faultfinder: see CRANK; CRITIC.

faultfinding: see CRITICAL.

faultless: see BLAMELESS; EXACT; PERFECT.

faultlessly: see EXACTLY.

faulty *adj*. defective, deficient, BROKEN, imperfect, damaged, UNRELIABLE.

favor *n*. KINDNESS, COURTESY, SERVICE, BENEFIT, GRACE, REGARD, ESTEEM.
— *v*. FANCY, PREFER, LIKE, APPROVE, OBLIGE, AID, SUPPORT.

favorable *adj*. KINDLY, advantageous, FRIENDLY, CONVENIENT, USEFUL, SUITABLE, WILLING, conducive.

favorably: see RIGHT.

favored *adj*. preferred, prized, approved, valued, praised, esteemed.
— *n*.: see BELOVED.

favorite *adj*. BELOVED, preferred, PET, CHOICE, cherished, treasured, adored.
— *n*.: see DARLING; PET.

fear *n*. FRIGHT, DREAD, TERROR, DISMAY, ALARM, HORROR.
— *v*. **1** *(to fear an earthquake)* DREAD, TREMBLE, cower, AVOID, shun; **2** *(to fear God)* revere, RESPECT, WORSHIP.

fearful *adj*. **1** *(a fearful bus ride)* DREADFUL, HORRIBLE, ghastly, frightening, terrifying, GRUESOME; **2** *(a fearful medical operation)* awesome, formidable, TREMENDOUS; **3** *(a fearful deserter)* TIMID, COWARDLY, base, dastardly, faint hearted, cringing.

fearless *adj*. BRAVE, BOLD, valorous, HEROIC, dauntless, DARING, COURAGEOUS, GALLANT.

feasibility: see POSSIBILITY.

feasible: see POSSIBLE; PRACTICAL.

feast *n*. FESTIVAL, HOLIDAY, MEAL, BANQUET, SPREAD, barbecue, picnic.
— *v*. EAT, DINE, FEED, ENTERTAIN.

feat: see ACHIEVEMENT; ACT; DEED; PERFORMANCE; STROKE; STUNT.

feather: see PLUME.

feathery: see SOFT.

feature *n*. ASPECT, CHARACTERISTIC, TRAIT, PART, innovation, specialty, highlight.
— *v*. star, SHOW, highlight, UNDERLINE, underscore, MARK.

features: see FACE.

federated: see ALLIED; CONFEDERATE.

federation: see ASSOCIATION; ORGANIZATION.

fee *n*. COST, PRICE, TOLL, charges, dues, compensation, pay, SALARY.

feeble *adj*. FRAIL, WEAK, puny, fragile, infirm, declining, POWERLESS.

feeble-minded *adj*. weak-minded, empty-headed, slow-witted, RETARDED, defective, subnormal.

feeble-mindedness: see STUPIDITY.

feebleness: see WEAKNESS.

feed *v*. NOURISH, nurture, FILL, SUSTAIN, subsist, SUPPLY, SATISFY.
— *n*. fodder, PASTURE, forage, provisions.

feel *v*. **1** *(she felt the new textiles)* TOUCH, HANDLE, fondle, FINGER, PROBE, EXPLORE; **2** *(she felt sorry for him)* SUFFER, EXPERIENCE, ENJOY, SENSE, perceive, CONSIDER.
— *n*.: see TEXTURE; TOUCH.

feeling *n*. SENSATION, perception, TENDERNESS, susceptibility, EMOTION, SYMPATHY, intuition.
— *adj*.: see HUMAN.

feign: see AFFECT; CAMOUFLAGE; DISGUISE.

fell: see FLOOR.

fellow *n*. BOY, LAD, YOUTH, PERSON, CHAP, MATE, COMPANION.

fellowship: see BROTHERHOOD; CHAIR; CLUB; COMPANIONSHIP; FRIENDSHIP; GRANT; SYMPATHY.

felon: see CONVICT; DELINQUENT.

felony: see CRIME.

felt: see MAT.

felt-tip: see PEN.

female *n*. WOMAN, GIRL, LADY.
— *adj*. FEMININE, womanlike, girlish, ladylike, maidenly, GENTLE, DELICATE, SOFT, MOTHERLY.

feminine *adj*. FEMALE, WOMANLY, MOTHERLY, matronly, DELICATE, TENDER, GENTLE, SOFT.

fen: see SWAMP.

fence *n*. ENCLOSURE, WALL, BARRIER, HEDGE, stockade, paling.
— *v*. **1** *(to fence the garden)* ENCLOSE, wall, GUARD,

PROTECT; **2** (*to fence an opponent*) duel, FIGHT, joust.

fence in: see CAGE; PEN.

fencing: see PEN.

ferment: see BOIL; TURN; WORK.

fermented: see SOUR.

ferocious: see FIERCE; VIOLENT; WILD.

ferocity: see CRUELTY; FURY; VIOLENCE.

ferry *v.* TRANSPORT, CARRY, CART, HAUL.
— *n.* BOAT, barge.

fertile *adj.* PRODUCTIVE, fruitful, prolific, potent, reproductive, creative.

fertility *n.* PRODUCTIVITY, fruitfulness, creativity, potency, RICHNESS.

fertilization: see GENERATION.

fertilize: see TILL.

fervent: see EAGER; EARNEST; ENTHUSIASTIC; INTENSE; WARM.

fervor: see HEAT; INTENSITY; WARMTH.

festival *n.* FEAST, carnival, CELEBRATION, HOLIDAY.

festive *adj.* jovial, GAY, MERRY, HAPPY, joyous, JOLLY.

festivity *n.* FUN, joyousness, gaiety, PARTY, gala, fiesta.

fetch: see GET.

feud *n.* FIGHT, QUARREL, DISPUTE, squabble, DISAGREEMENT, controversy, animosity.
— *v.*: see ARGUE.

fever *n.* TEMPERATURE, HEAT, FLUSH, FIRE, delirium, frenzy, EXCITEMENT.

feverish *adj.* HOT, flushed, delirious, hectic, frenzied, agitated, excited.

few *adj.* scantily, sparsely, RARELY, thinly, infrequently, minutely, insignificantly.
— *n.* HANDFUL, COUPLE, PAIR.

fewer: see LESS; LESSER.

fiancé: see BELOVED; GROOM; LOVER.

fiancée: see LOVER.

fiasco: see BLUNDER.

fib *n.* LIE, falsehood, untruth, STORY, TALE, YARN.
— *v.* LIE, INVENT, WITHHOLD.

fiber *n.* THREAD, strand, CORD, filament, wire, HAIR, nap.

fickle: see CHANGEABLE; UNFAITHFUL; UNRELIABLE.

fiction *n.* STORY, TALE, LEGEND, MYTH, NOVEL, INVENTION, fabrication, IMAGINATION.

fictional *adj.* MYTHICAL, anecdotal, narrative, invented, fanciful, IMAGINARY, novelized.

fictitious *adj.* MYTHICAL, FANTASTIC, contrived, concocted, legendary, FABULOUS, invented, fanciful.

fiddle: see DABBLE.

fiddlestick: see BOW.

fidelity: see ALLEGIANCE; EXACTNESS; FAITH; HONESTY; LOYALTY.

fidget: see SQUIRM.

fidgety: see FRISKY.

field *n.* LAND, PASTURE, RANGE, TRACT, plot, MEADOW, clearing. See also BUSINESS.

fiend: see ANIMAL; DEMON; DEVIL; MONSTER.

fierce *adj.* WILD, untamed, ferocious, SAVAGE, VICIOUS, VIOLENT, FURIOUS.

fiercely: see FORCIBLY.

fiery *adj.* burning, flaming, HOT, heated, ardent, PASSIONATE, hot-tempered.

fiesta: see FESTIVITY.

fiftieth: see GOLDEN.

fifty-fifty: see HALF.

fight *n.* BATTLE, COMBAT, strife, CONFLICT, QUARREL, FEUD, ARGUMENT.
— *v.* QUARREL, feud, DISPUTE, ARGUE, COMBAT, battle, brawl.

fighter *n.* contender, combatant, WARRIOR, SOLDIER, aggressor, attacker, boxer.

fighting: see ACTION; WAR; WARFARE.

figure *n.* **1** (*what are those figures in the dark?*) SHAPE, OUTLINE, APPEARANCE, FORM; **2** (*your figures are incorrect*) NUMBER, cipher, digit, CHARACTER, RATE, PRICE, QUOTATION; **3** (*she has a good figure*) SHAPE, BODY, torso, FORM, DEVELOPMENT.
— *v.* THINK, IMAGINE, DECIDE, ESTIMATE, CALCULATE, ADD, cipher.

figurine: see DOLL.

filament: see BULB; COBWEB; FIBER; HAIR; THREAD.

filch: see RUSTLE; SNEAK; STEAL.

file *n.* **1** (*in single file*) RANK, LINE, ROW, COLUMN; **2** (*to check the file*) RECORD, INDEX, REGISTER, CATALOG, ROLL, archive; **3** (*a nail file*) sander, sharpener.
— *v.* **1** (*to file into a room*) MARCH, align, line up, ARRANGE; **2** (*to file a letter*) STORE, DEPOSIT,

CATALOG, LIST, CLASSIFY; **3** *(to file smooth)* SMOOTH, SHARPEN, FINISH.

filibuster: see STALL.

fill *v.* **1** *(fill the tank)* PACK, cram, SUPPLY, LOAD, CHARGE, replenish; **2** *(to fill a hole)* PATCH, REPAIR, MEND, RESTORE.
— *n.*: see PADDING.

filled: see CHOCK-FULL; FULL.

filler: see PADDING.

filling: see PAD; PADDING.

filly: see HORSE.

film *n.* **1** *(a film of dirt)* LAYER, membrane, gauze, TISSUE, CLOUD, COATING; **2** *(a roll of film)* filmstrip, TAPE, roll, positive, negative; **3** *(the latest film)* motion picture, movie, photoplay, flick, cinema.
— *v.* photograph, SHOOT.

filmstrip: see FILM.

filter *n.* strainer, sieve, SCREEN.
— *v.* STRAIN, SCREEN, REFINE, SIFT, SEPARATE.

filth *n.* DIRT, rot, muck, MUD, foulness, corruption, nastiness.

filthiness: see COARSENESS.

filthy *adj.* DIRTY, soiled, NASTY, FOUL, unclean, IMPURE.

filtration: see CLARIFICATION.

final *adj.* ultimate, LAST, terminal, CONCLUSIVE, decisive.

finale: see FINISH.

finally *adv.* ultimately, lastly, EVENTUALLY, conclusively.

finance *v.* FUND, BACK, GUARANTEE, SUPPORT, PAY.
— *n.* banking, economics, BUSINESS, COMMERCE, REVENUE.

finances *pl.n.* CAPITAL, funds, MONEY, REVENUE.

financial *adj.* monetary, fiscal, COMMERCIAL.

find *v.* DISCOVER, ENCOUNTER, DETECT, ascertain, NOTICE, LOCATE.
— *n.* DISCOVERY, finding, treasure trove.

finding: see FIND; DISCOVERY; JUDGMENT; VERDICT.

find out *v.* LEARN, DISCOVER, ascertain, perceive, DETECT, SOLVE, decipher.

fine *adj.* **1** *(fine sand)* MINUTE, DELICATE, subtle, LIGHT, refined, powdery; **2** *(a fine gem)* RARE, EXQUISITE, EXCELLENT, FIRST-RATE.
— *n.* PENALTY, PUNISHMENT, damages.
— *v.* penalize, PUNISH, confiscate.

fine arts: see ART.

fineness: see TEXTURE.

finer: see BETTER; SUPERIOR.

finger *n.* digit, toe, index finger, thumb.
— *v.* **1** *(to finger a fabric)* FEEL, TOUCH, manipulate; **2** *(to finger the culprit)* ACCUSE, INDICATE, denounce, BETRAY, sell out.

fingernail: see NAIL.

fingerprint: see TRACK.

finicky: see CHOOSY; FUSSY; PARTICULAR.

finish *v.* CONCLUDE, CLOSE, END, CEASE, wrap up.
— *n.* **1** *(to bring to a finish)* END, CONCLUSION, finale, termination; **2** *(a glossy finish)* COAT, LAYER, POLISH, PAINT, GLOSS, SHINE.

finished: see COMPLETE; OVER; PAST.

fire *n.* **1** *(to start a fire)* FLAME, BLAZE, HEARTH, WARMTH, campfire, conflagration; **2** *(to have fire)* zeal, vehemence, PASSION, DASH, panache.
— *v.* **1** *(to fire a cannon)* KINDLE, ignite, DISCHARGE, set off; **2** *(to fire a shirker)* DISCHARGE, DISMISS, eject, let go. See also BAKE.

firearm *n.* WEAPON, GUN, PISTOL, REVOLVER, RIFLE.

firebrand: see TORCH.

fireplace: see HEARTH.

fireside: see HEARTH.

firewood: see WOOD.

fireworks: see ROCKET.

firm *adj.* SOLID, STEADY, SECURE, STRONG, HARD, STURDY, staunch, determined, CONSTANT, unmoved, unshakable.
— *n.* COMPANY, BUSINESS, enterprise, CORPORATION, ASSOCIATION, associates.
— *v.*: see HARDEN.

firmly *adv.* fixedly, fast, STEADILY, strongly, solidly, tightly, decisively.

firmness *n.* STRENGTH, stability, tenseness, stiffness, solidity, hardness, compactness.

first *adj.* INITIAL, ORIGINAL, beginning, CHIEF.

−*adv.* firstly, initially, primarily.
−*n.* winner, LEADER.

first-born: see SENIOR.

first-class: see FIRST-RATE; FOREMOST.

firsthand *adj.* DIRECT, IMMEDIATE, authoritative.
−*adv.* FIRST, DIRECTLY, INSTANTLY, EARLY.

firstly: see first; ORIGINALLY.

first-rate *adj.* EXCELLENT, first-class, FINE, CHOICE, SUPERIOR, top, top-notch.

fiscal: see FINANCIAL.

fish *v.* angle, cast, SEARCH, SEEK, PROBE, DIG.

fishy *adj.* suspect, SUSPICIOUS, DOUBTFUL, dubious, improbable, unlikely.

fissure: see RENT.

fist: see HAND.

fistful: see HANDFUL.

fit *adj.* **1** (*fit for service*) SUITABLE, suited, APT; **2** (*fit as a fiddle*) HEALTHY, robust.
−*v.* SUIT, CLOTHE, ADJUST, EQUIP, tailor.
−*n.* **1** (*a good fit*) suitability, FITNESS; **2** (*a fit of laughter*) ATTACK, seizure, BURST.

fitful: see RESTLESS.

fitness *n.* suitability, appropriateness, capability, aptitude.

fitted: see CONVENIENT.

fitting *adj.* PROPER, RIGHT, suited, seemly, DUE, congruent.
−*n.*: see PLUG.

fittings: see FURNITURE.

fix *v.* **1** (*to fix a date*) SET, SECURE, FASTEN, tighten, focus; **2** (*to fix a leak*) MEND, PATCH, REPAIR, ADJUST, PREPARE, ready. See also BRIBE.
−*n.*: see JAM.

fixed *adj.* **1** (*a fixed idea*) SET, FAST, arranged, settled; **2** (*my watch is fixed*) repaired, mended, rebuilt, READY.

fixedly: see FIRMLY.

fixing: see REPAIR.

fixture: see LAMP; LIGHT.

fixtures: see FURNITURE.

fizz: see HISS.

fizzy: see FOAMY.

flabbergast: see SURPRISE.

flabbiness: see LIMP.

flabby *adj.* SOFT, LIMP. WEAK, SLACK, inelastic, yielding.

flag *n.* BANNER, standard, colors, SIGNAL.
−*v.* SIGNAL, NOTIFY, WAVE, SALUTE, CALL, MARK, IDENTIFY; BAG; DECLINE; TIRE.

flagrant: see CONSPICUÓUS; EXTREME; NOTORIOUS.

flail: see THRASH.

flair: see ABILITY; GENIUS.

flake *n.* wafer, peel, LAYER, shaving, sliver.
−*v.* scale, PEEL, CHIP, WEAR.

flame *n.* FIRE, FLARE, FLASH, blaze, LIGHT.
−*v.* FLARE, FLASH, ignite, BURN, redden.

flaming: see FIERY; HOT.

flank *n.* SIDE, EDGE, BORDER, wing, loin.

flanking: see SIDE.

flap *v.* FLUTTER, waver, SWING, BEAT, SMACK.
−*n.* **1** (*the flap of a flag*) FLUTTER, slap, SWING; **2** (*to lick the flap*) tab, lapel, wing, STRIP; **3** (*to cause a flap*) COMMOTION, dither.

flare *v.* BLAZE, FLASH, FLAME, ignite, ERUPT.
−*n.* FLAME, SIGNAL, skyrocket, LIGHT, BURST, GLARE.

flare up: see BLAZE.

flare-up: see SCENE.

flash *n.* **1** (*a sudden flash*) STREAK, FLARE, GLEAM, outburst; **2** (*in a flash*) INSTANT, WINK, JIFFY, TWINKLE, SECOND.
−*v.* SPARK, BLAZE, GLARE, BURST.

flashing: see DAZZLING.

flashlight: see LANTERN; TORCH.

flask: see BOTTLE; CAPSULE; JUG.

flat *adj.* LEVEL, EVEN, SHALLOW, DULL, insipid, tasteless, broke.
−*n.* **1** (*the flat of the back*) PLAIN, PLANE, SIDE, WIDTH, expanse; **2** (*we had a flat*) blowout, BURST, EXPLOSION; **3** (*a new flat*) APARTMENT, ROOM, suite, LODGINGS.

flatboat: see RAFT.

flatiron: see IRON.

flatten: see PRESS; SMOOTH; SPREAD.

flatter *v.* butter up, glorify, PRAISE, adulate.

flattery: see COMPLIMENT.

flaunt: see BOAST; DISPLAY; PARADE.

flavor *n.* TASTE, savor, tang, essence.
  — *v.* SEASON, spice, SALT.

flavoring: see SPICE.

flaw: see BLEMISH; BLOT; DEFECT; SCAR; SPOT; VEIN.

flawless: see PERFECT.

fleck: see SPECK; SPOT.

fledgling: see YOUNGSTER.

flee *v.* RUN, ESCAPE, bolt, AVOID, DODGE.

fleece: see COAT; ROB; SWINDLE; THIEVE.

fleet *n.* NAVY, armada, GROUP, FORMATION. *adj.*:
  see QUICK; RAPID; SWIFT.

fleeting: see MOMENTARY.

flesh *n.* MEAT, TISSUE, BODY, SUBSTANCE, MAN.

fleshy: see FAT; STOUT.

flex: see ARCH; BEND.

flexibility *n.* pliability, pliancy, compliance,
  suppleness, limberness, adaptability, affability.

flexible *adj.* pliable, pliant, supple, LIMBER,
  elastic, compliant, yielding.

flick: see FILM; SNAP.

flicker *v.* SPARKLE, glimmer, TWINKLE, FLASH.
  — *n.* FLASH, TWINKLE, glimmer, HINT.

flier: see BIRD; PILOT.

flight *n.* **1** *(the flight of birds)* aviation, aeronautics,
  winging, soaring; **2** *(his sudden flight)* ESCAPE,
  disappearance, breakout, getaway; **3** *(one flight
  up)* stair, stairs, staircase, FLOOR, landing.

flighty: see CHANGEABLE; DIZZY.

flimsy *adj.* DELICATE, DAINTY, FRAIL, fragile,
  WEAK, SLIGHT, unsubstantial, POOR.

flinch: see SHRINK; STARTLE.

fling *v.* HURL, HEAVE, SLING, TOSS, CAST, THROW.

flint: see STEEL; STONE.

flinty: see ROCKY.

flirtation: see ROMANCE.

float *v.* skim, DRIFT, GLIDE, SOAR, SAIL, hover.
  — *n.*: see RAFT.

floater: see DRIFTER.

flock *n.* PACK, MASS, GROUP, throng, MULTITUDE.
  — *v.*: see CONGREGATE; TROOP.

flog: see LASH; SPANK; SWITCH; WHIP.

flood *n.* overflow, outpouring, TIDE, TORRENT,
  BATH, oversupply, EXCESS, glut.
  — *v.* deluge, SUBMERGE, OVERWHELM, DROWN.

floor *n.* BOTTOM, BASE, deck, GROUND, pavement,
  STORY, LEVEL, STAGE.
  — *v.* fell, down, drop, upset, topple.

floor-covering: see RUG.

floppy: see SLACK.

flounder: see FAIL; ROCK.

flour: see MEAL.

flourish *v.* **1** *(the flowers flourish)* THRIVE, FLOWER,
  PROSPER, SUCCEED; **2** *(to flourish a club)* WAVE,
  brandish, SWING.
  — *n.*: see TWIST.

flourishing: see GREEN; SUCCESSFUL.

flout: see DEFY; SCOFF.

flouting: see VIOLATION.

flow *v.* STREAM, GLIDE, SLIP, FLOAT, POUR, FLOOD,
  gush.
  — *n.* CURRENT, TIDE, movement, ISSUE, FLOOD.

flower *n.* BUD, BLOSSOM, bloom, posy, FRUIT.
  — *v.* BLOSSOM, OPEN, BLOOM, mature, PROSPER,
  DEVELOP.

flowing: see FLUID; GRACEFUL; RUNNING.

flow over: see SWEEP.

flu: see COLD.

flub: see GOOF.

fluctuate: see VARY; VIBRATE.

fluctuating: see VARIABLE.

fluctuation: see VIBRATION.

fluffy: see FUZZY; LIGHT.

fluid *n.* LIQUID, LIQUOR, SOLUTION, JUICE, SAP.
  — *adj.* FORMLESS, CHANGEABLE, flowing, watery,
  molten, amorphous.

fluidity: see MOBILITY, THICKNESS.

fluke: see LUCK.

flunk: see FAIL.

flunky: see ASSISTANT; FOLLOWER; PAWN.

flurry: see BREEZE; HURRY.

flush *n.* **1** *(a flush of water)* FLOOD, BATH, WASH,
  TIDE; **2** *(a straight flush)* HAND, SET,
  COMBINATION; **3** *(a delicate flush)* blush, GLOW,
  EXCITEMENT.

− *v.* FLOOD, DRAIN, EVACUATE, CLEAR, rout. See also BLUSH; COLOR.
− *adj.:* see EVEN; LEVEL.

flushed: see FEVERISH.

fluster: see UPSET.

flustered: see UPSET.

flutter *v.* FLAP, BEAT, SLAP, QUIVER, drum.
− *n.* FLAP, VIBRATION, BEAT, tizzy, EXCITEMENT.

flux: see MOBILITY; MOTION; TIDE.

fly *v.* 1 *(most birds fly)* SOAR, SAIL, GLIDE, FLOAT, wing; 2 *(to fly an airplane)* NAVIGATE, PILOT, maneuver; 3 *(to fly from danger)* FLEE, dart, RUSH, scurry, HIDE.
− *n.* housefly, horsefly, mosquito, INSECT.

flying: see SPEEDY.

foam *n.* lather, froth, suds, head.
− *v.* froth, bubble, effervesce.

foamy *adj.* fizzy, frothy, lathery, sudsy, creamy, bubbling, burbling.

focus: see CENTER; CONCENTRATE; CONCENTRATION; FIX; MIDDLE; SHARPEN.

fodder: see FEED; HAY.

foe *n.* ENEMY, OPPONENT, adversary, RIVAL, antagonist.

fog *n.* MIST, VAPOR, CLOUD, haze, bewilderment.

fogginess: see WETNESS.

foggy *adj.* 1 *(a foggy day)* CLOUDY, misty, DIM, blurry, HAZY; 2 *(a foggy idea)* confused, dazed, bewildered.

foil *v.* OUTWIT, frustrate, PREVENT, STOP, SPOIL, impede, thwart.
− *n.* plate, LEAF, FILM. See also SWORD.

fold *v.* 1 *(do not fold)* crease, BEND, WRINKLE; 2 *(the firm folded)* FAIL, COLLAPSE, default, go under.
− *n.* 1 *(a fold of flesh)* crease, WRINKLE, bend, overlap 2 *(to enter the fold)* corral, PEN, FLOCK, CONGREGATION.

folder *n.* portfolio, FILE, binder, wrapper.

folk *n.* NATION, TRIBE, clan, RACE, PEOPLE, kindred.

folklore: see MYTH; TRADITION.

folks: see FAMILY; HOUSEHOLD; KIN; PEOPLE.

folk tale: see MYTH.

folkway: see TRADITION.

follow *v.* 1 *(follow the leader)* PURSUE, CHASE, TRACK, TRAIL; 2 *(a long war followed)* ensue, result, SUCCEED; 3 *(to follow directions)* OBEY, HEED, OBSERVE, conform.

follower *n.* pursuer, partisan, SUPPORTER, FAN, DISCIPLE, CONVERT, MEMBER, flunky, yes-man, admirer.

following *adj.* subsequent, NEXT, ensuing.
− *n.* supporters, TRAIN, entourage, PUBLIC, AUDIENCE.
− *adv.:* see NEXT.
− *prep.:* see AFTER; BY; UNDER.

follow up: see CONTINUE.

follow-up: see CONTINUATION.

folly *n.* absurdity, NONSENSE, frivolity, STUPIDITY, BLUNDER, boner.

fond *adj.* PARTIAL, AFFECTIONATE, attached, FRIENDLY.

fondle: see CARESS; FEEL; PET.

fondly: see TENDERLY.

fondness: see AFFECTION; ATTACHMENT; CLOSENESS; DESIRE; RELISH.

food *n.* NOURISHMENT, sustenance, BREAD, FARE, foodstuff, provisions, grub, eats, chow.

foodstuff: see FOOD.

foodstuffs: see NOURISHMENT.

fool *n.* nitwit, dunce, oaf, nincompoop, ASS, ninny.
− *v.* clown, JOKE, dupe, DECEIVE, PRETEND.

foolhardy: see DARING; HASTY; RASH; RECKLESS.

foolish *adj.* inane, SENSELESS, STUPID, asinine, HALF-WITTED, unwise.

foolishness *n.* STUPIDITY, silliness, idiocy, imbecility, senselessness, witlessness.

foolscap: see PAPER.

foot *n.* 1 *(a sore foot)* PAW, HOOF, extremity, toe, sole; 2 *(the foot of the hill)* BOTTOM, BASE, EXTREME, pedestal.

footage: see AREA.

footfall: see STEP.

foothold: see ENTRANCE; ENTRY.

footing: see BASEMENT; FOUNDATION.

footlocker: see TRUNK.

footmark: see FOOTPRINT; FOOTSTEP.

footnote *n.* NOTE, notation, commentary, datum, REMARK, REMINDER, postscript, afterthought.

footpath *n.* PATH, way, pathway, TRAIL, footway, COURSE, sidewalk, PASSAGE.

footprint *n.* TRACE, TRAIL, TRACK, footmark.

footstep *n.* STEP, stride, FOOTPRINT, footmark, TRACK, TRACE.

footstool: see STOOL.

footway: see FOOTPATH.

footwear: see BOOT; SHOE.

for *prep.* TOWARD, pro, instead of, DURING, BY, CONCERNING, DESPITE, due to.
— *conj.* BECAUSE, SINCE, inasmuch as.

forage: see FEED; HAY.

foray: see RAID.

forbearance: see PATIENCE; TOLERANCE.

forbearing: see PATIENT.

forbid *v.* PROHIBIT, ban, disallow, PREVENT, STOP, outlaw, VETO.

forbidden *adj.* banned, outlawed, ILLEGAL, TABOO, unlawful, refused.

forbidding: see PREVENTION.

force *n.* **1** *(to take by force)* VIOLENCE, ARMS, compulsion, bloodshed; **2** *(an invasion in force)* POWER, MIGHT, STRENGTH; **3** *(armed forces)* ARMY, TROOPS, DIVISION, BAND, UNIT.
— *v.* COMPEL, OBLIGE, constrain, SHATTER, DRIVE.

forced: see UNNATURAL.

forceful *adj.* thrusting, pushing, ENERGETIC, VIGOROUS, MIGHTY, STRONG, VITAL, POWERFUL.

forces: see TROOPS.

forcibly *adv.* vigorously, strongly, powerfully, energetically, fiercely, vehemently, compellingly, compulsorily, convincingly, NECESSARILY.

ford: see CROSS.

forearm: see ARM.

forebear: see ANCESTOR; GRANDFATHER; GRANDMOTHER.

forebears: see FAMILY; FOREFATHERS.

forebode: see FOREWARN.

forecast: see AWAIT; FORESEE; FORESIGHT; FORETHOUGHT; OUTLOOK; PREDICTION; THREAT.

forefather: see ANCESTOR; GRANDFATHER.

forefathers *pl.n.* ancestors, predecessors, forebears, ancestry.

forego: see SACRIFICE.

foregoing *adj.* PRECEDING, aforesaid, PRIOR, FORMER.

foregone *adj.* decided, predetermined, FIXED, PAST, earlier.

foreground: see FRONT.

forehead: see BROW.

foreign *adj.* alien, exotic, immigrant, STRANGE, DISTANT, OUTSIDE, REMOTE.

foreigner *n.* ALIEN, IMMIGRANT, outsider, STRANGER, newcomer, TOURIST.

foreknowledge: see FORESIGHT.

foreman *n.* MANAGER, overseer, SUPERINTENDENT, SUPERVISOR, BOSS.

foremost *adj.* prime, FIRST, first-class, LEADING, front, CHIEF.

forenoon: see MORNING.

forepart: see FRONT.

forerunner: see ANCESTOR; PROPHET; SYMPTOM.

foresee *v.* preview, PREDICT, ANTICIPATE, forecast, foretell, prophesy.

foreseeing: see CAREFUL.

foresight *n.* vision, foreknowledge, PROSPECT, preconception, FORETHOUGHT, forecast, anticipation.

forest *n.* woods, timberland, WILDERNESS, WILD, JUNGLE.

forestall: see AVERT.

forestalling: see PREVENTIVE.

foretell: see FORESEE; PREDICT.

foretelling: see PREDICTION.

forethought *n.* forecast, FORESIGHT, prudence, PRECAUTION, providence, anticipation.

forever *adv.* infinitely, CONTINUALLY, continuously, EVER, EVERMORE, ALWAYS.

forewarn *v.* WARN, ALERT, admonish, CAUTION, forebode.

forewarning: see PRECAUTION.

foreword: see PREFACE.

forfeit: see LOSE; PENALTY; SACRIFICE.

forge *v.* **1** *(to forge a signature)* falsify, counterfeit, fabricate, IMITATE; **2** *(to forge a career)* SHAPE, MOLD, FORM, fashion, HAMMER.
— *n.:* see FURNACE; PLANT.

forged: see BEATEN.

forget *v.* NEGLECT, disremember, OVERLOOK, OMIT, IGNORE, disregard, FAIL, slight.

forgetful *adj.* ABSENT-MINDED, oblivious, preoccupied, unmindful.

forgetfulness *n.* inattention, heedlessness, absent-mindedness, carelessness, negligence, amnesia.

forgivable: see EXCUSABLE.

forgive *v.* PARDON, OVERLOOK, EXCUSE, DISMISS, acquit, remit, exonerate, FORGET.

forgiveness *n.* PARDON, absolution, acquittal, MERCY, clemency, reprieve.

forgiving: see MERCIFUL.

forgotten *adj.* overlooked, LOST, neglected, abandoned, gone, PAST.

fork *n.* **1** *(a salad fork)* holder, UTENSIL, pitchfork, SPEAR; **2** *(a fork in the road)* BRANCH, split, junction, crossroads, crossways, intersection.

forlorn: see ALONE; JOYLESS; LONELY; LONESOME; WRETCHED.

form *n.* **1** *(an elegant form)* SHAPE, FIGURE, contour, configuration; **2** *(shaped in a form)* MOLD, CAST, MODEL, PATTERN, BLOCK, dummy, mannequin; **3** *(fill out a form)* BLANK, ORDER, APPLICATION, questionnaire. See also CEREMONY.
— *v.* DESIGN, SHAPE, FASHION, ORGANIZE, MAKE, CREATE.

formal *adj.* CEREMONIAL, OFFICIAL, CORRECT, prescribed, STRICT, STIFF.

formality *n.* CEREMONY, etiquette, ORDER, CONVENTION, rite, CUSTOM, stiffness.

formation *n.* ARRANGEMENT, configuration, SHAPE, ORGANIZATION, ESTABLISHMENT, BEGINNING, CREATION.

former *adj.* **1** *(his former wife)* PREVIOUS, PRECEDING, LATE, onetime; **2** *(the former of two)* FIRST, OTHER.

formerly *adv.* PREVIOUSLY, BEFORE, ONCE, AGO.

formidable: see DREADFUL; FEARFUL.

forming: see ON.

formless *adj.* SHAPELESS, indefinite, VAGUE, indistinct, unmolded, undeveloped.

formula *n.* RECIPE, SPECIFICATION, PROCEDURE, PREPARATION, PRESCRIPTION, cliche, platitude.

formulate: see COMPOSE; CONSTRUCT; DESIGN.

formulation: see COMPOSITION; ORGANIZATION.

fornication: see SEX.

forsake: see DESERT; LEAVE.

forsaken: see ALONE; DESOLATE; LEFT; LONESOME.

fort *n.* FORTRESS, citadel, CASTLE, pillbox.

forth *adv.* FORWARD, OUT, AHEAD, ONWARD.

forthcoming: see NEAR, ONCOMING.

fortification: see TOWER.

fortify: see ARM; BARRICADE; CONFIRM; HARDEN; STRENGTHEN.

fortitude: see HEART; PATIENCE.

fortress *n.* stronghold, CASTLE, blockhouse, FORT.

fortunate *adj.* LUCKY, HAPPY, PROSPEROUS, FAVORED, well-off, FAVORABLE.

fortune *n.* WEALTH, RICHES, TREASURE, treasure-trove, ESTATE, LUCK, BREAK, DESTINY.

fortuneteller: see PROPHET.

fortunetelling: see PREDICTION.

forty winks: see SLUMBER.

forward *adv.* AHEAD, ON, ONWARD, FORTH.
— *adj.* LEADING, FOREMOST, AMBITIOUS, pushy.
— *v.* ADVANCE, SEND, SHIP, PAY.

foster *v.* RAISE, TEND, CARE, ENCOURAGE.
— *adj.* DEPUTY, SUBSTITUTE, stand-in.

foul *adj.* **1** *(foul air)* polluted, FILTHY, vile, IMPURE; **2** *(foul language)* disgusting, lewd, offensive, VULGAR, obscene; **3** *(a foul ball)* WRONG, ILLEGAL, improper, UNFAIR.
— *v.:* see SOIL.

fouling: see POLLUTION.

foul-mouthed: see CRUDE.

foulness: see FILTH; GRIME.

foul-up: see CONFUSION; TANGLE.

found *v.* set-up, ESTABLISH, BEGIN, initiate.
— *adj.:* see SITUATED.

foundation *n.* **1** *(a weakened foundation)* BASIS, BASE, BASEMENT, REASON, BOTTOM, footing,

underpinning; **2** *(a charitable foundation)*
INSTITUTION, CHARITY, endowment, BEGINNING.

founder *n.* MAKER, creator, ARCHITECT, AUTHOR,
FATHER, PATRON, INVENTOR.

founding: see ESTABLISHMENT.

foundry: see FACTORY; MILL; PLANT.

fountain *n.* SPRING, SOURCE, CAUSE, spout, JET.

fountainhead: see SPRING.

fountain pen: see PEN.

fowl *n.* BIRD, poultry, chicken, GAME.

fox *n.* canine, vixen, CHEAT, confidence man,
schemer, trickster, BEAUTY.

foxy *adj.* SLY, CLEVER, CUNNING, wily, devious,
good-looking, PRETTY, sensuous, sexy.

fraction *n.* PART, SECTION, BIT, segment,
DIVISION, PORTION, FRAGMENT.

fractional: see PART; PARTIAL.

fracture: see BREAK; CRACK.

fractured: see BROKEN.

fragile: see BRITTLE; CRISPY; DAINTY; DELICATE;
FEEBLE; FLIMSY; FRAIL; POWERLESS.

fragility: see WEAKNESS.

fragment *n.* SCRAP, REMNANT, leftover, BIT,
FRACTION.
— *v.*: see MINCE.

fragmentary: see PART; PARTIAL.

fragmentate: see CRUMBLE.

fragments: see REMAINS.

fragrance *n.* aroma, SCENT, essence, COLOGNE.

fragrant *adj.* aromatic, odorous, savory, SWEET,
redolent, scented.

frail *adj.* FEEBLE, WEAK, fragile, DELICATE, DAINTY.

frailty: see WEAKNESS.

frame *n.* **1** *(the frame is erected)* framework,
SKELETON, SUPPORT, ARCHITECTURE, physique;
2 *(a gilt frame)* MARGIN, BORDER, TRIM, FRINGE,
mounting, holder.
— *v.* **1** *(to frame a pact)* PLAN, DRAW, DRAFT; **2** *(to
frame a photo)* MOUNT; ENCASE; **3** *(to frame a
person)* ENTRAP, BETRAY.

frame of mind: see MOOD.

framework: see FRAME; RACK; SHELL; SKELETON;
STRUCTURE.

franchise: see CHAIN; CHARTER; LIBERTY; PERMIT.

frank *adj.* candid, OPEN, straightforward, HONEST,
outspoken.

frankly: see OPENLY.

frankness: see INNOCENCE; SINCERITY.

frantic *adj.* WILD, MAD, raving, frenzied, excited,
delirious.

fraternal: see BROTHERLY; CHUMMY.

fraternity: see BROTHERHOOD; CLUB; ORDER;
SOCIETY.

fraternization: see ASSOCIATION.

fraternize: see ASSOCIATE; BEFRIEND; MINGLE;
MIX.

fraud *n.* **1** *(the claim is a fraud)* deception, TRICK
TRICKERY, falsity; **2** *(he is a fraud)* CHEAT,
trickster, phony, IMPOSTER.

fraudulent: see CROOKED; MISLEADING.

fray: see BATTLE; RIP; WEAR.

frayed: see RAGGED; SHABBY.

freak *n.* malformation, deformation, abnormality,
monstrosity, MONSTER, ODDITY, CURIOSITY.

freakish: see ODD.

freckle: see DOT.

free *adj.* **1** *(the accused is free)* liberated, unbound,
INDEPENDENT, scot-free, VACANT; **2** *(the wrapping
is free)* complimentary; **3** *(a free manner)*
easygoing, candid, SHAMELESS.
— *v.* LIBERATE, loose, untie, let go.
— *adv.* FREELY, easily, voluntarily.

freedom *n.* LIBERTY, INDEPENDENCE, immunity,
self-government, LICENSE, leeway, LATITUDE.

freehanded: see LIBERAL.

freeing: see RESCUE.

freely *adv.* FREE, OPENLY, voluntarily,
unreservedly.

freeman: see NATIONAL.

freeway: see HIGHWAY.

freeze *v.* **1** *(water will freeze)* FROST, HARDEN,
solidify, NUMB, CHILL, REFRIGERATE; **2** *(to freeze
in one's tracks)* stiffen, STAND, REMAIN, ossify.
— *n.*: see FROST.

freight *n.* CARGO, shipment, LOAD, BURDEN,
GOODS, COST, CHARGE.
— *v.* LOAD, burden.

freighter: see SHIP.

freight load: see CARGO.

frenzied: see DESPERATE; FEVERISH; FRANTIC.

frenzy: see FEVER.

frequency: see CHANNEL; PITCH; REGULARITY.

frequent *adj.* recurrent, REGULAR, NUMEROUS.
— *v.* VISIT, revisit, ATTEND, haunt.

frequented: see HAUNTED.

frequenter: see GUEST; VISITOR.

frequently *adv.* OFTEN, REGULARLY, USUALLY.

fresh *adj.* **1** (*fresh eggs*) RECENT, NEW, CRISP,
brand-new, wholesome, unspoiled; **2** (*a fresh
child*) RUDE, impudent, disrespectful, snippy.

freshen *v.* enliven, revive, revivify, invigorate,
RENEW, rejuvenate, SWEETEN.

freshman: see BEGINNER.

freshness *n.* greenness, bloom, VIGOR, VITALITY,
currency, sparkle, FIRMNESS, recency.

fret *v.* WORRY, agonize, GRIEVE, BOTHER, STEW.
fume.

fretful: see FUSSY.

friar: see HERMIT; MONK.

fricassee: see FRY; SIMMER; STEW.

friction *n.* RESISTANCE, DISAGREEMENT, illwill,
CONFLICT, CLASH, grinding, scraping.

friend *n.* ACQUAINTANCE, ally, SUPPORTER, PAL,
COMPANION, COMRADE, crony, sidekick,
confidante, confidant.

friendless: see LONELY; SOLITARY.

friendliness: see AFFECTION; GOODNESS; WARMTH.

friendly *adj.* amiable, SYMPATHETIC, SOCIABLE,
likable, AFFECTIONATE, neighborly.

friendship *n.* ACQUAINTANCE, COMPANIONSHIP,
ASSOCIATION, BROTHERHOOD, fellowship,
intimacy, CLOSENESS.

frigate: see SHIP.

fright *n.* ALARM, FEAR, DREAD, HORROR, PANIC,
TERROR.

frighten *v.* SCARE, ALARM, SHOCK, DISMAY,
intimidate, TERRIFY, PANIC.

frightened: see AFRAID; BREATHLESS; COWARDLY;
PANICKY.

frightening: see FEARFUL; SCARY.

frightful *adj.* AWFUL, DREADFUL, shocking,
ghastly, appalling, horrendous, HORRIBLE.

frigid: see COLD; FROZEN; ICY.

frigidity: see COLD.

fringe *n.* EDGE, BORDER, HEM, trimming.

frisk: see PLAY.

frisky *adj.* nervous, twitching, fidgety, GAY,
ACTIVE, LIVELY, PLAYFUL.

frivolity: see FOLLY.

frivolous: see LIGHT; SHALLOW; SILLY.

frock: see GOWN.

frolic: see FUN; PLAY; SKIP; SPORT.

frolicsome: see PLAYFUL.

from *prep.* OF, OFF, OUTSIDE, SINCE, FOR, due to.

frond: see BLADE; NEEDLE.

front *n.* **1** (*in the front*) forepart, facade,
foreground, frontage, FACE, visage; **2** (*a solid
front*) UNITY, ALLIANCE, coalition; **3** (*at the front*)
battlefield, battleground.
— *v.* confront, FACE, LEAD.
— *adj.*: see FOREMOST.

frontage: see FRONT.

frontal: see FACIAL.

frontier *n.* BOUNDARY, BORDER, borderland,
hinterland, BUSH, boondocks.

frontiersman: see COLONIST; SETTLER.

frost *n.* hoarfrost, ICE, freeze, COLD, coolness,
aloofness.
— *v.* FREEZE, TOP, COAT, DECORATE, WHITEN.

frosty: see COLD; ICY.

froth; see FOAM.

frothy: see FOAMY.

frown *v.* scowl, GLARE, DISAPPROVE, SNEER.
— *n.* grimace, scowl, smirk, SNEER.

frozen *adj.* iced, COLD, frigid, chilled, hardened,
solidified, FIXED, fast.

frugal: see SPARE; SPARING; THRIFTY.

frugality: see THRIFT.

fruit *n.* **1** (*fruits and vegetables*) SEED, GRAIN, NUT,
berry; **2** (*the fruit of labor*) PRODUCE, PROFIT,
YIELD, OUTCOME, fruitage.

fruitage: see FRUIT.

fruitful: see FERTILE; PREGNANT; PRODUCTIVE; PROFITABLE; RICH.

fruitfulness: see FERTILITY.

fruitless: see UNSUCCESSFUL; USELESS; VAIN.

frustrate: see CROSS; DISAPPOINT; FOIL; PREVENT.

frustrating: see PREVENTIVE.

fry *v.* COOK, singe, brown, braise, fricassee.

fuel *n.* combustible, propellant, NOURISHMENT, FOOD, coal, petroleum, GAS, peat, WOOD.
— *v.* FEED, NOURISH, energize, activate.

fugitive: see OUTLAW.

fulfill *v.* ACHIEVE, SATISFY, ACCOMPLISH, FILL, EFFECT, carry out.

fulfilling: see SATISFACTORY.

fulfillment: see ACHIEVEMENT; REALIZATION.

full *adj.* filled, supplied, CHOCK-FULL, saturated, stocked, jam-packed, unlimited, abounding.

full-fledged: see REAL.

full-grown: see ADULT; GROWN; RIPE.

fullness *n.* completeness, entirety, roominess, expansiveness, profusion, ABUNDANCE, PLENTY.

fully *adv.* COMPLETELY, ENTIRELY, wholly, TOTALLY, ALTOGETHER, QUITE, ENOUGH.

fulminate: see CARRY ON.

fumble: see GOOF.

fume: see BOIL; FRET.

fumes: see GAS; SMOKE.

fun *n.* PLAY, SPORT, JEST, AMUSEMENT, diversion, frolic, merriment, DELIGHT, recreation.

function *n.* **1** *(what is its function?)* PURPOSE, MOTIVE, USE, EMPLOYMENT; **2** *(a social function)* PARTY, RECEPTION, AFFAIR.
— *v.* WORK, RUN, PERFORM, SERVE, ACT.

functional: see USEFUL.

functioning: see EFFECTIVE.

fund *n.* FINANCES, CAPITAL, endowment, RESERVE, SUPPLY, RESOURCE.
— *v.* FINANCE, PAY, BACK, GUARANTEE, SUPPORT.

fundamental *adj.* BASIC, radical, PRIMARY, elemental, ESSENTIAL, NECESSARY, ELEMENTARY.

fundamentally: see PRIMARILY; PRINCIPALLY.

fundamentals: see ALPHABET.

funds: see BUDGET; FINANCES; MONEY; SAVINGS.

funeral *n.* **1** *(to attend a funeral)* BURIAL, solemnity, rite, SERVICE; **2** *(a funeral passed by)* cortege, PROCESSION, mourners.

fungus: see MOLD.

funny *adj.* laughable, comic, COMICAL, humorous, HILARIOUS, ODD, PECULIAR, CURIOUS, ludicrous, RIDICULOUS.

fur *n.* HIDE, pelt, SKIN, COAT, stole, wrap.

furious *adj.* enraged, ANGRY, irate, MAD, VIOLENT, FRANTIC.

furlough: see ABSENCE; HOLIDAY; LEAVE; LIBERTY; VACATION.

furnace *n.* STOVE, heater, boiler, incinerator, kiln, forge.

furnish *v.* SUPPLY, EQUIP, appoint, DECORATE, rig, DISTRIBUTE.

furnishings: see EQUIPMENT; FURNITURE; KIT.

furniture *n.* furnishings, fittings, fixtures, effects, EQUIPMENT, gear.

furrow: see CHANNEL; GROOVE; RIDGE; TROUGH.

furry: see FUZZY.

further *adj.* MORE, ADDITIONAL, NEW, OTHER.
— *adv.* MORE, FARTHER, BEYOND, ALSO, BESIDES.
— *v.* ADVANCE, FOSTER, BACK, PROMOTE.

furthermore *adv.* MOREOVER, ALSO, TOO, YET.

furthest: see UTMOST.

fury *n.* RAGE, VIOLENCE, ferocity, wrath, ANGER, rampage, PASSION, vehemence.

fuse: see BLEND; MATCH; MELT; MIX; UNIFY; UNITE.

fusion: see BLEND.

fuss *n.* to-do, bother, UPSET, DISTURBANCE.
— *v.* OBJECT, RESIST, WHINE, FRET, crab.

fussy *adj.* worrisome, fretful, BOTHERSOME, bustling, finicky, CHOOSY, fastidious, overnice.

futile: see IMPOSSIBLE; UNSUCCESSFUL; USELESS; VAIN.

future *n.* futurity, hereafter, PROSPECT, tomorrow, DESTINY, FATE.
— *adj.* eventual, impending, expected, NEXT, later, subsequent, INEVITABLE.

futurity: see FUTURE.

fuzzy *adj.* **1** *(a fuzzy stuffed animal)* fluffy, furry, hairy, downy, woolly; **2** *(a fuzzy distinction)* unclear, blurred, incoherent, murky, FOGGY.

G

gab *v.* CHATTER, tattle, TELL, TALK, UTTER, gossip, BABBLE.
— *n.:* see CHIT-CHAT.

gabbing: see CACKLE.

gabble: see CACKLE.

gabby: see CHATTY; TALKATIVE.

gadget: see IMPLEMENT; THING; TOOL; TOY.

gag: see CHOKE; HUSH; JEST; SILENCE.

gaiety: see CHEER; CHEERFULNESS; FESTIVITY; HILARITY; JOY.

gaily: see CHEERFULLY.

gain *n.* PROFIT, ADVANTAGE, BENEFIT, ADDITION, INCREASE, IMPROVEMENT, profits.
— *v.* WIN, OBTAIN, EARN, REACH, BENEFIT, PROFIT.

gains: see EARNINGS.

gait: see PACE.

gala: see FESTIVITY.

gale *n.* STORM, tempest, hurricane.

gallant *adj.* **1** *(a gallant knight)* chivalrous, NOBLE, LOFTY, HONORABLE, POLITE, courteous; **2** *(a gallant rescue attempt)* BRAVE, HEROIC, COURAGEOUS, BOLD, DARING.

gallantry: see COURAGE; HEROISM.

gallery *n.* **1** *(the mine shaft led directly to the gallery)* passageway, CORRIDOR, walkway; **2** *(to play to the gallery)* balcony, loft, spectators, AUDIENCE; **3** *(those paintings were hung in the gallery)* salon, museum, HALL.

galosh: see BOOT.

galvanize: see STIR.

gamble *n.* BET, wager, PLAY, RISK, VENTURE, STAKE, GAME, lottery, raffle, HAZARD, CHANCE.
— *v.* BET, wager, PLAY, RISK, VENTURE, stake, game, raffle, HAZARD, chance.

game *n.* **1** *(life is not a game)* SPORT, AMUSEMENT, PLAY, pastime, ENTERTAINMENT, recreation; **2** *(the score of the game)* MATCH, TOURNAMENT, CONTEST, GAMBLE; **3** *(what's his game?)* PLAN, SCHEME; **4** *(to eat game)* quarry, PREY, venison.
— *adj.* **1** *(a game attempt)* BRAVE, valiant; **2** *(a game leg)* LAME, disabled; **3** *(I'm game!)* READY, WILLING.
— *v. see* GAMBLE.

games: see ENTERTAINMENT.

gang *n.* **1** *(a gang war)* BAND, MOB, crooks, gangsters; **2** *(a road gang)* COMPANY, CREW, SET, clique, squad, SHIFT.

gangster *n.* mobster, thug, goon, hoodlum, gunman, racketeer, CRIMINAL.

gangsters: see GANG.

gap *n.* **1** *(the Cumberland gap)* PASS, chasm, ravine; **2** *(to the bridge the gap)* OPENING, breach, rift, BREAK, cleft, SPACE, INTERVAL, crevice, SPLIT.

gape: see GAZE; WONDER.

garage: see STATION.

garb: see DRESS; HABIT; OUTFIT.

garbage *n.* WASTE, SCRAP, debris, LITTER, REFUSE, RUBBISH, TRASH, JUNK.

garden *n.* park, resort, zoo, plants, GROUNDS, plot.
— *v.* CULTIVATE, PLANT.

gardens: see GROUNDS.

garland: see WREATH.

garment *n.* clothing, COSTUME, CLOTHES, DRESS, rainment.

garments: see WARDROBE.

garnet: see MINERAL.

garrulous: see CHATTY; TALKATIVE.

gas *n.* **1** *(an agreement not to use poison gas)* VAPOR, fumes, AIR, STEAM, oxygen, nitrogen, hydrogen; **2** *(my car uses too much gas)* gasoline, FUEL, propane.

gash: see CUT; NOTCH; SLASH; SLIT; SPLIT.

gasoline: see GAS.

gasp *n.* panting, puffing, wheeze.
— *v.* **1** *(he was gasping for air)* PANT, PUFF, CHOKE; **2** *("Wow!" he gasped)* EXCLAIM, cry out.

gasping: see BREATHLESS.

gat: see GUN; PISTOL; REVOLVER.

gate *n.* **1** *(the gate of a fence)* ENTRANCE, entranceway, portal, door; **2** *(to open the gate of the dam)* DAM, BARRIER, valve; **3** *(a gate exceeding thousands of dollars)* proceeds, EARNINGS, TAKE.

gatekeeper: see PORTER.

gather *v.* **1** *(to gather all that one can)* PICK, COLLECT, GROUP, ASSEMBLE, ACCUMULATE, amass, hoard, PLUCK, REAP, come together, CONGREGATE; **2** *(the dress was gathered at the waist)* take in, DRAW, FOLD, pucker; **3** *(I gather that you are ill)* UNDERSTAND, CONCLUDE, infer.

gathering *n.* GROUP, ASSEMBLY, MEETING, COLLECTION.

gauge *v.* ESTIMATE, appraise, assess, MEASURE, rate, JUDGE.
— *n.* MEASURE, STANDARD, RULE, SCALE, norm, criterion.

gaunt: see LEAN.

gauze: see BANDAGE; COBWEB; FILM; TISSUE; VEIL.

gavel: see HAMMER.

gawk: see GAZE.

gawky: see CLUMSY; STIFF.

gay *adj.* **1** *(her lively, gay spirit)* MERRY, LIVELY, joyous, light-hearted, FESTIVE, JOLLY, jovial, showy, DASHING; **2** *(the gay liberation movement)* homosexual, lesbian.

gaze *v.* LOOK, STARE, gape, gawk, GLARE, PEER.
— *n.*: see REGARD; STARE.

gazette: see NEWSPAPER.

gaze upon: see REGARD.

gear: see ASSEMBLY; BAGGAGE; FURNITURE; HARNESS; KIT; OUTFIT; TACKLE.

gem *n.* JEWEL, STONE, TREASURE.

gems: see JEWELRY.

gender: see SEX.

general *adj.* **1** *(in general)* COMMON, USUAL, CUSTOMARY, FAMILIAR, ORDINARY, CURRENT, widespread, UNIVERSAL, POPULAR; **2** *(too general)* indefinite, VAGUE, undefined.
— *n.* commander in chief, generalissimo, CHIEF, LEADER.

generalissimo: see GENERAL.

generally *adv.* COMMONLY, USUALLY, customarily.

generate *v.* PRODUCE, FORM, MAKE, BREED, CREATE, ORIGINATE.

generation *n.* **1** *(the moral values of our generation)* OFFSPRING, descendants, RACE, TRIBE, FAMILY, ISSUE, contemporaries, ERA, epoch, AGE, colleagues; **2** *(the generation of new life)* breeding, fathering, propagation, reproduction, fertilization, conception, genesis; **3** *(the generation of electric power)* PRODUCTION, CREATION, FORMATION, fabrication, genesis, GROWTH, INCREASE, DEVELOPMENT, evolution.

generator *n.* alternator, dynamo, ENGINE, MACHINE, MAKER, creator.

generosity *n.* unselfishness, liberality, CHARITY, sharing.

generous *adj.* unselfish, LIBERAL, CHARITABLE, openhanded, ABUNDANT, AMPLE, munificent.

genesis: see BEGINNING; BIRTH; GENERATION.

genial: see CORDIAL; SOCIABLE.

genie: see FAIRY.

genius *n.* **1** *(we succeeded, thanks to her genius)* GIFT, flair, TALENT, aptitude, INTELLECT, brain, ingenuity, mastermind; **2** *(the genius of the English language)* NATURE, CHARACTERISTIC, SPIRIT.

genocide: see ASSASSINATION; MASSACRE.

gentle *adj.* **1** *(of gentle disposition)* MILD, SOFT, TENDER, KIND, QUIET, PEACEFUL, moderate, GRADUAL, EASY; **2** *(of gentle birth)* NOBLE, highborn, refined, well-bred.

gentleman: see ARISTOCRAT.

gentleness: see KINDNESS; MERCY; MILDNESS; TENDERNESS.

gently: see LIGHTLY; SMOOTHLY; SOFTLY; TENDERLY.

genuflect: see KNEEL.

genuine *adj.* REAL, AUTHENTIC, TRUE, PURE, HONEST, SINCERE, FRANK.

genuineness: see HONESTY; TRUTH.

genus: see CLASS; CLASSIFICATION; SPECIES; TYPE.

germ *n.* *(germs can cause disease)* microbe, bacterium, virus, bacillus, streptococcus; **2** *(the germ of an idea)* SEED, embryo, SPROUT, SOURCE, ORIGIN.

germ free: see SANITARY.

germinate: see SPROUT.

gesticulate: see BECKON; GESTURE.

gesture *n.* **1** *(the speaker's gestures were forceful)* SIGNAL, SIGN, movement, MOTION, mannerism; **2** *(a gesture of good will)* TOKEN, PROMISE, PLEDGE, COMPROMISE.
— *v.* gesticulate, MOTION, SIGNAL.

get *v.* **1** *(to get a glass of water)* RECEIVE, TAKE, fetch, OBTAIN, ACQUIRE, GAIN; **2** *(to get sick)* BECOME, GROW, BE, START, MOVE.

get along: see THRIVE.

getaway: see FLIGHT.

get back: see RECOVER.

get even: see AVENGE.

get there: see REACH.

get together: see MEETING; REUNION.

get up: see ARISE.

get up: see COSTUME; OUTFIT.

get well: see HEAL.

geyser: see JET; SPRING.

ghastly: see FEARFUL; FRIGHTFUL; GRUESOME; PALE.

ghost *n. specter, phantom,* spook, SPIRIT, apparition, SHADE.

giant *n.* MONSTER, colossus, muscleman, powerhouse, CELEBRITY.
— *adj.* HUGE, LARGE, ENORMOUS, colossal, IMMENSE, VAST, GIGANTIC.

gibber: see CHATTER.

gibberish: see CHATTER.

giddy: see DIZZY.

gift *n.* **1** *(a wedding gift)* PRESENT, DONATION, CONTRIBUTION, legacy; **2** *(a great gift for public speaking)* TALENT, ABILITY, aptitude, GENIUS, POWER.

gifted *adj.* talented, ABLE, INTELLIGENT.

gigantic *adj.* HUGE, LARGE, ENORMOUS, colossal, IMMENSE, VAST, prodigious.

giggle *v.* CHUCKLE, SNICKER, titter, CACKLE, chortle, LAUGH.
— *n.* titter, snicker, CHUCKLE, chortle.

gild: see PLATE.

gilt: see GOLD; GOLDEN.

gimlet: see BIT; DRILL.

gimmick: see THING.

gird: see BELT; GIRDLE; RING.

girder: see BEAM.

girdle *n.* BELT, BAND, sash, corset.
— *v.* SURROUND, gird, ENCLOSE, EMBRACE.

girl *n.* MAID, maiden, VIRGIN, miss, damsel, FEMALE, LADY, SWEETHEART.

girlish: see FEMALE.

girth: see THICKNESS.

gist: see HEART; MEAT.

give *v.* **1** *(to give a present)* PRESENT, bestow, bequeath, CONTRIBUTE, DONATE, FURNISH, SUPPLY, PAY, impart, PRODUCE, CAUSE; **2** *(to give way)* YIELD, BEND, RETREAT, SURRENDER, give up.

give back: see REFLECT; RETURN.

give in: see DESPAIR, SUBMIT; YIELD.

give off: see YIELD.

give up: see ABANDON; DESPAIR; GIVE; RESIGN; SURRENDER.

give way: see COLLAPSE; YIELD.

giving: see ADMINISTRATION.

gizmo: see THING.

glacé: see ICE.

glacial: see ICY.

glad *adj.* HAPPY, pleased, delighted, CHEERFUL, CONTENTED, JOYFUL, joyous, gratified.

gladden *v.* GRATIFY, PLEASE, SATISFY, DELIGHT, cheer, REJOICE.

gladly *adv.* willingly, CHEERFULLY, happily, joyfully, READILY, FREELY.

gladness *n.* JOY, joyfulness, DELIGHT, PLEASURE, gratification, rejoicing, HAPPINESS.

glamorous *adj.* charming, exciting, TEMPTING, enticing, fascinating, entrancing, captivating.

glamour *n.* CHARM, allure, APPEAL, INTEREST, enticement, enchantment, fascination.

glance *n.* GLIMPSE, LOOK, peek. *v.* **1** *(glance at this book)* LOOK, peek, GLIMPSE; **2** *(it glanced off the blackboard)* ricochet, rebound, reflect.

glare *n.* **1** *(the glare of the headlights)* FLARE, BRILLIANCE, blaze, FLAME, FLASH, dazzle; **2** *(his fierce glare when he's angry)* scowl, FROWN, STARE.
— *v.* **1** *(the spotlight glares)* FLARE, BLAZE, FLAME, FLASH, DAZZLE; **2** *(his opponent glared at him)* scowl, FROWN, STARE.

glaring: see CONSPICUOUS; DAZZLING.

glass *n.* crystal, MIRROR, tumbler, windowpane, telescope, glassful, lens.

glasses *pl.n.* eyeglasses, spectacles, glassware.

glassful: see GLASS.

glassware: see GLASSES.

glaze: see COAT; COATING; COVERING; ICE; VARNISH.

gleam *n.* GLOW, glint, glimmer, BEAM, RAY, GLITTER, GLANCE, FLASH, LUSTER, SPLENDOR.
— *v.* glimmer, SHINE, GLOW, glint, GLITTER, BEAM, FLASH, SPARKLE, GLANCE.

gleaming: see BRIGHT; BRILLIANT; SHINY.

glean: see HARVEST.

glee: see CHEER; HILARITY; JOY.

gleeful: see CHEERFUL; HILARIOUS.

glen: see DALE; VALLEY.

glib: see OILY; PAT; SMOOTH.

glide *v.* SLIP, SLIDE, run, FLOW, SHADE, SAIL, FLOAT, skim.
— *n.:* see SLIDE.

glider: see SWING.

glimmer: see FLICKER; GLEAM; GLISTEN; GLITTER; GLOW; RAY; TWINKLE.

glimmering: see SHINY.

glimpse *n.* GLANCE, FLASH, LOOK, peek, VIEW, SIGHT, glint.
— *v.* GLANCE, LOOK, peek, VIEW, glint.

glint: see GLEAM; GLIMPSE; GLISTEN; RAY; SPARK; SPARKLE; TWINKLE.

glisten *v.* SPARKLE, GLITTER, glint, glimmer, FLASH, SHINE, GLEAM.

glistening: see SHINY.

glitter *n.* sparkle, GLEAM, glimmer, FLASH, LUSTER, coruscation.
— *v.* SPARKLE, GLEAM, GLISTEN, glimmer, FLASH, coruscate.

gloaming: see DUSK; EVENING; TWILIGHT.

gloat: see BOAST; BRAG; REJOICE.

glob: see LUMP; MASS.

global: see EARTHLY; INTERNATIONAL; ROUND.

globally: see ROUND.

globe *n.* BALL, SPHERE, EARTH, MAP, BULB.

globe-trotter: see TRAVELER.

globule: see BUBBLE.

gloom *n.* DIMNESS, SHADOW, DARKNESS, SADNESS, gloominess, melancholy, DEPRESSION, murk.

gloominess: see GLOOM.

gloomy *adj.* DIM, DARK, dismal, CHEERLESS, SAD, melancholy, depressing.

glorify: see BLESS; DIGNIFY; FLATTER; IDOLIZE; PRAISE; WORSHIP.

glorious *adj.* SPLENDID, MAGNIFICENT, DELIGHTFUL, LOFTY, HIGH, FAMOUS, FAMED, illustrious, renowned.

glory *n.* SPLENDOR, magnificence, HONOR, FAME, eminence, renown.

gloss *n.* COMMENT, INTERPRETATION, NOTE, EXPLANATION.
— *v.* SHINE, GLOW, sheen, GLEAM.

glossary *n.* VOCABULARY, LIST, DICTIONARY, lexicon, commentary.

glossiness: see LUSTER.

glossy: see SHINY; SMOOTH.

glove: see MITTEN.

glow *n.* incandescence, WARMTH, PASSION, brightness, ENTHUSIASM, reddening, GLEAM, GLITTER, glimmer, luminosity.
— *v.* SHINE, RADIATE, BLUSH, GLEAM, GLITTER, glimmer.

glowing: see SHINY.

glue *n.* ADHESIVE, PASTE, CEMENT, epoxy.
— *v.* JOIN, FASTEN, cement, PASTE, adhere.

gluey: see ADHESIVE; THICK.

glum: see BLUE; CHEERLESS.

glut: see EXCESS; FLOOD.

glutinous: see ADHESIVE.

glutton: see HOG; PIG.

gnarl: see KNOT.

gnarled: see CROOKED.

gnaw *v.* BITE, nibble, crunch, corrode, CONSUME, TORMENT.

gnome: see DWARF.

go *v.* **1** *(to go to school)* TRAVEL, MOVE, PASS, PROCEED, ADVANCE, WALK, set out, REACH, EXTEND, LEAD, elapse; **2** *(the dishes go in the pantry)* BELONG, HARMONIZE, SUIT; **3** *(she goes her own way)* CONTINUE, STAY, PROCEED.
— *n.* ENERGY, endurance, animation, TRY.

go against: see DISAPPROVE.

go-ahead: see CLEARANCE.

goal *n.* OBJECT, AIM, END, design, DESTINATION, MARK, POST, SCORE.

go astray: see STRAY.

goatee: see BEARD.

go away: see LEAVE.

gob: see CLOT.

gobble: see CACKLE.

go-between: see AGENT.

goblet: see CUP.

goblin: see FAIRY; SPIRIT.

go by: see PASS.

go-cart: see CARRIAGE.

go crazy: see RAGE.

god *n.* divinity, deity, IDOL, God, Allah, Lord, Creator.

God: see GOD.

goddess: see IDOL.

God-fearing: see RELIGIOUS.

godlike: see DIVINE.

godliness: see HOLINESS.

godly *adj.* pious, HOLY, saintly, RELIGIOUS, SPIRITUAL, DIVINE, PURE.

godsend: see BLESSING.

goggle: see STARE.

go in: see ENTER.

going: see PASSAGE.

gold *n.* gilt, GOLDEN, WEALTH, MONEY, coins.

golden *adj.* **1** *(her golden hair)* GOLD, yellow, gilt; **2** *(a golden opportunity)* FAVORABLE, EXCELLENT, PRECIOUS, VALUABLE, HAPPY, PROSPEROUS, DELIGHTFUL, GLORIOUS, BRIGHT, SHINY; **3** *(their golden anniversary)* fiftieth.

go mad: see RAGE.

gondola: see CAR.

gone: see ABSENT; AGO; DEAD; FORGOTTEN; LOST; MISSING; NOWHERE; PAST.

gone by: see AGO.

gong: see ALARM; BELL.

goo: see GUM; MUD.

good *adj.* EXCELLENT, VALUABLE, PRECIOUS, SOUND, GENUINE, WORTHY, USEFUL, PROFITABLE, SUITABLE, PROPER, SATISFACTORY, competent, ABLE, READY, EXPERT, valid, wholesome, SINCERE, UPRIGHT, VIRTUOUS, righteous, HONORABLE, HONEST, KIND, FRIENDLY, benevolent, PLEASANT.
— *n.*: see BENEFIT; RIGHT; WELFARE.

good-bye *interj.* FAREWELL, adieu, adios, so long.

good-for-nothing: see WORTHLESS.

good-looking: see ATTRACTIVE; BEAUTIFUL; FOXY; HANDSOME; STUNNING.

goodly: see CONSIDERABLE; SIZABLE.

good-natured: see AGREEABLE.

goodness *n.* EXCELLENCE, VALUE, WORTH, usefulness, righteousness, HONESTY, VIRTUE, uprightness, integrity, purity, chastity, KINDNESS, friendliness, SYMPATHY, UNDERSTANDING, niceness, benevolence.

goods *pl.n.* MERCHANDISE, possessions, fabrics, EQUIPMENT, products.

gooey: see ADHESIVE; SLIMY.

goof *v.* err, FAIL, bungle, botch, flub.
— *n.* BLUNDER, FAILURE, abortion, fumble, MISTAKE.

goof-off: see CLOWN.

go on: see ADVANCE; LAST.

goon: see GANGSTER; HOOD.

gore: see BLOOD; BUTCHERY; STICK.

gorge: see CANYON; PASS; SWALLOW; STUFF; VALLEY.

gorgeous *adj.* SPLENDID, showy, BEAUTIFUL, RICH, FINE, SUPERB, DELIGHTFUL, ENJOYABLE.

gorilla: see APE.

gospel *n.* doctrine, CREED, PRINCIPLE, evangel, revelation.

gossamer: see COBWEB.

gossip: see BUZZ; CHAT; CHATTER; GAB; RUMOR; SCANDAL; TALK; TELLTALE.

gouge: see DENT; PENETRATE; SCOOP.

go under: see FOLD; SINK.

go up: see CLIMB.

govern *v.* RULE, DIRECT, MANAGE, CONTROL, RUN, COMMAND, REGULATE, administer.

government *n.* RULE, DIRECTION, MANAGEMENT, CONTROL, COMMAND, sway, ADMINISTRATION, restraint, CONDUCT, STATE, commonwealth, COUNTRY.

governmental: see POLITICAL.

governor *n.* RULER, DIRECTOR, MANAGER, COMMANDER, ADMINISTRATOR, SUPERINTENDENT, EXECUTIVE, regulator. See also BRAKE.

go with: see ACCOMPANY.

gown *n.* DRESS, ROBE, clothing, frock.

grab *v.* CLUTCH, SEIZE, SNATCH, GRASP, GRIP.
— *n.*: see GRASP.

grace *n.* **1** *(a dancer noted for her grace)* gracefulness, ELEGANCE, POLISH, CHARM, refinement, BEAUTY, EASE; **2** *(by divine grace)* PARDON, FORGIVENESS, MERCY, FAVOR, KINDNESS; **3** *(to say grace before meals)* PRAYER, BLESSING, THANKS; **4** *(three days' grace)* reprieve, RELIEF, TIME, LIMIT.

graceful *adj.* ELEGANT, EASY, NATURAL, flowing, BEAUTIFUL, charming, polished, TACTFUL.

gracefulness: see GRACE.

gracious: see CIVIL; HOSPITABLE; POLITE.

graciousness: see HOSPITALITY.

graduation: see SCALE.

grade *n.* RANK, degree, MEASURE, STEP, rating, SLOPE.
— *v.* SORT, rate, LEVEL.

gradient: see HILLSIDE.

gradual *adj.* REGULAR, CONTINUOUS, PROGRESSIVE, DELIBERATE, moderate, SLOW.

graduate *n.* alumna, alumnus, recipient.
— *v.* FINISH, MARK, ADJUST, proportion.

graduation *n.* commencement, CEREMONY, ADVANCEMENT. See also STEP.

grain *n.* **1** *(a grain of wheat)* SEED, kernel, PARTICLE, BIT; **2** *(against the grain)* TEXTURE, FIBER, ARRANGEMENT, DISPOSITION, HUMOR.

grand *adj.* stately, majestic, LOFTY, NOBLE, GREAT, eminent, illustrious, MAGNIFICENT, SPLENDID, SUPERB, GLORIOUS.

grandeur: see MAJESTY; SPLENDOR.

grandfather *n.* grandpapa, grandparent, ANCESTOR, forefather, forebear.

grandiose: see AMBITIOUS; TALL.

grandmama: see GRANDMOTHER.

grandmother *n.* grandmama, granny, grandparent, ANCESTOR, forebearer.

grandpapa: see GRANDFATHER.

grandparent: see GRANDFATHER; GRANDMOTHER.

grange: see RANCH.

granny: see GRANDMOTHER.

grant *n.* GIFT, PRESENT, boon, DONATION, fellowship, scholarship, AWARD.
— *v.* **1** *(to grant an extension of time)* GIVE, bestow, confer; **2** *(I'll grant you that)* ADMIT, ALLOW, concede, AGREE, YIELD.

granting: see SUPPOSING.

granulate: see MILL.

granules: see POWDER.

graph *n.* CHART, SKETCH, diagram, PLOT, OUTLINE, DESIGN, PLAN.

grapple: see CLAW; WRESTLE.

grasp *n.* CLASP, CLUTCH, grab, GRIP, embrace, REACH, UNDERSTANDING, HOLD, POSSESSION.
— *v.* CLASP, CLUTCH, GRAB, GRIP, EMBRACE, REACH, UNDERSTAND, HOLD, POSSESS.

grasping: see GREEDY.

grass *n.* LAWN, GREEN, vegetation, bluegrass, marijuana, POT.

grassland: see MEADOW; PASTURE; RANGE.

grate: see CLASH; GRIND; HEARTH; JAR; MILL; RUB; SCRAPE; SHRED.

grateful *adj.* THANKFUL, APPRECIATIVE, WELCOME, REFRESHING, soothing, AGREEABLE, PLEASING.

grater: see MILL.

gratification: see CONTENTMENT; DELIGHT; ENJOYMENT; GLADNESS; PLEASURE; SATISFACTION; TREAT.

gratified: see GLAD; HAPPY.

gratify *v.* PLEASE, SATISFY, indulge, humor, GRANT.

gratifying: see PLEASANT; PLEASURABLE.

grating: see HARSH; HOARSE; NOISY.

gratitude *n.* thankfulness, APPRECIATION.

grave *n.* TOMB, mausoleum, sepulcher, VAULT, DEATH.
— *adj.* SOLEMN, SOBER, SERIOUS, IMPORTANT, CRITICAL, DANGEROUS.

gravel *n.* stones, pebbles, GRAIN, GRIT, SAND, shale.

gravelly: see HOARSE.

gravestone: see STONE.

graveyard: see CEMETERY.

gravitate: see DESCEND; DRIFT; TEND.

gravitation: see GRAVITY.

gravity *n.* **1** *(the gravity of the crime)* SERIOUSNESS, IMPORTANCE; **2** *(the gravity of the earth)* gravitation, ATTRACTION, WEIGHT.

gravure: see PRINTING.

gravy: see SAUCE.

gray *adj.* ashen, leaden, CLOUDY, drab.

graze *v.* **1** *(the bullet grazed his skin)* SCRAPE, SCRATCH, RUB, BRUSH, GLANCE; **2** *(the cows were grazing)* pasture, FEED.

grease *n.* lubricant, FAT, OIL.
— *v.* LUBRICATE, OIL.

greasy *adj.* OILY, fatty, buttery, SMOOTH, SLIPPERY, SLICK, oleaginous.

great *adj.* BIG, LARGE, VAST, HUGE, GIGANTIC, GRAND, IMMENSE, IMPORTANT, ABUNDANT, FAMOUS, eminent, EXCELLENT, CONSIDERABLE, NUMEROUS.

greater: see MAJOR; SUPERIOR.

greatest: see MAXIMUM; SUPREME, UTMOST.

greatly *adj.* MUCH, considerably, largely.

greatness *n.* largeness, immensity, FAME, DISTINCTION, IMPORTANCE, MAJESTY, nobility.

greed *n.* greediness, selfishness, piggishness, egoism.

greediness: see GREED.

greedy *adj.* SELFISH, grasping, piggish, egoistic.

green *adj.* **1** *(of green color)* greenish, olive, emerald, aquamarine; **2** *(too green to be of use)* IMMATURE, untrained, naïve, UNRIPE, inexperienced; **3** *(green with envy)* wan, PALE, SICK; **4** *(the green countryside)* FRESH, flourishing, blooming.
— *n.* LAWN, MEADOW, GRASS.

greenback: see BILL; BUCK.

greenish: see GREEN.

greenness: see FRESHNESS.

greet *v.* WELCOME, HAIL, SALUTE, MEET, RECEIVE.

greeting: see RECEPTION; REGARD; SALUTATION; SALUTE; WELCOME.

greetings *pl.n.* WELCOME, SALUTATION, regards, compliments.

gregarious: see SOCIAL.

grief *n.* SORROW, SADNESS, affliction, TRIAL, DISTRESS, DISAPPOINTMENT, WOE.

grief-stricken: see BROKEN-HEARTED; SORROWFUL.

grievance: see COMPLAINT; INJURY; WRONG.

grieve *v.* sorrow, MOURN, SADDEN, REGRET, DISTRESS, afflict.

grieved: see SORE.

grieving: see MOURNFUL.

grill: see ROAST.

grim: see GRUESOME; MOURNFUL; SICK; SOLEMN; SULLEN; TRAGIC.

grimace: see FROWN; GRIN.

grime *n.* soot, smut, smudge, SLIME, DIRT, FILTH, foulness.

grimy: see DUSTY.

grin *n.* SMILE, smirk, grimace.
— *v.* SMILE, BEAM, LAUGH.

grind *v.* grate, pulverize, SHARPEN, CRUSH, oppress, harass.
— *n.* drudgery, LABOR, TOIL.

grinder: see MILL.

grinding: see FRICTION.

grindstone: see MILL.

grip *n.* GRASP, HOLD, CLUTCH, CONTROL. See also BAG; COLD.
— *v.* GRASP, HOLD, CLUTCH, SEIZE, CONTROL.

gripe: see COMPLAINT; GRUMBLE; KICK; MUTTER; PROTEST.

grisly: see GRUESOME.

grit *n.* SAND, GRAIN, GRAVEL, pebbles, DIRT, DUST. See also COURAGE.

gritty: see COARSE; STONY.

groan *n.* MOAN, COMPLAINT, creak, WHINE.
— *v.* MOAN, COMPLAIN, creak, bemoan, WHINE.

groggy: see DRUNK.

groom *n.* **1** *(the groom was late for the wedding)* bridegroom, fiancé, consort, HUSBAND, MAN; **2** *(the groom fed the horses)* stableboy, hostler.
— *v.* PREPARE, TRAIN, GROUND, ORDER, tidy, prim, spruce up, RUB, curry.

groove *n.* furrow, CHANNEL, CUT, rut, TRACK, scoring, TRENCH, DEPRESSION.
— *v.*: see NOTCH.

grooved: see HOLLOW.

grooves: see TREAD.

gross: see COARSE; DISAGREEABLE; NASTY; SHAMEFUL; VULGAR.

grossness: see COARSENESS.

grotesque: see MISSHAPEN; ODD; RIDICULOUS.

grotto: see CAVE.

grouch: see CRANK.

grouchy: see CRANKY.

ground *n.* **1** *(to fall to the ground)* EARTH, SOIL, LAND, sod, SURFACE, AREA, REGION, TERRITORY, FOUNDATION, BASE, BOTTOM, GROUNDWORK; **2** *(the ground of an antenna)* CONNECTION, connector, wiring. See also CAUSE.
— *v.* **1** *(well grounded in math)* TRAIN, SET, INSTRUCT, PREPARE, BASE, ESTABLISH; **2** *(the boat was grounded)* beach, strand, LAND.

grounded: see AGROUND; ASHORE.

ground floor: see BASEMENT.

grounds *n.pl.* **1** *(to walk around the grounds)* ESTATE, YARD, premises, PROPERTY, LAWN, LAND, gardens, TRACT; **2** *(grounds for divorce)* BASIS, ROOT, reasons, considerations, arguments, MOTIVE, EXCUSE; **3** *(coffee grounds)* sediment, WASTE.

groundwork *n.* FOUNDATION, BASE, background. See also PREPARATION.

group *n.* CROWD, BUNCH, COLLECTION, UNIT, GATHERING, CLUSTER, assemblage, ARRANGEMENT.
— *v.* GATHER, BUNCH, COLLECT, ASSEMBLE, CLUSTER, ARRANGE.

grouping: see ORGANIZATION.

grove *n.* WOOD, orchard, woodland, thicket.

grow *v.* **1** *(to grow large)* INCREASE, ENLARGE, DEVELOP, EXPAND, SWELL, FLOWER, bud, SPROUT, BECOME, wax; **2** *(to grow tomatoes)* RAISE, CULTIVATE, PRODUCE, PLANT.

growl *n.* snarl, snap, GRUMBLE, mumble, GROAN, BARK, ROAR, COMPLAINT.
— *v.* SNARL, SNAP, GRUMBLE, MUMBLE, MURMUR, MUTTER, GROAN, bark, ROAR, COMPLAIN.

grown *adj.* **1** *(grown-up)* ADULT, full-grown, MATURE, RIPE, developed; **2** *(grown beyond all belief)* increased, expanded, enlarged; **3** *(grown in rich soil)* cultivated, raised.

grown-up *n.* ADULT, WOMAN, MAN, PARENT.

growth *n.* **1** *(to reach full growth)* INCREASE, ENLARGEMENT, EXPANSION, DEVELOPMENT, evolution, PROGRESS, cultivation, sprouting, vegetation; **2** *(to remove a growth)* swelling, tumor, pimple, cancer, wart.

grub: see FOOD.

grudge *n.* ill will, HOSTILITY, RESENTMENT, malice, spite, HATRED, dislike, JEALOUSY, QUARREL, DISPUTE, BITTERNESS.
— *v.* begrudge, ENVY, covet, DISPUTE.

grudging: see ENVY; JEALOUS.

gruesome *adj.* FEARFUL, grim, grisly, TERRIBLE, FRIGHTFUL, ghastly, hideous.

gruff: see HOARSE.

grumble *n.* GROWL, grunt, COMPLAINT, gripe, FUSS.
— *v.* GROWL, GRUNT, COMPLAIN, gripe, FUSS.

grumbling: see WHINE.

grunt *n.* GRUMBLE, mumble, COMPLAINT, oink.
— *v.* GRUMBLE, MUMBLE, COMPLAIN, oink.

guarantee *v.* WARRANT, ASSURE, vouch, PROMISE, PLEDGE.
— *n.* WARRANTY, assurance, PROMISE, PLEDGE.

guaranteed: see ASSURED.

guaranty: see CERTIFICATION; PLEDGE; PROMISE; SECURITY; VOW; WARRANT.

guard *n.* **1** *(a guard against tooth decay)* PROTECTION, safeguard, DEFENSE, SHELTER, preservative, SHIELD, bulwark; **2** *(the guard was on duty)* PROTECTOR, bodyguard, watchman, sentry, PATROL, ESCORT, defender.
— *v.* PROTECT, safeguard, WATCH, DEFEND, SHELTER, PRESERVE, ESCORT, PATROL, BEWARE.

guarded: see CAREFUL; SAFE.

guardhouse: see PRISON.

guardian *n.* PROTECTOR, defender, preserver, watchdog, KEEPER, custodian, WARDEN, JAILER.

guardianship: see CARE; SUPERVISION.

guerrilla: see REBEL.

guess *n.* conjecture, hunch, hypothesis, THEORY, supposition, NOTION, OPINION, SUSPICION.
— *v.* conjecture, SUPPOSE, SUSPECT, THINK, BELIEVE, FANCY, IMAGINE, RECKON, surmise, fathom, SOLVE.

guest *n.* VISITOR, caller, COMPANY, invitee, visitant, houseguest, partygoer, frequenter, PASSENGER, habitué.

guidance: see DIRECTION; DISCIPLINE; LEADERSHIP.

guide *n.* PILOT, LEADER, CONDUCTOR, ESCORT, adviser, COUNSELOR, directory.
— *v.* PILOT, LEAD, CONDUCT, ESCORT, ADVISE, counsel, DIRECT.

guillotine: see EXECUTE.

guilt *n.* blame, CRIME, SIN, SHAME, WICKEDNESS, WRONG, FAULT, VIOLATION.

guiltless *adj.* INNOCENT, HARMLESS, FREE, HONEST, unstained, PURE, SPOTLESS.

guilty *adj.* blameworthy, CRIMINAL, sinful, SHAMEFUL, WICKED, WRONG, DELINQUENT, LIABLE, offending, RESPONSIBLE, convicted, indicted.

gulch: see PIT.

gulf *n.* **1** *(a gulf of misunderstanding)* abyss, chasm, DEPTH, hollow, CANYON, GAP, SEPARATION; **2** *(the Gulf of Mexico)* SEA, BAY, BASIN, ARM, inlet, SOUND, HARBOR, whirlpool.

gull: see CHEAT; OUTWIT.

gullible: see CHILDLIKE.

gully: see CHANNEL; DITCH; TRENCH.

gulp: see DEVOUR; SWALLOW.

gum *n.* rubber, ADHESIVE, GLUE, CEMENT, PASTE, mucilage, goo.
— *v.*: see SEAL.

gun *n.* handgun, FIREARM, sidearm, REVOLVER, PISTOL, gat, RIFLE, shotgun, musket, blunderbuss, BB gun, cannon, air rifle, WEAPON, ARM.

gunman: see ASSASSIN; GANGSTER; KILLER.

gunnery: see ARTILLERY.

gunny: see CANVAS.

gunpowder: see EXPLOSIVE.

guns: see ARMS.

gurgle: see BABBLE.

guru: see TEACHER.

gush: see EMERGE; FLOW; ISSUE; SPOUT; SPURT.

gushy: see SENTIMENTAL.

gust *n.* BREEZE, WIND, BLAST, squall, BLOW, BURST, outburst.

gusto: see RELISH.

gusty: see BREEZY; WINDY.

gut: see BELLY; INSIDE.

guts: see BACKBONE; BOLDNESS; BRAVERY; COURAGE; NERVE.

guttersnipe: see BRAT.

guy *n.* **1** *(he's a nice guy)* FELLOW, CHUM, mack, FRIEND, COMPANION, ACQUAINTANCE, PERSON, oddball, eccentric; **2** *(a guy rope)* ROPE, wire, SUPPORT, shroud, STAY.

guzzle: see DRINK.

gymnast: see ATHLETE.

gymnastic: see ATHLETIC.

gyp: see SWINDLE; THIEVE.

gypsum: see MINERAL.

gyrate: see CIRCLE; ROLL; WHIRL.

gyration: see ROLL; ROTATION.

H

habit *n.* **1** *(bad habits)* CUSTOM, PRACTICE, WAY, USAGE, RULE, MANNER, TENDENCY, FASHION, ROUTINE, addiction, compulsion; **2** *(a riding habit)* OUTFIT, DRESS, COSTUME, garb.

habitat: see ENVIRONMENT.

habitation: see HOUSE; RESIDENCE.

habitual *adj.* USUAL, CUSTOMARY, COMMON, REGULAR, routine, ORDINARY, FAMILIAR, EVERYDAY, confirmed.

habitually: see ALWAYS; ORDINARILY; REGULARLY; USUALLY.

habituate: see ACCUSTOM.

habitué: see GUEST.

hack: see AUTHOR; CHOP; COUGH.

hag: see BAG; WITCH.

haggard: see PALE.

haggle: see BARGAIN.

hail *v.* GREET, SALUTE, WELCOME, CALL, SIGNAL, holler.
— *n.* hailstone, ICE, pellet.

hailstone: see HAIL.

hair *n.* FUR, down, whiskers, BRISTLE, BEARD, coiffure, locks, tresses, mane, filament, FRACTION.

haircut: see TRIM.

hairy: see FUZZY.

half *n.* PART, DIVISION.
— *adj.* PARTIAL, INCOMPLETE, fifty-fifty.

half-breed: see CROSS.

halfway: see BETWEEN; CENTRAL.

half-wit *n.* blockhead, simpleton, MORON, nitwit, dunce, imbecile.

half-witted *adj.* FOOLISH, SILLY, moronic, STUPID, DULL, FEEBLE-MINDED.

hall *n.* BUILDING, manor, ROOM, auditorium, hallway, ENTRANCE, vestibule, lobby, CORRIDOR.

hallowed: see SACRED.

hallucinate: see DREAM.

hallucination: see DREAM; TRIP.

hallway: see CORRIDOR; HALL.

halt *n.* STOP, standstill, PAUSE, REST.
— *v.* STOP, PAUSE, REST, HESITATE.
— *adj.* LAME, crippled, disabled.

halve: see DIVIDE.

hamlet: see TOWN; VILLAGE.

hammer *n.* mallet, gavel, maul, striker, lever.
— *v.* HIT, BEAT, DRIVE, SHAPE, FORGE, drum, POUND.

hammered: see BEATEN.

hamper: see BASKET; HINDER.

hand *n.* **1** *(dirty hands)* palm, fist, extremity; **2** *(on the right hand)* SIDE, DIRECTION, PART; **3** *(the letter is written with a fine hand)* handwriting, penmanship, SIGNATURE; **4** *(the hired hands)* WORKER, LABORER, farmhand, helper; **5** *(give me a hand with this tire)* HELP, AID, SUPPORT; **6** *(he has quite a hand with the ladies)* SKILL, ABILITY, TALENT, faculty; **7** *(he was dealt a good hand with many face cards)* cards, ROUND, PLAYER; **8** *(he offered her his hand in marriage)* PROMISE, PLEDGE; **9** *(the hands of the clock)* pointer; **10** *(I had a hand in the work)* PART, participation, SHARE, CONCERN, INTEREST; **11** *(the actor got a good hand)* APPLAUSE, clapping, APPROVAL.
— *v.* GIVE, TRANSMIT, DELIVER, PRESENT.

handbag: see BILLFOLD, PURSE.

handbill: see ADVERTISEMENT; ANNOUNCEMENT; CIRCULAR; NOTICE; POSTER.

handcart: see CART.

handful *n.* fistful, QUANTITY, FEW, SEVERAL, sprinkling.

handgun: see GUN; PISTOL; REVOLVER.

handhold: see ARM.

handicap *n.* DISADVANTAGE, hindrance, OBSTACLE, DIFFICULTY, CONTEST, ADVANTAGE.
— *v.*: see PARALYZE.

handicapped: see cripple; lame.

handicraft: see HANDIWORK.

handiwork *n.* craftsmanship, workmanship, handicraft, CREATION.

handkerchief *n.* kerchief, bandanna, CLOTH, wiper, TISSUE, neckerchief, SCARF.

handle *n.* holder, hilt, HOLD, SHAFT, lever.
— *v.* HOLD, TOUCH, FINGER, FEEL, manhandle, PAW, manipulate, wield, MANAGE, USE, TREAT, maneuver.

handling: see MANAGEMENT; OPERATION; TREATMENT.

handout: see CHARITY.

hand over: see REACH.

hand-picked: see CHOSEN.

handsome *adj.* **1** *(a handsome actor)* ATTRACTIVE, good-looking, comely, well-formed, BEAUTIFUL; **2** *(a handsome sum)* GENEROUS, AMPLE, LIBERAL, ABUNDANT.

handwriting: see HAND; WRITING.

handy *adj.* **1** *(she is very handy at putting up curtains)* skillful, CLEVER, EXPERT, READY; **2** *(do you have a pliers handy?)* CONVENIENT, CLOSE, NEAR.

hang *v.* **1** *(to hang drapes)* ATTACH, FASTEN, SUSPEND, drape; **2** *(to hang one's head)* BEND, DROOP, incline; **3** *(to hang on)* HOLD, CLING, persevere; **4** *(to hang the horsethief)* EXECUTE, KILL, DIE.

hanger: see RACK; SLING.

hanging: see CURTAIN; EXECUTION; SUSPENSION.

hangman: see ASSASSIN.

hanker: see CRAVE; LUST; WANT.

hankering: see HUNGER.

haphazard: see RANDOM.

haphazardly: see ANYHOW.

happen *v.* OCCUR, take place, PASS, chance, transpire, ARISE, befall.

happening *n.* CIRCUMSTANCE, AFFAIR, OCCURRENCE, INCIDENT, EVENT, ADVENTURE, ACCIDENT.

happenings: see NEWS.

happily: see CHEERFULLY; GLADLY.

happiness *n.* **1** *(to express one's happiness)* JOY, DELIGHT, PLEASURE, ENJOYMENT, GLADNESS, CONTENTMENT, elation; **2** *(for his own happiness)* WELFARE, well-being, COMFORT, PROSPERITY.

happy *adj.* **1** *(happy to win)* delighted, GLAD, pleased, CONTENTED, gratified, ecstatic; **2** *(a happy face)* CHEERFUL, JOLLY, jovial, MERRY,

BRIGHT, GAY; **3** *(a happy ending)* LUCKY, FORTUNATE, JOYFUL, joyous, blissful, APPROPRIATE.

harangue: see SPEECH; SPOUT.

harass: see ANNOY; GRIND; HUSTLE; NAG; PERSECUTE; PESTER; WORRY.

harasser: see BULLY.

harassment: see ANNOYANCE; PERSECUTION.

harbor *n.* PORT, WHARF, marina, pier, DOCK, haven, SHELTER, PROTECTION, REFUGE. — *v.* **1** *(to harbor a criminal)* SHELTER, PROTECT, LODGE, KEEP; **2** *(to harbor thoughts)* CONSIDER, REGARD, THINK, ENTERTAIN.

hard *adj.* **1** *(a hard lesson)* ROUGH, TOUGH, DIFFICULT, toilsome, laborious; **2** *(hard wood)* SOLID, STRONG, FIRM, THICK; **3** *(a hard person)* STRICT, STERN, MEAN, unfeeling, unsympathetic; **4** *(hard liquor)* alcoholic, intoxicating, inebriating. — *adv.* laboriously, strenuously, diligently, energetically, vigorously, exhaustingly, solidly.

harden *v.* **1** *(to harden one's position)* firm, toughen, fortify, STRENGTHEN; **2** *(the ice cream hardened)* solidify, FREEZE, petrify.

hardened: see FROZEN.

hard-hearted: see MERCILESS.

hardly *adv.* **1** *(he hardly ate)* scarcely, SLIGHTLY, LITTLE; **2** *(he hardly got through)* NEARLY, BARELY, narrowly, JUST.

hardness: see FIRMNESS; STEEL.

hardship *n.* SUFFERING, BURDEN, MISFORTUNE, adversity, DISAPPOINTMENT, unhappiness, DIFFICULTY.

hardware: see ARM.

hardwood: see WOOD.

hard-working: see BUSY.

hardy *adj.* STRONG, HEALTHY, VIGOROUS, robust, COURAGEOUS, BRAVE, BOLD, DARING.

harebrained: see DIZZY.

hark: see HEAR.

harken: see LISTEN.

harm *n.* WRONG, hurt, MISCHIEF, DAMAGE, EVIL, WICKEDNESS, INJURY. — *v.* HURT, INJURE, DAMAGE, ABUSE.

harmful *adj.* hurtful, unhealthful, damaging, DESTRUCTIVE, injurious, noxious.

harmless *adj.* inoffensive, INNOCENT, PAINLESS, SURE, SAFE, POWERLESS, PURE.

harmonious *adj.* AGREEABLE, adaptable, congenial, amicable, compatible, conformable, blending, congruous.

harmonize *v.* **1** *(to harmonize a tune)* ARRANGE, orchestrate, SING, COMPOSE; **2** *(they harmonized with one another)* ADJUST, AGREE, conform, BLEND, accord.

harmony *n.* **1** *(the study of harmony)* MUSIC, sounds, tones, unison; **2** *(to live in harmony)* PEACE, FRIENDSHIP, AGREEMENT, UNITY, compatibility, accordance.

harness *n.* EQUIPMENT, gear, STRAP, YOKE. — *v.* yoke, saddle, CONTROL, CONTAIN, USE, COUPLE.

harsh *adj.* ROUGH, SHARP, SHRILL, discordant, grating, SOUR, ACID.

harshness *n.* sternness, strictness, severity, CRUELTY, brutality, roughness.

harvest *n.* YIELD, crops, PRODUCE, reaping, RETURN, PROFIT, intake, proceeds. — *v.* REAP, COLLECT, CUT, PICK, GATHER, GET, glean.

hash: see MINCE.

hasp: see BUCKLE.

hassle: see PESTER.

haste *n.* SPEED, promptness, QUICKNESS, RUSH, HURRY, DISPATCH, rapidity.

hasten *v.* HURRY, quicken, SPEED, expedite, RUSH, ACCELERATE.

hastening: see SCRAMBLE.

hasty *adj.* **1** *(a hasty exit)* HURRIED, QUICK, RAPID; **2** *(a hasty decision)* CARELESS, RASH, foolhardy, THOUGHTLESS, superficial.

hat *n.* headgear, head piece, CAP, bonnet, chapeau, sombrero.

hatch *v.* **1** *(to hatch in an incubator)* BREED, PRODUCE, incubate, BEAR; **2** *(to hatch a plan)* PREPARE, PLAN, DESIGN, concoct, PLOT, contrive. — *n.*: see DOOR.

hate *v.* detest, loathe, abhor, DESPISE, SCORN. — *n.*: see PASSION.

hateful *adj.* malevolent, detestable, malicious, abhorrent, obnoxious, loathesome, repulsive, rancorous.

hatred *n.* enmity, abhorrence, loathing, contempt, repugnance, GRUDGE, ill will, odium.

haughtiness: see PRIDE.

haughty: see CHILLY; PROUD; SUPERIOR.

haul *n.* **1** *(a haul of fish)* CATCH, TAKE; **2** *(a long

haul) DISTANCE, VOYAGE, ROUTE, TRIP; **3** *(a large haul)* LOOT, booty, TAKE, spoils, FIND.
— *v.* PULL, HEAVE, lug, TUG, TOW, DRAW, DRAG, CARRY, TRANSPORT, CATCH.

haulage: see TRANSPORTATION.

hauling: see TRANSPORTATION.

haunt *n.* DEN, RETREAT, DWELLING, stamping ground.
— *v.*: see FREQUENT.

haunted *adj.* frequented, inhabited, tormented.

have *v.* HOLD, RETAIN, KEEP, OWN, POSSESS, GET, RECEIVE, OBTAIN.

haven: see HARBOR; PORT; REFUGE.

have to: see MUST; OUGHT.

havoc: see BUTCHERY.

haw: see STAMMER.

hawk: see COUGH.

hawker: see PEDDLER.

hay *n.* GRASS, fodder, forage, FEED.

hayloft: see ATTIC.

hazard *n.* DANGER, peril, jeopardy, RISK, CHANCE, GAMBLE, STAKE.
— *v.* chance, RISK, GAMBLE, GUESS, VENTURE.

hazardous *adj.* DANGEROUS, perilous, UNSAFE, RISKY, UNCERTAIN, precarious.

haze: see BLUR; CLOUD; FOG; MIST; VAPOR.

hazy *adj.* CLOUDY, murky, DIM, GRAY, smoky, misty, overcast, nebulous.

he: see MALE.

head *n.* **1** *(our section head)* LEADER, EXECUTIVE, PRINCIPAL, COMMANDER, SUPERIOR, SUPERVISOR; **2** *(the head of a line)* START, BEGINNING, FRONT; **3** *(he has a good head)* faculty, reasoning; **4** *(at the head of our class)* TOP, SUMMIT, PEAK, pinnacle. See also FOAM.
— *v.* GO, LEAD, DOMINATE.

headcover: see CAP.

headcovering: see HOOD.

headgear: see HAT.

heading *n.* TITLE, subtitle, caption, HEADLINE, legend, ADDRESS, letterhead.

headline *n.* TITLE, HEADING, caption, TOPIC, BANNER, streamer.

headliner: see STAR.

headpiece: see HAT.

headquarters: see BASE.

headrest: see PILLOW.

headstone: see MEMORIAL; MONUMENT.

headstrong: see STUBBORN.

headway: see ADVANCEMENT; PROGRESS.

heal *v.* get well, MEND, CURE, RECOVER, regenerate, rejuvenate.

healer: see DOCTOR; PHYSICIAN.

healing: see MEDICINE.

health *n.* VIGOR, CONDITION, FITNESS, soundness, well-being.

healthful: see SANITARY.

healthy *adj.* HEARTY, robust, SOUND, FIT, TRIM, VIGOROUS, wholesome.

heap *n.* PILE, STACK, MASS, LUMP, accumulation, aggregation.
— *v.* LOAD, PILE, STACK, GATHER, ACCUMULATE, hoard, INCREASE.

hear *v.* LISTEN, HEED, hark, perceive, LEARN. See also TRY.

hearers: see AUDIENCE.

hearing: see AUDIENCE; SENSE; TRIAL.

hearsay: see REPORT; RUMOR; SCANDAL.

heart *n.* **1** *(the heart of the city)* CENTER, core, MIDDLE, nucleus; **2** *(the heart of the matter)* essence, gist, MEANING, ROOT; **3** *(she has a lot of heart)* EMOTION, FEELING, SYMPATHY, SOUL; **4** *(take heart)* COURAGE, SPIRIT, ENTHUSIASM, fortitude.

heartbeat: see PULSE; THROB.

heartburn: see ENVY; JEALOUSY.

hearten: see COMFORT; ENCOURAGE.

hearth *n.* fireside, fireplace, grate, HOME, abode, homestead.

heartily *adv.* cordially, enthusiastically, earnestly, SINCERELY, ardently.

heartiness: see ENTHUSIASM.

heartland: see INTERIOR.

heartless *adj.* CRUEL, MEAN, unfeeling, HARD, unsympathetic, PITILESS, MERCILESS.

heart-rending: see PITIFUL.

heartsick: see BROKEN-HEARTED.

hearty *adj.* WARM, cheery, jovial, congenial, GENUINE, exuberant, ABUNDANT.

heat *n.* **1** *(in the tropical heat)* WARMTH, torridity; **2** *(the heat of an argument)* EXCITEMENT, ardor, INTENSITY, fervor.
— *v.* WARM, inflame, FIRE, ignite, COOK, BOIL, BURN.

heated: see FIERY; WARM.

heater: see FURNACE; STOVE.

heathen: see SUPERSTITIOUS.

heave *v.* THROW, CAST, HURL, FLING, TOSS, LIFT, WAVE, RISE.
— *n.*: see THROW; TOSS.

heaven *n.* **1** *(the tree stood against a bright heaven)* SKY, SPACE, beyond, stratosphere; **2** *(it was seventh heaven to see her again)* rapture, bliss, ecstasy, PARADISE.

heavenly *adj.* DIVINE, angelic, GLORIOUS, ecstatic, blissful, WONDERFUL.

heavens: see SPACE.

heaviness: see THICKNESS; WEIGHT.

heavy *adj.* LARGE, HEFTY, MASSIVE, weighty, massy, BULKY, SERIOUS.

heavy-duty: see INDUSTRIAL.

heavy-hearted: see SAD.

heckle: see TEASE.

hectic: see FEVERISH.

hedge *n.* FENCE, bushes, shrubbery, BORDER, BOUNDARY, LIMIT, BARRIER.
— *v.* obstruct, HINDER, AVOID, DODGE, evade, side step, DUCK, pussyfoot.

heed *n.* ATTENTION, CARE, CAUTION, MIND, NOTICE, OBSERVATION.
— *v.* LISTEN, HEAR, NOTICE, CONSIDER, MIND, FOLLOW, OBEY.

heedful: see ATTENTIVE; CAREFUL; CAUTIOUS; OBSERVANT.

heedfulness: see CAUTION.

heedless: see BLIND, RECKLESS; THOUGHTLESS; UNAWARE.

heedlessness: see FORGETFULNESS.

heel *n.* SCOUNDREL, VILLAIN, louse, swine, skunk.
— *v.* FOLLOW, TAG, SHADOW, TILT, DIP, LEAN.

hefty *adj.* weighty, LARGE, substantial, burly, strapping, HUSKY.

height *n.* tallness, stature, ELEVATION, RISE, ALTITUDE, pinnacle.

heighten: see ELEVATE; RAISE.

heightening: see LIFT.

heir *n.* successor, inheritor, beneficiary, descendant, OFFSPRING.

heirloom: see ANTIQUE.

hell *n.* inferno, underworld, TORMENT, AGONY, MISERY, SUFFERING.

hello: see SALUTATION; WELCOME.

helmet: see ARMOR.

helmsman: see PILOT.

help *n.* **1** *(helping the aged)* ASSISTANCE, AID, RELIEF, COMFORT; **2** *(hired help)* SERVANT, aide.
— *v.* ASSIST, AID, SUPPORT, SHARE, SERVE.

helper: see ACCESSORY; AID; ASSISTANT; EMPLOYEE; HAND; MESSENGER; SECOND; SERVANT; SUPPORTER.

helpers: see STAFF.

helpful *adj.* beneficial, USEFUL, advantageous, SIGNIFICANT, IMPORTANT, supportive.

helpless *adj.* FEEBLE, incapable, impotent, disabled, DEFENSELESS, NAKED.

helplessness: see WEAKNESS.

hem *n.* BORDER, MARGIN, RIM, edging. See also COUGH.
— *v.* SEW, border, stitch, shut in. See also COUGH; STAMMER.

hem in: see MOB.

hemisphere: see DOME.

hemorrhage: see BLEED.

hence *adv.* THEREFORE, THUS, consequently.

henceforth: see HEREAFTER; THEREAFTER.

herald: see ANGEL; PROPHET.

herb *n.* vegetable, PLANT.

herd *n.* FLOCK, PACK, CROWD, drove, GATHERING.
— *v.* DRIVE, GATHER, ASSEMBLE, shepherd.

herder: see KEEPER.

herdsman: see KEEPER; SHEPHERD.

here *adv.* NOW, hither, PRESENT, herein, there, INSIDE.

hereafter *adv.* HENCE, henceforth, EVENTUALLY,
— *n.*: see FUTURE.

herein: see HERE.

heresy: see SUPERSTITION.

heretofore: see AGO.

heritage: see INHERITANCE.

hermit *n.* solitaire, shut-in, MONK, friar; recluse.

hero *n.* CHAMPION, CONQUEROR, WARRIOR, LEAD.

heroic *adj.* BRAVE, COURAGEOUS, valiant, BOLD, intrepid.

heroism *n.* BRAVERY, valor, gallantry, STRENGTH.

hesitancy: see RELUCTANCE.

hesitant: see RELUCTANT; UNCERTAIN.

hesitate *v.* WAIT, DELAY, PAUSE, falter, waver, vacillate.

hesitation *n.* indecision, DOUBT, skepticism, UNCERTAINTY, wavering.

heterogeneous: see DIFFERENT.

hew: see SCULPTURE.

hex: see CHARM; CURSE.

hi: see WELCOME.

hibernating: see ASLEEP.

hidden *adj.* PRIVATE, concealed, covered, cloaked, disguised, camouflaged.

hide *n.* SKIN, pelt, COAT.
 — *v.* CONCEAL, SCREEN, COVER, mask, SHELTER.

hideous: see GRUESOME; HORRIBLE; UGLY.

hideousness: see UGLINESS.

hideaway: see DEN; RETREAT.

hideout: see CONCEALMENT; NEST.

hiding: see CONCEALMENT; SECRECY.

high *adj.* **1** *(a high building)* TALL, towering, LOFTY, elevated, soaring; **2** *(high prices)* EXPENSIVE, COSTLY, DEAR; **3** *(he is high)* DRUNK, intoxicated, inebriated; **4** *(a high person)* IMPORTANT, eminent, esteemed.
 — *n.*: see TRIP.

highball: see DRINK.

highborn: see GENTLE; NOBLE.

highbrow: see INTELLECTUAL.

higher: see SUPERIOR.

highest: see CLASSIC; LAST; MAXIMUM; PRINCIPAL; SUPREME; UTMOST.

highland: see RIDGE.

highlands: see PLATEAU.

highlight: see FEATURE.

highly: see MOST; MUCH.

high-pitched: see SHRILL.

high-priced: see DEAR; EXPENSIVE; VALUABLE.

high-strung: see TEMPERAMENTAL.

highway *n.* parkway, freeway, expressway, turnpike, beltway, skyway, ROAD.

highwayman: see OUTLAW.

hijacker: see PIRATE.

hijacking: see PIRACY.

hike *n.* **1** *(a long hike)* TRIP, WALK, MARCH, backpack; **2** *(a hike in pay)* RAISE, INCREASE.
 — *v.* WALK, EXPLORE, tour.

hilarious *adj.* FUNNY, COMICAL, MERRY, gleeful, JOYFUL, GAY, JOLLY.

hilarity *n.* FUN, comedy, mirth, gaiety, merriment, glee, CHEERFULNESS, joyousness.

hill *n.* RISE, ELEVATION, MOUND, MOUNT, knoll, HEAP.

hillside *n.* SLOPE, gradient, ramp.

hilly *adj.* sloping, ABRUPT, STEEP, rising, elevated.

hilt: see HANDLE.

hind *adj.* REAR, BACK, posterior.
 — *n.*: see TAIL.

hind end: see REAR; TAIL.

hinder *v.* STOP, impede, hamper, obstruct, PREVENT, INTERRUPT.

hindering: see OPPOSING.

hindrance: see CHECK; DISADVANTAGE; DRAG; HANDICAP; OBSTACLE; RESISTANCE; STAY.

hinge *n.* swivel, joint, HOOK, LINK, LOCK, fastener.
 — *v.* TURN, pivot, HANG, REST, RELY ON.

hint *n.* TIP, CLUE, SUGGESTION, inkling, insinuation, implication.
 — *v.* IMPLY, infer, SUGGEST, tip.

hinterland: see BUSH; FRONTIER; INTERIOR.

hire *v.* ENGAGE, EMPLOY, RENT, CHARTER, lease.
 — *n.*: see EMPLOY; ENGAGEMENT.

hiss *v.* boo, hoot, fizz, seethe, SPIT.

historical *adj.* REAL, AUTHENTIC, factual, recorded, chronicled, biographical.

history *n.* RECORD, annals, chronicle, ACCOUNT, archives, narrative.

hit *n.* BLOW, slap, RAP, TAP, swat, clout, STROKE, COLLISION; MURDER.
— *v.* STRIKE, SMASH, CLASH, clonk, BEAT, KILL, FIND, DISCOVER.

hitch: see KNOT; TERM; TOUR.

hither: see HERE.

hitherto: see YET.

hitter: see BATTER.

hive *n.* SWARM, COLONY.

hoard: see ACCUMULATE; GATHER; HEAP; SAVINGS; STOCK; STORE.

hoarder: see MISER.

hoarfrost: see FROST.

hoarse *adj.* HUSKY, gruff, HARSH, ROUGH, gravelly, grating, raucous.

hoax: see CHEAT; SWINDLE.

hobble: see LIMP.

hobby *n.* pastime, diversion, recreation, PURSUIT.

hobbyist: see AMATEUR.

hobnail: see NAIL.

hobo: see BUM; DRIFTER; ROVER; TRAMP.

hock: see PAWN.

hodgepodge: see MESS.

hog *n.* PIG, SOW, swine, boar, glutton.

hoist *n.* LIFT, elevator, crane, derrick, pulley.
— *v.* RAISE, ELEVATE, HEAVE, LIFT.

hokum: see BUNK.

hold *n.* POSSESSION, keeping, retention, GRIP, GRASP, CONTROL, MAINTENANCE.
— *v.* **1** *(to hold a key)* GRASP, KEEP, GRIP, OWN, RETAIN; **2** *(to hold a mortgage)* MAINTAIN, CONTROL, CONTINUE; **3** *(to hold an idea)* THINK, adhere to, EMBRACE.

hold back: see WITHHOLD.

holder: see CONTAINER; FORK; FRAME; HANDLE; OWNER; PAIL; PROPRIETOR.

holding: see RESERVATION.

holdings: see EMPIRE.

hold on: see CLING.

hold out: see WITHSTAND.

holdup *n.* stick-up, ROBBERY, THEFT, ASSAULT, mugging.

hole *n.* OPENING, slot, GAP, SPACE, puncture, perforation, rip, CRACK, HOLLOW.

holiday *n.* VACATION, day off, FESTIVAL, CELEBRATION, LEAVE, furlough.

holiness *n.* sanctity, devoutness, piety, DEVOTION, sacredness, VIRTUE, godliness, righteousness.

holler: see HAIL; YELL.

hollow *adj.* **1** *(a hollow grave)* sunken, DEEP, concave, grooved; **2** *(a hollow stare)* EMPTY, VACANT, BLANK; **3** *(a hollow person)* FALSE, insincere, faithless, TREACHEROUS, deceitful.
— *n.*: see CAVITY; CAVE; CHAMBER; DENT; DEPRESSION; DIP; GULF; PIT; POCKET; RECESS; TROUGH.
— *v.*: see PIT.

holocaust: see MASSACRE.

holy *adj.* BLESSED, pious, saintly, SACRED, devout, PURE, RELIGIOUS.

homage: see ALLEGIANCE; ESTEEM; WORSHIP.

home *n.* **1** *(in our home)* HOUSE, FLAT, abode, RESIDENCE, domicile, HOUSEHOLD, birthplace; **2** *(she was placed in a home)* orphanage, asylum, INSTITUTION, sanitarium.
— *adv.*: see IN; INDOORS.

homecoming: see ARRIVAL; RETURN.

homeland: see COUNTRY.

homeliness: see UGLINESS.

homely *adj.* UNATTRACTIVE, UGLY, PLAIN, SIMPLE, ORDINARY, homespun, COMMON, uncultivated, uncomely.

homemaker: see HOUSEKEEPER; HOUSEWIFE.

homeowner: see LANDLORD.

home plate: see BASE

homespun: see HOMELY.

homestead: see FARM; HEARTH.

homesteader: see FARMER; PIONEER.

homework: see ASSIGNMENT.

homey: see DOMESTIC.

homicide: see ASSASSINATION; MURDER.

homosexual: see GAY.

hone: see SHARPEN.

honest *adj.* SINCERE, FAIR, TRUTHFUL, FRANK, OPEN, trustworthy, HONORABLE.

honestly: see FAIRLY; OPENLY; TRULY.

honesty *n.* integrity, SINCERITY, morality, truthfulness, uprightness, genuineness, fairness, fidelity, VIRTUE.

honey *n.* **1** *(bee's honey)* nectar, SWEETNESS; **2** *(she is his honey)* DEAR, DARLING, SWEETHEART, cutie.

honeycomb: see COMB.

honeyed: see SWEET.

honor *n.* **1** *(to show honor)* RESPECT, reverence, REGARD, ESTEEM, ADORATION, TRUST; **2** *(to bestow an honor)* DISTINCTION, TITLE, RECOGNITION, PRAISE.
— *v.* **1** *(to honor your father)* RESPECT, ADMIRE, PRAISE, ESTEEM, value, WORSHIP; **2** *(to honor a credit card)* ACCEPT, ACKNOWLEDGE, CLEAR.

honorable *adj.* FAMOUS, DISTINGUISHED, WORTHY, ADMIRABLE, trustworthy, reputable, respected, upstanding.

hood *n.* **1** *(a monk's hood)* headcovering, mantle, shawl, VEIL; **2** *(a car's hood)* COVER, canopy, LID, CAP, TOP; **3** *(a dangerous hood)* GANGSTER, mobster, CRIMINAL, racketeer, thug, hoodlum, goon, tough, ROWDY, CROOK.

hoodlum: see GANGSTER; HOOD; ROWDY.

hoodwink: see BLIND; CHEAT; DECEIVE.

hooey: see BUNK.

hoof *n.* FOOT, PAW.

hook *n.* CLASP, CATCH, latch, fastener, LOCK.
— *v.* CATCH, FASTEN, snare, entrap, NET.

hookup: see CIRCUIT.

hooligan: see ROWDY.

hoop: see RIM; ROUND; WHEEL.

hoot: see HISS.

hop *n.* JUMP, LEAP, skip, vault, SPRING. *v.* JUMP, SPRING, BOUNCE, SKIP, LEAP.

hope *n.* FAITH, BELIEF, WISH, EXPECTATION, DESIRE, anticipation, PROSPECT.
— *v.* TRUST, ANTICIPATE, EXPECT, DESIRE.

hopeful *adj.* optimistic, CONFIDENT, EXPECTANT, anticipating, encouraging, promising.

hopefulness: see OPTIMISM.

hopeless *adj.* LOST, despairing, DESPERATE, UNFORTUNATE, IMPOSSIBLE, incurable, irremediable.

hopelessness: see DESPAIR.

hoping: see EXPECTANT.

hopper: see BIN.

horde: see CROWD; HOST; LEGION; MOB; SWARM.

horizon: see DISTANCE.

horizontal: see EVEN; LEVEL; PLANE; STRAIGHT.

horizontally: see EVENLY.

horn: see BONE; SIGNAL; TRUMPET.

horoscope: see PREDICTION.

horrendous: see FRIGHTFUL.

horrible *adj.* AWFUL, TERRIBLE, repulsive, hideous, disgusting, revolting, DREADFUL.

horror *n.* **1** *(filled with horror)* FEAR, ALARM, TERROR, FRIGHT, PANIC; **2** *(his horror of spiders)* HATRED, DISGUST, loathing, aversion.

horse *n.* steed, stallion, mount, dobbin, pony, filly, thoroughbred.

horsefly: see FLY.

horse sense: see WISDOM.

horticulture: see AGRICULTURE.

hose *n.* **1** *(a woman's hose)* stockings, socks, anklets; **2** *(a garden hose)* TUBE, tubing, line, PIPE.
— *v.*: see RINSE.

hospitable *adj.* FRIENDLY, outgoing, amiable, CORDIAL, welcoming, gracious, receptive, unreserved.

hospital *n.* clinic, infirmary, sanitarium, dispensary.

hospitality *n.* WELCOME, cordiality, WARMTH, graciousness, KINDNESS, GENEROSITY.

hospitalization: see TREATMENT.

hospitalize: see COMMIT.

host *n.* **1** *(he was greeted by the host)* ENTERTAINER, RECEIVER, innkeeper; **2** *(a host of people)* horde, CROWD, throng, MULTITUDE, ARMY.
— *v.*: see TREAT.

hostage: see CAPTIVE; PRISONER.

hostel: see HOTEL.

hostelry: see INN.

hostile *adj.* antagonistic, UNFRIENDLY, opposed, HATEFUL, NASTY, VICIOUS, warlike, inimical.

hostilities: see WAR; WARFARE.

hostility *n.* repugnance, OPPOSITION, aversion, antagonism, belligerence, aggressiveness.

hostler: see GROOM.

hot *adj.* **1** *(hot coals)* burning, flaming, FIERY, blazing, boiling, spicy; **2** *(a hot temper)* PASSIONATE, excited, ANGRY, FURIOUS.

hotbed: see NEST.

hotel *n.* motel, roadhouse, INN, hostel, TAVERN, resort, spa.

hot-tempered: see FIERY; PEPPERY.

hound: see HUNT; PESTER; PURSUE.

hour *n.* TIME, MOMENT, PERIOD.

house *n.* RESIDENCE, domicile, HOME, abode, habitation, DWELLING, BUILDING.
— *v.* LODGE, SHELTER, PROTECT, HARBOR.

housebreaker: see BURGLAR; THIEF.

housefly: see FLY.

houseguest: see GUEST.

household *n.* HOME, HOUSE, FAMILY, folks.

housekeeper *n.* HOUSEWIFE, homemaker, SERVANT, housemaid, houseworker.

housemaid: see HOUSEKEEPER.

housemistress: see MISTRESS.

housemother: see MOTHER.

housewife *n.* MISTRESS, WIFE, HOUSEKEEPER, homemaker.

houseworker: see HOUSEKEEPER.

housing: see DEVELOPMENT.

hovel: see HUT; SHACK.

hover: see FLOAT.

how *adv.* whereby, whence, wherewith.

however *conj.* BUT, still, NEVERTHELESS, nonetheless, ALTHOUGH, DESPITE, notwithstanding.
— *adv.* WHATEVER, whatsoever.

howitzer: see ARTILLERY.

howl *n.* yowl, YELL, SHOUT, bawl, WAIL, CRY, lament, WHINE, MOAN, bark, yelp.
— *v.* SHOUT, BAWL, WAIL, CRY, lament, WHINE.

hub: see CENTER; MIDST.

hubbub: see CLAMOR; CLATTER; NOISE; RIOT; UPROAR.

huckster: see PEDDLER.

huddle *v.* CONGREGATE, ASSEMBLE, CLUSTER, GATHER, CROWD, MEET, CONSULT, DISCUSS.

— *n.* CROWD, DISORDER, CONFUSION, jumble, DISTURBANCE, tumult, CONFERENCE, DISCUSSION.

hue: see COLOR; SHADE; SHADOW; TINT; TONE.

huff: see PANT; PUFF.

hug *n.* SQUEEZE, embrace, caress.
— *v.* SQUEEZE, EMBRACE, CARESS, cuddle, SNUGGLE, enfold, PRESS.

huge *adj.* LARGE, BIG, GIANT, TREMENDOUS, ENORMOUS, GIGANTIC, IMMENSE, monumental, voluminous.

hugely: see VERY.

hull: see CRUST; POD.

hum *n.* buzzing, drone, murmuring.
— *v.* MURMUR, drone, buzz.

human *adj.* MORTAL, civilized, PERSONAL, humane, INDIVIDUAL, SYMPATHETIC, feeling.
— *n.* CREATURE, BEING, MORTAL, INDIVIDUAL, PERSON, MAN, WOMAN, SOMEONE, SOMEBODY.

humane: see HUMAN; KIND.

humanitarian: see CHARITABLE.

humanity *n.* **1** *(for service to humanity)* MANKIND, humankind, men, PEOPLE; **2** *(Gandhi's humanity was well known)* compassion, SYMPATHY, UNDERSTANDING, FEELING, KINDNESS, benevolence, CHARITY.

humankind: see HUMANITY; MANKIND; UNIVERSE.

humans: see PEOPLE.

humble *adj.* MODEST, meek, lowly, unpretending, unassuming, GENTLE, QUIET, courteous.
— *v.* downgrade, DEGRADE, SHAME, HUMILIATE, REDUCE, CRUSH, put down.

humbled: see BEATEN.

humbleness: see INFERIORITY.

humbug: see TRICK.

humdrum: see STALE.

humid *adj.* sticky, WET, DAMP, MOIST, MUGGY, stuffy.

humidity: see CLIMATE; DEW; MOISTURE; WETNESS.

humiliate *v.* DEGRADE, SHAME, HUMBLE, belittle, CRUSH, DISGRACE, EMBARRASS, INSULT.

humiliated: see ASHAMED.

humiliating: see DISGRACEFUL; SHAMEFUL.

humiliation *n.* degradation, EMBARRASSMENT, DISGRACE, INSULT, dishonor, SHAME, offense, mortification.

humility: see MODESTY.

humming: see BUZZ.

humor *n*. MOOD, DISPOSITION, TEMPER,
  AMUSEMENT, WIT, joking, FUN, merriment.
  — *v*.: see GRATIFY.

humorist: see COMEDIAN; JESTER; WIT.

humorous: see COMICAL; FUNNY.

hump: see BULGE.

hunch: see CROUCH; GUESS; IMPULSE; INSPIRATION.

hunger *n*. **1** *(they died from hunger)* starvation,
  FAMINE; **2** *(a hunger for love)* APPETITE, craving,
  DESIRE, yearning, longing, eagerness,
  hankering.
  — *v*.: see LUST; STARVE; THIRST.

hungry *adj*. starved, famished, ravenous, EAGER,
  craving, UNSATISFIED, longing.

hunt *v*. SEARCH, CHASE, PURSUE, hound, STALK,
  TRAIL, TRACK, TRAP.
  — *n*. chase, hunting, PURSUIT.

hunter *n*. sportsman, sportswoman, huntsman,
  trapper, tracker, chaser, pursuer.

hunting: see HUNT.

huntsman: see HUNTER.

hurdle: see BARRIER; CLEAR; JUMP; LEAP;
  OBSTACLE; WALL.

hurl *v*. HEAVE, FLING, THROW, PITCH, CAST, TOSS,
  chuck.

hurricane: see BLOW; GALE; STORM; WIND.

hurried *adj*. rushed, HASTY, superficial,
  accelerated, pressed.

hurry *v*. RUSH, HASTEN, SPEED, RUN, scurry, FLY,
  HUSTLE.
  — *n*. HASTE, RUSH, flurry, agitation, CONFUSION.

hurt *v*. HARM, INJURE, DAMAGE, impair, BRUISE,
  ACHE, pain.
  — *adj*.: see RESENTFUL; SORE; SUFFERING;
  WOUNDED.
  — *n*.: see BRUISE; DAMAGE; HARM; PAIN; STING;
  SUFFERING; WOUND.

hurtful: see DESTRUCTIVE; EVIL; HARMFUL.

hurting: see PAINFUL.

hurtle: see DASH; SPEED.

husband *n*. MATE, spouse, MAN, bridegroom
  consort, provider, breadwinner.
  — *v*. SAVE, economize.

husbandry: see AGRICULTURE.

hush *n*. QUIET, SILENCE, stillness, PEACE, CALM.
  — *v*. quiet, SILENCE, muffle, gag, stifle.

hushed: see LOW; SOUNDLESS; STILL.

husk: see BARK; POD; SHELL; SKIN.

husky *adj*. LARGE, weighty, STRONG, STURDY,
  SOLID, HEAVY, RUGGED, well-built.

hustle *v*. HASTEN, HURRY, SPEED, RUSH, URGE,
  FORCE, PUSH, PRESSURE, harass, PESTER.

hut *n*. COTTAGE, CABIN, bunkhouse, hovel,
  shanty, SHACK, SHED, HOUSE.

hybrid: see CROSS, MIXTURE.

hydrogen: see GAS.

hygiene: see SANITATION.

hygienic: see SANITARY.

hymn *n*. psalm, CHANT, chorale, CAROL,
  SPIRITUAL, canticle.

hyphen: see DASH.

hypothesis: see GUESS; THEORY.

hypothetical: see SUPPOSED.

hypothetically: see SUPPOSEDLY.

hysteria: see PANIC.

hysterical: see EMOTIONAL; PANICKY; SHRILL.

I

ice *n*. icicle, iceberg, glaze, FROST, glacé, HAIL,
  sleet, dry ice.
  — *v*.: see CHILL; REFRIGERATE.

iceberg: see ICE.

iced: see FROZEN; ICY.

icicle: see ICE.

icon: see IDOL.

icy *adj*. iced, frosty, frigid, FROZEN, arctic, glacial,
  SLIPPERY.

id: see SELF.

idea *n*. concept, NOTION, THOUGHT, SENSE,
  DESIGN, MEANING.

ideal *adj*. SUPREME, PERFECT, model, exemplary,
  COMPLETE.
  — *n*. MODEL, STANDARD, EXAMPLE.

idealistic: see ROMANTIC.

identical *adj.* like, ALIKE, SAME, selfsame, uniform, EQUAL, indistinguishable.

identification: see BADGE; CARD; IDENTITY; TAG.

identify *v.* DESCRIBE, NAME, CLASSIFY, CATALOG, DETERMINE.

identity *n.* individuality, SAMENESS, likeness, identification, NAME.

ideology: see SYSTEM.

idiocy: see FOOLISHNESS; MADNESS; STUPIDITY.

idiom: see LANGUAGE; PHRASE; TONGUE.

idiot *n.* FOOL, nincompoop, dunce, imbecile, MORON, cretin.

idiotic *adj.* moronic, STUPID, SENSELESS, asinine, FEEBLE-MINDED.

idle *adj.* inactive, inert, unoccupied, LAZY, unused, VACANT, VAIN.
— *v.*: see COAST.

idler: see LOAFER.

idol *n.* icon, STATUE, image, GOD, goddess, totem, HERO.

idolize *v.* WORSHIP, deify, ADORE, glorify, ADMIRE, HONOR.

if *conj.* provided, SUPPOSING, even if, THOUGH, whether.

iffy: see CHANCY.

if not: see UNLESS.

ignite: see BURN; FIRE; FLAME; FLARE; HEAT; KINDLE; LIGHT; STRIKE.

ignoramus: see SAP.

ignorance *n.* DARK, DULLNESS, illiteracy, STUPIDITY, blindness.

ignorant *adj.* UNAWARE, UNCONSCIOUS, illiterate, uneducated, uncultivated, empty-headed, naive, unmindful, nescient.

ignore *v.* DISREGARD, OVERLOOK, NEGLECT, OMIT, FORGET, slight.

ilk: see VEIN.

ill *adj.* SICK, unwell, UNHEALTHY, diseased, EVIL, unfavorable.
— *adv.* badly, POORLY, LITTLE.
— *n.*: see INJURY.

illegal *adj.* unlawful, WRONG, improper, taboo, FORBIDDEN, illegitimate, lawless.

illegality: see WRONG.

illegitimate: see ILLEGAL.

ill-fated: see CURSED; LUCKLESS; UNLUCKY.

ill-humored: see SULLEN.

illiberal: see NARROW-MINDED.

illiteracy: see IGNORANCE.

illiterate: see IGNORANT.

ill-made: see MISSHAPEN.

ill-mannered: see IMPOLITE.

illness *n.* SICKNESS, AILMENT, infirmity, DISEASE, DISORDER, maladjustment, phobia; malady.

ill-qualified: see RUSTY.

ill-treat: see PERSECUTE.

illume: see ILLUMINATE.

illuminate *v.* **1** *(to illuminate a space)* LIGHT, BRIGHTEN, illumine, illume; **2** *(to illuminate an issue)* EXPLAIN, CLARIFY, enlighten, INSPIRE.

illumination: see CLARIFICATION; LIGHT.

illumine: see BRIGHTEN; ILLUMINATE.

illusion *n.* **1** *(belief in magic is an illusion)* MISTAKE, misconception, delusion, fallacy; **2** *(illusions of grandeur)* fantasy, DREAM, FANCY, delusion.

illustrate *v.* PICTURE, portray, exemplify, EXPLAIN, REPRESENT, ADORN.

illustration *n.* REPRESENTATION, EXAMPLE, CASE, instance, CLARIFICATION, PICTURE, SKETCH.

illustrious: see CELEBRATED; DISTINGUISHED; FAMED; FAMOUS; GLORIOUS. GRAND.

ill will: see FRICTION; GRUDGE; HATRED.

image: see ASPECT; IDOL; PICTURE; REFLECTION; REPRESENTATION; SLIDE.

imaginable: see THINKABLE.

imaginary *adj.* FANTASTIC, MYTHICAL, legendary, FICTITIOUS, dreamy, fanciful, conceived, SUPPOSED.

imagination *n.* INSPIRATION, ORIGINALITY, insight, ingenuity, FANCY, fantasy.

imaginative: see INGENIOUS; INVENTIVE; ORIGINAL; ROMANTIC.

imagine *v.* visualize, conjure, FANCY, presume, PRETEND.

imbecile: see HALF-WIT; IDIOT; MORON.

imbecility: see FOOLISHNESS.

imbibe: see ABSORB; DRINK; SIP.

imitate *v.* COPY, mimic, impersonate, ape, DUPLICATE, counterfeit.

imitation *n.* DUPLICATE, COPY, counterfeit, facsimile, simulation, DUPLICATION, mimicry.

immaculate: see CLEAN; CLEANLY; PURE; SPOTLESS.

immaterial: see SPIRITUAL.

immature *adj.* YOUNG, undeveloped, UNRIPE, inexperienced, RAW, GREEN, CHILDISH.

immaturity: see YOUTH.

immeasurable *adj.* limitless, GREAT, boundless, ENDLESS, INFINITE, unlimited, IMMENSE.

immediate *adj.* INSTANT, PROMPT, DIRECT, SPEEDY, NEXT.

immediately *adv.* INSTANTLY, PROMPTLY, right away, DIRECTLY, speedily, SOON.

immense *adj.* VAST, HUGE, GIGANTIC, GREAT, ENDLESS.

immensity: see GREATNESS; INFINITY.

immerse: see ABSORB; BATHE; DIP; PLUNGE; SUBMERGE.

immersion: see DIP; WASHING.

immigrant *n.* newcomer, ALIEN, FOREIGNER, migrant, OUTSIDER.
— *adj.*: see FOREIGN.

immigrate *v.* ENTER, MIGRATE, SETTLE, colonize.

immigration *n.* migration, SETTLEMENT, ENTRY, colonization, naturalization.

immobile: see IMMOVABLE; MOTIONLESS; QUIET.

immobilize: see PIN.

immoderate: see EXCESSIVE; EXTREME; UNREASONABLE; WASTEFUL.

immoderation: see EXCESS.

immodest: see INDECENT; SHAMELESS.

immoral: see CRIMINAL; EVIL; LOOSE; SHAMEFUL; WICKED; WRONG.

immorality: see ABANDON; WRONG.

immortal *adj.* ETERNAL, ENDLESS, deathless, indestructible, everlasting, unceasing, timeless, eminent.

immortality *n.* permanence, durability, ETERNITY, INFINITY, perpetuity.

immovable *adj.* FIXED, immobile, STABLE, FIRM, steadfast, unyielding, stationary.

immunity: see FREEDOM; LIBERTY; RIGHT.

immutable: see UNCHANGEABLE.

imp: see BRAT; RASCAL; TERROR.

impact *n.* SHOCK, BLOW, STROKE, smash, CONTACT, INFLUENCE, EFFECT.

impair: see DAMAGE; HURT; SPOIL.

impaired: see BLIND; WORN.

impairment: see WEAR.

impart: see CAST; EXTEND; GIVE.

impartial: see EQUAL; EVEN; FAIR; JUST; NEUTRAL.

impartiality: see EQUALITY; JUSTICE.

impartially: see EVENLY; FAIRLY.

impatience *n.* restlessness, uneasiness, eagerness, ANXIETY, agitation, HASTE.

impatient *adj.* ANXIOUS, HASTY, RESTLESS, EAGER, agitated, UNEASY.

impeach: see ACCUSE.

impede: see BAR; BLOCK; CURB; DISCOURAGE; FOIL; HINDER; INTERRUPT; PREVENT; PROHIBIT.

impediment: see BAR; DRAG.

impel: see PUSH; URGE.

impend: see THREATEN.

impending: see FUTURE; ONCOMING.

imperative: see BINDING.

imperfect: see FAULTY; INCOMPLETE; UNSATISFACTORY.

imperfection: see DEFECT; FAULT; INFERIORITY.

imperial: see ROYAL.

imperil: see ENDANGER; MENACE.

impermanent: see MORTAL.

impersonate: see ACT; IMITATE; PLAY; REPRESENT.

impersonation: see CHARACTER; ROLE.

impersonator: see IMPOSTOR.

impertinence: see RUDENESS.

impertinent: see BOLD; IMPOLITE.

impervious: see AIRTIGHT.

impish: see MISCHIEVOUS.

implement *n.* TOOL, DEVICE, INSTRUMENT, gadget.
— *v.*: see ENABLE; ENFORCE.

implementation: see TRANSACTION.

implicated: see ENTANGLED.

implication: see HINT; IMPORT; THRUST.

implore: see PLEAD; PRAY; URGE.

imply *v.* HINT, SUGGEST, connote, ASSUME, MEAN, SIGNIFY, INVOLVE.

impolite *adj.* RUDE, insolent, impertinent, discourteous, disrespectful, ill-mannered, uncivil.

imponderable: see INFINITE; INVISIBLE.

import *v.* INTRODUCE, BRING, SHIP, TRANSPORT. See also MATTER.
— *n.* **1** *(a recent import)* PURCHASE, GOODS, MERCHANDISE; **2** *(of great import)* IMPORTANCE, CONSEQUENCE, WEIGHT; **3** *(the obvious import)* MEANING, signification, implication.

importance *n.* SIGNIFICANCE, CONCERN, WEIGHT, CONSEQUENCE.

important *adj.* substantial, SERIOUS. decisive, ESSENTIAL, eminent, INFLUENTIAL, PROMINENT, esteemed.

importune: see COAX; INVITE.

impose *v.* DICTATE, ORDER, COMPEL, burden, FIX, PLACE.

imposing: see MAGNIFICENT; MASSIVE; SPLENDID.

imposition: see INTRUSION.

impossible *adj.* VAIN, futile, unattainable, unthinkable, inconceivable, HOPELESS, infeasible.

impostor *n.* trickster, CHEAT, deceiver, FRAUD, pretender, faker, impersonator.

impotence: see WEAKNESS.

impotent: see HELPLESS; POWERLESS; WEAK.

impoverished: see BANKRUPT; POOR.

impractical: see USELESS.

impregnable: see AIRTIGHT.

impress *v.* **1** *(to impress a symbol)* STAMP, emboss, indent, imprint; **2** *(we are impressed)* AFFECT, INFLUENCE, MOVE, fascinate, overawe.

impressing: see PRINTING.

impression *n.* **1** *(the dart left an impression)* MARK, STAMP, DENT, imprint; **2** *(a bad impression)* EFFECT, REACTION, IMPACT, RESULT. See also ISSUE.

impressive: see AMBITIOUS; CONVINCING; EFFECTIVE; SUPERB.

impressiveness: see SPLENDOR.

imprint: see DENT; ENGRAVE; IMPRESS; INSCRIBE; IMPRESSION; MARK; STAMP; STRIKE.

imprinting: see PRINTING.

imprison: see ARREST; CAGE; CHAIN; CONFINE; JAIL; PUNISH; SENTENCE.

imprisonment: see PUNISHMENT.

improbable: see FISHY; INCREDIBLE; OUTSIDE; UNEXPECTED.

improbably: see EVEN.

impromptu: see OFFHAND.

improper: see FOUL; ILLEGAL; IRREGULAR; NAUGHTY; SUGGESTIVE; UNSUITABLE; WRONG.

improperly: see WRONG.

improve *v.* **1** *(to improve a product)* BETTER, AMEND, CORRECT, REFINE, purify; **2** *(his skill improves)* GROW, PROGRESS, RECOVER.

improved: see ADVANCED; ONWARD; UP-TO-DATE.

improvement *n.* betterment, CORRECTION, CHANGE, ADDITION, PROGRESS, RECOVERY.

improvised: see OFFHAND.

impudence: see DARING; RUDENESS.

impudent: see FRESH; SHAMELESS.

impulse *n.* surge, THROB, BURST, URGE, whim, FANCY, hunch.

impulsive *adj.* spontaneous, whimsical, SUDDEN, unpremeditated, OFFHAND, VIOLENT, HASTY, RASH.

impure *adj.* unclean, DIRTY, contaminated, polluted, FOUL, FILTHY, NASTY, corrupt.

impurity: see WICKEDNESS.

impute: see ATTRIBUTE; CHARGE.

in *prep.* WITHIN, into, INSIDE, ON, AMONG, DURING, AFTER.
— *adv.* INSIDE, within, home, accepted, STYLISH.

inaccurate: see WRONG.

inaccurately: see WRONG.

inactive: see IDLE; LAZY.

inactivity: see REST.

inadequacy: see INFERIORITY.

inadequate: see LIMITED; SCARCE; UNABLE; UNEQUAL; UNSATISFACTORY; WANTING; WRETCHED.

inadmissable: see INCREDIBLE; UNBEARABLE.

inadvertent: see UNCONSCIOUS.

inadvertently: see UNAWARES.

inalterable: see UNCHANGEABLE.

inamorata: see MISTRESS.

inane: see FOOLISH; SILLY; STUPID.

inappropriate: see UNSUITABLE; WRONG.

inappropriately: see WRONG.

inaptitude: see AWKWARDNESS.

inarticulate: see SPEECHLESS.

inasmuch as: see BECAUSE; FOR; SINCE.

inattention: see FORGETFULNESS.

inattentive: see ABSENT-MINDED; CARELESS; UNAWARE.

inaugural: see INITIAL.

inaugurate: see INSTITUTE; INTRODUCE.

inauguration: see INTRODUCTION.

inauspicious: see UNHAPPY.

inborn: see NATIVE; NATURAL.

inbred: see NATIVE.

incalculable: see INFINITE.

incandescence: see GLOW.

incandescent: see RADIANT.

incapable: see HELPLESS; UNABLE.

incapacitate: see CRIPPLE.

incarcerate: see CAGE.

incense *n.* SCENT, FRAGRANCE, PERFUME, essence.
— *v.*: see IRRITATE.

inception: see START.

incessant: see CONTINUAL; CONTINUOUS.

inch: see BUDGE; EDGE.

incident *n.* OCCURRENCE, EVENT, HAPPENING, CIRCUMSTANCE.

incidental: see OCCASIONAL; SIDE; STRAY.

incidentally *adv.* accidentally, casually, unexpectedly.

incinerate: see BURN.

incinerator: see FURNACE.

incise: see LANCE.

incision: see CUT; NOTCH; OPERATION; SCRATCH; SLASH; SLIT.

incisor: see TOOTH.

incite: see AROUSE; KINDLE; PROVOKE; RAISE.

incitement: see EXCITEMENT.

inclination *n.* **1** *(the inclination of the ladder)* SLANT, incline, HILL, SLOPE, TILT; **2** *(at the slightest inclination)* leaning, bias, bent, TREND, PREFERENCE.

incline: see BOW; DECLINE; HANG; INCLINATION; LEAN; NOD; PERSUADE; SLANT; SLOPE; SWAY; TEND; TILT.

inclined: see AGREEABLE; APT; BENT; WILLING.

include *v.* take in, CONTAIN, ADMIT, EMBRACE, INVOLVE, ACCOMMODATE, incorporate.

including *prep.* WITH, and, PLUS, inclusive.

inclusive: see INCLUDING.

incognito: see DISGUISE.

incoherent: see FUZZY.

income *n.* EARNINGS, SALARY, WAGES, REVENUE, receipts, PROFIT, proceeds, RENT, royalty, GAIN.

incomparable *adj.* peerless, unequaled, unmatched, unrivaled, unparalleled, inimitable.

incompetent: see UNABLE.

incomplete *adj.* unfinished, PARTIAL, imperfect, lacking, WANTING, deficient, unaccomplished.

incompletely: see PART; PARTLY.

inconceivable: see IMPOSSIBLE; UNHEARD OF.

inconsequential: see POINTLESS.

inconsiderate: see SHABBY; THOUGHTLESS.

inconsistent: see ABSURD; CHANGEABLE.

inconsistently: see VARIOUSLY.

inconstant: see VARIABLE.

inconvenience: see AWKWARDNESS; BOTHER; DISADVANTAGE; DISTURB; TROUBLE.

incorporate: see ASSOCIATE; INCLUDE; INVISIBLE.

incorporated: see CONFEDERATE.

incorrect: see FALSE; WRONG.

incorrectly: see WRONG.

incorrectness: see WRONG.

increase *v.* GROW, RISE, ENLARGE, EXPAND, escalate, IMPROVE, MULTIPLY.
— *n.* GROWTH, EXPANSION, DEVELOPMENT, PROFIT, BENEFIT.

increased: see GROWN.

increasingly *adv.* MORE, FURTHER, additionally, extra, EVER.

incredible *adj.* unbelievable, improbable, unlikely, far-fetched, EXTRAORDINARY; inadmissible.

increment: see MORE.

incubate: see HATCH; NEST.

incumbency: see REIGN.

incur: see OWE.

incurable: see HOPELESS.

incursion: see RAID.

indebted: see APPRECIATIVE; THANKFUL.

indecent *adj.* unbecoming, IMPROPER, unseemly, lewd, immodest, SHAMELESS, IMPURE.

indecision: see DOUBT; HESITATION; SUSPENSE; UNCERTAINTY.

indecisive: see TIMID.

indeed *adv.* CERTAINLY, TRULY, SURELY, REALLY, ACTUALLY.

indefinite: see ANY; DIM; FORMLESS; GENERAL; UNCERTAIN; UNDECIDED; VAGUE.

indelicate: see COARSE; CRUDE.

indemnity: see INSURANCE.

indent: see IMPRESS.

indentation: see DENT; NICK; NOTCH; PIT; RECESS.

independence *n.* FREEDOM, LIBERTY, emancipation, self-government, sovereignty, LICENSE.

independent *adj.* FREE, autonomous, liberated, uncontrolled, self-sufficient, self-reliant, SEPARATE.

indestructible: see IMMORTAL.

index *n.* **1** *(check the index)* table of contents, TABLE, CONTENTS, FILE, LIST, directory, CATALOG; **2** *(an index of progress)* INDICATION, MEASURE, GUIDE, indicator.
— *v.*: see CATALOG.

index finger: see FINGER.

indicate *v.* **1** *(to indicate a direction)* SHOW, DEMONSTRATE, point out, REVEAL, SUGGEST; **2** *(clouds may indicate rain)* MEAN, SIGNIFY, symbolize.

indicated: see EVIDENT.

indication *n.* SIGN, EVIDENCE, EXAMPLE, ILLUSTRATION, SUGGESTION, HINT.

indicative: see EXPRESSIVE.

indicator: see ARROW; INDEX.

indict: see ACCUSE; BLAME; PROSECUTE.

indicted: see GUILTY.

indictment: see CHARGE.

indifferent: see CARELESS; CASUAL; COLD; LUKEWARM; NEUTRAL.

indigenous: see DOMESTIC.

indignant: see ANGRY; RESENTFUL; SORE.

indignation: see ANGER; IRRITATION; RESENTMENT.

indirect: see CIRCULAR.

indispensable: see BASIC; ESSENTIAL; KEY; NECESSARY; VITAL.

indisposed: see RELUCTANT; SICK.

indisputable: see CERTAIN.

indisputably: see CERTAINLY; DOUBTLESS.

indistinct: see FAINT; FORMLESS; LOOSE.

indistinguishable: see IDENTICAL.

individual *adj.* SINGLE, ONLY, LONE, SINGULAR, DISTINCT, PARTICULAR, PERSONAL.
— *n.* PERSON, BEING, SOMEONE, SOMEBODY.

individuality: see IDENTITY; PERSONALITY; SELF.

individualize: see ITEMIZE.

indoctrinate: see CONVERT; TEACH.

indolent: see LAZY.

indoors *adv.* IN, INSIDE, within, home.

induce: see BRING; COAX; CONVINCE; LURE; PERSUADE.

inducement: see BAIT; TEMPTATION.

induct: see DRAFT; INSTALL.

induction: see DRAFT.

indulge: see BABY; GRATIFY; PET; SPOIL.

indulgence: see PARDON; TOLERANCE.

indulgent: see PERMISSIVE.

industrial *adj.* COMMERCIAL, manufacturing, business, MECHANICAL, heavy-duty.

industrious *adj.* diligent, AMBITIOUS, ACTIVE, ENERGETIC, BUSY, purposeful.

industry *n.* **1** *(the steel industry)* BUSINESS, PRODUCTION, COMMERCE, TRADE, CAPITAL; **2** *(he displays industry)* diligence, ENERGY, DRIVE; perseverance.

inebriated: see DRUNK; HIGH.

inebriating: see HARD.

inedible: see STALE.

ineffectual: see USELESS.

inelastic: see FLABBY.

inept: see AWKWARD; CLUMSY.

inequality: see DIFFERENCE.

inert: see ASLEEP; IDLE; LAZY; MOTIONLESS; SENSELESS.

inescapable: see INEVITABLE.

inestimable: see PRECIOUS.

inevitability: see FATE; NECESSARILY.

inevitable *adj.* unavoidable, inescapable, fated, predestined, CERTAIN.

inevitably: see CERTAINLY.

inexorable: see MERCILESS.

inexpensive *adj.* MODEST, REASONABLE, CHEAP, ECONOMICAL, THRIFTY, low-priced.

inexperienced: see CHILDISH; GREEN; IMMATURE; RAW; RUSTY; YOUNG; YOUTHFUL.

infallible: see PERFECT.

infamous: see NOTORIOUS.

infamy: see DISGRACE.

infancy: see CHILDHOOD.

infant *n.* BABY, babe, newborn, CHILD, tot, nursling, cub, pup.

infantile: see CHILDISH; CHILDLIKE.

infantry: see ARMY.

infatuated: see MAD.

infeasible: see IMPOSSIBLE.

infect *v.* **1** *(a fly infected him)* afflict, SICKEN, TRANSMIT, contaminate, POLLUTE; **2** *(the idea infected everyone)* INFLUENCE, corrupt, taint, SPOIL, blight.

infected: see SORE.

infection *n.* **1** *(a widespread virus infection)* affliction, contamination, COMMUNICATION, contagion, epidemic; **2** *(a skin infection)* DISEASE, DISORDER, virus, sore, ulcer.

infectious *adj.* contagious, CATCHING, communicable, inspiring.

infer: see CONCLUDE; GATHER; HINT; READ; UNDERSTAND.

inference: see CONCLUSION.

inferior *adj.* POOR, defective, secondary, mediocre, UNSATISFACTORY, subordinate, LOW, lowly, COMMON.
— *n.*: see SUBJECT.

inferiority *n.* deficiency, WEAKNESS, lowliness, baseness, humbleness, imperfection, inadequacy.

inferno: see HELL.

infertile: see BARREN.

infest: see POLLUTE.

infield: see DIAMOND.

infiltrate: see PENETRATE.

infinite *adj.* ENDLESS, limitless, boundless, ETERNAL, IMMENSE, incalculable, imponderable, SUPREME, ABSOLUTE.

infinitely: see FOREVER.

infinitesimal: see MINUTE.

infinitude: see INFINITY.

infinity *n.* vastness, immensity, infinitude, expanse, WEALTH, IMMORTALITY, continuum, ETERNITY, supremacy.

infirm: see FEEBLE.

infirmary: see HOSPITAL.

infirmity: see ILLNESS.

inflame: see ANGER; ENRAGE; EXCITE; HEAT.

inflamed: see ANGRY; SORE.

inflammation *n.* INFECTION, swelling, reddening, IRRITATION, sore, burning, HEAT, RAGE.

inflate *v.* blow up, FILL, EXPAND, SWELL, dilate, bloat, EXAGGERATE.

inflated: see LONG-WINDED.

inflation *n.* EXPANSION, swelling, GROWTH, build-up, INCREASE, RISE, crisis, boom.

inflexible: see BRITTLE; RIGID; STABLE; STIFF; STRICT; STUBBORN.

influence *v.* AFFECT, MOVE, SWAY, CHANGE, ALTER.
— *n.* EFFECT, IMPACT, SWAY, FORCE, CONTROL, POWER, prestige.

influential *adj.* IMPORTANT, POWERFUL, weighty, PROMINENT, dominant.

inform *v.* TELL, ADVISE, COMMUNICATE, INSTRUCT, NOTIFY, EXPLAIN, apprise.

informal *adj.* CASUAL, FAMILIAR, FRANK, straightforward, unrestrained, ORDINARY.

informant: see EDUCATOR.

information *n.* KNOWLEDGE, INTELLIGENCE, FACT, data, NOTICE, MESSAGE, REPORT, NEWS.

informative *adj.* instructive, EDUCATIONAL, advisory. See also TELLTALE.

infraction: see VIOLATION.

infrequency: see SCARCITY.

infrequent: see OCCASIONAL; RARE; SCARCE; UNCOMMON; UNUSUAL.

infrequently: see FEW; SELDOM.

infringe: see INVADE; TRESPASS.

infuriate *v.* PROVOKE, IRRITATE, aggravate, ENRAGE, madden, ANGER.

ingenious *adj.* INVENTIVE, creative, imaginative, CLEVER, skillful, GIFTED.

ingenuity: see ART; BRILLIANCE; CLEVERNESS; GENIUS; IMAGINATION; INVENTION; RESOURCE; SMARTNESS.

ingenuous: see OPEN.

ingrained: see NATURAL.

ingredient *n.* PART, ELEMENT, component, constituent.

inhabit *v.* OCCUPY, DWELL, RESIDE, LODGE, room, SETTLE.

inhabitant *n.* dweller, RESIDENT, LODGER, TENANT, CITIZEN, NATIVE.

inhabitants: see PEOPLE; POPULATION.

inhabited: see HAUNTED.

inhale *v.* BREATHE, respire, INSPIRE, DRAW, SUCK, GASP, PANT, PUFF.

inherit *v.* ACQUIRE, RECEIVE, GET, DERIVE, SUCCEED.

inheritance *n.* legacy, heritage, birthright, ESTATE, TRUST, endowment.

inheritor: see HEIR; RECEIVER.

inhibition: see MODESTY; RESERVATION.

inhospitable: see UNFRIENDLY.

inhuman *adj.* CRUEL, unfeeling, uncivilized, SAVAGE, barbarous, ruthless, BRUTAL, MERCILESS.

inhumane: see SAVAGE.

inhumanity: see CRUELTY.

inimical: see HOSTILE.

inimitable: see INCOMPARABLE.

initial *adj.* FIRST, beginning, BASIC, ELEMENTARY, inaugural, maiden.
— *n.* ABBREVIATION, LETTER.
— *v.* MARK, SIGN, APPROVE.

initially: see FIRST.

initiate: see ATTACK; BEGIN; COMMENCE; FOUND; INSTALL; START.

initiation: see START.

initiative: see DRIVE; ENERGY.

initiator: see AUTHOR; BEGINNER.

inject: see INTRODUCE.

injection: see INTRODUCTION; SHOT.

injure *v.* HURT, HARM, WOUND, DAMAGE, OFFEND, affront, tarnish.

injured: see CRIPPLE; SORE; WOUNDED.

injurious: see DESTRUCTIVE; EVIL; FATAL; HARMFUL; WRONG.

injury *n.* WOUND, HARM, DAMAGE, ill, affront, grievance, injustice.

injustice: see INJURY; WRONG.

inkling: see CLUE; HINT; NOTION.

inky: see BLACK.

inlet: see BAY; CANAL; GULF; MOUTH; PORT; SOUND.

in lieu of: see INSTEAD.

inmate: see CAPTIVE; PATIENT.

inn *n.* HOTEL, motel, hostelry, road house, TAVERN, LODGE.

inner *adj.* interior, inside, INTERNAL, CENTRAL, PRIVATE, HIDDEN.

innkeeper: see HOST.

innocence *n.* integrity, GOODNESS, purity, VIRTUE, righteousness, HONOR, naivete, VIRGINITY, frankness, uncorrupted.

innocent *adj.* GUILTLESS, sinless, BLAMELESS, unblemished, HONEST, PURE, naive, HARMLESS, inoffensive.

innovation: see DISCOVERY; FEATURE.

inoculation: see MEDICINE; SHOT.

inoffensive: see HARMLESS; INNOCENT.

inopportune: see PREMATURE.

inquest: see QUESTION.

inquire *v.* ASK, SEEK, QUESTION, INVESTIGATE, PROBE, EXPLORE.

inquiring: see CURIOUS.

inquiringness: see CURIOSITY.

inquiry *n.* INVESTIGATION, query, SEARCH, probe, EXAMINATION.

inquisitive: see CURIOUS, PERSONAL.

inquisitiveness: see CURIOSITY.

insane *adj.* **1** *(the sick and insane)* MAD, CRAZY, deranged, lunatic, demented, maniacal, psychopathic, psychotic, wacky; **2** *(an insane scheme)* madcap, FOOLISH, daft, RASH.

insanity *n.* **1** *(hopeless insanity)* MADNESS, schizophrenia, dementia praecox, lunacy, psychosis, delirium; **2** *(that fling was insanity)* FOLLY, rashness, ODDITY.

inscribe *v.* WRITE, MARK, ENGRAVE, IMPRESS, imprint, emblazon, STAMP.

inscription: see ENGRAVING; MEMORIAL; STAMP; WRITING.

insect *n.* bug, mite, FLY, spider, beetle, PEST, virus.

insecure *adj.* WEAK, tottering, SHAKY, UNSAFE, UNCERTAIN, unsure, RISKY.

insecurity: see UNCERTAINTY.

insensible: see ASLEEP; UNCONSCIOUS.

insensitive: see BLUNT; NUMB.

insert: see ENCLOSE; INTRODUCE; PANEL; PUT; THREAD.

inset: see PANEL.

inside *prep.* IN, WITHIN.
  — *adv.* within, INDOORS, inward, IN.
  — *n.* INDOORS, INTERIOR, core, CENTER, BELLY, bowels, gut, womb.
  — *adj.*: see INNER; INTERNAL.

inside of: see WITHIN.

insidious: see CROOKED; TREACHEROUS.

insight: see CLEVERNESS; IMAGINATION.

insignia: see CHARACTER; EMBLEM.

insignificant: see MINOR; TRASHY.

insignificantly: see FEW.

insincere: see EMPTY; HOLLOW.

insinuate: see SUGGEST; WORM.

insinuation: see HINT; SUGGESTION.

insipid: see FLAT.

insist *v.* URGE, DEMAND, COMMAND, REQUEST, MAINTAIN, emphasize.

insistent *adj.* affirmative, persistent, assertive, emphatic, FORCEFUL.

insolent: see IMPOLITE.

insolvent: see BANKRUPT.

insomniac: see WAKEFUL.

inspect *v.* EXAMINE, look over, scrutinize, CHECK, SURVEY, INVESTIGATE, EYE.

inspection *n.* EXAMINATION, CHECKUP, SURVEY, INVESTIGATION, INQUIRY, REVIEW.

inspector *n.* examiner, investigator, reviewer, detective, policeman, AGENT.

inspiration *n.* NOTION, IDEA, hunch, IMPULSE, FANCY, stimulus, brainstorm.

inspire *v.* invigorate, motivate, animate, IMPRESS, EXCITE, spur, ENCOURAGE.

inspiring: see INFECTIOUS; SPLENDID.

install *v.* set up, ESTABLISH, PLACE, FURNISH, induct, initiate.

installed: see SITUATED.

installment: see CREDIT; RENT.

instance: see CASE; ILLUSTRATION; PARTICULAR; SPECIMEN; TIME.

instant *adj.* instantaneous, IMMEDIATE, URGENT,

RAPID, DIRECT, PRESENT.
— *n*. SECOND, FLASH, WINK, twinkling, JIFFY.

instantaneous: see INSTANT; MOMENTARY.

instantly *adv*. IMMEDIATELY, right away, DIRECTLY, SWIFTLY.

instead *adv*. alternatively, RATHER, SOONER, alternately, contrariwise, conversely.
— *prep*. rather than, in lieu of.

instead of: see FOR.

instigate: see AROUSE; EXCITE.

instill: see BREATHE.

instinct *n*. intuition, IMPULSE, aptitude, TALENT.

instinctive: see AUTOMATIC.

institute *v*. ESTABLISH, set up, FOUND, LAUNCH, inaugurate.
— *n*.: see ACADEMY; COLLEGE; INSTITUTION; SCHOOL.

institution *n*. **1** *(soon after its institution)* ESTABLISHMENT, FOUNDATION, ORGANIZATION; **2** *(a charitable institution)* ORGANIZATION, FOUNDATION, SOCIETY, SCHOOL, ACADEMY, institute, asylum, sanitarium.

instruct *v*. INFORM, TEACH, EDUCATE, EXPLAIN, DIRECT, COMMAND.

instruction *n*. EDUCATION, DIRECTION, EXPLANATION, ORDER, directive.

instructional: see EDUCATIONAL.

instructive: see EDUCATIONAL; INFORMATIVE.

instructor *n*. TEACHER, TUTOR, PROFESSOR, MASTER, trainer, coach, EDUCATOR.

instrument *n*. TOOL, DEVICE, IMPLEMENT, apparatus, contrivance, MEANS, AGENT, PAWN.

instrumentalist: see ENTERTAINER; PERFORMER.

instrumentality: see MEDIUM.

instruments: see MEANS.

insubordinate: see DISOBEDIENT.

insubordination: see DISOBEDIENCE.

insufferable: see UNBEARABLE.

insufficiency: see SCARCITY; SHORTNESS.

insufficient: see LAME; LIMITED; POOR; SCARCE; SHORT; UNEQUAL; UNSATISFACTORY.

insufficiently: see POORLY.

insulate: see ISOLATE.

insulation: see ISOLATION.

insult *n*. offense, slight, outrage, slap.
— *v*. OFFEND, vilify, ABUSE, outrage, MOCK, malign.

insurance *n*. PROTECTION, assurance, SECURITY, indemnity, WARRANTY, PAYMENT, compensation.

insure *v*. ensure, ASSURE, SECURE, GUARANTEE, WARRANT, PROTECT.

insurrection: see REVOLT; REVOLUTION.

intact: see COMPLETE; WHOLE.

intake: see DIET; HARVEST.

intangible: see INVISIBLE.

integer: see ONE; UNIT.

integrated: see ONE.

integrity: see CHARACTER; GOODNESS; HONESTY; INNOCENCE; JUSTICE; SINCERITY; TRUTH; WORTH.

intellect *n*. INTELLIGENCE, UNDERSTANDING, comprehension, MIND, MENTALITY, REASON.

intellectual *adj*. cerebral, MENTAL, INVENTIVE, LEARNED, scholarly, highbrow, brainy.
— *n*. SCHOLAR, academician, GENIUS.

intelligence *n*. **1** *(of high intelligence)* UNDERSTANDING, INTELLECT, REASON, MIND; **2** *(recent intelligence)* INFORMATION, data, KNOWLEDGE, NEWS.

intelligent *adj*. BRIGHT, CLEVER, perceptive, SHARP, INGENIOUS, WISE, BRILLIANT, brainy, SMART, rational.

intelligible: see COMPREHENSIBLE; READABLE.

intemperance: see EXCESS.

intemperate: see SHRILL.

intend *v*. PLAN, DESIGN, AIM, EXPECT, aspire, contemplate.

intense *adj*. STRONG, ACUTE, DEEP, strenuous, fervent, EXTREME, vehement.

intensely: see EXTREMELY.

intensify: see CONCENTRATE; CONDENSE; DEEPEN; STRENGTHEN.

intensity *n*. FORCE, STRENGTH, CONCENTRATION, fervor, ENERGY, DEPTH, emphasis.

intent: see BOUND; EARNEST; INTENTION; MEANING; SPIRIT.

intention *n*. PURPOSE, intent, AIM, DESIGN, PLAN, MEANING.

intentional *adj.* DELIBERATE, willful, CONSCIOUS, purposeful, aforethought, premeditated.

intentionally: see DELIBERATELY; PURPOSELY.

intently: see SHARPLY.

interact: see RELATE.

intercepting: see PREVENTIVE.

interchange: see ALTERNATE; STAGGER; SUBSTITUTE; SUBSTITUTION.

intercourse: see ASSOCIATION; COMMERCE; COMMUNICATION; CORRESPONDENCE.

interest *n.* **1** *(full of interest)* ATTRACTION, IMPORTANCE; **2** *(of interest to us)* CONCERN, ATTENTION, CARE; **3** *(in one's interest)* WELFARE, ADVANTAGE, BENEFIT; **4** *(six percent interest)* RETURN, dividend, PREMIUM, usury; **5** *(a part interest)* SHARE, participation, CONTROL, ownership.
— *v.*: see AMUSE; APPEAL; CONCERN; ENTERTAIN.

interested: see CONCERNED.

interesting *adj.* ATTRACTIVE, engaging, PLEASING, alluring, absorbing, WINNING, enchanting, charming, colorful.

interfere *v.* INTRUDE, interpose, intervene, DISTURB, HINDER, PREVENT.

interference: see INTRUSION; OBSTACLE.

interfering: see MEDDLESOME.

interim: see BREAK; INTERVAL; MEANTIME; WHILE.

interior *n.* INSIDE, CENTER, core, HEART, BOSOM, heartland, hinterland.
— *adj.*: see INNER.

interject: see CHIRP.

interlace: see KNIT; LACE; TWINE.

interlaced: see TEXTILE.

interlock: see ENGAGE.

interlude: see INTERVAL; MEANTIME; PAUSE; SPELL.

intermediary: see BROKER.

intermediate: see NEUTRAL.

interminable: see LENGTHY.

intermission: see INTERVAL; PAUSE; RECESS; REST; SUSPENSION.

intermittent: see PERIODIC.

intermittently: see SOMETIMES.

intermix: see WEAVE.

intermixture: see CROSS; WEB.

intern: see COMMIT; CONFINE.

internal *adj.* INNER, INTERIOR, CENTRAL, inside, PRIVATE, intimate, HIDDEN, DOMESTIC.

international *adj.* global, worldly, world-wide, FOREIGN, UNIVERSAL, cosmopolitan.

interpose: see INTERFERE.

interpret *v.* EXPLAIN, DESCRIBE, REPRESENT, render, PERFORM, TRANSLATE, reword.

interpretation *n.* EXPLANATION, DESCRIPTION, REPRESENTATION, rendition, VERSION, TRANSLATION.

interrogate: see ASK; INTERVIEW; QUESTION.

interrogation: see CURIOSITY; QUIZ.

interrupt *v.* INTRUDE, INTERFERE, intervene, BUTT IN, meddle, impede, STOP, POSTPONE, DISCONTINUE.

interruption *n.* INTRUSION, BREAK, GAP, DELAY, INTERVAL, SUSPENSION.

intersect: see CROSS.

intersection: see ANGLE; FORK.

interspace: see SPACE.

intertwine: see ENTANGLE; INVOLVE; LACE; TWINE; TWIST; WEAVE.

intertwist: see TWIST.

interval *n.* GAP, SPACE, DISTANCE, PAUSE, lull, intermission, interlude, interim, MEANTIME.

intervene: see INTERFERE; INTERRUPT.

interview *n.* CONFERENCE, dialogue, AUDIENCE, CONVERSATION.
— *v.* QUESTION, interrogate, EXAMINE.

interweave: see ENTANGLE; TWINE.

interweaving: see WEB.

interwoven: see TEXTILE.

intimacy: see BROTHERHOOD; FRIENDSHIP; PRIVACY; SEX.

intimation: see WIND.

intimidate: see FRIGHTEN; MENACE; THREATEN.

intimidating: see SCARY.

into: see ABOARD; IN.

intolerable: see UNBEARABLE.

intolerance: see PERSECUTION.

intolerant: see NARROW-MINDED.

intonation: see PITCH.

intone: see CAROL; CHANT; SING.

intoxicated: see DRUNK; HIGH.

intoxicating: see HARD.

intoxication: see TRIP.

intrepid: see BOLD; BRAVE; HEROIC.

intricate: see COMPLEX; DIFFICULT; ELABORATE; FANCY.

intrigue *n.* PLOT, SCHEME, conspiracy, AFFAIR, ROMANCE, amour.
— *v.*: see SCHEME.

introduce *v.* PRESENT, ACQUAINT, set forth, insert, inject, INSTITUTE, inaugurate, COMMENCE.

introduction *n.* PRESENTATION, ADVANCEMENT, injection, INSTITUTION, BEGINNING, inauguration.

introductory: see ELEMENTARY; OPENING; PRELIMINARY.

intrude *v.* INTERFERE, CRASH, BUTT IN, cut in, meddle, INTERRUPT, INVADE, IMPOSE.

intruder: see INVADER.

intruding: see MEDDLESOME.

intrusion *n.* INVASION, interference, trespass, imposition, INTERRUPTION.

intuition: see FEELING; INSTINCT; KNOWLEDGE; TACT.

invade *v.* ENTER, PENETRATE, INTRUDE, ATTACK, overrun, TRESPASS, encroach, infringe.

invader *n.* intruder, trespasser, raider, marauder, assailant, aggressor.

invalid: see PATIENT.

invalidate: see CANCEL.

invaluable: see USEFUL.

invariable: see PERMANENT; UNCHANGEABLE.

invariably: see CONSTANTLY.

invasion *n.* ATTACK, RAID, INTRUSION, aggression, ASSAULT, INFECTION.

invent *v.* contrive, CREATE, DEVISE, DEVELOP, FASHION, fabricate, LIE, falsify, simulate.

invented: see FICTIONAL; FICTITIOUS; MADE-UP.

invention *n.* **1** (*endowed with invention*) IMAGINATION, GENIUS, ingenuity; **2** (*a time-saving invention*) CREATION, contrivance, NOVELTY, LIE, falsehood.

inventive *adj.* creative, imaginative, ORIGINAL, INGENIOUS, FERTILE.

inventiveness: see ORIGINALITY.

inventor *n.* developer, creator, ARCHITECT, designer, AUTHOR, MAKER, PIONEER.

inventory: see CATALOG; LIST.

inversion: see REVERSE.

invert: see TURN; UPSET.

inverted: see BACKWARD; REVERSE.

invest *v.* entrust, BUY, LEND, FINANCE, RISK, speculate, GAMBLE, vest, APPLY, bestow, DEDICATE.

investigate *v.* EXAMINE, EXPLORE, PROBE, INQUIRE, SEARCH, look into.

investigating: see CURIOUS.

investigation *n.* INQUIRY, EXAMINATION, probe, SEARCH, EXPLORATION.

investigator: see INSPECTOR.

investment *n.* EXPENDITURE, LOAN, speculation, securities, MORTGAGE.

invigorate: see CONFIRM; FRESHEN; INSPIRE; REFRESH; STIMULATE; STRENGTHEN.

invigorating: see BRACING; CRISP; REFRESHING.

invisible *adj.* unreal, abstract, SPIRITUAL, intangible, incorporate, imponderable, microscopic, UNSEEN, occult, supernatural.

invitation *n.* REQUEST, BID, SUMMONS, PROPOSAL, solicitation.

invite *v.* ASK, solicit, bid, BEG, call for, importune.

inviting *adj.* PLEASING, PLEASANT, ATTRACTIVE, appealing, TEMPTING, bewitching, promising, encouraging.

invocation: see PRAYER.

invoice: see BILL; STATEMENT.

invoke: see SUMMON.

involuntary: see AUTOMATIC; UNCONSCIOUS.

intimate: see CHUMMY; CLOSE; CONFIDENTIAL; INTERNAL; NEAR; PRIVATE; SEXUAL.

involve v. INCLUDE, EMBRACE, consist of, comprise, ENGAGE, JOIN, CONNECT, ENTANGLE, intertwine, IMPLY, COMPLICATE, WIND, COIL, ENVELOP, SURROUND.

involved: see COMPLEX; CONCERNED; ENTANGLED; TECHNICAL.

involvement: see RELATIONSHIP.

invulnerability: see SAFETY.

inward: see INSIDE.

ion: see MOLECULE.

iota: see PARTICLE; TRIFLE.

irascible: see IRRITABLE.

irate: see ANGRY; FURIOUS; MAD.

iris: see PUPIL.

irk: see BORE.

irksome: see BOTHERSOME; TROUBLESOME.

iron n. pig iron, STEEL, METAL, flatiron, mangle, WEAPON, CLUB, shackles.
—adj. ironlike, steely, STRONG, unbreakable.
—v. PRESS, SMOOTH, REMOVE, flatiron, mangle.

ironlike: see IRON.

irony: see RIDICULE.

irradiate: see RADIATE.

irrational: see ABSURD; SUPERSTITIOUS; UNREASONABLE.

irregular adj. VARIABLE, CHANGEABLE, erratic, spasmodic, UNUSUAL, ABNORMAL, disordered, disorderly, eccentric, improper, UNEVEN, RAGGED.

irregularity: see DISORDER; EXCEPTION; VARIATION.

irregularly: see SELDOM.

irrelevant: see POINTLESS; REMOTE; UNNECESSARY.

irremediable: see HOPELESS.

irresistible adj. compelling, moving, POWERFUL, overpowering, overwhelming.

irresponsible: see CHILDLIKE; UNRELIABLE.

irrigate: see WATER.

irritability: see MEANNESS.

irritable adj. CRANKY, touchy, peevish, snappish, irascible, IMPATIENT, petulant, EXCITABLE.

irritate v. ANGER, IRK, peeve, vex, OFFEND, ANNOY, incense, ruffle, displease, TEASE, PROVOKE, exasperate, sensitize, EXCITE.

irritated: see MAD; RAW.

irritating: see TROUBLESOME.

irritation n. **1** (an irritation on the skin) INFLAMMATION, ITCH, burn; **2** (his excuses were a great irritation to all) ANNOYANCE, ANGER, wrath, exasperation, displeasure, RESENTMENT, vexation, indignation, IMPATIENCE.

isle: see ISLAND; KEY.

islet: see ISLAND.

isolate v. SEPARATE, set apart, DETACH, insulate, quarantine, segregate.

isolated: see ALONE; DESOLATE; LONE; LONELY; PRIVATE; SOLITARY; UNIQUE.

isolation n. SEPARATION, detachment, insulation, quarantine, segregation, LONELINESS, solitude.

issuance: see ISSUE; PRINTING; PUBLICATION.

issue n. **1** (the real issue of the argument) PROBLEM, QUESTION, controversy, TOPIC, CONTEST, ARGUMENT; **2** (the issue of the contest was apparent) RESULT, OUTCOME, END, upshot, CONCLUSION, CONSEQUENCE, PRODUCT, FRUIT, EVENT, ESCAPE, OUTLET, EXIT, issuance, DISTRIBUTION; **3** (the latest issue of the paper) NUMBER, COPY, edition, PRINTING, impression; **4** (to die without issue) children, posterity, OFFSPRING.
—v. SEND, DELIVER, DISPATCH, send out, DISCHARGE, emit, come out, result, PUBLISH, bring out, FLOW, SPRING, SPURT, well, gush, PROCEED, ARISE, ensue, ORIGINATE.

italicize: see UNDERLINE.

itch: see TICKLE; TINGE; URGE.

item n. THING, OBJECT, POINT, NEWS, BULLETIN, ARTICLE, PARTICULAR, ENTRY, PARAGRAPH.

itemize v. LIST, DETAIL, SPECIFY, particularize, individualize, recount, RECITE, RELATE.

itinerary: see ROUTE.

ivory: see CHIP; WHITE.

J

jab: see NUDGE; PECK; POKE; PUNCH; THRUST.

jabber: see BABBLE; CACKLE; RAVE.

jackass: see ASS; DONKEY.

jacket n. COAT, jerkin, COVERING, SKIN, casing.

jackknife: see KNIFE.

jagged adj. zigzagged, CROOKED, POINTED, notched, serrated, RAGGED.

jail *n.* PRISON, penitentiary, reformatory, jug, dungeon, solitary, lockup.
— *v.* imprison, CONVICT, lock up.

jailbird: see CONVICT; PRISONER.

jailer *n.* WARDEN, KEEPER, GUARD.

jalopy: see AUTOMOBILE.

jam *n.* **1** (*I was eating jam*) jelly, preserves, conserves; **2** (*he's in a jam*) TROUBLE, fix, pickle, DIFFICULTY, OBSTACLE, encumbrance, jamming, CROWD, throng, MASS, PRESS.
— *v.* SQUEEZE, PRESS, wedge, pack in, CRUSH, BRUISE, INTERFERE.

jamming: see JAM.

jam-packed: see CHOCK-FULL; FULL.

jangle: see NOISE.

janitor *n.* SUPERINTENDENT, caretaker, ATTENDANT, custodian, PORTER, doorkeeper, watchman.

jar *n.* **1** (*put it in the jar*) CONTAINER, urn, VESSEL, beaker, GLASS, CONTENTS, QUANTITY; **2** (*the jars and bumps from the road*) SHAKE, JOLT, jounce, SHOCK, quiver, outrage, concussion, discord.
— *v.* SHAKE, JOLT, SHOCK, QUIVER, TREMBLE, VIBRATE, DISTURB, grate, CLASH, GRIND.

jargon: see LANGUAGE; SLANG.

jaundiced: see JEALOUS.

jaunt: see JOURNEY; RIDE; TRAVEL.

jaunty: see PERKY.

javelin: see LANCE; SPEAR.

jaw: see CHIT-CHAT; MOUTH.

jazz: see SWING.

jealous *adj.* envious, grudging, jaundiced, GREEDY, WATCHFUL, CAREFUL, vigilant.

jealousy *n.* ENVY, GREED, RESENTMENT, SUSPICION, heartburn.

jeans: see TROUSERS.

jeer: see RIDICULE; SCOFF; SNEER.

jell: see SETTLE.

jelly: see JAM; PULP.

jeopardize: see ENDANGER; RISK.

jeopardy: see DANGER; HAZARD; RISK; SERIOUSNESS.

jerk *n.* **1** (*give the rug a jerk*) yank, PUSH, PULL, JOLT, jiggle; **2** (*he's a jerk*) nitwit, clod, nobody, FOOL, retard.

— *v.* yank, PUSH, PULL, JOLT, TWITCH, jiggle.

jerkin: see JACKET.

jerky *adj.* ROUGH, bouncy, jiggly, UNEVEN.

jest *n.* JOKE, gag, quip, FUN, RIDICULE.
— *v.* JOKE, KID, spoof, TEASE.

jester *n.* CLOWN, joker, humorist, COMEDIAN, ENTERTAINER.

jet *n.* **1** (*black as jet*) BLACK, coal, raven; **2** (*a gas jet*) nozzle, spout, STREAM, geyser; **3** (*a jet plane*) jetliner, airplane.
— *v.*: see SPURT.

jetliner: see JET.

jewel *n.* GEM, STONE, ORNAMENT, PEARL, TREASURE, bearing.

jewelry *n.* jewels, gems, rings, bracelets, necklaces, earrings, beads, pins, brooches.

jewels: see JEWELRY.

jiffy *n.* MOMENT, INSTANT, minute, SECOND, FLASH.

jiggle: see JERK; TWITCH.

jiggly: see JERKY.

jigsaw: see PUZZLE.

jilt: see DITCH.

jingle: see RING; TINGLE.

jive: see SLANG.

job *n.* WORK, CHORE, TASK, DUTY, EMPLOYMENT, BUSINESS, POSITION, PLACE, POST.

jog: see NUDGE; RUN.

jogger: see RUNNER.

join *v.* CONNECT, COMBINE, UNITE, ASSOCIATE, consolidate, COUPLE, merge, abut, ADJOIN, weld.

jointed: see ALLIED; MARRIED.

joining: see MARRIAGE.

joint *adj.* combined, united, shared, collective.
— *n.*: see CONJUNCTION; ELBOW; HINGE; LINK; SEAM.

jointly: see TOGETHER.

joist: see BEAM; TIE.

joke *n.* jest, quip, witticism, laughingstock.
— *v.* KID, TEASE, josh, JEST.

joker: see CLOWN; COMEDIAN; JESTER; WIT.

joking: see HUMOR.

jolly *adj.* MERRY, jovial, CHEERFUL, GAY, PLAYFUL.

jolt *n.* JAR, shake, BUMP, SHOCK.
  — *v.* JAR, SHAKE, BUMP, STUN, SHOCK.

josh: see JOKE; KID.

jostle: see ELBOW; MOB; NUDGE; POKE; SHOVE.

jounce: see BOUNCE; BUMP; JAR.

journal *n.* NEWSPAPER, MAGAZINE, daybook, LOG, ledger, DIARY, minutes.

journalism: see PRESS.

journalist: see AUTHOR; CORRESPONDENT; EDITOR.

journey *n.* TRIP, VOYAGE, jaunt, excursion, EXPEDITION, TOUR, TRAVEL.
  — *v.*: see RIDE; TRAVEL.

joust: see FENCE.

jovial: see FESTIVE; GAY; HAPPY; HEARTY; JOLLY; JOYFUL.

joy *n.* HAPPINESS, GLADNESS, DELIGHT, glee, gaiety, bliss, rapture, ecstasy.

joyful *adj.* HAPPY, GLAD, joyous, overjoyed, GAY, MERRY, FESTIVE, JOLLY, jovial, elated.

joyfully: see CHEERFULLY; GLADLY.

joyfulness: see GLADNESS.

joyless *adj.* SAD, GLOOMY, CHEERLESS, forlorn. MOURNFUL, WRETCHED, despairing, disheartened.

joyous: see ALIVE; CHEERFUL; FESTIVE; GAY; GLAD; HAPPY; JOYFUL; MERRY; SUNNY; WELCOME.

joyousness: see FESTIVITY; HILARITY.

joy ride: see RIDE.

jubilee: see CELEBRATION.

judge *n.* JUSTICE, magistrate, referee, umpire, arbitrator, EXPERT, OFFICIAL, jurist, CRITIC.
  — *v.* DECIDE, DETERMINE, GUESS, CONSIDER, ESTEEM, RECKON, TRY, CONCLUDE, pronounce, ESTIMATE, BELIEVE, THINK, SETTLE, CONDEMN, SENTENCE.

judges: see JURY; PANEL.

judgment *n.* DECISION, VERDICT, OPINION, finding, AWARD, SENTENCE, CONCLUSION, ESTIMATION, WISDOM, SENSE, ESTIMATE, UNDERSTANDING, INTELLIGENCE, ORDER, decree, censure, discernment, discretion, CRITICISM, DEBT. See also PRISON.

judiciary: see JUSTICE.

judicious: see LEVEL; SELECTIVE; TACTFUL; WISE.

jug *n.* VESSEL, CONTAINER, PITCHER, JAR, BOTTLE, crock, flask, cooler. See also PEN.

juggle *v.* BALANCE, TOSS, TRICK, delude, DECEIVE, manipulate, maneuver, doctor.

juice *n.* FLUID, LIQUID, essence, SAP, FLOW, CURRENT, electricity.

juicy *adj.* **1** (*the orange was juicy*) WET, MOIST, watery, lush, luscious; **2** (*a juicy story*) spicy, scandalous, INTERESTING.

jumble *v.* SCRAMBLE, TANGLE, SNARL, muddle, MIX, clutter, MESS, CONFUSE.
  — *n.*: see DISORDER; HUDDLE; MESS; MIXTURE.

jumbled: see MISCELLANEOUS.

jump *n.* LEAP, SPRING, bound, HOP, somersault, skip, vault, RISE.
  — *v.* LEAP, SPRING, bound, HOP, somersault, SKIP, vault, RISE, CAPTURE, parachute, hurdle, CLEAR.

jumpy: see NERVOUS; RESTLESS.

junction: see COMBINATION; CONJUNCTION; CONNECTION; CONTACT; FORK.

juncture: see CONJUNCTION; POINT; STAGE.

jungle *n.* FOREST, WILDERNESS, BUSH, thicket, chaparral.

junior *adj.* younger, later, MINOR, subordinate, second-string.

junk *n.* RUBBISH, GARBAGE, TRASH, SCRAP, LITTER, debris.
  — *v.* DISCARD, can, DUMP, SCRAP.

junket: see TRAVEL.

junky: see TRASHY.

jurisdiction: see AUTHORITY; COMMAND; CONTROL; DEPARTMENT.

jurist: see JUDGE; JUSTICE.

jurors: see JURY; PANEL.

jury *n.* jurors, COURT, PANEL, COMMISSION, COMMITTEE, judges.

just *adj.* FAIR, impartial, equitable, HONEST, RIGHT, LAWFUL, ethical, TRUE, CORRECT, EXACT, SUITABLE, deserved, rightful, ACCURATE.
  — *adv.* EXACTLY, BARELY, ONLY, PRECISELY, QUITE, SIMPLY, perfectly, VERY, REALLY, justly.

justice *n.* **1** (*justice is blind*) fairness, RIGHT, justness, equity, legality, lawfulness, HONESTY, integrity, impartiality, accuracy; **2** (*the justice is in his chambers*) JUDGE, jurist, magistrate, OFFICIAL, judiciary.

justifiable: see EXCUSABLE.

justification *n*. REASON, EXPLANATION, EXCUSE, DEFENSE, adjustment, alignment.

justify *v*. EXPLAIN, DEFEND, EXCUSE, exonerate, ADJUST, STRAIGHTEN, align, BALANCE.

justly: see FAIRLY; JUST; RIGHT.

justness: see JUSTICE.

jut: see BULGE; PROJECT.

jutting: see PROMINENT.

juvenile: see CHILDISH; CHILDLIKE; KID; YOUNG.

K

keen *adj*. EAGER, EARNEST, INTENSE, ACUTE, SHARP, cutting, stinging, penetrating, shrewd, SEVERE, QUICK, astute, piercing, poignant.

keenness: see ALERTNESS; CLEVERNESS.

keep *v*. HOLD, RETAIN, detain, GUARD, PROTECT, MANAGE, SUPPORT, MAINTAIN, CONTAIN, CHECK, WAIT, REMAIN, CONTINUE, CELEBRATE, TEND. See also ABIDE BY.
− *n*.: see BOARD; LIVING.

keep back: see WITHHOLD.

keeper *n*. caretaker, custodian, GUARD, WARDEN, watchman, JAILER, herder, herdsman.

keeping: see CARE; HOLD.

keep on: see CONTINUE; PERSIST; RESUME.

keepsake: see SOUVENIR; TROPHY.

keep up: see SUSTAIN.

kerchief: see HANDKERCHIEF; SCARF.

kernel: see GRAIN; NUT; SEED.

kettle *n*. POT, teakettle, cauldron, boiler, urn, caldron.

key *n*. **1** (*the key in the door*) passkey, doorkey, opener; **2** (*the key to health*) GUIDE, ANSWERS, EXPLANATION, crib, CLUE, SOLUTION; **3** (*off key*) keynote, scale, clef, chord; **4** (*Key West*) isle, reef.
− *adj*. ESSENTIAL, FUNDAMENTAL, BASIC, crucial, indispensable, IMPORTANT.

keyed-up: see TENSE.

keynote: see KEY.

kick *v*. HIT, boot, punt, recoil, gripe, GRUMBLE.
− *n*.: see BANG; BOOT; CHARGE.

kicks: see ANIMATE.

kid *n*. CHILD, YOUNGSTER, BABY, juvenile.
− *v*. TEASE, josh, JOKE, spoof, FOOL.

kill *v*. MURDER, SLAUGHTER, ASSASSINATE, SLAY, MASSACRE, liquidate, EXECUTE, HANG, deaden, WEAKEN, DEFEAT, use up, cut off, SPOIL, FINISH.

killer *n*. MURDERER, ASSASSIN, cutthroat, gunman, executioner.

killing: see ASSASSINATION; BUTCHERY; EXECUTION; MASSACRE; MURDEROUS.

kiln: see FURNACE; OVEN.

kilt: see SKIRT.

kin *n*. relatives, parents, FAMILY, relations, folks, connections.
− *adj*. ALLIED, RELATED, PARALLEL, SIMILAR, akin.

kind *n*. TYPE, SORT, VARIETY, CLASS, SPECIES, SET, BREED, NATURE, CHARACTER.
− *adj*. KINDLY, loving, GENTLE, TENDER, GOOD, compassionate, humane, CHARITABLE, SYMPATHETIC.

kind-hearted: see TENDER; THOUGHTFUL.

kindle *v*. ignite, LIGHT, AROUSE, AWAKEN, EXCITE, incite.

kindliness: see KINDNESS; MILDNESS; SYMPATHY.

kindly *adj*. FRIENDLY, SYMPATHETIC, GENTLE, NICE, benevolent, AGREEABLE.
− *adv*. please, READILY.

kindness *n*. kindliness, SYMPATHY, gentleness, GOODNESS, TENDERNESS, thoughtfulness, MERCY, clemency.

kindred: see FOLK; RELATED.

king *n*. sovereign, MONARCH, MAJESTY, RULER.

kingdom *n*. MONARCHY, dominion, EMPIRE, realm, DIVISION, domain, GROUP, COUNTRY, LAND, PROVINCE.

kingly: see ROYAL.

kingship: see MONARCHY.

kink: see TWIST.

kinship: see RELATIONSHIP; RESEMBLANCE.

kinsman: see RELATION; RELATIVE.

kinswoman: see RELATION; RELATIVE.

kiss *v*. EMBRACE, CARESS, TOUCH, smack, PECK.
− *n*. smack, peck, embrace, caress, TOUCH.

kisser: see MOUTH.

kit *n.* packet, SET, gear, OUTFIT, EQUIPMENT, rig, furnishings.

kitty: see BANK.

knack: see ABILITY; TALENT; TECHNIQUE; TRICK.

knead: see MIX; SOFTEN.

kneel *v.* genuflect, WORSHIP.

knees: see LAP.

knife *n.* cutter, cleaver, machete, jackknife, pocketknife, penknife, switchblade.
— *v.* STAB, CUT, CHOP, CARVE, cleave, SPLIT, STRIKE, undermine, BETRAY.

knit *v.* WEAVE, interlace, crochet, JOIN, UNITE, CONNECT, HEAL, DRAW.

knob: see BULB; BUMP; LUMP.

knock *v.* RAP, HIT, bat, CLAP, BUMP, BEAT, SLAP, cuff, STRIKE, bash, PUNCH, CRITICIZE.
— *n.* RAP, HIT, BAT, CLAP, bump, slap, cuff, STROKE, bash, PUNCH, CRITICISM.

knock out: see DRUG; STUN.

knoll: see HILL.

knot *n.* splice, bend, hitch, fastening, TIE, CONNECTION, BUNCH, LUMP, gnarl, entanglement, CLUSTER, GATHERING, SWARM, COMPLICATION.
— *v.* splice, BEND, hitch, FASTEN, TIE, CONNECT, BUNCH, gnarl, CLUSTER, ENTANGLE.

know *v.* UNDERSTAND, comprehend, RECOGNIZE, SEE, perceive, DISTINGUISH, REALIZE, EXPERIENCE.

know-how: see KNOWLEDGE.

knowing: see AWARE; CONSCIOUS; LEARNED; UNDERSTANDING; WISE.

knowingly: see DELIBERATELY; PURPOSELY.

knowledge *n.* UNDERSTANDING, comprehension, RECOGNITION, SKILL, SCIENCE, enlightenment, intuition, INFORMATION, LEARNING, know-how, WISDOM, scholarship, ACQUAINTANCE, familiarity.

knowledgeable: see FAMILIAR.

known *adj.* understood, recognized, perceived, ascertained, CERTAIN, FAMILIAR, realized.

knurl: see THREAD.

L

label *n.* MARK, TAG, SLIP, TICKET, trademark, NAME, nickname, catchword, INDICATION.
— *v.* MARK, TAG, CLASSIFY, INDICATE, NAME.

labor *n.* **1** *(requiring much labor)* WORK, TOIL, EFFORT, SWEAT, STRUGGLE, drudgery; **2** *(labor and management)* workers, UNION, proletariat; **3** *(to be in labor)* childbirth, DELIVERY.
— *v.* WORK, TOIL, SWEAT, STRUGGLE, SUFFER.

laborer *n.* WORKER, WORKMAN, workingman, EMPLOYEE, HAND, proletarian.

laborious: see DIFFICULT; HARD.

laboriously: see HARD.

labor-saving: see AUTOMATIC.

labyrinth: see PUZZLE; WILDERNESS.

lace *n.* NET, CORD, WEB, webbing, COBWEB, mesh, trellis, latticework.
— *v.* TIE, LASH, WHIP, interlace, braid, intertwine, STREAK, MIX.

lack *n.* shortage, want, NEED, deficiency.
— *v.* WANT, NEED.

lackey: see ATTENDANT.

lacking: see ABSENT; INCOMPLETE; LESS; MINUS; MISSING; SHORT; SHY; WANTING; WITHOUT.

lacquer: see COAT; VARNISH.

lad *n.* laddie, shaver, YOUTH, BOY, YOUNGSTER.

ladder *n.* rungs, stairs, companionway.

laden: see CHOCK-FULL; LOADED.

ladle: see SCOOP.

lady *n.* WOMAN, miss, matron, dame, WIFE, spouse.

ladylike: see FEMALE; WOMANLY.

ladylove: see MISTRESS.

lag *v.* DELAY, tarry, loiter, LINGER, poke, dawdle, dilly-dally, procrastinate.
— *n.*: see DELAY.

laggard: see SLOW; TARDY.

lagoon: see BAY; LAKE; POND; POOL.

lair: see DEN.

lake *n.* POOL, POND, reservoir, BASIN, lagoon, DAM, millpond, loch, SEA, WATER.

lamb *n.* SHEEP, lambkin, mutton, babe, dove.

lambaste: see SLAM.

lambkin: see LAMB.

lame *adj.* **1** *(lame from birth)* crippled, limping, disabled, handicapped; **2** *(a lame excuse)* POOR, FLIMSY, WEAK, insufficient.

lameness: see LIMP.

lament: see BLUES; COMPLAIN; HOWL; MOAN; MOURN; REGRET; SADDEN; SIGH; WAIL; WEEP.

lamentable: see UNFORTUNATE.

lamentation: see MOURNING.

lamenting: see MOURNFUL.

laminate: see COAT; PLATE.

lamp *n.* LIGHT, LANTERN, fixture, BULB.

lampoon: see RIDICULE.

lance *n.* SPEAR, javelin, pike, KNIFE, scalpel.
— *v.* HURL, THROW, CUT, incise, PIERCE. See also BLEED.

land *n.* COUNTRY, NATION, PEOPLE, REGION, AREA, SOIL, EARTH, GROUND, LANDSCAPE, plot, SHORE, mainland.
— *v.* ARRIVE, alight, DESCEND, disembark, CATCH, FIND.

landing: see DOCK; FLIGHT; STORY; WHARF.

landlord *n.* OWNER, landowner, homeowner, PROPRIETOR.

landowner: see LANDLORD.

landscape *n.* scenery, VIEW, SCENE, panorama, APPEARANCE, ASPECT, contour.

landslide: see SLIDE.

lane *n.* ROAD, ROUTE, PATH, WAY, PASSAGE, ALLEY.

lang syne: see PAST.

language *n.* SPEECH, words, TALK, EXPRESSION, UTTERANCE, TONGUE, idiom, dialect, SLANG, jargon, lingo.

languish: see FAINT.

languor: see FATIGUE.

lanky: see SLENDER; TALL.

lantern *n.* LAMP, LIGHT, flashlight, TORCH, lighthouse, projector, skylight.

lap *n.* **1** (*he sat on her lap*) knees, waist, MIDDLE, FOLD, overlap; **2** (*one more lap around the track*) ROUND, CIRCUIT, CIRCLE.
— *v.* LICK, DRINK, SPLASH, COVER, FOLD.

lapel: see FLAP.

lapse: see BLUNDER; MISTAKE; PASSAGE; SLIP.

larceny: see BURGLARY; ROBBERY; THEFT.

lard: see FAT.

large *adj.* BIG, GREAT, BROAD, WIDE, AMPLE, FULL, ABUNDANT, substantial, BULKY, MASSIVE, HUGE, colossal, ENORMOUS, SPACIOUS, IMMENSE, EXTENSIVE.

largely: see GREATLY; MAINLY; MOSTLY.

largeness: see GREATNESS.

lark: see ADVENTURE.

lash *v.* **1** (*the waves lashed the deck*) STRIKE, BEAT, WHIP, flog, PUNISH, rebuke; **2** (*the posts were lashed together*) BIND, FASTEN, TIE.
— *n.* WHIP, ROPE, STRIKE, PUNCH, eyelash.

lassie: see YOUNGSTER.

lasso: see CATCH.

last *adj.* latest, FINAL, concluding, RECENT, highest, EXTREME, ultimate, unlikely.
— *adv.* FINALLY, RECENTLY.
— *v.* ENDURE, go on, REMAIN, CONTINUE.

lasting *adj.* continuing, remaining, PERMANENT, STABLE, enduring, durable, FIXED.

lastly: see EVENTUALLY; FINALLY.

latch: see CATCH; HOOK; LOCK.

latched: see SHUT.

late *adj.* **1** (*the train was late*) TARDY, SLOW, overdue, delayed; **2** (*the widow's late husband*) DEAD, deceased, FORMER; **3** (*a late model*) UP-TO-DATE, RECENT.
— *adv.* tardily, SLOWLY, LATELY, RECENTLY.

lately *adv.* RECENTLY, latterly.

latent: see ASLEEP; POTENTIAL.

later: see AFTER; AFTERWARDS; BEHIND; FUTURE; JUNIOR; SINCE.

lateral: see SIDE.

laterally: see ASIDE.

later than: see AFTER.

latest: see ACTUAL; LAST; NEW.

lather: see FOAM.

lathery: see FOAMY.

latitude *n.* LIBERTY, FREEDOM, SPACE, RANGE, scope, EXTENT.

latrine: see TOILET.

latter *adj.* LAST, SECOND, RECENT, MODERN.

latterly: see LATELY; RECENTLY.

latticework: see LACE.

laud: see PRAISE.

laugh *n.* LAUGHTER, CHUCKLE, CACKLE, GIGGLE, snicker.
— *v.* CHUCKLE, CACKLE, GIGGLE, SNICKER, titter.

laughable: see FUNNY; RIDICULOUS.

laughing: see LAUGHTER.

laughingstock: see JOKE.

laughs: see LAUGHTER.

laughter *n.* laughing, mirth, LAUGH, laughs.

launch *v.* START, BEGIN, INSTITUTE, SHOOT, THROW, HURL, catapult.
— *n.* BOAT, VESSEL, motorboat.

launching: see OPENING.

launder: see WASH.

laundromat: see LAUNDRY.

laundry *n.* WASHING, CLOTHES, laundromat, cleaner's.

lavatory: see TOILET.

lavish: see ABUNDANT; LUXURIOUS; MAGNIFICENT.

lavishness: see LUXURY; PLENTY.

law *n.* RULE, REGULATION, ordinance, PRINCIPLE, CODE, COMMANDMENT, courts, POLICE.

law-abiding: see ORDERLY.

lawful *adj.* LEGAL, legitimate, licit, PERMISSABLE, ALLOWABLE, PROPER, JUST, valid, rightful.

lawfulness: see JUSTICE.

lawless: see ILLEGAL.

law making: see LEGISLATION.

lawn *n.* GRASS, GROUNDS, GREEN, terrace.

laws: see LEGISLATION.

lawsuit: see ACTION; CASE; SUIT; TRIAL.

lawyer *n.* ATTORNEY, attorney at law, COUNSELOR, advocate.

lax: see CARELESS; SLACK.

lay *v.* PLACE, put down, IMPOSE, SPREAD.

lay away: see SPARE.

layer *n.* THICKNESS, SEAM, BED, ROW, COATING, SHEET, FILM, COVERING, FOLD, FLOOR, STAGE.

layman: see AMATEUR.

lay off: see DISMISS.

layout: see ARRANGEMENT; SPREAD.

lazy *adj.* IDLE, indolent, shiftless, slothful, inactive, sluggard, SLOW, sluggish, TIRED, inert.

lead *v.* GUIDE, CONDUCT, DIRECT, HEAD, star, SURPASS, excel, PERSUADE.
— *n.* **1** *(to take the lead)* LEADER, HEAD, STAR, CLUE, GAIN, FIRST; **2** *(heavy as lead)* METAL, ELEMENT, WEIGHT, bullet.

leaden: see GRAY.

leader *n.* GUIDE, CONDUCTOR, DIRECTOR, CHIEF, LEAD, PIONEER, SUPERIOR, winner, EDITORIAL, BARGAIN.

leadership *n.* guidance, DIRECTION, supremacy, domination.

leading *adj.* CHIEF, capital, PRINCIPAL, SUPREME, FIRST, stellar, directing, tending, suggesting.

leaf *n.* SHEET, PAGE, BLADE, petal, NEEDLE, membrane, FOIL, EXTENSION.
— *v.*: see PAGE.

leaflet: see CIRCULAR; PAMPHLET.

league *n.* ALLIANCE, UNION, confederation, COMBINATION, coalition, SOCIETY, ASSOCIATION.

leak *n.* drip, HOLE, CRACK, puncture, PIT, perforation, leaking, FLOW, trickle, dripping.
— *v.* OOZE, DRIP, seep.

leaking: see LEAK; RUNNING.

lean *v.* SLANT, incline, SLOPE, TILT, TEND, DEPEND, repose, REST.
— *adj.* THIN, SLENDER, gaunt, POOR, meager, scanty, BARREN.

leaning: see INCLINATION; TENDENCY.

lean-to: see SHED.

leap *n.* JUMP, SPRING, bound, HOP, somersault, skip, vault.
— *v.* JUMP, SPRING, bound, HOP, somersault, SKIP, vault, hurdle, CLEAR, caper.

learn *v.* MEMORIZE, MASTER, FIND OUT, HEAR, ascertain, ACQUIRE.

learned *adj.* educated, schooled, cultured, lettered, scholarly, trained, knowing, read, well-informed, WISE, skillful, EXPERT, acquired.

learner: see BEGINNER; DISCIPLE; PUPIL; STUDENT.

learning *n.* KNOWLEDGE, EDUCATION, scholarship, WISDOM, INFORMATION, lore.

lease: see CHARTER; HIRE; LET; MORTGAGE; RENT.

leash: see BRIDLE; CHAIN; REIN.

least *adj., n.* smallest, minutest, tiniest, slightest.

leather: see SADDLE; STRAP.

leave *v.* go away, DEPART, QUIT, WITHDRAW, STOP, forsake, COMMIT, bequeath, WILL.
— *n.* PERMISSION, LIBERTY, CONSENT, furlough, ABSENCE, DEPARTURE, FAREWELL.

leave off: see QUIT.

leave out: see ELIMINATE; OMIT.

leave-taking: see DEPARTURE; FAREWELL; PARTING.

leaving: see DEPARTURE; EXIT; PARTING.

leavings: see REFUSE; REMAINDER.

lectern: see DESK.

lecture *n.* SPEECH, ADDRESS, LESSON, reprimand, scolding, censure.
— *v.* TEACH, INSTRUCT, ADDRESS, reprimand, SCOLD, censure, moralize, sermonize.

lecturer *n.* speaker, talker, TEACHER.

ledge *n.* SHELF, bracket, BAR, RIDGE, BANK, CURB.

ledger: see ACCOUNT; JOURNAL.

leech: see SPONGE.

leer: see STARE.

leeway: see FREEDOM.

left *adj.* **1** (*on the left side*) left-hand, leftward, sinister; **2** (*something was left behind*) left-over, remaining, abandoned, forsaken.
— *n.* left side, liberals, left wing, radicals, socialists, revolutionaries.
— *adv.* leftward.

left-hand: see LEFT.

leftist: see LIBERAL.

leftover: see FRAGMENT; LEFT; SCRAP.

leftovers: see REMAINDER.

left side: see LEFT.

leftward: see LEFT.

left wing: see LEFT.

leg *n.* **1** (*a pair of nice legs*) LIMB, MEMBER, shank, extremity; **2** (*the last leg of a trip*) PART, STRETCH, SECTION, SIDE; **3** (*a table leg*) SUPPORT, PROP, POST, TIMBER, BAR.

legacy: see ESTATE; GIFT; INHERITANCE; WILL.

legal *adj.* LAWFUL, legitimate, licit, authorized.

legality: see JUSTICE.

legalize *v.* authorize, PERMIT, ALLOW, APPROVE.

legally: see RIGHT.

legation: see MISSION.

legend *n.* STORY, TALE, FABLE, MYTH, MOTTO. See also HEADING.

legendary: see FICTITIOUS; IMAGINARY; MYTHICAL; TRADITIONAL.

legible: see READABLE.

legion *n.* HOST, horde, MULTITUDE, ARMY, CROWD.

legislate *v.* enact, PASS, ordain, decree.

legislation *n.* lawmaking, enactment, laws.

legislator: see DEPUTY.

legislature: see CHAMBER.

legitimate: see CORRECT; LAWFUL; LEGAL.

leisure *n.* CONVENIENCE, EASE, FREEDOM, REST, RELAXATION, unemployment, retirement, recreation.

leisurely *adj.* unhurried, DELIBERATE, CASUAL, CALM, SLOW, relaxed, FREE, COMFORTABLE.

leitmotif: see THEME.

lend *v.* LOAN, ADVANCE, GRANT, FURNISH, AFFORD, PROVIDE, GIVE.

length *n.* longness, MEASURE, EXTENT, SPAN, REACH, STRETCH, DISTANCE, SIZE, duration, continuance.

lengthen *v.* STRETCH, elongate, PROLONG, GROW, INCREASE, EXTEND.

lengthened: see LENGTHY.

lengthwise: see ALONG.

lengthy *adj.* LONG, EXTENSIVE, prolonged, lengthened, drawn-out, interminable.

leniency: see CHARITY.

lenient: see MERCIFUL; PERMISSIVE; SOFT; UNDERSTANDING.

lens: see GLASS.

lesbian: see GAY.

lesion: see BRUISE.

less *adj.* fewer, LESSER, smaller, INFERIOR, MINOR.
— *prep.* MINUS, lacking.

lessee: see TENANT.

lessen *v.* REDUCE, DECREASE, DIMINISH, SHRINK, dwindle, LOWER, abate, CUT, lighten.

lessening: see REDUCTION; RELIEF.

lesser *adj.* fewer, smaller, INFERIOR, MINOR, secondary, diminished, curtailed.

lesson *n.* ASSIGNMENT, recitation, DRILL, EXERCISE, READING, INSTRUCTION, EXPERIENCE, EXAMPLE, WARNING, NOTICE, rebuke, scolding, LECTURE.

let *v.* ALLOW, PERMIT, tolerate, ASSIGN, LEAVE, GRANT, lease, RENT, HIRE.

letdown: see DISAPPOINTMENT.

let down: see BETRAY; DISAPPOINT.

let go: see FIRE; FREE; RELEASE.

lethal: see DEADLY; FATAL; MORTAL.

lethargy: see WEARINESS.

letter *n.* **1** *(to write a letter)* MESSAGE, NOTE, COMMUNICATION, epistle, MEANING; **2** *(a letter for football)* AWARD, EMBLEM, BADGE; **3** *(a letter of the alphabet)* CHARACTER, SYMBOL, TYPE.
— *v.*: see STAMP.

lettered: see LEARNED; LITERARY.

letterhead: see HEADING.

letters: see ALPHABET; CORRESPONDENCE; LITERATURE; MAIL; READING.

levee: see BANK; DAM.

level *adj.* horizontal, EVEN, FLAT, uniform, SMOOTH, flush, STEADY, well-balanced, cool-headed, judicious.
— *n.* GRADE, RANK, POSITION, HEIGHT, PLANE, FLOOR, STORY, ALTITUDE.
— *v.* **1** *(to level a gun)* AIM, DIRECT, POINT; **2** *(to level a building)* raze, DEMOLISH, tear down, equalize, SMOOTH, plane, PRESS, even.

level-headed: see CALM; EVEN.

lever: see CRANK; HAMMER; HANDLE.

levy: see CHARGE; DUTY; TARIFF; TAX; TOLL.

lewd: see FOUL; INDECENT; LOOSE.

lexicon: see DICTIONARY; GLOSSARY.

liability: see DEBT; DISADVANTAGE.

liable *adj.* LIKELY, RESPONSIBLE, answerable, ACCOUNTABLE, subject, susceptible.

libel: see ABUSE; LIE; SMEAR.

liberal *adj.* GENEROUS, openhanded, tolerant, broad-minded, unprejudiced, ABUNDANT, AMPLE, bounteous, free-handed.
— *n.* PROGRESSIVE, leftist.

liberality: see CHARITY; SHARING.

liberals: see LEFT.

liberate *v.* FREE, RELEASE, emancipate, loose, RESCUE, DISCHARGE, unfasten.

liberated: see FREE; INDEPENDENT.

liberation: see DELIVERY; DISCHARGE; RESCUE; SALVATION.

liberty *n.* FREEDOM, INDEPENDENCE, emancipation, OPPORTUNITY, LEISURE, franchise, exemption, LICENSE, immunity, LEAVE, furlough, PERMISSION.

library: see STUDIO; STUDY.

license *n.* PERMIT, PERMISSION, authorization, WARRANT, CONSENT, unconstraint, FREEDOM.
— *v.* PERMIT, ALLOW, authorize, CONSENT, APPROVE, endorse, WARRANT.

lichen: see MOLD.

licit: see ALLOWABLE; LAWFUL; LEGAL.

lick *v.* **1** *(the cat licked his wounds)* tongue, LAP, SUCK, TASTE, WASH; **2** *(the prizefighter licked his opponent)* BEAT, FIGHT, OVERCOME.

lid *n.* COVER, TOP, CAP, ROOF, STOPPER.

lie *v.* **1** *(he lied about his age)* DECEIVE, misinform, falsify, FIB, perjure, fabricate; **2** *(Mexico City lies on a plateau)* BE, LOCATE, repose, recline, STRETCH, REMAIN.
— *n.* falsehood, untruth, deception, libel, perjury, MYTH, fabrication.

lieutenant: see DEPUTY.

life *n.* **1** *(she had an unfortunate life)* BEING, EXISTENCE, essence, entity, PRESENCE; **2** *(the orchestra played with a lot of life)* SPIRIT, vivacity, VITALITY, VIGOR, animation, zeal.

lifeless *adj.* LIMP, sluggish, passive, spiritless, defunct, extinct, DEAD, BREATHLESS.

lift *n.* HOIST, pulley, ELEVATION, raising, boost, heightening, escalation.
— *v.* RAISE, ELEVATE, HOIST, escalate.

light *n.* **1** *(a ray of light)* illumination, SHINE, brightness, BRILLIANCE, radiance, clarity; **2** *(turn on the light)* fixture, LAMP, chandelier, BULB, CANDLE, MATCH; **3** *(he saw the light)* KNOWLEDGE, LEARNING, reasoning, comprehension, awareness.
— *adj.* **1** *(a light color)* BRIGHT, CLEAR, RADIANT, SUNNY; **2** *(a light pillow)* fluffy SOFT, airy, weightless, buoyant; **3** *(it was a light opera)* GAY, comic, MERRY, FUNNY, frivolous.
— *v.* ignite, FIRE, BURN, KINDLE, SHINE, ILLUMINATE, BRIGHTEN.

lighted: see BRIGHT.

lighten: see BLUNT; EASE; LESSEN; SWEETEN.

lighter: see MATCH.

light-headed: see DIZZY.

light-hearted: see GAY.

lighthouse: see LANTERN.

lightly *adv.* gently, carefully, SOFTLY, subtly, airily, nimbly, delicately.

lightness: see BRISKNESS.

lightning: see BOLT.

likable: see ENJOYABLE; FRIENDLY; LOVABLE.

like *prep.* same as, similar to, such as.
— *v.* ADMIRE, RELISH, ESTEEM, APPRECIATE, ADORE, LOVE, CHERISH, ENJOY.
— *n.* RESEMBLANCE, partiality, PREFERENCE.
— *adj.*: see CLOSE; IDENTICAL; SIMILAR; SUCH.

likelihood: see POSSIBILITY.

likely *adj.* believable, credible, POSSIBLE, PROBABLE, SUITABLE, presumable, REASONABLE.
— *adv.* seemingly, PROBABLY, aptly.

liken: see COMPARE.

likeness: see COMPARISON; IDENTITY; PARALLEL; PICTURE; PORTRAIT; REFLECTION; RESEMBLANCE; SIMILARITY.

likewise *adv.* ALSO, MOREOVER, similarly, BESIDES, FURTHERMORE.

liking: see DISH; FANCY; PREFERENCE; RELISH.

lilt: see SWING.

limb *n.* MEMBER, extremity, LEG, ARM, BRANCH, BOUGH, TWIG.

limber *adj.* supple, pliable, elastic, bending, wiry, lithe, FLEXIBLE.

limberness: see FLEXIBILITY.

limit *n.* BOUNDARY, FRONTIER, END, EXTREME, TIP, EXTENT, confine.
— *v.* RESTRICT, CONFINE, bound, CURB, restrain, HINDER, circumscribe.

limitation *n.* RESTRICTION, CONTROL, restraint, BOUNDARY, confinement, QUALIFICATION.

limited *adj.* restricted, confined, BOUND, LOCAL; restrained, checked, insufficient, inadequate.

limitless: see ENDLESS; IMMEASURABLE; INFINITE.

limousine: see AUTOMOBILE.

limp *adj.* SLACK, WEAK, SOFT, FLABBY, supple, LOOSE, LIMBER.
— *v.* hobble, falter, STAGGER, shuffle.

— *n.* lameness, hobble, suppleness, looseness, slackness, flabbiness.

limping: see LAME.

line *n.* **1** *(the customers waited in line)* ROW, FILE, RANGE, FORMATION, queue, COLUMN; **2** *(to hang clothes on a line)* CORD, STRING, ROPE, wire, CABLE; **3** *(the race began at the line)* marker, EDGE, BORDER, LIMIT, BOUNDARY; **4** *(what's your line of work?)* OCCUPATION, BUSINESS, PROFESSION, JOB, calling. See also BRAND; HOSE.
— *v.* **1** *(they lined the coat with fur)* PAD, STUFF, quilt, FILL, FACE; **2** *(line the glasses in a row)* ARRANGE, GROUP, SET, PLACE, FILE.

lineage: see BREED; PARENTAGE; RACE.

lineal: see STRAIGHT.

linen: see NAPKIN; SHEET; WASHING.

liner: see BOAT; SHIP.

lines: see REIN; STAFF.

line up: see FILE.

linger *v.* DELAY, STAY, tarry, LAG, HESITATE, loiter, dawdle.

lingerie: see SLIP.

lingo: see LANGUAGE; SLANG.

link *n.* joint, CONNECTION, TIE, COMBINATION.
— *v.* TIE, JOIN, UNITE, bridge, BIND, COUPLE, FASTEN, bracket.

links: see CHAIN.

lion: see CELEBRITY.

lip: see CURB; RIM.

lips: see MOUTH.

liquefy: see CONDENSE; DISSOLVE; MELT; THAW.

liquid *n.* FLUID, SOLUTION, secretion, SAP, JUICE, nectar, LIQUOR.

liquidate: see ASSASSINATE; CASH; ELIMINATE; KILL; MASSACRE.

liquor *n.* LIQUID, FLUID, BEVERAGE, spirits, alcohol, whiskey.

lisp: see MINCE.

list *n.* TABLE, ROLL, RECORD, roster, REGISTER, inventory, enumeration.
— *v.* ENTER, RECORD, FILE, INDEX, POST, tabulate. See also SLOPE; TILT.

listen *v.* HEAR, HEED, harken, MONITOR, eavesdrop.

listener: see OBSERVER.

listing: see CATALOG.

literacy: see READING.

literal: see EXACT; VERBAL.

literally: see EXACTLY.

literary *adj.* bookish, lettered, LEARNED, educated.

literature *n.* books, letters, WRITING, PUBLICATION, LEARNING.

lithography: see PRINTING.

litigate: see SUE.

litter *n.* **1** *(the street was filled with litter)* MESS, clutter, RUBBISH, TRASH, JUNK; **2** *(the wounded were brought by litter)* stretcher, COT; pallet; **3** *(the cat had a litter of five)* OFFSPRING, brood.
— *v.* clutter, SCATTER, STREW, MESS, JUMBLE, derange.

little *adj.* **1** *(a little child)* SMALL, TINY, MINUTE, diminutive, wee; **2** *(a little paragraph)* SHORT, BRIEF, concise.
— *adv.* SLIGHTLY, briefly, concisely.

live *v.* **1** *(they live in poverty)* BE, EXIST, subsist, SURVIVE, BREATHE, ENDURE; **2** *(we live in New York)* DWELL, RESIDE, INHABIT, STAY.
— *adj.* LIVING, existing, ACTIVE, VITAL, VIVID, animated, ENERGETIC.

livelihood: see BUSINESS; LIVING; MAINTENANCE.

liveliness: see ACTIVITY; QUICKNESS; SPARK; SPIRIT; VITALITY.

lively *adv.* CHEERFUL, spirited, animated, vibrant, spry, GAY, ACTIVE, exciting, VIGOROUS.

liven: see PERK.

live off: see SPONGE.

livestock: see STOCK.

living *adj.* existing, ALIVE, surviving, enduring, breathing.
— *n.* livelihood, EXISTENCE, SUPPORT, keep, MAINTENANCE, sustenance.

living room: see PARLOR.

load *n.* WEIGHT, BURDEN, PACK, CARGO, FREIGHT, shipment, HAUL.
— *v.* PACK, FILL, STUFF, cram, STACK, PILE, weigh, CHARGE.

loaded *adj.* FULL, charged, burdened, laden, packed, stuffed, RICH, WEALTHY, DRUNK.

loaf *v.* lounge, RELAX, IDLE, loiter, putter, dawdle, dally.
— *n.*: see BREAD.

loafer *n.* lounger, loiterer, idler, wanderer, vagabond, vagrant, BUM.

loam: see SOIL.

loan *n.* advance, CREDIT, TRUST, MORTGAGE.
— *v.* LEND, ADVANCE, GIVE.

loath: see RELUCTANT.

loathe: see DESPISE; HATE.

loathesome: see HATEFUL; NASTY.

loathing: see DISGUST; HATRED; HORROR; REVOLT.

lob: see TOSS.

lobby: see ENTRY; HALL; LOUNGE.

local *adj.* regional, sectional, territorial, provincial, LIMITED, restricted.
— *n.*: see TRAIN.

locale: see NEIGHBORHOOD; REGION.

locality *n.* POSITION, LOCATION, SITUATION, REGION AREA, PLACE, environs.

locate *v.* DISCOVER, FIND, FIX, SET, PLACE, PUT, RESIDE, situate, DETERMINE.

located: see SITUATED.

locating: see ON.

location *n.* SPOT, PLACE, POSITION, REGION, AREA, SITE, SITUATION. See also DISCOVERY; STRIKE.

loch: see LAKE.

lock *n.* **1** *(the key for this lock)* padlock, BOLT, latch, BAR, clamp, fastener; **2** *(a lock of baby's hair)* tress, tuft, braid, ringlet, BUNCH.
— *v.* FASTEN, SECURE, CLASP, bolt, BAR, latch.

locker: see BIN; CLOSET.

locks: see HAIR.

lock up: see JAIL.

lockup: see JAIL.

locomotive: see ENGINE.

locus: see ORBIT; SITE.

locution: see PHRASE.

lode: see DEPOSIT; ORE.

lodge *n.* **1** *(a mountain lodge)* CAMP, CABIN, COTTAGE, chalet, bungalow, INN; **2** *(a member of the lodge)* CLUB, ORGANIZATION, SOCIETY.
— *v.* RESIDE, DWELL, LIVE, OCCUPY, board, room. See also ANCHOR.

lodger *n.* roomer, GUEST, boarder, RESIDENT.

lodging: see ACCOMMODATION; REST; ROOM.

lodgings *pl. n.* ACCOMMODATION, DWELLING, rooms, quarters, ADDRESS, RESIDENCE, HOME.

loft: see ATTIC; GALLERY.

loftiness: see ELEVATION.

lofty *adj.* **1** (*lofty heights*) HIGH, TALL, towering, soaring, elevated, raised, commanding, majectic; **2** (*a lofty ambition*) VAIN, conceited, exalted, GRAND, PROUD, arrogant.

log *n.* **1** (*a log in the fireplace*) BLOCK, WOOD, LUMBER; **2** (*a ship's log*) JOURNAL, DIARY, ACCOUNT, RECORD, REGISTER.

log cabin: see CABIN.

logic *n.* REASON, THOUGHT, SENSE, rationality, deduction.

logical *adj.* SOUND, SENSIBLE, rational, REASONABLE, SANE, coherent, consistent, valid.

logs: see LUMBER.

loin: see FLANK.

loiter: see LAG; LINGER, LOAF.

loiterer: see LOAFER.

lone *adj.* SOLITARY, ALONE, SOLE, isolated, secluded, deserted, DESOLATE.

loneliness *n.* ISOLATION, solitude, seclusion, aloneness, SEPARATION, desolation, dreariness.

lonely *adj.* SOLITARY, ALONE, friendless, secluded, isolated, deserted, forlorn.

lonesome *adj.* forsaken, forlorn, DESOLATE, companionless, SOLITARY, ALONE.

long *adj.* LENGTHY, extended, protracted, elongated, drawn-out, outstretched, expanded.
— *v.*: see ACHE; MISS; SIGH.

longbow: see BOW.

long for: see DESIRE; WISH.

longhand: see WRITING.

longing: see ACHE; AMBITION; APPETITE; HUNGER; HUNGRY; THIRST; WISH; YEARN.

longitude: see PARALLEL.

longitudinally: see ALONG.

longness: see LENGTH.

long-suffering: see PATIENT.

long-winded *adj.* boring, DULL, wordy, verbose, TALKATIVE, tedious, inflated.

look *v.* **1** (*look into the mirror*) SEE, VIEW, GLANCE, SCAN, PEER, STARE; **2** (*he looks sick*) SEEM, APPEAR, RESEMBLE; **3** (*look for your wallet*) SEARCH, SEEK, PRY.
— *n.* GAZE, GLANCE, squint, STARE, EXAMINATION, OBSERVATION. See also AIR.

look after: see PROTECT; REAR.

look at: see OBSERVE; REGARD.

looking glass: see MIRROR.

look into: see INVESTIGATE.

look like: see RESEMBLE.

look out: see BEWARE; PATROL.

lookout: see WATCH.

look over: see INSPECT; SURVEY.

looks: see APPEARANCE.

loom: see APPEAR; EMERGE; MENACE.

loop *n.* noose, RING, FOLD, crease, bend, CURVE.
— *v.*: see CURL.

loophole: see ESCAPE.

loose *adj.* **1** (*a loose buckle*) unfastened, unattached, relaxed, SLACK, LIMP, baggy; **2** (*a loose interpretation*) FREE, VAGUE, HAZY, indistinct; **3** (*a loose person*) lewd, immoral.
— *v.*: see FREE; LIBERATE.

loosen *v.* untie, unfasten, SLACKEN, RELEASE, unleash, unpin, unlace.

looseness: see LIMP.

loot *n.* booty, plunder, spoils, HAUL.
— *v.* ROB, STEAL, plunder, burglarize, ransack, rifle.

looting: see PIRACY.

lop: see CROP.

loquacious: see TALKATIVE.

lord *n.* MASTER, PROPRIETOR, RULER, COMMANDER, GOVERNOR, sovereign.

Lord: see GOD.

lordly: see NOBLE; PROUD.

lore: see LEARNING; SCIENCE.

lose *v.* **1** (*they lost their tickets*) misplace, MISLAY, FORGET, MISS; **2** (*they lost the war*) forfeit, succumb, FALL, FAIL. See also DIET; REDUCE.

losing: see OUT.

loss *n.* DAMAGE, RUIN, INJURY, DEATH, bereavement, deprivation, degeneration, detriment.

lost *adj.* misplaced, MISSING, vanished, gone, ruined, devastated, destroyed. See also ABSENT-MINDED.

lot *n.* **1** *(the land was divided into lots)* PORTION, PART, PARCEL, DIVISION, SHARE; **2** *(he had an unfortunate lot)* FATE, DESTINY, CHANCE, LUCK; **3** *(a lot of people)* ABUNDANCE, GROUP, BUNDLE, BUNCH.

lotion *n.* salve, cream, balm, OINTMENT.

lottery: see GAMBLE.

loud *adj.* NOISY, resounding, roaring, deafening, SHRILL, piercing.

loudly: see ALOUD; OUT.

loudness *n.* VOLUME, INTENSITY, NOISE, CLAMOR, rumpus, din, pandemonium, UPROAR.

lounge *n.* salon, lobby, PARLOR, waiting room, BAR, restaurant.
— *v.:* see LOAF.

lounger: see LOAFER.

louse: see HEEL.

lovable *adj.* ADORABLE, warm-hearted, amiable, likable, SWEET, WINNING, captivating.

love *n.* AFFECTION, adoration, ATTACHMENT, ATTRACTION, PASSION, FEELING. See also BELOVED.
— *v.* ADORE, WORSHIP, CHERISH, IDOLIZE, revere, FANCY.

lovely *adj.* charming, ATTRACTIVE, BEAUTIFUL, HANDSOME, DELIGHTFUL, appealing.

lover *n.* SWEETHEART, steady, fiancé, fiancée, admirer, FAN, FOLLOWER, wooer.

loving: see AFFECTIONATE; KIND; PASSIONATE; TENDER.

low *adj.* **1** *(a low table)* low-lying, FLAT, SHORT, prostrate; **2** *(a low comment)* VULGAR, debased, MEAN, CHEAP; **3** *(a low noise)* WEAK, softened, muffled, hushed. See also MOODY.
— *n.:* see ZERO.

low-cost: see CHEAP.

lower *v.* depress, DECREASE, SHORTEN, LESSEN, REDUCE, DIMINISH, take down.
— *adj.:* see UNDER.

lowland: see PLAIN.

lowliness: see INFERIORITY.

lowly: see HUMBLE; INFERIOR.

low-lying: see LOW.

lowness: see DEPTH.

low-priced: see CHEAP; INEXPENSIVE.

loyal *adj.* FAITHFUL, DEVOTED, TRUE, CONSTANT, staunch, UNFAILING.

loyalty *n.* fidelity, DEVOTION, constancy, ALLEGIANCE, trustworthiness.

lozenge: see DIAMOND; PILL; TABLET.

LSD: see ACID.

lubricant: see GREASE; OIL.

lubricate *v.* OIL, GREASE, WAX, cream, SMOOTH.

Lucifer: see DEVIL.

luck *n.* FORTUNE, CHANCE, LOT, FATE, fluke, SUCCESS.

luckless *adj.* UNLUCKY, UNHAPPY, UNFORTUNATE, UNSUCCESSFUL, unprosperous, unfavorable, ill-fated.

lucky *adj.* FORTUNATE, FAVORED, BLESSED, SUCCESSFUL, WEALTHY, promising.

ludicrous: see FUNNY; RIDICULOUS.

lug: see CARRY; CART; HAUL; TOW.

luggage *n.* bags, valises, suitcases, trunks, BAGGAGE, things.

lukewarm *adj.* tepid, COOL, CHILLY, unconcerned, indifferent, uninterested.

lull: see CALM; INTERVAL; PAUSE; SOOTHE; STILL; TRUCE.

lullaby: see SONG.

lumber *n.* WOOD, TIMBER, logs, boards, planks.

luminosity: see GLOW.

luminous: see RADIANT.

lump *n.* **1** *(a lump on the head)* BUMP, swelling, knob; **2** *(the mix had too many lumps)* glob, MASS, chunk, BLOCK, solid.

lunacy: see INSANITY; MADNESS.

lunatic: see CRAZY; INSANE; MAD; MANIAC.

lunch: see DINE; EAT; MEAL; REFRESHMENTS; SNACK.

lunchroom: see CAFE.

lunge: see PASS.

lurch: see DUCK; STUMBLE; SWAY; TOTTER.

lure *n.* ATTRACTION, enticement, TEMPTATION, seduction, entrapment.

−*v.* entice, ATTRACT, TEMPT, seduce, induce, BEWITCH.

lurk: see PROWL.

luscious: see DELICIOUS; JUICY; SWEET; TASTY.

lush: see DRUNK; JUICY.

lust *n.* DESIRE, APPETITE, craving, PASSION, sensuality.
  −*v.* DESIRE, hanker, CRAVE, hunger, WANT.

luster *n.* glossiness, GLOSS, SHINE, sheen, GLITTER, brightness, GLOW, radiance, BRILLIANCE.

lusterless: see DEAD.

lustful: see PASSIONATE.

luxuriance: see RICHNESS.

luxuriant: see RICH.

luxurious *adj.* extravagant, ELEGANT, lavish, MAGNIFICENT, sumptuous, voluptuous.

luxury *n.* ELEGANCE, lavishness, ABUNDANCE, PLENTY, affluence, WEALTH.

lying: see TREACHERY.

lyrical: see MUSICAL.

lyrics: see MUSIC.

M

machete: see KNIFE.

machine *n.* MECHANISM, MOTOR, ENGINE, APPLIANCE, TOOL, IMPLEMENT.

macho: see MALE; MASCULINE.

mack: see GUY.

mackinaw: see COAT.

mad *adj.* **1** (*are you mad at me?*) annoyed, irritated, irate, ANGRY, FURIOUS, enraged, exasperated; **2** (*a mad composer*) INSANE, CRAZY, lunatic, deranged, delirious; **3** (*a mad party*) WILD, FRANTIC, GAY, riotous; **4** (*she's mad about him*) WILD, infatuated.

madcap: see INSANE.

madden: see ANGER; ENRAGE; INFURIATE.

made-up *adj.* **1** (*a made-up story*) invented, contrived, thought-up, fabricated, untrue, FICTITIOUS, concocted; **2** (*a made-up woman*) rouged, powdered.

madhouse: see CONFUSION.

madman: see MANIAC; NUT.

madness *n.* **1** (*he was hospitalized for his madness*) INSANITY, craziness, lunacy, delirium, derangement; **2** (*his idea was pure madness*) FOOLISHNESS, FOLLY, silliness, idiocy.

madrigal: see CAROL.

maestro: see MASTER.

magazine *n.* periodical, JOURNAL, PAMPHLET, booklet, REVIEW, PUBLICATION. See also WAREHOUSE.

magic *n.* enchantment, CHARM, witchcraft, wizardry, sorcery, voodoo, RELIGION, SUPERSTITION.

magical *adj.* enchanting, MIRACULOUS, mystical, MYSTERIOUS, bewitching, weird, occult, diabolical.

magician *n.* enchanter, WIZARD, sorcerer, WITCH, warlock, trickster.

magistrate: see COURT; JUDGE; JUSTICE.

magnanimous: see CHARITABLE.

magnet *n.* lodestone, ATTRACTION, captivation, CHARM, fascination.

magnetic: see ATTRACTIVE.

magnetism: see DRAW.

magnification: see ENLARGEMENT; EXAGGERATION.

magnificence: see GLORY; MAJESTY; SPLENDOR.

magnificent *adj.* MARVELOUS, SPLENDID, majestic, lavish, GRAND, stately, imposing, SUPERB.

magnify *v.* INCREASE, ENLARGE, EXPAND, BROADEN, amplify, augment.

magnitude *n.* EXTENT, SIZE, bulk, dimension, VOLUME, MASS.

magnum opus: see MONUMENT.

maid *n.* **1** (*leave the clean-up for the maid*) domestic, SERVANT, HELP, HOUSEKEEPER; **2** (*Joan of Arc, the Maid of Orleans*) GIRL, VIRGIN, maiden, miss.

maiden: see GIRL; INITIAL; MAID; VIRGIN.

maidenly: see FEMALE.

maidservant: see SERVANT.

mail *n.* CORRESPONDENCE, letters, cards, COMMUNICATION. See also ARMOR.
  −*v.* SEND, POST, TRANSMIT, DISPATCH.

mailing: see DELIVERY.

maim: see MISTREAT.

main *adj.* CHIEF, IMPORTANT, PRINCIPAL, LEADING,

FOREMOST, PRIMARY, FIRST, dominant.
— *n.*: see OCEAN.

mainland: see LAND.

mainly *adv.* largely, PRIMARILY, CHIEFLY, PRINCIPALLY, essentially.

mainstay: see PILLAR; STAPLE.

mainstream: see SWIM.

maintain *v.* **1** (*let's maintain a close vigil*) KEEP, SUSTAIN, UPHOLD, RETAIN, GUARD; **2** (*he maintains that it is not true*) SAY, STATE, contend, assert, CLAIM, INSIST.

maintenance *n.* upkeep, SUPPORT, sustenance, livelihood, CONTINUATION, preservation, subsistence.

majestic: see DIGNIFIED; GRAND; LOFTY; MAGNIFICENT; NOBLE; SPLENDID.

majesty *n.* nobility, grandeur, stateliness, DIGNITY, GREATNESS, magnificence.

major *adj.* greater, dominant, PRINCIPAL, LEADING, CHIEF, overshadowing.
— *n.*: see OFFICER.

majority *n.* bulk, MASS, plurality.

make *v.* **1** (*did you make the cookies?*) PREPARE, DO, CONSTRUCT, FORM, PRODUCE, manufacture, CREATE; **2** (*he made me do it*) COMPEL, REQUIRE, FORCE, CAUSE.
— *n.* MODEL, STYLE, BRAND, KIND, TYPE, SORT.

make good: see PROSPER.

make known: see PRESENT.

make love: see PET.

maker *n.* doer, producer, MANUFACTURER, fabricator, executer, preparer, creator.

makeshift: see SUBSTITUTE.

make up: see PRETEND.

makeup: see ANATOMY; CHARACTER; COMPACT; COMPLEXION; COMPOSE; COMPOSITION; DISPOSITION; NATURE; ORGANIZATION; PERSONALITY; TEMPERAMENT; TEXTURE; TOILET.

maladjustment: see ILLNESS.

malady: see DISEASE; ILLNESS.

malcontent: see DISOBEDIENT; UNSATISFIED.

male *n.* he, BOY, MAN.
— *adj.* MASCULINE, MANLY, virile, potent, POWERFUL, macho.

malefactor: see CRIMINAL; DELINQUENT; VILLAIN.

malevolence: see REVENGE; WICKEDNESS.

malevolent: see CRUEL; HATEFUL; WICKED.

malfeasance: see CRIME.

malformation: see FREAK.

malfunction: see BREAKDOWN; DISORDER.

malice: see GRUDGE; RESENTMENT.

malicious: see HATEFUL; MISCHIEVOUS.

maliciousness: see MEANNESS.

malign: see INSULT.

mall: see MARKET; STORE.

malleable: see SOFT.

mallet: see HAMMER.

maltreat: see ABUSE; PERSECUTE; WRONG.

mamma: see MOTHER.

mammal: see ANIMAL.

man *n.* **1** (*man is a rational animal*) HUMAN, BEING, MORTAL, PERSON, INDIVIDUAL, CREATURE; **2** (*a working man*) MALE, BOY, FELLOW, CHAP, WORKER, spouse, PARTNER.

manage *v.* administer, HANDLE, DIRECT, GOVERN, CONTROL, CONDUCT, SUPERVISE.

manageable: see EASY; PORTABLE.

management *n.* ADMINISTRATION, DIRECTION, CONTROL, handling, SUPERVISION, REGULATION, superintendence.

manager *n.* BOSS, DIRECTOR, administrator, SUPERINTENDENT, SUPERVISOR, overseer, comptroller.

mandate: see COMMAND; COMMANDMENT.

mane: see HAIR.

maneuver: see FLY; HANDLE; JUGGLE; STRATEGY.

maneuvers: see TACTICS.

manger: see CRIB; TROUGH.

mangle: see IRON.

manhandle: see HANDLE; MAUL; MISTREAT.

mania: see COMPLEX.

maniac *n.* madman, lunatic, psychotic, NUT, screwball, CRANK.

maniacal: see INSANE.

manifest: see APPARENT.

manifestation: see SYMPTOM.

manifesto: see ANNOUNCEMENT; EDITORIAL; PROCLAMATION.

manipulate: see FINGER; HANDLE; JUGGLE; TOUCH; WORK.

mankind *n.* humankind, MAN, SOCIETY, HUMANITY, PEOPLE.

man-made: see CHEMICAL.

mannequin: see DOLL; FORM.

manner *n.* WAY, HABIT, CUSTOM, KIND, FORM, modus, METHOD, STYLE.

mannerism: see CHARACTER; GESTURE.

mannerly *adj.* courteous, respectful, POLITE, THOUGHTFUL, refined, well-bred.

manners *pl. n.* breeding, CONDUCT, morals, bearing, COURTESY, POLITENESS.

manor: see ESTATE; HALL.

mansion *n.* PALACE, villa, RESIDENCE, DWELLING, abode, HOUSE.

manslaughter: see ASSASSINATION; MURDER.

mantle: see CLOAK; HOOD; ROBE.

mantelpiece: see SHELF.

manual: see BOOK; TEXT.

manufacture *n.* PRODUCTION, CONSTRUCTION, FORMATION, BUILDING, PREPARATION, assembling.
− *v.*: see MAKE; MINT; PRODUCE.

manufacturer *n.* MAKER, creator, producer, builder, preparer, OPERATOR, CORPORATION.

manufacturing: see INDUSTRIAL.

manuscript *n.* WRITING, PAPER, COMPOSITION, parchment, DOCUMENT, ORIGINAL.

many *adj.* NUMEROUS, PLENTIFUL, DIVERSE, VARIOUS, FREQUENT.
− *n.* ABUNDANCE, PLENTY, MULTITUDE, CROWD.

map *n.* PLAN, diagram, PLOT, CHART, SKETCH, blueprint.
− *v.* CHART, delineate, OUTLINE, PLOT, diagram, SKETCH, DRAFT.

mar: see BLEMISH; DAMAGE; NICK, NOTCH; SOIL; SPOT; STREAK; STROKE.

marathon: see RACE; RUN.

marauder: see INVADER; PIRATE.

march *v.* WALK, PACE, trek, HIKE, PARADE, ADVANCE.
− *n.* TRIP, JOURNEY, WALK, HIKE, PARADE.

margin *n.* BORDER, EDGE, FRINGE, RIM, brink, verge.

marginal *adj.* bordering, verging, edging, rimming.

marijuana: see GRASS; POT.

marina: see HARBOR.

marine *adj.* oceanic, SEA, nautical, maritime, naval, seagoing, seafaring.

mariner: see SAILOR.

marionettte: see DOLL.

marital: see BRIDAL.

maritime: see MARINE.

mark *n.* **1** *(he put a mark on the form)* STAMP, imprint, IMPRESSION, NOTE, SPOT, STAIN; **2** *(to hit the mark)* GOAL, TARGET, bull's-eye; **3.** *(he got high marks in algebra)* GRADE, rating, MERIT, RECOGNITION; **4** *(the medal was a mark of courage)* SYMBOL, BADGE, SIGN, EMBLEM, INDICATION.
− *v.* imprint, CHECK, STROKE, SIGNIFY, INDICATE, rate, GRADE, STAMP, brand, NOTE.

marked: see CONSIDERABLE; NOTICEABLE.

marker: see BADGE; BASE; CHALK; LINE; PENCIL; STAKE.

market *n.* mart, STORE, SHOP, mall, bazaar, FAIR, stall.
− *v.* SELL, merchandise, vend.

marketing: see COMMERCE.

marketplace: see SQUARE.

maroon: see RED.

marred: see DEFORMED.

marriage *n.* wedlock, matrimony, WEDDING, pledging, UNION, joining, ALLIANCE.

married *adj.* mated, joined, wedded, coupled, matrimonial.

marry *v.* wed, betroth, JOIN, MATE, UNITE.

marsh *n.* quagmire, bog, SWAMP, mire.

marshal *n.* DIRECTOR, GUIDE, ESCORT, LEADER, CONDUCTOR, OFFICER.
− *v.*: see USHER.

mart: see MARKET.

martial: see MILITARY.

martyr: see VICTIM.

marvel *n.* MIRACLE, WONDER, CURIOSITY, AMAZEMENT, SURPRISE, ASTONISHMENT.
− *v.*: see PUZZLE.

marvel at: see WONDER.

marvelous adj. WONDERFUL, astonishing, stupendous, MIRACULOUS, AMAZING, astounding, wondrous.

mascot: see PET.

masculine adj. MANLY, COURAGEOUS, VIGOROUS, virile, POWERFUL, macho, MALE.

mash v. CRUSH, SQUEEZE, squash, GRIND, MIX, thresh, BEAT, pulverize, crunch, CRUMBLE.
— n. mix, PASTE, PULP.

mask: see CAMOUFLAGE; CONCEAL; COVER; DISGUISE; HIDE; SCREEN; VEIL.

masked: see UNSEEN.

masquerade: see CAMOUFLAGE.

mass n. **1** (a mass of people) CROWD, BUNCH, assemblage, BODY, slew, MOB; **2** (a mass of batter) LUMP, glob, CLOT, bulk; **3** (a mass of rubble) HEAP, accumulation, MOUND.
— v. SWARM, JAM, CROWD, BLOCK, MOB.

massacre n. MURDER, killing, SLAUGHTER, BUTCHERY, extermination, holocaust, genocide.
— v. MURDER, KILL, SLAY, butcher, SLAUGHTER, exterminate, liquidate.

massage; see STROKE.

massive adj. HUGE, IMMENSE, HEAVY, BULKY, SOLID, GIGANTIC, imposing.

mast n. POST, POLE, ROD, STICK, TRUNK.

master n. **1** (the master of the manor) LORD, OWNER, DIRECTOR, MANAGER, BOSS, overseer; **2** (a master at chess) EXPERT, GENIUS, winner, CHAMPION, maestro.
— v. **1** (he mastered his opponents) OVERCOME, CONQUER, OVERPOWER, subdue; **2** (to master a subject) excel, LEARN, ACQUIRE.

masterful adj. EXCELLENT, skillful, ruling, domineering, commanding, controlling.

masterly: see ABLE; CLASSIC.

mastermind: see GENIUS.

master of ceremonies: see CHAIRMAN.

masterpiece: see ART; MONUMENT.

mastery: see COMMAND; TRIUMPH; UNDERSTANDING; VICTORY.

mat n. COVERING, RUG, CLOTH, felt, place setting.

match n. **1** (he is no match for his father) equal, PEER, EQUIVALENT, DUPLICATE, MATE; **2** (children should not play with matches) FIRE, LIGHT, lighter, fuse; **3** (are you going to the match?) COMPETITION, CONTEST, GAME.
— v. DUPLICATE, COMPARE, CONTRAST, PAIR, COUPLE, MATE, equate.

matching: see EQUAL; EQUIVALENT; EVEN.

matchless: see UNIQUE.

mate n. COMPANION, ASSOCIATE, spouse, PEER, co-worker, BUDDY, COMRADE.
— v. COUPLE, equalize, PAIR, TEAM, MATCH.

mated: see MARRIED.

mater: see MOTHER.

material n. MATTER, SUBSTANCE, BODY, component, STUFF, FABRIC, GOODS.
— adj.: see ESSENTIAL.

materialistic: see WORLDLY.

materialize: see APPEAR.

materials: see EQUIPMENT.

materiel: see equipment.

maternal: see MOTHERLY; PARENTAL; PROTECTIVE.

mates: see PAIR; TWO.

mathematical adj. NUMERICAL, arithmetical, ACCURATE, PRECISE.

matriarch: see QUEEN.

matrimonial: see MARRIED.

matrimony: see BRIDAL; MARRIAGE; UNION; WEDDING.

matrix: see MOLD.

matron: see LADY; MISTRESS.

matronly: see FEMININE; WOMANLY.

matter n. **1** (the study of matter and energy) BODY, SUBSTANCE, MATERIAL, STUFF; **2** (what is the matter with him?) DIFFICULTY, TROUBLE; **3** (it's no matter of yours) CONCERN, BUSINESS, AFFAIR.
— v. SIGNIFY, WEIGH, COUNT, value, import.

mattress: see BED.

maturation: see DEVELOPMENT.

mature adj. RIPE, READY, MELLOW, AGED, GROWN, cultivated, cultured.
— v.: see DEVELOP; FLOWER; MELLOW; RIPEN.

matured: see OWING.

maturity n. aging, ripening, mellowness, PERFECTION, cultivation, adulthood, DEVELOPMENT.

maul *v.* manhandle, BRUISE, BATTER, BEAT, ABUSE, disfigure, MISTREAT.
— *n.*: see HAMMER.

mausoleum: see GRAVE; TOMB.

maverick: see MISFIT.

mawkish: see SENTIMENTAL.

maxim: see PROVERB.

maximum *n.* PEAK, HEIGHT, highest, greatest, supreme, LIMIT.

may *v.* CAN, WILL, shall.

maybe *adv.* PERHAPS, POSSIBLY, perchance, conceivably.

mayhem: see BUTCHERY; SLAUGHTER.

maze: see PUZZLE.

meadow *n.* FIELD, PASTURE, grassland, PLAIN, prairie, RANGE.

meadows: see COUNTRY.

meager: see BARE; LEAN; POOR; SLENDER; SLIM; SMALL; SPARE; THIN.

meagerly: see BARELY.

meagerness: see SCARCITY.

meal *n.* **1** *(to grind meal)* FEED, GRAIN, bran, flour; **2** *(three meals a day)* repast, SPREAD, collation, breakfast, lunch, DINNER, supper, SNACK, brunch.

meals: see BOARD.

mealy: see COURSE.

mealy-mouthed: see VAGUE.

mean *v.* denote, INDICATE, INTEND, SIGNIFY, purpose, IMPLY.
— *adj.* **1** *(a mean disposition)* NASTY, EVIL, ornery, VICIOUS, unkindly, unkind, CRUEL, IRRITABLE; **2** *(they lived in mean conditions)* POOR, WRETCHED, MISERABLE, PITIFUL. See also AVERAGE.
— *n.*: see AVERAGE.

meander: see ROAM; ROVE; STROLL; WANDER; WIND.

meanie: see VILLAIN.

meaning *n.* purport, SENSE, denotation, intent, connotation, SIGNIFICANCE, signification.

meaningful: see CONSIDERABLE; EXPRESSIVE; PREGNANT; SIGNIFICANT; TELLTALE.

meaningless: see POINTLESS.

meanness *n.* testiness, maliciousness, irritability, unkindness, CRUELTY, vileness, sordidness.

means *pl.n.* resources, AID, MECHANISM, MEDIUM, instruments, TACTICS, techniques, MONEY.

meantime *n.* interim, INTERVAL, interlude, INTERRUPTION, PAUSE.

meanwhile *adv.* MEANTIME, DURING, UNTIL.

measure *n.* dimension, SIZE, WEIGHT, CAPACITY, VOLUME, LENGTH, WIDTH, HEIGHT, RULE, GAUGE. See also ACT; BAR; STEP.
— *v.* ESTIMATE, RULE, WEIGH, GAUGE, LEVEL. See also BEAT.

measurement *n.* SIZE, SCALE, WEIGHT, HEIGHT, GRADE, RANK, appraisal, ESTIMATION.

measurer: see RULER.

meat *n.* basics, essentials, essence, SUBSTANCE, gist, HEART.

meat cutter: see BUTCHER.

mechanic: see OPERATOR; WORKMAN.

mechanical *adj.* AUTOMATIC, routine, engineered, mechanized, actuated, TECHNICAL, contrived, HANDY, adept.

mechanism *n.* MACHINE, DEVICE, works, MOVEMENT, PROGRAM.

mechanized: see AUTOMATIC; MECHANICAL.

medal *n.* BADGE, decoration, AWARD, REWARD, citation, medallion, plaque.

medalist: see CHAMPION.

medallion: see MEDAL; TOKEN.

meddle: see BUTT IN; INTERRUPT; INTRUDE; MESS; MONKEY; PRY; TAMPER.

meddlesome *adj.* BOTHERSOME, prying, nosy, interfering, intruding, trespassing, obtrusive.

median: see AVERAGE; MEDIUM; MIDDLE.

medic: see NURSE.

medical *adj.* medicinal, therapeutic, PREVENTIVE, CORRECTIVE.

medicament: see MEDICINE; TREATMENT.

medicate: see DOCTOR.

medication: see CURE; REMEDY.

medicinal: see MEDICAL.

medicine *n.* **1** *(the practice of medicine)* therapeutics, curing, healing, therapy; **2** *(to take medicine)* REMEDY, CURE, DRUG, potion, LOTION, antibiotic, medicament, inoculation.

mediocre: see AVERAGE; COARSE; COMMON; FAIR; INFERIOR; MEDIUM; PASSABLE.

meditate: see CONCENTRATE; THINK; WONDER.

meditation *n.* THOUGHT, REFLECTION, STUDY, contemplation, deliberation, pondering, PRAYER.

medium *adj.* AVERAGE, mediocre, middling. — *n.* **1** (*the medium of the range*) midpoint, MEAN, median, AVERAGE; **2** (*the medium of radio*) MEANS, mode, MECHANISM, VEHICLE, instrumentality; **3** (*in one's medium*) milieu, ENVIRONMENT, atmosphere; **4** (*the artist's medium*) MATERIAL, SUBSTANCE. See also PROPHET.

medley: see MIXTURE.

meek: see HUMBLE; MILD; MODEST; OBEDIENT; TAME.

meet *v.* **1** (*to meet by chance*) ENCOUNTER, come upon; **2** (*to meet through a friend*) KNOW, ACQUAINT; **3** (*the club meets here*) GATHER, ASSEMBLE, RALLY, converge. — *n.*: see RACE.

meeting *n.* ENCOUNTER, PRESENTATION, CONFERENCE, ASSEMBLY, GATHERING, SESSION, get together, COMPETITION.

melancholy: see BLUES; GLOOM; GLOOMY; SAD; SADNESS; UNHAPPY.

meld: see BLEND.

mellow *adj.* SOFT, SWEET, GENTLE, SMOOTH, RIPE, MATURE. — *v.* SOFTEN, RIPEN, mature.

mellowness: see MATURITY.

melodious *adj.* tuneful, MUSICAL, HARMONIOUS, SWEET, MELLOW.

melodrama: see TRAGEDY.

melodramatic: see SENTIMENTAL.

melody *n.* TUNE, HARMONY, THEME, MUSIC.

melt *v.* liquefy, DISSOLVE, THAW, RUN, SOFTEN, disintegrate, fuse BLEND, relent, VANISH.

member *n.* **1** (*a severed member*) PART, PORTION, segment, LIMB, ORGAN; **2** (*an honorary member*) ASSOCIATE, FELLOW, affiliate, charter member, BROTHER, sister.

members: see MEMBERSHIP.

membership *n.* **1** (*to renew membership*) ASSOCIATION, affiliation, acceptance, ADMISSION; **2** (*the vote of the membership*) members, BROTHERHOOD, COMMUNITY, rank and file, roster, REGISTER, INDEX, ROLL.

membrane: see ENVELOPE; FILM; LEAF; TISSUE.

memento: see REMEMBRANCE; SOUVENIR; TOKEN; TROPHY.

memo: see DIARY; NOTE; RECEIPT; RECORD.

memoirs: see MEMORY.

memorandum: see RECEIPT.

memorial *n.* REMEMBRANCE, SOUVENIR, TOKEN, headstone, TRIBUTE, testimonial, inscription, RECORD.

memorize *v.* LEARN, REMEMBER, RECORD, RETAIN.

memory *n.* **1** (*to lose one's memory*) recall, recollection; **2** (*a childhood memory*) REMEMBRANCE, recollection, MEMORIAL, memoirs, memento, SOUVENIR.

men: see HUMANITY.

menace *n.* THREAT, HAZARD, DANGER, peril. — *v.* intimidate, THREATEN, imperil, loom, ALARM.

mend *v.* REPAIR, PATCH, FIX, RESTORE, CORRECT, REFORM.

mended: see FIXED.

mending: see PATCH.

menses: see PERIOD.

mental *adj.* cerebral, rational, INTELLECTUAL, psychotic, INSANE.

mentality *n.* MIND, INTELLECT, comprehension, ATTITUDE, TEMPERAMENT, point of view.

mention *v.* NOTE, REMARK, STATE, REFER, cite. — *n.* REFERENCE, citation, STATEMENT, allusion.

mentioning: see REFERENCE.

mentor: see COUNSELOR; DIRECTOR; EDUCATOR; SCHOLAR; TEACHER.

menu: see FARE; TABLE.

mercantile: see COMMERCIAL.

mercenary: see SOLDIER.

merchandise *n.* GOODS, wares, STOCK, PRODUCE. — *v.*: see MARKET; SELL.

merchandizing: see COMMERCE.

merchant *n.* TRADER, tradesman, retailer, shopkeeper, wholesaler, DEALER, businessman, seller, middleman.

merciful *adj.* THANKFUL, compassionate, SYMPATHETIC, KIND, GENTLE, lenient, forgiving, clement.

merciless *adj.* PITILESS, unfeeling, CRUEL,

hard-hearted, unsparing, relentless, SEVERE, inexorable.

mercurial: see CHANGEABLE.

mercy *n.* KINDNESS, clemency, PITY, compassion, FORGIVENESS, TOLERANCE, TENDERNESS, gentleness.

mere *adj.* SIMPLE, MINOR, ONLY, JUST, sheer, PURE.

merely *adv.* SIMPLY, solely, JUST, ONLY, ABSOLUTELY.

merge: see ASSOCIATE; COMBINE; JOIN; MINGLE; UNIFY; UNITE.

merit *n.* VALUE, WORTH, QUALITY, VIRTUE, BENEFIT, DUE.
— *v.* DESERVE, WARRANT, EARN, RATE.

merited: see DUE.

meritorious: see ADMIRABLE; EXCELLENT; WORTHY.

merrily: see CHEERFULLY.

merriment: see CHEERFULNESS; FUN; HILARITY; HUMOR.

merry *adj.* GAY, HAPPY, joyous, JOLLY, FESTIVE, entertaining, PLEASANT.

mesh: see ENGAGE; LACE; NET; TISSUE; WEB.

meshing: see ENGAGEMENT.

mess *n.* **1** (*the room is a mess*) DISORDER, jumble, hodgepodge, CONFUSION; **2** (*a mess of beans*) PORTION, BATCH, BLEND, HEAP, LOT; **3** (*officers' mess*) MEAL, FOOD, rations.
— *v.* mess up, botch, disorder, TRIFLE, PLAY, FOOL, meddle.

message *n.* COMMUNICATION, NEWS, DISPATCH, LETTER, REPORT, communiqué.

messenger *n.* carrier, courier, RUNNER, PAGE, emissary, helper, BOY.

mess up: see CONFUSE; MESS.

messy *adj.* untidy, CARELESS, slovenly, DIRTY, disorderly, tangled.

metal *n.* MINERAL, ELEMENT, ORE, VEIN, bullion, IRON, GOLD, silver, copper, nickel, LEAD, platinum, zinc, tin, chromium, tungsten.

metamorphosis: see TRANSFORMATION.

meteorology: see CLIMATE.

meter *n.* GAUGE, dial, SCALE, MEASURE. See also POETRY, VERSE.

method *n.* PROCEDURE, PROCESS, WAY, mode, DESIGN, SCHEME, PLAN.

methodical: see ORDERLY; RELIGIOUS; SCIENTIFIC; SYSTEMATIC.

methodically: see ORDERLY, SYSTEMATICALLY.

methods: see TACTICS.

meticulous: see CAREFUL; PRECISE; THOROUGH.

meticulously: see PRECISELY.

meticulousness: see PRECISION.

metropolis: see CAPITAL.

microbe: see GERM.

microscopic: see INVISIBLE; MINUTE; TINY.

mid: see CENTRAL.

midday: see NOON.

middle *n.* midpoint, CENTER, core, MEAN, median, AVERAGE, focus, bull's-eye, waist, BELLY.
— *adj.*: see CENTRAL.

middleman: see BROKER; MERCHANT.

middling: see MEDIUM.

midget: see DWARF.

midpoint: see AVERAGE; CENTER; MEDIUM; MIDDLE.

midst *n.* MIDDLE, CENTER, core, HEART, hub, BOSOM, nucleus.

midway: see BETWEEN.

might *n.* FORCE, STRENGTH, POWER, domination.

mighty *adj.* STRONG, POWERFUL, MUSCULAR, GREAT, LARGE.
— *adv.* VERY, EXTREMELY, strongly.

migrant: see IMMIGRANT.

migrate *v.* MOVE, emigrate, IMMIGRATE, resettle, DRIFT, ROVE, WANDER, ROAM.

migration: see IMMIGRATION.

mild *adj.* SOFT, suave, GENTLE, MELLOW, meek, bland, tepid.

mildew: see MOLD; RUST.

mildness *n.* gentleness, WARMTH, TENDERNESS, compassion, kindliness, moderation, TRANQUILLITY.

milestone: see EVENT.

milieu: see ENVIRONMENT; MEDIUM.

military *adj.* warlike, martial, combative, rigorous.
— *n.* armed forces, ARMY, NAVY, air force, militia.

militia: see ARMY; MILITARY.

milksop: see COWARD.

milky: see WHITE.

mill *n.* grinder, grindstone, press, grater,
millstone, windmill, FACTORY, foundry, PLANT.
— *v.* **1** *(to mill coffee)* GRIND, grate, pulverize,
granulate; **2** *(to mill about the streets)* WANDER,
ROAM, MOVE.

millpond: see LAKE.

millstone: see MILL.

mimic: see DUPLICATE; IMITATE; MOCK.

mimicry: see IMITATION.

mince *v.* CUT, dice, CHOP, cube, CRUSH, hash,
fragment, pussyfoot, lisp, POSE.

mind *n.* MENTALITY, REASON, INTELLECT, brain,
ATTENTION, awareness, CONSCIOUSNESS,
INTENTION.
— *v.* CARE, OBEY, ATTEND, care for, baby-sit,
TROUBLE, BOTHER, OBJECT.

mindful: see APPRECIATIVE; AWARE.

mine *n.* **1** *(a silver mine)* VEIN, PIT, WELL, DEPOSIT,
quarry, excavation, WEALTH, TREASURE, STORE,
QUANTITY; **2** *(a land mine)* bomb, booby trap,
EXPLOSIVE.
— *pron.* my.
— *v.* undermine, EXTRACT, quarry, excavate.

mineral *n.* ROCK, ORE, VEIN, magma, crystal,
coal, quartz, mica, garnet, gypsum, bauxite.

mingle *v.* MIX, BLEND, COMBINE, merge, socialize,
fraternize.

mingled: see COMPOSITE; MISCELLANEOUS.

miniature *adj.* TINY, SMALL, LITTLE, MINUTE,
minuscule, diminutive, bantam.
— *n.*: see MODEL; TOY.

minimal: see SEVERE.

minimize: see DWARF; REDUCE.

minimum *n.* LEAST, BOTTOM, TRIFLE, JOT, BIT,
SPECK.

minister *n.* **1** *(a Protestant minister)* cleric,
clergyman, PREACHER, PRIEST, PASTOR,
reverend; **2** *(the minister of the interior)*
AMBASSADOR, consul, representative,
OFFICIAL, SECRETARY, prime minister,
premier.

ministry: see CABINET.

minor *adj.* LESSER, insignificant, trivial, SLIGHT,
paltry.

— *n.* CHILD, BOY, GIRL, adolescent, YOUTH.

minority: see CHILDHOOD.

minstrel: see SINGER.

mint *v.* FORGE, INVENT, fashion, MAKE,
manufacture, STAMP, COIN.

minus *prep.* LESS, WITHOUT, wanting, lacking.
— *adj.* deficient, WANTING, INFERIOR, LESS,
negative.
— *n.* deficiency, ·negative, DEBT, failing, LACK,
demerit.

minuscule: see MINIATURE; MINUTE.

minute *adj.* TINY, minuscule, microscopic,
infinitesimal, EXACT, PRECISE, trivial.
— *n.*: see JIFFY.

minutely: see FEW.

minutes: see JOURNAL.

minutest: see LEAST.

miracle *n.* WONDER, MARVEL, rarity, revelation,
phenomenon.

miracle-worker: see WIZARD.

miraculous *adj.* wondrous, WONDERFUL,
MARVELOUS, supernatural, phenomenal,
EXTRAORDINARY, unaccountable.

mirage: see SIGHT.

mire: see MARSH; MUD; SLIME.

mirror *n.* GLASS, looking glass, reflector.
— *v.* REFLECT, ECHO, IMITATE, REPRESENT.

mirth: see HILARITY; LAUGHTER; SPORT.

misanthrope: see MISER.

misapply: see ABUSE.

misbehave: see CARRY ON; SIN.

misbehavior: see VIOLATION.

miscalculate: see MISS.

miscarry: see MISS.

miscellaneous *adj.* diverse, VARIOUS, mixed,
mingled, combined, selected, ASSORTED,
diversified, motley, COMPOSITE, jumbled,
scrambled.

miscellany: see ASSORTMENT; MIXTURE; STUFF.

mischance: see MISFORTUNE; TROUBLE.

mischief *n.* wrongdoing, devilment, EVIL,
INJURY, TROUBLE, prank.

mischief-maker: see RASCAL.

mischievous *adj.* impish, devilish, roguish,

rascally, HARMFUL, malicious, waggish, vexatious.

misconception: see ILLUSION.

misdeed: see CRIME; WRONG.

misdemeanor: see CRIME.

misdirect: see MISLEAD.

misdirecting: see MISLEADING.

miser *n.* hoarder, skinflint, penny pincher, tightwad, misanthrope.

miserable *adj.* UNHAPPY, afflicted, pathetic, UNFORTUNATE, WRETCHED, WORTHLESS.

miserably: see POORLY.

miserly: see CHEAP; CLOSE.

misery *n.* DISTRESS, SUFFERING, dejection, POVERTY, GRIEF, ANXIETY, wretchedness.

misfit *n.* nonconformist, dropout, maverick, paranoid, psychotic, pervert.

misfortune *n.* affliction, mischance, mishap, TRAGEDY, SORROW, DISASTER.

misgiving: see ANXIETY; DISTRUST; DOUBT; MISTRUST.

misguide: see MISLEAD.

misguided: see MISTAKEN.

misguiding: see MISLEADING.

mishap: see ACCIDENT; BREAKDOWN; MISFORTUNE; TROUBLE.

mishmash: see MIXTURE.

misinform: see LIE; MISLEAD.

misinforming: see MISLEADING.

misinterpret: see CONFUSE.

misjudge: see MISTAKE.

mislay *v.* misplace, displace, LOSE, FORGET.

mislead *v.* delude, misinform, DECEIVE, misdirect, CHEAT, defraud, misguide.

misleading *adj.* deluding, deceptive, fraudulent, fallacious, misdirecting, misinforming, misguiding.

misplace: see LOSE; MISLAY.

misplaced: see LOST.

misrepresent: see STRETCH.

miss *v.* **1** (*to miss the target*) FAIL, ERR, miscalculate, miscarry, fall short; **2** (*to miss a turn*) OVERLOOK, PASS, FORGET; **3** (*we miss you*)

YEARN, LACK, DESIRE, long.
— *n.*: see GIRL; LADY; MAID; VIRGIN.

misshapen *adj.* grotesque, DEFORMED, UGLY, disfigured, disproportioned, ill-made.

missile *n.* **1** (*he hurled a missile*) SHOT, bullet, SHELL, cartridge, dart, ARROW, boomerang; **2** (*to launch a missile*) ROCKET, space ship, space probe.

missing *adj.* ABSENT, lacking, WANTING, LOST, astray, gone.

mission *n.* **1** (*my life's mission*) ERRAND, TASK, JOB, ASSIGNMENT, vocation, PURPOSE, END; **2** (*a Spanish mission*) delegation, legation, CHURCH, chapel, CENTER.

missionary: see PREACHER.

missus: see MISTRESS; WIFE.

mist *n.* FOG, haze, SPRAY, drizzle, CLOUD, smog.

mistake *v.* blunder, err, OVERLOOK, MISS, FORGET, misjudge.
— *n.* error, misunderstanding, BLUNDER, SLIP, lapse.

mistaken *adj.* WRONG, erroneous, FALSE, misguided, INCORRECT, fallacious.

mistakenly: see WRONG.

mistiness: see WETNESS.

mistreat *v.* MAUL, manhandle, HARM, maim, molest, ABUSE, BRUISE.

mistreatment: see ABUSE; PUNISHMENT.

mistress *n.* **1** (*a wardrobe mistress*) HOUSEWIFE, housemistress, WIFE, schoolmistress, schoolmarm, MANAGER, matron, missus; **2** (*to keep a mistress*) LOVER, inamorata, ladylove, SWEETHEART.

mistrust *v.* DOUBT, QUESTION, SUSPECT, DISTRUST, disbelieve.
— *n.* skepticism, DOUBT, questioning, SUSPICION, misgiving, DISTRUST.

misty: see FOGGY; HAZY.

misunderstand: see CONFUSE; RESENT.

misunderstanding: see DISAGREEMENT; MISTAKE; QUARREL.

misuse: see ABUSE; WASTE.

mite: see INSECT; PARTICLE; SPECK.

mitt: see MITTEN.

mitten *n.* glove, mitt, muff.

mix *v.* BLEND, STIR, COMBINE, fuse, BEAT, knead,

cross, COMPOUND, fraternize.
— *n.*: see BATTER; MASH; MIXTURE.

mixed: see ASSORTED; COMPOSITE; COMPOUND; MISCELLANEOUS; SHAKEN.

mixture *n.* mix, BLEND, COMBINATION, medley, miscellany, hybrid, BATTER, mishmash, jumble.

mix-up: see CONFUSION; MUSS; TANGLE.

moan *n.* GROAN, WAIL, lament, RUMBLE, creak.
— *v.* bemoan, GROAN, GRIEVE, WAIL, lament, deplore.

moat: see DITCH; TRENCH.

mob *n.* SWARM, horde, MASS, CROWD, MULTITUDE, rabble, riffraff.
— *v.* hem in, CROWD, SURROUND, jostle.

mobile *adj.* movable, PORTABLE, wheeled, FREE, CHANGEABLE, volatile.

mobility *n.* movement, fluidity, FLOW, flux, ACTIVITY, FREEDOM.

mobster: see GANGSTER; HOOD.

mock *v.* RIDICULE, SCORN, deride, taunt, TEASE, mimic, IMITATE.
— *adj.* sham, FALSE, counterfeit, fake.

mockery: see RIDICULE; SCORN; SPORT.

mod: see STYLISH.

mode: see MEDIUM; METHOD; PRACTICE; STYLE; SYSTEM; TECHNIQUE.

model *n.* PATTERN, FORM, exemplar, prototype, IDEAL, miniature.
— *v.* **1** *(to model clay)* FASHION, SHAPE, COPY, DUPLICATE, MOLD; **2** *(to model clothes)* POSE, SIT, EXHIBIT, DEMONSTRATE.
— *adj.*: see IDEAL.

modeling: see SCULPTURE.

moderate: see CONSERVATIVE; COOL; ECONOMICAL; GENTLE; GRADUAL; PASSABLE; REASONABLE; SEASON; SLACKEN; SOBER; SOFTEN.

moderately: see FAIRLY.

moderation: see MILDNESS.

moderator: see CHAIRMAN.

modern *adj.* UP-TO-DATE, CONTEMPORARY, RECENT, FASHIONABLE, modernistic, prevailing.

modernistic: see MODERN.

modernize *v.* refurbish, renovate, RENEW, IMPROVE, refit, RESTORE, rejuvenate.

modest *adj.* BASHFUL, HUMBLE, unaffected, meek, chaste, PURE, unobtrusive, SMALL, ECONOMICAL, INEXPENSIVE.

modesty *n.* humility, shyness, inhibition, decency, INNOCENCE.

modification: see CORRECTION; VARIATION.

modify *v.* ALTER, remodel, CHANGE, ADAPT, restrain, CURB.

modish: see FASHIONABLE.

modulate: see VARY.

modulation: see PITCH.

modus: see MANNER.

moist *adj.* WET, DAMP, SODDEN, HUMID, MUGGY, clammy.

moisten: see WASH; WATER; WET.

moisture *n.* WETNESS, dampness, humidity, MIST, drizzle.

moistureless: see DRY.

moisturizer: see OINTMENT.

molar: see TOOTH.

mold *n.* **1** *(formed in a mold)* SHAPE, FORM, die, matrix, CAST, PATTERN; **2** *(rust and mold)* fungus, parasite, decay, lichen, smut.
— *v.* **1** *(to mold in clay)* SHAPE, FASHION, FORM, CARVE, CAST; **2** *(it molds quickly)* DECAY, rust, corrode, mildew, ROT.

moldy: see ROTTEN.

mole: see BLEMISH.

molecule *n.* PARTICLE, FRAGMENT, BIT, ATOM, electron, ion.

molest: see MISTREAT; PERSECUTE; PLAGUE.

molestation: see DISTURBANCE.

molt: see SHED.

molten: see FLUID.

mom: see MOTHER.

moment *n.* INSTANT, PERIOD, FLASH, twinkling, JIFFY.

momentarily: see AWHILE.

momentary *adj.* BRIEF, fleeting, instantaneous, passing, ABRUPT.

momento: see MEMORY.

momentous: see OUTSTANDING.

mommy: see MOTHER.

monarch *n.* KING, QUEEN, EMPEROR, empress, sovereign, autocrat, TYRANT, despot, czar, kaiser, shah.

monarchy *n.* KINGDOM, kingship, principality, EMPIRE, royalty, REIGN.

monastery: see CONVENT.

monetary: see COMMERCIAL; FINANCIAL.

money *n.* COIN, CASH, EXCHANGE, CURRENCY, CAPITAL, funds, WEALTH, dough.

moneyed: see WEALTHY.

money order: see DRAFT.

monger: see DEALER.

monition: see WARNING.

monitor *n.* GUARD, custodian, COUNSELOR, SUPERVISOR, detector, REGISTER, CONTROL.
   — *v.* GUARD, oversee, WATCH, SUPERVISE, TRACE, SCORE, DETECT, REGISTER, CONTROL.

monk *n.* friar, PRIEST, BROTHER, HERMIT, prior, abbot.

monkey *n.* ape, chimpanzee, gorilla, baboon, primate.
   — *v.* meddle, TAMPER, INTERFERE.

monopoly: see CHAIN; TRUST.

monorail: see RAIL.

monotone: see SAMENESS.

monotonous *adj.* tiresome, tedious, DULL, dreary, repetitious, boring.

monotony *n.* DULLNESS, BOREDOM, tedium, SAMENESS.

monster *n.* BEAST, monstrosity, FREAK, ODDITY, GIANT, titan, fiend.

monstrosity: see FREAK; MONSTER; ODDITY.

monstrous *adj.* ENORMOUS, HUGE, GIGANTIC, bestial, shocking, ABNORMAL.

monument *n.* **1** (*to raise a monument*) STATUE, TOMB, COLUMN, PILLAR, headstone, BUILDING, MEMORIAL; **2** (*a literary monument*) magnum opus, masterpiece, ACCOMPLISHMENT, ACHIEVEMENT, CONTRIBUTION.

monumental: see BIG; HUGE.

mooch: see BUM.

moocher: see BEGGAR.

mood *n.* STATE, CONDITION, DISPOSITION, frame of mind, INCLINATION.

moody *adj.* TEMPERAMENTAL, CHANGEABLE, pensive, touchy, SENSITIVE, SAD, low.

moon: see SATELLITE.

moonbeam: see SHAFT.

moonshine: see NONSENSE.

moor: see CALL.

mop *n.* swab, duster, sweeper.
   — *v.* WIPE, swab, SPONGE, WASH, DUST, CLEAN.

moppet: see CHILD.

moral *adj.* PROPER, ethical, RIGHT, DECENT, JUST, UPRIGHT, VIRTUOUS.
   — *n.* LESSON, MEANING, SIGNIFICANCE, THEME.

morale: see ATTITUDE.

morality: see CHARACTER; CODE; CONSCIENCE; HONESTY, VIRTUE.

moralize: see LECTURE; PREACH.

moralizer: see PREACHER.

morals: see CONSCIENCE; MANNERS.

morbid: see SICK.

more *adj.* ADDITIONAL, EXTRA, OTHER, FRESH, NEW.
   — *n.* INCREASE, increment, dividend, BONUS.
   — *adv.* additionally, ALSO, TOO, BEYOND, FURTHERMORE, MOREOVER.

moreover *adv.* FURTHERMORE, ALSO, BESIDES, YET.

morn: see MORNING.

morning *n.* morn, forenoon, DAWN, sunrise, daylight, daybreak, sunup, A. M.

moron *n.* IDIOT, JERK, imbecile, cretin, simpleton, dunce, blockhead, mushhead, clunkhead, cheesehead.

moronic: see HALF-WITTED; IDIOTIC.

morose: see SULLEN.

morsel: see BIT; BITE; MOUTHFUL; PAT; SNACK.

mortal *adj.* **1** (*man is mortal*) impermanent, PERISHABLE, transient, passing, FRAIL; **2** (*a mortal blow*) DEADLY, lethal, FATAL.
   — *n.* HUMAN, MAN, HUMANITY, BEING, PERSON, CREATURE.

mortar: see ARTILLERY; CEMENT; PLASTER.

mortgage *n.* DEBT, lease, LOAN, CONTRACT, encumbrance, PLEDGE.

mortification: see EMBARRASSMENT; HUMILIATION.

mortify: see EMBARRASS.

mosque: see CHURCH; TEMPLE.

mosquito: see FLY.

mossback: see CONSERVATIVE.

most *adj.* MAXIMUM, UTMOST, unsurpassed, BEST.
— *adv.* VERY, EXTREMELY, highly.
— *n.* MAJORITY, MASS, bulk, plurality.

mostly *adv.* largely, CHIEFLY, GENERALLY, MAINLY.

mote: see SPECK.

motel: see HOTEL; INN.

moth-eaten: see OLD.

mother *n.* PARENT, MAMA, mommy, mom, mater, housemother, SUPERINTENDENT, ORIGIN.
— *v.* nurture, NURSE, RAISE, CHERISH, FOSTER, BABY.

motherland: see COUNTRY.

motherly *adj.* maternal, PROTECTIVE, PARENTAL, WATCHFUL, TENDER.

mother-of-pearl: see PEARL.

motility: see MOTION.

motion *n.* movement, ACTION, flux, CHANGE, motility, PROPOSAL, SUGGESTION.
— *v.* GESTURE, WAVE, POINT, SIGNAL.

motionless *adj.* STILL, QUIET, immobile, inert, stagnant.

motion picture: see FILM.

motivate: see INSPIRE.

motivation: see EXCITEMENT; REASON.

motive *n.* REASON, CAUSE, PURPOSE, END, GROUNDS.

motley: see MISCELLANEOUS.

motor *n.* ENGINE, POWER, dynamo.

motorboat: see LAUNCH.

motorcade: see PARADE.

motorcar: see AUTOMOBILE.

motorman: see DRIVER.

motto *n.* saying, PROVERB, byword, slogan.

mound *n.* PILE, HEAP, BANK, HILL, STACK, SHOCK.

mount *v.* **1** *(to mount a fence)* CLIMB, SCALE, straddle, ASCEND, INCREASE, GROW; **2** *(to mount photos)* set up, FRAME, DISPLAY.
— *n.* FRAME, BASE, pedestal, HILL. See also HORSE.

mountain *n.* HILL, MOUNT, PEAK, HEIGHT, PILE, HEAP.

mounting: see FRAME.

mourn *v.* GRIEVE, lament, FRET, CRY, MISS.

mourners: see FUNERAL.

mournful *adj.* SYMPATHETIC, SORROWFUL, grieving, lamenting, bemoaning, downcast, grim, doleful.

mourning *n.* GRIEF, SORROW, lamentation.

mousy: see DULL.

mouth *n.* **1** *(close your mouth)* lips, jaw, teeth, kisser; **2** *(the mouth of the river)* OPENING, ENTRANCE, access, delta, SOUND, inlet.

mouthful *n.* PORTION, BITE, morsel, assertion, STATEMENT.

mouthpiece: see ATTORNEY; BIT.

mouthy: see TALKATIVE.

movable: see ADJUSTABLE; CHANGEABLE; MOBILE; PORTABLE.

move *v.* **1** *(to move about)* GO, TRAVEL, TRANSFER, SHIFT, PROGRESS, PUSH; **2** *(it moved me deeply)* TOUCH, INFLUENCE, ROUSE, PERSUADE; **3** *(I move we adjourn)* PROPOSE, SUGGEST.
— *n.* movement, TRANSFER, SHIFT, CHANGE, tactic, PLAY.

move along: see PROGRESS.

movement: see ACTION; ACTIVITY; CIRCULATION; FLOW; GESTURE; MOBILITY; MOTION; MOVE; PASSAGE; PROGRESS; TRANSPORTATION.

movie: see FILM; PICTURE; SHOW.

movies: see SCREEN.

moving: see CONVINCING; DRAMATIC; EMOTIONAL; EXCITABLE; IRRESISTIBLE; TRANSPORT.

mow: see CLIP; REAP; SHEAR.

moxie: see COURAGE.

much *adj.* AMPLE, ABUNDANT, VARIOUS, SIZABLE, SUFFICIENT.
— *adv.* VERY, GREATLY, OFTEN, highly, amply, repeatedly.
— *n.* AMOUNT, QUANTITY, LOT, SUPPLY, scads.

mucilage: see ADHESIVE; CEMENT; GUM; PASTE.

muck: see FILTH; MUD; SLIME.

mucky: see SLIMY.

mud *n.* muck, silt, SLIME, ooze, sludge, goo, mire.

muddle: see COMPLICATE; CONFUSE; JUMBLE; TANGLE.

muddy *adj.* DIRTY, SLIMY, MESSY, FOUL, murky, DARK, obscure, confused, disorderly, bespattered.

muff: see MITTEN.

muffle: see DROWN; HUSH; MUMBLE; SOFTEN; STILL.

muffled: see LOW; SOUNDLESS.

muffler: see SCARF.

mug *n.* **1** *(a mug of beer)* CUP, stein, VESSEL; **2** *(a hideous mug)* FACE, visage, ASPECT.
— *v.*: see ASSAULT; ATTACK.

mugging: see HOLDUP.

muggy *adj.* HUMID, MOIST, DAMP, dank, WET, oppressive, stuffy.

mule: see SHOE.

mulish: see STUBBORN.

mull: see THINKING.

multifarious: see VARIOUS.

multiple: see COMPLEX.

multiply *v.* INCREASE, amplify, DOUBLE, square, cube, compound, REPRODUCE, mushroom.

multitude *n.* CROWD, throng, MOB, FLOCK, ABUNDANCE, QUANTITY.

mum: see SILENT.

mumble *v.* MUTTER, MURMUR, muffle, GRUMBLE, whimper, WHINE.
— *n.*: see GROWL; GRUNT; WHISPER.

mummer: see CLOWN.

munch *v.* EAT, CHEW, nibble, crunch, BITE, CRUSH.

municipal: see CIVIL; PUBLIC.

municipality: see TOWN; VILLAGE.

munificent: see GENEROUS.

munitions: see ARMS; WEAPON.

murder *n.* homicide, ASSASSINATION, SLAUGHTER, manslaughter, MASSACRE, EXECUTION.
— *v.* SLAY, KILL, ASSASSINATE, EXECUTE, rub out, SLAUGHTER, DEFEAT, OVERWHELM.

murderer *n.* KILLER, slayer, ASSASSIN, BUTCHER, executioner.

murderous *adj.* BRUTAL, killing, DEADLY, bloody, bloodthirsty, CRUEL, SAVAGE.

murk: see GLOOM.

murkiness: see DARK; DARKNESS.

murky: see CLOUDY; DARK; DULL; FUZZY; HAZY; MUDDY.

murmur *n.* WHISPER, GRUMBLE, MOAN, RUSTLE.
— *v.* WHISPER, HUM, drone, MUMBLE, RUSTLE, swish.

murmuring: see HUM; WHINE.

muscle: see TISSUE.

muscleman: see GIANT.

muscular *adj.* brawny, HUSKY, STRONG, POWERFUL, robust, sinewy, ATHLETIC.

muse: see REFLECT.

museum: see GALLERY.

mush: see PULP.

mushhead: see MORON.

mushroom: see MULTIPLY.

mushy: see ROMANTIC; SENTIMENTAL.

music *n.* HARMONY, MELODY, STRAIN, SONG, TUNE, lyrics, CONCERT, opera, symphony, sonata.

musical *adj.* tuneful, HARMONIOUS, MELODIOUS, MELLOW, rhythmic, lyrical, symphonic, operatic.
— *n.* SHOW, operetta.

musicale: see CONCERT.

musician: see ARTIST; PERFORMER.

musing: see ABSENT-MINDED; REFLECTION.

musk: see ODOR.

musket: see GUN; RIFLE.

muss *n.* MESS, mix-up, clutter, disarray, SCRAMBLE, DISORDER.
— *v.* rumple, MESS, clutter, disorganize, LITTER.

must *v.* have to, ought to, should.

muster: see ASSEMBLE; CONGREGATE.

mutable: see CHANGEABLE.

mute: see SILENT; SOUNDLESS; SPEECHLESS.

mutilate: see SLAUGHTER.

mutilation: see BUTCHERY.

mutineer: see REBEL; TRAITOR.

mutiny: see DISOBEDIENCE; REBEL; REBELLION; REVOLT; REVOLUTION.

mutter *v.* MURMUR, MUMBLE, WHISPER, GRUMBLE, COMPLAIN, gripe.

mutton: see LAMB; SHEEP.

muzzle: see SILENCE.

muzzleloader: see RIFLE.

my: see MINE.

mysterious *adj.* STRANGE, ODD, RARE, UNUSUAL, UNNATURAL, mystic, occult, weird, uncanny, spooky.

mysteriousness: see DIMNESS.

mystery *n.* RIDDLE, PUZZLE, SECRET, subtlety, perplexity, ODDITY, complexity, intricacy, sphinx.

mystic: see MYSTERIOUS.

mystical: see MAGICAL.

mystify: see BEWILDER; PUZZLE.

myth *n.* FABLE, TALE, folk tale, fairy tale, FICTION, fantasy, TRADITION, LEGEND, folklore.

mythical *adj.* TRADITIONAL, legendary, FICTITIOUS, FABULOUS, FANTASTIC.

N

nab: see CAPTURE; CATCH; NAIL.

nadir: see BOTTOM.

nag *v.* harass, BOTHER, PESTER, dwell, ANNOY, CRITICIZE.

nagging: see CRITICAL.

nail *n.* **1** *(a ten-penny nail)* spike, PIN, TACK, hobnail, PEG; **2** *(a nail file)* fingernail, toenail, CLAW, spur, talon.
— *v.* **1** *(to nail down)* TACK, SECURE, FASTEN; **2** *(to nail a thief)* CAPTURE, CATCH, COLLAR, nab, ARREST.

naive: see GREEN; IGNORANT; INNOCENT.

naiveté: see INNOCENCE.

naked *adj.* **1** *(to go naked)* NUDE, BARE, unclothed, stripped, exposed, HELPLESS;
2 *(the naked truth)* PLAIN, SIMPLE, MERE, straightforward, bald.

namby-pamby: see WEAK.

name *n.* **1** *(name and address)* TITLE, patronymic, designation, denomination, nickname, pen name, alias; **2** *(my good name)* REPUTATION, HONOR, CREDIT, FAME; **3** *(a big name)* CELEBRITY, STAR, HERO.
— *v.* CALL, LABEL, christen, IDENTIFY.

nameless *adj.* UNKNOWN, obscure, unlabeled, undistinguished, untitled, untagged.

nap *n.* sleep, cat nap, siesta, snooze. See also FIBER.
— *v.* doze, snooze, SLEEP.

napkin *n.* linen, CLOTH, TOWEL, RAG.

napping: see ASLEEP.

narcotic: see DRUG.

narrate *v.* TELL, RELATE, RECITE, recount, REPORT.

narration *n.* TALE, ACCOUNT, STORY, chronicle, narrative, recitation, PRESENTATION, DELIVERY.

narrative: see FICTIONAL; HISTORY; NARRATION; RELATION; STORY; TALE.

narrow *adj.* **1** *(a narrow path)* THIN, SLIM, SLENDER, TIGHT, CLOSE; **2** *(of narrow views)* NARROW-MINDED, dogmatic, CONSERVATIVE, bigoted, prejudiced.
— *v.*: see RESTRICT.

narrowly: see HARDLY.

narrow-minded *adj.* NARROW, illiberal, bigoted, prejudiced, dogmatic, intolerant.

narrows: see SOUND.

nastiness: see FILTH.

nasty *adj.* MEAN, sarcastic, UNPLEASANT, gross, loathsome, revolting, DIRTY, vile.

nation *n.* COUNTRY, STATE, LAND, commonwealth, REPUBLIC, SOCIETY, populace, PUBLIC, FOLK.

national *adj.* nationwide, GENERAL, NATIVE, SOCIAL, POLITICAL, CIVIL, civic, DOMESTIC.
— *n.* CITIZEN, SUBJECT, NATIVE, freeman.

nationalism: see NATIONALITY.

nationality *n.* citizenship, LOYALTY, ALLEGIANCE, nationalism, STATE, NATION, commonwealth.

nationwide: see NATIONAL.

native *adj.* native-born, NATURAL, inborn, inbred, LOCAL, DOMESTIC, FUNDAMENTAL.
— *n.* NATIONAL, CITIZEN, INHABITANT, countryman.

native-born: see NATIVE.

natural *adj.* NATIVE, inborn, ORIGINAL, NORMAL, CUSTOMARY, ingrained, SIMPLE, artless.

naturalization: see IMMIGRATION.

naturalness: see EASE.

nature *n.* **1** *(Mother Nature)* UNIVERSE, WORLD, CREATION, ENVIRONMENT, OUTSIDE, OUTDOORS; **2** *(a pleasant nature)* PERSONALITY, makeup, CHARACTER, DISPOSITION, kind. See also ANATOMY.

naughty *adj.* **1** *(a naughty boy)* MISCHIEVOUS, BAD, DISOBEDIENT, uruly, WICKED; **2** *(a naughty word)* INDECENT, obscene, improper.

nausea: see DISGUST.

nauseate: see REVOLT; SICKEN.

nautical: see MARINE.

naval: see MARINE.

navel: see CENTER.

navigate v. STEER, GUIDE, PILOT, SAIL, cruise.

navigation n. seamanship, piloting, sailing.

navigator: see SAILOR.

navy n. warships, FLEET, armada, sailors.

nay: see NO; VETO.

near adj. **1** (the near side) CLOSE, NEARBY, neighboring, adjacent, adjoining; **2** (the day is near) forthcoming, approaching; **3** (a near relative) intimate, CLOSE, FAMILIAR, DEAR; **4** (the nearest road) SHORT, DIRECT, STRAIGHT.
— adv. NEARLY, closely, ABOUT, PRACTICALLY.
— prep. next to, adjacent to, close to, close by, nigh.
— v.: see COME.

nearby adv. beside, AROUND, closely.

nearest: see NEXT.

nearing: see ONCOMING.

nearly adv. ALMOST, ABOUT, APPROXIMATELY, roughly, GENERALLY, closely, well-nigh.

nearness: see CLOSENESS; PRESENCE; VICINITY.

neat adj. **1** (a neat desk) TIDY, ORDERLY, well-kept, CLEAN, spic-and-span, prim, well-organized, shipshape, SMART, ELEGANT; **2** (a neat trick) CLEVER, skillful; **3** (to take one's whiskey neat) undiluted, PLAIN; **4** (that's neat!) GREAT, FINE, WONDERFUL.

neatness n. ORDER, orderliness, tidiness.

neb: see BILL.

nebulous: see CLOUDY; HAZY.

necessarily adv. unavoidably, inevitably, essentially, urgently.

necessary adj. needed, needful, required, ESSENTIAL, indispensable, requisite, URGENT, obligatory, compulsory, unavoidable, INEVITABLE.

necessitate: see COMPEL; DEMAND; NEED.

necessity n. NEED, requirement, prerequisite, essential, requisite, compulsion, URGENCY.

neckband: see COLLAR.

neckerchief: see HANDKERCHIEF.

necklaces: see JEWELRY.

neckpiece: see COLLAR.

necktie: see TIE.

nectar: see HONEY; LIQUID.

need n. **1** (no need for panic) NECESSITY, REQUIREMENT, prerequisite, compulsion, URGENCY; **2** (a refugee in great need) LACK, want, POVERTY, pennilessness, DISTRESS.
— v. necessitate, REQUIRE, COMPEL, FORCE, DEMAND, WANT, CRAVE, MISS, LACK.

needed: see ESSENTIAL; NECESSARY.

needful: see ESSENTIAL; NECESSARY.

needle n. pointer, PIN, ROD, TUBE, PRICK, SHOT, STING, SPINE, spur, LEAF, frond.
— v.: see TEASE.

needless: see UNNECESSARY.

needy adj. POOR, penniless, poverty-stricken, destitute.

negate: see DENY.

negative: see FILM; MINUS; RESISTANT.

neglect v. disregard, slight, OVERLOOK, MISS, SKIP, IGNORE, by-pass.
— n.: see OMISSION.

neglected: see FORGOTTEN.

neglectful: see THOUGHTLESS.

negligence: see FAILURE; FAULT; FORGETFULNESS; OMISSION.

negligent: see CARELESS; DELINQUENT.

negligible: see SLIGHT.

negotiate: see BARGAIN; CONSULT; TREAT.

negotiation: see SALE; TRANSACTION.

neighbor n. FRIEND, FELLOW, ACQUAINTANCE, COMRADE, ASSOCIATE.
— v.: see ADJOIN.

neighborhood n. VICINITY, DISTRICT, SECTION, quarter, locale, AREA, COMMUNITY, LOCALITY, ENVIRONMENT, environs, SURROUNDINGS.

neighboring: see NEAR.

neighborly: see BROTHERLY; FRIENDLY.

neologism: see WORD.

nerve n. **1** (to strain every nerve) FIBER, CORD, sinew, tendon, rib, VEIN; **2** (it takes a lot of nerve) COURAGE, BOLDNESS, guts, GRIT, VIGOR, ENERGY; **3** (you have your nerve!) RUDENESS, brass, cheek.

nerveless: see COWARDLY.

nervous adj. UNEASY, TENSE, uptight, jumpy, JERKY, RESTLESS, excited.

nervously: see COWARDLY.

nescient: see IGNORANT.

nest *n.* **1** *(a bird's nest)* birdhouse, SHELTER, POCKET; **2** *(a nest of vice)* hideout, hotbed, DEN, RETREAT.
— *v.* SETTLE, incubate.

nest egg: see RESERVE; SAVINGS.

nestle *v.* LIE, SIT, REST, REMAIN, cuddle, SNUGGLE, nuzzle.

net *adj.* CLEAR, PURE, FREE, FINAL.
— *n.* snare, dragnet, NETWORK, mesh, WEB.
— *v.* **1** *(to net fish)* CATCH, ensnare, entrap, COVER, SCREEN, PROTECT; **2** *(to net fifty dollars)* clear, GAIN, EARN, YIELD, PRODUCE.

nettle: see ANGER; OFFEND.

network *n.* COMBINATION, SYSTEM, CHAIN.

neurotic: see ANXIOUS.

neutral *adj.* **1** *(a neutral nation)* uncommitted, impartial, unbiased, indifferent; **2** *(in neutral position)* intermediate, UNDECIDED, uncharged, sexless, colorless, DULL, drab, disengaged.

neutralize: see CANCEL; COMPENSATE.

never: see NO.

nevertheless *adv.* notwithstanding, nonetheless, HOWEVER, YET.

new *adj.* MODERN, RECENT, FRESH, latest, NOVEL, changed, DIFFERENT, ORIGINAL, unused, renewed, refreshed, UNFAMILIAR, STRANGE.

newborn: see BABY; INFANT; YOUNG.

newcomer: see BEGINNER; FOREIGNER; IMMIGRANT; STRANGER.

newly *adv.* LATELY, RECENTLY, anew.

newlyweds: see COUPLE.

newness: see ORIGINALITY; VIRGINITY.

news *n.* INFORMATION, INTELLIGENCE, REPORT, TIDINGS, KNOWLEDGE, happenings.

newsletter: see NEWSPAPER.

newspaper *n.* PAPER, JOURNAL, daily, weekly, gazette, tabloid, newsletter.

newspapers: see PRESS.

next *adj.* FOLLOWING, succeeding, after, nearest, adjoining, adjacent.
— *adv.* following, succeedingly.

next to: see BESIDE; NEAR.

nib: see BEAK.

nibble : see CHEW; GNAW; MUNCH; PECK.

nice *adj.* **1** *(oh, that's nice!)* PLEASANT, AGREEABLE, PLEASING; **2** *(a nice reception)* CORDIAL, FRIENDLY, KIND; **3** *(a nice girl)* chaste, RESPECTABLE, PROPER, SUITABLE, courteous, refined, fastidious; **4** *(a nice distinction)* FINE, EXACT, PRECISE, ACCURATE; **5** *(a nice car)* FINE, GOOD; **6** *(a nice amount)* AMPLE, GENEROUS.

niceness: see GOODNESS.

niche: see CORNER; PLACE; RECESS.

nick *n.* NOTCH, mar, SCRATCH, MARK, HOLE, GROOVE, indentation.
— *v.* NOTCH, mar, SCRATCH, CUT, DASH, SLIT.

nickel: see COIN; METAL.

nickname: see CALL; LABEL; NAME.

nifty: see CLASSY.

nigh: see AROUND; NEAR.

night *n.* nighttime, EVENING, DARKNESS, GLOOM.

nightcap: see CAP.

night club: see CAFE.

nightfall: see DUSK; EVENING; TWILIGHT.

nightmare *n.* ordeal, TRIAL, TERROR, HORROR, PANIC.

nightstick: see CLUB.

nighttime: see DARKNESS; EVENING; NIGHT.

nihil: see NOTHING.

nil: see NOTHING.

nimble: see ACTIVE; RAPID.

nimbly: see LIGHTLY.

nincompoop: see ASS; FOOL; IDIOT.

ninny: see FOOL.

nip: see BEVERAGE; BITE; PINCH; SHOT; SNIP.

nippy: see COOL.

nirvana: see TRANQUILLITY.

nitrogen: see GAS.

nitwit: see FOOL; HALF-WIT; JERK.

nix: see NO.

no *adv.* not, never, nay, nope, nix, noway, noways, nowise.
— *n.* nay, VETO, nix, OBJECTION, dissent, PROTEST.

nobby: see ELEGANT.

nobility: see DIGNITY; GREATNESS; MAJESTY; TITLE.

noble *adj.* aristocratic, titled, highborn, blue-blooded, lordly, LOFTY, majestic, GREAT, DIGNIFIED, MAGNIFICENT, VIRTUOUS, GENEROUS, self-sacrificing, HONORABLE, HONEST, UPRIGHT.

nobleman: see ARISTROCRAT.

nobody: see JERK; NOTHING.

nod *v.* BECKON, SIGNAL, incline, BEND, drowse, NAP, SLUMBER. See also BOB.
  − *n.* nodding, shake, SIGNAL, APPROVAL.

nodding: see NOD.

noël: see CAROL.

noise *n.* SOUND, RACKET, din, CLATTER, jangle, hubbub, UPROAR, CLAMOR, tumult, OUTCRY.

noiseless: see SOUNDLESS; STILL.

noisily: see ALOUD.

noisy *adj.* LOUD, clamorous, boisterous, uproarious, tumultuous, riproaring, rackety, screechy, creaky, squeaky, grating.

nominal: see CHEAP.

nominate *v.* SELECT, APPOINT, ASSIGN, NAME, designate, CHOOSE, PROPOSE.

nomination *n.* SELECTION, APPOINTMENT.

nominee: see CANDIDATE.

nonattendance: see ABSENCE.

nonce: see PRESENT.

nonchalance: see EASE.

nonchalant: see CASUAL.

noncitizen: see ALIEN.

noncompliance: see DISOBEDIENCE.

nonconformist: see MISFIT; REBEL.

nonentity: see ZERO.

nonessential: see TRIFLE.

nonetheless: see HOWEVER; NEVERTHELESS.

nonexistent: see NOWHERE.

nonprofessional: see AMATEUR.

nonsense *n.* silliness, absurdity, FOLLY, tomfoolery, STUPIDITY, claptrap, poppycock, moonshine.

nonsensical *adj.* SILLY, ABSURD, FOOLISH, STUPID, RIDICULOUS, SENSELESS, brainless.

nonstop: see CONSTANT.

nook: see CORNER; RECESS.

noon *n.* noontime, noonday, midday.

noonday: see NOON.

noontime: see NOON.

noose: see LOOP.

nope: see NO.

norm: see AVERAGE; GAUGE.

normal *adj.* REGULAR, TYPICAL, USUAL, NATURAL, AVERAGE, STANDARD, GENERAL, HABITUAL, CUSTOMARY, ROUTINE, SANE, SOUND, HEALTHY.

normally: see ORDINARILY; REGULARLY; USUALLY.

nose: see BEAK; PRY; STEM; TRUNK.

nosh: see SNACK.

nosy: see MEDDLESOME.

not: see NO.

notable *adj.* FAMOUS, PROMINENT, OUTSTANDING, NOTED, signal, eminent, noteworthy, EVIDENT, REMARKABLE, RARE, UNUSUAL, UNCOMMON, CONSPICUOUS, distinctive, DISTINGUISHED.
  − *n.* somebody, CELEBRITY, PERSONALITY, STAR.

notably: see ESPECIALLY; PARTICULARLY; PRIMARILY.

notarize: see CERTIFY.

notation: see FOOTNOTE; NOTE; SIGNATURE.

notch *n.* NICK, mar, SCRATCH, MARK, HOLE, indentation, incision.
  − *v.* NICK, gash, CUT, chisel, groove, SCORE, SCRATCH.

notched: see JAGGED.

note *n.* **1** *(to sign a note for money owed)* I.O.U., DEBT, PAPER, bank note, BILL; **2** *(to enclose a note in an envelope)* LETTER, memo, MESSAGE, FOOTNOTE, commentary, REMARK, NOTICE; **3** *(to strike the wrong note)* SOUND, TONE, notation, KEY; **4** *(men of note)* IMPORTANCE, REPUTATION, DISTINCTION.
  − *v.* WRITE, RECORD, REMARK, point out, MENTION, OBSERVE, NOTICE, DISCOVER.

notebook: see PAD; TABLET.

noted *adj.* FAMOUS, CELEBRATED, WELL-KNOWN.

noteworthy: see NOTABLE; NOTICEABLE; REMARKABLE.

nothing *n.* ZERO, nil, nought, nobody, TRIFLE, nothingness, nihil.

nothingness: see NOTHING.

notice *v.* SEE, NOTE, OBSERVE, HEED, REMARK.
  − *n.* NOTE, OBSERVATION, ATTENTION, ADVICE,

WARNING, NOTIFICATION, ANNOUNCEMENT, POSTER, CIRCULAR, handbill, ADVERTISEMENT. See also RECEIPT.

noticeable *adj.* APPARENT, CONSPICUOUS, marked, SIGNIFICANT, striking, noteworthy.

noticeability: see VISIBILITY.

noticeably: see DISTINCTLY; VISIBLY.

notification *n.* ANNOUNCEMENT, COMMUNICATION, INFORMATION, INSTRUCTION, ADVICE, WARNING, REPORT.

notify *v.* INFORM, ADVISE, WARN, ANNOUNCE, MENTION, REVEAL, DECLARE, ACQUAINT.

notion *n.* IDEA, BELIEF, OPINION, IMPRESSION, conception, VIEW, inkling, whim, FANCY.

notorious *adj.* NOTED, infamous, scandalous, disreputable, CONSPICUOUS, flagrant.

notwithstanding: see ALTHOUGH; BUT; DESPITE; HOWEVER; NEVERTHELESS; STILL; YET.

nought: see NOTHING; ZERO.

nourish *v.* FEED, nurture, SUSTAIN, SUPPLY, SUPPORT, FOSTER.

nourishing: see EDIBLE.

nourishment *n.* FOOD, nutrition, nutriment, foodstuffs, sustenance, DIET, SUPPORT, manna, vittles.

novel *adj.* FRESH, ORIGINAL, UNUSUAL, offbeat, NEW, RECENT, DIFFERENT, UNIQUE, ODD, STRANGE.
— *n.* FICTION, novelette, STORY, ROMANCE.

novelette: see NOVEL.

novelist: see WRITER.

novelized: see FICTIONAL.

novelty *n.* FRESHNESS, ORIGINALITY, WRINKLE, NOTION, IDEA, ITEM.

novice: see AMATEUR; APPRENTICE; BEGINNER.

now *adv.* presently, IMMEDIATELY, RECENTLY, SOMETIMES, NOWADAYS, REALLY.
— *n.* PRESENT, MOMENT.
— *conj.* SINCE.

nowadays *adv.* NOW, presently, today, ALREADY.

now and then: see RARELY.

noway: see NO.

noways: see NO.

nowhere *adv.* ABSENT, gone, nonexistent.

nowise: see NO.

noxious: see HARMFUL.

nozzle: see JET.

nuclear: see CENTRAL.

nucleus: see ATOM; HEART; MIDST.

nude *adj.* NAKED, BARE, uncovered, unclothed, exposed, undressed.

nudge *v.* PUSH, TAP, jostle, jab, prod, prompt, ENCOURAGE.
— *n.* shove, TAP, PUSH, POKE, prod, jog.

nuisance *n.* ANNOYANCE, bother, IRRITATION, PEST, pain in the neck.

null: see WORTHLESS.

numb *adj.* SENSELESS, unfeeling, SLEEPY, DULL, deadened, insensitive.
— *v.* deaden, DULL, stupefy, DRUG, STUN, PARALYZE.

number *n.* **1** *(quite a number)* AMOUNT, QUANTITY, SUM, TOTAL, COLLECTION; **2** *(an Arabic number)* numeral, FIGURE, digit; **3** *(don't miss her number)* SONG, SELECTION, ACT, PIECE, copy, ISSUE, ITEM, ARTICLE; **4** *(we count her among our number)* GROUP, CLASS, LOT, caste.
— *v.* ENUMERATE, numerate, COUNT, compute, RECKON, tally, total, ADD, CALCULATE, MARK, ESTIMATE, designate, INCLUDE.

numbered: see NUMERICAL.

numbness: see TINGLE.

numeral: see NUMBER; NUMERICAL.

numerate: see NUMBER.

numeric: see NUMERICAL.

numerical *adj.* numbered, numeral, numeric.

numerous *adj.* FREQUENT, countless, MANY, LARGE.

nunnery: see CONVENT.

nuptial: see BRIDAL.

nurse *n.* ATTENDANT, AIDE, sister, midwife, medic, ORDERLY, corpsman, wet nurse.
— *v.* TEND, care for, suckle, nurture, REAR, NOURISH, ENCOURAGE, FOSTER.

nursling: see INFANT.

nurture: see CHERISH; CULTIVATE; FEED; MOTHER; NOURISH; NURSE; RAISE; REAR.

nut *n.* **1** *(to eat nuts)* kernel, PIT; **2** *(nuts and bolts)* BLOCK, tightener; **3** *(a hard nut to crack)* PROBLEM, DIFFICULTY; **4** *(a camera nut)* enthusiast, fanatic, FOOL, madman.

nutriment: see NOURISHMENT.

nutrition: see DIET; NOURISHMENT.

nuzzle: see NESTLE; SNUGGLE.

O

oaf: see FOOL.

oath *n.* VOW, PROMISE, PLEDGE, CURSE, curseword, swearword.

obedience *n.* compliance, dutifulness, DUTY, submission, RESPECT, docility.

obedient *adj.* dutiful, respectful, yielding, submissive, well-behaved, meek, obliging, COOPERATIVE.

obelisk: see COLUMN.

obese: see FAT; PLUMP; STOUT.

obey *v.* comply, YIELD, SUBMIT, SERVE, FOLLOW, KEEP, OBSERVE.

object *v.* DISAPPROVE, PROTEST, COMPLAIN.
— *n.* **1** (*the object of her trip*) END, AIM, objective, REASON, GOAL, TARGET, MISSION, PURPOSE, DESIGN, MOTIVE, INTENTION; **2** (*two objects on the table*) THING, ARTICLE, MATTER, MATERIAL, SUBSTANCE, phenomenon.

objection *n.* DISAPPROVAL, PROTEST, COMPLAINT, EXCEPTION, dislike, DIFFICULTY, DOUBT, DISAGREEMENT.

objectionable: see UNSUITABLE.

objective: see AIM; DESTINATION; DIRECTION; OBJECT; SCIENTIFIC; TARGET.

obligate: see BIND; OWE.

obligation *n.* DUTY, RESPONSIBILITY, PROMISE, CONTRACT, AGREEMENT, VOW, REQUIREMENT, DEBT, TASK.

obligatory: see BINDING; NECESSARY.

oblige *v.* **1** (*obliged to work*) REQUIRE, COMPEL, FORCE, FIND, constrain; **2** (*much obliged*) PLEASE, GRATIFY, ACCOMMODATE, FAVOR, SERVE, ASSIST.

obliged: see THANKFUL.

obliging: see CIVIL; COOPERATIVE; OBEDIENT; WILLING.

oblique: see SIDE.

obliterate: see ABOLISH; CROSS OUT; DEMOLISH; ERASE.

oblivious: see FORGETFUL; SENSELESS.

obnoxious: see DISAGREEABLE; HATEFUL.

obscene: see FOUL; NAUGHTY; VULGAR.

obscure: see BLUR; CLOUD; CONCEAL; DIFFICULT; MUDDY; NAMELESS; SHADE; UNSEEN; VAGUE.

obscurity: see DARK; DARKNESS; DIMNESS; DULLNESS.

observable: see REMARKABLE; VISIBLE; VISUAL.

observance: see CEREMONIAL; CEREMONY; SERVICE.

observant *adj.* WATCHFUL, ATTENTIVE, vigilant, ALERT, KEEN, heedful, OBEDIENT.

observation *n.* SUPERVISION, EXAMINATION, awareness, NOTICE, COMMENT, MENTION, REMARK, OPINION.

observe *v.* **1** (*to observe carefully*) WATCH, SEE, NOTICE, look at, REGARD, WITNESS, perceive, scrutinize, INVESTIGATE; **2** (*to observe the speed limit*) HONOR, KEEP, CELEBRATE, OBEY, FOLLOW, ABIDE BY; **3** (*he observed frequently that the weather was warm*) SAY, COMMENT, MENTION, REMARK, NOTE.

observer *n.* watcher, commentator, spotter, listener, DELEGATE, SPECTATOR, WITNESS, onlooker.

obsession: see COMPLEX.

obsolete: see ANTIQUE; OLD; OLD-FASHIONED.

obstacle *n.* BARRIER, obstruction, hindrance, hurdle, DIFFICULTY, interference, BLOCK, BARRIER.

obstinate: see STUBBORN.

obstruct: see BARRICADE; BLOCK; CROSS; HEDGE; HINDER; OPPOSE; PLUG; STOP.

obstruction: see BAR; BARRIER; DAM; OBSTACLE; PREVENTION; WALL.

obtain *v.* GET, secure, ACQUIRE, GAIN, ACHIEVE, CAPTURE.

obtainable: see AVAILABLE.

obtainer: see RECEIVER.

obtrusive: see MEDDLESOME.

obtuse: see BLUNT; DULL.

obviate: see REMOVE.

obvious *adj.* EVIDENT, APPARENT, CLEAR, PLAIN, unmistakable, OPEN, unconcealed, CONSPICUOUS, striking, understandable, commonplace.

obviously: see APPARENTLY; DEFINITELY; EVIDENTLY; VISIBLY.

occasion *n.* AFFAIR, CIRCUMSTANCE, episode, CELEBRATION, OCCURRENCE, HAPPENING, TIME, OPPORTUNITY, CHANCE, EXCUSE.
— *v.*: see CAUSE.

occasional *adj.* infrequent, UNCOMMON, CASUAL, incidental, IRREGULAR, RANDOM.

occasionally: see SELDOM; SOMETIMES.

occult: see INVISIBLE; MAGICAL; MYSTERIOUS; SUPERSTITIOUS.

occupancy: see ENJOYMENT; OCCUPATION; POSSESSION.

occupant: see RESIDENT; TENANT.

occupation *n.* **1** *(her occupation was dentistry)* vocation, BUSINESS, calling, LINE, TRADE, PROFESSION, JOB, EMPLOYMENT; **2** *(the occupation of France by the Germans)* seizure, CONTROL, capture; **3** *(the occupation of an apartment)* occupancy, POSSESSION, tenancy.

occupational: see PROFESSIONAL.

occupied: see BUSY.

occupy *v.* **1** *(to occupy the house)* OWN, HOLD, POSSESS, INHABIT, USE; **2** *(to occupy one's mind)* busy, FILL, EMPLOY.

occur *v.* HAPPEN, take place, turn up, befall, result, APPEAR, SUGGEST.

occurrence *n.* EVENT, HAPPENING, CIRCUMSTANCE, INCIDENT, ACCIDENT, APPEARANCE, phenomenon, DEVELOPMENT, EXPERIENCE.

occurring: see ON.

ocean *n.* SEA, DEEP, main, brine, expanse, mare.

oceanic: see MARINE.

odd *adj.* **1** *(odd manners)* STRANGE, PECULIAR, UNUSUAL, UNCOMMON, QUEER, CURIOUS, QUAINT, EXTRAORDINARY, FUNNY, whimsical, outlandish, erratic, eccentric, freakish, grotesque, FANTASTIC, weird, ABNORMAL; **2** *(an odd number)* UNEVEN, unmatched, EXTRA, surplus, INDIVIDUAL, SINGLE.

oddball: see CHARACTER; GUY; ODDITY.

oddity *n.* eccentricity, PECULIARITY, quirk, strangeness, abnormality, oddball, monstrosity, rarity, FREAK.

oddly: see BACKWARD.

oddness: see PECULIARITY.

odds: see CHANCE.

ode: see POEM.

odium: see HATRED.

odor *n.* SCENT, FRAGRANCE, bouquet, PERFUME, SMELL, aroma, STINK, stench, reek, musk.

odorous: see FRAGRANT.

of *prep.* FROM, BY, CONCERNING, AMONG, containing, possessing, BEFORE, ON.

of course: see CERTAINLY; SURE; YES.

off *adv.* AWAY, FROM, OVER, done, against, NEAR, discontinued, COMPLETELY.
— *prep.* away from, BELOW, AGAINST, ALONG, opposite to, facing.
— *adj.* FARTHER, disconnected, completing, starting, AWAY, REMOTE, WRONG, CRAZY, SLOW.

offbeat: see NOVEL.

off-color: see SUGGESTIVE.

offend *v.* INSULT, slight, antagonize, snub, SHOCK, displease, IRRITATE, PROVOKE, nettle, ANNOY, outrage.

offended: see ANGRY; RESENTFUL; WOUNDED.

offender: see CRIMINAL; DELINQUENT.

offending: see DERELICT; GUILTY.

offense: see CRIME; EXCEPTION; HUMILIATION; INSULT; RESENTMENT; WRONG.

offensive: see AWFUL; DISAGREEABLE; FOUL; UNPLEASANT.

offer *v.* PRESENT, SUGGEST, PROPOSE, SACRIFICE, EXTEND, ADVANCE, SUBMIT, VOLUNTEER, GIVE.
— *n.* PROPOSAL, BID, SUGGESTION, advance, PRESENTATION, PROPOSITION, overture.

offering: see DONATION; PAYMENT; PRESENT; PRESENTATION; SACRIFICE.

offhand *adv.* spur-of-the-moment, extempore, casually, cavalierly.
— *adj.* CASUAL, easygoing, extemporaneous, impromptu, INFORMAL, unprepared, improvised, spontaneous.

office *n.* BUREAU, DEPARTMENT, AGENCY, POSITION, POST, SITUATION.

officer *n.* OFFICIAL, EXECUTIVE, LEADER, MANAGER, DIRECTOR, administrator, dignitary, GENERAL, CAPTAIN, major, policeman, cop, trooper, patrolman, sheriff.

officers: see POLICE.

official *n.* OFFICER, dignitary, EXECUTIVE, DIRECTOR, administrator, bureaucrat.
— *adj.* authorized, authoritative, administrative, red-tape, approved.

officials: see ADMINISTRATION.

officiate: see ACT; PRESIDE.

offish: see FRIENDLY.

off-key: see SOUR.

offset: see BALANCE; COMPENSATE.

offshoot: see BOUGH; BRANCH; OFFSPRING.

offspring *n*. descendants, children, ISSUE, PRODUCT, RESULT, offshoot, HEIR.

often *adv*. FREQUENTLY, recurrently, ofttimes, oftentimes, REGULARLY, USUALLY.

oftentimes: see OFTEN.

ofttimes: see OFTEN.

ogle: see STARE.

oil *n*. petroleum, lubricant, OINTMENT, GREASE, PAINTING.
   — *v*. GREASE, LUBRICATE, SMEAR, anoint.

oily *adj*. GREASY, SLICK, SMOOTH, glib, SLIPPERY.

oink: see GRUNT.

ointment *n*. OIL, balm, salve, LOTION, pomade, moisturizer.

OK: see SATISFACTORY; YES.

old *adj*. ANCIENT, AGED, elderly, ANTIQUE, time-honored, olden, FORMER, OLD-FASHIONED, unfashionable, out-of-date, antiquated, obsolete, decrepit, superannuated, aging, STALE, rancid, moth-eaten, RUSTY, threadbare, stock, overused, timeworn, USED, WORN, faded, RAGGED, broken-down.

olden: see ANCIENT; OLD.

older: see ELDER; SENIOR.

old-fashioned *adj*. UNFASHIONABLE, out-of-date, antiquated, superannuated, ANCIENT, OLD, aging, outmoded, overused, obsolete, outdated, unchanging.

oldster: see VETERAN.

oleaginous: see GREASY.

olive: see GREEN.

omen: see PREDICTION.

omission *n*. oversight, neglect, exclusion, disregard, negligence.

omit *v*. OVERLOOK, SKIP, EXCEPT, by-pass, exclude, leave out, pass over, disregard, NEGLECT, IGNORE.

omitting: see EXCEPT.

omniscient: see WISE.

on *prep*. covering, located, at, forming, ABOUT.
   — *adv*. FORWARD, FORTH, continuously, ONWARD, steady, attached.
   — *adj*. operating, occurring, performing, planned.

once *adv*. FORMERLY, aforetime, EVER, singly.
   — *conj*. whenever, whensoever.

oncoming *adj*. approaching, nearing, impending, forthcoming, anticipated, expected.

one *n*. UNIT, INDIVIDUAL, PERSON, HUMAN, ace, integer.
   — *pron*. ANYONE, SOMEONE.
   — *adj*. INDIVIDUAL, SINGLE, united, CERTAIN, SAME, COMMON, undivided, integrated, SOME, ANY.

oneness: see UNION; UNITY.

one-sided: see PARTIAL; UNFAIR; UNJUST.

onetime: see FORMER; THEN.

onion: see BULB.

onionskin: see PAPER; TISSUE.

onlooker: see OBSERVER; SPECTATOR.

only *adj*. SOLE, SOLITARY, SINGLE, ONE, ALONE, UNIQUE, SUPERIOR.
   — *adv*. exclusively, MERELY, singly, JUST, solely, BARELY, SIMPLY, BUT.

onset: see ASSAULT; ATTACK.

onslaught: see ASSAULT; ATTACK; SIEGE.

onto *prep*. ON, to, upon, aware of.

onward *adv*. FORWARD, AHEAD, ON.
   — *adj*. advancing, FORWARD, ADVANCED, improved, conducting.

oodles: see ABUNDANCE.

ooze: see BLEED; LEAK; MUD; PERSPIRE; SLIME; SWEAT; TRICKLE.

oozing: see RUNNING.

open *adj*. **1** *(an open door)* unclosed, unlocked, unbarred, exposed, uncovered, unhidden, unsealed, unfolded; **2** *(an open manner)* FRANK, candid, PLAIN, SINCERE, TRUTHFUL, HONEST, FAIR, FREE, EASY, ingenuous, aboveboard; **3** *(an open mind)* UNDECIDED, unprejudiced, receptive, GENEROUS; **4** *(an open meeting)* PUBLIC, FREE, unrestricted, accessible; **5** *(an open field)* VACANT, unfilled, unoccupied.
   — *v*. **1** *(to open the meeting)* BEGIN, START, COMMENCE; **2** *(to open the door)* unbar, unlock, CRACK, SPRING; **3** *(to open one's hand)* SPREAD,

EXTEND, EXPAND, REVEAL, EXPOSE, UNCOVER,
UNFOLD, DEVELOP; **4** *(to open a can)* puncture,
uncork, unseal, PIERCE.
— *n.* open air, OUTDOORS, OPENING, clearing,
CONTEST.

open air: see OPEN; OUTDOORS.

opener: see KEY.

openhanded: see GENEROUS; LIBERAL.

open-hearted *adj.* welcoming, FRIENDLY, OPEN,
HOSPITABLE, warm-hearted, HONEST, GENEROUS,
SINCERE.

opening *n.* **1** *(the opening of the music festival)*
debut, INTRODUCTION, START, BEGINNING; **2** *(an
opening in the wall)* BREAK, TEAR, CRACK.
— *adj.* beginning, starting, FIRST, INITIAL,
ORIGINAL, launching, introductory.

openly *adv.* publicly, candidly, frankly, plainly,
truthfully, SINCERELY, honestly.

open-minded: see PROGRESSIVE.

openness: see SIMPLICITY.

open up: see PIONEER.

opera: see MUSIC.

operate *v.* **1** *(to operate a machine)* RUN, DRIVE,
MANAGE, FUNCTION, WORK, USE, PERFORM,
INFLUENCE; **2** *(to operate on a patient)* cut open,
cut out, REMOVE, amputate.

operatic: see MUSICAL.

operating: see ON.

operation *n.* **1** *(no longer in operation)* USE,
working, PERFORMANCE, FUNCTION, ACTION,
handling, MANAGEMENT, SUPERVISION; **2** *(a
surgical operation)* surgery, KNIFE, incision.

operations: see CAMPAIGN.

operative: see EFFECTIVE; EFFICIENT; OPERATOR;
WORKER; WORKMAN.

operator *n.* DRIVER, mechanic, operative,
SPECIALIST, DIRECTOR.

operetta: see MUSICAL.

opinion *n.* VIEW, IDEA, NOTION, SENTIMENT,
ESTIMATE, IMPRESSION, JUDGMENT, BELIEF,
CONVICTION, CONCLUSION, viewpoint.

opinionated: see STUBBORN.

opponent *n.* adversary, COMPETITOR, RIVAL,
antagonist, contestant, FOE, ENEMY.

opportune: see APPROPRIATE.

opportunity *n.* CHANCE, OCCASION, TIME,
LEISURE, FREEDOM.

oppose *v.* RESIST, WITHSTAND, obstruct, thwart,
DEFY, COMBAT.

opposed: see CONTRARY; HOSTILE; OPPOSITE;
RELUCTANT.

opposing *adj.* OPPOSITE, antagonistic, resisting,
hindering, conflicting, contradicting,
counteracting.

opposite *adj.* CONTRARY, opposed, DIFFERENT,
contradictory, REVERSE, facing, OPPOSING.
— *n.* contrary, REVERSE, converse, antonym.

opposite to: see ACROSS; AGAINST; OFF.

opposition *n.* RESISTANCE, counteraction,
OBJECTION, antagonism, COMPETITION, ENEMY,
adversary, contestant, FOE, antagonist.

oppress: see GRIND; PERSECUTE; WRONG.

oppression: see ABUSE; PERSECUTION.

oppressive: see MUGGY.

oppressor: see TYRANT.

opt: see CHOOSE.

optic: see VISUAL.

optimism *n.* hopefulness, CONFIDENCE, HOPE,
buoyancy, assurance.

optimistic: see HOPEFUL; SUNNY.

option: see CHOICE; PREFERENCE; VOICE.

optional: see VOLUNTARY.

opulence: see WEALTH.

oracle: see PROPHET.

oracular: see WISE.

oral *adj.* vocal, spoken, said, uttered, told,
VERBAL, sounded, voiced, vocalized, articulated.

oration: see ADDRESS; PRESENTATION; SPEECH;
TALK.

orator *n.* speaker, LECTURER, spellbinder.

orbit *n.* CIRCUIT, REVOLUTION, PATH, COURSE,
cycle, CIRCLE, scope, realm, locus.
— *v.* CIRCLE, TRAVEL, FOLLOW, REVOLVE.

orchard: see GROVE.

orchestra: see BAND.

orchestrate: see ARRANGE; HARMONIZE.

orchestration: see ARRANGEMENT; SCORE.

ordain: see LEGISLATE.

ordeal: see EXPERIENCE; NIGHTMARE; SESSION;
TEST; TRIAL.

order *n.* **1** (*in good order*) SYSTEM, ARRANGEMENT, CLASSIFICATION, SEQUENCE, NEATNESS, PATTERN, DISPOSITION; **2** (*to give an order*) COMMAND, INSTRUCTION, REQUEST, REQUIREMENT, DIRECTION, directive, REGULATION, CONTRACT, requisition; **3** (*to receive the invoice of an order*) GOODS, MERCHANDISE, shipment, PURCHASE; **4** (*the Order of the Garter*) SOCIETY, ASSOCIATION, BADGE, sorority, fraternity, sisterhood, BROTHERHOOD, RANK, GRADE, HONOR, AWARD. — *v.* COMMAND, DIRECT, MANAGE, REGULATE, RESERVE, REQUEST, ARRANGE, BUY.

orderliness: see NEATNESS; SYSTEM.

orderly *adj.* methodical, EFFICIENT, REGULAR, SYSTEMATIC, TRIM, NEAT, shipshape, PEACEABLE, law-abiding, disciplined, well-behaved. — *adv.* PROPERLY, methodically, SYSTEMATICALLY. — *n.* AIDE, ATTENDANT, MESSENGER, NURSE.

ordinance: see LAW; REGULATION.

ordinarily *adv.* USUALLY, habitually, normally, REGULARLY.

ordinary *adj.* USUAL, HABITUAL, NORMAL, REGULAR, CUSTOMARY, COMMON, AVERAGE, MEDIOCRE, workaday, commonplace, EVERYDAY, undistinguished.

ore *n.* MINERAL, ROCK, VEIN, lode.

organ *n.* INSTRUMENT, MEDIUM, MEANS, PART, VOICE.

organic *adj.* LIVING, BODILY, biotic, VITAL, FUNDAMENTAL, constitutional.

organization *n.* **1** (*Organization of American States*) ASSOCIATION, SOCIETY, ESTABLISHMENT, COMPANY, BUSINESS, federation, GROUP, LEAGUE, syndicate; **2** (*faulty organization*) planning, ARRANGEMENT, DISPOSITION, grouping, STRUCTURE, constitution, PLAN, formulation, makeup, CHARACTER.

organize *v.* ESTABLISH, FOUND, constitute, FORM, set up, ARRANGE, ORDER, COMPOSE, coordinate, SHAPE, systematize.

organized: see SYSTEMATIC.

origin *n.* BEGINNING, SOURCE, GERM, derivation, ROOT, RISE, START, BIRTH, CAUSE, PARENTAGE, commencement, OCCASION.

original *adj.* FIRST, EARLY, prime, beginning, PRIMARY, PRIMITIVE, FRESH, NOVEL, creative, imaginative, INVENTIVE, DIFFERENT, UNIQUE. — *n.* WORK, PAINTING, MANUSCRIPT, MODEL, CREATION.

originality *n.* newness, NOVELTY, uniqueness, FRESHNESS, inventiveness, creativeness, IMAGINATION.

originally *adv.* PRIMARILY, preliminarily, firstly, distinctively.

originate *v.* START, BEGIN, ARISE, SPRING, stem, father, GENERATE, CREATE, INVENT.

origination: see CREATION.

originator: see ARCHITECT; AUTHOR.

ornament *n.* decoration, adornment, enrichment. — *v.* DECORATE, ADORN, ENRICH, BEAUTIFY.

ornamental: see DECORATIVE.

ornamented: see ELABORATE.

ornate: see DECORATIVE; ELABORATE.

ornery: see MEAN.

orphanage: see HOME.

orthodox: see STANDARD.

oscillate: see BEAT; SWING.

oscillation: see RIPPLE; SWING; VIBRATION.

ossify: see FREEZE.

ostensible: see APPARENT.

ostentation: see PARADE; SHOW.

ostentatious: see VAIN.

ostracism: see EXILE.

ostracize: see BANISH.

other *adj.* DIFFERENT, ADDITIONAL, MORE, remaining, FORMER. — *pron.* other one, SOMETHING, others. — *adv.* OTHERWISE, differently.

other one: see OTHER.

others: see OTHER.

otherwise *adv.* differently, POSSIBLY, OTHER. — *adj.* DIFFERENT, OTHER, SPECIAL.

otherworldly: see SPIRITUAL.

ought *v.* should, MUST, have to.

ought to: see MUST.

ounce *n.* TRIFLE, SPECK, BIT.

oust: see DISCARD; EXPEL.

out *adv.* OUTSIDE, ABROAD, AWAY, FORTH, loudly, FINALLY, IDLE, disclosed, extended, blotted, COMPLETELY. — *adj.* ABSENT, AWAY, MISTAKEN, losing, UNCONSCIOUS, retired, ended, extinguished, unfashionable.

out-and-out: see UTTER.

outbreak *n.* BURST, ERUPTION, outburst, DISTURBANCE, RIOT, REBELLION, uprising, PROTEST.

outburst: see ERUPTION; FLASH; GUST; OUTBREAK; SCENE; TORRENT.

outcast: see OUTLAW.

outclass: see SURPASS.

outcome *n.* RESULT, aftermath, CONSEQUENCE, EFFECT, ISSUE, upshot, END.

outcry *n.* CRY, HOWL, YELL, ROAR, CLAMOR, SCREAM, SCREECH.

outdated: see OLD-FASHIONED.

outdo *v.* SURPASS, outshine, excel, BEAT, DEFEAT, outstrip, EXCEED.

outdoors *n.* OUTSIDE, open air, OPEN.

outer *adj.* OUTSIDE, exterior, EXTERNAL, FARTHER.

outermost: see EXTERNAL.

outfit *n.* EQUIPMENT, gear, kit, supplies, rig, rigging, TACKLE, CLOTHING, COSTUME, WARDROBE, get-up, garb.
− *v.* EQUIP, SUPPLY, FURNISH, PROVIDE.

outflow: see DRAIN.

outgoing: see HOSPITABLE.

outgrowth: see RESULT.

outing: see DRIVE; EXPEDITION.

outlander: see STRANGER.

outlandish: see ODD.

outlast: see ENDURE; SURVIVE.

outlaw *n.* bandit, CRIMINAL, highwayman, fugitive, outcast.
− *v.*: see EXILE; FORBID.

outlawed: see FORBIDDEN.

outlay: see EXPENDITURE.

outlet *n.* **1** (*an outlet to the hall*) BREAK, CRACK, TEAR, OPENING, HOLE, EXIT, vent; **2** (*an electric outlet*) socket, PLUG, CONNECTION, terminal.

outline *n.* PLAN, SKETCH, DRAFT, diagram, contour, PROFILE, FEATURE, silhouette, BORDER, EDGE, FRAME.
− *v.* DESCRIBE, SUMMARIZE, DRAFT, PLAN, SHAPE, SKETCH, diagram, DRAW.

outlive: see SURVIVE.

outlook *n.* PROSPECT, forecast, FUTURE, VIEW, PICTURE, perspective, OPPORTUNITY, viewpoint, speculation.

outmaneuver: see OUTWIT.

outmoded: see OLD-FASHIONED.

out of: see OUTSIDE; WITHOUT.

out-of-date: see OLD; OLD-FASHIONED.

out-of-the-way: see REMOTE.

outplay: see DEFEAT.

outpost: see COLONY.

outpouring: see FLOOD.

output *n.* PRODUCTION, YIELD, PRODUCTIVITY, HARVEST, POWER, amperage.

outrage: see INSULT; JAR; OFFEND.

outrageous: see DISGRACEFUL; TREMENDOUS.

outrank: see EXCEED; RANK.

outright: see ALTOGETHER; TOTAL.

outset: see BEGINNING; BIRTH; DAWN; START.

outshine: see OUTDO.

outside *n.* exterior, SURFACE, COVERING, LIMIT, bounds, UTMOST, OUTDOORS.
− *adv.* externally, OUTDOORS.
− *prep.* BEYOND, excepting, out of.
− *adj.* OUTER, REMOTE, MAXIMUM, improbable, exterior, EXTERNAL, OUTWARD, superficial.

outside of: see WITHOUT.

outsider: see FOREIGNER; STRANGER.

outsmart: see TRICK.

outspoken: see FRANK.

outstanding *adj.* **1** (*an outstanding teacher*) REMARKABLE, IMPORTANT, WONDERFUL, LEADING, WELL-KNOWN, FAMOUS, PROMINENT, CONSPICUOUS, striking, momentous;
2 (*outstanding debts*) unpaid, OWING, unsettled, overdue, DUE.

outstandingly: see ESPECIALLY.

outstretched: see LONG.

outstrip: see EXCEED; OUTDO.

outward *adj.* EXTERNAL, OUTER, VISIBLE, superficial.

outwit *v.* TRICK, BAFFLE, DECEIVE, CHEAT, dupe, best, worst, gull, outmaneuver, FOIL.

outworn: see USELESS.

ovation: see APPLAUSE.

oven *n.* bakery, FURNACE, STOVE, kiln.

over *prep.* ABOVE, ACROSS, THROUGH,

THROUGHOUT, DURING, upon, CONCERNING, covering.
— *adv.* AGAIN, BESIDES, anew, ABOVE, ACROSS, BEYOND, UPSET.
— *adj.* finished, settled, concluded, LEFT, remaining.

overabundance: see EXCESS.

overabundant: see EXCESSIVE.

overact: see OVERDO.

overage: see EXCESS.

overall *adj.* WHOLE, ENTIRE, COMPLETE, undivided, TOTAL, comprehensive, GENERAL.

overalls *pl.n.* coveralls, dungarees.

overarch: see ARCH.

overarched: see ARCHED.

overawe: see IMPRESS.

overcast: see CLOUDY; HAZY.

overcoat: see COAT.

overcome *v.* OVERWHELM, subdue, CONQUER, DEFEAT, STUN, surmount.

overdo *v.* EXAGGERATE, overact, EXCEED, MAGNIFY, SURPASS, ENLARGE, STRETCH, overplay, EXHAUST.

overdoing: see EXCESS.

overdue: see BEHIND; LATE; OUTSTANDING; SLOW; TARDY.

overestimate: see EXAGGERATE.

overestimation: see EXAGGERATION.

overflow *v.* overrun, deluge, runover, FLOOD, FLOW.
— *n.*: see EXCESS; FLOOD.

overhaul: see REPAIR.

overhead: see ABOVE; UPWARD.

overindulge: see BABY.

overjoyed: see JOYFUL.

overlap: see FOLD; LAP.

overlay: see COATING.

overlook *v.* disregard, MISS, NEGLECT, IGNORE. See also TOWER.

overlooked: see FORGOTTEN.

overly: see TOO.

overmaster: see DEFEAT.

overnice: see FUSSY.

overpass: see BRIDGE.

overplay: see OVERDO.

overpower *v.* OVERCOME, OVERTHROW, OVERWHELM, BEAT, CRUSH, DEFEAT, CONQUER.

overpowering: see DAZZLING; IRRESISTIBLE; STUNNING.

overreact: see PANIC.

overrule *v.* contradict, REJECT, REVOKE, repeal, VETO.

overrun: see INVADE; OVERFLOW; RAID.

overseas: see ABROAD.

oversee: see BOSS; MONITOR; SUPERVISE; TEND; WATCH.

overseer: see DIRECTOR; FOREMAN; MANAGER; MASTER; SUPERINTENDENT; SUPERVISOR; WARDEN.

overshadow: see CLOUD; DWARF; SHADE; SHADOW.

overshadowing: see MAJOR.

overshoe: see BOOT.

oversight: see BLUNDER; OMISSION.

overspread: see ENVELOP.

overstate: see EXAGGERATE.

overstatement: see EXAGGERATION.

overstep: see TRESPASS.

oversupply: see FLOOD.

overtake: see CATCH.

overtax: see STRAIN.

overthrow *v.* OVERPOWER, OVERCOME, overturn, DEFEAT, DESTROY, CONQUER, UPSET.
— *n.* DEFEAT, DESTRUCTION, REMOVAL, unseating.

overthrown: see BEATEN; FALLEN.

overtone: see SUGGESTION.

overture: see OFFER.

overturn: see OVERTHROW; UPSET.

overused: see OLD; OLD-FASHIONED.

overweight: see STOUT.

overwhelm *v.* OVERCOME, OVERPOWER, CONQUER, rout, astound.

overwhelmed: see PANICKY.

overwhelming: see IRRESISTIBLE; OVERWHELMING; TEMPTING.

overwork: see CHORE.

overworked: see TIRED.

owe *v.* incur, CONTRACT, PROMISE, PLEDGE, obligate, BORROW.

owed: see DUE.

owing *adj.* unpaid, payable, OUTSTANDING, DUE, matured.

owing to: see BECAUSE.

own *v.* POSSESS, OCCUPY, HOLD, HAVE, CONTAIN. See also ADMIT.
— *adj.*: see PERSONAL.

owner *n.* PROPRIETOR, holder, possessor.

ownership: see INTEREST; POSSESSION; RIGHT; TITLE.

own up: see CONFESS.

oxford: see SHOE.

oxidation: see RUST.

oxidized: see RUSTY.

oxygen: see GAS.

P

pace *n.* STEP, gait, FOOTSTEP, RATE, tempo.
— *v.* step, WALK, TREAD, MARCH, STRIDE, GO, ROAM.

pacific: see PEACEABLE.

pacify: see CALM; SOOTHE.

pack *n.* **1** (*the pack on his back*) BUNDLE, LOAD, BURDEN, backpack, PACKAGE; **2** (*the wolf pack*) BAND, GANG, drove, HERD, GROUP, carton; **3** (*a pack of cards*) deck, SET, cards.
— *v.* LOAD, stow, FILL, put in, CARRY, WEAR, CROWD, cram, PRESS, package, BUNDLE.

package *n.* PARCEL, packet, BOX, PACK, BUNDLE.
— *v.*: see PACK.

packed: see CHOCK-FULL; LOADED; THICK.

packet: see BALE; KIT; PACKAGE; PARCEL.

pack in: see JAM.

pact: see AGREEMENT; ALLIANCE; ARRANGEMENT; COMPACT; CONTRACT; DEAL; TREATY.

pad *n.* **1** (*a soft pad*) CUSHION, wadding, stuffing, filling, rubber, MAT, bedpad; **2** (*a writing pad*) TABLET, BLOCK, PAPER, notebook, quire, ream; **3** (*a launching pad*) platform, BASE, strip; **4** (*a roomy pad*) ROOM, DEN, APARTMENT, HOME, BED.
— *v.* STUFF, FILL, ADD, INCREASE.

padding *n.* filling, stuffing, fill, filler.

paddle: see RACKET; SPANK; SWIM.

paddock: see PEN.

padlock: see LOCK.

page *n.* **1** (*to turn the page*) PAPER, LEAF, SHEET, signature; **2** (*the message brought by the page*) page boy, MESSENGER, bellboy, ATTENDANT, SERVANT, squire, errand boy.
— *v.* CALL, SUMMON, leaf, NUMBER.

pageant: see PROCESSION; SHOW; SPECTACLE; SPLENDOR.

pageantry: see PARADE.

pageboy: see PAGE.

pagoda: see TEMPLE.

pail *n.* BUCKET, POT, tub, CONTAINER, holder, receptacle.

pain *n.* SUFFERING, hurt, AGONY, ACHE, DISTRESS, smart, STING, anguish, pang, affliction.
— *v.*: see ACHE; AIL; BITE; HURT; SMART; WOUND.

pained: see WOUNDED.

painful *adj.* hurting, aching, agonizing, SORE, TENDER, distressing, DIFFICULT.

pain in the neck: see NUISANCE.

painkiller: see DRUG.

painless *adj.* unpainful, COMFORTABLE, EASY; HARMLESS.

painstaking: see PARTICULAR; THOROUGH.

paint *n.* COLOR, pigment, OIL, STAIN, VARNISH, enamel, rouge, cosmetic.
— *v.* COLOR, COAT, COVER, STAIN, VARNISH, enamel, daub, DRAW, portray, DESIGN, depict, DESCRIBE, DECORATE.

painter: see ARTIST.

painting *n.* CANVAS, OIL, PICTURE, DRAWING, coloring, DESIGN, ILLUSTRATION, ART, BEAUTIFY.

paintings: see ART.

pair *n.* TWO, COUPLE, brace, TEAM, MATCH, partners, mates.
— *v.* COUPLE, MATCH, DOUBLE.

paired: see TWIN.

pair off: see AVERAGE.

pal *n.* CHUM, crony, COMRADE, COMPANION, FRIEND.

palace *n.* MANSION, CASTLE, chateau, RESIDENCE, HOUSE, BUILDING.

palatable: see APPETIZING.

pale *adj.* whitish, LIGHT, colorless, DIM, wan, FEEBLE, ashen, bloodless, haggard, ghastly.
   — *v.*: see FADE; WHITEN.

paling: see FENCE.

palisade: see CLIFF.

pall: see CLOUD.

pallet: see LITTER.

palliate: see SOFTEN.

palm: see HAND.

palpitate: see THROB.

palsy walsy: see CHUMMY.

paltry: see MINOR, PETTY; TRASHY.

pampas: see PLAIN.

pamper: see BABY.

pamphlet *n.* brochure, leaflet, booklet, TRACT, treatise, ESSAY.

pan *n.* saucepan, DISH, PLATE, TRAY, VESSEL, receptacle.
   — *v.* **1** *(to pan gold)* STRAIN, WASH, SETTLE, SORT; **2** *(the critics panned the play)* RIDICULE, CRITICIZE; **3** *(to pan for a wide landscape shot)* SWING, TURN.

panache: see DASH; FIRE.

pandemonium: see LOUDNESS.

pane *n.* SHEET, PANEL, GLASS, window, SIDE, FRAME.

panel *n.* **1** *(made up of panels)* paneling, PANE, SECTION, PIECE, insert, inset, divider, WALL, partition, DIVISION, STRIP, CLOTH, switchboard; **2** *(a panel on TV)* round table, DISCUSSION, GROUP; **3** *(the panel of jurors)* LIST, SELECTION, jurors, judges, advisers, COMMISSION, COMMITTEE.

paneling: see PANEL.

pang: see PAIN; WRENCH.

panhandle: see BIG; BUM.

panhandler: see BEGGAR.

panic *n.* ALARM, FRIGHT, FEAR, hysteria, DREAD, TERROR, stampede, RUSH, CRASH.
   — *v.* ALARM, FRIGHTEN, TERRIFY, stampede, overreact.

panicky *adj.* alarmed, frightened, FEARFUL, hysterical, terrified, panic-stricken, AFRAID, overwhelmed.

panic-stricken: see PANICKY.

pannier: see BASKET.

panorama: see LANDSCAPE; VIEW.

pant *v.* GASP, wheeze, PUFF, whiff, huff, BREATHE, THROB.
   — *n.*: see PUFF.

pantheon: see CHURCH; TEMPLE.

panting: see BREATHLESS; GASP.

pantry: see CABINET; CLOSET.

pap: see PULP.

papa: see DADDY; FATHER.

paper *n.* stationery, SHEET, PIECE, PAGE, LEAF, parchment, onionskin, TISSUE, foolscap, PAD, TABLET, REPORT, ESSAY, ARTICLE, dissertation, thesis, WRITING, DOCUMENT, CERTIFICATE, bills, bank notes, NEWSPAPER, JOURNAL, wallpaper.

paper clip: see CLIP.

par: see AVERAGE.

parable: see FABLE.

parachute: see JUMP.

parade *n.* PROCESSION, review, MARCH, LINE, FILE, motorcade, DISPLAY, pageantry, pomp, SHOW, ostentation.
   — *v.* MARCH, FILE, PASS, FORM, DISPLAY, flaunt, show off.

paradise *n.* HEAVEN, utopia, BLISS.

paradox: see RIDDLE.

paragraph *n.* ITEM, SECTION, ARTICLE, DIVISION, WRITING, DISCUSSION, passage.

parallel *adj.* corresponding, equidistant, LIKE, SIMILAR, resembling.
   — *n.* COMPARISON, counterpart, CORRESPONDENCE, likeness, SIMILARITY, conformity, RESEMBLANCE, longitude.
   — *v.*: see RESEMBLE.

parallelogram: see DIAMOND.

paralyze *v.* CRIPPLE, disable, STOP, deaden, NUMB, WEAKEN, handicap.

paramount: see BEST; CHIEF; SUPERIOR.

paranoid: see MISFIT.

parasite: see MOLD; SATELLITE.

parcel *n.* PACKAGE, packet, BUNDLE, PART, SHARE, DIVISION, SECTION, LOT, PLOT, PROPERTY.
   — *v.* DIVIDE, apportion.

parch: see DRY; SCORCH; WITHER.

parched: see DRY.

parchment: see MANUSCRIPT; PAPER.

pardon *n.* FORGIVENESS, amnesty, acquittal, GRACE, MERCY, remission, exoneration, release, indulgence.
— *v.* FORGIVE, acquit, exonerate, RELEASE, condone, EXCUSE, FREE, OVERLOOK.

pardonable: see EXCUSABLE.

pare: see PEEL; SHAVE; SKIN; TRIM.

parent *n.* FATHER, sire, MOTHER, ANCESTOR, GUARDIAN, AUTHOR, ORIGIN, SOURCE, producer, creator.

parentage *n.* lineage, extraction, DESCENT, ancestry, pedigree, stock, FAMILY.

parental *adj.* FATHERLY, MOTHERLY, paternal, maternal, TENDER, caring, PROTECTIVE.

parents: see KIN.

parish: see CHURCH.

park: see GARDEN; SQUARE.

parkway: see HIGHWAY.

parley: see CONFERENCE; CONVERSATION.

parlor *n.* living room, salon, LOUNGE, HALL, anteroom.

parrot: see RECITE.

parson: see PASTOR.

part *n.* SHARE, SECTION, PIECE, ITEM, DETAIL, component, ELEMENT, PORTION, SIDE, PARTY, FRACTION, FRAGMENT, PARTICLE, FUNCTION, CONCERN, INTEREST, RESPONSIBILITY, CHARACTER, ROLE, DUTY, participation, UNIT, MELODY.
— *v.* DIVIDE, SEPARATE, SPLIT, DETACH, REMOVE, disjoin, sever, allot, apportion, DISCONNECT, LEAVE, QUIT, DEPART, GO.
— *adj.* PARTIAL, INCOMPLETE, fragmentary, fractional, bipartite.
— *adv.* PARTLY, partially, incomplete.

partake *v.* savor, SAMPLE, SIP, SHARE, CONTRIBUTE, PARTICIPATE, ATTEND.

partial *adj.* **1** (*a partial rundown*) INCOMPLETE, unfinished, fragmentary, fractional, sectional; **2** (*a partial witness*) prejudiced, biased, one-sided, partisan, UNFAIR, UNJUST, FOND, disposed.

partiality: see LIKE; PREFERENCE.

partially: see PART; PARTLY; SOMEWHAT.

participant: see ACTOR; PARTNER.

participate *v.* SHARE, take part, PARTAKE, COOPERATE.

participation: see ATTENDANCE; COOPERATION; HAND, INTEREST; PART; PARTNERSHIP; REPRESENTATION.

particle *n.* BIT, SPECK, SCRAP, ATOM, mite, MOLECULE, GRAIN, SPOT, CRUMB, SHRED, jot, iota.

particles: see DUST; POWDER.

particular *adj.* **1** (*a particular subject*) SPECIAL, DISTINCT, APPROPRIATE, UNUSUAL, SINGULAR, PECULIAR, NOTABLE, exclusive; **2** (*my editor is very particular*) exacting, STRICT, CHOOSY, fastidious, FUSSY, EXACT, PRECISE, painstaking, finicky, CRITICAL.
— *n.* ITEM, DETAIL, ASPECT, instance, SUBJECT, INDIVIDUAL, SIDE.

particularize: see DETAIL; ITEMIZE; SPECIFY.

particularly *adv.* ESPECIALLY, specially, PRINCIPALLY, notably, specifically, EXACTLY, PRECISELY.

parting *adj.* separating, departing, dividing, declining, breaking.
— *n.* leave-taking, leaving, FAREWELL, EXIT, DEPARTURE, withdrawal, DEATH.

partisan: see CHAMPION; FOLLOWER; PARTIAL.

partition: see DIVISION; PANEL; SCREEN.

partly *adv.* partially, incompletely.

partner *n.* ASSOCIATE, coowner, co-worker, colleague, COMPANION, ally, participant, MATE, spouse, dancer.

partners: see PAIR; PARTNERSHIP.

partnership *n.* partners, ASSOCIATION, associates, BUSINESS, FIRM, UNION, participation, PROFESSION.

parturition: see DELIVERY.

party *n.* **1** (*a wild party*) CELEBRATION, AFFAIR, FESTIVITY, GATHERING, dance; **2** (*the communist party*) ORGANIZATION, faction, GROUP, BAND, sect, CIRCLE, FORCE, CAUSE, SIDE, politicians, plaintiff, defendant, INTEREST; **3** (*your party is on the phone*) PERSON, INDIVIDUAL, speaker, SOMEBODY, SOMEONE.
— *v.*: see CELEBRATE.

partygoer: see GUEST.

pass *n.* **1** (*a mountain pass*) defile, GAP, gorge, ravine, BREAK; **2** (*a press pass*) ADMISSION, TICKET, PERMIT, safe-conduct, PASSPORT, credentials, LEAVE; **3** (*a long pass to the left*) THROW, TOSS, TRANSFER, THRUST, lunge.
— *v.* GO, PROCEED, MOVE, go by, ADVANCE,

THROW, CONTINUE, CIRCULATE, HAPPEN, EXCEED, SURPASS, enact, SPEND, DISCHARGE. See also DELIVER; REACH.

passable *adj.* SUFFICIENT, acceptable, ADEQUATE, ALLOWABLE, admissible, moderate, RESPECTABLE, TOLERABLE, mediocre.

passage *n.* **1** *(a narrow passage)* passageway, CHANNEL, PATH, WAY, GAP, VOYAGE, movement, ENTRY, CORRIDOR, HALL, going; **2** *(the passage of the bill)* enactment, APPROVAL, PERMISSION, passing; **3** *(the passage of time)* lapse, expiration, DEPARTURE, DEATH. See also PARAGRAPH.

passageway: see AISLE; ALLEY; CORRIDOR; GALLERY; PASSAGE; PATH; TUNNEL.

pass away: see DIE; PERISH.

passenger *n.* voyager, rider, TRAVELER, wayfarer, COMPANION.

passing: see DEATH; MOMENTARY; MORTAL; PASSAGE; TEMPORARY.

passion *n.* EMOTION, FEELING, EXCITEMENT, RAGE, ANGER, craze, APPETITE, FANCY, DESIRE, LUST, LOVE, hate, FLAME, HEAT, FIRE, SEX, upheaval, ENTHUSIASM, AFFECTION, vehemence, fad.

passionate *adj.* EMOTIONAL, demonstrative, sexy, amorous, lustful, sensual, loving, vehement, EARNEST, SINCERE.

passive: see LIFELESS.

pass on: see DIE; EXPIRE.

pass over: see OMIT.

passport *n.* PASS, PERMIT, PERMISSION, visa, safe-conduct, authorization, authentication, credentials, DOCUMENT, OPPORTUNITY, WAY, ADMISSION.

password: see WORD.

past *adj.* FORMER, PREVIOUS, finished, OVER, done, earlier, PRIOR, gone, bygone, LATTER.
— *n.* HISTORY, antiquity, annals, yesterday, yesteryear, yore, lang syne, experiences.
— *adv.* BY, BEYOND, FORMERLY.
— *prep.* BEYOND, AFTER, ABOVE, exceeding.

paste *n.* GLUE, CEMENT, mucilage, GUM, ADHESIVE.
— *v.* GLUE, cement, STICK, ATTACH, COVER, MEND.

pasteboard: see CARD.

pastime: see AMUSEMENT; GAME; HOBBY; SPORT.

pastor *n.* MINISTER, PRIEST, reverend, parson, clergyman, churchman, ecclesiastic.

pastry *n.* CRUST, pies, tarts, DESSERT.

pasturage: see PASTURE.

pasture *n.* pasturage, grassland, MEADOW, FIELD.
— *v.*: see GRAZE.

pat *n.* TAP, RAP, STROKE, PIECE, morsel, LUMP.
— *v.* TAP, RAP, STRIKE, TOUCH, SHAPE.
— *adj.* APT, FITTING, pertinent, glib.
— *adv.* perfectly, COMPLETELY, conveniently, advantageously.

patch *n.* PLOT, PARCEL, STRIP, PIECE, mending.
— *v.* REPAIR, MEND, darn, SEW, SETTLE, reinforce.

patent *n.* PERMIT, PROTECTION, copyright, RIGHT, PRIVILEGE, PROPERTY.

patently: see CLEARLY.

paternal: see FATHERLY; PARENTAL, PROTECTIVE.

path *n.* pathway, passageway, LANE, TRACK, FOOTPATH, WALK, WAY, ROAD, PASS, COURSE, ROUTE, DIRECTION.

pathetic: see MISERABLE; PITIFUL; WRETCHED.

pathfinder: see PIONEER.

pathway: see AISLE; FOOTPATH; PATH.

patience *n.* endurance, perseverance, CALMNESS, quietness, fortitude, forbearance, peacefulness.

patient *adj.* uncomplaining, persevering, CALM, QUIET, forebearing, long-suffering.
— *n.* invalid, shut-in, inmate, sufferer, CASE, SUBJECT.

patio: see COURT; PORCH.

patriarch: see SENIOR.

patrician: see ARISTOCRAT.

patrol *v.* POLICE, WATCH, GUARD, SCOUT, INSPECT.
— *n.* POLICE, WATCH, GUARD, lookout, spotter, PROTECTION.

patrolman: see OFFICER.

patrolmen: see POLICE.

patron *n.* CUSTOMER, CLIENT, purchaser, buyer, SUPPORTER, CHAMPION, backer, donor.

patronize: see BEFRIEND; TRADE.

patronymic: see NAME.

pattern *n.* MODEL, STANDARD, DESIGN, EXAMPLE, METHOD, SHAPE, STYLE, MOLD, IMPRESSION.
— *v.* MODEL, DESIGN, fashion, SHAPE, style, IMITATE, COPY, MOLD.

paunch: see BELLY.

paunchy: see CHUBBY.

pauper: see BEGGAR.

pauperism: see POVERTY.

pause *n.* STOP, REST, DELAY, STAY, lull,
SUSPENSION, interlude, intermission.
— *v.* STOP, REST, WAIT, HESITATE, HALT, CEASE,
DELAY, STAY.

pave *v.* surface, SMOOTH, PREPARE.

pavement: see CURB; FLOOR.

pavilion *n.* platform, canopy, TENT, STAND,
SHELTER, wing, BUILDING.

paving: see CEMENT.

paw *n.* FOOT, PAD, CLAW.
— *v.* SCRAPE, RUB, HANDLE, TOUCH.

pawn *v.* hock, PLEDGE, DEPOSIT, stake, wager,
BET.
— *n.* flunky, stooge, INSTRUMENT.

pay *v.* COMPENSATE, recompense, remit,
DISCHARGE, SETTLE, defray, GIVE, MAKE, TIP,
REWARD.
— *n.*: see EARNINGS; FEE; SALARY; WAGES,
compensation.

payable: see DUE; OWING.

payment *n.* compensation, recompense, offering,
OFFER, TIP, SETTLEMENT, REWARD, FEE, SALARY,
SATISFACTION, defrayment.

peace *n.* CONCORD, quiet, CALM, TRANQUILLITY,
REST, ORDER, TRUCE, ARMISTICE, amity,
FRIENDSHIP, AGREEMENT.

peaceable *adj.* PEACEFUL, pacific, CALM, QUIET,
ORDERLY, TRANQUIL, GENTLE, MILD, FRIENDLY,
diplomatic.

peaceful *adj.* PEACEABLE, FRIENDLY, COOPERATIVE,
NEUTRAL, untroubled, undisturbed, amicable,
placid, serene, CALM, QUIET, TRANQUIL,
stormless.

peacefulness: see PATIENCE.

peach: see DOLL.

peacock: see COCK.

peak *n.* TOP, POINT, SUMMIT, apex, CROWN, CREST,
pinnacle, MAXIMUM.

peal: see CACKLE: RESOUND; RING; STRIKE; STROKE.

pearl *n.* GEM, JEWEL, BEAD, mother-of-pearl,
TREASURE.

peasant *n.* FARMER, WORKER, commoner, rustic.

peat: see FUEL.

pebble *n.* STONE, ROCK, GRAVEL, pellet.

pebbles: see GRAVEL; GRIT.

peck *v.* STRIKE, POKE, jab, TAP, nibble, PAT, KISS.
— *n.*: see KISS.

peculiar *adj.* ODD, STRANGE, QUEER, eccentric,
CURIOUS, SINGULAR, UNUSUAL.

peculiarity *n.* eccentricity, oddness, ODDITY,
curiousness.

peddle *v.* SELL, vend, retail, canvass, solicit,
DISTRIBUTE.

peddler *n.* vender, seller, hawker, huckster,
salesman.

pedestal: see FOOT; MOUNT; POST.

pedicle: see STALK; STEM.

pedigree: see PARENTAGE.

peek: see GLANCE; GLIMPSE; PEEP; PEER.

peel *v.* STRIP, pare, UNCOVER, take off, come off.
— *n.*: see FLAKE.

peep *v.* **1** *(to peep through the hole)* peek, PEER,
GLANCE, GLIMPSE, LOOK; **2** *(the chicks were
peeping)* CHIRP, cheep, squeak, CRY.
— *n.* peek, GLIMPSE, GLANCE, LOOK, chirp,
cheep, squeak, CRY.

peephole: see EYE.

peer *n.* equal, SAME, MATCH, EQUIVALENT, MATE,
contemporary, ASSOCIATE, colleague. See also
ARISTOCRAT.
— *v.* peek, PRY, STARE, PEEP.

peerless: see BEST; INCOMPARABLE; UNIQUE.

peeve: see IRRITATE.

peevish: see CRANKY; IRRITABLE.

peg *n.* PIN, BOLT, ROD, STICK, STAKE.

pellet: see BEAD; HAIL; PEBBLE; PILL.

pelt: see BATTER; BOMBARD; COAT; FUR; HIDE; SKIN.

pen *n.* **1** *(the cow in the pen)* ENCLOSURE, COOP,
pound, paddock, corral, fencing; **2** *(the convict
in the pen)* penitentiary, PRISON, JAIL, jug; **3** *(to
write with a pen)* ballpoint, felt-tip, stylograph,
quill, fountain pen.
— *v.* **1** *(to pen a letter)* WRITE, INSCRIBE,
autograph, COMPOSE; **2** *(she felt penned in)*
ENCLOSE, coop up, fence in, CONFINE, box in.

penal: see CORRECTIVE.

penalization: see CORRECTION.

penalize: see FINE; PUNISH.

penalty *n.* PUNISHMENT, FINE, forfeit, SENTENCE, DISADVANTAGE.

penance: see PUNISHMENT.

pencil *n.* crayon, BRUSH, marker, ROD, RAY.
— *v.* WRITE, scribble, OUTLINE, SKETCH, depict, INSCRIBE.

pending: see DURING; UNDECIDED.

penetrate *v.* PIERCE, BORE, permeate, SOAK, infiltrate, FILTER, pervade, discern, DETECT, gouge.

penetrating: see DEEP; KEEN.

penetration: see UNDERSTANDING; VISION.

penitentiary: see JAIL; PEN; PRISON.

penknife: see KNIFE.

penman: see WRITER.

penmanship: see HAND.

pen name: see NAME.

pennant: see BANNER.

penniless: see BANKRUPT; NEEDY; POOR.

pennilessness: see NEED; POVERTY.

penny: see COIN.

penny pincher: see MISER.

pen pal: see CORRESPONDENT.

pension *n.* retirement, annuity, INCOME, SUPPORT, allotment, subsidy, PAY.

pensive: see MOODY.

people *pl.n.* inhabitants, POPULATION, populace, PUBLIC, persons, RACE, TRIBE, NATION, FAMILY, folks, CROWD, proletariat, MOB, rabble.
— *n.* NATION, COUNTRY, RACE, TRIBE, FOLK. humans.

pep: see BRISKNESS.

pepper: see BOMBARD; SHELL; SPICE.

peppery *adj.* pungent, SHARP, spicy, spirited, piquant, IRRITABLE, hot-tempered.

peppy: see BRISK.

per *prep.* FOR, BY, THROUGH, via.
— *pron.* EACH, EVERY.

perceivably: see VISIBLY.

perceive: see FEEL, FIND OUT; HEAR; KNOW; OBSERVE; REMARK; SEE; SENSE; TELL; UNDERSTAND; WITNESS.

perceived: see KNOWN.

percentage *n.* RATE, PROPORTION, SHARE, PORTION, PART, ADVANTAGE.

perceptibility: see VISIBILITY.

perceptible: see SENSIBLE; VISUAL.

perception: see CLEVERNESS; CONSCIOUSNESS; FEELING; SENSATION, SENSE; UNDERSTANDING; VISION.

perceptive: see INTELLIGENT; SENSIBLE; SENSITIVE; SHARP; UNDERSTANDING; VISIBLE; WISE.

perch *n.* roost, REST, STAND, SEAT, POLE, HEIGHT.
— *v.* roost, REST, BALANCE, SIT, SETTLE, situate.

perchance: see MAYBE; POSSIBLY.

percolate: see BOIL; BREW.

percolating: see RUNNING.

per diem: see DAILY.

perennial: see ANNUAL.

perfect *adj.* flawless, faultless, unblemished, COMPLETE, ENTIRE, FULL, WHOLE, unequaled, BEST, IDEAL, ACCURATE, infallible, EXACT, PRECISE, ABSOLUTE, PURE, sinless.
— *v.* COMPLETE, FINISH, IMPROVE, ACCOMPLISH, ACHIEVE.

perfection *n.* EXCELLENCE, completeness, FINISH, wholeness, purity, utopia.

perfectly: see COMPLETELY; JUST; PAT; THOROUGHLY.

perforate: see BORE; DRILL; PIERCE; PRICK; PUNCH.

perforation: see HOLE; LEAK; PIT; PRICK.

perform *v.* ACHIEVE, COMPLETE, DISCHARGE, MEET, carry out, DO, ACT, EXECUTE, render, PLAY, REPRESENT.

performance *n.* **1** *(two performances on Saturday)* PRESENTATION, SHOW, PRODUCTION, PLAY, DEED, feat, EXHIBITION, APPEARANCE; **2** *(not up to her usual performance)* BEHAVIOR, EXECUTION, EFFICIENCY, ACHIEVEMENT, ACCOMPLISHMENT.

performer *n.* ACTOR, actress, PLAYER, ARTIST, ENTERTAINER, instrumentalist, musician, SINGER.

performing: see ON.

perfume *n.* SCENT, FRAGRANCE, ODOR, LOTION, COLOGNE, essence, EXTRACT.

perhaps *adv.* MAYBE, POSSIBLY, conceivably.

peril: see DANGER; HAZARD; MENACE; RISK; SERIOUSNESS.

perilous: see DANGEROUS; HAZARDOUS; RISKY; UNSAFE.

period *n.* TERM, TIME, AGE, PHASE, cycle, menses, timing, duration, punctuation, DOT, MARK.

periodic *adj.* repeated, recurrent, intermittent, OCCASIONAL, cyclic, seasonal, REGULAR, clocklike.

periodical: see MAGAZINE.

periodicity: see REGULARITY.

perish *v.* DIE, SPOIL, DECAY, EXPIRE, pass away. VANISH.

perishable *adj.* destructible, decaying, dying, spoiling, FRESH.

perjure: see LIE.

perjury: see LIE.

perk *v.* prank, DRESS, TRIM, liven, revive, enliven, RECUPERATE.

perky *adj.* TRIM, jaunty, LIVELY, SHARP, SMART, dressy.

permanence: see ETERNITY; IMMORTALITY.

permanent *adj.* LASTING, durable, ENDLESS, timeless, perpetual, enduring, STABLE, FIXED, steadfast, invariable, UNCHANGEABLE, CONSTANT, established.

permeate: see PENETRATE.

permissible *adj.* ALLOWABLE, TOLERABLE, LEGAL, LAWFUL, admissible.

permission *n.* ALLOWANCE, CONSENT, APPROVAL, LEAVE, AUTHORITY, LICENSE, FREEDOM.

permissive *adj.* tolerant, lenient, indulgent, AGREEABLE.

permit *v.* ALLOW, CONSENT, tolerate, LICENSE, empower, authorize, LET.
    — *n.* LICENSE, PASS, WARRANT, AUTHORITY, franchise, PATENT.

perpendicular: see ALTITUDE; ERECT; RIGHT; STEEP; UPRIGHT; VERTICAL.

perpetrate: see COMMIT.

perpetual: see CONTINUAL; CONTINUOUS; ENDLESS; ETERNAL; PERMANENT; UNBROKEN; UNENDING.

perpetually: see EVERMORE.

perpetuity: see IMMORTALITY.

perplex: see AMAZE; BAFFLE; BEWILDER; DISTRACT; PUZZLE; SURPRISE.

perplexing: see DIFFICULT; SURPRISING.

perplexity: see AMAZEMENT; DIFFICULTY; MYSTERY.

persecute *v.* harass, oppress, TORMENT, PLAGUE, molest, ANNOY, ill-treat, maltreat, ABUSE, victimize, HARM.

persecution *n.* harassment, oppression, TORMENT, ANNOYANCE, ABUSE, HARM, intolerance, INJURY, SUFFERING.

perseverance: see INDUSTRY; PATIENCE; RESOLUTION; STEADINESS.

persevere: see CONTINUE; HANG; PERSIST.

persevering: see PATIENT.

persist *v.* ENDURE, CONTINUE, persevere, recur, LAST, keep on.

persistence: see CONTINUATION.

persistent: see INSISTENT; STUBBORN; URGENT.

person *n.* INDIVIDUAL, BODY, SELF, ONE, SOMEONE, SOMEBODY, BEING, personage, SOUL, CHARACTER, HUMAN.

personable: see PLEASANT.

personage: see CELEBRITY; PERSON.

personal *adj.* **1** *(a personal problem)* PRIVATE, INDIVIDUAL, exclusive, PARTICULAR, PECULIAR, own; **2** *(he gets too personal)* inquisitive, prying, FRESH.

personality *n.* individuality, IDENTITY, makeup, characteristics, emotions, CELEBRITY.

personify: see REPRESENT.

personnel: see STAFF.

persons: see EVERYONE; PEOPLE.

perspective: see ASPECT; OUTLOOK; SLANT.

perspiration: see BEAD; SWEAT.

perspire *v.* SWEAT, swelter, ooze, transpire, secrete.

persuade *v.* CONVINCE, induce, URGE, wheedle, INFLUENCE, incline, entice, COAX, prompt, CONVERT, brainwash, win over.

persuasion *n.* **1** *(it will take some persuasion)* convincing, urging, persuasiveness, brainwashing; **2** *(of a similar persuasion)* CONVICTION, BELIEF, sect, RELIGION.

persuasive *adj.* convincing, INFLUENTIAL, valid, compelling, cogent, WINNING, seductive, alluring, stimulating.

persuasiveness: see PERSUASION.

pertain: see BELONG; CONCERN; RELATE.

pertaining: see RELATIVE.

pertinent: see PAT; RELATIVE.

perturbed: see UPSET.

pervade: see PENETRATE.

perverse: see STUBBORN; WRONG.

pervert: see BEAST; MISFIT.

perverted: see ABNORMAL.

pest *n.* NUISANCE, ANNOYANCE, TROUBLE, PLAGUE, CURSE, INSECT, bug.

pester *v.* BOTHER, ANNOY, hound, hassle, badger, NAG, harass, aggravate, PLAGUE.

pestilence: see DISEASE; PLAGUE.

pet *n.* ANIMAL, mascot, favorite, BELOVED, DARLING.
— *adj.* FAVORITE, DARLING, DEAR, cherished.
— *v.* PAT, CARESS, fondle, STROKE, make love, indulge.

petal: see LEAF.

petition: see APPEAL; ASK; DEMAND; PLEA; PRAY; PRAYER; SUE.

petitioner: see BEGGAR.

petrify: see HARDEN.

petroleum: see FUEL; OIL.

petticoat: see SKIRT.

petty *adj.* trifling, trivial, paltry, unimportant, SMALL, MEAN, stingy, NARROW-MINDED, small-minded.

petulant: see IRRITABLE.

pew: see BENCH.

phantom *n.* GHOST, SPIRIT, spook, ILLUSION, fantasy, VISION, apparition.

phase *n.* STAGE, PERIOD, STATE, ASPECT, VIEW, CONDITION, POSITION, SIDE, PART, ANGLE, facet, INCIDENT.

phenomenal: see MIRACULOUS; REMARKABLE.

phenomenon: see CURIOSITY; MIRACLE; OBJECT; OCCURRENCE.

philosopher: see SCHOLAR; SCIENTIST.

philosophical: see SCIENTIFIC.

phlebotomize: see BLEED.

phobia: see COMPLEX; ILLNESS.

phone *n.* telephone, radiophone, radiotelephone.
— *v.* telephone, CALL, radio.

phone call: see RING.

phonics: see READING.

phony: see BLANK; CHEAT; FRAUD.

photo: see PICTURE.

photograph: see FILM; MAP; PORTRAIT; SHOOT; SLIDE; TAKE.

photoplay: see FILM.

photostat: see COPY.

phrase *n.* locution, idiom, EXPRESSION.

physical *adj.* BODILY, EXTERNAL, MUSCULAR, ATHLETIC.

physician *n.* DOCTOR, practitioner, healer, consultant, SPECIALIST.

physique: see BUILD; FRAME.

pick *v.* CHOOSE, SELECT, cull, winnow, GATHER, DRAW, PLUCK. See also PUNCH.
— *n.* CHOICE, BEST, SELECTION.

picket *n.* **1** *(a fence made of pickets)* STAKE, WALL, BAR, ENCLOSURE, FENCE; **2** *(to form a picket)* boycott, STRIKE, DEMONSTRATION, sit-in, REVOLT.
— *v.* **1** *(to picket a corral)* FENCE, ENCLOSE; **2** *(to picket a factory)* STRIKE, DEMONSTRATE, boycott.

pickle: see JAM; RELISH; SALT.

pickpocket: see THIEF.

pick up: see TAKE.

pickup: see TRUCK.

picky: see CHOOSY.

picnic: see FEAST; SNACK; SPREAD.

picture *n.* photo, PAINTING, DRAWING, movie, likeness, image.
— *v.* IMAGINE, FANCY, DESCRIBE, REPRESENT, portray, depict, ILLUSTRATE.

pidgin: see SLANG.

piece *n.* SECTION, FRAGMENT, PORTION, PART, SHEET, OBJECT, counter, COIN, GUN, ARTICLE.
— *v.* JOIN, ENLARGE, MEND.

pier: see DOCK; HARBOR; PORT; WHARF.

pierce *v.* STAB; PENETRATE, perforate, puncture, PRICK, THRUST, EXCITE, THRILL, ROUSE, AFFECT.

piercing: see KEEN; LOUD; SHRILL.

pies: see PASTRY.

piety: see HOLINESS; RELIGION.

pig *n.* swine, HOG, boar, SOW, porker, pork, glutton.

pigeonhole: see COMPARTMENT.

piggish: see GREEDY.

piggishness: see GREED.

pig-headed: see STUBBORN.

pig iron: see IRON.

pigment: see COLOR; DYE; PAINT.

pike: see LANCE; SPEAR.

pikestaff: see STAFF.

pile *n.* HEAP, STACK, MASS, accumulation, POST, FOUNDATION, COLLECTION, BATCH, LOAD.
— *v.* HEAP, STACK, amass, ACCUMULATE, LOAD, COLLECT, STORE.

pile up: see ACCUMULATE.

pilfer: see PINCH; STEAL; THIEVE.

pilferer: see CROOK; ROBBER.

pilgrim *n.* worshiper, TRAVELER, wanderer, wayfarer, crusader.

pill *n.* MEDICINE, pellet, CAPSULE, lozenge, TABLET, CURE.

pillage: see PIRACY; PREY; RIOT; ROBBERY.

pillar *n.* COLUMN, SHAFT, mainstay, SUPPORT, SUPPORTER, TOWER, MAST, PROP.

pillbox: see FORT.

pillow *n.* headrest, CUSHION, PAD, bolster, SUPPORT.

pilot *n.* GUIDE, LEADER, helmsman, steersman, flier, aviator, DRIVER, OPERATOR.
— *v.* GUIDE, STEER, CONTROL, NAVIGATE, HANDLE.

piloting: see NAVIGATION.

pimple: see BLISTER; BOIL; GROWTH.

pin *n.* fastener, CLIP, CLASP, CATCH, brooch, PEG, BOLT, NEEDLE.
— *v.* FASTEN, CLASP, HOLD, secure, PRESS, immobilize.

pincer: see CLAW.

pinch *v.* SQUEEZE, nip, PRESS, pilfer, GRAB, ARREST.
— *n.*: see CRUMB; DASH; SITUATION; URGENCY; DISCOMFORT.

pinch-hit: see SUBSTITUTE.

pinch hitter: see SUBSTITUTE.

pine: see ACHE.

pink: see RED.

pinnacle: see HEAD; HEIGHT; PEAK; SUMMIT; TOP.

pins: see JEWELRY.

pioneer *n.* EXPLORER, pathfinder, adventurer, homesteader, SETTLER, COLONIST, GUIDE, LEADER.
— *v.* EXPLORE, SETTLE, colonize, open up, DISCOVER, GUIDE, LEAD.

pious: see GODLY; HOLY; SACRED; UPRIGHT.

pip: see SPOT.

pipe *n.* TUBE, HOSE, duct, conduit, CANAL, CHANNEL, windpipe, corncob, bagpipe, reed, whistle, bird call.
— *v.*: see CHIRP.

piquant: see PEPPERY.

piracy *n.* pillage, plundering, privateering, ROBBERY, THEFT, thievery, looting, hijacking.

pirate *n.* buccaneer, privateer, marauder, plunderer, sea robber, corsair, hijacker, desperado.

pistol *n.* REVOLVER, handgun, automatic, GUN, gat, FIREARM, WEAPON.

pit *n.* **1** *(clay pits)* DITCH, excavation, HOLE, CAVITY, crater, WELL, gulch, SHAFT, abyss, hollow, pitfall, DEPRESSION, DENT, puncture, perforation, LEVEL, indentation, POCK, pockmark, NOTCH; **2** *(a fruit pit)* STONE, SEED, NUT.
— *v.* MARK, SCAR, hollow, pockmark.

pitch *v.* THROW, HURL, FLING, TOSS, vault, CAST, HEAVE, ROLL.
— *n.* **1** *(the house was on a slight pitch)* SLOPE, INCLINE, SLANT, ANGLE; **2** *(her voice had a high pitch)* frequency, TONE, intonation, modulation. See also COMMERCIAL.

pitch-black: see BLACK.

pitcher *n.* VESSEL, JUG, CONTAINER, JAR, urn, vase.

pitchfork: see FORK.

pitfall: see PIT; TRAP.

pitiful *adj.* MISERABLE, pathetic, touching, distressing, heart-rending, WRETCHED.

pitifully: see POORLY.

pitiless *adj.* unsympathetic, MERCILESS, HARSH, unfeeling, ruthless, HEARTLESS.

pity *n.* compassion, SYMPATHY, MERCY, CHARITY, benevolence, HUMANITY.
— *v.* SPARE, console, COMFORT, PARDON.

pivot: see AXIS; CENTER; HINGE; ROTATE, ROUND; WHIRL.

pivotal: see CENTRAL.

pixy: see FAIRY.

placard: see ANNOUNCEMENT; POSTER, SIGN.

placate: see SATISFY.

place *n.* LOCATION, POSITION, POST, STATION, SPOT, AREA, SPACE, SEAT, SITE, city, REGION, niche, ROOM, quarter, RANK, COURT, BUSINESS, DUTY, SITUATION.
   — *v.* PUT, SET, STATION, LOCATE, situate, ASSIGN, APPOINT, PLANT, LAY, STAND, FIX, ARRANGE, CLASSIFY, IDENTIFY, CONNECT, SETTLE, HIRE, EMPLOY, ENGAGE.

placed: see SITUATED.

place setting: see MAT.

placid: see CALM; PEACEFUL; QUIET; TRANQUIL.

plague *n.* DISEASE, pestilence, PEST, epidemic.
   — *v.* BOTHER, ANNOY, DISTURB, molest, TROUBLE, PESTER, TORMENT.

plain *adj.* **1** *(the plain truth)* CLEAR, HONEST, unadulterated, SINCERE; **2** *(a plain house)* MODEST, COMMON, ORDINARY, unadorned.
   — *n.* LEVEL, PLATEAU, lowland, mesa, prairie, pampas.

plainly: see CLEARLY; EVIDENTLY; OPENLY; SIMPLY.

plainness: see SIMPLICITY.

plaintiff: see PARTY; SIDE.

plait: see TUCK.

plan *n.* PROJECT, PLOT, SCHEME, DRAFT, PROPOSAL, OUTLINE.
   — *v.* PREPARE, DESIGN, DRAFT, concoct, SHAPE, DEVISE, conceive.

plane *n.* **1** *(an unobstructed plane)* LEVEL, horizontal, FLAT; **2** *(a supersonic plane)* aircraft, airliner, airplane.
   — *adj.*: see EVEN.
   — *v.*: see LEVEL; SMOOTH.

planet: see EARTH; SPHERE; STAR.

planetary: see EARTHLY.

plank *n.* BOARD, WOOD, LUMBER.

planks: see LUMBER.

planned: see DELIBERATE; ON; STUDIED.

planner: see ARCHITECT.

planning: see ARCHITECTURE; ORGANIZATION; STRATEGY.

plans: see DESIGN.

plant *n.* **1** *(to raise plants in a greenhouse)* vegetation, HERB; **2** *(an automobile plant)*

FACTORY, SHOP, foundry, forge, MILL; **3** *(the police set up a plant)* TRAP, TRICK, snare.
   — *v.* SOW, SEED, root, GROW, pot, START, ESTABLISH.

plantation: see FARM; RANCH.

planter: see FARMER; RANCHER.

plants: see GARDEN.

plaque: see MEDAL; TABLET; TROPHY.

plasma: see BLOOD.

plaster *n.* PASTE, CEMENT, mortar, binding.
   — *v.* PASTE, cement, COVER.

plastic: see CEMENT; CHEMICAL.

plat: see CHART.

plate *v.* COAT, laminate, gild, silver.
   — *n.*: see BASE; DISH; FOIL; TRAY.

plateau *n.* mesa, ELEVATION, highlands, tableland, PLAIN.

platform: see DOCK; PAD; PAVILION; STAGE; STAND.

platinum: see METAL.

platitude: see FORMULA.

platter: see DISH; RECORD; TRAY.

plausible: see POSSIBLE; REASONABLE.

plausibly: see PROBABLY.

play *v.* **1** *(they played around the pool)* frolic, sport, frisk, dally; **2** *(to play a role)* PERFORM, impersonate, ACT, REPRESENT; **3** *(to play a game)* PARTICIPATE, COMPETE, engage.
   — *n.* DRAMA, comedy, REPRESENTATION, SHOW, PERFORMANCE, ACTIVITY, GAME.

player *n.* ACTOR, PERFORMER, ATHLETE, COMPETITOR.

playful *adj.* GAY, LIVELY, sportive, frolicsome, FRISKY, MISCHIEVOUS.

playgoers: see AUDIENCE.

playhouse: see THEATER.

plays: see THEATER.

plaything: see DOLL; SPORT; TOY.

playtime: see RECESS.

playwright: see WRITER.

plaza: see SQUARE.

plea *n.* REQUEST, petition, asking, APPEAL, supplication, PRAYER.

plead *v.* APPEAL, REQUEST, implore, BEG, entreat, supplicate.

pleasant *adj.* AGREEABLE, ENJOYABLE, amiable, gratifying, congenial, personable.

pleasantly: see SMOOTHLY.

pleasantness: see SWEETNESS.

please *v.* SATISFY, GRATIFY, GLADDEN, DELIGHT, CHARM, OBLIGE.
— *adv.*: see KINDLY.

pleased: see CONTENTED; GLAD; HAPPY; PROUD; THANKFUL.

pleasing *adj.* appealing, DESIRABLE, WELCOME, engaging, charming, DELIGHTFUL.

pleasurable *adj.* DELIGHTFUL, PLEASING, JOYFUL, gratifying, AGREEABLE, LUXURIOUS, sensual.

pleasure *n.* ENJOYMENT, gratification, JOY, GLADNESS, DELIGHT, CHEER, elation, recreation.

pleat: see SEAM; TUCK.

pledge *n.* OATH, PROMISE, AGREEMENT, VOW, guaranty, commitment.
— *v.* PROMISE, SWEAR, vouch, VOW, ASSURE, GUARANTEE.

pledging: see MARRIAGE.

plenteous: see AMPLE.

plentiful *adj.* ABUNDANT, ENOUGH, AMPLE, SUFFICIENT, bountiful.

plenty *n.* sufficiency, ENOUGH, ABUNDANCE, profusion, lavishness.

pliability: see FLEXIBILITY.

pliable: see FLEXIBLE; LIMBER; SOFT.

pliancy: see FLEXIBILITY.

pliant: see FLEXIBLE.

plight: see CASE.

plop: see THUMP.

plot *n.* **1** *(a plot to overthrow the government)* PLAN, PROJECT, SCHEME, conspiracy, DESIGN; **2** *(the plot of the play)* STORY, OUTLINE, THEME, SKETCH. See also FIELD; GARDEN; LAND; TRACT.
— *v.* SCHEME, PLAN, conspire, contrive.

plow *v.* TILL, BREAK, WORK, CULTIVATE.

pluck *v.* JERK, PULL, yank, SNATCH, cull, unfeather.

plug *n.* STOPPER, cork, wadding, wedge, fitting, CONNECTION. See also COMMERCIAL; PROMOTION; PUBLICITY.

— *v.* STOP, BLOCK, cork, wedge, clog, RAM, obstruct. See also PROMOTE; PUSH.

plumb: see SOUND.

plume *n.* feather, quill.

plump *adj.* FAT, CHUBBY, pudgy, stocky, STOUT, obese.

plunder: see LOOT; PREY; RAID; ROB; STRIP; THEFT.

plunderer: see PIRATE; ROBBER.

plundering: see PIRACY.

plunge *v.* immerse, DIVE, SUBMERGE, DIP, SINK, DESCEND.
— *n.* dive, LEAP, JUMP, FALL, DROP.

plurality: see MAJORITY; MOST.

plus *prep.* added to, WITH.
— *n.* ADVANTAGE, BENEFIT, OPPORTUNITY, GAIN.
— *conj.* and, ALSO.

ply: see TRAVEL; TWIST.

poach: see RUSTLE.

pocket *n.* HOLE, CAVITY, POUCH, hollow, CHAMBER.
— *v.*: see CASH.

pocketbook: see BAG; BILLFOLD; POUCH; PURSE.

pocketknife: see KNIFE.

pockmark: see BLEMISH; PIT.

pod *n.* CAPSULE, hull, husk, sheath, CASE.

poem *n.* rhyme, VERSE, ode, ballad, sonnet.

poet: see WRITER.

poetry *n.* lyric, rhyme, VERSE, meter, epic.

poignant: see KEEN.

point *n.* **1** *(a point on a map)* POSITION, LOCATION, PLACE, SITE, SPOT; **2** *(what is his point?)* PURPOSE, MEANING, AIM, GOAL, IDEA, essence, OBJECT; **3** *(at this point in time)* MOMENT, PERIOD, juncture. See also ANGLE; BASKET; SPINE; TOOTH.
— *v.* SHOW, DIRECT, GUIDE, LEAD, AIM, INDICATE, STEER.

pointed *adj.* SHARP, ACUTE, FINE, caustic, ACID, biting, sarcastic.

pointedly: see SHARPLY.

pointer: see ARROW; COMPASS; HAND; NEEDLE; TIP.

pointing: see AIM.

pointless *adj.* ABSURD, aimless, meaningless, SENSELESS, inconsequential, REMOTE, irrelevant.

point of view: see MENTALITY.

point out: see INDICATE; NOTE; SHOW.

poise *n.* assurance, composure, CONFIDENCE, CALM, CONTROL, BALANCE.

poised: see ASSURED; CALM.

poison *n.* toxic, venom, virus, PEST, malignancy.
  — *v.* INFECT, taint, envenom, KILL, corrupt.

poisonous *adj.* toxic, venomous, DEADLY.

poke *v.* jab, RAM, SHOVE, PUSH, THRUST, PUNCH. See also LAG.
  — *n.* STAB, jab, jostle, NUDGE. See also BAG; POUCH.

pole *n.* STICK, SHAFT, STAFF, ROD, POST, BAR, STAKE, PILE.

polestar: see COMPASS.

police *n.* patrolmen, cops, officers, FORCE.
  — *v.* PATROL, CONTROL, WATCH, OBSERVE, GUARD, REGULATE.

policeman: see INSPECTOR; OFFICER.

policy *n.* PROCEDURE, SYSTEM, doctrine, RULE, STRATEGY, TACTICS, WAY, METHOD.

polish *v.* SHINE, BRIGHTEN, SCOUR, RUB, buff, SMOOTH.
  — *n.* SHINE, LUSTER, BRILLIANCE, sheen, GLOSS, FINISH.

polished: see ACCOMPLISHED; CIVIL; CLASSIC; ELEGANT; GRACEFUL; SHINY; SMOOTH.

polite *adj.* courteous, CONSIDERATE, THOUGHTFUL, respectful, MANNERLY, gracious, refined.

politeness *n.* COURTESY, CONSIDERATION, civility, thoughtfulness, TACT, refinement, comity.

politic: see TACTFUL.

political *adj.* civic, CIVIL, PUBLIC, governmental, administrative, diplomatic, bureaucratic.

politicians: see PARTY.

poll *n.* SURVEY, canvass, consensus, BALLOT, VOTE, ELECTION.
  — *v.* QUESTION, SURVEY, ENROLL, REGISTER, ASSEMBLE.

pollute *v.* dirty, contaminate, infest, tarnish, taint, VIOLATE, corrupt.

polluted: see DIRTY; FOUL; IMPURE.

pollution *n.* contamination, soiling, fouling, ABUSE, corruption, VIOLATION.

pomade: see OINTMENT.

pommel: see CLUB.

pomp: see PARADE; SPLENDOR.

poncho: see CLOAK.

pond *n.* LAKE, POOL, BASIN, lagoon.

ponder: see CONCENTRATE; CONSIDER; REFLECT; WEIGH; WONDER.

ponderable: see THINKABLE.

pondering: see MEDITATION.

pony: see HORSE.

pool *n.* **1** *(a pool of water)* LAKE, POND, lagoon, reservoir, puddle; **2** *(is there money in the pool?)* FUND, GROUP, combine.
  — *v.*: see COOPERATE.

poor *adj.* **1** *(the poor immigrants)* NEEDY, destitute, impoverished, penniless; **2** *(the play had a poor showing)* PITIFUL, MISERABLE, meager, UNSATISFACTORY, insufficient.

poorly *adv.* ILL, miserably, badly, pitifully, unsuccessfully, insufficiently.

pop *v.* detonate, EXPLODE, FIRE, BURST, CRACK.
  — *n.* **1** *(the bottle opened with a pop)* EXPLOSION, BANG, BURST, SHOT; **2** *(they drank pop with their hamburgers)* soda, soft drink, BEVERAGE.

poppycock: see NONSENSE.

populace: see NATION; PEOPLE; POPULATION.

popular *adj.* FAMOUS, CELEBRATED, admired, well-liked, FAMILIAR, CURRENT.

popularity *n.* FAME, vogue, FASHION, DEMAND, FOLLOWING, prevalence.

popularly: see CURRENTLY.

population *n.* PEOPLE, populace, inhabitants, residents, citizenry, NATION.

porch *n.* veranda, stoop, deck, patio.

pore: see COMB.

pork: see PIG.

porker: see PIG.

port *n.* HARBOR, haven, inlet, BAY, anchorage, DOCK, pier, WHARF.

portable *adj.* movable, transferable, manageable, HANDY, CONVENIENT.

portage: see TRANSPORTATION.

portal: see DOOR; ENTRANCE; GATE.

porter *n.* carrier, bearer, redcap, doorman, gatekeeper, JANITOR, SUPERINTENDENT.

portfolio: see BILLFOLD; FOLDER.

portion *n.* PART, PIECE, allotment, SHARE, segment, DIVISION, SECTION.
— *v.* DIVIDE, allot, PARCEL, section, DISTRIBUTE.

portly: see STOUT.

portrait *n.* likeness, REPRESENTATION, PAINTING, PICTURE, photograph, snapshot, DESCRIPTION, RESEMBLANCE.

portraiture: see REPRESENTATION.

portray: see DESCRIBE; ILLUSTRATE; PAINT; PICTURE; REPRESENT.

portrayal: see DESCRIPTION.

pose *v.* **1** *(he posed for a picture)* PLACE, PUT, SET, SIT, position, MODEL; **2** *(he posed as a man of the world)* PRETEND, posture, AFFECT, simulate.
— *n.* POSITION, stance, pretense, POSTURE, PRESENCE.

posh: see CLASSY.

position *n.* **1** *(a panoramic position)* LOCATION, SPOT, SITE, PLACE, AREA, REGION; **2** *(an erect position)* POSTURE, bearing, POSE, CARRIAGE; **3** *(a university position)* JOB, POST, ROLE, EMPLOYMENT, SITUATION, FUNCTION, OFFICE; **4** *(what is the candidate's position?)* STAND, BELIEF, OPINION, ATTITUDE, STATEMENT.
— *v.*: see POSE; STATION.

positive *adj.* DEFINITE, CERTAIN, ACTUAL, REAL, AUTHENTIC, ABSOLUTE, concrete, ASSURED.
— *n.*: see FILM.

positively *adv.* CERTAINLY, DEFINITELY, SURELY, ABSOLUTELY, decidedly, CLEARLY, undoubtedly, SURELY.

possess *v.* HAVE, HOLD, OWN, KEEP, OCCUPY, RETAIN, MAINTAIN.

possessing: see OF.

possession *n.* ownership, occupancy, retention, MAINTENANCE, CONTROL, PROPERTY.

possessions: see ESTATE; GOODS; RICHES; WEALTH.

possessive *adj.* retentive, dominating, controlling, SELFISH.

possessor: see OWNER; PROPRIETOR.

possibility *n.* likelihood, workability, feasibility, probability, potentiality, eventuality.

possible *adj.* conceivable, LIKELY, LIABLE, POTENTIAL, PROBABLE, plausible, eventual, feasible.

possibly *adv.* MAYBE, PERHAPS, perchance, conceivably, PROBABLY, potentially, EVENTUALLY.

post *n.* **1** *(a hitching post)* POLE, PILLAR, COLUMN, pedestal, SUPPORT, STAKE, stud; **2** *(a teaching post)* POSITION, SITUATION, JOB, EMPLOYMENT; **3** *(a military post)* BASE, CAMP, STATION, LOCATION, AREA, REGION, SITE; **4** *(to send the letter through the post)* MAIL, DISPATCH.
— *v.* **1** *(to post an announcement)* DISPLAY, affix, LIST, ANNOUNCE; **2** *(the letter was posted)* SEND, MAIL, DISPATCH, FORWARD.

poster *n.* PRINT, placard, BILL, handbill, billboard, NOTICE, SIGN.

posterior: see BACK; HIND; REAR.

posterity: see ISSUE.

postpone *v.* DELAY, defer, retard, shelve, TABLE, procrastinate.

postponement: see DELAY; EXTENSION.

postscript: see FOOTNOTE.

posture *n.* POSITION, stance, ATTITUDE, POSE, SITUATION, CONDITION, STATE.
— *v.*: see POSE.

pot *n.* **1** *(a cooking pot)* VESSEL, saucepan, KETTLE, cauldron, PAN, crock, urn, CONTAINER; **2** *(to smoke pot)* marijuana, GRASS, weed, dope. See also BANK; PURSE.
— *v.*: see PLANT.

potency: see FERTILITY; PRODUCTIVITY; STRENGTH.

potent: see FERTILE; MALE.

potential *adj.* POSSIBLE, LIKELY, conceivable, latent, dormant, promising.
— *n.* CAPACITY, capability, ABILITY, PROMISE.

potentiality: see POSSIBILITY.

potentially: see POSSIBLY.

potion: see BEVERAGE; DRINK; MEDICINE.

potter's field: see CEMETERY.

pouch *n.* POCKET, BAG, SACK, poke, CONTAINER, pocketbook.

poultry: see BIRD; FOWL.

pounce: see SWOOP.

pound *v.* HAMMER, BEAT, KNOCK, STRIKE, HIT, BATTER, CRUSH, pulverize.
— *n.*: see CAGE; PEN.

pounded: see BEATEN.

pour *v.* FLOW, SPILL, spew, splash, drain, drench, FLOOD, STREAM. See also CAST.

poverty *n.* want, NEED, pennilessness, pauperism, starvation, FAMINE.

poverty-stricken: see NEEDY.

powder *n.* DUST, GRIT, SAND, granules, particles.
— *v.* DUST, SPRINKLE, dredge.

powdered: see MADE-UP.

powdery: see DUSTY; FINE.

power *n.* FORCE, STRENGTH, VIGOR, domination,
GOVERNMENT, AUTHORITY, COMMAND.
— *v.* vest, ENABLE, RUN, RULE, CONTROL, PERMIT.

power-driven: see ELECTRIC.

powerful *adj.* STRONG, ENERGETIC, MUSCULAR,
MIGHTY, VIGOROUS, FORCEFUL, INFLUENTIAL,
overwhelming.

powerfully: see FORCIBLY.

powerhouse: see GIANT.

powerless *adj.* HELPLESS, impotent, WEAK,
FEEBLE, fragile.

powwow: see DISCUSSION.

pox: see DISEASE.

practical *adj.* usable, USEFUL, workable, feasible,
SOUND, attainable, achievable, SENSIBLE.

practically *adv.* **1** (*his idea was practically thought
out*) sensibly, economically, advantageously,
soundly, rationally; **2** (*he practically stopped
breathing*) NEARLY, ALMOST, virtually, basically.

practice *v.* EXERCISE, TRAIN, DRILL, REPEAT,
REHEARSE, USE, FOLLOW.
— *n.* **1** (*a religious practice*) TRADITION, USAGE,
CUSTOM, HABIT, MANNER, mode; **2** (*piano
practice*) REPETITION, REHEARSAL, DRILL,
EXERCISE.

practiced *adj.* trained, schooled, EXPERT, drilled,
rehearsed, SKILLED, adept.

practicing: see REHEARSAL.

practitioner: see DOCTOR; PHYSICIAN.

prairie: see MEADOW; PLAIN; RANGE.

praise *n.* APPLAUSE, COMPLIMENT, commendation,
ESTEEM, ADMIRATION.
— *v.* COMPLIMENT, acclaim, CELEBRATE,
commend, ADMIRE, glorify, laud.

praised: see FAVORED.

praiseworthy: see ADMIRABLE.

pram: see CARRIAGE.

prance: see SKIP.

prank: see MISCHIEF; PERK; STUNT; TRICK.

prattle: see BABBLE; CHAT; CHATTER; RATTLE.

pray *v.* ASK, BEG, PLEAD, APPEAL, supplicate,
entreat, implore, petition.

prayer *n.* REQUEST, APPEAL, petition, solicitation,
supplication, invocation, summoning.

preach *v.* DECLARE, PRONOUNCE, INFORM, TEACH,
LECTURE, sermonize, moralize.

preacher *n.* LECTURER, moralizer, evangelist,
missionary, MINISTER, PRIEST.

preamble: see PREFACE.

precarious: see CHANCY; CRITICAL; DANGEROUS;
HAZARDOUS; RISKY; TICKLISH; UNSAFE.

precaution *n.* CARE, REGARD, prudence,
wariness, FORESIGHT, forewarning, anticipation,
discretion.

precautionary: see PREVENTIVE.

precede: see RANK.

preceding *adj.* PRELIMINARY, FOREGOING,
PREVIOUS, earlier, aforesaid.

precept: see COMMANDMENT; PROVERB.

preceptive: see QUICK.

preceptor: see TUTOR.

precinct: see DISTRICT.

precious *adj.* VALUABLE, COSTLY, EXPENSIVE,
priceless, prized, cherished, inestimable.
— *n.*: see DARLING.

precipice: see CLIFF.

precipitation: see CLIMATE; DEW; RAIN.

précis: see SUMMARY.

precise *adj.* EXACT, DEFINITE, ACCURATE, SPECIFIC,
CORRECT, SEVERE, meticulous, unmistakable.

precisely *adv.* EXACTLY, DEFINITELY, correctly,
POSITIVELY, strictly, carefully, meticulously,
specifically.

precision *n.* correctness, accuracy, sureness,
EXACTNESS, DETAIL, meticulousness, rigidity,
PERFECTION.

preconception: see FORESIGHT.

predecessor: see ANCESTOR; ELDER.

predecessors: see FOREFATHERS.

predestination: see DESTINY; DOOM.

predestined: see INEVITABLE.

predetermined: see DELIBERATE; FOREGONE.

predicament: see PROBLEM.

predict *v.* envision, ANTICIPATE, foretell, FORESEE, divine, prophesy, augur.

prediction *n.* anticipation, foretelling, forecast, divination, prophecy, fortunetelling, horoscope, soothsaying, omen, speculation.

predominantly: see PRIMARILY.

predominate: see DOMINATE; REIGN.

preen: see BEAUTIFY.

preface *n.* INTRODUCTION, BEGINNING, foreword, preamble, prelude, prologue, preliminary, OPENING.

prefer *v.* FAVOR, FANCY, CHOOSE, SELECT, PICK, ADOPT, ELECT.

preferable *adj.* choicest, SUPERIOR, BETTER, WORTHY, DESIRABLE.

preferably: see RATHER.

preference *n.* CHOICE, liking, option, SELECTION, ELECTION, partiality, priority.

preferred: see CHOICE; CHOSEN; FAVORED; FAVORITE.

pregnant *adj.* expecting, FERTILE, fruitful, FULL, weighty, PRODUCTIVE, creative, charged, meaningful, SUGGESTIVE.

prehistoric: see PRIMITIVE.

prejudiced: see NARROW; NARROW-MINDED; PARTIAL; UNJUST.

preliminarily: see ORIGINALLY.

preliminary *adj.* beginning, introductory, PRIOR, PRECEDING, preparatory.
— *n.*: see PREFACE.

prelude: see PREFACE.

premature *adj.* EARLY, unprepared, untimely, RASH, HASTY, FORWARD, inopportune, UNRIPE, undeveloped.

premeditated: see INTENTIONAL; STUDIED.

premier: see MINISTER.

premise: see BASIS; THEORY.

premises: see GROUNDS.

premium *n.* REWARD, GIFT, recompense, PRIZE, BONUS, ENCOURAGEMENT, APPRECIATION, enhancement.

premonition: see WARNING.

preoccupation: see COMPLEX.

preoccupied: see ABSENT-MINDED; CONCERNED; FORGETFUL.

preparation *n.* readiness, groundwork, FORMATION, REHEARSAL, FOUNDATION, PRODUCT, ARRANGEMENT. See also BATTER.

preparations: see EQUIPMENT.

preparatory: see PRELIMINARY; TRIAL.

prepare *v.* ARRANGE, ready, FIX, concoct, REHEARSE, DEVELOP, DEVISE.

prepared: see WATCHFUL.

preparer: see MAKER; MANUFACTURER.

preposterous: see ABSURD.

prerequisite: see NECESSITY; NEED; REQUIREMENT.

prescribe *v.* COMMAND, DICTATE, ORDER, DIRECT, GUIDE, SUGGEST, RECOMMEND.

prescribed: see FORMAL.

prescription *n.* DIRECTION, SUGGESTION, RECOMMENDATION, ORDER, FORMULA, RECIPE, REMEDY.

presence *n.* **1** *(the enemy's presence caused concern)* nearness, VICINITY, CLOSENESS, proximity, COMPANY, ATTENDANCE; **2** *(his personality gives him a good presence)* bearing, CARRIAGE, APPEARANCE.

present *adj.* IMMEDIATE, existing, CURRENT, MODERN, CONTEMPORARY, ACTUAL.
— *v.* **1** *(he presented her with a ring)* GIVE, SUBMIT, OFFER, DONATE, GRANT, AWARD; **2** *(the emcee presented the guest of honor)* NOMINATE, INTRODUCE, SHOW, make known, ACQUAINT.
— *n.* **1** *(a birthday present)* GIFT, DONATION, offering, FAVOR; **2** *(no time like the present)* NOW, today, INSTANT, nonce.

presentation *n.* **1** *(he gave a stirring presentation)* SPEECH, oration, DELIVERY, INTRODUCTION, EXHIBITION; **2** *(a presentation to charity)* offering, DONATION, GIFT, GRANT, AWARD.

presently: see ALREADY; CURRENTLY; EARLY; NOW; NOWADAYS; SHORTLY; SOON.

preservation: see MAINTENANCE; SAFETY; SALVATION.

preservative: see GUARD.

preserve *v.* SAVE, PROTECT, secure, safeguard, conserve, MAINTAIN, SUPPORT, SUSTAIN.

preserved: see SAFE.

preserver: see GUARDIAN.

preserves: see JAM.

preside *v.* officiate, DIRECT, GOVERN, CONTROL, MANAGE, administer.

president *n.* HEAD, COMMANDER, CHAIRMAN, DIRECTOR, administrator.

press *v.* **1** *(press the button)* PUSH, SQUEEZE, PIN, FORCE, COMPRESS; **2** *(the crowd pressed on)* CRUSH, PUSH, RUSH, HURRY, HASTEN; **3** *(he pressed for an answer)* INSIST, URGE, COMPEL, constrain, STRESS, emphasize; **4** *(to press clothes)* IRON, flatten, SMOOTH.
— *n.* **1** *(the press printed one million copies)* printer, roller; **2** *(the power of the press)* publishing, journalism, newspapers, publications; **3** *(the press for time)* PRESSURE, URGENCY, STRAIN, TENSION. See also MILL.

pressed: see HURRIED.

pressing: see URGENT.

pressure *n.* **1** *(water pressure)* FORCE, WEIGHT, BURDEN, LOAD, MASS, TENSION; **2** *(political pressure)* POWER, INFLUENCE, PERSUASION, coercion, repression.
— *v.* URGE, COMPEL, PERSUADE, INFLUENCE, INSIST, PRESS.

prestige: see AUTHORITY; FAME; INFLUENCE.

presumable: see LIKELY; PROBABLE; THINKABLE.

presumably: see PROBABLY; SUPPOSEDLY.

presume: see ASSUME; CONCLUDE; EXPECT; IMAGINE; SUPPOSE; SUSPECT.

presumed: see SUPPOSED.

presumption: see CONCLUSION.

presumptuous: see BOLD.

pretend *v.* simulate, AFFECT, MISLEAD, delude, IMITATE, fake, counterfeit, DECEIVE, make up.

pretender: see IMPOSTOR.

pretense: see ACT; CAMOUFLAGE; POSE; SHOW.

pretty *adj.* BEAUTIFUL, ATTRACTIVE, comely, FINE, DAINTY, appealing, PLEASING, becoming, INVITING.

prevail: see REIGN; RESIST, TRIUMPH.

prevailing: see CURRENT; FASHIONABLE; MODERN; UNIVERSAL; USUAL.

prevalence: see POPULARITY.

prevalent: see CURRENT; EXISTENT; UNIVERSAL.

prevent *v.* STOP, HINDER, HALT, thwart, impede, frustrate, BLOCK. See also ANTICIPATE.

prevention *n.* avoidance, INTERRUPTION, PROHIBITION, forbidding, hindrance, thwarting, obstruction.

preventive *adj.* precautionary, forestalling, frustrating, checking, intercepting, prohibitive.

preview: see FORESEE.

previous *adj.* earlier, PRIOR, FORMER, PRECEDING, PRELIMINARY, aforementioned.

previously: see ALREADY; BEFORE.

prey *n.* VICTIM, sufferer, GAME, pillage, LOOT, SPOIL.
— *v.* plunder, LOOT, ROB, RAID, pillage, DEVOUR, CONSUME.

price *n.* EXPENSE, COST, VALUE, CHARGE, FIGURE, WORTH, AMOUNT.
— *v.* appraise, value, assess, ESTIMATE, rate.

priceless: see PRECIOUS.

prick *v.* puncture, PIERCE, perforate, STAB, STICK, STING, SMART.
— *n.* puncture, stab, perforation, POINT, MARK, CUT.

prickle: see STING; THORN; TINGLE.

pride *n.* DIGNITY, vanity, conceit, egotism, haughtiness, arrogance, SUPERIORITY.

priest *n.* MINISTER, clergyman, PASTOR, churchman, ecclesiastic.

prim: see GROOM; NEAT.

primarily *adv.* PRINCIPALLY, MAINLY, CHIEFLY, essentially, fundamentally, notably, predominantly.

primary *adj.* PRINCIPAL, CHIEF, dominant, MAIN, BASIC, LEADING, FUNDAMENTAL.

primate: see MONKEY.

prime *n.* zenith, HEIGHT, apex, SUMMIT.
— *adj.*: see BEST; FOREMOST; ORIGINAL; RIPE.

prime minister: see MINISTER.

primitive *adj.* ORIGINAL, PRIMARY, prehistoric, BASIC, FUNDAMENTAL, uncivilized, uncultured.

primp: see BEAUTIFY.

prince *n.* RULER, sovereign, MONARCH.

principal *n.* CHIEF, LEADER, HEAD, MASTER, chieftain. See also CAPITAL.
— *adj.* MAIN, CHIEF, LEADING, BASIC, FIRST, PRIMARY, highest, FOREMOST, ESSENTIAL, PROMINENT, capital.

principality: see MONARCHY.

principally *adv.* MAINLY, CHIEFLY, essentially, PRIMARILY, ESPECIALLY, fundamentally, PARTICULARLY.

principle *n.* REGULATION, LAW, RULE, REASON, teaching, STANDARD, doctrine, METHOD.

print *v.* IMPRESS, ENGRAVE, etch, STAMP, ISSUE, PUBLISH.
— *n.* IMPRESSION, ENGRAVING, etching, STAMP, PUBLICATION.

printer: see PRESS.

printing *n.* **1** (*a beautifully detailed printing*) lithography, stamping, typography, gravure, impressing, imprinting, ENGRAVING; **2** (*this is the tenth printing*) edition, issuance, DISTRIBUTION, PUBLICATION, VERSION.

prior *adj.* PRECEDING, earlier, PREVIOUS, FORMER, FOREGOING.
— *n.*: see MONK.

priority: see PREFERENCE.

prison *n.* JAIL, penitentiary, PEN, reformatory, guardhouse, stockade, clink, cooler, jug, slammer.

prisoner *n.* CONVICT, con, jailbird, CAPTIVE, prisoner of war, hostage.

prisoner of war: see PRISONER.

privacy *n.* SECRECY, intimacy, CONCEALMENT, seclusion, RETREAT, ISOLATION, solitude, apartness.

private *adj.* **1** (*a private matter*) PERSONAL, CONFIDENTIAL, PARTICULAR, INDIVIDUAL, SECRET; **2** (*a private room*) secluded, QUIET, isolated, intimate, SEPARATE.
— *n.*: see SOLDIER.

privateering: see PIRACY.

privilege *n.* RIGHT, LICENSE, CLAIM, CHARTER, exemption, PERMISSION, GRANT.

privileged: see ELECT.

privy: see TOILET.

prize *n.* REWARD, AWARD, HONOR, PREMIUM, BONUS, recompense.
— *v.* CHERISH, ESTEEM, VALUE, WORSHIP, IDOLIZE, ADORE, RESPECT.

prized: see FAVORED; PRECIOUS.

pro: see FOR.

probability: see POSSIBILITY; THREAT.

probable *adj.* LIKELY, presumable, LIABLE, APT, REASONABLE, APPARENT, seeming.

probably *adv.* presumably, undoubtedly, APPARENTLY, plausibly, seemingly, DOUBTLESS, LIKELY, conceivably, MAYBE.

probe *v.* INVESTIGATE, EXAMINE, RESEARCH, SEARCH, EXPLORE, VERIFY, TEST, SIFT.
— *n.*: see EXPLORATION; INQUIRY; INVESTIGATION; ROCKET.

problem *n.* DIFFICULTY, predicament, OBSTACLE, dilemma, PUZZLE, QUESTION, quandary.

procedure *n.* OPERATION, PLAN, PROGRAM, SYSTEM, METHOD, PROCESS, COURSE.

proceed *v.* ADVANCE, PROGRESS, CONTINUE, MOVE, FOLLOW, FLOW, COME, GO.

proceeding: see TRANSACTION.

proceeds: see GATE; HARVEST; INCOME; PROFIT; TAKE.

process *n.* PROCEDURE, METHOD, TECHNIQUE, ROUTINE, PRACTICE, PROGRESS, DEVELOPMENT.
— *v.*: see COOK.

procession *n.* PARADE, COLUMN, MARCH, TRAIN, cavalcade, pageant, ADVANCE.

proclaim: see ANNOUNCE; CROWN; DECLARE.

proclamation *n.* ANNOUNCEMENT, decree, NOTICE, manifesto.

procrastinate: see DELAY; LAG; POSTPONE; WAIT.

procrastination: see DELAY.

procure: see ENLIST; RAISE.

prod: see DRIVE; NUDGE; REMIND; URGE.

prodigious: see ENORMOUS; GIGANTIC.

produce *v.* bring forth, YIELD, FLOWER, GIVE, FURNISH, CREATE, fabricate, manufacture, conceive, EFFECT.
— *n.* PRODUCT, HARVEST, CROP, RETURN, GATHERINGS.

producer: see FARMER; MAKER; MANUFACTURER; PARENT.

product *n.* RESULT, OUTPUT, PRODUCE, artifact, CREATION.

production *n.* **1** (*mass production*) OUTPUT, CONSTRUCTION, DEVELOPMENT, ASSEMBLY, CREATION; **2** (*a Hollywood production*) SHOW, PLAY, PROGRAM, SPECTACLE, extravaganza.

productive *adj.* prolific, FERTILE, creative, fruitful, PROFITABLE, beneficial.

productivity *n.* FERTILITY, PRODUCTION, EFFICIENCY, potency, usefulness, ABUNDANCE, RICHNESS, OUTPUT.

products: see GOODS.

profane: see WORLDLY.

profession *n.* **1** (*to learn a profession*) FIELD, vocation, specialty, OCCUPATION, CAREER; **2** (*the profession of faith*) DECLARATION, STATEMENT, ADMISSION, credo.

professional *adj.* vocational, occupational, specialized, LEARNED, certified.
— *n.* SPECIALIST, EXPERT, AUTHORITY, MASTER, connoisseur.

professor *n.* academician, TEACHER, EDUCATOR, SCHOLAR, SAGE, DOCTOR, LECTURER.

professorship: see CHAIR.

proficient: see ABLE; ACCOMPLISHED; CAPABLE; EFFICIENT; EXPERT; SKILLED.

profile *n.* silhouette, OUTLINE, SHADOW, SHAPE, FORM, FIGURE.

profit *n.* GAIN, RETURN, ADVANTAGE, EARNINGS, proceeds.
— *v.* BENEFIT, GAIN, SERVE, REAP.

profitable *adj.* PRODUCTIVE, fruitful, beneficial, advantageous.

profits: see GAIN.

profound: see DEEP; SOUND.

profoundness: see DEPTH.

profundity: see DEPTH.

profusion: see ABUNDANCE; FULLNESS; PLENTY; RICHNESS.

program *n.* **1** (*the day's program*) ACTIVITY, BUSINESS, PRESENTATION, PERFORMANCE, SHOW, PROCEDURE; **2** (*a printed program*) SCHEDULE, ANNOUNCEMENT, PLAN, LIST.
— *v.*: see SCHEDULE.

progress *n.* ADVANCEMENT, GROWTH, movement, headway, JOURNEY.
— *v.* ADVANCE, PROCEED, move along, IMPROVE, ACCELERATE.

progression: see SCALE; SUCCESSION.

progressive *adj.* **1** (*a progressive platform*) LIBERAL, open-minded, tolerant, radical; **2** (*progressive improvement*) FORWARD, REGULAR, uniform, consecutive.

prohibit *v.* FORBID, ban, OUTLAW, impede, BAR, BLOCK, EXCEPT, exclude, REMOVE.

prohibition *n.* ban, RESTRICTION, embargo, VETO, BLOCK, PREVENTION.

prohibitive: see PREVENTIVE.

project *n.* DESIGN, SCHEME, PLAN, PROGRAM, enterprise, UNDERTAKING.

— *v.* **1** (*we project higher prices*) FORESEE, ANTICIPATE, PLAN; **2** (*the bow projects proudly*) jut, protrude, EXTEND, BULGE; **3** (*to project a space probe*) LAUNCH, CAST, emit, propel, SCREEN.

projectile: see ARROW; BALL; ROCKET; SHELL.

projection: see ANGLE; BULGE.

projector: see LANTERN.

proletarian: see LABORER.

proletariat: see LABOR; PEOPLE.

prolific: see FERTILE; PRODUCTIVE.

prologue: see PREFACE.

prolong *v.* CONTINUE, LENGTHEN, EXTEND, DELAY.

prolonged: see LENGTHY.

promenade *n.* WALK, STROLL, MARCH, saunter, dance.
— *v.*: see WALK.

prominence: see DISTINCTION; FAME; VISIBILITY.

prominent *adj.* **1** (*a prominent jaw*) jutting, OUTSTANDING, protruding, CONSPICUOUS, NOTICEABLE; **2** (*a prominent citizen*) NOTABLE, WELL-KNOWN, FAMOUS.

promise *n.* **1** (*to keep a promise*) PLEDGE, VOW, assurance, guaranty; **2** (*a person of promise*) TALENT, HOPE, EXPECTATION, POTENTIAL, OUTLOOK.
— *v.* VOW, PLEDGE, SWEAR, augur, SUGGEST, GUARANTEE.

promising: see HOPEFUL; INVITING, LUCKY; POTENTIAL.

promote *v.* ELEVATE, ADVANCE, upgrade, BACK, FINANCE, FOSTER, ADVERTISE, plug.

promotion *n.* **1** (*her promotion to a higher grade*) ADVANCEMENT, ELEVATION, HONOR; **2** (*the promotion of products*) PUBLICITY, ADVERTISEMENT, ballyhoo, plug.

prompt *adj.* timely, punctual, ALERT, QUICK.
— *v.*: see NUDGE; PERSUADE.

promptly *adv.* right away, IMMEDIATELY, quickly.

promptness: see HASTE; QUICKNESS.

promulgate: see DICTATE.

prong: see TOOTH.

pronounce *v.* **1** (*pronounce this word*) SAY, enunciate, articulate, UTTER; **2** (*to pronounce a speech*) DELIVER, SPEAK, declaim. See also JUDGE.

pronouncement: see DECISION; UTTERANCE; VERDICT.

pronunciation *n.* UTTERANCE, articulation, enunciation, diction, EXPRESSION.

proof *n.* EVIDENCE, GROUNDS, CERTIFICATION, VERIFICATION, TRIAL, TEST, SAMPLE.

proofreader: see EDITOR.

prop *n.* strengthener, BRACE, SUPPORT, truss, buttress, STAY, PIN.
 — *v.* BRACE, SUPPORT, SUSTAIN, UPHOLD, truss, BEAM.

propaganda: see CAMPAIGN; COMMERCIAL; PUBLICITY.

propagate: see REPRODUCE.

propagation: see GENERATION.

propane: see GAS.

propel: see DRIVE; PROJECT; PUSH; SLING; SMASH; START.

propellant: see FUEL.

proper *adj.* CORRECT, RIGHT, JUST, ethical, DECENT, STRICT, prudish, CUSTOMARY.

properly *adv.* RIGHT, rightly, correctly, WELL, accurately.

property *n.* **1** *(private property)* POSSESSION, belongings, assets, LAND, acreage, ESTATE, GROUNDS; **2** *(a property of a substance)* CHARACTERISTIC, TRAIT, FEATURE.

prophecy: see PREDICTION.

prophesy: see FORESEE, PREDICT.

prophet *n.* **1** *(a prophet of doom)* soothsayer, oracle, medium, fortuneteller; **2** *(the prophet Isaiah)* herald, MESSENGER, spokesman, forerunner.

proportion *n.* **1** *(a certain proportion)* PART, PORTION, FRACTION, QUANTITY; **2** *(in proper proportion)* RATIO, SCALE, HARMONY, BALANCE.
 — *v.*: see GRADUATE.

proportional: see RELATIVE.

proposal *n.* PLAN, SUGGESTION, OFFER, MOTION, PROPOSITION.

propose *v.* SUGGEST, OFFER, tender, INTEND, NOMINATE.

proposition *n.* OFFER, SUGGESTION, MOTION, PLAN, PROPOSAL, SCHEME.

proprietor *n.* OWNER, possessor, holder, LANDLORD.

propulsion: see PUSH.

prosecute *v.* **1** *(to prosecute one's plan)* EXECUTE,

CONTINUE, carry out; **2** *(to prosecute a felon)* ACCUSE, CHARGE, indict, SUE.

prospect *n.* OUTLOOK, VIEW, POTENTIAL, CHANCE, expectancy, OPPORTUNITY.
 — *v.* EXPLORE, SEARCH, HUNT.

prospectus: see DRAFT.

prosper *v.* THRIVE, SUCCEED, FLOURISH, make good, BLOSSOM.

prosperity *n.* SUCCESS, FORTUNE, PLENTY, WEALTH, affluence, well-being.

prosperous *adj.* WEALTHY, SUCCESSFUL, well-off, well-to-do, affluent.

prostrate: see LOW.

protagonist: see CANDIDATE.

protect *v.* SHELTER, GUARD, SHIELD, PRESERVE, look after.

protected: see SAFE; SECURE; SNUG.

protection *n.* **1** *(the protection of the trees)* SHELTER, DEFENSE, ARMOR; **2** *(the protection of assets)* surety, SECURITY, INSURANCE; **3** *(the protection racket)* extortion, shake-down, RACKET, syndicate.

protective *adj.* defensive, WATCHFUL, armored, maternal, paternal, PARENTAL, PREVENTIVE, safeguarding.

protector *n.* GUARDIAN, defender, PATRON, CHAMPION, bodyguard, watchman, conserver, ESCORT.

protectorate: see COLONY.

protégé: see CLIENT.

protest *v.* OBJECT, DISAGREE, COMPLAIN, gripe.
 — *n.* OBJECTION, COMPLAINT, dissent, RALLY, DEMONSTRATION, sit-in.

protestation: see DEMONSTRATION; EXCEPTION.

protocol: see CEREMONY.

protoplasm: see CELL.

prototype: see MODEL.

protracted: see LONG.

protrude: see BULGE; PROJECT.

protruding: see PROMINENT.

protrusion: see BULGE.

proud *adj.* haughtly, lordly, DIGNIFIED, VAIN, self-centered, spirited, egotistic, chesty, pleased.

prove *v.* **1** *(I will prove it)* DEMONSTRATE, SHOW,

DETERMINE, deduce, substantiate, VERIFY; **2** *(the test proved negative)* result, turn out, CONCLUDE.

proven: see ASSURED; EVIDENT.

proverb *n.* saying, maxim, adage, precept, byword, MOTTO, MORAL, QUOTATION.

provide *v.* SUPPLY, FURNISH, CONTRIBUTE, AFFORD, render, administer, cater.

provided: see IF; SUPPOSING.

providence: see FORETHOUGHT.

provider: see HUSBAND; SUPPORTER; WIFE.

province *n.* **1** *(in the provinces)* TERRITORY, DIVISION, DEPARTMENT, STATE, COUNTY, REGION; **2** *(it is not my province)* CONCERN, SPHERE, realm, domain, RESPONSIBILITY, TASK, scope.

provinces: see COUNTRYSIDE.

provincial: see LOCAL.

provision: see TERM.

provisional: see TEMPORARY.

provisions: see BOARD; EQUIPMENT; FARE; FEED; FOOD; SUPPLY.

provocation: see ANNOYANCE; EXCITEMENT.

provoke *v.* AROUSE, CAUSE, incite, bring about, VEX, ANGER.

provoking: see EXCITABLE.

prow: see BEAK.

prowl *v.* slink, SNEAK, lurk, CREEP, ROVE, ROAM, ramble.

proximity: see PRESENCE; VICINITY.

proxy: see AGENT; SUBSTITUTE.

prudence: see FORETHOUGHT; PRECAUTION; TACT; THRIFT.

prudent: see CAREFUL; CAUTIOUS; WATCHFUL; WISE.

prudish: see PROPER; STRICT.

prune: see CLIP; CROP; TRIM.

pry *v.* **1** *(to pry open)* jimmy, FORCE, LOOSEN, LIFT, PUSH; **2** *(it is rude to pry)* meddle, SEEK, SEARCH, snoop, nose, PEEP.

prying: see MEDDLESOME; PERSONAL.

psalm: see HYMN.

psyche: see SELF; SOUL; SPIRIT.

psychoanalysis: see ANALYSIS.

psychopathic: see INSANE.

psychosis: see INSANITY.

psychotic: see INSANE; MANIAC; MENTAL; MISFIT.

pub: see TAVERN.

public *adj.* OPEN, COMMON, POPULAR, FREE, communal, municipal, NATIONAL, WELL-KNOWN. — *n.* PEOPLE, POPULATION, COMMUNITY, SOCIETY, citizenry, electorate, MASS.

publication *n.* **1** *(the publication of textbooks)* PRINTING, issuance, APPEARANCE, broadcast, PROCLAMATION, edition; **2** *(a recent publication)* BOOK, PRINT, ARTICLE, JOURNAL, MAGAZINE, NEWSPAPER, serial, edition.

publications: see PRESS.

publicity *n.* ADVERTISEMENT, propaganda, PROMOTION, RELEASE, plug, ballyhoo.

publicize: see AIR; REVEAL.

publicly: see ABROAD; OPENLY.

publish *v.* **1** *(to publish a book)* PRINT, ISSUE, RELEASE; **2** *(to publish a fact)* ANNOUNCE, AIR, BROADCAST, PROMOTE, REPORT.

publisher: see EDITOR.

publishing: see PRESS.

pucker: see GATHER; WRINKLE.

puddle: see POOL.

pudgy: see FAT; PLUMP; STUBBY.

puff *n.* pant, BLOW, BREATH, GUST, BURST, drag. — *v.* PANT, EXHALE, ENLARGE, SWELL, INFLATE, huff.

puffing: see GASP.

pugnacious: see AGGRESSIVE.

pull *v.* TOW, DRAW, DRAG, HAUL, TUG, JERK, EXTRACT, REMOVE. — *n.* TOW, DRAG, STRAIN, INFLUENCE, clout, POWER.

pulley: see HOIST; LIFT; TACKLE.

pulp *n.* pap, mush, FLESH, MASH, PASTE, JAM, jelly.

pulsate: see BEAT; THROB.

pulse *n.* **1** *(a rapid pulse)* BEAT, heartbeat, THROB, VIBRATION; **2** *(the public pulse)* MOOD, TEMPER, INCLINATION.

pulverize: see CRUMBLE; GRIND; MASH; MILL; POUND.

pummel: see BATTER; BEAT.

pump: see TAP.

punch *n.* **1** *(a punch in the nose)* sock, smash, POKE, uppercut, jab, VIGOR; **2** *(a metal punch)* bore, STAMP, pick, PRESS, NEEDLE; **3** *(fruit punch)* cocktail, DRINK, BEVERAGE.
— *v.* sock, wallop, POKE, PIERCE, perforate, DRILL.

punctual: see EXACT; PROMPT.

punctuality: see REGULARITY.

punctually: see SHARP.

punctuate: see DOT.

punctuation: see PERIOD.

puncture: see HOLE; LEAK; OPEN; PIERCE; PIT; PRICK.

pungent: see PEPPERY.

punish *v.* penalize, CORRECT, DISCIPLINE, FINE, imprison, EXILE, TORTURE, EXECUTE, MISTREAT, ABUSE, chastise.

punishment *n.* PENALTY, SENTENCE, FINE, DISCIPLINE, penance, imprisonment, ABUSE, mistreatment.

punster: see WIT.

punt: see BOOT; KICK.

puny: see FEEBLE; UNHEALTHY; WEAK.

pup: see INFANT.

pupil *n.* **1** *(a new pupil)* STUDENT, learner, FOLLOWER, DISCIPLE, adherent; **2** *(the pupil of the eye)* EYE, eyeball, iris.

puppet: see DOLL.

purblind: see BLIND.

purchase *v.* BUY, ACQUIRE, GET, OBTAIN.
— *n.* BUY, acquisition, DEAL, TRANSACTION, POSSESSION, BARGAIN.

purchaser: see CUSTOMER; PATRON.

pure *adj.* **1** *(pure gold)* GENUINE, unmixed, unstained, unblemished, immaculate, sinless, VIRTUOUS, vestal, chaste; **2** *(pure nonsense)* UTTER, TOTAL, COMPLETE, ABSOLUTE.

purely *adv.* wholly, ENTIRELY, COMPLETELY, utterly, SIMPLY.

pureness: see SIMPLICITY.

purge: see CLEANSE.

purify: see AIR; CLEAN; CLEANSE; IMPROVE; REFINE.

purity: see CLEANLINESS; GOODNESS; INNOCENCE; PERFECTION; VIRGINITY.

purport: see MEANING.

purpose *n.* MOTIVE, REASON, END, PLAN, design, RESOLUTION, DETERMINATION.
— *v.*: see AIM; MEAN.

purposeful: see DELIBERATE; INDUSTRIOUS; INTENTIONAL; SINGLE-MINDED.

purposely *adv.* DELIBERATELY, knowingly, designedly, intentionally, advisedly.

purse *n.* **1** *(a change purse)* pocketbook, BAG, handbag, POUCH; **2** *(the winner's purse)* PRIZE, BANK, treasury, STAKE, pot, POOL, PROFIT, TAKE.

pursue *v.* **1** *(to pursue a criminal)* CHASE, TRACK, TRAIL, PERSECUTE, hound; **2** *(to pursue a goal)* SEEK, FOLLOW, STRIVE, PRACTICE, CRAVE.

pursuer: see FOLLOWER; HUNTER.

pursuit *n.* chase, RACE, SEARCH, quest, CAREER, PROFESSION.

push *v.* THRUST, impel, propel, SHOVE, PRESS, STRAIN, PROMOTE, plug.
— *n.* DRIVE, THRUST, propulsion, PRESSURE, ENERGY, PROMOTION.

pushcart: see CART.

pushing: see FORCEFUL.

pushover: see SAP.

pushy: see FORWARD.

pussyfoot: see HEDGE; MINCE.

put *v.* PLACE, LOCATE, situate, SET, ESTABLISH, INSTALL, POSE, insert, EMPLOY.

put back: see RESTORE.

put down: see DAMN; HUMBLE; LAY.

put in: see PACK.

put off: see ADJOURN; CHARGE.

put on: see STAGE.

put out: see QUENCH.

putter: see DABBLE; LOAF.

put up: see CAN; CONSTRUCT; ERECT.

puzzle *n.* RIDDLE, MYSTERY, PROBLEM, maze, enigma, GAME, jigsaw, crossword, cryptogram, labyrinth, sphinx, UNKNOWN, SECRET.
— *v.* CONFUSE, mystify, perplex, BEWILDER, stump, BAFFLE, marvel, WONDER.

puzzling: see DOUBTFUL.

pygmy: see DWARF.

Q

qua: see AS.

quadrangle: see COURT; SQUARE; YARD.

quadrilateral: see SQUARE.

quagmire: see MARSH; SWAMP.

quaint *adj.* ODD, RARE, QUEER, UNUSUAL, OLD-FASHIONED, fanciful, whimsical.

quake: see SHUDDER; VIBRATE.

qualification *n.* **1** *(to have the qualifications)* aptitude, FITNESS, essential, NEED, REQUIREMENT; **2** *(to impose a qualification)* CONDITION, RESERVATION, EXCEPTION. See also RESTRICTION.

qualified: see ABLE.

qualify *v.* SUIT, FIT, FULFILL, PASS, LIMIT, temper, MODIFY.

quality *n.* CHARACTERISTIC, NATURE, TRAIT, CLASS, caliber, EXCELLENCE, VALUE, DISTINCTION.

qualm: see RELUCTANCE.

quandary: see PROBLEM, UNCERTAINTY.

quantity *n.* VOLUME, AMOUNT, ABUNDANCE, SUPPLY, LOT, NUMBER.

quarantine: see ISOLATE; ISOLATION.

quarrel *n.* DISPUTE, ARGUMENT, FEUD, squabble, FIGHT, OBJECTION.
  — *v.* FIGHT, ARGUE, contend, DISPUTE, OBJECT, misunderstanding.

quarrelsome: see DISAGREEABLE; UGLY.

quarry: see GAME; MINE; TARGET.

quarter: see ACCOMMODATE; COIN; NEIGHBORHOOD; PLACE; REGION; SHELTER.

quarterly: see BULLETIN.

quarters: see APARTMENT; LODGINGS; ROOM.

quartz: see MINERAL.

quaver: see TREMBLE.

queen *n.* RULER, MONARCH, matriarch, empress, czarina, queen consort, queen regent.

queen consort: see QUEEN.

queen regent: see QUEEN.

queer *adj.* ODD, PECULIAR, STRANGE, RARE, QUAINT, SUSPICIOUS.

quench *v.* **1** *(to quench the thirst)* SATISFY, appease, remedy, DRINK; **2** *(to quench flames)* SMOTHER, stifle, douse, put out.

query: see ASK; DOUBT; INQUIRY; QUESTION; QUIZ.

quest: see EXPEDITION; PURSUIT; SEARCH; SEEK.

question *n.* INQUIRY, query, inquest, PROBLEM, PUZZLE.
  — *v.* query, ASK, interrogate, PROBE, DOUBT, EXAMINE.

questionable *adj.* DOUBTFUL, disputable, debatable, unlikely, SUSPICIOUS.

questioning: see CURIOUS; CURIOSITY; MISTRUST; QUIZ; SUSPICIOUS.

questionnaire: see BLANK; FORM; QUIZ; SURVEY.

queue: see LINE; STRING.

quibble: see STALL.

quick *adj.* fleet, FAST, RAPID, IMMEDIATE, DIRECT, PROMPT, ALERT, quick-witted, perceptive.

quicken: see ACCELERATE; HASTEN.

quickly: see PROMPTLY; READILY; SOON; SWIFTLY.

quickness *n.* SPEED, rapidity, swiftness, BRISKNESS, liveliness, promptness, HASTE, ALERTNESS.

quick-witted: see QUICK; SMART.

quiet *adj.* CALM, STILL, immobile, SILENT, SOUNDLESS, placid, MODEST, SHY, taciturn.
  — *n.* SILENCE, PEACE, quietude.
  — *v.*: see CALM; HUSH; PEACE; SOOTHE; STILL.

quietly: see SOFTLY.

quietness: see CALMNESS; PATIENCE; TRANQUILLITY.

quietude: see CALMNESS; QUIET.

quill: see BRISTLE; PEN; PLUME; SPINE.

quilt: see CUSHION; LINE.

quip: see JEST; JOKE.

quire: see PAD.

quirk: see ODDITY.

quisling: see TRAITOR.

quit *v.* CEASE, DISCONTINUE, desist, leave off, LEAVE, DEPART, RESIGN.

quite *adv.* considerably, RATHER, TRULY, VERY, ENTIRELY, COMPLETELY.

quitting: see RESIGNATION; STRIKE.

quiver *v.* TREMBLE, SHUDDER, SHAKE, VIBRATE.
  — *n.*: see JAR; TINGLE; TWITCH; VIBRATION.

quivering: see SHAKY.

quiz *n.* TEST, exam, interrogation, query, questioning, questionnaire, RIDDLE.
  — *v.*: see TEST.

quizzical: see SUSPICIOUS.

quota: see RATIO; RATION.

quotation *n.* citation, EXTRACT, excerpt, SELECTION, PRICE.

quote *v.* REPEAT, cite, excerpt, RECITE, evidence.

R

rabble: see MOB; PEOPLE.

race *n.* **1** (*the human race*) SPECIES, BREED, VARIETY, PEOPLE, lineage, TRIBE, FOLK; **2** (*a foot race*) CONTEST, COMPETITION, meet, ENGAGEMENT, marathon, sprint, derby, regatta.
 — *v.* SPEED, DASH, sprint, CHASE, COMPETE.

racer: see RUNNER.

rack *n.* FRAME, STAND, framework, SHELF, hanger, stretcher, TORTURE.

racket *n.* **1** (*an unbearable racket*) din, NOISE, CLATTER, DISTURBANCE; **2** (*a tennis racket*) paddle, BAT; **3** (*the protection racket*) extortion, shake-down, corruption, CRIME, confidence game, syndicate.

racketeer: see GANGSTER; HOOD.

rackety: see NOISY.

radiance: see BRILLIANCE; LIGHT; LUSTER.

radiant *adj.* luminous, BRIGHT, incandescent, BRILLIANT, HAPPY, beaming, delighted, aglow.

radiate *v.* **1** (*the spokes radiate from the hub*) diffuse, spread, disperse, BROADCAST, irradiate; **2** (*heat radiates from the sun*) BEAM, LIGHT, ILLUMINE, GLOW, GLARE.

radical: see EXTREME; FUNDAMENTAL; PROGRESSIVE; REBEL.

radicals: see LEFT.

radio: see CABLE; PHONE.

radiophone: see PHONE.

radiotelephone: see PHONE.

raffle: see GAMBLE.

raft *n.* barge, BOAT, flatboat, float.

rafter: see BEAM; TIMBER.

rafters: see ATTIC.

rag *n.* CLOTH, washrag, washcloth, dishrag, dishcloth, MOP, wiper, tatter.

rage *n.* **1** (*to fly into a rage*) FURY, ANGER, wrath, rampage; **2** (*it's the rage*) FASHION, fad, vogue, STYLE, craze.
 — *v.* rant, bluster, storm, RAVE, EXPLODE, go mad, go crazy.

ragged *adj.* tattered, frayed, torn, SHABBY, WORN, scraggly.

raging: see EXPLOSIVE; VIOLENT.

raid *n.* ATTACK, INVASION, incursion, foray, seizure.
 — *v.* overrun, INVADE, ATTACK, plunder, break in.

raider: see INVADER.

rail *n.* **1** (*a hand rail*) RAILING, BAR, BARRIER, banister, FENCE; **2** (*to travel by rail*) railroad, railway, TRACK, monorail.

railing *n.* BARRIER, FENCE, banister, BAR, GUARD.

railroad: see RAIL; TRACK.

railway: see RAIL.

raiment: see GARMENT.

rain *n.* rainfall, raindrop, precipitation, drizzle, MIST, shower, STORM, cloudburst.
 — *v.* DROP, POUR, SPRINKLE, shower, deluge.

raindrop: see RAIN.

rainfall: see RAIN.

rainless: see FAIR.

raise *v.* **1** (*to raise a structure*) LIFT, UPLIFT, ELEVATE, HOIST, ERECT, AROUSE, incite, EXCITE, heighten; **2** (*to raise children*) REAR, nurture, BREED, GROW, CULTIVATE; **3** (*to raise money*) COLLECT, GATHER, procure, BORROW.
 — *n.* INCREASE, RISE, ELEVATION, PROMOTION.

raised: see GROWN; LOFTY.

raising: see LIFT.

rake *v.* SCRAPE, CLEAR, SMOOTH, TILL, GRADE, SEARCH, COMB.

rally *v.* GATHER, convene, ASSEMBLE, DEMONSTRATE, RECUPERATE.
 — *n.* ASSEMBLY, DEMONSTRATION, PROTEST, sit-in.

ram *v.* **1** (*to ram a ship*) CRASH, STRIKE, butt, BATTER; **2** (*to ram a wad*) cram, PACK, STUFF, tamp.
 — *n.*: see SHEEP.

ramble: see PROWL; ROAM; ROVE; STROLL; WALK; WANDER.

rambler: see DRIFTER; ROVER.

rambunctious: see ROWDY.

ramification: see TWIG.

ramp: see HILLSIDE.

rampage: see FURY; RAGE.

ranch *n.* FARM, plantation, grange, ESTATE, rancho.

rancher *n.* FARMER, cattleman, sheepman, breeder, planter, ranchero.

ranchero: see RANCHER.

rancho: see RANCH.

rancid: see OLD; ROTTEN; SOUR.

rancor: see RESENTMENT.

rancorous: see HATEFUL.

random *adj.* CASUAL, chance, haphazard, accidental.

randomly: see ANYHOW, AROUND.

range *n.* **1** (*long-range signals*) SPAN, EXTENT, REACH, AREA, WIDTH, LENGTH, DISTANCE, LIMIT, VARIATION; **2** (*home on the range*) PLAIN, PASTURE, MEADOW, prairie, grassland; **3** (*a range of mountains*) CHAIN, sierra; **4** (*a cooking range*) STOVE, cooker. See also SIGHT.
— *v.* VARY, EXTEND, REACH, encompass, ROVE.

rank *n.* ROW, ORDER, COLUMN, POSITION, status, GRADE.
— *v.* ARRANGE, CLASSIFY, align, precede, outrank.

rank and file: see MEMBERSHIP.

ranking: see ELDER.

ransack: see LOOT; SEARCH.

ransom *n.* PRICE, compensation, redemption, expiation.
— *v.* REDEEM, RESCUE, DELIVER, LIBERATE, BUY, RECOVER.

rant: see RAGE; RAVE; SHOUT.

rap *n.* **1** (*a rap on the door*) TAP, KNOCK, whack, slap; **2** (*to take the rap*) blame, FAULT, RESPONSIBILITY, CRITICISM.
— *v.* **1** (*to rap for silence*) TAP, SLAP, STRIKE, KNOCK; **2** (*to rap for a while*) TALK, CONVERSE, CHAT.

rape: see ASSAULT.

rapid *adj.* SPEEDY, SWIFT, IMMEDIATE, nimble, LIVELY, fleet.

rapidity: see HASTE; QUICKNESS; SPEED.

rapidly: see SWIFTLY.

rapier: see SWORD.

rapport: see RELATION.

rapture: see HEAVEN; JOY.

rare *adj.* **1** (*with rare modesty*) UNCOMMON, UNACCUSTOMED, infrequent, SCARCE, select, EXCEPTIONAL; **2** (*make mine rare*) RAW, underdone, uncooked.

rarely *adv.* SELDOM, HARDLY, scarcely, now and then.

rarity: see ANTIQUE; CURIOSITY; MIRACLE; ODDITY; SCARCITY.

rascal *n.* scamp, scalawag, imp, rogue, mischief-maker, SCOUNDREL.

rascally: see MISCHIEVOUS.

rash *adj.* RECKLESS, IMPULSIVE, CARELESS, FOOLISH, foolhardy.
— *n.* OUTBREAK, epidemic, ERUPTION, INFLAMMATION.

rashness: see INSANITY.

rate *n.* **1** (*what is the rate?*) AMOUNT, PRICE, SPEED, RATIO, EXCHANGE; **2** (*third rate*) RANK, status, QUALITY.
— *v.*: see CALCULATE; DESERVE; ESTIMATE; GAUGE; GRADE; MARK; PRICE; SCORE.

rather *adv.* **1** (*it is rather hot*) QUITE, INDEED, CERTAINLY, considerably; **2** (*I would rather not say*) sooner, preferably, INSTEAD, MORE.

rather than: see INSTEAD.

ratification: see APPROVAL.

ratify: see APPROVE; CONFIRM; STRIKE; SUSTAIN.

rating: see GRADE; MARK.

ratio *n.* RELATIONSHIP, PROPORTION, RATE, quota.

ration *n.* SHARE, PROPORTION, quota, PORTION, allotment.
— *v.* DISTRIBUTE, allot, apportion, LIMIT, CONTROL.

rational: see INTELLIGENT, LOGICAL; MENTAL; SANE.

rationality: see LOGIC.

rationally: see PRACTICALLY.

rationing: see DISTRIBUTION.

rations: see FARE; MESS.

rattle *v.* **1** (*the windows rattled*) clatter, clack, SHAKE, CHATTER, prattle; **2** (*to rattle a person*) UPSET, unnerve, CONFUSE, disconcert.
— *n.*: see CLATTER.

rattlesnake: see SNAKE.

raucous: see HOARSE.

ravage: see DESTROY.

rave v. **1** (*to rant and rave*) BABBLE, jabber, splutter, RAGE, rant; **2** (*they raved about us*) exalt, extol, FLATTER.

raven: see JET.

ravenous: see HUNGRY.

ravine: see CANYON; FRANTIC; GAP; PASS; VALLEY.

ravish: see ABUSE; ASSAULT.

ravishing: see BEAUTIFUL; STUNNING.

raw adj. **1** (*a raw egg*) uncooked, RARE, underdone, unprepared, NATURAL, CRUDE; **2** (*raw recruits*) NEW, inexperienced, GREEN, untrained; **3** (*a raw day*) COLD, wintry, biting, bleak; **4** (*the raw flesh*) exposed, SORE, irritated, WOUNDED, PAINFUL.

ray n. BEAM, STREAM, GLEAM, glimmer, FLICKER, glint, SUGGESTION, BIT, TRACE.

raze: see DESTROY; LEVEL.

razor: see BLADE.

reach v. **1** (*to reach a goal*) ARRIVE, get there, ATTAIN, ACHIEVE, EXTEND, LAST, suffice; **2** (*I can't reach it*) hand over, pass, STRETCH, TOUCH, GRASP, CONTACT. See also AMOUNT.
— n. RANGE, EXTENT, scope, COMPASS, GRASP, CAPACITY.

reaching: see RUNNING.

react: see RESPOND.

reaction n. ANSWER, RESPONSE, reflex, rebound, RETURN, recoil, RESULT.

reactionary: see CONSERVATIVE.

read v. decipher, SCAN, GRASP, comprehend, INTERPRET, infer.
— adj.: see LEARNED.

readable adj. legible, DISTINCT, intelligible, COMPREHENSIBLE, INTERESTING, engaging, PLEASURABLE.

reader: see EDITOR.

readers: see CIRCULATION.

readily adv. easily, quickly, PROMPTLY, GLADLY, FREELY.

readiness: see ALERTNESS; EASE; EFFICIENCY; PREPARATION.

reading n. **1** (*reading and writing*) literacy, EDUCATION, phonics, letters; **2** (*a public reading*) recitation, DELIVERY, VERSION, excerpt, EXTRACT, PASSAGE; **3** (*to take a reading*) readout, RECORD, INDICATION, SCORE, status, OBSERVATION.

readout: see READING.

ready adj. **1** (*dinner is ready*) AVAILABLE, SUITABLE, RIPE, accessible, HANDY; **2** (*a ready answer*) ALERT, PROMPT, QUICK, IMMEDIATE, CONVENIENT. See also ABOUT.
— v.: see COCK; COOK; FIX; PREPARE; SET.

real adj. ACTUAL, TRUE, AUTHENTIC, GENUINE, ORIGINAL, factual, full-fledged.

real estate: see DEVELOPMENT.

reality n. actuality, TRUTH, EXISTENCE, DEED, FACT, certainty.

realization n. **1** (*the realization of goals*) fulfillment, ACHIEVEMENT, completion, EXECUTION; **2** (*the realization of his failure*) CONSCIOUSNESS, KNOWLEDGE, comprehension, awareness.

realize v. **1** (*to realize a fact*) UNDERSTAND, comprehend, GRASP, SEE, RECOGNIZE; **2** (*to realize a plan*) carry out, FULFILL, ACHIEVE, ACCOMPLISH; **3** (*to realize a gain*) REAP, EARN, clear, BENEFIT, PROFIT.

realized: see KNOWN.

really adv. TRULY, INDEED, ABSOLUTELY, POSITIVELY, SURELY, VERY, EXTREMELY.

realm: see KINGDOM; ORBIT; PROVINCE; REGION; SPHERE; TERRITORY.

ream: see PAD.

reap v. **1** (*to reap a crop*) HARVEST, GATHER, CUT, mow; **2** (*to reap a gain*) GAIN, EARN, PROFIT, BENEFIT, DERIVE.

reaping: see HARVEST.

rear n. BACK, posterior, backside, TAIL, hind end, rear end, END, rump.
— adj. HIND, BACK, posterior, after.
— v. RAISE, nurture, care for, look after, TRAIN, uprear, ELEVATE, LIFT.

rear end: see REAR; TAIL.

rearrangement: see TRANSFORMATION.

rearward: see BACKWARD.

reason n. **1** (*the age of reason*) INTELLIGENCE, INTELLECT, common sense, LOGIC; **2** (*a good reason*) CAUSE, MOTIVE, END, motivation.
— v. THINK, ANALYZE, REFLECT, deduce.

reasonable adj. **1** (*a reasonable excuse*) plausible, SENSIBLE, LOGICAL, WISE; **2** (*a reasonable price*) moderate, JUST, FAIR, acceptable.

reasonableness: see SANITY.

reasoned: see DELIBERATE.

reasoning: see DEBATE; HEAD; LIGHT; THINKING.

reasons: see GROUNDS.

reassure: see ASSURE; COMFORT.

rebate: see REFUND.

rebel *n.* dissenter, nonconformist, radical, revolutionist, mutineer, guerrilla.
− *v.* REVOLT, RESIST, mutiny, OBJECT, BETRAY, OVERTHROW.

rebellion *n.* REVOLT, REVOLUTION, defiance, mutiny, RESISTANCE, uprising, coup d'état.

rebound: see ECHO; GLANCE; REACTION.

rebuild: see REPRODUCE.

rebuilt: see FIXED.

rebuke: see CHECK; DISAPPROVAL; LASH; LESSON; SCOLD.

recall *v.* **1** (*I can't recall*) REMEMBER, RECOLLECT, reminisce; **2** (*to recall an official*) DISCHARGE, SUSPEND, revoke, retract, repeal, WITHDRAW. See also RETAIN.
− *n.*: see MEMORY; REMEMBRANCE.

recant: see APOLOGIZE; REPENT.

recapitulation: see REVIEW.

recapture: see RECOVER; RECOVERY; REGAIN; RESCUE.

recast: see REFORM; REVISE.

recede: see CONTRACT; RETREAT.

receipt *n.* **1** (*to pay on receipt*) receiving, DELIVERY, acceptance; **2** (*to sign a receipt*) acknowledgment, NOTICE, I.O.U., memo, memorandum, STUB, voucher.
− *v.*: see SIGN.

receipts: see EARNINGS; INCOME; REVENUE.

receive *v.* **1** (*to receive a salary*) GET, GAIN, ACCEPT, ACQUIRE, COLLECT, WIN; **2** (*to receive a blow*) undergo, SUFFER, BEAR, SUSTAIN; **3** (*to receive guests*) WELCOME, ADMIT, GREET, usher in.

receiver *n.* accepter, obtainer, recipient, collector, acquirer, retriever, inheritor.

receiving: see RECEIPT; RECEPTION.

recency: see FRESHNESS.

recent *adj.* LATE, NEW, FRESH, MODERN, CURRENT, CONTEMPORARY, UP-TO-DATE.

recently *adv.* LATELY, NEWLY, latterly.

receptacle: see BIN; BOWL; BOX; CAN; CASE; CHAMBER; CONTAINER; PAN; PAIL; TANK; TRAY; VESSEL.

reception *n.* RECEIPT, receiving, acceptance, WELCOME, ADMISSION, greeting, ENTERTAINMENT, PARTY, GATHERING.

receptive: see HOSPITABLE; OPEN; SENSATIONAL.

recess *n.* **1** (*a recess in the wall*) niche, nook, hollow, indentation, slot; **2** (*it's time for recess*) BREAK, playtime, intermission, PAUSE.

recession: see DEPRESSION.

recipe *n.* directions, FORMULA, PRESCRIPTION, METHOD, PROCEDURE.

recipient: see GRADUATE; RECEIVER.

reciprocate: see ALTERNATE.

recital: see ACCOUNT; CONCERT.

recitation: see LESSON; NARRATION; READING; REPETITION.

recite *v.* REPEAT, parrot, REHEARSE, REPORT, SPEAK, NARRATE, RELATE, recount, ITEMIZE.

reckless *adj.* heedless, CARELESS, foolhardy, RASH, THOUGHTLESS, DARING.

reckon *v.* COUNT, tally, FIGURE, CALCULATE, ESTIMATE, compute, THINK, SUPPOSE, JUDGE.

reclaim: see REDEEM; REFORM; RESCUE; RESTORE.

reclaimed: see SECOND-HAND.

reclamation: see REFORM.

recline: see LIE.

recluse: see HERMIT.

recognition *n.* REMEMBRANCE, recollection, acknowledgment, NOTICE, acceptance, ALLOWANCE, commendation, HONOR.

recognize *v.* REMEMBER, RECOLLECT, RECALL, ACKNOWLEDGE, NOTICE, ACCEPT, ADMIT, APPROVE, IDENTIFY, SALUTE, COMPREHEND, UNDERSTAND.

recognized: see KNOWN; WELL-KNOWN.

recoil: see BOUNCE; KICK; REACTION.

recollect *v.* REMEMBER, RECALL, RECOGNIZE.

recollection: see MEMORY; RECOGNITION; REMEMBRANCE.

recommence: see RESUME.

recommend *v.* ADVISE, SUGGEST, URGE, entrust, APPROVE, PRAISE, commend.

recommendation *n.* ADVICE, SUGGESTION, APPROVAL, PRAISE, commendation, testimonial, REFERENCE.

recompense: see PAY; PAYMENT; PREMIUM; PRIZE; RIGHT.

reconcile: see ADAPT; ADJUST; BALANCE; UNIFY; UNITE.

reconciliation: see COMPROMISE; REUNION.

recondition: see REPAIR.

reconnoiter: see SCOUT.

reconstruct: see REFORM; REPRODUCE.

reconstruction: see REPAIR.

record *n.* recording, disk, platter, release, album, TAPE, HISTORY, chronicle, ACCOUNT, memo, NOTE, JOURNAL, allusion, SCORE. See also CEILING.
  — *v.* REGISTER, ENTER, transcribe, REPORT, set down, WRITE.

recorded: see HISTORICAL.

recorder: see CLERK.

recording: see RECORD; TAPE.

recount: see ITEMIZE; NARRATE; RECITE; REHEARSE; RELATE; REPEAT; REPORT.

recounting: see REHEARSAL.

recover *v.* REGAIN, retake, get back, retrieve, repossess, recapture, salvage, RECUPERATE, convalesce, HEAL, IMPROVE.

recovery *n.* RETURN, retrieval, recapture, repossession, recuperation, convalescence, IMPROVEMENT.

recreation: see AMUSEMENT; ENTERTAINMENT; FUN; GAME; HOBBY; LEISURE; PLEASURE; RELAXATION; SPORT.

recreational: see ATHLETIC.

recruit: see DRAFT; VOLUNTEER.

rectangle: see SQUARE.

rectification: see CORRECTION; REFORM.

rectify: see ADJUST; AMEND; CORRECT; EDIT; REFORM; REPAIR; REVISE; RIGHT; STRAIGHTEN.

recuperate *v.* REST, RECOVER, RALLY, revive, HEAL, IMPROVE, REGAIN.

recuperation: see RECOVERY.

recur: see PERSIST; REPEAT; RETURN.

recurrence: see CONTINUATION; REPETITION; RETURN.

recurrent: see CONTINUAL; FREQUENT; PERIODIC.

recurrently: see OFTEN.

recurring: see ROUND.

red *adj.* reddish, ruddy, rosy, blushing, bloody, red-faced, red-haired, sandy, pink, crimson, ruby, scarlet, vermilion, CARDINAL, cherry, maroon, magenta.

redcap: see PORTER.

redden: see BLUSH; COLOR; FLAME.

reddening: see GLOW; INFLAMMATION.

reddish: see RED.

redeem *v.* RECOVER, REGAIN, RESTORE, reclaim, DELIVER, FREE, RESCUE, COMPENSATE, buy back, RANSOM, LIBERATE.

redemption: see RANSOM.

red-faced: see RED.

red-haired: see RED.

redo: see REPRODUCE.

redolent: see FRAGRANT.

redress: see RIGHT.

red-tape: see OFFICIAL.

reduce *v.* DIMINISH, LESSEN, CUT, curtail, minimize, SHRINK, lose, DECREASE, WEAKEN, CONQUER, SUBJECT, alleviate.

reduction *n.* lessening, cutting, diminishing, shrinking, LOSS, decrease, subjection.

reed: see PIPE.

reef: see ISLAND; KEY; ROCK; SHELF.

reek: see ODOR; SMELL; SMOKE; STINK.

reel *n.* SPOOL, bobbin, spindle, axle.
  — *v.* SWAY, STAGGER, TOTTER, waver, TURN, WIND, SPIN, WHIRL.

reestablish: see RESTORE; TRANSPLANT.

refashion: see REFORM.

refer *v.* MENTION, DIRECT, POINT, allude, SEEK, ATTRIBUTE, CONCERN, REGARD.

referee: see JUDGE; TRY.

reference *n.* MENTION, mentioning, ascription, allusion, INFORMATION, RECOMMENDATION, CERTIFICATE.

referendum: see ELECTION; VOTE.

referring: see RELATIVE.

refer to: see REGARD.

refine *v.* CLARIFY, purify, SHARPEN, IMPROVE.

refined: see CLASSIC; DELICATE; ELEGANT; FINE; GENTLE; MANNERLY; NICE; POLITE.

refinement: see CIVILIZATION; CLARIFICATION; CULTURE; ELEGANCE; GRACE; POLITENESS; REFORM; STYLE.

refit: see MODERNIZE.

reflect *v.* MIRROR, COPY, throw back, give back, REVERSE, REPRODUCE, SHOW, discredit, ponder, MEDITATE, contemplate, muse. See also GLANCE.

reflection *n.* image, likeness, COPY, APPEARANCE, CRITICISM, reproach, THOUGHT, MEDITATION, contemplation, musing.

reflective: see THOUGHTFUL.

reflex: see REACTION.

reform *v.* BETTER, IMPROVE, rectify, reclaim, CORRECT, REPAIR, HELP, regenerate, DEVELOP, remodel, reshape, recast, refashion, UPLIFT, reconstruct.
— *n.* betterment, IMPROVEMENT, rectification, reclamation, CORRECTION, REPAIR, HELP, regeneration, DEVELOPMENT, REVISION, CHANGE, refinement, enrichment.

refrain: see AVOID; CEASE; CHANT; REPETITION; STOP; WITHHOLD.

refresh *v.* FRESHEN, invigorate, reinvigorate, enliven, rejuvenate, RENEW, renovate, cheer, STRENGTHEN.

refreshed: see NEW.

refreshing *adj.* satisfying, restful, soothing, cooling, calming, invigorating, COMFORTABLE.

refreshment: see BEVERAGE.

refreshments *pl.n.* tonic, stimulant, bracer, beverages, drinks, cocktails, beer, wine, FOOD, lunch, buffet, SNACK.

refrigerate *v.* COOL, CHILL, FREEZE, air-condition.

refuge *n.* shelter, haven, RETREAT, sanctuary, asylum, PROTECTION, COVER, resort.

refund *v.* RETURN, remit, repay, rebate, reimburse, ADJUST, RESTORE.

refurbish: see MODERNIZE; RENEW.

refusal: see RESISTANCE; VETO.

refuse *v.* REJECT, DECLINE, disallow, DENY, renounce, turn down.
— *n.* GARBAGE, RUBBISH, TRASH, scraps, WASTE, slops, scum, leavings.

refused: see FORBIDDEN.

regain *v.* RECOVER, retrieve, recapture, repossess, reobtain.

regal: see ROYAL.

regard *v.* CONSIDER, SCAN, OBSERVE, look at, gaze upon, contemplate, HEED, RESPECT, relate to, concern, refer to, NOTICE.
— *n.* CONSIDERATION, greeting, RESPECT, HEED, CARE, ESTEEM, AFFECTION, FAVOR, LOOK, gaze, ATTENTION, NOTICE.

regarding: see CONCERNING; TOWARD.

regardless of: see DESPITE.

regards: see GREETINGS.

regatta: see RACE.

regenerate: see HEAL; REFORM.

regime: see REIGN.

regimen: see DIET.

regiment: see CORPS.

region *n.* AREA, VICINITY, LOCALITY, TERRITORY, DISTRICT, ZONE, locale, NEIGHBORHOOD, quarter, realm, SPHERE, COUNTRY.

regional: see LOCAL.

register *n.* RECORD, LIST, ROLL, roster, CATALOG, HISTORY, annals, archives.
— *v.* RECORD, INSCRIBE, ENTER, ENROLL, SIGN, SHOW, INDICATE.

registrar: see CLERK.

regret *v.* bewail, deplore, lament, MOURN, REPENT, APOLOGIZE.
— *n.* SORROW, SADNESS, GRIEF, CONCERN, DISAPPOINTMENT, contrition, remorse, APOLOGY.

regretful: see AFRAID; APOLOGETIC; ASHAMED; SORRY.

regrettable: see UNFORTUNATE.

regular *adj.* CUSTOMARY, HABITUAL, NORMAL, USUAL, COMMON, TYPICAL, STEADY, uniform, EVEN, LOYAL, ACTIVE, FIXED, AVERAGE, PERMANENT, LAWFUL, GOOD, SMOOTH, symmetrical, SYSTEMATIC, SET, equidistant.

regularity *n.* HABIT, ROUTINE, SYSTEM, ORDER, RULE, METHOD, CUSTOM, HARMONY, symmetry, BALANCE, CORRESPONDENCE, punctuality, cycle, frequency, periodicity, uniformity.

regularly *adv.* USUALLY, habitually, normally, customarily, typically, FREQUENTLY.

regulate *v.* ADJUST, DETERMINE, DIRECT, CONTROL, MANAGE, DISPOSE, GOVERN, systematize, LEGISLATE, REPAIR.

regulation *n.* RULE, directive, ordinance, LAW, statute, COMMAND, ORDER, PRINCIPLE, SUPERVISION.

regulator: see CONTROL; GOVERNOR.

rehabilitate: see CURE.

rehabilitating: see CORRECTIVE.

rehearsal *n.* PRACTICE, practicing, PREPARATION, DRILL, REPETITION, recounting, PERFORMANCE.

rehearse *v.* REPEAT, PRACTICE, TRAIN, recount, DESCRIBE, RELATE, DETAIL.

rehearsed: see PRACTICED.

reign *n.* RULE, dominion, sovereignty, POWER, sway, CONTROL, regime, incumbency.
− *v.* RULE, prevail, GOVERN, DOMINATE, COMMAND, CONTROL, predominate.

reimburse: see COMPENSATE; REFUND.

rein *n.* leash, BRIDLE, lines, STRAP, CONTROL, restraint, deterrent, GUIDE.
− *v.* restrain, CURB, GUIDE, CONTROL, GOVERN, CHECK, repress, deter.

reinforce: see BRACE; BUILD; PATCH.

reins: see BRIDLE.

reinstate: see REPLACE; RESTORE.

reinstatement: see REPLACEMENT.

reinvigorate: see REFRESH.

reiteration: see REPETITION.

reject *v.* REFUSE, spurn, DECLINE, DENY, repel, turn down, renounce, ELIMINATE, EXPEL, disdain, DISCARD, disbelieve, discredit.

rejection: see BOOT; ELIMINATION; SCORN; VETO.

rejoice *v.* DELIGHT, GLADDEN, ENJOY, CELEBRATE, exult, gloat.

rejoicing: see GLADNESS.

rejuvenate: see FRESHEN; HEAL; MODERNIZE; REFRESH; RENEW.

relate *v.* REPORT, RECITE, TELL, NARRATE, recount, DETAIL, DESCRIBE, REHEARSE, REFER, CONNECT, correlate, ALLY, COMPARE, interact, pertain, REGARD, AFFECT.

related *adj.* connected, ALLIED, affiliated, associated, belonging, kindred.

relate to: see REGARD.

relating: see RESPECTIVE.

relation *n.* **1** *(the relation between those two)* CONNECTION, REFERENCE, RESPECT, ASSOCIATION, REGARD, rapport, SIMILARITY; **2** *(the relation of the event)* narrative, ACCOUNT, telling; **3** *(poor relations)* RELATIVE, PARENT, cousin, kinsman, kinswoman.

relations: see KIN.

relationship *n.* CONNECTION, involvement, ASSOCIATION, SIMILARITY, PARENTAGE, kinship, clan, TRIBE, RACE, STOCK, STRAIN, BREED, KIN.

relative *n.* RELATION, PARENT, cousin, KIN, kinsman, kinswoman.
− *adj.* comparative, comparable, pertaining, referring, relevant, proportional, DEPENDENT, pertinent, circumstantial.

relatively *adv.* comparatively, RATHER, SOMEWHAT.

relatives: see FAMILY; KIN.

relax *v.* SLACKEN, LOOSEN, YIELD, RELIEVE, OPEN, EASE, REST, unbend, UNWIND.

relaxation *n.* REST, repose, PEACE, RELIEF, COMFORT, EASE, recreation, diversion.

relaxed: see COMFORTABLE; CONTENTED, COOL; LEISURELY; LOOSE.

release *v.* unloose, unfasten, relinquish, SURRENDER, DISCHARGE, exempt, acquit, let go, LIBERATE, PERMIT, PUBLISH, DISTRIBUTE.
− *n.*: see DISCHARGE; ESCAPE; PARDON; RECORD; RELIEF; RESCUE; SALVATION.

relent: see MELT; THAW.

relentless: see MERCILESS; RIGID.

relevant: see RELATIVE.

reliable *adj.* DEPENDABLE, RESPONSIBLE, STABLE, trustworthy, believable, TRUTHFUL, veracious.

reliance: see DEPENDENCE; TRUST.

relic: see ANTIQUE; SOUVENIR.

relics: see REMAINS.

relief *n.* **1** *(relief for the poor)* ASSISTANCE, HELP, AID, SUPPORT, CHARITY, COMFORT, RESCUE; **2** *(relief from a headache)* alleviation, EASE, RELAXATION, release, DISCHARGE, FREEDOM, lessening; **3** *(to show in relief)* OUTLINE, cameo, SCULPTURE, sharpness, vividness, definition, distinctness.

relieve *v.* **1** *(to relieve a headache)* COMFORT, EASE, alleviate, REDUCE, RELAX, RELEASE, AID, ASSIST,

HELP, FREE, set off, BREAK; **2** *(to relieve a pitcher)* REPLACE, REMOVE, spell, DISCHARGE.

religion *n.* BELIEF, FAITH, PERSUASION, CREED, DEVOTION, piety, SUPERSTITION, CHURCH, WORSHIP, voodoo.

religious *adj.* believing, FAITHFUL, PIOUS, devout, reverent, HOLY, saintly, GODLY, god-fearing, SUPERSTITIOUS, STRICT, methodical.

relinquish: see ABANDON; DELIVER; RELEASE; RESIGN; SACRIFICE; SURRENDER; VACATE.

relinquishing: see SPARING.

relish *n.* **1** *(I have no relish for long calls)* ENJOYMENT, fondness, DELIGHT, zest, gusto, TASTE, FLAVOR, APPETITE, stomach, liking, SATISFACTION; **2** *(a hot dog with relish)* SAUCE, pickle, appetizer.
  − *v.* LIKE, ENJOY, TASTE, APPRECIATE.

reluctance *n.* unwillingness, disinclination, dislike, qualm, HESITATION, hesitancy.

reluctant *adj.* unwilling, hesitant, loath, indisposed, averse, opposed, BACKWARD.

rely on *v.* depend on, count on, believe in, trust in, confide in.

remain *v.* STAY, REST, LINGER, CONTINUE, LAST, ENDURE, LIVE, RESIDE, LODGE, SURVIVE.

remainder *n.* REMNANT, leavings, residue, REMAINS, leftovers, SURPLUS, REST, balance.

remaining: see LASTING; LEFT; OTHER; OVER.

remains *pl.n.* **1** *(the remains of plant life)* REMNANT, residue, ashes, fragments, relic, ruin; **2** *(to view the remains at the funeral home)* CORPSE, cadaver, stiff.

remark *v.* MENTION, OBSERVE, SAY, COMMENT, EXPRESS, perceive, NOTICE.
  − *n.* MENTION, STATEMENT, COMMENT, NOTE, NOTICE, OBSERVATION.

remarkable *adj.* EXTRAORDINARY, noteworthy, NOTABLE, OUTSTANDING, phenomenal, PROMINENT, eminent, WONDERFUL, observable, CURIOUS.

remarkably: see EXCEEDINGLY; EXTREMELY.

remedial: see CORRECTIVE.

remedy *n.* CORRECTIVE, RELIEF, medication, MEDICINE, CURE, TREATMENT.
  − *v.*: see CURE; QUENCH; REPAIR; RIGHT; TREAT.

remember *v.* RECOLLECT, RECALL, MEMORIZE, RETAIN, GREET.

remembrance *n.* SOUVENIR, memento, TOKEN, REMINDER, recollection, recall, retrospect, reminiscence.

remind *v.* prod, SUGGEST, HINT, cue, REPEAT.

reminder *n.* SUGGESTION, HINT, REPETITION.

remindful: see SUGGESTIVE.

reminisce: see RECALL.

reminiscence: see REMEMBRANCE; SOUVENIR.

remission: see PARDON.

remit: see FORGIVE; PAY; REFUND.

remnant *n.* REMAINS, residue, FRAGMENT, vestige, SCRAP, PORTION.

remodel: see MODIFY; REFORM; REPAIR.

remodeling: see REPAIR.

remorse: see REGRET; SHAME; SORROW.

remorseful: see APOLOGETIC; ASHAMED; SORRY.

remote *adj.* DISTANT, FAR, secluded, alien, out-of-the-way, FOREIGN, unrelated, SLIGHT, irrelevant, FAINT.

remotely: see AFAR; APART; FAR.

remoteness: see DISTANCE.

removal *n.* ELIMINATION, REPLACEMENT, dismissal, TRANSFER, SHIFT, DEPARTURE, CHANGE.

remove *v.* take away, TRANSFER, MOVE, displace, TRANSPLANT, WITHDRAW, ELIMINATE, ERASE, obviate, STRIP, take off.

remuneration: see EXPENDITURE.

render: see INTERPRET; PERFORM; PROVIDE.

rendezvous: see DATE.

rendition: see INTERPRETATION; VERSION.

renew *v.* renovate, rejuvenate, refurbish, REPLACE, replenish, revitalize, revive, RESUME.

renewal: see CONTINUATION.

renewed: see NEW; SECOND-HAND.

renounce: see REFUSE; REJECT; RESIGN.

renouncement: see RESIGNATION.

renovate: see MODERNIZE; REFRESH; RENEW.

renown: see AUTHORITY; FAME; GLORY.

renowned: see CELEBRATED; FAMOUS; GLORIOUS; WELL-KNOWN.

rent *n.* **1** *(a rent in his coat)* rip, TEAR, tatter, BREAK, breach, schism, DIVISION, rupture,

fissure; **2** *(the rent is due)* rental, PAYMENT, installment, tenancy, INCOME, PROFIT.
— *v.* lease, LET, HIRE.

rental: see RENT.

renter: see TENANT.

reobtain: see REGAIN.

repair *v.* FIX, overhaul, RESTORE, CORRECT, MEND, PATCH, ADJUST, rectify, remedy, RENEW, remodel, recondition.
— *n.* fixing, overhaul, restoration, reconstruction, remodeling, REPLACEMENT.

repaired: see FIXED.

repartee: see RESPONSE; WIT.

repast: see BANQUET; DINNER; MEAL.

repay: see AVENGE; COMPENSATE; REFUND; RETURN; REVENGE.

repayment: see REVENGE; VENGEANCE.

repeal: see OVERRULE; RECALL.

repeat *v.* REPEAT, recount, DUPLICATE, REPRODUCE, PERSIST, recur.
— *n.*: see DUPLICATE; ECHO.

repeated: see CONTINUAL; PERIODIC.

repeatedly: see AGAIN; MUCH.

repeating: see REPETITION.

repel: see REJECT; REVOLT; SHED; SICKEN.

repent *v.* REGRET, REFORM, recant, APOLOGIZE.

repentance: see SORROW.

repentant: see APOLOGETIC.

repercussion: see ECHO; RESULT.

repetition *n.* repeating, restatement, refrain, recitation, reiteration, ECHO, recurrence.

repetitious: see MONOTONOUS.

replace *v.* RESTORE, RETURN, reinstate, supplant, supersede, SUBSTITUTE.

replacement *n.* restoration, reinstatement, TRANSFER, SUBSTITUTION, understudy.

replenish: see FILL; RENEW.

replica: see COPY; DUPLICATE.

replication: see DUPLICATION.

reply *v.* ANSWER, RESPOND, ACKNOWLEDGE, REPEAT, retort, SAY, ECHO.
— *n.* ANSWER, RESPONSE, acknowledgment, retort, ECHO.

report *n.* **1** *(the report of its activities)* ACCOUNT, STATEMENT, RECORD, STORY, RUMOR, hearsay, ANNOUNCEMENT; **2** *(a loud report)* BANG, EXPLOSION.
— *v.* TELL, RELATE, recount, REVEAL, RECORD, NARRATE, disclose, EXPOSE, PUBLISH. See also ARRIVE.

reporter: see CORRESPONDENT.

reports: see TALK.

repose: see LEAN; LIE; RELAXATION; REST.

repository: see BANK.

repossess: see RECOVER; REGAIN.

repossession: see RECOVERY.

represent *v.* **1** *(the article represents him as a dictator)* depict, DESCRIBE, portray, PICTURE, symbolize, CORRESPOND; **2** *(to represent the voters)* SERVE, stand for, personify, impersonate.

representation *n.* **1** *(a representation of a flower)* PICTURE, image, EMBLEM, portraiture; **2** *(the representation of our district in Congress)* delegation, deputation, agents, emissaries, participation, MISSION.

representative: see AGENT; AMBASSADOR; CHARACTERISTIC; CLASSIC; DELEGATE; MINISTER; TYPE; TYPICAL.

repress: see CONFINE; REIN.

repression: see PRESSURE.

reprieve: see FORGIVENESS; GRACE; STAY.

reprimand: see DISAPPROVE; LECTURE.

reprint: see COPY; ENGRAVING.

reprisal: see REVENGE.

reproach: see ABUSE; REFLECTION.

reproduce *v.* **1** *(to reproduce a speech)* COPY, DUPLICATE, redo, REPEAT, TRACE, reconstruct, rebuild; **2** *(can those animals reproduce?)* BREED, propagate, MULTIPLY, MATE, BEAR, beget.

reproduced: see DUPLICATE.

reproduction: see COPY; DUPLICATE; DUPLICATION; GENERATION; SEX; TRANSCRIPT.

reproductive: see FERTILE; SEXUAL.

reptile: see SNAKE.

republic *n.* STATE, commonwealth, democracy, NATION, GOVERNMENT.

repudiate: see DENY.

repugnance: see HATRED; HOSTILITY; REVOLT.

repulsive: see AWFUL; HATEFUL; HORRIBLE; UGLY; UNPLEASANT.

reputable: see FAMOUS; HONORABLE; WELL-KNOWN.

reputation *n.* FAME, standing, repute, RANK, DISTINCTION, MARK, NAME, OPINION.

repute: see REPUTATION.

request *n.* DEMAND, APPEAL, asking, APPLICATION.
— *v.* DEMAND, APPEAL, ASK, APPLY.

require *v.* NEED, DEMAND, WANT, call for, ORDER, entail, COMPEL, CAUSE.

required: see BINDING; ESSENTIAL; NECESSARY.

requirement *n.* NEED, DEMAND, prerequisite, requisite, NECESSITY, CONDITION, ORDER, RULE, REGULATION.

requisite: see CONDITION; ESSENTIAL; NECESSARY; NECESSITY; REQUIREMENT.

requisition: see APPLICATION; ORDER.

rescue *v.* SAVE, FREE, RELEASE, LIBERATE, DELIVER, recapture, reclaim, retake, RECOVER.
— *n.* rescuing, liberation, release, freeing, SALVATION, deliverance.

rescuing: see RESCUE.

research *n.* INVESTIGATION, INQUIRY, SEARCH, HUNT, EXPLORATION, STUDY.
— *v.* INVESTIGATE, INQUIRE, SEARCH, HUNT, EXPLORE, STUDY.

researcher: see SCIENTIST; STUDENT.

resemblance *n.* likeness, SIMILARITY, similitude, approximation, CORRESPONDENCE, kinship.

resemble *v.* look like, take after, IMITATE, FAVOR, ECHO, MATCH, parallel, DUPLICATE.

resembling: see ALIKE; PARALLEL; SIMILAR.

resent *v.* take amiss, begrudge, ENVY, disfavor, DISLIKE, misunderstand.

resentful *adj.* angry, offended, BITTER, spiteful, envious, indignant, hurt.

resentment *n.* ANGER, offense, rancor, umbrage, BITTERNESS, GRUDGE, spite, ENVY, malice, indignation, animosity.

reservation *n.* **1** *(to declare without reservation)* reserve, restraint, RESTRICTION, inhibition, CONTROL; **2** *(a room reservation)* booking, ASSIGNMENT, scheduling, holding, ARRANGEMENT, ENGAGEMENT; **3** *(an Indian reservation)* TRACT, LAND, CAMP, AREA.

reserve *v.* set aside, SAVE, HOLD, KEEP, book, ENGAGE, SCHEDULE, secure, ARRANGE, GET.
— *n.* **1** *(his annoying reserve)* shyness, BASHFULNESS, coyness, coldness, LIMITATION, reticence, PRIDE, backwardness; **2** *(in reserve)* STORE, SUPPLY, backlog, STOCK, SAVINGS, nest egg.
— *adj.*: see EXTRA; SPARE.

reserved: see BASHFUL, CONFIDENTIAL; DEVOTE; DIGNIFIED; STRANGE.

reserves: see ARMY.

reservoir: see LAKE; POOL; SPRING; TANK.

reset: see SET.

resettle: see MIGRATE.

reshape: see REFORM.

reside *v.* LIVE, DWELL, OCCUPY, INHABIT.

residence *n.* HOME, HOUSE, DWELLING, MANSION, domicile, habitation.

resident *n.* INHABITANT, occupant, TENANT, dweller.

residents: see POPULATION.

residue: see ASHES; REMAINDER; REMAINS; REMNANT.

resign *v.* QUIT, LEAVE, WITHDRAW, RETIRE, YIELD, give up, relinquish, renounce, abdicate.

resignation *n.* quitting, DEPARTURE, retirement, renouncement.

resilience: see SPRING.

resilient: see TOUGH.

resist *v.* OPPOSE, DEFY, WITHSTAND, REFUSE, weather, prevail.

resistance *n.* OPPOSITION, defiance, hindrance, antagonism, refusal.

resistant *adj.* negative, unbowed, defiant, resisting.

resisting: see OPPOSING, RESISTANT.

resolute: see COURAGEOUS; STEADY; STURDY.

resolutely: see STEADILY.

resolution *n.* **1** *(a New Year's resolution)* DECISION, DETERMINATION, INTENTION, PURPOSE, steadfastness, perseverance, solving; **2** *(the resolution received three votes)* MOTION, PROPOSAL, PROPOSITION. See also ANALYSIS.

resolve *v.* DECIDE, DETERMINE, CONCLUDE, SETTLE, SOLVE, EXPLAIN, dispel, clear up, INTEND.
— *n.* RESOLUTION, DETERMINATION, CONCLUSION, INTENTION, WILL.

resonance: see ROAR.

resort: see GARDEN; HOTEL; REFUGE; RESOURCE.

resound *v.* reverberate, VIBRATE, ECHO, RING, chime, peal.

resounding: see LOUD.

resource *n.* RESERVE, STORE, STOCK, SUPPLY, WEALTH, MEANS, resort, contrivance, SKILL, ingenuity, expedient, SOURCE.

resources: see CAPITAL; MEANS; RICHES; SAVINGS.

respect *v.* HONOR, ADMIRE, ESTEEM, REVERE, OBEY. — *n.* HONOR, ADMIRATION, ESTIMATION, REGARD, deference, CONSIDERATION, ESTEEM, NOTICE, COURTESY, OBEDIENCE, veneration.

respectable *adj.* DECENT, WORTHY, deserving, PROPER, FAIR, acceptable, PASSABLE, NUMEROUS.

respected: see FAMED; HONORABLE.

respectful: see MANNERLY; OBEDIENT; POLITE.

respecting: see CONCERNING.

respective *adj.* PARTICULAR, SEVERAL, EACH, relating.

respectively: see APIECE.

respiration: see BREATH.

respire: see BREATHE; INHALE.

respite: see EXTENSION; STAY; TRUCE.

respond *v.* REPLY, ANSWER, react, ACKNOWLEDGE.

response *n.* REPLY, ANSWER, REACTION, ECHO, acknowledgment, repartee.

responsibility *n.* OBLIGATION, DUTY, blame, accountability, BURDEN.

responsible *adj.* **1** *(a responsible driver)* ABLE, CAPABLE, RELIABLE, DEPENDABLE, trustworthy, STABLE, HONEST; **2** *(who is responsible for his death?)* ACCOUNTABLE, answerable, LIABLE, GUILTY, blameworthy.

responsive: see ALIVE; SENSITIVE.

rest *v.* SLEEP, repose, NAP, RELAX, PAUSE, PUT, SETTLE, LAY, DEPOSIT. See also BE. — *n.* **1** *(to get some rest)* SLEEP, repose, NAP, RELAXATION, inactivity, PAUSE, BREAK, QUIET, PEACE, DEATH, intermission, lodging; **2** *(the rest of the money)* REMAINDER, REMNANT, SURPLUS, EXCESS, BALANCE. See also ARM.

restart: see RESUME.

restatement: see REPETITION.

restaurant: see CAFE; LOUNGE.

restful: see CALM; COMFORTABLE; REFRESHING.

restive: see RESTLESS.

restless *adj.* UNEASY, NERVOUS, fitful, jumpy, troubled, unsettled, DISCONTENTED, agitated, wandering, restive, unquiet.

restlessness: see DISCONTENT; IMPATIENCE.

restoration: see CURSE; REPAIR; REPLACEMENT.

restore *v.* reinstate, REPLACE, RETURN, REFUND, reestablish, reclaim, REPAIR, put back.

restrain: see ARREST; BIND; CHAIN; CHECK; CONFINE; CURB; LIMIT; MODIFY; REIN; RESTRICT; SMOTHER; STILL; STOP; WITHHOLD.

restrained: see LIMITED.

restraint: see BRIDLE; CHECK; COLLAR; DRAG; GOVERNMENT; LIMITATION; REIN; RESERVATION.

restrict *v.* CONFINE, LIMIT, narrow, restrain, crimp.

restricted: see LIMITED; LOCAL.

restriction *n.* LIMIT, BOUNDARY, RESERVATION, CONDITION, qualification, taboo.

result *n.* OUTCOME, upshot, CONSEQUENCE, sequel, CONSEQUENCES, ISSUE, EFFECT, repercussion, PRODUCT, outgrowth, DEVELOPMENT, end. — *v.*: see BECOME; FOLLOW; ISSUE; OCCUR; PROVE.

resume *v.* recommence, CONTINUE, PROCEED, restart, BEGIN, keep on.

resumé: see REVIEW.

resumption *n.* RECOVERY, REPETITION, BEGINNING, START.

retail: see COMMERCIAL; PEDDLE; SELL.

retailer: see MERCHANT.

retain *v.* **1** *(to retain a prisoner)* HOLD, KEEP, WITHHOLD, REMEMBER, recall; **2** *(to retain a lawyer)* HIRE, EMPLOY, ENGAGE.

retake: see RECOVER; RESCUE.

retaliate: see ANSWER; AVENGE; REVENGE.

retaliation: see REVENGE; VENGEANCE.

retard: see CHECK; CHOKE; CURB; JERK; POSTPONE.

retarded *adj.* BACKWARD, SLOW, defective, subnormal, slow-witted, FEEBLE-MINDED, DULL.

retention: see HOLD; POSSESSION.

retentive: see POSSESSIVE.

reticence: see RESERVE.

retire *v.* WITHDRAW, RESIGN, LEAVE, abdicate, DEPART, RETREAT, SLEEP, REST, REMOVE.

retired: see OUT; SOLITARY.

retirement: see LEISURE; PENSION; RESIGNATION; RETREAT.

retiring: see SHY.

retort: see ANSWER; REPLY.

retract: see RECALL.

retraction: see APOLOGY.

retreat *v.* RETIRE, WITHDRAW, SURRENDER, ebb, recede, draw back.
— *n.* withdrawal, retirement, seclusion, solitude, SHELTER, hideaway, sanctuary.

retrieval: see RECOVERY.

retrieve: see RECOVER; REGAIN.

retriever: see RECEIVER.

retrospect: see REMEMBRANCE.

return *v.* RESTORE, give back, recur, come back, REPLY, ANSWER, repay, YIELD, PRODUCE.
— *n.* homecoming, ANSWER, REPLY, recurrence, YIELD, PROFIT.

returns: see TAKE.

reunion *n.* MEETING, get-together, GATHERING, ASSEMBLY, RECEPTION, reconciliation, CONVENTION.

reveal *v.* disclose, divulge, EXPOSE, SHOW, ANNOUNCE, PUBLISH, BROADCAST, publicize.

revealed: see VISIBLE.

revelation: see CONFESSION; EXPOSURE; GOSPEL; MIRACLE.

revelry: see RIOT.

revenge *v.* AVENGE, retaliate, repay.
— *n.* VENGEANCE, retaliation, repayment, reprisal, malevolence.

revenue *n.* INCOME, PROFIT, receipts, EARNINGS.

reverberate: see ECHO; RESOUND.

reverberation: see RUMBLE.

revere: see FEAR; LOVE.

reverence: see ESTEEM; HONOR; WORSHIP.

reverend: see MINISTER; PASTOR.

reverent: see RELIGIOUS.

reverse *adj.* OPPOSITE, BACKWARD, CONTRARY, inverted, upended.
— *n.* OPPOSITE, contradiction, inversion, UPSET, adversity, TURN.

review *v.* EXAMINE, INSPECT, scrutinize, STUDY, CRITICIZE, SURVEY.

— *n.* EXAMINATION, INSPECTION, SURVEY, STUDY, CRITICISM, commentary, scrutiny, resumé, recapitulation, MAGAZINE, JOURNAL. See also PARADE.

reviewer: see CRITIC; INSPECTOR.

revise *v.* CHANGE, CORRECT, AMEND, EDIT, recast, POLISH, rectify, doctor, emend.

reviser: see EDITOR.

revision *n.* CHANGE, CORRECTION, AMENDMENT, edition, VERSION, conversion, emendation.

revisit: see FREQUENT.

revitalize: see RENEW.

revive: see FRESHEN; PERK; RECUPERATE; RENEW; STRENGTHEN.

revivify: see FRESHEN.

revoke: see CANCEL; RECALL.

revolt *n.* **1** *(to be in revolt)* REBELLION, mutiny, insurrection, REVOLUTION, uprising, sedition; **2** *(the revolt I feel at that sight)* DISGUST, repugnance, distaste, loathing, aversion.
— *v.* **1** *(to revolt against authority)* REBEL, mutiny, RIOT, RISE; **2** *(that sight revolts me)* disgust, nauseate, repel.

revolting: see HORRIBLE; NASTY.

revolution *n.* **1** *(the French Revolution)* REVOLT, REBELLION, mutiny, insurrection, sedition, RIOT, anarchy, uprising, OVERTHROW; **2** *(one revolution around the sun)* ROTATION, TURN, ORBIT, cycle, CIRCLE.

revolutionaries: see LEFT.

revolutionary: see DISOBEDIENT; TRAITOR.

revolutionist: see REBEL.

revolutionize: see TRANSFORM.

revolve *v.* ROTATE, TURN, ORBIT, CIRCLE, SPIN, WHIRL, ROLL.

revolver *n.* PISTOL, handgun, automatic, gat, six-shooter, FIREARM, sidearm.

revulsion: see DISGUST.

reward *n.* PRIZE, AWARD, BONUS, CROWN, TIP, PAYMENT.
— *v.* PAY, AWARD, RETURN, TIP.

rewarding: see SUCCESSFUL.

reword: see INTERPRET; TRANSLATE.

rewrite: see EDIT.

rhinitis: see COLD.

rhombus: see DIAMOND.

rhyme: see POEM; POETRY.

rhythm: see BEAT; SWING.

rhythmic: see MUSICAL.

rib: see BONE; NERVE; RIDGE.

ribbon: see BAND; BELT; BOW; STRIP; TAPE.

rich *adj.* **1** *(a rich man)* WEALTHY, affluent, well-off, well-to-do; **2** *(a rich harvest)* ABUNDANT, PLENTIFUL, fruitful, FERTILE, BOUNTIFUL, PRODUCTIVE; **3** *(rich colors)* deep, FULL, VIVID, MELLOW, sonorous, MELODIOUS, luxuriant, LUXURIOUS, COSTLY, EXPENSIVE, VALUABLE.

riches *pl.n.* WEALTH, possessions, PLENTY, assets, resources, SUBSTANCE, ABUNDANCE.

richness *n.* WEALTH, affluence, ABUNDANCE, LUXURY, luxuriance, profusion, PROSPERITY.

ricochet: see BOUNCE; GLANCE.

rid *v.* FREE, DELIVER, ELIMINATE, CLEAR, REMOVE.

riddance: see ELIMINATION.

riddle *n.* enigma, PUZZLE, cryptogram, PROBLEM, QUESTION, dilemma, paradox, MYSTERY, sphinx.

ride *v.* TRAVEL, journey, TOUR, DRIVE.
— *n.* JOURNEY, RUN, jaunt, joy ride.

rider: see PASSENGER; TRAVELER.

ridge *n.* corrugation, GROOVE, furrow, SPINE, rib, LEDGE, SADDLE, RANGE, CHAIN, highland.

ridicule *v.* satirize, deride, MOCK, jeer, SNEER, lampoon, banter, TEASE.
— *n.* satire, sarcasm, derision, mockery, irony.

ridiculous *adj.* ABSURD, NONSENSICAL, ludicrous, grotesque, laughable, COMICAL, FUNNY.

riffraff: see MOB.

rifle *n.* shotgun, musket, blunderbuss, GUN, air rifle, BB gun, FIREARM, muzzleloader, carbine.
— *v.*: see LOOT; ROB.

rift: see GAP; SEPARATION.

rig: see CARRIAGE; FURNISH; KIT; OUTFIT.

rigging: see OUTFIT; TACKLE.

right *adj.* **1** *(in right field)* right-hand, dexter; **2** *(the right dictionary for one's work)* CORRECT, PRECISE, PROPER, EXACT, GOOD, ACCURATE, COMPLETE, TRUE, SUITABLE, HONEST, VIRTUOUS, JUST, righteous, LAWFUL; **3** *(a right angle)* perpendicular, STRAIGHT.
— *adv.* correctly, PRECISELY, EXACTLY, justly, PROPERLY, suitably, PROMPTLY, favorably, COMPLETELY, legally, righteously.
— *n.* **1** *(freedom of speech is a right)* PRIVILEGE, LICENSE, immunity, ADVANTAGE, INTEREST, ownership, good, JUSTICE, VIRTUE, righteousness, HONOR, TITLE, CLAIM, GOODNESS, authorization; **2** *(the politicians of the right)* conservativism, fascism, capitalism, anticommunism, authoritarianism, right wing.
— *v.* CORRECT, RESTORE, redress, AVENGE, remedy, recompense, rectify, ADJUST, FIX, REGULATE, ORDER, upright.

right away: see AWHILE; IMMEDIATELY; INSTANTLY; PROMPTLY.

righteous: see GOOD; RIGHT; UPRIGHT; VIRTUOUS.

righteously: see RIGHT.

righteousness: see GOODNESS; HOLINESS; INNOCENCE; RIGHT; TRUTH; VIRTUE.

rightful: see CORRECT; JUST; LAWFUL; TRUE.

rightist: see CONSERVATIVE.

rightly: see PROPERLY.

right wing: see RIGHT.

rigid *adj.* STIFF, inflexible, unyielding, HARD, FIRM, TENSE, unbending, HARSH, FIXED, STRICT, relentless, SEVERE, static, STERN.

rigidity: see PRECISION.

rigor: see DIFFICULTY.

rigorous: see EXACT; MILITARY; SEVERE; STERN; STRICT.

rill: see BROOK.

rim *n.* EDGE, BORDER, MARGIN, brink, verge, lip, BRIM, hoop, RING, CIRCLE.
— *v.*: see RING.

rimming: see MARGINAL.

rind: see BARK; CRUST.

ring *n.* **1** *(to enter the ring)* CIRCLE, ARENA, LOOP, RIM; **2** *(a wedding ring)* BAND, ringlet, GEM; **3** *(a ring of thieves)* GANG, clique, LEAGUE; **4** *(the ring of a bell)* chime, peal, TOLL, tinkle, jingle, ring-a-ling, BUZZ; **5** *(a telephone ring)* CALL, buzz, phone call.
— *v.* **1** *(to ring the bell)* chime, peal, toll, buzz, jingle, SOUND; **2** *(to ring the city)* ENCIRCLE, SURROUND, ENCLOSE, gird, rim.

ringlet: see LOCK; RING; WREATH.

rings: see JEWELRY.

ring up: see CALL.

rinse *v.* SPRAY, hose, shampoo, WASH, CLEANSE, SOAK, REMOVE.

riot *n.* UPROAR, tumult, COMMOTION, DISTURBANCE, DEMONSTRATION, REVOLUTION, REVOLT, hubbub, CONFUSION, revelry.
— *v.* REBEL, REVOLT, DEMONSTRATE, ARISE, RISE, pillage, carouse.

riotous: see MAD.

rip *v.* SHRED, fray, TEAR, rupture, SPLIT, CUT, SEPARATE, BREAK.
— *n.*: see HOLE; RENT; TEAR.

ripe *adj.* MATURE, full-grown, PERFECT, prime, GROWN, ADULT, seasoned, READY, MELLOW, WISE, developed.

ripen *v.* mature, evolve, DEVELOP, COMPLETE, PERFECT, AGE, GROW, MELLOW.

ripening: see MATURITY.

ripple *n.* ruffle, undulation, oscillation, WAVE, billow, VIBRATION.
— *v.*: see WAVE.

riproaring: see NOISY.

rise *v.* ASCEND, MOUNT, ADVANCE, PROGRESS, APPEAR, GROW, PROSPER.
— *n.* ascent, MOUNT, INCREASE, upgrade, GROWTH, LIFT, INFLATION.

risen: see AWAKE.

rising: see HILLY.

risk *n.* DANGER, HAZARD, GAMBLE, VENTURE, CHANCE, jeopardy, peril.
— *v.* HAZARD, GAMBLE, wager, BET, speculate, ENDANGER, jeopardize.

risky *adj.* CHANCY, UNSAFE, perilous, HAZARDOUS, precarious, UNCERTAIN.

rite: see CEREMONY; FORMALITY; FUNERAL; TRADITION.

rites: see BURIAL; WORSHIP.

ritual: see CEREMONIAL; CEREMONY; SERVICE; TRADITION.

rival *n.* COMPETITOR, adversary, antagonist, OPPONENT, contestant, MATCH.

rivalry: see COMPETITION; CONTEST.

river *n.* STREAM, watercourse, tributary, CANAL, CHANNEL, waterway.

rivet: see BOLT.

rivulet: see BROOK.

road *n.* thoroughfare, HIGHWAY, ROUTE, COURSE, boulevard, STREET, AVENUE, ALLEY.

roadblock: see BARRICADE; BLOCKADE.

roadhouse: see HOTEL; INN; TAVERN.

roam *v.* WANDER, ROVE, STROLL, saunter, straggle, meander, ramble.

roamer: see DRIFTER; ROVER.

roar *v.* RESOUND, THUNDER, boom, TRUMPET, SHOUT, RUMBLE, HOWL.
— *n.* THUNDER, bluster, CRASH, BOOM, resonance, SHOUT, bellow.

roaring: see LOUD.

roast *v.* COOK, broil, barbecue, BAKE, TOAST, grill.

rob *v.* STEAL, plunder, LOOT, fleece, SWINDLE, burglarize, rifle, sack.

robber *n.* THIEF, BURGLAR, bandit, desperado, thug, plunderer, pilferer.

robbery *n.* THEFT, HOLDUP, pillage, sack, BURGLARY, larceny, stick-up.

robe *n.* GOWN, HABIT, mantle, cape, COSTUME, GARMENT, attire.
— *v.* DRESS, cloak, shroud, attire, array, VEIL.

robust: see ATHLETIC; FIT; HARDY; HEALTHY; MUSCULAR; RUGGED; SOUND; STURDY.

robustness: see STRENGTH.

rock *n.* boulder, STONE, PEBBLE, slab, cobble, crag, reef.
— *v.* SWAY, REEL, wobble, SWING, PITCH, flounder, VIBRATE. See also SWING.

rocker: see CRADLE.

rocket *n.* MISSILE, projectile, probe, spacecraft, thruster, fireworks.

rocking: see SWING.

rocky *adj.* STONY, flinty, calcified, craggy, RUGGED, HARD. See also SHAKY.

rod *n.* **1** (*an iron rod*) POLE, BAR, STAFF, wand, BATON; **2** (*a shooting rod*) PISTOL, REVOLVER, side arm, FIREARM, GUN.

roebuck: see BUCK.

rogue: see RASCAL; SCOUNDREL; SWINDLER; VILLAIN.

roguish: see MISCHIEVOUS.

role *n.* CHARACTER, PART, REPRESENTATION, impersonation, FUNCTION, POSITION, TASK.

roles: see CAST.

roll *v.* SPIN, WHIRL, TURN, REVOLVE, ROTATE, gyrate, wheel.
— *n.* **1** *(the roll of a ball)* spin, ROTATION, REVOLUTION, gyration, whirl, TURN; **2** *(a dinner roll)* bun, BREAD, biscuit, TWIST; **3** *(to call the roll)* roster, REGISTER, LIST, TABLE. See also CASH; FILM; RUMBLE.

rolled up: see WOUND.

roller: see PRESS; WAVE; WHEEL.

romance *n.* **1** *(a passionate romance)* AFFAIR, enchantment, flirtation; **2** *(a paperback romance)* STORY, TALE, NOVEL, FICTION, ADVENTURE.

romantic *adj.* ADVENTUROUS, DARING, mushy, SENTIMENTAL, fanciful, imaginative, idealistic.

roof *n.* SHELTER, PROTECTION, HOUSE, DWELLING, COVER, TOP, CEILING.

room *n.* **1** *(is there room?)* SPACE, AREA, scope, VOLUME, CAPACITY, expanse; **2** *(a private room)* ENCLOSURE, CHAMBER, quarters, lodging, APARTMENT.
— *v.*: see INHABIT; LODGE.

roomer: see LODGER; TENANT.

roomette: see COMPARTMENT.

roominess: see FULLNESS.

rooms: see LODGINGS.

roomy *adj.* SPACIOUS, VAST, EXTENSIVE, AMPLE, expansive, BROAD, WIDE, commodious.

roost: see PERCH; SQUAT.

rooster: see COCK.

root *n.* BASIS, GROUND, FOUNDATION, MOTIVE, CAUSE, SOURCE, ORIGIN.
— *v.*: see PLANT.

rope *n.* CABLE, CORD, STRING, TWINE, LINE.

ropes: see TACKLE.

roster: see CARD; LIST; MEMBERSHIP; REGISTER; ROLL.

rosy: see RED.

rot *v.* DECAY, SPOIL, decompose, MOLD, WASTE.
— *n.*: see FILTH; RUST.

rotate *v.* TURN, REVOLVE, TWIST, ORBIT, pivot, swivel, wheel.

rotation *n.* turning, twisting, whirl, swirl, ORBIT, REVOLUTION, gyration, spin.

rotisserie: see SPIT; STOVE.

rotten *adj.* **1** *(rotten vegetables)* spoiled, decayed, decomposed, moldy, rancid, STALE; **2** *(a rotten*

person) corrupt, DIRTY, IMPURE, IMMORAL, dishonest.

rotund: see ROUND.

rotunda: see DOME.

route: see COMPACT; PAINT.

rouged: see MADE-UP.

rough *adj.* COARSE, UNEVEN, bumpy, ROCKY, IRREGULAR, choppy, turbulent, ungentle.

roughen: see CHAP.

roughly: see APPROXIMATELY; NEARLY.

roughneck: see ROWDY.

roughness: see COARSENESS; HARSHNESS.

round *n.* CIRCLE, hoop, RING, WHEEL, TURN, cylinder, ROTATION.
— *adj.* CIRCULAR, spherical, global, rotund, curved, ARCHED, cylindrical.
— *adv.* circularly, globally, cylindrically, COMPLETELY, FULLY, AROUND, recurring.
— *v.* SPIN, TURN, curve, CIRCLE, REVOLVE, pivot, ROTATE.
— *prep.*: see ABOUT; AROUND.

roundabout: see CIRCULAR.

rounded: see CHUBBY; CIRCULAR.

rounds: see BEAT.

round table: see PANEL.

rouse *v.* RAISE, awake, STIR, STIMULATE, EXCITE, PROVOKE, KINDLE.

roused: see AWAKE.

rout: see CONQUEST; DEFEAT; FLUSH; OVERWHELM.

route *n.* itinerary, ROAD, PATH, TRACK, COURSE, DIRECTION, way.

routine *n.* CUSTOM, HABIT, MANNER, WAY, SYSTEM, METHOD, USAGE.
— *adj.*: see ACCUSTOMED; CUSTOMARY; EVERYDAY; HABITUAL; MECHANICAL; NORMAL.

rove *v.* ROAM, WANDER, ramble, DRIFT, LOAF, meander, TRAMP, STRAY.

rover *n.* roamer, wanderer, rambler, DRIFTER, TRAMP, vagrant, BUM, hobo.

row *n.* **1** *(in the first row)* LINE, FILE, RANK, SERIES, tier; **2** *(they got clobbered in a row)* FIGHT, spat, DISPUTE, ARGUMENT.

rowdy *n.* BULLY, tough, ruffian, hoodlum, HOOD, roughneck, hooligan.
— *adj.* unruly, disorderly, boisterous, rambunctious, MISCHIEVOUS.

royal *adj.* regal, stately, DIGNIFIED, LOFTY, aristocratic, kingly, imperial.

royalty: see INCOME; MONARCHY.

rub *v.* BRUSH, STROKE, SCOUR, GRIND, grate, SCRAPE, POLISH.
— *n.*: see STROKE.

rubber: see BOOT; GUM; PAD.

rubbish *n.* TRASH, WASTE, GARBAGE, JUNK, LITTER, debris, REFUSE.

rubble: see TRASH.

rub out: see ERASE; MURDER.

ruby: see RED:

ruddy: see RED.

rude *adj.* ROWDY, uncouth, untaught, ROUGH, VIOLENT, COARSE, PRIMITIVE.

rudeness *n.* unmannerliness, discourtesy, disrespect, impudence, impertinence.

ruffian: see BULLY; ROWDY.

ruffle: see IRRITATE; RIPPLE; WRINKLE.

rug *n.* CARPET, MAT, floor-covering, runner.

rugged *adj.* HARDY, robust, ROUGH, HUSKY, STURDY, HARD, DIFFICULT.

ruin *v.* DESTROY, SPOIL, WRECK, devastate, DEMOLISH, SMASH, SHATTER, OVERTHROW.
— *n.* DESTRUCTION, devastation, decay, DEFEAT, WRECK, LOSS, undoing.

ruined: see BANKRUPT; FALLEN; LOST.

ruinous: see DESTRUCTIVE.

rule *n.* GOVERNMENT, CONTROL, POWER, COMMAND, REGULATION, ORDER, GUIDE.
— *v.* GOVERN, REIGN, DIRECT, REGULATE, MANAGE, COMMAND, ADVISE.

ruler *n.* **1** *(measure it with a ruler)* straightedge, yardstick, measurer, T square; **2** *(a tyrannical ruler)* LEADER, GOVERNOR, CHIEF, HEAD, COMMANDER.

ruling: see MASTERFUL.

rumble *n.* THUNDER, reverberation, ECHO, roll.
— *v.*: see THUNDER.

rummage: see SEARCH.

rummy: see DRUNK.

rumor *n.* SUGGESTION, hearsay, gossip, LIE, SCANDAL, REPORT, STORY.

rump: see REAR.

rumple: see MUSS.

rumpus: see COMMOTION; LOUDNESS.

run *v.* **1** *(to run around)* jog, trot, RACE, RUSH, HURRY, bound; **2** *(the machine is running)* WORK, OPERATE, GO, FUNCTION; **3** *(he runs a deli)* MANAGE, OPERATE, MAINTAIN. See also GLIDE.
— *n.* **1** *(an exhausting run)* RACE, sprint, DASH, PACE, marathon, RUSH; **2** *(the kids have the run of the house)* USE, CONTROL, COMMAND, DIRECTION; **3** *(the crisis caused a run on gasoline)* DEMAND, PRESSURE, MARKET, URGENCY. See also CREEK.

run-down: see UNHEALTHY.

rungs: see LADDER.

run-in: see CLASH.

runner *n.* jogger, sprinter, racer, courier, MESSENGER. See also CARPET; RUG.

runner up: see SECOND.

running *adj.* **1** *(the running head of a page)* CONTINUOUS, uninterrupted, UNBROKEN, CONSECUTIVE, sustained, connected, ENTIRE; **2** *(a running cable)* extending, reaching, stretching, spreading, CONTINUOUS; **3** *(running water)* flowing, dripping, leaking, oozing, percolating.

run off: see DESERT.

runover: see OVERFLOW.

runt: see DWARF.

runway: see CHANNEL.

rupture: see ERUPT; ERUPTION; RENT; RIP; SPLIT.

rural *adj.* agricultural, backwoods, country, PRIMITIVE, unsophisticated. PLAIN.

rush *v.* HURRY, HASTEN, SPEED, DASH, RUN, PUSH, PRESSURE.
— *n.* HASTE, HURRY, RUN.

rushed: see HURRIED.

rust *n.* oxidation, tarnish, corrosion, decay, rot, MOLD, mildew.
— *v.*: see EAT; MOLD.

rustic: see CRUDE; PEASANT.

rustle *v.* **1** *(to rustle a page)* swish, WHISPER, whir, MURMUR, HUM; **2** *(to rustle cattle)* STEAL, ROB, filch, poach.
— *n.* bustle, whir, HUM, swish.

rusty *adj.* **1** *(a rusty nail)* corroded, tarnished, oxidized, mildewed, STALE; **2** *(a rusty ball player)* unpracticed, sluggish, ill-qualified, inexperienced, GREEN.

rut: see GROOVE.

ruthless: see CRUEL; INHUMAN; PITILESS; SAVAGE.

ruthlessness: see CRUELTY.

S

saber: see STEEL; SWORD.

sable: see BLACK.

sabotage: see DAMAGE.

saboteur: see VANDAL.

sac: see BLISTER; BUBBLE.

saccharine: see SWEET.

sack *n.* PACK, BAG, POUCH, duffle. See also
ROBBERY.
— *v.*: see ROB.

sacred *adj.* HOLY, hallowed, sanctified, DIVINE,
pious, saintly, sacrosanct, RELIGIOUS, taboo.

sacredness: see HOLINESS.

sacrifice *v.* relinquish, SURRENDER, YIELD, forfeit,
forego, LOSE, OFFER.
— *n.* offering, SURRENDER, self-denial, VICTIM,
LOSS.

sacrificing: see SPARING.

sacroiliac: see BACKBONE.

sacrosanct: see SACRED.

sad *adj.* UNHAPPY, melancholy, depressed,
DOWNHEARTED, GLOOMY, dismal, SORRY, woeful,
heavy-hearted.

sadden *v.* DISCOURAGE, dishearten, GRIEVE,
MOURN, lament, bemoan.

saddle *n.* YOKE, HARNESS, SEAT, leather.
— *v.*: see HARNESS.

sadism: see CRUELTY.

sadist: see BEAST.

sadness *n.* SORROW, SYMPATHY, melancholy,
DEPRESSION, GRIEF, GLOOM, unhappiness,
doldrums.

safari: see EXPEDITION.

safe *adj.* SECURE, protected, shielded, guarded,
supervised, preserved, UNHARMED.
— *n.* VAULT, strongbox, CHEST, coffer, CASE,
cache.

safe-conduct: see PASS; PASSPORT.

safeguard: see GUARD; PRESERVE; SCREEN; SHIELD.

safeguarding: see PROTECTIVE.

safekeeping: see CHARGE.

safely: see SURELY; WELL.

safety *n.* PROTECTION, SECURITY, SHELTER, REFUGE,
sanctuary, preservation, invulnerability.

sag: see BAG; BUCKLE; BULGE; DANGLE; DROOP;
WILT.

saga: see STORY.

said: see ORAL; VERBAL.

sail *n.* NAVIGATION, cruise, excursion, VOYAGE,
TRIP, JOURNEY.
— *v.* NAVIGATE, cruise, PILOT, voyage, FLOAT,
GLIDE.

sailcloth: see CANVAS.

sailing: see NAVIGATION.

sailor *n.* seaman, mariner, seafarer, navigator,
boatman, voyager.

sailors: see NAVY.

saint: see ANGEL.

saintly: see GODLY; HOLY; RELIGIOUS; SACRED.

sake *n.* CAUSE, CONSEQUENCE, REASON, MOTIVE,
END, PURPOSE, ACCOUNT.

salaam: see BOW.

salary *n.* pay, WAGES, compensation, PAYMENT,
INCOME, EARNINGS, ALLOWANCE.

sale *n.* EXCHANGE, TRADE, TRANSACTION, vending,
COMMERCE, BUSINESS, negotiation.

salesclerk: see CLERK.

salesman: see BROKER; PEDDLER; TRADER;
TRAVELER.

salesperson: see TRADER.

saleswoman: see TRADER.

salivate: see SLOBBER; SPIT.

salon: see GALLERY; LOUNGE; PARLOR.

saloon: see BAR; TAVERN.

salt *n.* brine, seasoning, savor, zest, SPICE,
RELISH.
— *v.* SEASON, FLAVOR, spice, pickle, cure.

salutation *n.* greeting, hello, WELCOME, ADDRESS,
SALUTE, bow, RECEPTION.

salutations: see WELCOME.

salute *v.* GREET, WELCOME, HAIL, ADDRESS,
CONGRATULATE, APPLAUD, RECEIVE.
— *n.* greeting, SALUTATION, bow, ADDRESS,
RECEPTION, PRAISE.

salvage: see RECOVER; SAVE.

salvation *n.* emancipation, liberation, release, deliverance, RESCUE, preservation, conservation.

salve: see LOTION; OINTMENT.

salver: see TRAY.

same *adj.* IDENTICAL, ALIKE, DUPLICATE, EQUIVALENT, SIMILAR.
— *pron.* EQUIVALENT, EQUAL, SUBSTITUTE.

same as: see LIKE.

sameness *n.* SIMILARITY, consistency, alikeness, equivalence, RESEMBLANCE, MONOTONY, monotone.

sample *n.* SPECIMEN, EXAMPLE, MODEL, PATTERN, swatch, TASTE, TRY.
— *v.* TASTE, SIP, savor, EXAMINE, INSPECT, TRY.

sanctified: see BLESSED; SACRED.

sanctify: see BLESS.

sanctity: see HOLINESS.

sanctuary: see ALTAR; CHURCH; REFUGE; RETREAT; SAFETY; SHELTER; SHRINE; TEMPLE.

sand *n.* DUST, silt, POWDER, GRIT, GRAVEL, DIRT.
— *v.* SMOOTH, GRIND, FILE.

sandal: see SHOE.

sander: see FILE.

sandpaper: see SMOOTH.

sandstorm: see STORM.

sandy: see RED.

sane *adj.* rational, balanced, SOUND, NORMAL, SENSIBLE, REASONABLE, HEALTHY, well-conditioned.

saneness: see SANITY.

sanitarium: see HOME; HOSPITAL; INSTITUTION.

sanitary *adj.* germ-free, disinfected, sterile, hygienic, uncontaminated, wholesome, healthful.

sanitation *n.* hygiene, CLEANLINESS, HEALTH, wholesomeness.

sanity *n.* REASON, clearmindedness, saneness, reasonableness, BALANCE.

sap *n.* **1** (*the sap of a tree*) FLUID, secretion, JUICE, latex; **2** (*only a sap would believe that*) FOOL, simpleton, pushover, ignoramus, dope, JERK.

sappy: see SILLY.

sarcasm: see RIDICULE.

sarcastic: see NASTY; POINTED; SHARP.

sarcastically: see SHARPLY.

sarcophagus: see COFFIN.

sash: see BELT; GIRDLE.

Satan: see DEVIL.

satanic: see WICKED.

sate: see SATISFY.

satellite *n.* **1** (*Jupiter has numerous satellites*) moon, asteroid, sputnik, ROCKET; **2** (*weak countries are often satellites of powerful ones*) FOLLOWER, subordinate, parasite, DEPENDENT.

satiate: see SATISFY.

satiety: see SATISFACTION.

satiny: see SMOOTH; SOFT.

satire: see RIDICULE.

satirize: see RIDICULE.

satisfaction *n.* gratification, PLEASURE, DELIGHT, CONTENTMENT, COMFORT, ENJOYMENT, satiety.

satisfactorily: see WELL.

satisfactory *adj.* PLEASING, ADEQUATE, OK, all right, SUFFICIENT, fulfilling, ENOUGH, CONVINCING.

satisfied: see COMFORTABLE; CONTENTED.

satisfy *v.* DELIGHT, PLEASE, COMFORT, GRATIFY, SUIT, BENEFIT, appease, sate, satiate, placate.

satisfying: see ENJOYABLE; REFRESHING.

saturate: see SOAK; SWAMP.

saturated: see FULL.

sauce *n.* gravy, seasoning, condiment, RELISH, JUICE.

saucepan: see PAN; POT.

saucer: see BOWL.

saucy: see SHAMELESS.

saunter: see PROMENADE; ROAM; STROLL.

savage *adj.* WILD, FIERCE, uncivilized, barbarous, CRUEL, inhumane, ruthless.
— *n.* barbarian, VANDAL, BEAST, BRUTE, ANIMAL.

savagery: see CRUELTY.

save *v.* **1** (*to save someone from drowning*) RESCUE, DELIVER, DEFEND, PRESERVE; **2** (*to save money*) KEEP, ACCUMULATE, economize, GATHER; **3** (*to*

save leftovers) REDEEM, salvage, RECOVER, STORE.
— *prep.:* see BUT.

saved: see ELECT.

saving: see ECONOMICAL; ECONOMY; EFFICIENT; EXCEPT.

savings *pl.n.* funds, resources, INVESTMENT, RESERVE, hoard, nest-egg.

savor: see FLAVOR; PARTAKE; SALT; SAMPLE; SIP; SPICE; TASTE.

savory: see APPETIZING; DELICIOUS; FRAGRANT; TASTY.

say *v.* STATE, DECLARE, TELL, SPEAK, REMARK, UTTER, PRONOUNCE.
— *n.* AUTHORITY, DECISION, RIGHT, POWER, VOICE, VOTE.

saying: see MOTTO; PROVERB; WORD.

say-so: see VOICE.

scab: see CLOT.

scads: see MUCH.

scalawag: see RASCAL.

scald: see BURN.

scale *n.* BALANCE, RULER, MEASUREMENT, SYSTEM, RANGE, PROPORTION, progression, gradation. See also KEY.
— *v.* **1** *(they scaled Mt. Everest)* CLIMB, ASCEND, MOUNT; **2** *(he scaled the blueprints to the original size)* COMPARE, BALANCE, MEASURE, COMPUTE. See also FLAKE.

scalp: see SKIN.

scalpel: see LANCE.

scamp: see BRAT; RASCAL; SCOUNDREL.

scamper *v.* DASH, DART, scurry, RUN, RACE, RUSH, HUSTLE.

scan *v.* CONSIDER, EXAMINE, OBSERVE, STUDY, INSPECT, INVESTIGATE, scrutinize.

scandal *n.* **1** *(the scandal forced him to resign)* DISGRACE, SHAME, dishonor, HUMILIATION; **2** *(she loved to make up scandals)* gossip, hearsay, RUMOR, TALK, defamation, DIRT, disparagement.

scandalize: see SHOCK.

scandalous: see DISGRACEFUL; JUICY; NOTORIOUS.

scant: see BARE; THIN.

scantily: see BARELY; FEW.

scanty: see LEAN; SCARCE; SPARE.

scapegoat: see TARGET; VICTIM.

scar *n.* MARK, BLEMISH, DEFECT, disfigurement, flaw, INJURY.
— *v.* HURT, deface, WOUND, MARK, BLEMISH, disfigure.

scarce *adj.* insufficient, scanty, deficient, UNCOMMON, infrequent, RARE, sparse, inadequate.

scarcely: see BARELY; HARDLY; RARELY; SELDOM; SLIGHTLY.

scarcity *n.* LACK, sparsity, deficiency, insufficiency, rarity, infrequency, meagerness.

scare *v.* FRIGHTEN, TERRIFY, STARTLE, ALARM, PANIC, SURPRISE.
— *n.* FEAR, FRIGHT, PANIC, TERROR.

scared: see AFRAID.

scarf *n.* muffler, shawl, stole, kerchief, bandanna, babushka.

scarlet: see RED.

scary *adj.* frightening, terrifying, startling, ALARMING, SURPRISING, intimidating.

scatter *v.* DISTRIBUTE, SPREAD, disperse, strew, SPRINKLE, SPRAY, SOW, disseminate.

scattered: see STRAY.

scattering: see SPRINKLE.

scene *n.* **1** *(the scene of the play)* PLACE, SPOT, LOCATION, background, VIEW, DISPLAY, EXHIBITION; **2** *(the irate woman made a scene in the store)* outburst, SPECTACLE, flare-up, tantrum, DISTURBANCE.

scenery: see COUNTRYSIDE; LANDSCAPE; SET.

scent *n.* ODOR, SMELL, FRAGRANCE, essence, aroma, PERFUME.
— *v.* TRACK, TRAIL, DETECT, SMELL, SNIFF, snift, snuff.

scented: see FRAGRANT.

schedule *n.* PROGRAM, CALENDAR, agenda, PLAN, timetable, REGISTER, CATALOG.
— *v.* LIST, PLAN, program, REGISTER, RECORD, slate.

scheduled: see DUE.

scheduling: see RESERVATION.

scheme *n.* PLOT, PLAN, PROJECT, PURPOSE, DESIGN, PROGRAM, AIM.
— *v.* PLOT, intrigue, conspire, contrive, DESIGN, PROJECT, AIM, ASPIRE.

schemer: see FOX.

schism: see RENT.

schizophrenia: see INSANITY.

scholar *n.* TEACHER, PROFESSOR, mentor, philosopher, STUDENT, DISCIPLE.

scholarly: see INTELLECTUAL; LEARNED.

scholarship: see GRANT; KNOWLEDGE; LEARNING.

scholastic: see EDUCATIONAL.

school *n.* **1** *(a school of instruction)* ACADEMY seminary, COLLEGE, institute; **2** *(a school of thought)* CIRCLE, GROUP, sect, FOLLOWING; **3** *(a school of fish)* shoal, GROUP, FLOCK, HERD.
— *v.*: see EDUCATE; TEACH.

schoolboy: see STUDENT.

schooldays: see CHILDHOOD.

schooled: see LEARNED; PRACTICED.

schoolgirl: see STUDENT.

schooling: see EDUCATION, TRAINING.

schoolmarm: see MISTRESS.

schoolmaster: see TEACHER.

schoolmistress: see MISTRESS.

science *n.* KNOWLEDGE, INFORMATION, LEARNING, enlightenment, craftsmanship, SKILL, ART, lore.

scientific *adj.* CLEAR, PRECISE, objective, ACCURATE, LOGICAL, METHODICAL, PHILOSOPHICAL.

scientist *n.* SPECIALIST, EXPERT, technician, researcher, SCHOLAR, craftsman, philosopher.

scoff *v.* deride, MOCK, jeer, RIDICULE, belittle, SNEER, flout.

scold *v.* chide, censure, rebuke, berate, CRITICIZE, LECTURE, NAG.

scolding: see DISAPPROVAL; LECTURE; LESSON.

scoop *v.* shovel, DIG, excavate, ladle, bail, gouge.
— *n.*: see BUCKET.

scoot: see SPEED.

scope: see AREA; CIRCLE; EXTENT; LATITUDE; ORBIT; PROVINCE; REACH; ROOM.

scorch *v.* singe, sear, char, parch, BURN, swelter.

score *n.* **1** *(the winning score of a team)* COUNT, POINT, TOTAL, tally, RECORD; **2** *(the score of a play)* MUSIC, ARRANGEMENT, orchestration, TRANSCRIPT. See also scratch.
— *v.* **1** *(she scored the highest grade in the exam)* rate, RECORD, tabulate, RECEIVE, EARN, WIN, GET; **2** *(he scored the desk with a knife)* MARK, NOTCH, NICK, CUT; **3** *(to score an exam)* GRADE, CORRECT, CHECK, tally, RECORD, NOTE. See also ARRANGE; COMPOSE.

scoring: see GROOVE.

scorn *n.* HATRED, contempt, rejection, mockery, RIDICULE.
— *v.* DESPISE, HATE, REJECT, spurn.

scot-free: see FREE.

scoundrel *n.* rogue, RASCAL, VILLAIN, DEVIL, scamp, CHEAT, SWINDLER.

scour: see POLISH; RUB; SCRAPE; SCRUB; SEARCH.

scout *n.* PIONEER, EXPLORER, spotter, PATROL.
— *v.* EXPLORE, PATROL, SEARCH, HUNT, reconnoiter.

scowl: see FROWN; GLARE.

scowling: see UGLY.

scrabble: see CLAW.

scraggly: see RAGGED.

scramble *v.* **1** *(to scramble eggs)* MIX, BLEND, COMBINE, JUMBLE, MINGLE; **2** *(to scramble for the exit)* DASH, dart, RUSH, PUSH, HASTEN.
— *n.* STRUGGLE, CONTEST, RUSH, PUSH, hastening, climb.

scrambled: see MISCELLANEOUS.

scrap *n.* **1** *(production scrap)* WASTE, leftover, JUNK, debris, LITTER, TRASH; **2** *(the dispute led to a bloody scrap)* QUARREL, FIGHT, brawl, tiff.
— *v.* REJECT, DISMISS, JUNK, ABANDON, DISCARD.

scrape *v.* BRUSH, GRIND, FILE, grate, scour, SCRATCH.

scraping: see FRICTION.

scraps: see REFUSE.

scratch *v.* SCRAPE, SCAR, SCORE, CLAW. See also cancel.
— *n.* INJURY, MARK, score, SCAR, incision, WOUND.

scratchy: see COARSE.

scrawl: see WRITE.

scream *v.* SHRIEK, YELL, HOWL, SCREECH.
— *n.* shriek, SCREECH, YELL, HOWL, OUTCRY.

screech *v.* SCREAM, SHRIEK, YELL, CRY, SHOUT.
— *n.* shriek, YELL, SCREAM, OUTCRY, HOWL.

screechy: see NOISY.

screen *n.* **1** *(a folding screen)* SEPARATION, partition, SHADE, COVER, CONCEALMENT, safeguard; **2** *(the motion-picture screen)* movies, FILM, cinema.
— *v.* **1** *(they screened the evidence)* HIDE, CONCEAL, mask, SHIELD, VEIL; **2** *(to screen applications)* REVIEW, SORT, FILTER, FILE.

screw n. fastener, spiral, BOLT, PIN.
— v. TWIST, ROTATE, TURN, DRIVE.

screwball: see MANIAC.

scribble: see PENCIL; WRITE.

scribbler: see AUTHOR.

scribe: see AUTHOR; WRITER.

scriber: see COMPASS.

scrub v. WASH, CLEAN, CLEANSE, scour, SCRAPE.
— n.: see BUSH.

scrubbing: see WASH.

scrumptious: see DELICIOUS; TASTY.

scrutinize: see EXAMINE; INSPECT; OBSERVE;
REVIEW; SCAN; SURVEY.

scrutinizing: see CURIOUS.

scrutiny: see CHECKUP; EXAMINATION; REVIEW.

sculptor: see ARTIST.

sculpture n. carving, STATUE, modeling.
— v. CARVE, hew, chisel, fashion, MODEL, SHAPE.

scum: see REFUSE; SLIME.

scummy: see SLIMY.

scurry: see FLY; HURRY; SCAMPER.

scuttle: see BUCKET; SINK.

sea n. OCEAN, DEEP, WATER, LAKE.

seafarer: see SAILOR.

seafaring: see MARINE.

seagoing: see MARINE.

seal n. **1** (a seal of approval) confirmation,
assurance, endorsement, PERMIT, PERMISSION,
authorization; **2** (Christmas seals) STAMP, sticker,
TAPE, fastener.
— v. CLOSE, FASTEN, secure, PASTE, gum, attest,
CONFIRM.

sealed: see AIRTIGHT; SHUT.

seam n. stitching, WRINKLE, HEM, TUCK, pleat,
joint, crevice.

seaman: see SAILOR.

seamanship: see NAVIGATION.

sear: see DRY; SCORCH.

search v. EXPLORE, HUNT, rummage, ransack,
ROOT, scour, PROBE.
— n. EXPLORATION, quest, seeking, INQUIRY,
PURSUIT, HUNT, chase.

sea robber : see PIRATE.

seashore: see SHORE.

seaside: see BEACH; COAST; SHORE.

season n. TERM, PERIOD, INTERVAL, SPELL, TIME.
— v. **1** (to season with garlic) FLAVOR, spice, SALT;
2 (he seasoned his words with care) QUALIFY,
moderate. See also ACCUSTOM.

seasonal: see PERIODIC.

seasoned: see RIPE; VETERAN.

seasoning: see SALT; SAUCE; SPICE.

seat n. CHAIR, BENCH, STOOL, PLACE, POSITION,
SITUATION, SITE.
— v. SET, PLACE, LOCATE, FIX.

secede: see WITHDRAW.

seclude: see SEPARATE.

secluded: see LONE; LONELY; PRIVATE; REMOTE;
SECRET.

seclusion: see LONELINESS; PRIVACY; RETREAT;
SECRECY.

second adj. NEXT, OTHER, secondary, INFERIOR,
FOLLOWING.
— n. **1** (a split second) MOMENT, INSTANT, FLASH,
twinkling, WINK; **2** (a duelist's second)
SUPPORTER, helper, FOLLOWER, stand-in,
runner-up.
— v. AGREE, endorse, UPHOLD, BACK, HELP.

secondary: see INFERIOR; LESSER; SECOND.

second-hand adj. USED, renewed, reclaimed,
WORN.

second-rate: see COMMON.

second-string: see JUNIOR.

secrecy n. CONCEALMENT, hiding, PRIVACY,
ISOLATION, solitude, seclusion, SEPARATION,
MYSTERY.

secret adj. UNKNOWN, HIDDEN, concealed,
MYSTERIOUS, PRIVATE, secluded, ulterior.
— n. MYSTERY, CONFIDENCE, CONCEALMENT.

secretary n. **1** (United Nations Secretary General)
EXECUTIVE, OFFICER, DIRECTOR, MANAGER,
SUPERINTENDENT; **2** (a secretary to handle
correspondence) CLERK, typist, CORRESPONDENT,
stenographer, ASSISTANT. See also DESK.

secrete: see CONCEAL; PERSPIRE.

secretive: see SILENT.

sect: see PARTY; PERSUASION; SCHOOL.

section n. PART, PORTION, FRACTION, DIVISION,
segment, AREA, sector.
— v.: see PORTION.

sectional: see LOCAL; PARTIAL.

sector: see DISTRICT; SECTION; SIDE.

secure *adj.* SAFE, SURE, SOUND, UNHARMED, defended, protected, sheltered.
– *v.* FASTEN, tighten, TIE, BIND, CLOSE. See also ACQUIRE; COLLECT; OBTAIN; PRESERVE; RESERVE; SEAL; TAKE; WIN.

securities: see INVESTMENT.

security *n.* PROTECTION, SAFETY, assurance, BOND, PLEDGE, guaranty, WARRANTY.

sedan: see AUTOMOBILE.

sedate: see SOBER.

sediment: see DEPOSIT; GROUNDS.

sedition: see REVOLT; REVOLUTION.

seduce: see BRIBE; LURE; TEMPT.

seduction: see ATTRACTION; LURE.

seductive: see ATTRACTIVE; PERSUASIVE; SEXUAL; TEMPTING.

see *v.* LOOK, VIEW, perceive, OBSERVE, NOTICE, RECOGNIZE, UNDERSTAND.

seeable: see VISUAL.

seed *n.* **1** *(to plant a seed)* GRAIN, PIT, NUT, kernel, PARTICLE; **2** *(the seed of the parents)* OFFSPRING, ISSUE, children, descendants.
– *v.* PLANT, SOW, SCATTER, disseminate, DISTRIBUTE.

seek *v.* SEARCH, HUNT, EXPLORE, quest, PURSUE, ATTEMPT, TRY.

seeking: see SEARCH.

seem *v.* APPEAR, LOOK, SHOW, RESEMBLE.

seeming: see APPARENT; PROBABLE.

seemingly: see APPARENTLY; LIKELY; PROBABLY.

seemly: see DECENT; FITTING.

seen: see VISUAL.

seep: see LEAK; TRICKLE.

seethe: see BOIL; HISS; SIMMER.

segment: see COMMUNITY; FRACTION; MEMBER; PORTION; SECTION; SLICE.

segregate: see ISOLATE; WEED.

segregation: see ISOLATION.

seize *v.* GRAB, GRASP, SNATCH, HOLD, RETAIN, KEEP, appropriate, usurp.

seizure: see ARREST; ATTACK; CATCH; CLUTCH; FIT; OCCUPATION; RAID; SIEGE; STROKE.

seldom *adv.* RARELY, HARDLY, scarcely, infrequently, irregularly, occasionally.

select *v.* CHOOSE, PICK, DECIDE, ELECT, PREFER, designate.
– *adj.*: see CHOSEN; ELECT; EXCELLENT; RARE.

selected: see CHOSEN; MISCELLANEOUS.

selection *n.* CHOICE, PICK, ELECTION, DETERMINATION, designation, PREFERENCE, differentiation.

selective *adj.* CAREFUL, PARTICULAR, judicious, discriminating, CHOOSY, FUSSY.

self *n.* **1** *(her better self)* individuality, PERSON, CONSCIOUSNESS, CHARACTER, NATURE, psyche, SOUL, SPIRIT, CONSCIENCE, superego; **2** *(putting self first)* selfishness, ego, id, egoism.

self-centered: see PROUD.

self-confidence: see CONFIDENCE.

self-conscious: see UNCOMFORTABLE; UNEASY.

self-consciousness: see EMBARRASSMENT.

self-control: see BEHAVIOR; CALMNESS; DISCIPLINE; WILL.

self-denial: see SACRIFICE.

self-government: see FREEDOM; INDEPENDENCE.

selfish *adj.* POSSESSIVE, egoistic, NARROW, venal, GREEDY, ungenerous.

selfishness: see GREED; SELF.

self-possession: see CALMNESS.

self-reliant: see INDEPENDENT; SINGLE-HANDED; SINGLE-MINDED.

self-respect: see DIGNITY.

self-sacrificing: see NOBLE.

selfsame: see IDENTICAL.

self-sufficient: see INDEPENDENT.

sell *v.* vend, MARKET, retail, TRADE, barter, EXCHANGE, merchandise.

seller: see DEALER; MERCHANT; PEDDLER; TRADER.

sell out: see BETRAY; FINGER.

semaphore: see SIGNAL.

semblance: see FACE.

semester: see SESSION; TERM.

seminary: see ACADEMY; COLLEGE; SCHOOL.

send *v.* MAIL, SHIP, DISPATCH, convey, FORWARD, TRANSMIT, COMMUNICATE.

send away: see DISPATCH.

sending: see TRANSPORT.

send out: see ISSUE.

senior *adj.* ELDER, older, SUPERIOR, ADVANCED.
— *n.* upperclassman, SUPERIOR, first-born,
VETERAN, patriarch.

sensation *n.* **1** *(a strange sensation)* FEELING,
CONSCIOUSNESS, perception, IMPRESSION; **2** *(he is
a sensation)* SUCCESS, CELEBRITY, HERO, DARLING,
HIT, STAR, IDOL, WONDER, thrill.

sensational *adj.* SUCCESSFUL, exciting,
MARVELOUS, sensory, receptive.

sense *n.* **1** *(the five senses)* FEELING, SENSATION,
perception, MEANING, IMPORT, SIGHT, hearing,
TOUCH, SPEECH, SMELL; **2** *(an artistic sense)*
APPRECIATION, TALENT, GIFT, CAPACITY; **3** *(to
have sense)* WISDOM, LOGIC, INTELLIGENCE,
REASON; **4** *(the sense of the membership)*
consensus, FEELING, INCLINATION, OPINION.
— *v.* perceive, FEEL, DETECT, RECOGNIZE.

senseless *adj.* **1** *(a senseless act)* STUPID, FOOLISH,
SILLY, asinine, IDIOTIC, witless, UNREASONABLE;
2 *(a senseless body)* LIFELESS, UNCONSCIOUS,
oblivious, inert, unfeeling.

senselessness: see FOOLISHNESS; STUPIDITY.

sensible *adj.* REASONABLE, discerning, WISE,
perceptive, AWARE, perceptible.

sensibly: see PRACTICALLY.

sensitive *adj.* perceptive, subtle, responsive,
TEMPERAMENTAL, touchy, thin-skinned,
DELICATE.

sensitize: see IRRITATE.

sensory: see SENSATIONAL.

sensual: see PASSIONATE; PLEASURABLE; SEXUAL.

sensuality: see LUST.

sensuous: see FOXY.

sentence *n.* **1** *(a declarative sentence)* PHRASE,
STATEMENT, PROPOSITION, THOUGHT; **2** *(a jail
sentence)* JUDGMENT, ORDER, decree, PENALTY,
censure.
— *v.* JUDGE, CONVICT, DOOM, PUNISH, FINE,
imprison.

sentiment *n.* EMOTION, FEELING, SENSATION,
delicacy.

sentimental *adj.* EMOTIONAL, ROMANTIC,
melodramatic, gushy, mush, mawkish.

sentinel: see WATCH.

sentry: see GUARD.

separate *v.* PART, DEPART, BREAK, undo, ISOLATE,
seclude, CLASSIFY.
— *adj.* INDIVIDUAL, APART, SINGLE, DISTINCT,
INDEPENDENT.

separated: see DISTANT.

separately: see APART; APIECE.

separating: see PARTING.

separation *n.* **1** *(the separation of fluids)* PARTING,
DIVISION, disintegration, GAP; **2** *(a legal
separation)* DIVORCE, ISOLATION, SPLIT, rift.

sepulcher: see GRAVE; TOMB; VAULT.

sequel: see CONTINUATION; RESULT.

sequence *n.* ORDER, SUCCESSION, ARRANGEMENT,
FLOW, SERIES, CHAIN.

sequential: see SUCCESSIVE.

serene: see CALM; CLEAR; CONTENTED; PEACEFUL;
TRANQUIL.

serenity: see CALM; CONTENTMENT; TRANQUILLITY.

serf: see SLAVE.

serial: see PUBLICATION; SUCCESSIVE.

series *n.* ROW, SEQUENCE, SET, CHAIN, STRING,
concatenation, ORDER, PROGRAM.

serious *adj.* EARNEST, GRAVE, substantial,
IMPORTANT, SEVERE, dire, complicated.

seriously: see SINCERELY; TERRIBLY.

seriousness *n.* **1** *(the seriousness of the economic
problem)* IMPORTANCE, SIGNIFICANCE, GRAVITY,
solemnity, austerity; **2** *(the seriousness of
mountain climbing)* DANGER, peril, RISK,
jeopardy, HAZARD.

sermon *n.* LECTURE, TALK, ADDRESS, LESSON,
admonition, exhortation.

sermonize: see LECTURE; PREACH.

serpent: see SNAKE.

serrated: see JAGGED.

serum: see BLOOD.

servant *n.* domestic, ATTENDANT, MAID, valet,
maidservant, HOUSEKEEPER, COOK, butler,
helper.

serve *v.* ASSIST, HELP, WORK, wait on, DELIVER,
ENROLL, ENLIST, FOLLOW, SUPPORT, suffice,
SATISFY, THROW.

server: see TRAY; WAITER.

service *n.* **1** *(a delivery service)* ASSISTANCE, HELP, WORK, DUTY, MAINTENANCE, REPAIR; **2** *(the armed services)* armed forces, ARMY, NAVY, air force; **3** *(a religious service)* CEREMONY, observance, FUNERAL, ritual.

serviceable: see EFFICIENT; USEFUL.

serviceman: see SOLDIER.

services: see WORSHIP.

serving: see SHARE.

servitude: see SLAVERY.

session *n.* ASSEMBLY, sitting, MEETING, DISCUSSION, PERFORMANCE, ordeal, semester.

set *n.* SERIES, GROUP, suite, GAME, KIT, scenery, setting, POSITION.
— *adj.* READY, FIXED, DEFINITE, USUAL, HABITUAL, STUBBORN.
— *v.* PLACE, MOUNT, FIX, reset, ADJUST, ready, ARRANGE.

set apart: see ISOLATE.

set aside: see RESERVE.

setback: see BLOW; DISAPPOINTMENT.

set down: see RECORD.

set forth: see INTRODUCE.

set off: see COMMENCE; FIRE; RELIEVE.

set out: see COMMENCE; DEPART; GO; START.

settee: see BENCH; COUCH; SOFA.

setting: see ENVIRONMENT; SET.

settle *v.* ARRANGE, RESOLVE, ESTABLISH, DECIDE, colonize, PAY, REST, SINK, HARDEN, jell, COMPROMISE.

settled: see CERTAIN; FIXED; OVER.

settlement *n.* **1** *(the settlement of differences)* RESOLUTION, AGREEMENT, terms; **2** *(settlement of a debt)* PAYMENT, ACCOMMODATION, compensation; **3** *(a frontier settlement)* COLONY, encampment, TOWN, ESTABLISHMENT.

settler *n.* COLONIST, PIONEER, frontiersman.

set up: see ARRANGE; ASSEMBLE; ESTABLISH; FOUND; INSTALL; INSTITUTE; MOUNT; ORGANIZE.

sever: see BREAK; CUT; DISCONNECT; DIVORCE; PART; SLASH; SLIT; SNIP; SPLIT.

several *adj.* SOME, FEW, sundry, VARIOUS, diverse, DIFFERENT, SINGLE, SEPARATE.

severally: see APIECE; VARIOUSLY.

severe *adj.* STRICT, STERN, HARSH, exacting, rigorous, PLAIN, minimal.

severity: see HARSHNESS.

sew *v.* stitch, FASTEN, tailor, baste, MEND, FIX.

sewer: see DRAIN; SINK.

sex *n.* **1** *(the male sex)* gender, MALE, FEMALE, MAN, WOMAN, BOY, GIRL; **2** *(attitudes toward sex)* reproduction, sexual intercourse, copulation, coitus, intimacy, fornication.

sexless: see NEUTRAL.

sexual *adj.* reproductive, sensual, seductive, erotic, carnal, intimate.

sexual intercourse: see SEX.

sexy: see FOXY; PASSIONATE; SULTRY.

shabby *adj.* **1** *(a shabby appearance)* RAGGED, frayed, threadbare, PITIFUL; **2** *(a shabby treatment)* inconsiderate, RUDE, MEAN, THOUGHTLESS.

shack *n.* hovel, HUT, shanty, SHED, DUMP.

shackle: see BOND.

shackled: see BOUND.

shackles: see IRON.

shade *n.* **1** *(the shade of an oak)* SHADOW, DARKNESS, DIMNESS, DUSK, PROTECTION; **2** *(pull the shade)* BLIND, CURTAIN, SCREEN, shutter, COVER; **3** *(the skin shade)* TONE, tinge, hue, shading, chiaroscuro.
— *v.* darken, SCREEN, overshadow, VEIL, obscure, BLEND.

shadiness: see DUSK.

shading: see SHADE.

shadow *n.* DARK, DIMNESS, SHADE, silhouette, eyeshadow, hue, TRACE, SUSPICION.
— *v.* **1** *(to shadow a sketch)* SHADE, DARKEN, tone, overshadow; **2** *(to shadow a suspect)* FOLLOW, TAIL, TRAIL, TRACK, OBSERVE.

shadowy: see DARK; DIM.

shaft *n.* **1** *(a warped shaft)* ROD, POLE, SPEAR, ARROW, BAR, STEM; **2** *(a mine shaft)* PASSAGE, TUNNEL, WELL, PIT; **3** *(a shaft of light)* RAY, BEAM, STREAM, sunbeam, moonbeam.

shah: see EMPEROR; MONARCH.

shake *v.* TREMBLE, RATTLE, SHUDDER, VIBRATE, agitate, STIR, MIX.
— *n.*: see JOLT; NOD; TOSS; VIBRATION.

shake-down: see PROTECTION; RACKET.

shaken *adj.* mixed, stirred, UPSET, unnerved, disturbed, agitated, NERVOUS, unsettled.

shaky *adj.* UNCERTAIN, unsure, unstable, rocky, JERKY, quivering, shivering.

shale: see GRAVEL.

shall: see MAY.

shallow *adj.* superficial, trivial, frivolous, SLIGHT, skin-deep.

sham: see MOCK; SHOW.

shame *n.* DISGRACE, EMBARRASSMENT, dishonor, discredit, GUILT, remorse.
— *v.* dishonor, HUMILIATE, DISGRACE, vilify, dissatisfy.

shamed: see ASHAMED.

shameful *adj.* INDECENT, corrupt, immoral, IMPURE, DISGRACEFUL, gross, EVIL, despicable, humiliating.

shamefulness: see WICKEDNESS.

shameless *adj.* brazen, BOLD, audacious, impudent, immodest, saucy, brassy.

shampoo: see RINSE.

shank: see LEG.

shanty: see CABIN; HUT; SHACK; SHED.

shape *n.* FORM, FIGURE, OUTLINE, contour, PATTERN, CONDITION, STATE, HEALTH.
— *v.* fashion, FORM, MOLD, ADJUST, DEVELOP, CONSTRUCT.

shapeless *adj.* FORMLESS, unformed, DEFORMED, MISSHAPEN, disfigured, IRREGULAR, amorphous.

shapely *adj.* well-built, well-formed, well-proportioned, TRIM, comely, ATTRACTIVE, GRACEFUL.

shard: see CHIP.

share *n.* PORTION, allotment, PART, serving, RATION, apportionment, PERCENTAGE.
— *v.* DIVIDE, allot, MEASURE, PARTICIPATE, PARTAKE.

shared: see JOINT.

sharing: see GENEROSITY.

shark: see WIZARD.

sharp *adj.* 2 *(a sharp tool)* ACUTE, POINTED, KEEN; 2 *(a sharp whistle)* CLEAR, DISTINCT, SHRILL, audible; 3 *(a sharp mind)* ACUTE, ALERT, BRIGHT, perceptive, astute; 4 *(a sharp retort)* cutting, sarcastic, biting, NASTY; 5 *(a sharp taste)* SOUR, tart, tangy, BITTER; 6 *(a sharp dresser)* STYLISH, CHIC, FASHIONABLE.
— *adv.* EXACTLY, punctually, PRECISELY.

sharpen *v.* FILE, whet, hone, GRIND, focus, CLARIFY.

sharpener: see FILE.

sharply *adv.* CLEARLY, pointedly, acutely, intently, sarcastically, smartly, stylishly, vividly.

sharpness: see ALERTNESS; EDGE; RELIEF.

sharp-witted: see SLICK.

shatter *v.* SMASH, SPLIT, BURST, BREAK, splinter, DESTROY, RUIN.

shattered: see BROKEN.

shattering: see BURST.

shave *v.* CUT, SHEAR, STRIP, BARE, SLICE, pare, skim.

shaver: see LAD; YOUNGSTER.

shaving: see FLAKE.

shawl: see CLOAK; HOOD; SCARF.

shay: see CARRIAGE.

sheaf: see STACK.

shear *v.* CLIP, CUT, TRIM, CROP, SHAVE, mow, SNIP.

sheath: see CASE; POD.

shed *n.* lean-to, HUT, SHACK, shanty.
— *v.* cast off, DROP, DISCARD, repel, CAST, disown, molt, slough, SCATTER, RADIATE, ABANDON.

sheen: see GLOSS; LUSTER; POLISH; SHINE.

sheep *n.* LAMB, ewe, ram, mutton, FOLLOWER, DISCIPLE.

sheepherder: see SHEPHERD.

sheepish: see ASHAMED; BASHFUL; TIMID.

sheepman: see RANCHER.

sheer: see ABRUPT; MERE; STEEP; THIN; THOROUGH; TRANSPARENT.

sheet *n.* LAYER, LEAF, PAGE, FOIL, COAT, FILM, PANE, bedclothes, linen, expanse.

shelf *n.* LEDGE, shoals, reef, RACK, bracket, mantelpiece.

shell *n.* 1 *(a nut shell)* husk, POD, CRUST, CASE, NUT, ARMOR; 2 *(a live shell)* bullet, cartridge, ROUND, SHOT, projectile; 3 *(the shell of a house)* FRAME, framework, SKELETON.
— *v.* 1 *(to shell peas)* husk, PEEL, STRIP, shuck; 2 *(to shell a stronghold)* BOMBARD, bomb, strafe, pepper.

shellac: see COAT; VARNISH.

shelter n. PROTECTION, ROOF, HOUSE, LODGINGS, SECURITY, SHADE, sanctuary, DEFENSE.
— v. PROTECT, HARBOR, DEFEND, HOUSE, LODGE, quarter.

sheltered: see SECURE.

sheltering: see CONCEALMENT.

shelve: see POSTPONE; TABLE.

shepherd n. sheepherder, herdsman, GUARDIAN, PROTECTOR, GUIDE, PASTOR.
— v.: see ESCORT; HERD.

sheriff: see OFFICER.

shield n. PROTECTION, safeguard, buckler, buffer, ARMOR. See also BADGE.
— v. PROTECT, safeguard, DEFEND, SCREEN, CONCEAL.

shielded: see SAFE.

shift v. TRANSFER, MOVE, CHANGE, ADJUST.
— n. 1 (a shift in plans) CHANGE, MOVE, TRANSFER; 2 (the day shift) PERIOD, SPELL, TURN; 3 (the cleaning shift) TEAM, GROUP, CREW, COMPANY.

shifting: see VARIABLE.

shiftless: see LAZY.

shifty adj. SLY, sneaky, CUNNING, TRICKY, evasive.

shilling: see COIN.

shine v. GLOW, RADIATE, GLEAM, REFLECT, BEAM, POLISH, buff, excel.
— n. GLEAM, LUSTER, GLOSS, POLISH, sheen.

shining: see DAZZLING.

shiny adj. glossy, glimmering, gleaming, glowing, glistening, sparkling, silvery, polished.

ship n. BOAT, VESSEL, liner, freighter, battleship, destroyer, cruiser, frigate, airplane, airship.
— v. SEND, TRANSPORT, DISPATCH, MAIL.

shipment: see CARGO; DELIVERY; FREIGHT; LOAD; ORDER; TRANSPORT; TRANSPORTATION.

shipshape: see NEAT; ORDERLY.

shipwrecked: see AGROUND.

shirk: see DODGE.

shiver v. TREMBLE, SHAKE, SHUDDER, QUIVER.
— n.: see SHUDDER.

shivering: see SHAKY.

shoal: see SCHOOL.

shoals: see SHELF.

shock n. 1 (an electric shock) JOLT, CLASH, IMPACT, UPSET, SURPRISE, stupor, tremor; 2 (a shock of corn) BUNCH, STACK, BUNDLE.
— v. STUN, JOLT, daze, scandalize, SCARE, SURPRISE.

shocking: see FRIGHTFUL; MONSTROUS; TERRIFIC.

shoe n. footwear, BOOT, sneaker, oxford, clog, slipper, sandal, mule.

shoot v. 1 (to shoot a gun) FIRE, DISCHARGE, HURL, INJURE, MURDER; 2 (to shoot a picture) FILM, photograph; 3 (to shoot out the door) DASH, dart, RUN, SPURT.
— n.: see BLADE; BUD; SPRAY; SPROUT; SWITCH; TWIG.

shop n. STORE, boutique, workshop, BUSINESS.
— v. BUY, MARKET, SEEK.

shopkeeper: see MERCHANT.

shoplift: see STEAL; TAKE.

shoplifter: see THIEF.

shopper: see CONSUMER; CUSTOMER.

shore n. BEACH, COAST, seashore, seaside, EDGE, waterside.

shoreline: see BEACH; COAST.

short adj. BRIEF, concise, curt, LOW, LITTLE, squat, undersized, insufficient, lacking, MISSING.

shortage: see LACK; SHORTNESS.

shortcoming: see FAULT.

shorten v. LESSEN, DIMINISH, curtail, REDUCE, abridge, ABBREVIATE, TRIM.

shortening: see ABBREVIATION; CONTRACTION.

shortly adv. SOON, DIRECTLY, PROMPTLY, presently.

shortness n. conciseness, brevity, shortage, REDUCTION, insufficiency, deficiency.

short-sighted: see CHILDLIKE.

shot n. 1 (to take a shot) DISCHARGE, BLAST, bullet, cartridge, bird shot, MISSILE, CHANCE; 2 (a flu shot) injection, innoculation, dose DRINK, nip. See also ATTEMPT.
— adj. WORN, USELESS, BROKEN, spent.

shotgun: see GUN; RIFLE.

should: see MUST; OUGHT.

shoulder: see CARRY; SHOVE.

shout v. YELL, CRY, BELLOW, rant, CALL, SCOLD.
— n. CALL, YELL, ROAR, OUTCRY, bellow, EXCLAMATION.

shouting: see CLAMOR.

shove *v.* jostle, PUSH, THRUST, DRIVE, shoulder.
— *n.*: see NUDGE; THRUST.

shovel: see SCOOP.

show *v.* point out, INDICATE, DEMONSTRATE,
DISPLAY, EXHIBIT, EXPLAIN.
— *n.* **2** *(a stage show)* PLAY, PERFORMANCE,
PROGRAM, PRESENTATION, movie, pageant; **2** *(a
flower show)* EXHIBITION, exposition, DISPLAY;
3 *(a show of force)* ostentation, pretense,
APPEARANCE, ILLUSION, sham.

showcase: see COUNTER.

shower: see BATH; BATHE; RAIN; SPRAY; SPRINKLE.

showiness: see SPLENDOR.

showing: see EXPOSURE; SYMPTOM.

show off: see DISPLAY; PARADE.

show up: see ARRIVE; ATTEND; COME.

showy: see AMBITIOUS; GAY; GORGEOUS; VAIN.

shred *n.* PIECE, tatter, STRIP, sliver, BIT,
FRAGMENT.
— *v.* TEAR, RIP, grate, SLICE, SLIT.

shrew: see WITCH.

shrewd: see ACUTE; CLEVER; CUNNING; CUTE;
KEEN; SLY; WISE.

shriek *v.* SCREECH, SCREAM, whoop, SQUEAL,
YELL.
— *n.*: see SCREAM; SCREECH.

shrill *adj.* piercing, SHARP, high-pitched,
hysterical, intemperate.

shrine *n.* sanctuary, CHURCH, TEMPLE,
synagogue, MEMORIAL, tabernacle.

shrink *v.* CONTRACT, DIMINISH, DECREASE,
REDUCE, WITHDRAW, flinch, cower.

shrinkage: see CONTRACTION.

shrinking: see REDUCTION.

shrivel: see WITHER.

shriveled: see DRY.

shroud: see CLOUD; GUY; ROBE.

shrub *n.* BUSH, HEDGE, bramble, BRUSH.

shrubbery: see BUSH; HEDGE.

shuck: see SHELL.

shudder *v.* SHAKE, TREMBLE, quake, SHIVER.
— *n.* shiver, tremor, VIBRATION, TWITCH,
agitation.

shuffle: see LIMP.

shun: see AVOID; DISLIKE; FEAR.

shunt: see SWITCH.

shut *v.* CLOSE, SEAL, CAP, LOCK, clog, PLUG, SLAM.
— *adj.* closed, sealed, fastened, bolted, latched.

shut-eye: see SLEEP.

shut in: see CAGE; HEM; SURROUND.

shut-in: see CAPTIVE; HERMIT; PATIENT.

shutter: see SHADE.

shy *adj.* **1** *(a shy child)* BASHFUL, retiring, MODEST;
2 *(a nickel shy)* SHORT, deficient, lacking.

shyness: see BASHFULNESS; MODESTY; RESERVE;
TIMIDITY.

sibling: see BROTHER; CHILD.

sick *adj.* **1** *(to feel sick)* ILL, unwell, sickly,
diseased, LAME, indisposed; **2** *(sick and tired)*
disgusted, WEARY; **3** *(a sick joke)* morbid, grim,
GRUESOME, ABNORMAL, bizarre, weird.

sicken *v.* UPSET, afflict, nauseate, AIL, disgust,
repel, REVOLT.

sickly: see SICK; UNHEALTHY; WEAK.

sickness *n.* ILLNESS, AILMENT, DISEASE,
INFECTION, disability, COMPLAINT.

side *n.* **1** *(the side of the page)* FACE, EDGE, FLANK,
SURFACE, PLANE, PART, ASPECT, facet, sector,
HAND; **2** *(the winning side)* PARTY, TEAM,
combatant, plaintiff, adversary; **3** *(a side of an
issue)* ARGUMENT, viewpoint, SLANT, POSITION.
— *adj.* lateral, flanking, oblique, incidental.

sidearm: see GUN; ROD; REVOLVER.

sidekick: see BUDDY; CHUM; FRIEND.

side step: see HEDGE.

sidetrack: see AVERT.

sidewalk: see FOOTPATH.

sidewise: see ASIDE.

siege *n.* ATTACK, ASSAULT, BATTLE, SESSION, bout,
onslaught, seizure, SPELL.

sierra: see RANGE.

siesta: see NAP; SLEEP; SLUMBER.

sieve: see FILTER.

sift *v.* SCREEN, STRAIN, GRADE, SORT, PROBE,
INVESTIGATE, EXAMINE.

sigh *v.* MURMUR, lament, SOB, MOAN, long;
— *n.* MOAN, SOB, MURMUR, BREATH, RUSTLE.

sight *n.* **1** *(the power of sight)* VISION, eyes, eyesight, range; **2** *(a sight to behold)* VIEW, SPECTACLE, GLIMPSE, SCENE, DISPLAY, mirage, vista, eyeful, eyesore.
— *v.* SEE, NOTICE, WITNESS, FIND.

sighting: see AIM.

sightless: see BLIND.

sightseeing: see TOUR.

sightseer: see TOURIST.

sign *n.* **1** *(a sign of strength)* SYMBOL, SIGNAL, GESTURE, WARNING, MARK; **2** *(to post a sign)* placard, NOTICE, signboard, ADVERTISEMENT, POSTER; **3** *(to leave a sign)* INDICATION, TRACE, REMINDER, EVIDENCE, TOKEN.
— *v.* endorse, ACKNOWLEDGE, receipt, attest, SUBSCRIBE.

signal *n.* SIGN, WARNING, NOTICE, GESTURE, cue, beacon, whistle, buzzer, BELL, siren, horn, semaphore, emission, transmission.
— *v.* GESTURE, FLAG, BECKON, INDICATE, WARN.
— *adj.*: see NOTABLE.

signature *n.* NAME, endorsement, autograph, notation, STAMP, MARK, trademark. See also PAGE.

signboard: see SIGN.

significance *n.* MEANING, MESSAGE, SENSE, CONSEQUENCE, IMPORTANCE, VALUE, INTEREST, MOMENT.

significant *adj.* meaningful, substantial, NOTABLE, IMPORTANT.

signification: see IMPORT; MEANING.

signify *v.* REPRESENT, REVEAL, INDICATE, MEAN, IMPLY, denote.

sign up: see ENLIST; ENROLL.

silence *n.* stillness, PEACE, CALM, HUSH.
— *v.* HUSH, STILL, muzzle, gag, stifle, SOFTEN.

silent *adj.* STILL, QUIET, SOUNDLESS, mute, SPEECHLESS, tight-lipped, secretive, mum, concluded.

silhouette: see OUTLINE; PROFILE; SHADOW.

silky: see SOFT.

silliness: see FOOLISHNESS; MADNESS; NONSENSE.

silly *adj.* SENSELESS, FOOLISH, SIMPLE, inane, RIDICULOUS, frivolous, sappy.

silt: see DEPOSIT; MUD; SAND.

silver: see COIN; METAL; PLATE; WHITEN.

silvery: see SHINY; WHITE.

similar *adj.* like, ALIKE, SAME, comparable, resembling.

similarity *n.* likeness, SAMENESS, RESEMBLANCE, COMPARISON, coincidence, analogy.

similarly: see AS; LIKEWISE.

similar to: see LIKE.

similitude: see RESEMBLANCE.

simmer *v.* BOIL, bubble, FOAM, COOK, STEW, fricassee, seethe.

simple *adj.* EASY, facile, OBVIOUS, unmixed, PLAIN, unaffected, simple-minded, MERE, effortless.

simple-minded: see SIMPLE.

simpleton: see HALF-WIT; MORON; SAP.

simplicity *n.* clearness, clarity, pureness, plainness, austerity, INNOCENCE, IGNORANCE, openness.

simplified: see ELEMENTARY.

simplify: see EASE; EXPLAIN.

simply *adv.* CLEARLY, plainly, easily, MERELY, TOTALLY, JUST.

simulate: see AFFECT; ASSUME; BLUFF; INVENT; POSE; PRETEND.

simulation: see IMITATION.

simultaneous: see CONTEMPORARY.

simultaneously: see ALONG; TOGETHER.

sin *n.* WRONG, error, CRIME, wrongdoing, trespass, vice.
— *v.* TREPASS, err, WRONG, OFFEND, STRAY, misbehave.

since *prep.* AFTER, FOLLOWING.
— *conj.* BECAUSE, inasmuch as, FOR, whereas.
— *adv.* THEREAFTER, AFTERWARDS, AFTER, THEN, thereupon, later, subsequently.

sincere *adj.* GENUINE, ACTUAL, HONEST, EARNEST, TRUTHFUL, straightforward.

sincerely *adv.* TRULY, REALLY, seriously, SIMPLY, PURELY, cordially.

sincerity *n.* HONESTY, frankness, veracity, HONOR, directness, integrity.

sinew: see NERVE.

sinewy: see MUSCULAR; STRONG.

sinful: see CRIMINAL; EVIL; FALLEN; GUILTY; VILLAINOUS; WRONG.

sinfulness: see WICKEDNESS.

sing *v.* CHANT, croon, warble, vocalize, HARMONIZE, intone, CHIRP, TWITTER, SQUEAL, BETRAY, double-cross, CONFESS.

singe: see BURN; FRY; SCORCH.

singer *n.* vocalist, songster, crooner, diva, minstrel, troubadour.

singing: see CHANT.

single *adj.* LONE, SOLE, SINGULAR, INDIVIDUAL, ONE, PRIVATE, unmarried, unattached.

single-handed *adj.* ALONE, unaided, self-reliant, DARING.

single-minded *adj.* purposeful, determined, DEVOTED, self-reliant, SELFISH, STUBBORN.

singly: see ALONE; APART; ONCE; ONLY.

singular *adj.* SINGLE, SOLE, ONE, ODD, UNIQUE, OUTSTANDING, NOTABLE.

sinister: see DARK; LEFT.

sink *v.* **1** (*profits are sinking*) DECLINE, SET, subside, dwindle, go under, FAIL, scuttle, WRECK; **2** (*to flounder and sink*) SUBMERGE, DROWN.
— *n.* BASIN, washbowl, tub, sewer, cesspool, washtub.

sinless: see INNOCENT; PERFECT; PURE.

sinner: see DELINQUENT.

sinus: see CAVITY.

sip *v.* PARTAKE, imbibe, DRINK, SWALLOW, TASTE, SAMPLE, savor.
— *n.*: see BEVERAGE; DRINK.

siphon: see STRAW; TAP.

sire: see ANCESTOR; DADDY; FATHER; PARENT.

siren: see ALARM; SIGNAL.

sister: see CHILD; MEMBER; NURSE; TWIN.

sisterhood: see ORDER.

sit *v.* SEAT, SET, REST, PERCH, WAIT, MEET, convene.

sit-down: see STRIKE.

site *n.* LOCATION, PLACE, locus, LOT, SCENE, NEIGHBORHOOD.

sit-in: see DEMONSTRATION; PICKET; PROTEST; RALLY.

sitting: see SESSION.

situate: see LOCATE; PERCH; PLACE; PUT.

situated *adj.* SET, located, found, placed, installed.

situation *n.* LOCATION, SPOT, pinch, CIRCUMSTANCE, CONDITION, STATE.

six-shooter: see REVOLVER.

sizable *adj.* LARGE, biggish, CONSIDERABLE, goodly.

size *n.* MEASUREMENT, dimension, EXTENT, MAGNITUDE, bigness, VOLUME.
— *v.*: see VARNISH.

sizing: see VARNISH.

skate: see SLIDE.

skedaddle: see SPEED.

skeleton *n.* FRAME, framework, SHELL, OUTLINE, basics, MINIMUM.

skeptical: see SUSPICIOUS.

skepticism: see HESITATION; MISTRUST; SUSPICION.

sketch *n.* DRAWING, PICTURE, PLAN, PROFILE, PLAY, skit.
— *v.* DRAW, DRAFT, DESCRIBE, DESIGN, PLAN, SUMMARIZE.

skewer: see SPIT.

skid: see SLIDE; SLIP.

skill *n.* ABILITY, facility, TALENT, CRAFT, TRADE, virtuosity.

skilled *adj.* skillful, trained, proficient, ABLE, adept, versed.

skillful: see ABLE; ARTISTIC; CAPABLE; CLEVER; CUNNING; EFFICIENT; EXPERT; HANDY; INGENIOUS; LEARNED; MASTERFUL; NEAT; SKILLED.

skim: see COAST; FLOAT; GLIDE; SHAVE.

skin *n.* HIDE, epidermis, pelt, BARK, COAT, COVERING, exterior.
— *v.* PEEL, pare, scalp, STRIP, husk, BARE, ROB, CHEAT.

skin-deep: see SHALLOW.

skinflint: see MISER.

skinny: see THIN.

skin-tight: see TIGHT.

skip *v.* OMIT, MISS, PASS, by-pass, IGNORE, prance, LEAP, frolic, FLEE, DESERT, ESCAPE.
— *n.*: see HOP; JUMP; LEAP.

skipper: see CAPTAIN; SUPERVISOR.

skirmish: see COMBAT; ENCOUNTER.

skirt *n.* BORDER, MARGIN, FRINGE, kilt, DRESS, underskirt, petticoat, tutu.
— *v.*: see DODGE.

skit: see SKETCH.

skullcap: see CAP.

skunk: see HEEL; WRETCH.

sky *n.* HEAVEN, AIR, atmosphere, SPACE, welkin, ether.

skylight: see LANTERN.

skyrocket: see ASCEND; FLARE.

skyway: see HIGHWAY.

slab: see BAR; BLOCK; BOARD; ROCK; SLICE; STONE; TABLET.

slack *adj.* DULL, SLOW, lax, LOOSE, floppy, baggy, droopy.

slacken *v.* RELAX, LOOSEN, SLOW, slow down, abate, moderate, stagnate.

slackness: see LIMP.

slacks: see TROUSERS.

slam *v.* SHUT, BANG, sock, wallop, HURL, CRITICIZE, lambaste.
　－ *n.*: see THUMP.

slammer: see PRISON.

slander: see ABUSE; SMEAR.

slang *n.* jargon, jive, lingo, colloquial, pidgin, vulgate, vernacular.

slant *n.* incline, INCLINATION, TILT, ANGLE, viewpoint, perspective.
　－ *v.* TILT, incline, LEAN, COLOR, distort.

slap *v.* SMACK, HIT, pat, swat, SPANK, INSULT.
　－ *n.*: see BOX; CLAP; HIT; INSULT; FLAP; KNOCK; RAP.

slash *v.* CUT, SLIT, gash, KNIFE, sever, LOWER.
　－ *n.* gash, SLIT, CUT, incision, REDUCTION, BREAK.

slate: see BOARD; SCHEDULE; TICKET.

slaughter *n.* BUTCHERY, bloodshed, MURDER, MASSACRE, mayhem, DEFEAT.
　－ *v.* butcher, SLAY, mutilate, DEFEAT.

slave *n.* CAPTIVE, bondman, serf.
　－ *v.* LABOR, TOIL, SWEAT.

slaver: see SPIT.

slavery *n.* bondage, captivity, servitude, exploitation, drudgery, TOIL.

slay *v.* KILL, MURDER, ASSASSINATE.

slayer: see MURDERER.

slaying: see ASSASSINATION.

sleek: see SLICK.

sleep *v.* REST, SLUMBER, snooze, NAP, doze.
　－ *n.* SLUMBER, REST, NAP, siesta, cat nap, shut-eye.

sleeping: see ASLEEP.

sleepless: see WAKEFUL.

sleepy *adj.* drowsy, WEARY, TIRED, DULL, somnolent.

sleet: see ICE.

slender *adj.* SLIM, THIN, LEAN, lanky, NARROW, SLIGHT, meager, SCARCE, willowy.

slew: see MASS.

slice *n.* slab, sliver, PIECE, segment, SAMPLE.
　－ *v.* CUT, CARVE, apportion, dissect.

slick *adj.* **1** (*slick roads*) SMOOTH, sleek, OILY, SLIPPERY, ICY, GREASY; **2** (*a slick operator*) FOXY, SMOOTH, sharp-witted.
　－ *v.*: see SMOOTH.

slicker: see COAT.

slide *v.* GLIDE, SLIP, skid, skate, PUSH, DRAG.
　－ *n.* **1** (*to take a slide*) SLIP, skid, glide, DECLINE, landslide, avalanche; **2** (*to project slides*) image, transparency, photograph, SPECIMEN.

slight *adj.* MINOR, SMALL, FRAIL, SLIM, PETTY, negligible.
　－ *v.*: see CUT; FORGET; IGNORE; NEGLECT; OFFEND.
　－ *n.*: see INSULT.

slightest: see LEAST.

slightly *adv.* LITTLE, LIGHTLY, HARDLY, scarcely, SOMEWHAT.

slim *adj.* SLENDER, THIN, LEAN, meager, SLIGHT, SPARE.

slime *n.* MUD, muck, mire, scum, slush, sludge, ooze.

slimy *adj.* slithery, oozy, muddy, mucky, scummy, clammy, gooey, FOUL, vile, ROTTEN.

sling *n.* HOIST, hanger, strap, BANDAGE, SUPPORT, slingshot, catapult.
　－ *v.* HURL, FLING, propel, FIRE.

slingshot: see SLING.

slink: see PROWL; SNEAK; STEAL.

slip *v.* SLIDE, skid, GLIDE, STUMBLE.
　－ *n.* **1** (*to take a slip*) skid, SLIDE, slump; **2** (*to make a slip*) error, MISTAKE, lapse; **3** (*a nylon slip*) undergarment, underclothes, lingerie; **4** (*a slip of paper*) SHEET, LEAF, STRIP; **5** (*a ferry slip*) berth, WHARF, DOCK.

slipper: see SHOE.

slippery *adj.* SLICK, ICY, OILY, GREASY, SLY, elusive, SHIFTY.

slipshod: see CARELESS; SLOPPY.

slit *v.* CUT, SLICE, SLASH, sever, TEAR.
— *n.* gash, TEAR, SPLIT, OPENING, crevice, incision.

slither: see SNEAK.

slithery: see SLIMY.

sliver: see CHIP; FLAKE; SHRED; SLICE.

slobber *v.* salivate, drool, DRIBBLE, DRIP, sputter.

slog: see TOIL.

slogan: see CHANT; MOTTO.

slop: see SPILL.

slope *n.* HILL, HILLSIDE, SLANT, incline, GRADE.
— *v.* SLANT, incline, TILT, LEAN, RISE, list, ASCEND, DESCEND.

sloping: see HILLY.

sloppy *adj.* MUDDY, DIRTY, MESSY, untidy, CARELESS, unkempt, slipshod, substandard, splattered.

slops: see REFUSE.

slosh: see SPILL.

slot: see HOLE; RECESS.

slothful: see LAZY.

slough: see SHED.

slovenly: see MESSY.

slow *adj.* **1** (*a slow train*) sluggish, laggard, GRADUAL, DELIBERATE, belated, overdue, LATE; **2** (*a slow pupil*) DULL, STUPID, RETARDED.

slow down: see SLACKEN.

slowdown: see STRIKE.

slowly *adv.* SLOW, LEISURELY, DELIBERATELY.

slow-witted: see FEEBLE-MINDED; RETARDED; STUPID.

sludge: see MUD; SLIME.

slug: see TOKEN.

sluggard: see LAZY.

slugger: see BATTER.

sluggish: see LAZY; LIFELESS; RUSTY; SLOW; STUPID.

slumber *v.* SLEEP, REST, snooze, doze, NAP.
— *n.* SLEEP, NAP, siesta, forty winks, SUSPENSE.

slumbering: see ASLEEP.

slump: see DESCENT; DROOP; SLIP.

slur: see BLOT.

slush: see SLIME.

sly *adj.* CLEVER, FOXY, canny, CUNNING, cagey, SLICK, shrewd, wily.

smack *v.* HIT, BEAT, STRIKE, SLAP, PUNCH, CRACK, whack. See also KISS.
— *n.*: see KISS.

small *adj.* LITTLE, diminutive, TINY, teeny, MINIATURE, YOUNG, trivial, meager, PETTY, DAINTY.

smaller: see LESS; LESSER.

smallest: see LEAST.

small-minded: see PETTY.

smart *adj.* BRIGHT, ALERT, CLEVER, INTELLIGENT, quick-witted, NEAT, TRIM, STYLISH.
— *v.* pain, STING, HURT, BURN, wince.
— *n.*: see PAIN; STING.

smartly: see SHARPLY.

smartness *n.* CLEVERNESS, ALERTNESS, acuteness, INTELLIGENCE, ingenuity, ELEGANCE, NEATNESS.

smash *v.* **1** (*to smash a window*) SHATTER, splinter, DESTROY, RUIN, COLLIDE; **2** (*to smash a ball*) DRIVE, sock, wallop, propel.
— *n.*: see IMPACT; PUNCH.

smashed: see BROKEN.

smash-up: see COLLISION; CRASH.

smear *v.* **1** (*to smear with mud*) COVER, COAT, SPREAD, daub, smudge; **2** (*to smear a person*) slander, libel, defame, discredit, vilify.
— *n.*: see BLOTCH; BLUR; DAB.

smell *v.* **1** (*the meat smells*) STINK, reek; **2** (*I smell onions*) SNIFF, SENSE, DETECT; **3** (*to smell a rat*) DETECT, SUSPECT.
— *n.* ODOR, PERFUME, SCENT, STINK, stench, FRAGRANCE.

smidgen: see TOUCH; TRACE; TRIFLE.

smile *n.* GRIN, smirk, GLOW.
— *v.* GRIN, BEAM, smirk, FAVOR, BENEFIT.

smiling: see CHEERFUL.

smirch: see BLOT.

smirk: see FROWN; GRIN; SMILE.

smitten: see STRICKEN.

smog: see MIST; VAPOR.

smoke *n.* VAPOR, STEAM, fumes, CLOUD.
— *v.* smolder, reek, PUFF, INHALE.

smokestack: see STACK.

smoky: see HAZY.

smolder: see SMOKE.

smooth *adj.* FLAT, EVEN, STEADY, unwrinkled, polished, satiny, velvety, glossy, unruffled, CALM, CLEVER, urbane, glib, creamy, bland.
— *v.* flatten, EVEN, LEVEL, plane, POLISH, PRESS, IRON, sandpaper, ROLL, GREASE, wax, slick, SHAVE, CALM.

smoothly *adv.* easily, EVENLY, READILY, FREELY, STEADILY, SOFTLY, gently, pleasantly.

smother *v.* suffocate, throttle, stifle, CHOKE, asphyxiate, restrain, suppress, CONCEAL, SILENCE.

smudge: see BLOT; BLOTCH; BLUR; GRIME; SMEAR.

smut: see DIRT; DUST; GRIME; MOLD.

snack *n.* lunch, picnic, BITE, MOUTHFUL, morsel, nosh.

snag: see CATCH; TANGLE.

snake *n.* serpent, viper, reptile, rattlesnake.
— *v.*: see COIL.

snap *v.* CLICK, CATCH, CRACK, flick, bang, BREAK, CLOSE, bark, GROWL, FLASH, SPARKLE, SHOOT, photograph.
— *n.*: see CLICK; CRACK; GROWL.

snappish: see IRRITABLE.

snapshot: see PORTRAIT.

snare: see CATCH; CORNER; HOOK; NET; PLANT; TRAP.

snarl *v.* GROWL, GRUMBLE, SNAP, bark, THUNDER, TANGLE.
— *n.*: see GROWL; TANGLE.

snarled: see ENTANGLED.

snatch *v.* GRAB, CLUTCH, GRASP, GRIP, SEIZE, CAPTURE.

sneak *v.* PROWL, slink, slither, SLIDE, GLIDE, CONCEAL, STEAL, filch.
— *n.*: see COWARD; WORM; WRETCH.

sneaker: see SHOE.

sneaky: see SHIFTY.

sneer *v.* SCORN, MOCK, jeer, taunt, SCOFF, snort.
— *n.* jeer, snort, GRIN, disdain.

snicker *v.* LAUGH, titter, GIGGLE, CHUCKLE.
— *n.*: see GIGGLE; LAUGH.

sniff *v.* SMELL, snuff, snuffle, INHALE, SCENT.
— *n.* SMELL, sniffle, snuffle, snuff.

sniffle: see SNIFF.

sniffles: see COLD.

snift: see SCENT.

snip *v.* nip, SNAP, CLIP, SLICE, sever, CUT.
— *n.*: see BRAT.

snippy: see FRESH.

snitch: see SQUEAL.

snoop: see PRY; SPY.

snooze: see NAP; SLEEP; SLUMBER.

snort: see SNEER.

snout: see BEAK; TRUNK.

snowdrift: see DRIFT.

snowy: see WHITE.

snub: see CUT; OFFEND.

snuff: see SCENT; SNIFF.

snuffle: see SNIFF.

snug *adj.* TIGHT, CLOSE, COMFORTABLE, COZY, SAFE, protected.

snuggle *v.* CUDDLE, NESTLE, nuzzle.

so *adv.* AS, LIKEWISE, THEREFORE, THEN, TOO, VERY, THUS, ACCORDINGLY.

soak *v.* drench, douse, saturate, steep, WET.
— *n.*: see BATH.

soaked: see WET.

soap: see BRIBE.

soar *v.* GLIDE, FLY, RISE, CLIMB, ASCEND.

soaring: see FLIGHT; HIGH; LOFTY.

sob *v.* whimper, WAIL, WEEP, CRY.
— *n.* whimper, WAIL, weeping, CRY.

sobbing: see TEARFUL.

sober *adj.* SERIOUS, GRAVE, SOLEMN, staid, STEADY, sedate, THOUGHTFUL, moderate, somber, unintoxicated, uninebriated.
— *v.*: see CALM.

sociable *adj.* FRIENDLY, SOCIAL, HOSPITABLE, CHATTY, JOLLY, genial, affable.

social *adj.* SOCIABLE, gregarious, companionable, PUBLIC, POPULAR, HUMAN.

socialists: see LEFT.

socialize: see MINGLE.

society *n.* ASSOCIATION, ORGANIZATION, GROUP, CLUB, CIRCLE, fraternity, COMPANIONSHIP, COMPANY, COMMUNITY, CIVILIZATION, PEOPLE, HUMANITY.

sock: see PUNCH; SLAM; SMASH; STOCKING.

socket: see CHAMBER; OUTLET.

socks: see HOSE.

sod: see GROUND.

soda: see POP.

sofa *n.* COUCH, davenport, divan, settee, SEAT, love seat.

soft *adj.* GENTLE, TENDER, pliable, FLEXIBLE, elastic, FLABBY, SLACK, supple, spongy, soggy, malleable, ductile, yielding, SMOOTH, velvety, silky, satiny, downy, feathery, cottony, QUIET, lenient, courteous, WEAK.

soft drink: see POP.

soften *v.* moderate, muffle, WEAKEN, palliate, chasten, subdue, MASH, knead, DISSOLVE, MELT, THAW, MELLOW, tenderize.

softened: see LOW.

softly *adv.* gently, TENDERLY, SMOOTHLY, quietly.

soggy: see SOFT; WET.

soil *n.* EARTH, DIRT, GROUND, loam, DUST, LAND, COUNTRY, TERRITORY.
   — *v.* dirty, STAIN, contaminate, POLLUTE, mar, besmear, foul, daub.

soiled: see DIRTY; FILTHY.

soiling: see POLLUTION.

sojourn: see STAY.

sojourner: see VISITOR.

soldier *n.* serviceman, FIGHTER, WARRIOR, private, mercenary, adventurer, stalwart.

soldiers: see TROOPS.

sole *adj.* ONLY, LONE, UNIQUE, SINGLE, ALONE.
   — *n.*: see BALL; FOOT.

solely: see ALONE; BUT; MERELY; ONLY.

solemn *adj.* SERIOUS, GRAVE, EARNEST, grim, somber, FORMAL, SACRED.

solemnity: see FUNERAL; SERIOUSNESS.

solemnize: see CELEBRATE.

solicit: see APPLY; BEG; COLLECT; COURT; INVITE; PEDDLE.

solicitation: see APPLICATION; INVITATION; PRAYER.

solid *adj.* HARD, COMPACT, DENSE, FIRM, RIGID, TIGHT, STURDY, STABLE, SOUND, STRONG, stalwart, UNBROKEN, substantial, MASSIVE, three-dimensional, unmixed, PLAIN.
   — *n.*: see LUMP.

solidified: see FROZEN.

solidify: see FREEZE; HARDEN.

solidity: see FIRMNESS; STEADINESS.

solidly: see COMPLETELY; FIRMLY; HARD.

solitaire: see DIAMOND; HERMIT.

solitarily: see ALONE.

solitary *adj.* ALONE, LONE, LONESOME, SOLE, ONLY, INDIVIDUAL, friendless, deserted, REMOTE, retired, DESOLATE, isolated.
   — *n.*: see JAIL.

solitude: see DESERT; ISOLATION; LONELINESS; PRIVACY; RETREAT; SECRECY.

solo: see CONCERT.

so long: see FAREWELL; GOOD-BY.

solution *n.* **1** *(the solution to the puzzle)* ANSWER, EXPLANATION, CLARIFICATION, RESOLUTION; **2** *(to pour in the solution)* MIXTURE, FLUID, BLEND.

solve *v.* ANSWER, EXPLAIN, clear up, RESOLVE, unravel, untangle.

solving: see RESOLUTION.

somber: see DARK; SOBER; SOLEMN; SULLEN.

sombrero: see HAT.

some *adj.* CERTAIN, SEVERAL, ANY, ONE, A, AN, ABOUT, NEAR, REMARKABLE.
   — *pron.* CERTAIN, SEVERAL, PART, PORTION, PEOPLE, FRAGMENT, FRACTION, MINIMUM.

somebody *pron.* SOMEONE, ANYONE, anybody, ONE, PEOPLE, INDIVIDUAL, PERSON.
   — *n.*: see CELEBRITY; NOTABLE.

somehow *adv.* someway, ANYWAY.

someone *pron.* SOMEBODY, ANYONE, anybody, ONE, PEOPLE, PERSON, INDIVIDUAL.

someplace: see SOMEWHERE.

somersault: see JUMP; LEAP.

something *pron.* THING, ARTICLE, entity, OBJECT, commodity.

sometime *adv.* ONCE, FORMERLY, SOMETIMES.

sometimes *adv.* occasionally, intermittently, ONCE, FREQUENTLY, FORMERLY.

someway: see SOMEHOW.

somewhat *adv.* PARTLY, partially, RATHER, FAIRLY, TOLERABLY, SLIGHTLY, adequately. See also ALMOST.

somewhere *adv.* someplace, ANYWHERE, anyplace, ELSEWHERE.

somnolent: see SLEEPY.

son *n.* CHILD, BOY, HEIR, OFFSPRING, descendant, PRODUCT, OUTCOME.

sonata: see MUSIC.

song *n.* MUSIC, MELODY, TUNE, air, NUMBER, HYMN, CHANT, lullaby, CAROL, ballad, aria.

songster: see SINGER.

sonnet: see POEM.

sonorous: see RICH.

soon *adv.* SHORTLY, presently, PROMPTLY, quickly, READILY, willingly.

sooner: see BEFORE; RATHER.

soot: see DUST; GRIME.

soothe *v.* RELIEVE, COMFORT, CALM, tranquilize, lull, pacify, quiet, HEAL, console.

soothing: see CALM; GRATEFUL; REFRESHING.

soothsayer: see PROPHET.

soothsaying: see PREDICTION.

sophistication: see STYLE.

sorcerer: see MAGICIAN; WIZARD.

sorceress: see WITCH.

sorcery: see CHARM; MAGIC; SUPERSTITION.

sordidness: see MEANNESS.

sore *adj.* **1** *(a sore foot)* PAINFUL, SENSITIVE, TENDER, aching, injured, inflamed, bruised, infected; **2** *(sore at heart)* hurt, grieved, distressed, annoyed, RESENTFUL, indignant, ANGRY, MAD.
— *n.*: see BLISTER; BRUISE; INFECTION; INFLAMMATION.

sorority: see ORDER.

sorrow *n.* SADNESS, REGRET, GRIEF, remorse, repentance, TRIAL, WOE, DEPRESSION, GLOOM.
— *v.*: see GRIEVE.

sorrowful *adj.* SAD, MOURNFUL, grief-stricken, SUFFERING, troubled, MISERABLE, agonizing, DOWNHEARTED.

sorry *adj.* SAD, SORROWFUL, APOLOGETIC, regretful, remorseful, MOURNFUL, WRETCHED, MISERABLE, SHABBY.

sort *n.* KIND, VARIETY, TYPE.
— *v.* CLASSIFY, ORDER, SEPARATE, GROUP, ARRANGE.

soul *n.* SPIRIT, psyche, PERSON, SUBSTANCE, MORTAL.

sound *n.* **1** *(a harsh sound)* NOISE, RACKET, din, CLAMOR, UPROAR, static; **2** *(Long Island Sound)* inlet, strait, narrows, PASSAGE.
— *v.* **1** *(to sound a warning)* UTTER, SPEAK, PRONOUNCE, articulate, ECHO, RESOUND, VIBRATE; **2** *(to sound the depths)* plumb, PROBE.
— *adj.* **1** *(of sound body)* STRONG, WELL, robust, HEALTHY, HARDY, WHOLE; **2** *(sound reasons)* REASONABLE, SENSIBLE, RELIABLE, DEEP, profound, DEPENDABLE, trustworthy, COMPLETE, THOROUGH; **3** *(safe and sound)* uninjured, UNHARMED, SECURE, SAFE.

sounded: see ORAL.

soundless *adj.* noiseless, SPEECHLESS, SILENT, voiceless, dumb, mute, hushed, subdued, muffled.

soundly: see PRACTICALLY; WELL.

soundness: see HEALTH.

sounds: see HARMONY.

soupy: see THICK.

sour *adj.* **1** *(a sour taste)* tart, ACID, rancid, curdled, GREEN, spoiled, fermented; **2** *(a sour disposition)* CRANKY, CROSS, SHARP, BITTER, touchy, bad-tempered, DISAGREEABLE, UNPLEASANT, SAD, off-key.
— *v.* TURN, curdle, SPOIL.

source *n.* ORIGIN, BEGINNING, SPRING, START, derivation.

soused: see DRUNK.

souvenir *n.* REMINDER, REMEMBRANCE, keepsake, TOKEN, momento, relic, reminiscence.

sovereign: see EMPEROR; KING; LORD; MONARCH; PRINCE; SUPREME.

sovereignty: see INDEPENDENCE; REIGN.

sow *v.* SEED, PLANT, SCATTER, disseminate.
— *n.* swine, PIG, HOG, FEMALE.

spa: see HOTEL.

space *n.* DISTANCE, expanse, AREA, LOCATION, ROOM, STRETCH, TERRITORY, RANGE, EXTENT, blank, INFINITY, UNIVERSE, heavens, WORLD, SPHERE, PERIOD, INTERVAL.
— *v.* interspace, SPREAD, ARRANGE, SEPARATE.

spacecraft: see CAPSULE; ROCKET.

space probe: see CAPSULE; MISSILE.

spaceship: see MISSILE.

spacious *adj.* ROOMY, LARGE, AMPLE, BROAD, VAST, expansive, GENEROUS.

spaciously: see EVERYWHERE.

spade: see DIG.

span *v.* COVER, bridge, EXTEND, REACH, STRETCH, EXPAND, MEASURE.
— *n.* **1** *(a span over a river)* BRIDGE, viaduct, EXTENSION; **2** *(a span of time)* PERIOD, SPELL, INTERVAL; **3** *(a large span of water)* DISTANCE, expanse.

spangle: see BOW.

spank *v.* flog, paddle, WHIP, cane, HIT, SLAP, PUNISH, DISCIPLINE.

spare *v.* AFFORD, PROVIDE, RESERVE, lay away, WITHHOLD, SAVE, PROTECT, EXCUSE, FORGIVE.
— *adj.* **1** *(some spare cash)* EXTRA, ADDITIONAL, reserve, excess; **2** *(a spare frame)* LEAN, THIN, scanty, meager, BARE, frugal, POOR.

sparing *adj.* **1** *(a tolerant and sparing master)* MERCIFUL, yielding, PERMISSIVE, FOREGOING, relinquishing, sacrificing; **2** *(be frugal and sparing)* frugal, ECONOMICAL, THRIFTY, TIGHT, CAUTIOUS.

spark *n.* FLASH, FLICKER, glint, LIGHT, FIRE, SPIRIT, liveliness.
— *v.* FLASH, FLICKER, glint, GLITTER, INSPIRE, ENCOURAGE, expedite.

sparkle *v.* GLITTER, TWINKLE, FLASH, FLICKER, glint, GLIMMER, GLISTEN, bubble, effervesce.
— *n.*: see FRESHNESS; GLITTER; SPIRIT; TWINKLE; WINK.

sparkling: see BRIGHT; BRILLIANT; DAZZLING; SHINY.

sparse: see SCARCE; THIN.

sparsely: see FEW.

sparsity: see SCARCITY.

spasm: see TWIST.

spasmodic: see IRREGULAR; UNEVEN.

spat: see ROW.

spatter: see DOT; SPLASH; SPRINKLE.

spawn: see BEAR.

speak *v.* TALK, UTTER, SAY, CONVERSE, EXPRESS, PRONOUNCE, articulate, STATE, TESTIFY, LECTURE, RECITE.

speaker: see ENTERTAINERS; LECTURER; ORATOR; PARTY.

speak to: see ADDRESS.

spear *n.* pike, LANCE, javelin, BLADE, WEAPON.
— *v.*: see STAB; STICK.

special *adj.* especial, EXTRAORDINARY, UNIQUE, EXCEPTIONAL, distinctive, CERTAIN, SPECIFIC, INDIVIDUAL, DIFFERENT, UNCOMMON.
— *n.* BARGAIN, SALE, edition, ITEM.

specialist *n.* EXPERT, SCHOLAR, AUTHORITY, connoisseur, MASTER, VETERAN, technician, PROFESSIONAL.

speciality: see FEATURE.

specialization: see STUDY.

specialize: see STUDY.

specialized: see PROFESSIONAL; TECHNICAL.

specially: see ESPECIALLY; PARTICULARLY.

specialty: see CAREER; PROFESSION.

species *n.* KIND, SORT, TYPE, FAMILY, BREED, genus, subgroup.

specific *adj.* EXACT, PRECISE, DEFINITE, clear-cut, explicit, PARTICULAR, UNIQUE, SOLE, SPECIAL.

specifically: see PARTICULARLY; PRECISELY.

specification *n.* PLAN, REQUIREMENT, STATEMENT, PARTICULAR, ORDER, DETAIL, technicality, DESCRIPTION.

specify *v.* DESCRIBE, particularize, ITEMIZE, designate, enumerate, DEFINE, MENTION, NAME, cite, STATE.

specimen *n.* SAMPLE, EXAMPLE, instance, TYPE, ILLUSTRATION, PATTERN, MODEL, cross section, SLIDE.

speck *n.* SPOT, DOT, fleck, mite, BIT, TRACE, mote.

spectacle *n.* SIGHT, EXHIBITION, SHOW, DISPLAY, pageant, PARADE.

spectacles: see GLASSES.

spectacular: see WONDERFUL.

spectator *n.* OBSERVER, viewer, onlooker, WITNESS.

spectators: see GALLERY.

specter: see SPIRIT.

speculate: see BET; INVEST; RISK.

speculation: see INVESTMENT; OUTLOOK; PREDICTION; THEORY; THINKING.

speech *n.* LANGUAGE, talking, words, TALK, LECTURE, oration, ADDRESS, SERMON, discourse, harangue, disquisition, CONVERSATION, diction, ACCENT, TONE, PRONUNCIATION, enunciation, articulation, TONGUE, dialect.

speeches: see CAMPAIGN.

speechless *adj.* mute, wordless, SILENT, dumb, STILL, inarticulate, surprised.

speed *n.* HASTE, rapidity, swiftness, velocity, HURRY, RUSH, MOTION, RATE, PACE, tempo.
— *v.* HASTEN, HURRY, RUSH, SPURT, hurtle, skedaddle, SHOOT, SWOOP, scoot, dart, sprint, CHARGE, stampede.

speedily: see IMMEDIATELY.

speedway: see TRACK.

speedy *adj.* QUICK, RAPID, flying, HASTY, FAST, SWIFT, HURRIED.

spell *v.* NAME, EXPLAIN, DETAIL, INDICATE, SIGNIFY, write out. See also RELIEVE.
— *n.* **1** *(under her spell)* MAGIC, INFLUENCE, CHARM, fascination; **2** *(a spell of dizziness)* ATTACK, FIT, bout; **3** *(a spell of bad weather)* SPACE, TIME, TERM, interlude, PERIOD, TURN.

spellbinder: see ORATOR.

spend *v.* expend, PAY, disburse, USE, squander, CONSUME, EXHAUST, WASTE, PASS.

spent: see BROKEN; BUSHED; SHOT; USED.

spew: see POUR; SPURT.

sphere *n.* BALL, GLOBE, EARTH, planet, WORLD, realm, ORBIT, PROVINCE, ZONE, domain, RANGE, FIELD, GROUND, POSITION, STATION, EXTENT, ENVIRONMENT, AREA, SURROUNDINGS.

spherical: see CIRCULAR; ROUND.

spheroid: see CIRCULAR.

sphinx: see MYSTERY; PUZZLE; RIDDLE.

spice *n.* flavoring, seasoning, RELISH, SALT, zest, savor, ENJOYMENT, pepper, aromatic.
— *v.*: see FLAVOR; SALT; SEASON.

spick-and-span: see CLEAN; NEAT.

spicy: see HOT; JUICY; PEPPERY; SUGGESTIVE.

spider: see INSECT.

spigot: see TAP.

spike: see BOLT; NAIL; TOOTH.

spill *v.* DROP, FALL, TUMBLE, SCATTER, FLOW, POUR, RUN, STREAM, SPLASH, SPRAY, slop, slosh.

spin *v.* WHIRL, REVOLVE, TWIRL, ROTATE, TWIST, TELL, RELATE.
— *n.*: see DRIVE; ROLL; ROTATION; TURN.

spindle: see AXLE; REEL.

spine *n.* BACKBONE, vertebrae, COLUMN, stamina, THORN, spur, point, quill.

spiral: see COIL; CURL; SCREW; TWIST; WREATH.

spire: see TOWER.

spirit *n.* SOUL, psyche, PERSONALITY, FORCE, DASH, ENTHUSIASM, sparkle, VITALITY, MOOD, liveliness, TEMPER, disposition, ATTITUDE, INTENTION, intent, MEANING, GHOST, specter, goblin, DEMON, DEVIL, ANGEL, FAIRY, PHANTOM, elf.

spirited: see ALERT; EAGER; ENERGETIC; LIVELY; PEPPERY; PROUD; VIGOROUS.

spiritless: see LIFELESS.

spirits: see LIQUOR.

spiritual *adj.* immaterial, otherwordly, DIVINE, HOLY, RELIGIOUS.

spit *v.* salivate, slaver, SPURT, sputter, SNARL.
— *n.* ROD, skewer, rotisserie, barbecue.

spite: see BITTERNESS; GRUDGE; RESENTMENT.

spiteful: see RESENTFUL.

splash *v.* spatter, splatter, SPRAY, SPRINKLE.
— *n.*: see DASH; SPRAY.

splatter: see SPLASH; SPRAY; SPRINKLE.

splattered: see SLOPPY.

splendid *adj.* MAGNIFICENT, GLORIOUS, GRAND, GORGEOUS, majestic, imposing, inspiring, MARVELOUS, FINE, SUPERB, EXCELLENT.

splendidly: see WELL.

splendor *n.* magnificence, GLORY, MAJESTY, LUSTER, PARADE, sumptuousness, DISPLAY, pomp, pageant, showiness, grandeur, BRILLIANCE, impressiveness.

splice: see KNOT.

splinter: see CHIP; CHOP; CRACK; CRASH; SHATTER; SMASH.

split *v.* SEPARATE, DIVIDE, CLEAR, CRACK, SNAP, CUT, TEAR, sever, gash.
— *n.* SEPARATION, rupture, SLIT, CRACK, gash. See also FORK.

splotch: see STAIN.

splutter: see RAVE.

spoil *v.* DAMAGE, impair, INJURE, DESTROY, RUIN, ROT, decompose, MOLD, corrupt, indulge, disfigure.

spoiled: see BAD; ROTTEN; SOUR; STALE.

spoiling: see PERISHABLE.

spoils: see HAUL; LOOT.

spoken: see ORAL; VERBAL.

spokesman: see PROPHET.

sponge *v.* **1** *(to sponge off the sink)* WIPE, swab, RUB, CLEAN, dampen, SOAK; **2** *(to sponge on a friend)* live off, leech.

spongy: see SOFT.

spontaneous: see AUTOMATIC; IMPULSIVE; OFFHAND; VOLUNTARY.

spoof: see JEST; KID.

spook: see GHOST; PHANTOM.

spooky: see MYSTERIOUS.

spool *n.* REEL, bobbin, cylinder.

sport *n.* pastime, PLAY, recreation, diversion, ENTERTAINMENT, athletics, frolic, mirth, plaything, mockery, RIDICULE, JEST. See also ATHLETE.
— *v.*: see PLAY.

sportive: see PLAYFUL.

sportsman: see ATHLETE; HUNTER.

sportswoman: see HUNTER.

sporty: see CASUAL.

spot *n.* **1** *(a spot on the rug)* STAIN, BLOTCH, BLEMISH, BLOT, flaw; **2** *(the spots on the dice)* PIP, DOT, SPECK, fleck, BIT, dapple, spotlight; **3** *(a pleasant spot)* SITE, LOCALITY, POST, PLACE.
— *v.* **1** *(to spot the rug)* STAIN, BLEMISH, mar, MARK, tarnish, dirty, BLOT; **2** *(to spot an airplane)* LOCATE, TRACE, FIND, DISCOVER, IDENTIFY, PLACE.

spotless *adj.* CLEAN, TIDY, unsoiled, immaculate, stainless, unblemished, untarnished.

spotlight: see SPOT.

spotter: see OBSERVER; PATROL; SCOUT.

spouse: see HUSBAND; MAN; MATE; PARTNER; WIFE.

spout *v.* gush, POUR, STREAM, SPURT, ROLL, SPILL. harangue.
— *n.*: see FOUNTAIN; JET.

sprain *v.* STRAIN, WRENCH, TWIST, contort.
— *n.*: see TWIST; WRENCH.

sprawl: see SPREAD.

spray *n.* **1** *(the ocean spray)* MIST, SPRINKLE, shower, splash, squirt JET, FOUNTAIN; **2** *(the spray gun)* vaporizer, atomizer, sprinkler, sprayer; **3** *(the spray in the vase)* BRANCH, shoot, TWIG, bouquet.
— *v.* SPRINKLE, shower, SPLASH, squirt, splatter, SCATTER, SPREAD, SMEAR.

sprayer: see SPRAY.

spread *n.* **1** *(a spread of four points)* STRETCH, EXTENSION, layout, DISPLAY; **2** *(the spread on the bed)* bedspread, coverlet, counterpane, tablecloth; **3** *(a delicious spread)* FEAST, buffet, picnic, COATING, topping.
— *v.* STRETCH, sprawl, UNFOLD, unroll, OPEN, PUBLISH, CIRCULATE, disseminate, COAT, SMEAR, disperse, SCATTER, divulge, flatten.

spreading: see RUNNING.

sprig: see SWITCH; TWIG.

sprightly: see ACTIVE; ALIVE; BREEZY; CHEERFUL.

spring *n.* **1** *(water from the spring)* FOUNTAIN, POND, reservoir, FLOW, JET, geyser; **2** *(a spring of inspiration)* fountainhead, SOURCE, ORIGIN, BEGINNING, PRIME, springtime, SEASON, springtide; **3** *(a spring in his walk)* bounce, bound, LEAP, vault, resilience, elasticity.
— *v.* **1** *(to spring from)* ORIGINATE, DERIVE, BEGIN; **2** *(to spring into the air)* LEAP, bound, BOUNCE, HOP; **3** *(to spring a leak)* SNAP, WARP, CRACK, RELEASE, disclose, PRODUCE.

springtide: see SPRING.

springtime: see SPRING; YOUTH.

spring up: see ARISE.

sprinkle *v.* splatter, spatter, SPRAY, SPLASH, SPILL, squirt, SCATTER, shower, spread, strew.
— *n.* RAIN, drizzle, sprinkling, scattering.

sprinkler: see SPRAY.

sprinkling: see DASH; HANDFUL; SPRINKLE.

sprint: see DASH; RACE; RUN; SPEED.

sprinter: see RUNNER.

sprout *v.* GROW, SHOOT, bud, DEVELOP, branch, FLOURISH, germinate.
— *n.* shoot, BRANCH, PLANT.

sprouting: see GROWTH.

spruce up: see BEAUTIFY; GROOM.

spry: see LIVELY.

spunk: see BACKBONE; BOLDNESS; BRAVERY.

spur: see ACCELERATE; INSPIRE; MAIL; NEEDLE; SPINE; STIMULATE; URGE.

spurn: see REJECT; SCORN.

spur-of-the-moment: see OFFHAND.

spurt *v.* squirt, gush, spew, jet, ERUPT, EXPEL, SPOUT.
— *n.*: see BURST.

sputnik: see SATELLITE.

sputter: see SLOBBER; SPIT.

spy *n.* AGENT, detective, SCOUT, snoop.
— *v.* OBSERVE, WATCH, SEE, DISCOVER, DETECT, snoop, PRY, PEEP, GLIMPSE, SEARCH.

squabble: see FEUD; QUARREL.

squad: see GANG; TEAM.

squadron: see COMPANY.

squall: see BLAST; GUST.

squally: see WINDY.

squander: see SPEND; WASTE.

squandering: see WASTE; WASTEFUL.

square *n.* rectangle, quadrilateral, quadrangle, marketplace, plaza, park, GREEN.
— *v.*: see CORRESPOND; MULTIPLY.

squash: see CRUSH; MASH; TRAMPLE.

squat *v.* HUDDLE, CROUCH, roost, PERCH, cower, SETTLE, DWELL.
— *adj.*: see SHORT; STUBBY.

squatter: see COLONIST.

squawk: see COMPLAIN.

squeak: see PEEP; SQUEAL.

squeaky: see NOISY.

squeal *v.* **1** (*pigs often squeal*) squeak, SCREECH, YELL, CRY; **2** (*to squeal on someone*) tattle, INFORM, snitch, blab.

squeeze *v.* PRESS, COMPRESS, PUSH, extort, exact, wrest, HUG, cuddle, EMBRACE.

squeezing: see COMPRESSION.

squint: see LOOK.

squire: see PAGE.

squirm *v.* fidget, TWIST, TURN, wiggle, wriggle, writhe.

squirt: see DRIBBLE; SPRAY; SPRINKLE; SPURT.

stab *v.* STICK, KNIFE, spear, THRUST, bayonet, PIERCE, WOUND.
— *n.*: see PRICK.

stability: see FIRMNESS; STEADINESS.

stabilize: see BALANCE.

stable *adj.* STEADY, staunch, stalwart, FIRM, steadfast, inflexible, STURDY, STRONG, STIFF, substantial, SOLID.

stableboy: see GROOM.

stack *n.* **1** (*a stack of books*) PILE, HEAP, MOUND, sheaf, BUNDLE, RACK, SHELF; **2** (*smoke came out of the stack*) smokestack, chimney.
— *v.* ARRANGE, PILE, ACCUMULATE, HEAP, LOAD, GATHER.

stadium: see ARENA.

staff *n.* **1** (*on the staff*) FORCE, crew, helpers, assistants, employees, personnel, faculty, cadre; **2** (*to lean on the staff*) cane, STICK, POLE, pikestaff; **3** (*to write a note on the staff*) staves, lines.
— *v.* HIRE, EMPLOY, APPOINT.

staffer: see EMPLOYEE.

stag: see BUCK.

stage *n.* **1** (*on the stage*) platform, dais, ARENA, SCENE, THEATER; **2** (*at this stage*) POINT, MOMENT, juncture, PHASE, PERIOD, STEP, SECTION, status; **3** (*to take the stage to Dallas*) coach, stagecoach, buggy.
— *v.* PRODUCE, PLAN, PRESENT, put on, DIRECT.

stagecoach: see CARRIAGE; STAGE.

stagger *v.* waver, TOTTER, wobble, REEL, SWAY, falter, STUN, STARTLE, zigzag, interchange, ALTERNATE, VARY.

stagnant: see MOTIONLESS.

stagnate: see SLACKEN.

stagnation: see DEPRESSION.

staid: see CALM; SOBER.

stain *n.* VARNISH, PAINT, DYE, TINT, splotch.
— *v.* PAINT, VARNISH, SPOT, tarnish, MARK, BLEMISH, taint, DISGRACE.

stainless: see SPOTLESS.

stair: see FLIGHT.

staircase: see FLIGHT.

stairs: see FLIGHT; LADDER.

stake *n.* **1** (*move the stake by six inches*) POST, POLE, STICK, marker, SUPPORT; **2** (*what's at stake here?*) PRIZE, wager, BET, PURSE, INTEREST, CONCERN, ISSUE.
— *v.*: see BET; GAMBLE; PAWN.

stale *adj.* spoiled, inedible, OLD, DRY, HARD, tasteless, FLAT, DULL, WORN, trite, uninteresting, humdrum, stereotyped.

stalemate: see DRAW.

stalk *n.* STEM, TRUNK, pedicle, SUPPORT.
— *v.* HUNT, TRACK, SHADOW, FOLLOW, APPROACH, STRIDE.

stall *v.* STOP, HESITATE, DELAY, tarry, POSTPONE, quibble, filibuster.
— *n.*: see CRIB; COMPARTMENT; MARKET.

stallion: see HORSE.

stalwart: see SOLDIER; SOLID; STABLE; STURDY.

stamina: see SPINE.

stammer *v.* stutter, STUMBLE, falter, hem, haw, HESITATE.

stamp *v.* **1** (*to stamp on the floor*) TRAMPLE, CRUSH, step; **2** (*to stamp the letter*) MARK, INSCRIBE, letter. See also COIN.
— *n.* SEAL, cachet, imprint, die, block, inscription.

stampede: see PANIC; SPEED.

stamping: see PRINTING.

stamping ground: see HAUNT.

stance: see POSE; POSTURE.

stand *v.* **1** (*to stand up*) RISE, ARISE; **2** (*to stand it on end*) PUT, LOCATE, DISPOSE; **3** (*to stand in one place*) ENDURE, LAST, STAY; **4** (*to stand the insults*) tolerate, ABIDE BY, ACCEPT.
— *n.* **1** (*to take a stand*) POSITION, ATTITUDE, OPINION, standpoint, SENTIMENT, POSTURE; **2** (*the fruit stand*) TABLE, COUNTER, platform.

standard *n.* yardstick, GAUGE, criterion, MODEL, MEASURE, TYPE, TEST, COMPARISON, IDEAL. See also BANNER; FLAG.
— *adj.* REGULAR, NORMAL, orthodox, stock, authoritative.

stand for: see REPRESENT.

stand-in: see DOUBLE; FOSTER; SECOND; SUBSTITUTE.

standing: see ERECT; ESTATE; REPUTATION.

stand-offish: see UNFRIENDLY.

standpoint: see ATTITUDE; STAND.

standstill: see HALT.

stanza: see VERSE.

staple *n.* **1** (*use staples to hold it together*) fastener, binder, connector, CLASP; **2** (*what staples does the*

country produce?*) PRODUCT, basics, essentials, mainstay, commodity, RESOURCE, SUBSTANCE, ITEM.

star *n.* planet, comet, meteor, CELEBRITY, LEAD, HERO, PRINCIPAL, NAME, headliner, asterisk.
— *v.*: see FEATURE; LEAD.

stare *v.* GAZE, LOOK, leer, glare, goggle, ogle.
— *n.* LOOK, leer, gaze, GLARE, goggle, ogle.

start *n.* **1** (*a good start*) BEGINNING, inception, commencement, outset, initiation; **2** (*a head start*) LEAD, ADVANTAGE; **3** (*to awake with a start*) JUMP, JERK, SHOCK, SCARE, TWITCH, TURN, SURPRISE.
— *v.* **1** (*to start the motor*) BEGIN, LAUNCH, propel, FOUND, COMMENCE, initiate; **2** (*to start on a journey*) LEAVE, SET OUT.

starter: see BEGINNER.

starting: see OFF; OPENING.

startle *v.* SHOCK, ALARM, FRIGHTEN, EXCITE, SURPRISE, agitate, SCARE, JOLT, STUN, flinch, unnerve.

startling: see ALARMING; SCARY; SURPRISING; UNEXPECTED.

starvation: see FAMINE; HUNGER; POVERTY.

starve *v.* hunger, famish, WANT.

starved: see HUNGRY.

state *n.* **1** (*affairs of state*) NATION, COUNTRY, COMMUNITY; **2** (*a sorry state*) status, RANK, LEVEL, SITUATION, CONDITION, FORM.
— *v.* DECLARE, assert, UTTER, affirm, TELL, SAY, EXCLAIM, allege, NARRATE, voice, EXPRESS.

stated: see VERBAL.

stateliness: see MAJESTY.

stately: see CEREMONIAL; DIGNIFIED; GRAND; MAGNIFICENT; ROYAL; SUPERB.

statement *n.* DECLARATION, assertion, COMMENT, UTTERANCE, affirmation, MENTION, REMARK, ANNOUNCEMENT, COMMUNICATION, ADMISSION, BILL, invoice.

stateroom: see CABIN.

static: see RIGID; SOUND.

station *n.* POST, SPOT, POSITION, LEVEL, ORDER, RANK, SEAT, depot, terminal, garage.
— *v.* SET, PLACE, POST, LOCATE, position, ESTABLISH, PLANT, INSTALL.

stationary: see IMMOVABLE; STILL.

stationery: see PAPER.

statue *n.* SCULPTURE, FIGURE, PIECE, bust.

statuette: see TROPHY.

stature: see ALTITUDE; HEIGHT.

status: see CONDITION; RANK; RATE; READING; STAGE; STATE.

statute: see ACT; REGULATION.

staunch: see DEPENDABLE; FIRM; LOYAL; STABLE; STURDY; TRUE.

staves: see STAFF.

stay *v.* REMAIN, CONTINUE, ENDURE, LINGER, tarry, REST, LAST, DWELL, ABIDE BY, CHECK, suppress.
— *n.* **1** *(a brief stay)* STOP, sojourn, HALT, DELAY, VACATION; **2** *(a stay of execution)* reprieve, respite, SUSPENSION, CHECK, hindrance; **3** *(the stay holding the mast)* ROPE, LINE, BRACE, SUPPORT.

staying: see WAITING.

steadfast: see DEPENDABLE; FAITHFUL; IMMOVABLE; PERMANENT; STABLE; STEADY; UNFAILING.

steadfastness: see RESOLUTION; STEADINESS.

steadily *adv.* EVENLY, REGULARLY, CONSTANTLY, FIRMLY, resolutely.

steadiness *n.* stability, REGULARITY, evenness, steadfastness, constancy, FIRMNESS, solidity, perseverance, DETERMINATION.

steady *adj.* STABLE, REGULAR, EVEN, CONSTANT, resolute, FIRM, SOLID, unfaltering, steadfast, unchanging, unvarying, SOBER, CALM, unexcited.
— *n.*: see LOVER.

steal *v.* **1** *(to steal money)* ROB, swipe, pilfer, filch, SWINDLE, shoplift, embezzle; **2** *(to steal away)* slink, SLIP, SNEAK, PROWL.
— *n.*: see BARGAIN; BUY.

steam *n.* VAPOR, MIST, FOG, GAS, CLOUD, ENERGY.
— *v.*: see EVAPORATE.

steamer: see BOAT.

steed: see HORSE.

steel *n.* IRON, alloy, METAL, flint, WEAPON, SWORD, KNIFE, saber, BLADE, hardness, VIGOR.
— *v.*: see STRENGTHEN.

steely: see IRON.

steep *adj.* sheer, ABRUPT, HIGH, perpendicular.
— *v.*: see SOAK; WATER.

steeple: see TOWER.

steer *v.* DRIVE, PILOT, NAVIGATE, DIRECT, GUIDE, CONTROL.

steersman: see PILOT.

stein: see CUP; MUG.

stellar: see LEADING.

stem *n.* **1** *(the stem of a plant)* TRUNK, STALK, STOCK, pedicle; **2** *(the stem of a word)* ROOT, FAMILY, BASE; **3** *(the stem of a boat)* bow, nose.
— *v.*: see ORIGINATE.

stench: see ODOR; SMELL; STINK.

stenographer: see SECRETARY.

stenography: see DICTATION.

step *n.* **1** *(a quick step)* TREAD, stride, PACE, footfall; **2** *(a step higher)* STAGE, gradation, GRADE; **3** *(the government will take the necessary steps)* measure, MOVE, ACTION.
— *v.*: see PACE; STAMP; STRIDE; TREAD; WALK.

stepping: see TREAD.

stereotyped: see STALE.

sterile: see BARREN; SANITARY.

stern *adj.* SEVERE, HARSH, rigorous, STRICT, HARD, unyielding, RIGID.
— *n.*: see BACK.

sternness: see HARSHNESS.

stew *v.* **1** *(to stew the meat)* BOIL, SIMMER, fricassee; **2** *(to stew about one's grades)* WORRY, FUSS, FRET.

steward: see ATTENDANT; WAITER.

stick *n.* TWIG, BRANCH, STALK, cane, ROD, STAFF
— *v.* **1** *(to stick one's head out)* PLACE, PUT, LAY, SET; **2** *(to stick to the paper)* adhere, CATCH, CLING, HOLD; **3** *(to stick a marshmallow)* STAB, PIERCE, spear, gore.

sticker: see SEAL; TAG.

stick-up: see HOLDUP; ROBBERY; THEFT.

sticky: see ADHESIVE; HUMID; SULTRY.

stiff *adj.* **1** *(a stiff collar)* RIGID, inflexible, unyielding, FIRM, unbending; **2** *(a stiff sentence)* SEVERE, HARSH, DIFFICULT; **3** *(his stiff manner)* FORMAL, COLD, UNFRIENDLY, COOL, AWKWARD, gawky, wooden.
— *n.*: see CORPSE; REMAINS.

stiffen: see FREEZE; TENSE.

stiffness: see FIRMNESS; FORMALITY.

stifle: see CHOKE; DROWN; HUSH; QUENCH; SILENCE; SMOTHER; STRANGLE.

stifling: see SULTRY.

stigma: see BLOT; BLOTCH.

still *adj.* MOTIONLESS, stationary, QUIET, CALM, PEACEFUL, TRANQUIL, SILENT, hushed, noiseless.
—*adv.* EVEN, YET, AS, ALWAYS, EVER, AGAIN, NEVERTHELESS, notwithstanding, HOWEVER.
—*v.* STOP, STALL, restrain, ARREST, lull, tranquilize, SILENCE, quiet, HUSH, muffle.
—*conj.*: see BUT; HOWEVER.

stillness: see CALM; CALMNESS; HUSH; SILENCE.

stimulant: see REFRESHMENTS.

stimulate *v.* AROUSE, INSPIRE, activate, URGE, invigorate, spur, PROVOKE.

stimulating: see APPETIZING; BRACING; BRISK; CRISP; EXCITABLE; PERSUASIVE.

stimulation: see EXCITEMENT; THRILL.

stimulus: see EXCITEMENT; INSPIRATION; URGE.

sting *v.* PRICK, BITE, WOUND, SMART, INSPIRE.
—*n.* PRICK, prickle, TINGLE, hurt, smart, anguish.

stinging: see ACID; KEEN.

stingy: see CHEAP; CLOSE; PETTY; TIGHT.

stink *v.* SMELL, reek.
—*n.* SMELL, ODOR, stench, reek.

stint: see TERM.

stipend: see COMMISSION.

stipple: see DOT.

stipulate: see CONTRACT.

stipulation: see CONDITION; DEMAND; TERM; WARRANTY.

stir *v.* WHIP, MIX, BLEND, agitate, TOSS, MOVE, BUDGE, AROUSE, STIMULATE, electrify, galvanize.

stirred: see SHAKEN.

stirring: see ELECTRIC; EMOTIONAL; EXCITABLE.

stitch: see HEM; SEW; TACK.

stitching: see SEAM.

stock *n.* **1** (*a stock of provisions*) SUPPLY, RESERVE, backlog, STORE, GOODS; **2** (*to feed the stock*) livestock, cattle, BREED; **3** (*the stock of a company*) SHARE, CAPITAL; **4** (*the stock of a gun*) HANDLE, butt. See also BLOOD; PARENTAGE; STRAIN; TRIBE.
—*v.* STORE, KEEP, hoard, RESERVE, carry, SUPPLY, PROVIDE, FURNISH.
—*adj.*: see OLD; STANDARD; TYPICAL; USUAL.

stockade: see ENCLOSURE; FENCE; PRISON.

stocked: see FULL.

stocking *n.* anklet, sock, HOSE.

stockings: see HOSE.

stockpile: see STORE; SUPPLY.

stockroom: see WAREHOUSE.

stocky: see PLUMP; STUBBY.

stole: see FUR; SCARF.

stomach: see ABIDE BY; BELLY; RELISH; SWALLOW.

stone *n.* ROCK, boulder, PEBBLE, GRAVEL, flint, cobblestone, slab, tombstone, gravestone, marble, GEM, JEWEL, PIT, SEED.

stones: see GRAVEL.

stony *adj.* ROCKY, gritty, HARD, FIRM, RESISTANT, SOLID, unyielding.

stooge: see PAWN.

stool *n.* SEAT, BENCH, footstool, campstool. See also TOILET.

stoop *v.* CROUCH, BEND, LEAN, KNEEL, BOW.
—*n.*: see PORCH.

stooped: see BENT.

stop *v.* HALT, PAUSE, STALL, restrain, ARREST, STILL, DISCONTINUE, SUSPEND, obstruct, HOLD, CHECK, refrain, PREVENT, QUIT, CEASE.
—*n.* **1** (*to come to a stop*) HALT, END, PAUSE, DELAY; **2** (*to make a stop at her office*) VISIT, STAY, CALL; **3** (*to pull out the stop*) STOPPER, PLUG, cork.

stoppage: see BREAKDOWN; STRIKE.

stopper *n.* PLUG, cork, stopple, LID, COVER.

stopple: see STOPPER.

stopwatch: see CLOCK.

store *n.* **1** (*to shop at that store*) SHOP, mall, MARKET, supermarket, boutique, emporium; **2** (*a large store of toothbrushes*) STOCK, SUPPLY, stockpile, deposit, hoard, RESERVE, TREASURE.
—*v.* STOCK, SAVE, stockpile, RESERVE, BANK, ACCUMULATE, COLLECT, hoard, cache.

storehouse: see WAREHOUSE.

storeroom: see CELLAR; CLOSET.

storm *n.* thunderstorm, tempest, hurricane, cyclone, tornado, blizzard, sandstorm, windstorm, GALE, FURY, RAGE, bluster, upheaval, whirlwind.
—*v.*: see ASSAULT; CARRY ON; RAGE.

stormless: see PEACEFUL.

stormy: see EXPLOSIVE.

story *n.* **1** (*to tell a story*) narrative, PLOT, NOVEL, anecdote, saga, MYTH, LEGEND, TALE, LIE, FIB; **2** (*on the second story*) FLOOR, LEVEL, landing.

storyteller: see COMEDIAN.

stout *adj.* FAT, fleshy, overweight, obese, strapping, portly, PLUMP, HEAVY.

stove *n.* RANGE, cookstove, rotisserie, OVEN, FURNACE, heater.

stow: see PACK.

straddle: see MOUNT.

strafe: see SHELL.

straggle: see ROAM.

straight *adj.* DIRECT, lineal, EVEN, horizontal, UNBROKEN, TRUE, ORDERLY, straightforward, UPRIGHT, HONEST.
— *adv.*: see DIRECTLY.

straightedge: see RULER.

straighten *v.* CORRECT, rectify, JUSTIFY, even, RIGHT.

straighten out: see CLARIFY.

straightforward: see BLUNT; DIRECT; FRANK; INFORMAL; NAKED; SINCERE; STRAIGHT.

strain *v.* **1** (*to strain one's back*) STRETCH, tighten, overtax, TAX, INJURE, HARM, SPRAIN, STRUGGLE, TOIL, LABOR; **2** (*to strain out the seeds*) SIFT, FILTER, SCREEN.
— *n.* **1** (*the strain of hard work*) TENSION, STRESS, EXERTION, EFFORT; **2** (*a strain of wheat*) SPECIES, BREED, RACE, stock; **3** (*the strains of a hymn*) TUNE, MELODY; **4** (*a strain of insanity*) STREAK, SUSPICION, SUGGESTION, TONE, SPIRIT, STYLE.

strained: see UNNATURAL.

strainer: see FILTER.

strait: see SOUND.

strand: see BEACH; FIBER; GROUND.

stranded: see AGROUND; ASHORE.

strange *adj.* UNUSUAL, ODD, PECULIAR, CURIOUS, eccentric, bizarre, EXTRAORDINARY, UNNATURAL, IRREGULAR, QUEER, FANTASTIC, exotic, alien, FOREIGN, UNFAMILIAR, REMOTE, COLD, reserved, SHY, UNACCUSTOMED, unacquainted, unskilled.

strangeness: see ODDITY.

stranger *n.* newcomer, outsider, outlander, FOREIGNER, ALIEN.

strangle *v.* CHOKE, SMOTHER, suffocate, stifle, SQUEEZE, suppress.

strap *n.* BAND, BELT, STRIP, leather, thong.
— *v.* **1** (*to strap the box*) FASTEN, BIND, TIE, LASH, tether; **2** (*to strap the robber*) WHIP, BELT, BEAT, PUNISH, SPANK.

strapped: see BANKRUPT.

strapping: see HEFTY; STOUT.

strategy *n.* planning, TECHNIQUE, approach, MANAGEMENT, DIRECTION, FORESIGHT, SYSTEM, SCHEME, maneuvre.

stratosphere: see HEAVEN.

straw *n.* **1** (*a bed of straw*) STALK, STEM, FIBER, HAY, BALE, BED; **2** (*to sip with a straw*) TUBE, siphon, PIPE.

stray *v.* WANDER, ROVE, ROAM, go astray, err.
— *adj.* strayed, scattered, LOST, wandering, CASUAL, incidental.

strayed: see STRAY.

streak *n.* **1** (*streaks of mud*) STRIPE, LINE, BAND, STROKE, BAR, RULE, LAYER, RAY, BEAM, STREAM, FLASH; **2** (*a streak of humor*) STRAIN, VEIN, TENDENCY, SUGGESTION, SUSPICION; **3** (*a winning streak*) RUN, SPELL, PERIOD, TIME, STRETCH.
— *v.* MARK, mar, STAIN.

stream *n.* BROOK, CREEK, RIVER, waterway, COURSE, DRIFT, CURRENT, RUSH, TORRENT, RAY, BEAM.
— *v.* RUN, FLOW, RUSH, GUSH, MOVE, POUR, DRIP.

streamer: see HEADLINE.

street *n.* AVENUE, boulevard, ROAD, ROUTE, ALLEY, alleyway, PROMENADE, LANE, HIGHWAY, way, thoroughfare.

strength *n.* FORCE, VIGOR, MIGHT, POWER, ENERGY, INTENSITY, potency, CONCENTRATION, vehemence, toughness, robustness, sturdiness, durability.

strengthen *v.* fortify, PROP, BRACE, buttress, REINFORCE, STIFFEN, steel, invigorate, revive, HARDEN, toughen, intensify.

strengthener: see PROP.

strenuous: see DIFFICULT; INTENSE.

strenuously: see HARD.

streptococcus: see GERM.

stress *v.* emphasize, ACCENT, accentuate, MARK, UNDERLINE, underscore, FEATURE, STRAIN, TAX, PRESSURE.
— *n.* emphasis, ACCENT, WEIGHT, IMPORTANCE, STRAIN, TENSION, PRESSURE, compulsion.

stretch *v.* PULL, draw out, elongate, LENGTHEN, EXTEND, SPREAD, REACH, EXPAND, RANGE, bridge, RELAX, STRAIN, economize, EXAGGERATE, distort, misrepresent.
— *n.* **1** (*too much stretch*) elasticity, STRAIN,

TENSION; **2** *(a stretch of three years)* TIME, PERIOD, COMPASS, SPACE, LINE, DISTANCE.

stretcher: see LITTER; RACK.

stretching: see RUNNING.

strew: see SCATTER; SPRINKLE.

stricken *adj.* smitten, afflicted.

strict *adj.* EXACT, PRECISE, STIFF, inflexible, RIGID, STERN, HARSH, SEVERE, HARD, NARROW, authoritarian, CAREFUL, rigorous, prudish, ACCURATE.

strictly: see PRECISELY.

strictness: see HARSHNESS.

stride *v.* step, TREAD, STALK, PARADE, WALK.
— *n.*: see FOOTSTEP; STEP; TREAD.

strife: see BATTLE; COMBAT; CONFLICT; FIGHT; STRUGGLE; WAR.

strike *v.* **1** *(don't strike me!)* HIT, BEAT, ASSAULT, ATTACK, SLAP, SMACK; **2** *(how does that strike you?)* AFFECT, IMPRESS, STUN, ASTONISH, OVERWHELM; **3** *(to strike a match)* ignite, LIGHT, RUB; **4** *(to strike oil)* DISCOVER, UNCOVER, unearth; **5** *(to strike twelve)* chime, RING, peal, SOUND; **6** *(to strike a bargain)* CONCLUDE, MAKE, ratify; **7** *(to strike a manufacturing plant)* QUIT, STOP, WALK; **8** *(to strike a medal)* STAMP, IMPRESS, imprint; **9** *(to strike the flag)* LOWER, take down, REMOVE.
— *n.* BLOW, THRUST, DISCOVERY, location, stoppage, quitting, walkout, sit-down, slowdown.

striker: see HAMMER.

striking: see CONSPICUOUS; NOTICEABLE; OBVIOUS; OUTSTANDING; STUNNING.

string *n.* **1** *(to tie with string)* CORD, TWINE, THREAD, ROPE; **2** *(a string of victories)* SERIES, queue, ROW, STRETCH.

strip *v.* tear off, take apart, REMOVE, PEEL, UNCOVER, EXPOSE, UNDRESS, disrobe, empty, plunder, ROB.
— *n.* BAND, STRIPE, ribbon, STREAK, PIECE. See also ALLEY; PAD.

stripe *n.* STREAK, BAND, STRIP, LINE, BAR, RULE, braid, KIND.

stripped: see NAKED.

strive *v.* TRY, STRUGGLE, COMPETE, FIGHT, ATTEMPT, ENDEAVOR.

stroke *n.* **1** *(a stroke of the pen)* mar, STREAK, LINE, DASH, SCORE, BAR, RULE, STEP, MEASURE, rub, KNOCK, TAP, BLOW, RAP, peal, chime; **2** *(a stroke of genius)* feat, ACHIEVEMENT, ACCOMPLISHMENT, IMPACT; **3** *(recovery from a stroke)* seizure, FIT, convulsion.
— *v.* HIT, KNOCK, TAP, RAP, RUB, PET, CARESS, massage, COMFORT, SMOOTH.

stroll *v.* saunter, amble, ramble, meander, WANDER, WALK.
— *n.* PROMENADE, TURN, WALK, ramble.

stroller: see CARRIAGE.

strong *adj.* POWERFUL, MIGHTY, MUSCULAR, HARDY, brawny, sinewy, HEALTHY, SOUND, RESISTANT, durable, FIRM, uncompromising, FAVORABLE, PERSUASIVE, compelling, concentrated, COMPACT, VIOLENT.

strongbox: see SAFE; VAULT.

stronghold: see CASTLE; FORTRESS.

strongly: see FIRMLY; FORCIBLY; MIGHTY.

structure *n.* BUILDING, edifice, CONSTRUCTION, framework, FORM, ARRANGEMENT.

struggle *n.* FIGHT, BATTLE, CONFLICT, CONTEST, ENCOUNTER, strife, ATTEMPT, EFFORT, ENDEAVOR.
— *v.* FIGHT, OPPOSE, TRY, ATTEMPT, STRIVE, QUARREL.

stub *n.* END, stump, TAG, TAIL, butt, RECEIPT.

stubble: see BEARD; BRISTLE.

stubborn *adj.* obstinate, pig-headed, unbending, opinionated, headstrong, unyielding, STIFF, inflexible, RIGID, FIRM, perverse, persistent, mulish, wrong-headed.

stubby *adj.* BLUNT, SHORT, squat, stocky, CHUBBY, pudgy, chunky.

stud: see POST.

student *n.* PUPIL, SCHOLAR, schoolgirl, coed, schoolboy, cadet, researcher, INTELLECTUAL, bookworm, undergraduate, thinker, learner, BEGINNER, APPRENTICE.

students: see CLASS.

studied *adj.* DELIBERATE, INTENTIONAL, designed, premeditated, calculated, THOROUGH, planned, PRECIOUS, ARTIFICIAL.

studio *n.* STUDY, workshop, workroom, atelier, SHOP, APARTMENT, library.

study *n.* **1** *(in the study)* STUDIO, DEN, OFFICE, library, workroom; **2** *(to require study)* LEARNING, RESEARCH, EXAMINATION, REVIEW, INSPECTION, ATTENTION, THOUGHT, REFLECTION, contemplation; **3** *(a field of study)* SUBJECT,

COURSE, specialization; **4** *(to prepare a study)* INVESTIGATION, REPORT, SKETCH.
— *v.* LEARN, INVESTIGATE, CONSIDER, WEIGH, REVIEW, INSPECT, PREPARE, cram, MEMORIZE, specialize, TRAIN, ENROLL.

stuff *n.* things, GOODS, miscellany, FABRIC, MATERIAL, SUBSTANCE.
— *v.* cram, JAM, PACK, CROWD, FILL, congest, gorge.

stuffed: see CHOCK-FULL; LOADED.

stuffing: see PAD; PADDING.

stuffy: see CLOSE; HUMID; MUGGY.

stumble *v.* TRIP, SLIP, FALL, falter, lurch, stutter, STAMMER.

stump: see PUZZLE; STUB; TRUNK.

stun *v.* knock out, daze, benumb, STAGGER, CONFUSE, AMAZE, SHOCK, SURPRISE, astound, discombobulate.

stunning *adj.* astonishing, astounding, WONDERFUL, overpowering, ravishing, striking, good-looking, ATTRACTIVE.

stunt *n.* TRICK, antic, caper, prank, JOKE, exploit, feat, DEED.
— *v.*: see CHECK; CHOKE; DWARF.

stupefy: see AMAZE; DRUG; NUMB.

stupendous: see ENORMOUS; MARVELOUS; VAST.

stupid *adj.* dumb, DULL, unintelligent, SLOW, slow-witted, RETARDED, benumbed, sluggish, brainless, SIMPLE, inane, FOOLISH, IDIOTIC, FEEBLE-MINDED, HALF-WITTED, ABSURD, SENSELESS.

stupidity *n.* dumbness, foolishness, idiocy, absurdity, senselessness, unintelligence, feeble-mindedness, DULLNESS.

stupor: see SHOCK.

sturdiness: see STRENGTH.

sturdy *adj.* STRONG, RUGGED, HARDY, robust, MUSCULAR, well-built, STOUT, stalwart, staunch, FIRM, resolute.

stutter: see STAMMER; STUMBLE; TALK.

sty: see ENCLOSURE.

style *n.* DESIGN, KIND, SORT, FORM, CLASS, TYPE, delicacy, refinement, sophistication, MANNER, ELEGANCE, SMARTNESS, FASHION, vogue, mode.
— *v.*: see ENTITLE; PATTERN.

stylish *adj.* FASHIONABLE, UP-TO-DATE, SMART, ELEGANT, mod.

stylishly: see SHARPLY.

stylograph: see PEN.

suave: see MILD.

subconscious: see UNCONSCIOUS.

subdivision: see CHAPTER; CLASS.

subdue: see BLUNT; DEFEAT; MASTER; OVERCOME; SOFTEN; SUBJECT; TAME.

subdued: see SOUNDLESS; TAME.

subgroup: see SPECIES.

subject *n.* **1** *(the subject of study)* TOPIC, THEME, content, AREA, domain, STUDY, COURSE; **2** *(the king's loyal subjects)* commoner, CITIZEN, dependent, inferior.
— *v.* DOMINATE, CONQUER, subdue, EXPOSE.
— *adj.*: see LIABLE; UNDER.

subjection: see CONQUEST; REDUCTION.

subject matter: see CONTENTS; TEXT.

sublime: see DIVINE; SUPERB.

subliminal: see UNCONSCIOUS.

submerge *v.* DIP, PLUNGE, immerse, SINK.

submission: see DEPENDENCE; OBEDIENCE; SURRENDER.

submissive: see OBEDIENT.

submit *v.* SURRENDER, YIELD, give in, OFFER, advance, PROPOSE.

subnormal: see FEEBLE-MINDED; RETARDED.

subordinate: see ASSISTANT; DEPENDENT; DEPUTY; INFERIOR; JUNIOR; SATELLITE; UNDER.

subpoena: see CHARGE; SUE; SUMMONS; WARRANT.

subscribe *v.* AGREE, CONSENT, PROMISE, SIGN, endorse, ORDER, ENROLL, REGISTER.

subsequent: see FOLLOWING; FUTURE.

subsequently: see AFTER; AFTERWARDS; BEHIND; SINCE; THEREAFTER.

subsequent to: see AFTER.

subservience: see DEPENDENCE.

subside: see DECREASE; SINK; TAPER.

subsidiary: see BRANCH; SUPPLEMENTARY.

subsidize: see AID; SUPPLEMENT; SUPPORT.

subsidy: see AID; ALLOWANCE; PENSION; SUPPLEMENT.

subsist: see BE; EXIST; FEED; LIVE.

subsistence: see EXISTENCE; MAINTENANCE.

subsistent: see EXISTENT.

substance *n.* MATTER, MATERIAL, STUFF, THING, tangibility.

substandard: see SLOPPY.

substantial: see AMPLE; HEFTY; IMPORTANT; LARGE; SERIOUS; SIGNIFICANT; SOLID; STABLE; WEALTHY.

substantiate: see ESTABLISH; PROVE; SUPPORT; SUSTAIN; VERIFY.

substantiation: see VERIFICATION.

substitute *n.* REPLACEMENT, proxy, stand-in, pinch hitter, alternate, understudy, successor, expedient, makeshift.
 − *v.* REPLACE, pinch-hit, interchange, swap, EXCHANGE, SWITCH, SUCCEED.

substitution *n.* REPLACEMENT, EXCHANGE, swap, SWITCH, interchange, displacement.

subterfuge: see CAMOUFLAGE; SWINDLE.

subterranean: see DEEP.

subtitle: see ENTITLE; HEADING.

subtle: see FAINT; FINE; SENSITIVE.

subtlety: see CUNNING; MYSTERY.

subtly: see LIGHTLY.

subtract *v.* deduct, take away, LESSEN, REMOVE, WITHDRAW, REDUCE, DIMINISH.

suburb: see COMMUNITY.

subway: see TUNNEL.

succeed *v.* **1** *(to succeed in business)* PROSPER, FLOURISH, TRIUMPH, WIN, THRIVE; **2** *(to succeed the dead king)* REPLACE, FOLLOW.

succeeding: see NEXT.

succeedingly: see NEXT.

success *n.* VICTORY, TRIUMPH, PROSPERITY, FORTUNE, LUCK, attainment, ACCOMPLISHMENT, ACHIEVEMENT.

successful *adj.* VICTORIOUS, HAPPY, PROSPEROUS, flourishing, LUCKY, FAVORABLE, rewarding.

succession *n.* SEQUENCE, SERIES, CHAIN, COURSE, progression.

successive *adj.* sequential, consecutive, serial, FOLLOWING.

successor: see HEIR; SUBSTITUTE.

succumb: see DECEASE; LOSE.

such *adj.* like, SIMILAR.
 − *adv.* VERY, EXTREMELY.

such as: see LIKE.

suck *v.* SIP, suckle, ABSORB, DRAW.

suckle: see NURSE; SUCK.

sudden *adj.* QUICK, SWIFT, HASTY, SPEEDY, ABRUPT, UNEXPECTED, unforeseen.

suddenly: see SWIFTLY; UNAWARES.

suds: see FOAM.

sudsy: see FOAMY.

sue *v.* litigate, PROSECUTE, subpoena, petition, ACCUSE.

suffer *v.* agonize, writhe, ENDURE, undergo, EXPERIENCE, SUPPORT, tolerate, ALLOW, PERMIT, GRIEVE.

sufferer: see PATIENT; PREY; VICTIM.

suffering *n.* AGONY, MISERY, TORMENT, PAIN, hurt, DISTRESS, ACHE.
 − *adj.* hurt, aching, tormented, distressed.

suffice: see DO; REACH; SERVE; SUIT.

sufficiency: see PLENTY.

sufficient *adj.* ENOUGH, ADEQUATE, AMPLE, PLENTY, ABUNDANT.

sufficiently: see ENOUGH.

suffocate: see DROWN; SMOTHER; STRANGLE.

sugar: see SWEETEN.

sugar-coat: see SWEETEN.

sugariness: see SWEETNESS.

sugary: see SWEET.

suggest *v.* RECOMMEND, PROPOSE, advance, OFFER, ADVISE, INDICATE, HINT, IMPLY, insinuate, counsel.

suggesting: see LEADING.

suggestion *n.* RECOMMENDATION, PROPOSAL, PLAN, IDEA, OFFER, ADVICE, TIP, PROPOSITION, HINT, TRACE, overtone, insinuation.

suggestive *adj.* **1** *(a sky suggestive of spring)* remindful, thought-provoking, symbolic, PREGNANT; **2** *(too suggestive for the whole family)* improper, VULGAR, off-color, spicy.

suit *n.* **1** *(to wear a suit)* CLOTHES, COSTUME, WARDROBE; **2** *(a suit in chancery)* lawsuit, CASE, ACTION; **3** *(which suit is trump?)* SET, GROUP, SERIES, COLLECTION.
 − *v.* SATISFY, PLEASE, AGREE, FIT, conform, suffice, ADAPT, ACCOMMODATE, SERVE.

suitability: see CONVENIENCE; FIT; FITNESS.

suitable *adj.* usable, FITTING, APT, PROPER, SATISFACTORY, APPROPRIATE, compatible, CONVENIENT, ADEQUATE, becoming.

suitably: see RIGHT.

suitcase: see BAG.

suitcases: see BAGGAGE; LUGGAGE.

suite: see FLAT; SET.

suited: see FIT; FITTING; USEFUL.

sulky: see SULLEN.

sullen *adj.* sulky, morose, ill-humored, QUIET, SILENT, unsociable, MOODY, GLOOMY, BITTER, grim, somber, depressing, dismal, brooding, clouded.

sultry *adj.* **1** (*a sultry day*) HOT, HUMID, MUGGY, sticky, CLOSE, stifling; **2** (*a sultry blond*) sexy, erotic, PASSIONATE.

sum *n.* TOTAL, WHOLE, AMOUNT, SUMMARY. −*v.* add up, total, SUMMARIZE.

summarize *v.* sum up, add up, total, REVIEW, OUTLINE, epitomize, CONDENSE, DIGEST.

summary *n.* REVIEW, ACCOUNT, OUTLINE, synopsis, précis, DIGEST, compendium, abridgment, summation.

summation: see SUMMARY.

summit *n.* TOP, PEAK, CROWN, POINT, pinnacle, aspiration.

summon *v.* CALL, INVITE, bid, ROUSE, call forth, invoke, COMMAND, cite.

summoning: see PRAYER.

summons *n.* CALL, REQUEST, INVITATION, NOTICE, ORDER, COMMAND, subpoena, citation.

sump: see TANK.

sumptuous: see LUXURIOUS.

sumptuousness: see SPLENDOR.

sum up: see ADD; SUMMARIZE.

sunbeam: see SHAFT.

sundown: see DUSK; EVENING.

sundry: see ASSORTED; SEVERAL.

sunken: see HOLLOW.

sunny *adj.* sunshiny, unclouded, BRIGHT, CLEAR, CHEERFUL, joyous, WARM, optimistic, beaming, RADIANT.

sunrise: see DAWN; MORNING.

sunset: see DUSK; EVENING.

sunshiny: see SUNNY.

sunup: see MORNING.

sup: see DINE.

superb *adj.* FINE, EXCELLENT, SPLENDID, GRAND, MARVELOUS, MAGNIFICENT, SUPERIOR, WONDERFUL, EXTRAORDINARY, impressive, stately, ELEGANT, sublime.

superannuated: see OLD; OLD-FASHIONED.

superego: see CONSCIENCE; SELF.

superficial: see CASUAL; EXTERNAL; FACIAL; HASTY; HURRIED; OUTSIDE; OUTWARD; SHALLOW; SURFACE.

superfluous: see EXCESSIVE; UNNECESSARY; USELESS.

superhuman: see DIVINE.

superintend: see BOSS; SUPERVISE.

superintendence: see MANAGEMENT; SUPERVISION.

superintendent *n.* **1** (*the superintendent of schools*) SUPERVISOR, administrator, HEAD, overseer, DIRECTOR, MANAGER, FOREMAN; **2** (*the superintendent of an apartment building*) custodian, caretaker, JANITOR.

superior *adj.* BETTER, higher, greater, MORE, finer, EXCELLENT, upper, above, paramount, dominant, PRINCIPAL, FOREMOST, haughty. −*n.* BOSS, CHIEF, HEAD, EMPLOYER, SUPERVISOR.

superiority *n.* BEST, MOST, LEAD, POSITION, RANK, EXCELLENCE, ADVANTAGE, eminence.

superlative: see DIVINE.

supermarket: see STORE.

supernatural: see INVISIBLE; MIRACULOUS; SUPERSTITION; SUPERSTITIOUS.

supersede: see REPLACE.

superstition *n.* witchcraft, sorcery, witchery, MAGIC, RELIGION, deviltry, voodoo, heresy, supernatural.

superstitious *adj.* irrational, supernatural, MYTHICAL, RELIGIOUS, MAGICAL, demoniac, occult, heathen.

supervise *v.* oversee, superintend, MANAGE, DIRECT.

supervised: see SAFE.

supervision *n.* superintendence, MANAGEMENT, surveillance, DIRECTION, CONTROL, INSPECTION, guardianship.

supervisor *n*. SUPERINTENDENT, HEAD, DIRECTOR, overseer, MANAGER, FOREMAN, administrator, skipper.

supper: see DINNER; MEAL.

supplant: see REPLACE.

supple: see FLEXIBLE; LIMBER; LIMP; SOFT.

supplement *n*. ADDITION, subsidy, BONUS, EXTENSION, APPENDIX, additive, SECTION, addenda, errata.
  — *v*. ADD, COMPLETE, subsidize.

supplementary *adj*. ADDITIONAL, auxiliary, subsidiary.

suppleness: see FLEXIBILITY; LIMP.

supplicant: see BEGGAR.

supplicate: see PLEAD; PRAY.

supplication: see PLEA; PRAYER.

supplied: see FULL.

supplies: see EQUIPMENT; OUTFIT.

supply *v*. FURNISH, PROVIDE, STOCK, EQUIP.
  — *n*. STOCK, STORE, RESERVE, provisions, GOODS, backlog, stockpile.

support *v*. HOLD, MAINTAIN, KEEP, BEAR, PROP, SUSTAIN, CARRY, ENDURE, AID, HELP, FINANCE, PROVIDE, ASSIST, BACK, PROMOTE, ENCOURAGE, subsidize, BRACE, advocate, CONFIRM, VERIFY, substantiate, APPROVE, STRENGTHEN, CHERISH.
  — *n*. PROP, BRACE, STAY, BASE, FOUNDATION, BASIS, MAINTENANCE, upkeep, ASSISTANCE, AID.

supporter *n*. upholder, advocate, FAN, devotee, backer, PATRON, ANGEL, PROTECTOR, provider, breadwinner, helper, ally, CHAMPION.

supporters: see FOLLOWING.

supportive: see HELPFUL.

suppose *v*. IMAGINE, ASSUME, presume, GUESS, BELIEVE, THINK, surmise, PRETEND, JUDGE, IMPLY, INVOLVE.

supposed *adj*. IMAGINED, assumed, presumed, believed, accepted, LIKELY, PROBABLE, theoretical, hypothetical.

supposedly *adv*. presumably, APPARENTLY, PROBABLY, theoretically, hypothetically.

supposing *conj*. IF, provided, whether, granting.

supposition: see GUESS; THINKING.

suppress: see CONCEAL; SMOTHER; STAY; STRANGLE.

supremacy: see INFINITY; LEADERSHIP.

supreme *adj*. highest, greatest, FIRST-RATE, top-drawer, BEST, UTMOST, CHIEF, FINAL, dominant, sovereign.
  — *n*.: see MAXIMUM.

sure *adj*. CERTAIN, ACTUAL, POSITIVE, DEFINITE, REAL, AUTHENTIC, STABLE, SAFE, DEPENDABLE, RELIABLE, trustworthy, FIRM, SOLID, KNOWN, ASSURED, convinced, unavoidable, INEVITABLE.
  — *adv*. YES, of course, CERTAINLY, DEFINITELY, DOUBTLESS, POSITIVELY.

surely *adv*. CERTAINLY, DEFINITELY, POSITIVELY, true, DOUBTLESS, undoubtedly, assuredly, FIRMLY, safely.

sureness: see PRECISION.

surety: see PROTECTION; WARRANT.

surface *n*. TOP, COVERING, COVER, OUTSIDE, FACE, exterior, PLANE. See also TREAD.
  — *adj*. TOP, exterior, EXTERNAL, OUTWARD, superficial, SHALLOW.
  — *v*.: see EMERGE; PAVE; VARNISH.

surge *v*. SWELL, HEAVE, SWEEP, RUSH, RISE, MOVE, ROLL, BILLOW.
  — *n*.: see IMPULSE; WAVE.

surgeon: see DOCTOR.

surgery: see OPERATION.

surmise: see GUESS; SUPPOSE; SUSPECT.

surmount: see OVERCOME.

surpass *v*. EXCEED, excel, OUTDO, transcend, BETTER, PASS, OUTCLASS.

surplus *n*. EXCESS, extra, REMAINDER, balance.
  — *adj*.: see EXTRA; ODD.

surprise *v*. AMAZE, astound, ASTONISH, CATCH, perplex, dumfound, BEWILDER, flabbergast.
  — *n*. AMAZEMENT, ASTONISHMENT, SHOCK, JOLT, bewilderment, WONDER, bombshell.

surprised: see SPEECHLESS.

surprising *adj*. AMAZING, astonishing, startling, perplexing, UNEXPECTED, awesome, breathtaking.

surrender *v*. give up, QUIT, concede, SUBMIT, YIELD, RESIGN, ABANDON, relinquish.
  — *n*. submission, DEFEAT, abandonment.

surrendered: see FALLEN.

surrey: see CARRIAGE.

surround *v*. ENCIRCLE, RING, GIRDLE, ENCLOSE, encompass, shut in.

surrounded by: see AMIDST; AMONG.

surrounding: see ABOUT.

surroundings *pl.n.* ENVIRONMENT, environs, circumstances, NEIGHBORHOOD, conditions.

surveillance: see SUPERVISION.

survey *v.* REVIEW, EXAMINE, INSPECT, OBSERVE, VIEW, SCAN, scrutinize, look over, MEASURE.
— *n.* REVIEW, EXAMINATION, INSPECTION, VIEW, LOOK, PROSPECT, POLL, questionnaire, TEST, OBSERVATION.

survival: see EXISTENCE.

survive *v.* outlive, outlast, PERSIST, ENDURE, REMAIN, CONTINUE, LIVE, EXIST.

surviving: see EXISTENT; LIVING.

susceptibility: see FEELING; TENDENCY.

susceptible: see CAPABLE; LIABLE.

suspect *v.* IMAGINE, GUESS, presume, SUPPOSE, ASSUME, surmise, DOUBT, DISTRUST, disbelieve.
— *n.* defendant, accused, DELINQUENT, culprit.
— *adj.*: see FISHY; SUSPICIOUS.

suspecting: see SUSPICIOUS.

suspend *v.* **1** *(to suspend in midair)* HANG, HOLD, DANGLE, SWING, DEPEND; **2** *(to suspend the hearing)* POSTPONE, defer, DELAY, INTERRUPT, ARREST, DISCONTINUE, STOP, REMOVE, WITHHOLD.

suspense *n.* UNCERTAINTY, indecision, DOUBT, ANXIETY, expectancy, anticipation.

suspension *n.* hanging, INTERRUPTION, intermission, adjournment.

suspicion *n.* DOUBT, skepticism, JEALOUSY, STRAIN, STREAK, SUGGESTION, TRACE, BIT, disbelief.

suspicious *adj.* doubting, suspecting, dubious, skeptical, questioning, quizzical, DOUBTFUL, distrusting, UNUSUAL, far-fetched, FISHY, IRREGULAR, suspect.

sustain *v.* SUPPORT, BEAR, CARRY, MAINTAIN, KEEP, keep up, ENCOURAGE, NOURISH, ratify, APPROVE, COMFORT, CONFIRM, substantiate, ENDURE, undergo, SUFFER, ENCOUNTER.

sustained: see RUNNING.

sustenance: see DIET; FOOD; LIVING; MAINTENANCE; NOURISHMENT.

swab: see DRY; MOP; SPONGE; WIPE.

swagger: see BOAST; BRAG.

swallow *v.* gulp, EAT, gorge, ABSORB, ACCEPT, BITE, stomach.

swamp *v.* FLOOD, deluge, drench, saturate, SOAK, OVERFLOW, OVERWHELM, SUBMERGE, ENTANGLE.
— *n.* MARSH, bog, fen, quagmire.

swanky: see CLASSY.

swap: see SUBSTITUTION; SWITCH; TRADE.

swarm *n.* HOST, CROWD, horde, HERD, BODY.
— *v.* CROWD, throng, JAM, MOB, abound.

swat: see HIT; SLAP.

swatch: see SAMPLE.

sway *v.* SWING, waver, incline, LEAN, BEND, ROCK, REEL, lurch, IMPRESS, CONVINCE, PERSUADE, DOMINATE, CONTROL.
— *n.*: see EMPIRE; GOVERNMENT; INFLUENCE; REIGN; SWING.

swaying: see SWING.

swear *v.* CURSE, DAMN, blaspheme, PROMISE, vow, vouch, vouchsafe, WARRANT, DECLARE, assert, STATE, TESTIFY, affirm.

swearword: see OATH.

sweat *v.* PERSPIRE, swelter, broil, OOZE, TOIL, LABOR, WORK, EXTRACT.
— *n.* perspiration, WORK, ANXIETY.

sweep *v.* BRUSH, VACUUM, REMOVE, CLEAN, flow over, SCAN, RANGE, EMBRACE, PASS.

sweeper: see MOP.

sweet *adj.* **1** *(a sweet taste)* sugary, saccharine, honeyed, TASTY, AGREEABLE, luscious; **2** *(sweet butter)* unsalted, FRESH, PURE, CLEAN, MILD, FRAGRANT; **3** *(a sweet disposition)* GENTLE, SYMPATHETIC, LOVABLE, TENDER, KIND, winsome, CHARMING, ATTRACTIVE, BELOVED, DARLING; **4** *(a sweet song)* PLEASANT, AGREEABLE, DELIGHTFUL, HARMONIOUS, MELODIOUS.

sweeten *v.* sugar, candy, sugar-coat, SOFTEN, FRESHEN, lighten, IMPROVE.

sweetheart *n.* LOVER, BELOVED, DARLING, DEAR, HONEY.

sweetmeats: see DESSERT.

sweetness *n.* sugariness, SYMPATHY, KINDNESS, TENDERNESS, MILDNESS, HARMONY, FRESHNESS, pleasantness.

sweets: see DESSERT.

swell *v.* INCREASE, GROW, ENLARGE, RISE, PUFF, EXPAND, INFLATE, dilate, BULGE, SURGE.
— *adj.* GRAND, GREAT, FINE, EXCELLENT, SMART, STYLISH, well-dressed, ELEGANT.
— *n.*: see WAVE.

swelling: see BELLY; BLISTER; BULGE; BUMP; EXPANSION; GROWTH; INFLAMMATION; INFLATION; LUMP.

swelter: see PERSPIRE; SCORCH; SWEAT.

swerve: see SWING; TURN.

swift *adj.* FAST, QUICK, RAPID, SPEEDY, fleet, SUDDEN, HASTY, ABRUPT, UNEXPECTED.

swiftly *adv.* quickly, rapidly, suddenly, PROMPTLY.

swiftness: see QUICKNESS; SPEED.

swig: see BEVERAGE.

swim *v.* BATHE, wade, paddle, DIVE, CRAWL, SUBMERGE, FLOOD, GLIDE, WHIRL.
— *n.* swimming, bathing, DIP, CURRENT, STREAM, mainstream.

swimming: see SWIM.

swindle *v.* CHEAT, defraud, STEAL, embezzle, THIEVE, ROB, fleece, gyp.
— *n.* FRAUD, CHEAT, deception, hoax, TRICK, subterfuge.

swindler *n.* cheater, embezzler, FRAUD, THIEF, ROBBER, trickster, rogue.

swine: see HEEL; HOG; PIG; SOW.

swing *v.* SWAY, ROCK, oscillate, WAVE, FLAP, HANG, DANGLE, STRIKE, TURN, swerve.
— *n.* **1** *(the swing of a pendulum)* oscillation, sway, swaying, rocking, dangle, swerve, TURN; **2** *(that band plays swing)* jazz, bop, rock, boogie-woogie, rhythm, tempo, lilt, **3** *(a porch swing)* glider, SEAT, RIDE.

swipe: see STEAL.

swirl: see ROTATION; WHIRL.

swish: see MURMUR; RUSTLE.

switch *n.* **1** *(to make a switch to a new brand)* TRADE, EXCHANGE, swap, CHANGE, SHIFT, MOVE, circuit breaker, button, switch box, shunt, by-pass; **2** *(to whip with a switch)* ROD, STICK, WHIP, STRAP, BELT, birch, sprig, shoot.
— *v.* TRADE, EXCHANGE, CHANGE, MOVE, SHIFT, TURN, divert, CONVERT, SWING, JERK, WAG, MAKE, BREAK, WHIP, THRASH, flog, LASH.

switchblade: see KNIFE.

switchboard: see PANEL.

switch box: see SWITCH.

swivel: see AXIS; HINGE; ROTATE.

swoon: see FAINT.

swoop *v.* zoom, pounce, FALL, DIVE, PLUNGE, DROP, SEIZE.

sword *n.* STEEL, BLADE, saber, rapier, foil, cutlass, broadsword.

symbol *n.* SIGN, FIGURE, REPRESENTATION, TOKEN, EMBLEM, MARK, BADGE, TYPE, LETTER.

symbolic: see SUGGESTIVE; TYPICAL.

symbolize: see EXPRESS; INDICATE; REPRESENT.

symmetrical: see REGULAR.

symmetry: see BALANCE; BEAUTY; REGULARITY.

sympathetic *adj.* UNDERSTANDING, warm-hearted, considerate, KIND, compassionate, WARM, TENDER, congenial.

sympathize *v.* UNDERSTAND, FEEL, PITY, condole, HARMONIZE.

sympathy *n.* UNDERSTANDING, empathy, FEELING, AGREEMENT, HARMONY, WARMTH, SENTIMENT, MERCY, compassion, TENDERNESS, kindliness, PITY, fellowship.

symphonic: see MUSICAL.

symphony: see MUSIC.

symptom *n.* EVIDENCE, manifestation, NOTICE, SIGN, TOKEN, MARK, forerunner, TROUBLE, SHOW, showing, APPEARANCE.

synagogue: see CHURCH; SHRINE; TEMPLE.

synchronize: see TIME.

syndicate: see ORGANIZATION; PROTECTION; RACKET; TRUST.

synonym: see WORD.

synonymous: see ALIKE.

synopsis: see SUMMARY.

synthetic: see ARTIFICIAL; CHEMICAL; COMPOSITE.

system *n.* METHOD, PROCEDURE, ORGANIZATION, ARRANGEMENT, ORDER, PLAN, STRATEGY, SCHEME, ideology, RULE, mode, orderliness.

systematic *adj.* methodical, organized, ORDERLY, EFFICIENT, COMPLETE, THOROUGH, REGULAR, steady.

systematically *adv.* methodically, efficiently, COMPLETELY, THOROUGHLY, REGULARLY.

systematize: see ARRANGE; ORGANIZE; REGULATE.

T

tab: see CHECK; FLAP.

tabernacle: see CHURCH; SHRINE.

table *n.* **1** *(to set the table)* COUNTER, STAND, BOARD, LEVEL; **2** *(the table of contents)* SUMMARY, INDEX, LIST, CATALOG, SCHEDULE; **3** *(to set a good table)* menu, FARE, FOOD.
— *v.* POSTPONE, defer, shelve, ADJOURN.

tablecloth: see CLOTH; SPREAD.

table of contents: see CONTENTS; INDEX.

tablet *n.* **1** *(take two tablets with water)* PILL, lozenge, CAPSULE, wafer, cake; **2** *(to write notes on a tablet)* PAD, notebook, PAPER; **3** *(a memorial tablet)* PANEL, slab, plaque.

tabloid: see NEWSPAPER.

taboo: see FORBIDDEN; ILLEGAL; RESTRICTION; SACRED.

tabulate: see CATALOG; CHART; LIST; SCORE.

tabulation: see CATALOG; COUNT.

taciturn: see QUIET.

tack *n.* **1** *(to hammer a tack)* thumbtack, NAIL, stitch; **2** *(to begin on the wrong tack)* DIRECTION, SET, AIM, bent.
— *v.* NAIL, FASTEN, stitch, SET, DIRECT, SHIFT, AIM.

tackle *n.* EQUIPMENT, gear, apparatus, OUTFIT, rigging, ropes, pulley, appliances.
— *v.* **1** *(to tackle a job)* take on, ACCEPT, undertake, TRY; **2** *(to tackle the halfback)* CATCH, GRAB, SEIZE, down.

tacky: see ADHESIVE.

tact *n.* diplomacy, discretion, SENSE, JUDGMENT, delicacy, intuition, prudence.

tactful *adj.* diplomatic, discreet, polite, CAREFUL, judicious, SENSITIVE.

tactic: see MOVE.

tactics *pl.n.* methods, maneuvers, approach, PLAN, expedient, STRATEGY, MANNERS.

tactless: see CLUMSY.

tag *n.* LABEL, identification, TICKET, SLIP, sticker, END, STUB, TIP.
— *v.* LABEL, NAME, MARK, title, TERM, SELECT, PICK, TAP, TOUCH, TRAIL.

tail *n.* END, CONCLUSION, TRAIN, REAR, DOCK, STUB, hind, hind end, rear end.
— *v.* FOLLOW, train, LAG.

tailor: see FIT; SEW.

taint: see CLOUD; INFECT; POISON; POLLUTE; STAIN.

take *v.* **1** *(to take a pen and begin to write)* GET, HOLD, GRIP, GRAB, SEIZE; **2** *(to take firewood into the house)* CARRY, GATHER, pick up, HEAP; **3** *(to take the best one)* PICK, CHOOSE, SELECT; **4** *(to take a complement)* ACCEPT, RECEIVE; **5** *(taken in the act)* CATCH, CAPTURE, TRAP, collar, ensnare, WIN, ACQUIRE; **6** *(the thief took money out of the register)* STEAL, REMOVE, shoplift, ROB; **7** *(to take a course)* ENROLL, ATTEND, FOLLOW; **8** *(to take a pill)* EAT, SWALLOW, CONSUME; **9** *(to take a magazine)* SUBSCRIBE, secure; **10** *(to take sugar in one's coffee)* USE, EMPLOY; **11** *(to take the train)* BOARD, TRAVEL, RIDE; **12** *(to take a girl to a dance)* ESCORT, LEAD, BRING, CONDUCT, GUIDE; **13** *(to take a picture)* SNAP, photograph; **14** *(to take a letter in shorthand)* WRITE, RECORD, NOTE, REGISTER; **15** *(to take a lot of attention)* REQUIRE, NEED, DEMAND; **16** *(to take his own life)* END, KILL; **17** *(the hat took her fancy)* CHARM, ATTRACT; **18** *(do you take my meaning?)* UNDERSTAND, GRASP.
— *n.* proceeds, returns, GATE, CATCH. See also VERSION.

take after: see RESEMBLE.

take amiss: see RESENT.

take apart: see ANALYZE; STRIP.

take away: see REMOVE; SUBTRACT.

take back: see WITHDRAW.

take down: see LOWER; STRIKE.

take in: see ABSORB; ADMIT; GATHER; INCLUDE.

take off: see ASCEND; PEEL; REMOVE.

take on: see TACKLE.

take over: see ASSUME.

take part: see PARTICIPATE.

take place: see HAPPEN; OCCUR.

tale *n.* STORY, ACCOUNT, REPORT, narrative, anecdote, YARN, falsehood, LIE, LEGEND, MYTH.

talent *n.* ABILITY, aptitude, GIFT, SKILL, knack, GENIUS, facility, CLEVERNESS.

talented: see ABLE; CLEVER; EFFICIENT; GIFTED.

talk *n.* **1** *(to give a talk)* SPEECH, ADDRESS, LECTURE, CONFERENCE, oration, CONVERSATION, DISCUSSION, dialogue, UTTERANCE, CHAT; **2** *(oh, that's just talk!)* gossip, RUMOR, reports.
— *v.* SPEAK, SAY, UTTER, ADDRESS, PRONOUNCE, CONVERSE, CONFER, DISCUSS, CONSULT, CONFAB, CHATTER, CHAT, WHISPER, drawl, stutter, gossip.

talkative *adj.* CHATTY, chattering, garrulous, gabby, mouthy, loquacious, voluble.

talker: see LECTURER.

talking: see SPEECH.

tall *adj.* HIGH, towering, lanky, exaggerated, grandiose.

tallness: see HEIGHT.

tallow: see CANDLE.

tally: see BALLOT; BILL; CALCULATE; CHECK; COUNT; NUMBER; RECKON; SCORE.

talon: see CLAW; NAIL.

tam: see CAP.

tame *adj.* **1** *(tame animals)* domesticated, trained, DOMESTIC, subdued, GENTLE, meek; **2** *(a very tame party)* DULL, boring, flat, unexciting, uninteresting, commonplace.
− *v.* domesticate, TRAIN, subdue, DISCIPLINE, MASTER.

tamp: see RAM.

tamper *v.* ALTER, tinker, FOOL, DABBLE, INTERFERE, meddle.

tang: see FLAVOR; TASTE.

tangibility: see SUBSTANCE.

tangle *v.* SNARL, snag, TWIST, ensnare, CONFUSE, COMPLICATE, FIGHT, vie.
− *n.* KNOT, snarl, MESS, muddle, mix-up, foul-up, entanglement.

tangled: see MESSY.

tangy: see SHARP.

tank *n.* CONTAINER, VESSEL, receptacle, tub, cistern, reservoir, sump.

tantalizing: see TEMPTING.

tantrum: see ANGER; SCENE.

tap *v.* **1** *(to tap on a door)* RAP, SLAP, PAT, drum; **2** *(to tap a tank)* DRAW, DRAIN, siphon, pump, eavesdrop, LISTEN.
− *n.* **1** *(a tap on the door)* RAP, KNOCK, PAT; **2** *(open the tap)* faucet, spigot.

tape *n.* ribbon, ROPE, CORD, SEAL, BAND, REEL, recording, transcription.
− *v.* **1** *(to bind with tape)* FASTEN, FIX, MEND, BANDAGE, WRAP; **2** *(to make a tape)* RECORD, transcribe, REGISTER, PRESERVE.

taper *v.* thin, subside, DECREASE, whittle, SHARPEN.
− *n.*: see CANDLE.

taproom: see TAVERN.

tardily: see LATE.

tardy *adj.* LATE, SLOW, laggard, BEHIND, behindhand, overdue.

target *n.* GOAL, DESTINATION, objective, MARK, bull's-eye, butt, scapegoat, quarry.

tariff *n.* TAX, DUTY, levy, CHARGE, RATE, FEE.

tarnish: see BLEMISH; INJURE; POLLUTE; RUST; SPOT; STAIN.

tarnished: see DIM; RUSTY.

tarpaulin: see CANVAS; TENT.

tarry: see DELAY; LAG; LINGER; STALL; STAY; WAIT.

tarrying: see WAITING.

tart: see ACID; BITTER; COOKIE; SHARP; SOUR.

tartness: see BITTERNESS.

tarts: see PASTRY.

task *n.* JOB, CHORE, DUTY, ASSIGNMENT, ERRAND, ENGAGEMENT.

taskmaster: see BOSS.

taste *v.* savor, TRY, TEST, RELISH, EXPERIENCE.
− *n.* **1** *(a bitter taste)* FLAVOR, savor, tang; **2** *(a person of taste)* JUDGMENT, discrimination, TONE, STYLE, TENDENCY.

tasteful: see ARTISTIC; ELEGANT.

tasteless: see FLAT; STALE.

tasty *adj.* savory, APPETIZING, DELICIOUS, luscious, scrumptious.

tatter: see RAG; RENT; SHRED.

tattered: see RAGGED.

tattle: see GAB; SQUEAL.

tattletale: see TELLTALE.

taunt: see MOCK; SNEER; TEASE.

taut: see TIGHT; UPTIGHT.

tavern *n.* saloon, BAR, INN, taproom, pub, roadhouse, cabaret.

tax *n.* levy, TARIFF, DUTY, taxation, TOLL, customs, excise, assessment.
− *v.* assess, exact, levy, DRAIN, TIRE.

taxation: see TAX.

taxi: see CARRIAGE.

taxicab: see AUTOMOBILE.

teach *v.* EDUCATE, INSTRUCT, school, guide, indoctrinate, TRAIN, DRILL, coach.

teacher *n.* INSTRUCTOR, EDUCATOR, PROFESSOR, TUTOR, schoolmaster, coach, guru, mentor, LEADER.

teaching: see PRINCIPLE.

teakettle: see KETTLE.

team *n.* squad, CREW, GANG, troupe, PAIR, YOKE.
— *v.* JOIN, COMBINE, COUPLE, yoke.

teamwork: see COOPERATION.

tear *v.* RIP, SPLIT, SHRED, INJURE, SPEED.
— *n.* **1** *(wear and tear)* SPLIT, rip, OPENING, RENT,
ABUSE; **2** *(to shed tears)* teardrop, droplet,
WATER.

tear down: see LEVEL.

teardrop: see TEAR.

tearful *adj.* SAD, weeping, crying, sobbing,
blubbering, bawling, whimpering.

tear off: see STRIP.

tease *v.* taunt, ANNOY, MOCK, heckle, needle,
PESTER.

technical *adj.* SCIENTIFIC, MECHANICAL,
specialized, detailed, involved.

technicality: see SPECIFICATION.

technician: see SCIENTIST; SPECIALIST.

technique *n.* METHOD, mode, FASHION,
PROCEDURE, STYLE, SKILL, knack.

techniques: see MEANS.

tedious: see DRY; DULL; LONG WINDED;
MONOTONOUS.

tedium: see BOREDOM; MONOTONY.

teen-ager: see MINOR; YOUNGSTER.

teeny: see SMALL; TINY.

teeter: see TOTTER.

teeth: see MOUTH.

telegraph: see CABLE.

telephone: see CALL; PHONE.

telescope: see GLASS.

televise: see AIR; BROADCAST.

tell *v.* SAY, INFORM, ORDER, NARRATE, DESCRIBE,
EXPLAIN, perceive, RECOGNIZE, AFFECT.

telling: see EFFECTIVE; RELATION; TELLTALE.

telltale *adj.* informative, telling, SUGGESTIVE,
meaningful.
— *n.* gossip, tattletale, blabbermouth.

temper *n.* DISPOSITION, STATE, MOOD, HUMOR,
ANGER, FURY, RAGE.
— *v.*: see BLUNT; QUALIFY.

temperament *n.* DISPOSITION, TEMPER, NATURE,
makeup, PERSONALITY, HUMOR.

temperamental *adj.* MOODY, touchy, SENSITIVE,
high-strung, volatile, EMOTIONAL.

temperate: see WARM.

temperature *n.* WARMTH, HEAT, COLD, FEVER,
ILLNESS.

tempest: see GALE; STORM.

tempestuous: see EXPLOSIVE.

temple *n.* CHURCH, synagogue, mosque, pagoda,
SHRINE, sanctuary, pantheon.

tempo: see PACE; SPEED; SWING; TIME.

temporal: see EARTHLY.

temporarily: see AWHILE.

temporary *adj.* BRIEF, passing, MOMENTARY,
transitory, provisional, ephemeral.

tempt *v.* LURE, entice, ATTRACT, bait, seduce,
captivate.

temptation *n.* ATTRACTION, LURE, BAIT, come-on,
fascination, inducement.

tempter: see DEVIL.

tempting *adj.* enticing, enchanting, INVITING,
overwhelming, tantalizing, seductive.

tenacity: see DETERMINATION.

tenancy: see OCCUPATION; RENT.

tenant *n.* renter, occupant, LODGER, roomer,
GUEST, lessee.

tend *v.* **1** *(to tend shop)* ATTEND, WATCH, care for,
oversee, OPERATE; **2** *(to tend to exaggerate)*
incline, LEAN, gravitate.

tendency *n.* leaning, INCLINATION, bias, HABIT,
susceptibility.

tender *adj.* **1** *(the tender years)* YOUNG, INNOCENT,
CHILDISH; **2** *(tender meat)* SOFT, DELICATE, WEAK,
SENSITIVE; **3** *(a tender person)* loving, GENTLE,
kind-hearted; **4** *(tender skin)* SORE, SENSITIVE,
PAINFUL.
— *n.*: see BID; CAR.
— *v.*: see PROPOSE; VOLUNTEER.

tenderize: see SOFTEN.

tenderly *adv.* SOFTLY, gently, KINDLY, fondly.

tenderness *n.* gentleness, AFFECTION, LOVE,
MILDNESS, SYMPATHY.

tending: see LEADING.

tendon: see NERVE.

tenet: see BELIEF.

tense *adj.* TIGHT, taut, STIFF, NERVOUS, uptight, keyed-up.
— *v.* tighten, strain, stiffen, HARDEN.

tenseness: see FIRMNESS.

tension *n.* STRAIN, STRESS, PRESSURE, ANXIETY, worry.

tent *n.* canopy, tarpaulin, SHELTER, PAVILION, tepee, wigwam.
— *v.*: see CAMP.

tentative: see UNDECIDED.

tepee: see TENT.

tepid: see LUKEWARM; MILD.

term *n.* **1** (*a school term*) PERIOD, INTERVAL, SESSION, semester, hitch, stint; **2** (*a vulgar term*) WORD, EXPRESSION, designation, LABEL; **3** (*terms and conditions*) CONDITION, clause, provision, stipulation.
— *v.* CALL, NAME, dub, TAG, characterize.

terminal: see CONCLUSIVE; FINAL; OUTLET; STATION.

terminate: see ADJOURN; CEASE; CONCLUDE; END; EXPIRE.

termination: see CONCLUSION; END; ENDING; FINISH.

terminology: see VOCABULARY.

terminus: see DESTINATION.

terms: see SETTLEMENT.

terrace: see LAWN.

terrain: see ENVIRONMENT; TERRITORY.

terrible *adj.* AWFUL, FEARFUL, awesome, DREADFUL, UNFORTUNATE, SEVERE, EXTREME.

terribly *adv.* dreadfully, awfully, badly, seriously, EXTREMELY.

terrific *adj.* GREAT, IMMENSE, TREMENDOUS, MARVELOUS, SENSATIONAL, TERRIBLE, shocking.

terrified: see PANICKY.

terrify *v.* FRIGHTEN, appall, ALARM, STUN.

terrifying: see FEARFUL; SCARY.

territorial: see LOCAL.

territory *n.* LAND, terrain, GROUND, PROPERTY, DISTRICT, REGION, domain, realm, COLONY, NEIGHBORHOOD.

terror *n.* **1** (*full of terror*) DREAD, FEAR, HORROR,

PANIC; **2** (*Joey is a terror*) RASCAL, BRAT, imp, NUISANCE.

terry: see TOWEL.

terse: see BRIEF; COMPACT.

test *n.* EXAMINATION, QUIZ, INSPECTION, CHECK, ANALYSIS, TRIAL, dry run, ordeal.
— *v.* EXAMINE, quiz, VERIFY, TRY, TASTE, ANALYZE.

testament: see WILL.

testify *v.* DECLARE, assert, INDICATE, PROVE, WITNESS, SWEAR, CERTIFY, WARRANT.

testimonial: see MEMORIAL; RECOMMENDATION; TRIBUTE.

testimony *n.* DECLARATION, EVIDENCE, PROOF, WITNESS.

testiness: see MEANNESS.

testing: see TRIAL.

tether: see CHAIN; STRAP.

tethered: see BOUND.

text *n.* **1** (*the text for the course*) BOOK, textbook, manual; **2** (*a few pages of text*) CONTENTS, subject matter, BODY, writings; **3** (*the text to be discussed*) TOPIC, THEME, VERSE, PASSAGE.

textbook: see TEXT.

textile *n.* CLOTH, FABRIC, MATERIAL, GOODS.
— *adj.* WOVEN, interwoven, interlaced, FIBER.

texture *n.* QUALITY, makeup, fineness, feel, essence, STRUCTURE, COMPOSITION.

thank *v.* ACKNOWLEDGE, APPRECIATE, RECOGNIZE, BLESS.

thankful *adj.* APPRECIATIVE, GRATEFUL, obliged, pleased, beholden, indebted.

thankfulness: see GRATITUDE.

thanks *pl.n.* APPRECIATION, GRATITUDE, acknowledgment, thanksgiving.

thanksgiving: see THANKS.

thaw *v.* MELT, liquefy, DISSOLVE, warm up, SOFTEN, relent.

theater *n.* **1** (*I love the theater*) DRAMA, STAGE, theatrics, dramatics, plays; **2** (*a small theater*) playhouse, amphitheater, cinema, HALL, auditorium; **3** (*theater of war*) battleground, FRONT, FIELD, ARENA, AREA.

theatric: see DRAMATIC.

theatrics: see THEATER.

theft *n.* thievery, larceny, ROBBERY, stick-up, BURGLARY, plunder.

theme *n.* TOPIC, SUBJECT, MOTIVE, MESSAGE, MORAL, PAPER, ESSAY, MELODY, leitmotif, concept.

then *adv.* thereupon, thence, AFTERWARDS, FORMERLY, BEFORE, NEXT.
— *conj.* THEREFORE, consequently.
— *adj.* onetime, FORMER, PREVIOUS, PAST.

thence: see THEN; THEREAFTER; THEREFORE.

theoretical: see SUPPOSED.

theoretically: see SUPPOSEDLY.

theorize: see ASSUME.

theory *n.* **1** *(the guiding theory)* hypothesis, premise, assumption; **2** *(I have a theory)* speculation, GUESS, SUSPICION, IDEA.

therapeutic: see CORRECTIVE; MEDICAL.

therapeutics: see MEDICINE.

there: see HERE.

thereafter *adv.* AFTERWARDS, thence, henceforth, subsequently.

therefore *adv.* consequently, thence, THEN, HENCE.

thereupon: see SINCE; THEN.

thermos: see BOTTLE.

thesaurus: see DICTIONARY; VOCABULARY.

thesis: see ESSAY; PAPER.

thick *adj.* **1** *(a thick book)* HEFTY, WIDE, LARGE, HEAVY; **2** *(a thick paste)* DENSE, soupy, gluey; **3** *(a thick jungle)* DENSE, packed, cramped, COMPACT; **4** *(thick and stubborn)* STUPID, DULL, RETARDED, SLOW. See also CHUMMY.

thicken: see CONDENSE.

thicket: see BUSH; GROVE; JUNGLE.

thickness *n.* **1** *(the thickness of batter)* density, heaviness, fluidity; **2** *(the thickness of a tree)* breadth, WIDTH, girth, DIAMETER, DEPTH, SIZE.

thief *n.* ROBBER, CROOK, BURGLAR, housebreaker, shoplifter, pickpocket, CRIMINAL, yegg.

thieve *v.* STEAL, pilfer, embezzle, defraud, SWINDLE, CHEAT, fleece, gyp.

thievery: see BURGLARY; PIRACY; THEFT.

thin *adj.* NARROW, SLIM, SLENDER, skinny, FLIMSY, WEAK, sheer, sparse, meager, scant, wispy.
— *v.*: see TAPER.

thing *n.* OBJECT, MATTER, AFFAIR, ITEM, DEED, SITUATION, IDEA, POSSESSION, SOMETHING, thingumabob, gadget, gimmick, gizmo, contraption.

things: see LUGGAGE; STUFF.

thingumabob: see THING.

think *v.* meditate, REFLECT, contemplate, CONSIDER, CALCULATE, EXPECT, BELIEVE, GUESS, IMAGINE, REMEMBER, conceive, mull.

thinkable *adj.* POSSIBLE, believable, imaginable, ponderable, assumable, presumable, conceivable.

thinker: see STUDENT.

thinking *n.* THOUGHT, reasoning, contemplation, REFLECTION, supposition, speculation, cognition, cerebration.

think up: see DEVISE.

thinly: see FEW.

thin-skinned: see SENSITIVE.

thirst *n.* dryness, craving, DESIRE, longing.
— *v.* CRAVE, DESIRE, YEARN, hunger, covet.

thirsty: see DRY.

thong: see BAND; STRAP.

thorax: see BREAST; CHEST.

thorn *n.* NEEDLE, SPINE, barb, prickle, ANNOYANCE, NUISANCE, WOE.

thorough *adj.* COMPLETE, TOTAL, ABSOLUTE, sheer, meticulous, painstaking, diligent.

thoroughbred: see HORSE.

thoroughfare: see ROAD; STREET.

thoroughly *adv.* VERY, COMPLETELY, ENTIRELY, PURELY, perfectly, utterly.

though *conj.* DESPITE, ALTHOUGH, even if.
— *adv.* HOWEVER, NEVERTHELESS.

thought *n.* **1** *(the power of thought)* THINKING, CONSIDERATION, REFLECTION; **2** *(a thought occurred to me)* IDEA, NOTION, concept, CONCERN, REGARD; **3** *(that was my thought)* INTENTION, PLAN, HOPE, AIM.

thoughtful *adj.* considerate, CAREFUL, KINDLY, CONCERNED, kind-hearted, contemplative, reflective.

thoughtfulness: see KINDNESS; POLITENESS.

thoughtless *adj.* inconsiderate, CARELESS, unconcerned, unthinking, neglectful, heedless, unreflective.

thought-provoking: see SUGGESTIVE.

thought-up: see MADE-UP.

thrash *v.* **1** *(the fish thrashed about)* flail, TOSS, writhe, FLUTTER, STRUGGLE; **2** *(I'll thrash you)* BEAT, WHIP, PUNISH, BATTER, STRIKE.

thread *n.* STRING, YARN, FIBER, filament, RIDGE, TRACK, knurl, THEME, IDEA.
— *v.* insert, wire, ATTACH.

threadbare: see OLD; SHABBY; USED.

threat *n.* **1** *(to make a threat)* MENACE, RISK, WARNING, DANGER; **2** *(the threat of rain)* POSSIBILITY, CHANCE, probability, forecast.

threaten *v.* MENACE, intimidate, WARN, SCARE, impend, APPROACH.

threatening: see ALARMING; ANGRY; DANGEROUS; UGLY.

three-demensional: see SOLID.

thresh: see MASH.

threshold: see BORDER.

thrift *n.* ECONOMY, austerity, frugality, prudence.

thriftless: see WASTEFUL.

thrifty *adj.* frugal, ECONOMICAL, austere, SPARING.

thrill *v.* ROUSE, animate, EXCITE, TINGLE.
— *n.* EXCITEMENT, stimulation, kicks, BANG, VIBRATION.

thrive *v.* LIVE, GROW, BLOSSOM, PROSPER, SUCCEED, get along.

throb *v.* pulsate, BEAT, palpitate.
— *n.* BEAT, PULSE, heartbeat.

thrombus: see CLOT.

throng: see CONGREGATE; CROWD; FLOCK; HOST; JAM; MULTITUDE; SWARM; TROOP.

throttle: see CHOKE; SMOTHER; WRING.

through *prep.* via, BY, DURING, THROUGHOUT, FOR.
— *adv.* THROUGHOUT, COMPLETELY, ALONG.

throughout *prep.* THROUGH, AMIDST, ALONG, DURING.
— *adv.* EVERYWHERE, TOTALLY, ALWAYS.

throw *v.* HURL, CAST, PITCH, TOSS, HEAVE.
— *n.* TOSS, PITCH, SHOT, heave.

throw back: see REFLECT.

throw off: see CAST.

throw out: see DISCARD.

thrust *v.* PUSH, POKE, SHOVE, jab, RAM, DRIVE.
— *n.* PUSH, jab, shove, DRIVE, ATTACK, FORCE, implication, SENSE, DIRECTION.

thruster: see ROCKET.

thrusting: see FORCEFUL.

thud: see THUMP.

thug: see GANGSTER; HOOD; ROBBER.

thumb: see FINGER.

thumbtack: see TACK.

thump *n.* thud, CRASH, clunk, slam, BLOW.
— *v.* clunk, plop, FALL, BEAT, clobber, POUND, drub.

thunder *n.* ROAR, RUMBLE, CLAP, NOISE, BOOM.
— *v.* ROAR, rumble, EXPLODE, SHOUT.

thunderbolt: see BOLT.

thunderclap: see CLAP.

thunderstorm: see STORM.

thus *adv.* THEREFORE, HENCE, SO, accordingly.

thwart: see AVERT; CROSS; DISCOURAGE; FOIL; OPPOSE; PREVENT.

thwarting: see PREVENTION.

tiara: see CROWN.

tick *n.* CLICK, TAP, BEAT, THROB, PULSE.
— *v.* CLICK, BEAT, CHECK, SCORE.

ticket *n.* FARE, ADMISSION, CHECK, TAG, LABEL, STUB, PASS, SUMMONS, slate, CARD.
— *v.* TAG, LABEL, SUMMON, RESERVE, book.

tickle *v.* TINGLE, itch, STROKE, AMUSE, DELIGHT.
— *n.*: see TINGLE.

ticklish *adj.* DELICATE, unstable, unsteady, DANGEROUS, UNCERTAIN, precarious, RISKY, touchy.

tide *n.* flux, RISE, FALL, FLOOD, WAVE, MULTITUDE.

tidiness: see CLEANLINESS; NEATNESS.

tidings *pl.n.* NEWS, REPORT, INFORMATION, WORD.

tidy *adj.* NEAT, ORDERLY, TRIM, CONSIDERABLE, SIZABLE, LARGE.
— *v.*: see ARRANGE; GROOM.

tie *v.* LINK, FASTEN, KNOT, ATTACH, CONNECT, RELATE, even, equal, MATCH.
— *n.* LINK, CONNECTION, BAND, necktie, TIMBER, joist. See also DRAW.

tied: see BOUND; EVEN.

tier: see ROW.

tiff: see SCRAP.

tight *adj.* fast, SECURE, taut, SHUT, SNUG, skin-tight, FULL, stingy, SCARCE.

tighten: see FIX; SECURE; STRAIN; TENSE.

tightener: see NUT.

tight-lipped: see SILENT.

tightly: see CLOSE; FIRMLY.

tightwad: see MISER.

tile: see BOARD.

till *conj.* UNTIL, before.
— *prep.* UNTIL, up to, to, BEFORE.
— *v.* CULTIVATE, PLOW, WORK, FARM, fertilize, PREPARE.

tilt *v.* incline, TIP, LEAN, list.
— *n.* SLANT, INCLINATION, SLOPE, bias, TENDENCY.

timber *n.* **1** (*acres of timber*) LUMBER, WOOD, GROVE, FOREST, woodland; **2** (*the roof timber*) BEAM, rafter, BOARD, LOG, LUMBER.

timberland: see FOREST.

time *n.* duration, PERIOD, AGE, ERA, HOUR, OCCASION, instance, EXPERIENCE, OPPORTUNITY, LIBERTY, LEISURE, SPEED, PACE, tempo.
— *v.* MEASURE, CHECK, clock, synchronize.

time-honored: see ANCIENT; OLD.

timekeeper: see CLOCK.

timeless: see IMMORTAL; PERMANENT.

timelessness: see ETERNITY.

timely: see PROMPT.

timepiece: see CLOCK.

timer: see CLOCK.

timetable: see CALENDAR; SCHEDULE.

timeworn: see OLD.

timid *adj.* SHY, HUMBLE, FEARFUL, indecisive, sheepish, COWARDLY.

timidity *n.* shyness, MODESTY, RESERVE, FEAR, HESITATION, cowardice.

timidly: see COWARDLY.

timing: see PERIOD.

tin: see CAN; METAL.

ting-a-ling: see RING.

tinge: see CAST; COLOR; DASH; SHADE; TINT.

tingle *v.* prickle, TICKLE, THRILL, SHIVER, itch, jingle.
— *n.* tickle, itch, quiver, numbness.

tiniest: see LEAST.

tinker: see DABBLE; TAMPER.

tinkle: see RING.

tint *n.* COLOR, SHADE, tinge, hue, DYE, HINT, SUGGESTION.
— *v.* SHADE, COLOR, DYE.

tiny *adj.* LITTLE, MINIATURE, teeny, diminutive, microscopic.

tip *n.* **1** (*the finger tip*) POINT, END, PEAK, extremity; **2** (*to leave a tip*) GIFT, bribe, baksheesh; **3** (*a hot tip*) ADVICE, pointer, HINT, INFORMATION, tipoff.
— *v.* **1** (*to tip the waiter*) REWARD, BRIBE; **2** (*to tip over*) LEAN, TILT, FALL, topple, UPSET. See also HINT.

tip off: see ALERT.

tipoff: see CLUE; TIP.

tippled: see DRUNK.

tipsy: see DRUNK.

tire *v.* flag, DROOP, weary, fatigue, wear out, TAX, EXHAUST, ANNOY, BORE.

tired *adj.* exhausted, fatigued, WEARY, overworked, SLEEPY, drowsy, droopy.

tiredness: see EXHAUSTION; FATIGUE; WEARINESS.

tiresome: see DRY; MONOTONOUS; TROUBLESOME.

tissue *n.* WEB, mesh, FABRIC, gauze, onionskin, HANDKERCHIEF, membrane, muscle, FLESH, BONE.

titan: see MONSTER.

title *n.* **1** (*a book title*) NAME, designation, caption; **2** (*to hold title*) ownership, DEED, RIGHT; **3** (*to confer a title*) HONOR, RANK, nobility, MERIT, DISTINCTION, championship.
— *v.*: see CALL; ENTITLE; TAG.

titled: see NOBLE.

titles: see CATALOG.

titter: see CHUCKLE; GIGGLE; LAUGH; SNICKER.

tittle: see DOT.

tizzy: see FLUTTER.

TNT: see EXPLOSIVE.

to: see ONTO; TILL; TOWARD.

toast *n.* PRAISE, HONOR, SALUTE, PROPOSAL. See also BREAD.
— *v.* **1** (*to toast bread*) brown, HEAT, WARM; **2** (*to toast a guest*) SALUTE, HONOR, PRAISE.

toastmaster: see CHAIRMAN.

today: see NOWADAYS; PRESENT.

to-do: see COMMOTION; FUSS.

toe: see FINGER; FOOT.

toenail: see NAIL.

together *adv.* jointly, collectively, simultaneously, continuously.

toil *v.* LABOR, drudge, slog, STRAIN, SWEAT, SLAVE.
— *n.* LABOR, drudgery, EXERTION, EFFORT, travail.

toiler: see WORKER.

toilet *n.* **1** *(to flush the toilet)* stool, latrine, commode, urinal; **2** *(a public toilet)* bathroom, lavatory, washroom, privy; **3** *(she has finished her toilet)* dressing, DRESS, attire, apparel, BATH, makeup.

toilsome: see HARD.

token *n.* SYMBOL, SIGN, COIN, medallion, slug, memento, TROPHY, MINIMUM.

told: see ORAL; VERBAL.

tolerable *adj.* bearable, endurable, DECENT, RESPECTABLE, acceptable.

tolerance *n.* forbearance, PATIENCE, CHARITY, indulgence, RESISTANCE.

tolerant: see CHARITABLE; LIBERAL; PERMISSIVE; PROGRESSIVE.

tolerate: see ABIDE BY; ACCEPT; ALLOW; ENDURE; LET; PERMIT; STAND; SUFFER.

toll *n.* FEE, TAX, levy, COST, PRICE, DUTY.
— *v.*: see RING.

tomb *n.* GRAVE, sepulcher, VAULT, crypt, mausoleum.

tombstone: see STONE.

tombstones: see CEMETERY.

tomfoolery: see NONSENSE.

tomorrow: see FUTURE.

tone *n.* **1** *(a musical tone)* NOTE, PITCH; **2** *(a color tone)* SHADE, hue, TINT; **3** *(his ideas lend tone)* STYLE, QUALITY, atmosphere, ELEGANCE.
— *v.*: see SHADOW.

tones: see HARMONY.

tongue *n.* LANGUAGE, SPEECH, dialect, idiom.
— *v.*: see LICK.

tonic: see REFRESHMENTS.

too *adv.* ALSO, FURTHERMORE, MOREOVER, LIKEWISE, EXCEEDINGLY, overly, EXTREMELY.

tool *n.* IMPLEMENT, UTENSIL, DEVICE, gadget, contrivance, MEANS, MEDIUM.
— *v.*: see CARVE.

tools: see EQUIPMENT.

tooth *n.* fang, tusk, prong, cog, RIDGE, point, spike, incisor, molar, bicuspid.

top *n.* **1** *(the top of the hill)* TIP, PEAK, SUMMIT, HEAD, ROOF; **2** *(a bottle top)* CAP, LID, STOPPER, COVER; **3** *(to reach the top)* zenith, acme, pinnacle, HEAD, LEAD, FRONT.
— *v.* **1** *(to top an opponent)* SURPASS, best, EXCEED, OUTDO; **2** *(to top something off)* CAP, COVER, CROWN, FINISH, COMPLETE.
— *adj.*: see FIRST-RATE.

top-drawer: see SUPREME.

toper: see DRUNK.

topic *n.* SUBJECT, ISSUE, MATTER, POINT, THEME, OPINION.

top-notch: see FIRST-RATE.

topping: see SPREAD.

topple: see COLLAPSE; FLOOR; TIP; UPSET.

toppling: see DESTRUCTION.

tops: see BEST.

torch *n.* LAMP, flashlight, beacon, firebrand.

torment *v.* TORTURE, MISTREAT, TEASE, vex.
— *n.* ABUSE, PAIN, AGONY, SUFFERING.

tormented: see HAUNTED; SUFFERING.

tormenting: see CURSED.

tormentor: see BULLY.

torn: see RAGGED.

tornado: see STORM; WIND.

torpid: see ASLEEP.

torque: see TWIST.

torrent *n.* FLOOD, downpour, FLOW, RUSH, cascade, outburst, DISCHARGE.

torridity: see HEAT.

torso: see BODY; FIGURE; TRUNK.

tort: see WRONG.

torture *n.* TORMENT, ABUSE, PAIN, SUFFERING, AGONY.
— *v.* TORMENT, MISTREAT, ABUSE, afflict, distort, TWIST.

toss *v.* CAST, HURL, PITCH, FLING, SWAY, SQUIRM.
— *n.* PITCH, THROW, heave, lob, shake.

toss-up: see CHANCE.

tot: see BABY; INFANT.

total *adj.* COMPLETE, ENTIRE, WHOLE, FULL, outright.
— *n.* WHOLE, SUM, entirety, aggregation, totality, ALL.
— *v.*: see ADD; AMOUNT; NUMBER; SUM; SUMMARIZE.

totality: see ALL; TOTAL; WHOLE.

totally *adv.* FULLY, ENTIRELY, COMPLETELY, utterly.

tote: see CARRY; CART.

totem: see IDOL.

totter *v.* teeter, SWAY, lurch, STAGGER.

tottering: see INSECURE.

touch *v.* FEEL, CONTACT, FINGER, HANDLE, manipulate, INVOLVE, AFFECT, MOVE.
— *n.* FEELING, CONTACT, feel, COMMUNICATION, STYLE, trace, BIT, smidgen.

touched: see CRAZY.

touching: see CONCERNING; PITIFUL.

touchy: see CROSS; IRRITABLE; MOODY; SENSITIVE; SOUR; TEMPERAMENTAL; TICKLISH.

tough *adj.* STRONG, RUGGED, resilient, STURDY, LASTING, STUBBORN, unyielding, FIERCE, ROUGH.
— *n.*: see BULLY; HOOD; ROWDY.

toughen: see HARDEN; STRENGTHEN.

toughness: see STRENGTH.

tour *n.* **1** *(to take a tour)* TRIP, VOYAGE, VISIT, sightseeing, excursion, VACATION; **2** *(to serve a tour)* SHIFT, hitch, STRETCH, enlistment.
— *v.*: see CAMPAIGN; HIKE; TRAVEL.

tourist *n.* TRAVELER, sightseer, vacationer, VISITOR.

tournament *n.* CONTEST, GAME, MATCH, tourney, COMPETITION, CLASH, duel.

tourney: see TOURNAMENT.

tow *v.* PULL, TUG, DRAG, HAUL, lug.
— *n.* PULL, DRAG, LIFT, ASSISTANCE.

toward *prep.* to, FOR, regarding, NEAR.

towel *n.* drier, wiper, NAPKIN, CLOTH, RAG, terry.
— *v.*: see DRY.

tower *n.* turret, fortification, spire, steeple, watchtower, crow's-nest.
— *v.* DOMINATE, overlook, RISE, excel.

towering: see HIGH; LOFTY; TALL.

town *n.* VILLAGE, hamlet, municipality, township, COMMUNITY, SETTLEMENT.

township: see TOWN.

toxic: see POISON; POISONOUS.

toy *n.* plaything, GAME, DOLL, gadget, TRIFLE, miniature, MODEL.
— *v.*: see DABBLE; TRIFLE.

trace *n.* **1** *(a trace of sadness)* BIT, TOUCH, DAB, HINT, smidgen; **2** *(without a trace)* SIGH, EVIDENCE, TRACK, TRAIL.
— *v.* **1** *(to trace stolen goods)* TRACK, HUNT, PURSUE, ascertain; **2** *(to trace a silhouette)* OUTLINE, COPY, DRAW, SKETCH.

track *n.* **1** *(a mountain track)* TRAIL, ROAD, RAIL, railroad, PATH; **2** *(to leave a track)* TRACE, MARK, FOOTPRINT, fingerprint, SCENT; **3** *(a race track)* COURSE, speedway.
— *v.* TRACE, PURSUE, TAIL, HUNT, MONITOR, SHADOW.

tracker: see HUNTER.

tract *n.* plot, LOT, PARCEL, acreage, PROPERTY, TERRITORY.

trade *n.* COMMERCE, BUSINESS, barter, EXCHANGE, DEAL, clientele, OCCUPATION, CRAFT.
— *v.* EXCHANGE, barter, patronize, swap, BUY, SELL.

trademark: see BRAND; LABEL; SIGNATURE.

trader *n.* buyer, seller, MERCHANT, DEALER, businessman, salesman, saleswoman, salesperson.

tradesman: see MERCHANT.

tradition *n.* CUSTOM, PRACTICE, ritual, rite, LEGEND, TALE, folklore, folkway.

traditional *adj.* CUSTOMARY, HABITUAL, age-old, legendary, MYTHICAL.

traffic *n.* **1** *(vehicular traffic)* transit, MOVEMENT, TRAVEL, PASSAGE; **2** *(illicit drug traffic)* COMMERCE, TRADE, BUSINESS.

trafficker: see DEALER.

tragedy *n.* MISFORTUNE, DISASTER, calamity, DOOM, HARDSHIP, DRAMA, melodrama.

tragic *adj.* FATAL, UNLUCKY, SAD, disastrous, grim.

trail *v.* FOLLOW, PURSUE, TRACK, TAIL, SHADOW.
— *n.* PATH, TRACK, ROAD, FOOTPRINT, SCENT, CHAIN, SERIES.

train *n.* **1** *(a train of events)* SERIES, CHAIN, SEQUENCE; **2** *(a night train)* express, local, FREIGHT, el, caravan; **3** *(the queen's train)*

entourage, cortege, FOLLOWER.
— *v.* TEACH, EDUCATE, DRILL, coach, POINT. See
also TAIL.

trained: see LEARNED; PRACTICED; SKILLED; TAME.

trainer: see EDUCATOR; INSTRUCTOR; TUTOR.

training *n.* schooling, EDUCATION, DRILL,
PRACTICE, EXERCISE.

trainman: see CONDUCTOR.

trait *n.* CHARACTERISTIC, QUALITY, PROPERTY,
FEATURE, CHARACTER.

traitor *n.* betrayer, turncoat, quisling, SPY,
deserter, deceiver, REBEL, mutineer,
revolutionary.

traitorous: see TREACHEROUS.

tramp *v.* WANDER, HIKE, MARCH, WALK, ROAM,
STAMP, TRAMPLE, tromp.
— *n.* wanderer, BUM, hobo, BEGGAR, vagrant,
DRIFTER.

trample *v.* TRAMP, CRUSH, crunch, squash,
tromp.

tranquil *adj.* QUIET, PEACEFUL, serene, placid,
CALM, unruffled, undisturbed, STEADY.

tranquilize: see CALM; SOOTHE; STILL.

tranquillity *n.* quietness, PEACE, serenity,
CALMNESS, STEADINESS, nirvana.

transaction *n.* TRADE, negotiation, BUSINESS,
DEAL, ACTION, DEED, PROCESS, proceeding,
implementation.

transcend: see SURPASS.

transcendent: see UPWARD.

transcribe: see RECORD; TAPE.

transcript *n.* COPY, IMITATION, DUPLICATE,
reproduction, RECORD, transcription.

transcription: see DICTATION; DUPLICATION; TAPE;
TRANSCRIPT.

transfer *v.* EXCHANGE, TRADE, MOVE, CHANGE,
SHIFT, TRANSPORT, CARRY, TRANSMIT, ASSIGN,
transpose, TRANSPLANT, SELL, GIVE.
— *n.* EXCHANGE, TRADE, TRANSPORT, TICKET,
ASSIGNMENT, transference, transplantation,
transmittance.

transferable: see PORTABLE.

transferal: see EXCHANGE.

transference: see TRANSFER.

transfigure: see TRANSFORM.

transform *v.* CHANGE, CONVERT, revolutionize,
transmute, transfigure.

transformation *n.* CHANGE, conversion,
metamorphosis, changeover, REVOLUTION,
rearrangement.

transformer: see ENGINE.

transient: see DRIFTER; MORTAL.

transit: see BRIDGE; TRAFFIC; TRANSPORTATION.

transitory: see TEMPORARY.

translate *v.* **1** *(to translate a foreign language)*
INTERPRET, reword, decipher, decode, EXPLAIN;
2 *(to translate wishes into deeds)* CHANGE,
CONVERT, MOVE, TRANSFORM, transpose.

translation *n.* INTERPRETATION, EXPLANATION,
VERSION, transposition.

translucent: see TRANSPARENT.

transmission: see BEAM; SIGNAL.

transmit *v.* SEND, PASS, DISPATCH, convey,
TRANSFER, MAIL, ISSUE, CONDUCT.

transmittance: see TRANSFER.

transmitter: see CONDUCTOR.

transmute: see TRANSFORM.

transparency: see SLIDE.

transparent *adj.* CLEAR, translucent, crystal,
sheer, EVIDENT, APPARENT, OBVIOUS, PLAIN,
undisguised.

transpire: see HAPPEN; PERSPIRE.

transplant *v.* CHANGE, MOVE, REMOVE, TRANSFER,
reestablish, SHIFT, displace, transpose.

transplantation: see TRANSFER.

transport *v.* CARRY, MOVE, TRANSFER, convey.
— *n.* carrying, moving, sending, TRANSFER,
shipment.

transportation *n.* carrying, TRANSFER,
movement, transit, haulage, hauling, FARE,
portage, shipment.

transpose: see TRANSFER; TRANSLATE;
TRANSPLANT.

transposition: see TRANSLATION.

transversely: see ACROSS.

trap *n.* snare, pitfall, deadfall, NET, ambush,
TRICK, deception.
— *v.* ensnare, entrap, snare, NET, bag, CATCH,
TRICK, FOOL, DECEIVE.

trapped: see ENTANGLED.

trapper: see HUNTER.

trash *n.* GARBAGE, JUNK, debris, RUBBISH, SCRAP, LITTER, rubble.

trashy *adj.* junky, INFERIOR, paltry, WORTHLESS, USELESS, unimportant, insignificant.

travail: see CHORE; TOIL.

travel *v.* GO, PASS, MOVE, journey, cruise, SAIL, CROSS, commute, tour, ply.
— *n.* tourism, TRIP, TOUR, VOYAGE, excursion, JOURNEY, jaunt, junket, cruise, EXPEDITION.

traveler *n.* voyager, wayfarer, TOURIST, rider, PASSENGER, commuter, globe-trotter, PILGRIM, salesman.

traverse: see CROSS.

tray *n.* plate, platter, server, salver, DISH, receptacle, CONTAINER, waiter.

treacherous *adj.* TRICKY, SHIFTY, FALSE, untrue, deceitful, dishonest, disloyal, traitorous, deceiving, insidious, DANGEROUS, INSECURE, MISLEADING.

treachery *n.* TRICKERY, deceit, dishonesty, deception, disloyalty, TREASON, faithlessness, unfaithfulness, lying.

tread *v.* step, WALK, PRESS, CRUSH, TRAMPLE.
— *n.* **1** (*his tread resounded*) STEP, FOOTSTEP, stepping, TRAMP, walking, stride; **2** (*the tread of a tire*) surface, PATTERN, grooves.

treason *n.* betrayal, TREACHERY, disloyalty, REBELLION, desertion.

treasure *n.* WEALTH, RICHES, ABUNDANCE, PRIZE, valuables, MONEY, GOLD.
— *v.*: see CHERISH; ESTEEM.

treasured: see FAVORITE.

treasure-trove: see FIND; FORTUNE.

treasury: see BANK; PURSE.

treat *v.* **1** (*to treat a guest*) ENTERTAIN, host, GRATIFY, DELIGHT, REWARD; **2** (*to treat a cough*) CURE, HEAL, DOCTOR, TEND, ATTEND, remedy; **3** (*to treat a question*) CONSIDER, DISCUSS, REGARD, HANDLE, MANAGE, negotiate.
— *n.* PLEASURE, JOY, DELIGHT, GIFT, REWARD, PRESENT, ENTERTAINMENT, gratification.

treatise: see PAMPHLET.

treatment *n.* **1** (*the treatment we received in the hospital*) CARE, CURE, ATTENTION, REMEDY, MEDICINE, medicament, therapy, doctoring, hospitalization; **2** (*the teacher's treatment of equations*) handling, approach, MANNER.

treaty *n.* pact, AGREEMENT, COMPACT, COMPROMISE, TRUCE.

trek: see MARCH; TRUDGE.

trellis: see LACE.

tremble *v.* SHAKE, SHIVER, SHUDDER, QUIVER, quaver, waver, FLUTTER, VIBRATE, THROB.
— *n.*: see VIBRATION.

tremendous *adj.* IMMENSE, ENORMOUS, GIGANTIC, colossal, VAST, HUGE, GREAT, FINE, EXCELLENT, outrageous.

tremor: see SHOCK; SHUDDER.

trench *n.* DITCH, gully, dike, moat, OPENING, CHANNEL.

trend *n.* TENDENCY, DIRECTION, INCLINATION, DRIFT.

trespass *v.* infringe, overstep, INTRUDE, encroach, INVADE, SIN, err.
— *n.*: see INTRUSION; SIN.

trespasser: see INVADER.

trespassing: see MEDDLESOME.

tress: see LOCK.

tresses: see HAIR.

trestle: see BENCH; BRIDGE.

trial *n.* **1** (*witness at the trial*) hearing, lawsuit, SUIT, CASE, CONTEST; **2** (*two weeks' free trial*) TEST, testing, EXPERIMENT, PROOF, ANALYSIS, TRY, ENDEAVOR, EFFORT; **3** (*comfort in the hour of trial*) HARDSHIP, DIFFICULTY, SUFFERING, ordeal, TROUBLE, AFFLICTION.
— *adj.* PRELIMINARY, TEMPORARY, preparatory, TEST.

tribe *n.* CLASS, GROUP, DIVISION, clan, FAMILY, NATION, PEOPLE, KIND, TYPE, stock.

tribunal: see COURT.

tributary: see BRANCH; RIVER.

tribute *n.* PAYMENT, COMPLIMENT, testimonial, RECOGNITION.

trick *n.* **1** (*to play tricks*) JOKE, JEST, prank, FRAUD, ILLUSION, deception; **2** (*the trick of keeping afloat*) knack, SKILL, ART, TECHNIQUE.
— *v.* FOOL, DECEIVE, beguile, dupe, humbug, CHEAT, bamboozle, defraud, SWINDLE, outsmart.

trickery *n.* ILLUSION, deception, cheating, FRAUD, knavery, chicanery.

trickle *v.* DRIBBLE, DROP, LEAK, seep, ooze.
— *n.*: see LEAK.

trickster: see CHEAT; FOX; FRAUD; IMPOSTOR; MAGICIAN; SWINDLER.

tricky *adj.* crafty, wily, SHIFTY, SLY, TREACHEROUS, DIFFICULT, confusing.

trifle *n.* BIT, TRACE, PARTICLE, iota, trinket, smidgen, nonessential, NOTHING.
 — *v.* dawdle, WASTE, toy, dally, PLAY.

trifling: see PETTY.

trigger: see CAUSE.

trim *v.* **1** *(to trim a hedge)* CLIP, pare, CROP, prune, SHORTEN, curtail, ADJUST, BALANCE; **2** *(to trim the Christmas tree)* DECORATE, ORNAMENT, ADORN.
 — *n.* **1** *(in fine trim)* CONDITION, FITNESS, STATE; **2** *(to paint the trim)* trimming, decoration, ORNAMENT, edging, woodwork; **3** *(to have a trim)* haircut, CUT.
 — *adj.* NEAT, TIDY, ORDERLY.

trimming: see FRINGE; TRIM.

trinket: see TRIFLE.

trip *v.* STUMBLE, FALL, SKIP, SLIP, bungle, blunder, err, RELEASE.
 — *n.* **1** *(to take a trip)* JOURNEY, excursion, VOYAGE, VACATION, cruise, TOUR; **2** *(a bad trip on LSD)* high, hallucination, intoxication.

trite: see STALE; USED.

triumph *n.* VICTORY, SUCCESS, exultation, ACHIEVEMENT, CONQUEST, mastery.
 — *v.* SUCCEED, WIN, prevail, ACHIEVE, ATTAIN, OVERCOME.

triumphant: see SUCCESSFUL; VICTORIOUS.

trivial: see MINOR; MINUTE; PETTY; SHALLOW; SMALL; VAIN.

tromp: see TRAMP; TRAMPLE.

troop *n.* CROWD, COMPANY, GROUP, BAND, UNIT.
 — *v.* MARCH, CONGREGATE, throng, flock.

trooper: see OFFICER; VETERAN.

troops *pl.n.* soldiers, ARMY, forces.

trophy *n.* PRIZE, AWARD, memento, keepsake, statuette, plaque, MEDAL.

trot: see RUN.

troubadour: see SINGER.

trouble *v.* BOTHER, PLAGUE, PESTER, WORRY, DISTURB, DISTRESS, CONCERN, UPSET.
 — *n.* DIFFICULTY, inconvenience, EFFORT, CARE, EXERTION, MISFORTUNE, mishap, mischance, ILLNESS, affliction.

troubled: see ANXIOUS; CURSED; RESTLESS; SORROWFUL; UPSET.

troublesome *adj.* BOTHERSOME, annoying, tiresome, irksome, burdensome, irritating, disturbing, distressing, unruly, ungovernable.

trough *n.* BIN, manger, TRAY, DEPRESSION, hollow, CHANNEL, furrow.

troupe: see BAND; TEAM.

trousers *pl.n.* PANTS, slacks, breeches, britches, jeans.

truce *n.* ARMISTICE, PEACE, HALT, lull, respite, AGREEMENT.

truck *n.* barrow, CART, WAGON, pickup, van.
 — *v.*: see CARRY; CART.

trudge *v.* TREAD, wade, STUMBLE, trek.

true *adj.* CORRECT, EXACT, RIGHT, rightful, REAL, ACCURATE, ACTUAL, GENUINE, SINCERE, HONEST, UPRIGHT, MORAL, PURE, GOOD, TRUTHFUL, JUST, LOYAL, staunch, STEADY, FAITHFUL.
 — *adv.*: see CERTAINLY; SURE; SURELY; YES.

truly *adv.* truthfully, honestly, SINCERELY, REALLY, ACTUALLY, PRECISELY, INDEED.

trumpet *n.* bugle, cornet, clarion, horn, brass.

trunk *n.* **1** *(to pack the trunk)* CHEST, BOX, footlocker, WARDROBE; **2** *(the tree trunk)* stump, STOCK, STEM, torso; **3** *(the elephant's trunk)* nose, snout.

trunks: see LUGGAGE.

truss: see BIND; BRACE; PROP.

trussed: see BOUND.

trust *n.* **1** *(a position of trust)* reliance, CONFIDENCE, assurance, credence, EXPECTATION, FAITH, BELIEF, HOPE, CREDIT, DUTY; **2** *(left in trust)* INVESTMENT, PROPERTY, custody, CHARGE, CARE; **3** *(the big trusts)* monopoly, syndicate.
 — *v.* entrust, accredit, RELY ON, BELIEVE, HOPE, EXPECT.

trustful *adj.* trusting, believing.

trust in: see RELY ON.

trusting: see TRUSTFUL.

trustworthiness: see LOYALTY.

trustworthy: see AUTHENTIC; CERTAIN; CONVINCING; DEPENDABLE; FAITHFUL; HONEST; HONORABLE; RELIABLE; RESPONSIBLE; SOUND; SURE; TRUTHFUL.

truth *n.* accuracy, correctness, FACT, facts, actuality, REALITY, genuineness, verity, veracity, integrity, HONESTY, faithfulness, RIGHT, righteousness.

truthful *adj.* ACCURATE, DEPENDABLE, RELIABLE, trustworthy, HONEST, GENUINE, REAL.

truthfully: see OPENLY; TRULY.

truthfulness: see HONESTY.

try *v.* ATTEMPT, ENDEAVOR, essay, STRIVE, TEST, EXAMINE, EXPERIMENT, ANALYZE, INVESTIGATE, PROVE, JUDGE, hear, arbitrate, referee, IRRITATE, ANNOY.
— *n.* ATTEMPT, EFFORT, ENDEAVOR, BID, TEST, CHANCE.

trying *adj.* annoying, DIFFICULT, TROUBLESOME.

T square: see RULER.

tub: see BASIN; PAIL; SINK; TANK.

tubby: see CHUBBY.

tube *n.* PIPE, cylinder, duct, TUNNEL.

tubing: see HOSE.

tuck *v.* FOLD, GATHER, pleat, plait, SEAM.

tuckered: see BUSHED.

tuft: see BRUSH; LOCK.

tug *v.* PULL, yank, JERK, STRUGGLE, DRAG, TOW.
— *n.*: see WRENCH.

tulip: see BULB.

tumble *v.* FALL, DROP, DESCEND, STUMBLE, TRIP, SLIP, ROLL.

tumbler: see CUP; GLASS.

tummy: see BELLY.

tumor: see BOIL; BUMP; GROWTH.

tumult: see CLAMOR; COMMOTION; HUDDLE; NOISE; RIOT; UPROAR.

tumultuous: see NOISY.

tune *n.* MELODY, STRAIN, SONG, MUSIC.

tuneful: see MELODIOUS; MUSICAL.

tungsten: see METAL.

tunic: see COAT.

tunnel *n.* underpass, subway, passageway, TUBE.
— *v.* DIG, BURROW.

turbine: see ENGINE.

turbulent: see ROUGH.

tureen: see BOWL.

turmoil: see COMMOTION.

turn *v.* **1** (*the world turns*) SPIN, ROTATE, REVOLVE; **2** (*to turn on a lathe*) CHANGE, SHAPE, FASHION; **3** (*turn at the next light*) veer, swerve, MOVE, BEND, curve, SEND, DRIVE, invert, REVERSE; **4** (*the milk is turning*) SOUR, SPOIL, ferment, TRANSFORM, BECOME.
— *n.* **1** (*at the next turn*) bend, CORNER, CURVE, turning, swerve; **2** (*to take a turn around the block*) WALK, RIDE, STROLL, SPIN, ROUND, REVOLUTION, ROTATION; **3** (*it's my turn*) SHIFT, OCCASION, NEED, OPPORTUNITY, CHANCE; **4** (*a turn for the worst*) CHANGE, alteration, bent, TENDENCY, INCLINATION, aptitude; **5** (*it gave me quite a turn*) SURPRISE, SHOCK.

turnbuckle: see BUCKLE.

turncoat: see CONVERT; TRAITOR.

turn down: see REFUSE; REJECT.

turned: see WOUND.

turning: see ROTATION; TURN.

turn out: see BECOME; PROVE.

turn over: see UPSET.

turnpike: see HIGHWAY.

turn up: see OCCUR.

turret: see TOWER.

tusk: see TOOTH.

tussle: see WRESTLE.

tutor *n.* TEACHER, coach, INSTRUCTOR, MASTER, trainer, GUIDE, preceptor.
— *v.* TEACH, coach, INSTRUCT, TRAIN, GUIDE, EDUCATE.

tutu: see SKIRT.

tweak: see TWIST.

twelvemonth: see ANNUAL.

twice *adv.* doubly, twofold, bis, encore.

twiddle: see DABBLE.

twig *n.* sprig, shoot, SPRAY, SWITCH, BRANCH, ramification.

twilight *n.* nightfall, DUSK, gloaming, EVENING, DARKNESS, GLOOM, END, decay, DECLINE.

twin *adj.* DOUBLE, biform, paired, coupled, DUPLICATE, binary, SIMILAR, IDENTICAL, SAME.
— *n.* MATCH, MATE, FELLOW, BROTHER, sister, COMPANION.

twine *v.* entwine, intertwine, interweave, WIND, interlace, WEAVE, TWIST, WIND, COIL, ENCIRCLE.
— *n.* STRING, CORD, ROPE, THREAD.

twinkle *v.* SPARKLE, GLITTER, glint, GLISTEN, FLASH, GLEAM, glimmer, SHINE.
— *n.* SPARKLE, GLITTER, glint, FLASH, GLEAM, twinkling, INSTANT.

twinkling: see INSTANT; MOMENT; SECOND; TWINKLE.

twirl *v.* WHIRL, TWIST, REEL, SPIN, CURL, ROTATE, TURN, PITCH, TOSS.

twist *v.* TWIRL, TWINE, entwist, intertwist, intertwine, braid, entwine, WARP, wreathe, WIND, curve, BEND, ROTATE, REVOLVE, distort, writhe, SQUIRM, wriggle, WRENCH, WRING, tweak.
— *n.* bend, ply, braid, warp, sprain, WRENCH, kink, spiral, curlicue, flourish, torque, TENDENCY, distortion, dance, THREAD.

twisted: see BENT; CROOKED.

twisting: see ROTATION.

twitch *v.* JERK, PULL, SHUDDER, jiggle.
— *n.* JERK, PULL, SHUDDER, jiggle, spasm, quiver, CONTRACTION.

twitching: see FRISKY.

twitter: see CHIRP; SING.

two *n.* PAIR, twosome, COUPLE, DOUBLE, couplet, brace, deuce, binary, SPAN, YOKE, TEAM, mates.

two bits: see COIN.

two-faced: see FALSE.

twofold: see DOUBLE; DUPLICATE; TWICE.

twosome: see TWO.

two-time: see BETRAY.

type *n.* **1** *(a type of dictionary)* KIND, SORT, VARIETY, CLASS, genus, SPECIES, representative, EXAMPLE, MODEL, PATTERN; **2** *(bold-face type)* LETTER, PRINT, SYMBOL, CHARACTER.

typescript: see WRITING.

typewrite: see WRITE.

typhoon: see WIND.

typical *adj.* representative, CHARACTERISTIC, symbolic, REGULAR, NORMAL, stock, commonplace, unexceptional, ORDINARY.

typically: see REGULARLY.

typist: see SECRETARY.

typography: see PRINTING.

tyrant *n.* dictator, oppressor, RULER.

U

ugliness *n.* uncomeliness, homeliness, unattractiveness, unsightliness, eyesore, hideousness, deformity.

ugly *adj.* hideous, unsightly, repulsive, PLAIN, HOMELY, UNPLEASANT, displeasing, DISAGREEABLE, bad-natured, VICIOUS, NASTY, DANGEROUS, EVIL, WICKED, scowling, threatening, quarrelsome.

ulcer: see INFECTION.

ulterior: see SECRET.

ultimate: see EXTREME; FINAL; LAST.

ultimately: see EVENTUALLY; FINALLY.

ultimatum: see WARNING.

ultra: see EXTREME.

umbrage: see RESENTMENT.

umpire: see JUDGE.

unable *adj.* incapable, POWERLESS, HELPLESS, inadequate, incompetent, WEAK, CLUMSY.

unabridged: see COMPLETE; ENTIRE.

unacceptable: see UNBEARABLE; UNSATISFACTORY; UNSUITABLE.

unaccommodating: see DIFFICULT.

unaccomplished: see INCOMPLETE.

unaccustomed *adj.* UNFAMILIAR, UNUSUAL, unused, untrained, unskilled, FOREIGN, STRANGE.

unacquainted: see STRANGE.

unadjusted: see UNBALANCED.

unadorned: see PLAIN.

unadulterated: see AUTHENTIC; PLAIN.

unaffected: see CHILDLIKE; MODEST; SIMPLE.

unafraid: see BRAVE.

unaided: see SINGLE-HANDED.

unalluring: see UNATTRACTIVE.

unambiguous: see DIRECT.

unanimity: see AGREEMENT.

unanimous *adj.* united, agreeing, HARMONIOUS, SOLID.

unappeased: see UNSATISFIED.

unarmed: see DEFENSELESS.

unassuming: see HUMBLE.

unattached: see LOOSE; SINGLE.

unattainable: see IMPOSSIBLE.

unattended: see ALONE.

unattractive *adj.* HOMELY, UGLY, undesirable, uninviting, unalluring.

unattractiveness: see UGLINESS.

unauthentic: see CHEMICAL.

unavoidable: see INEVITABLE; NECESSARY; SURE.

unavoidably: see NECESSARILY.

unaware *adj.* UNCONSCIOUS, unsuspecting, unknowing, IGNORANT, unwarned, heedless, inattentive.

unawares *adv.* suddenly, unexpectedly, abruptly, inadvertently, unconsciously, accidentally, unintentionally.

unbalanced *adj.* unadjusted, unsettled, unsound, unsteady, deranged, CRAZY, INSANE, INSECURE.

unbar: see OPEN.

unbarred: see OPEN.

unbearable *adj.* intolerable, unsupportable, unacceptable, insufferable, unendurable, inadmissible.

unbecoming: see INDECENT; UNSUITABLE.

unbelief: see DOUBT.

unbelievable: see FABULOUS; INCREDIBLE; UNHEARD OF.

unbend: see RELAX.

unbending: see RIGID; STIFF; STUBBORN.

unbiased: see NEUTRAL.

unblemished: see INNOCENT; PERFECT; PURE; SPOTLESS.

unblocked: see CLEAR.

unbound: see FREE.

unbowed: see RESISTANT.

unbreakable: see IRON.

unbroken *adj.* INTACT, CONTINUOUS, CONSTANT, uninterrupted, STEADY, perpetual, REGULAR, changeless.

uncanny: see MYSTERIOUS.

uncaring: see CARELESS.

unceasing: see CONTINUOUS; IMMORTAL.

uncertain *adj.* unsure, DOUBTFUL, QUESTIONABLE, indefinite, UNDECIDED, hesitant, dubious, doubting, INSECURE, VARIABLE, VAGUE, unpredictable.

uncertainty *n.* DOUBT, QUESTION, indecision, HESITATION, insecurity, dilemma, quandary.

unchangeable *adj.* immutable, inalterable, PERMANENT, CONSTANT, STEADY, invariable, ETERNAL.

unchanging: see OLD-FASHIONED; STEADY.

uncharged: see NEUTRAL.

uncivil: see IMPOLITE; UNGRACIOUS.

uncivilized: see INHUMAN; PRIMITIVE; SAVAGE; WILD.

unclean: see FILTHY; IMPURE.

unclear: see CLOUDY; FUZZY; VAGUE.

unclosed: see OPEN.

unclothe: see UNDRESS.

unclothed: see BARE; NAKED; NUDE.

unclouded: see CLEAR; SUNNY.

uncomeliness: see UGLINESS.

uncomely: see HOMELY.

uncomfortable *adj.* UNEASY, self-conscious, SUFFERING, DISAGREEABLE, UNPLEASANT, UNHAPPY.

uncommitted: see NEUTRAL.

uncommon *adj.* RARE, UNUSUAL, ODD, UNIQUE, UNFAMILIAR, STRANGE, infrequent.

uncommonly: see EXTREMELY.

uncomplaining: see PATIENT.

uncompliant: see DISOBEDIENT.

uncomplicated: see EASY; ELEMENTARY.

uncompromising: see STRONG.

unconcealed: see OBVIOUS.

unconcerned: see CARELESS; LUKEWARM; THOUGHTLESS.

unconditional: see BINDING; CONCLUSIVE.

unconditionally: see ABSOLUTELY.

unconscious *adj.* UNAWARE, unmindful, unheeding, IGNORANT, SENSELESS, insensible, inadvertent, involuntary, subconscious, subliminal.

unconsciously: see UNAWARES.

unconstraint: see LICENSE.

uncontaminated: see CLEAN; SANITARY.

uncontrolled: see ADRIFT; INDEPENDENT; WILD.

uncooked: see RARE; RAW.

uncordial: see UNFRIENDLY.

uncork: see OPEN.

uncorrupted: see INNOCENT.

uncouth: see CRUDE; RUDE.

uncover *v.* unearth, EXPOSE, REVEAL, unmask, OPEN, disclose, unveil.

uncovered: see BARE; NUDE; OPEN.

uncovering: see EXPOSURE.

uncultivated: see HOMELY; IGNORANT; WILD.

uncultured: see PRIMITIVE.

uncut: see COMPLETE; WHOLE.

undamaged: see UNHARMED; WHOLE.

undaunted: see BRAVE.

undecided *adj.* pending, DOUBTFUL, UNCERTAIN, indefinite, unsettled, undetermined, tentative.

undefended: see UNGUARDED.

undefined: see GENERAL.

undeniable: see CERTAIN.

under *prep.* BENEATH, BELOW, UNDERNEATH, following, IN.
—*adj.* lower, BOTTOM, subject, subordinate, INFERIOR.
—*adv.* BENEATH, UNDERNEATH, BELOW, DOWNWARD, DOWN, underfoot, underground.

underbrush: see BRUSH.

underclothes: see SLIP.

underdeveloped: see BACKWARD.

underdone: see RARE; RAW.

underfoot: see UNDER.

undergarment: see SLIP.

undergo: see ENDURE; EXPERIENCE; RECEIVE; SUFFER; SUSTAIN.

undergraduate: see STUDENT.

underground: see UNDER.

underhanded: see CROOKED.

underline *v.* emphasize, underscore, INDICATE, MARK, italicize, STRESS.

underlying: see BASIC.

undermine: see KNIFE; MINE; WEAKEN.

underneath *prep.*, *adv.* BENEATH, BELOW.

underpass: see TUNNEL.

underpinning: see FOUNDATION.

underscore: see FEATURE; STRESS; UNDERLINE.

underside: see BOTTOM.

undersized: see SHORT.

underskirt: see SKIRT.

understand *v.* KNOW, LEARN, GRASP, SEE, HEAR, REALIZE, GATHER, RECOGNIZE, comprehend, infer, BELIEVE, perceive, PENETRATE, MASTER, discern.

understandable: see CLEAR; OBVIOUS.

understanding *n.* KNOWLEDGE, LEARNING, GRASP, comprehension, AGREEMENT, SYMPATHY, knowing, mastery, penetration, GRIP, perception, MIND, CONSCIOUSNESS, apprehension, JUDGMENT, IMPRESSION.
—*adj.* perceptive, discerning, SYMPATHETIC, lenient, KIND.

understood: see KNOWN.

understudy: see REPLACEMENT; SUBSTITUTE.

undertake: see ASSUME; ATTEMPT; COMMENCE; ENDEAVOR; TACKLE.

undertaking *n.* TASK, VENTURE, PROJECT, AFFAIR, enterprise, ENDEAVOR, ATTEMPT, BUSINESS, WORK, PURSUIT, RESPONSIBILITY, ADVENTURE.

undertone: see WHISPER.

undertow: see CURRENT.

underworld: see HELL.

undesirable: see UNATTRACTIVE.

undetermined: see UNDECIDED.

undeveloped: see FORMLESS; IMMATURE; PREMATURE.

undeviating: see DIRECT.

undiluted: see NEAT.

undiscovered: see UNKNOWN; UNSEEN.

undisguised: see TRANSPARENT.

undistinguished: see NAMELESS; ORDINARY.

undisturbed: see PEACEFUL; TRANQUIL; VIRGIN.

undivided: see COMPLETE; ENTIRE; ONE; OVERALL.

undo: see SEPARATE.

undoing: see RUIN.

undone: see APART.

undoubtedly: see CERTAINLY; DEFINITELY; DOUBTLESS; POSITIVELY; PROBABLY; SURELY; YES.

undrape: see UNDRESS.

undress *v.* disrobe, denude, unclothe, undrape, STRIP, PEEL.

undressed: see NUDE.

undulate: see WAVE.

undulation: see RIPPLE; WAVE.

undying: see ETERNAL.

unearth: see DIG; EXPOSE; STRIKE; UNCOVER.

uneasiness: see EMBARRASSMENT; IMPATIENCE.

uneasy *adj.* RESTLESS, disturbed, ANXIOUS, UPSET, UNCOMFORTABLE, AWKWARD, self-conscious, STIFF, constrained, unstable, UNCERTAIN.

uneducated: see IGNORANT.

unemployment: see LEISURE.

unending *adj.* ENDLESS, ceaseless, CONTINUAL, CONTINUOUS, perpetual, INFINITE, everlasting, ETERNAL.

unendurable: see UNBEARABLE.

unenthusiastic: see DIM.

unequal *adj.* UNEVEN, UNBALANCED, INFERIOR, IRREGULAR, disproportioned, inadequate, insufficient.

unequaled: see INCOMPARABLE; PERFECT; UNIQUE.

unerring: see ACCURATE.

unessential: see UNNECESSARY.

uneven *adj.* **1** *(an uneven surface)* IRREGULAR, ROUGH, bumpy, UNEQUAL, UNBALANCED, VARIABLE, CHANGEABLE, spasmodic, disparate; **2** *(an uneven number)* ODD, unmatched.

unexceptional: see TYPICAL.

unexcited: see CALM; STEADY.

unexciting: see TAME.

unexpected *adj.* unforeseen, improbable, ABRUPT, SUDDEN, SURPRISING, astonishing, startling.

unexpectedly: see INCIDENTALLY; UNAWARES.

unexpired: see ACTIVE.

unexplained: see UNKNOWN.

unexplored: see UNKNOWN.

unfailing *adj.* CONSTANT, CONTINUOUS, steadfast, LOYAL, FAITHFUL, TRUE, DEPENDABLE, RELIABLE, LASTING.

unfair *adj.* UNJUST, PARTIAL, one-sided, UNEQUAL, dishonest, ILLEGAL, UNREASONABLE, CROOKED.

unfairness: see WRONG.

unfaithful *adj.* FALSE, fickle, untrue, INCONSTANT, disloyal, UNRELIABLE, dishonest.

unfaithfulness: see TREACHERY.

unfaltering: see STEADY.

unfamiliar *adj.* unknowing, STRANGE, UNUSUAL, UNIQUE, RARE, NEW, bizarre.

unfashionable: see OLD; OUT.

unfasten: see DETACH; LIBERATE; LOOSEN; RELEASE.

unfastened: see LOOSE.

unfavorable: see CONTRARY; ILL; LUCKLESS.

unfavorableness: see DISADVANTAGE.

unfeather: see PLUCK.

unfeeling: see ASLEEP; BLUNT; HARD; HEARTLESS; INHUMAN; MERCILESS; NUMB; PITILESS; SENSELESS.

unfilled: see EMPTY; OPEN; VACANT.

unfinished: see INCOMPLETE; PARTIAL; UNRIPE.

unfit: see UNSUITABLE; WRONG.

unfix: see DETACH.

unfold *v.* UNCOVER, divulge, disclose, REVEAL, unmask, unravel, decipher.

unfolded: see OPEN.

unfolding: see DEVELOPMENT.

unformed: see SHAPELESS.

unforseen: see SUDDEN; UNEXPECTED.

unfortunate *adj.* UNLUCKY, SAD, regrettable, deplorable, lamentable, calamitous, TRAGIC, adverse, disastrous, UNSUCCESSFUL.

unfriendly *adj.* stand-offish, COOL, uncordial, aloof, unsociable, inhospitable, DISTANT, offish.

unfurnished: see BARE.

ungenerous: see SELFISH.

ungentle: see ROUGH.

ungodliness: see WICKEDNESS.

ungovernable: see TROUBLESOME.

ungracious *adj.* RUDE, ROUGH, IMPOLITE, discourteous, unkind, uncivil, unmannerly.

ungrateful: see UNPLEASANT.

unguarded *adj.* unprotected, unwatched, unsheltered, UNSAFE, unshielded, DEFENSELESS, undefended.

unhappiness: see HARDSHIP; SADNESS.

unhappy *adj.* SAD, melancholy, WRETCHED, JOYLESS, MISERABLE, distressed, CHEERLESS, UNFORTUNATE, UNLUCKY, inauspicious, UNSUITABLE.

unharmed *adj.* SAFE, SOUND, uninjured, unhurt, undamaged, unscathed.

unhealthful: see HARMFUL.

unhealthy *adj.* sickly, ILL, puny, WEAK, FRAIL, ailing, run-down.

unheard-of *adj.* UNUSUAL, UNCOMMON, RARE, UNIQUE, STRANGE, unbelievable, inconceivable.

unhearing: see DEAF.

unheeding: see DEAF; UNCONSCIOUS.

unhelpful: see USELESS.

unhidden: see OPEN.

unhinge: see UPSET.

unhitch: see DETACH.

unhook: see DISCONNECT.

unhurried: see LEISURELY.

unhurt: see UNHARMED.

unification: see COMBINATION; UNION; UNITY.

uniform: see EQUAL; EVEN; IDENTICAL; LEVEL; PROGRESSIVE; REGULAR.

uniformity: see EQUALITY; REGULARITY; UNITY.

uniformly: see CONSTANTLY; EVENLY.

unify *v.* UNITE, JOIN, COMBINE, merge, fuse, BLEND, consolidate, HARMONIZE, reconcile.

unilluminated: see DARK.

unimportant: see PETTY; TRASHY.

uninebriated: see SOBER.

uninjured: see SOUND; UNHARMED.

uninspired: see DULL.

unintelligence: see STUPIDITY.

unintelligent: see STUPID.

unintentional: see CASUAL.

unintentionally: see UNAWARES.

uninterested: see LUKEWARM.

uninteresting: see DRY; DULL; STALE; TAME.

uninterrupted: see CONTINUAL; CONTINUOUS; RUNNING; UNBROKEN.

unintoxicated: see SOBER.

uninviting: see UNATTRACTIVE.

union *n.* COMBINATION, uniting, unification, BLEND, UNITY, oneness, coalition, LINK, confederation, consolidation, CONJUNCTION, ASSOCIATION, ALLIANCE, LEAGUE, MARRIAGE, matrimony, wedlock, coitus, CONNECTION.

unique *adj.* SINGLE, SOLE, ONLY, SOLITARY, RARE, exclusive, unmatched, unequaled, INCOMPARABLE, unprecedented, EXCEPTIONAL, UNUSUAL, NOVEL, ORIGINAL, UNCOMMON, isolated, peerless, matchless.

uniqueness: see DISTINCTION; ORIGINALITY.

unison: see HARMONY.

unit *n.* GROUP, DIVISION, QUANTITY, DISTANCE, integer, ASSOCIATION, ORGANIZATION, wing, detachment, apparatus, MACHINE.

unite *v.* UNIFY, COMBINE, JOIN, fuse, blend, mix, merge, LINK, COUPLE, CONNECT, conjoin, cohere, reconcile, consolidate, amalgamate.

united: see ALLIED; CONFEDERATE; JOINT; ONE; UNANIMOUS.

uniting: see UNION; UNITY.

unity *n.* uniting, unification, AGREEMENT, UNION, oneness, uniformity, CONNECTION, IDENTITY, SAMENESS, HARMONY.

universal *adj.* widespread, COMMON, prevalent, GENERAL, prevailing, ENTIRE, WHOLE, unlimited, diffuse, EVERYWHERE, catholic, cosmic, all-embracing.

universally: see EVERYWHERE.

universe *n.* CREATION, NATURE, WORLD, ALL, EVERYTHING, SPACE, COSMOS, MANKIND, humankind.

unjust *adj.* UNFAIR, PARTIAL, one-sided, UNEQUAL, prejudiced.

unjustly: see WRONG.

unkempt: see SLOPPY.

unkind: see MEAN; UNGRACIOUS.

unkindly: see MEAN.

unkindness: see MEANNESS.

unknowing: see UNAWARE; UNFAMILIAR.

unknown *adj.* UNSEEN, unexplored, undiscovered, UNHEARD-OF, unexplained,

UNFAMILIAR, STRANGE, concealed, HIDDEN, unlearned.
— *n.* MYSTERY, SECRET, RIDDLE, PUZZLE, beyond.

unlabeled: see NAMELESS.

unlace: see LOOSEN.

unlawful: see CRIMINAL; FORBIDDEN; ILLEGAL.

unlearned: see UNKNOWN.

unleash: see LOOSEN.

unless *conj.* except if, except, if not.

unlike *adj.* DIFFERENT, dissimilar, diverse.

unlikely: see FISHY; INCREDIBLE; LAST; QUESTIONABLE.

unlimited: see ABSOLUTE; FULL; IMMEASURABLE; UNIVERSAL.

unload: see DISCHARGE; DUMP.

unlock: see OPEN.

unlocked: see OPEN.

unloose: see RELEASE.

unlucky *adj.* UNFORTUNATE, unprosperous, UNSUCCESSFUL, LUCKLESS, ill-fated, disastrous.

unmannerliness: see RUDENESS.

unmannerly: see UNGRACIOUS.

unmarried: see SINGLE.

unmask: see EXPOSE; UNCOVER; UNFOLD.

unmasking: see EXPOSURE.

unmatched: see INCOMPARABLE; ODD; UNEVEN; UNIQUE.

unmellowed: see UNRIPE.

unmerciful: see BRUTAL.

unmindful: see FORGETFUL; IGNORANT; UNCONSCIOUS.

unmistakable: see OBVIOUS; PRECISE.

unmistakenly: see DEFINITELY.

unmixed: see ENTIRE; PURE; SIMPLE; SOLID.

unmolded: see FORMLESS.

unmoved: see FIRM.

unnamed: see CERTAIN.

unnatural *adj.* UNCOMMON, UNUSUAL, RARE, IRREGULAR, ABNORMAL, forced, strained, FOREIGN.

unnecessary *adj.* needless, unneeded, USELESS, POINTLESS, irrelevant, superfluous, excess, expendable, unessential.

unneeded: see UNNECESSARY.

unnerve: see RATTLE; STARTLE.

unnerved: see SHAKEN.

unobstructed: see CLEAR.

unobtrusive: see MODEST.

unoccupied: see EMPTY; IDLE; OPEN; VACANT.

unpaid: see DUE; OUTSTANDING; OWING.

unpainful: see PAINLESS.

unparalleled: see INCOMPARABLE.

unpin: see LOOSEN.

unplanned: see CASUAL.

unpleasant *adj.* DISAGREEABLE, distasteful, UNCOMFORTABLE, UNFRIENDLY, ungrateful, offensive, repulsive, annoying, unwelcome.

unplug: see DISCONNECT.

unpracticed: see RUSTY.

unprecedented: see UNIQUE; UNUSUAL.

unpredictable: see UNCERTAIN.

unprejudiced: see LIBERAL; OPEN.

unpremeditated: see IMPULSIVE.

unprepared: see OFFHAND; PREMATURE; RAW.

unpretending: see HUMBLE.

unproductive: see BARREN.

unprofitable: see USELESS.

unprosperous: see LUCKLESS; UNLUCKY; UNSUCCESSFUL.

unprotected: see DEFENSELESS; UNGUARDED; UNSAFE.

unqualified: see ABSOLUTE.

unquestionable: see ABSOLUTE; CERTAIN.

unquestionably: see ABSOLUTELY; DOUBTLESS.

unquiet: see RESTLESS.

unravel: see SOLVE; UNFOLD; UNWIND.

unreal: see INVISIBLE.

unreasonable *adj.* SENSELESS, irrational, NONSENSICAL, unsound, discourteous, EXCESSIVE, immoderate, extravagant.

unrefined: see COARSE; COMMON; CRUDE.

unreflective: see THOUGHTLESS.

unrelated: see REMOTE.

unreliable *adj.* untrustworthy, fickle, irresponsible, unsure, unstable, UNCERTAIN.

unreserved: see HOSPITABLE.

unreservedly: see FREELY.

unrestrained: see INFORMAL.

unrestricted: see OPEN.

unrighteous: see WICKED.

unripe *adj.* IMMATURE, unmellowed, GREEN, PREMATURE, unfinished.

unrivalled: see INCOMPARABLE.

unroll: see SPREAD.

unruffled: see CALM; EVEN; SMOOTH; TRANQUIL.

unruly: see NAUGHTY; ROWDY; TROUBLESOME.

unsafe *adj.* DANGEROUS, perilous, UNGUARDED, unprotected, unsheltered, HAZARDOUS, RISKY, precarious, INSECURE.

unsalted: see SWEET.

unsatisfactory *adj.* INFERIOR, inadequate, insufficient, unacceptable, disappointing, FAULTY, imperfect.

unsatisfied *adj.* dissatisfied, unappeased, malcontent, displeased, DISCONTENTED.

unscathed: see UNHARMED.

unseal: see OPEN.

unsealed: see OPEN.

unseating: see OVERTHROW.

unseemly: see INDECENT.

unseen *adj.* HIDDEN, INVISIBLE, veiled, UNKNOWN, concealed, undiscovered, masked, obscure.

unselfish: see GENEROUS.

unselfishness: see GENEROSITY.

unsettled: see CHANGEABLE; OUTSTANDING; RESTLESS; SHAKEN; UNBALANCED; UNDECIDED.

unshakable: see FIRM.

unsheltered: see UNGUARDED; UNSAFE.

unshielded: see UNGUARDED.

unsightliness: see UGLINESS.

unsightly: see UGLY.

unskilled: see STRANGE; UNACCUSTOMED.

unskillful: see AWKWARD.

unsnap: see DETACH.

unsociable: see SULLEN; UNFRIENDLY.

unsoiled: see CLEAN; SPOTLESS.

unsophisticated: see RURAL.

unsound: see UNBALANCED; UNREASONABLE.

unsparing: see MERCILESS.

unspeakable: see WICKED.

unspecified: see ANY; CERTAIN.

unspoiled: see EDIBLE; FRESH.

unspotted: see BLANK.

unstable: see SHAKY; TICKLISH; UNEASY; UNRELIABLE.

unstained: see CLEAN; GUILTLESS; PURE.

unsteady: see DIZZY; TICKLISH; UNBALANCED; VARIABLE.

unsubstantial: see FLIMSY.

unsuccessful *adj.* abortive, UNFORTUNATE, fruitless, VAIN, futile, unprosperous, LUCKLESS.

unsuccessfully: see POORLY.

unsuitable *adj.* inappropriate, unacceptable, unfit, improper, unbecoming, objectionable, UNSATISFACTORY.

unsuited: see USELESS.

unsupportable: see UNBEARABLE.

unsure: see DOUBTFUL; INSECURE; SHAKY; UNCERTAIN; UNRELIABLE.

unsurpassed: see MOST.

unsuspecting: see UNAWARE.

unswerving: see DIRECT.

unsympathetic: see HARD; HEARTLESS; PITILESS.

untagged: see NAMELESS.

untamed: see FIERCE; WILD.

untangle: see COMB; SOLVE; UNWIND.

untarnished: see SPOTLESS.

untaught: see RUDE.

unthinkable: see IMPOSSIBLE.

unthinking: see CHILDLIKE; THOUGHTLESS.

unthoughtful: see CARELESS.

untidy: see MESSY; SLOPPY.

untie: see FREE; LOOSEN.

until *prep.* TILL, to, BEFORE.
 – *conj.* TILL, before.

untimely: see CONTRARY; EARLY; PREMATURE.

untitled: see NAMELESS.

untouched: see VIRGIN.

untrained: see GREEN; RAW; UNACCUSTOMED.

untroubled: see CLEAR; EASY; PEACEFUL.

untrue: see MADE-UP; TREACHEROUS; UNFAITHFUL.

untrustworthy: see UNRELIABLE.

untruth: see FIB; LIE.

untruthful: see FALSE; WRONG.

untruthfully: see WRONG.

unused: see BLANK; IDLE; NEW; UNACCUSTOMED; VIRGIN.

unusual *adj.* UNCOMMON, infrequent, UNFAMILIAR, STRANGE, unprecedented, UNEXPECTED, NOVEL, FRESH, SCARCE, EXTRAORDINARY, ABNORMAL, OUTSTANDING, EXCEPTIONAL.

unusually: see ESPECIALLY.

unvarying: see STEADY.

unveil: see UNCOVER.

unwarned: see UNAWARE.

unwashed: see DIRTY.

unwatched: see UNGUARDED.

unwelcome: see UNPLEASANT.

unwell: see ILL; SICK.

unwholesome: see BAD.

unwieldy: see AWKWARD; BULKY.

unwilling: see RELUCTANT.

unwillingness: see RELUCTANCE.

unwind *v.* REST, RELAX, disentangle, untangle, unravel.

unwise: see FOOLISH.

unwrinkled: see SMOOTH.

unyielding: see IMMOVABLE; RIGID; STERN; STIFF; STONY; STUBBORN; TOUGH.

up: see UPWARD.

upend: see UPSET.

upended: see REVERSE.

upgrade: see ELEVATE; PROMOTE; RISE.

upheaval: see PASSION; STORM.

uphill: see UPWARD.

uphold *v.* SUPPORT, MAINTAIN, DEFEND, endorse.

upholder: see SUPPORTER.

upkeep: see MAINTENANCE; SUPPORT.

uplift *v.* LIFT, RAISE, ERECT, ELEVATE, RISE, IMPROVE, INSPIRE.

upon: see ONTO; OVER; WITH.

upper: see ADVANCED; SUPERIOR; UPWARD.

upperclassman: see SENIOR.

uppercut: see PUNCH.

upper hand: see EDGE.

uprear: see REAR.

upright *adj.* **1** *(an upright post)* STRAIGHT, VERTICAL, ERECT, perpendicular, STEEP; **2** *(an upright person)* HONEST, HONORABLE, ethical, JUST, TRUE, MORAL, GOOD, pious, righteous. — *v.*: see RIGHT.

uprightness: see GOODNESS; HONESTY.

uprising: see DISTURBANCE; OUTBREAK; REBELLION; REVOLT; REVOLUTION.

uproar *n.* DISTURBANCE, din, tumult, hubbub, RACKET, COMMOTION, CLAMOR, NOISE.

uproarious: see NOISY.

upset *v.* overturn, turn over, topple, capsize, upend, invert, OVERTHROW, DEFEAT, derange, unhinge, CONFUSE, disquiet, fluster, BOTHER, DISTURB. — *adj.* disturbed, distressed, flustered, UNEASY, NERVOUS, troubled, perturbed, uptight. — *n.* DEFEAT, ACCIDENT, SURPRISE, OVERTHROW, upsetting, DISORDER.

upsetting: see ALARMING; UPSET.

upshot: see CONSEQUENCE; ISSUE; OUTCOME; RESULT.

upstanding: see HONORABLE.

uptight: see NERVOUS; TENSE; UPSET.

up to: see TILL.

up-to-date *adj.* MODERN, RECENT, improved, NEW, POPULAR.

upward *adj.* upper, uphill, ascending, transcendent, SUPERIOR. — *adv.* aloft, up, ABOVE, overhead.

urbane: see SMOOTH.

urchin: see BRAT.

urge *v.* ENCOURAGE, INVITE, COAX, PERSUADE, spur, ADVISE, RECOMMEND, BEG, implore, INSIST,

PUSH, PROMOTE, PERSIST, DRIVE, impel, prod, PRESS.
— *n.* IMPULSE, DESIRE, itch, stimulus.

urgency *n.* EMERGENCY, crisis, pinch, crux, NECESSITY, PROBLEM, NEED, DEMAND.

urgent *adj.* pressing, demanding, INSISTENT, IMMEDIATE, persistent.

urgently: see NECESSARILY.

urging: see ENCOURAGEMENT; PERSUASION.

urinal: see TOILET.

urn: see JAR; KETTLE; PITCHER; POT.

usable: see AVAILABLE; PRACTICAL; SUITABLE.

usage *n.* TREATMENT, CUSTOM, HABIT, PRACTICE, USE, METHOD, TRADITION, CONVENTION, SPEECH, APPLICATION.

use *v.* utilize, EMPLOY, ADOPT, CONSUME, expend, SPEND, wear out, exploit, EXERCISE, OPERATE, WORK, wield, HANDLE, PRACTICE.
— *n.* utilization, EMPLOYMENT, ADOPTION, PRACTICE, EXERCISE, METHOD, TREATMENT, CUSTOM, NEED, SERVICE, exploitation, ADVANTAGE, POINT, PROFIT, BENEFIT, APPLICATION, WEAR.

used *adj.* SECOND-HAND, WORN, worn out, SHABBY, threadbare, spent, consumed, STALE, trite.

useful *adj.* HELPFUL, serviceable, VALUABLE, invaluable, advantageous, PROFITABLE, WORTHY, beneficial, suited, PRACTICAL, functional.

usefulness: see EFFICIENCY; GOODNESS; PRODUCTIVITY; UTILITY; WORTH.

useless *adj.* valueless, WORTHLESS, unprofitable, fruitless, ineffectual, unhelpful, unsuited, impractical, superfluous, futile, outworn.

user: see CONSUMER.

use up: see KILL.

usher *n.* MARSHAL, GUIDE, doorkeeper, ATTENDANT, GUARD, CONDUCTOR.
— *v.* marshal, GUIDE, CONDUCT, DIRECT.

usher in: see RECEIVE.

usual *adj.* COMMON, REGULAR, FAMILIAR, STANDARD, commonplace, FREQUENT, ACCUSTOMED, prevailing, POPULAR, TYPICAL, stock, ORDINARY, NORMAL, HABITUAL, CUSTOMARY, AVERAGE, wonted, expected.

usually *adv.* REGULARLY, FREQUENTLY, customarily, ORDINARILY, habitually, normally.

usurp: see SEIZE.

usury: see INTEREST.

utensil *n.* IMPLEMENT, INSTRUMENT, DEVICE, apparatus, TOOL, APPLIANCE, VESSEL.

utensils: see EQUIPMENT.

utility *n.* USE, usefulness, FUNCTION, PURPOSE, SERVICE, AID, BENEFIT.

utilization: see APPLICATION; USE.

utilize: see APPLY; CONSUME; EMPLOY; EXERT; USE.

utmost *adj.* greatest, furthest, farthest, LAST, uttermost, highest, EXTREME.
— *n.* LIMIT, BEST, MOST.

utopia: see PARADISE; PERFECTION.

utter *v.* SPEAK, PRONOUNCE, SAY, SOUND, DELIVER.
— *adj.* COMPLETE, TOTAL, ABSOLUTE, THOROUGH, UNQUALIFIED, out-and-out.

utterance *n.* STATEMENT, EXPRESSION, COMMENT, pronouncement, REMARK, DECLARATION, assertion, EXCLAMATION.

uttered: see ORAL.

utterly: see ALTOGETHER; ENTIRELY; EXTREMELY; PURELY; THOROUGHLY; TOTALLY.

uttermost: see UTMOST.

V

vacancy *n.* OPENING, OPPORTUNITY, void, emptiness, VACUUM.

vacant *adj.* EMPTY, OPEN, void, CLEAR, unfilled, unoccupied, FREE.

vacate *v.* relinquish, SURRENDER, FREE, QUIT, ABANDON, LEAVE, EVACUATE.

vacation *n.* HOLIDAY, LEAVE, furlough, REST.
— *v.*: see CAMP.

vacationer: see TOURIST.

vacillate: see HESITATE.

vacuous: see EMPTY.

vacuum *n.* emptiness, void, VACANCY.
— *v.*: see CLEAN.

vagabond: see BUM; LOAFER.

vagrant: see BUM; DRIFTER; LOAFER; ROVER; TRAMP.

vague *adj.* obscure, unclear, UNCERTAIN, HAZY, QUESTIONABLE, indefinite, blurred, mealy-mouthed.

vaguely: see ANYWHERE.

vagueness: see DIMNESS.

vain *adj.* conceited, egotistic, arrogant, PROUD, ostentatious, showy, deceitful, void, EMPTY, USELESS, fruitless, futile, trivial, WORTHLESS.

vale: see DALE; VALLEY.

valediction: see FAREWELL.

valet: see SERVANT; WAITER.

valiant: see BRAVE; COURAGEOUS; DARING; GAME; HEROIC.

valid: see GOOD; LAWFUL; LOGICAL; PERSUASIVE.

validate: see VERIFY.

validation: see VERIFICATION.

valise: see BAG.

valises: see LUGGAGE.

valley *n.* vale, DALE, glen, gorge, CANYON, ravine, BASIN.

valor: see BRAVERY; COURAGE; DARING; HEROISM.

valorous: see FEARLESS.

valuable *adj.* EXPENSIVE, COSTLY, PRECIOUS, high-priced, SIGNIFICANT, IMPORTANT.

valuables: see TREASURE.

valuation: see APPRECIATION; ESTIMATE.

value *n.* PRICE, COST, WORTH, EXCELLENCE, MERIT, IMPORTANCE, SIGNIFICANCE.
  — *v.*: see CHERISH; ESTEEM; HONOR; MATTER; PRICE.

valued: see BELOVED; FAVORED.

valueless: see USELESS; WORTHLESS.

valve: see GATE.

vampire: see BAT.

van: see TRUCK; WAGON.

vandal *n.* destroyer, saboteur, wrecker, THIEF, barbarian, BRUTE, BEAST.

vandalism: see DAMAGE.

vane: see BLADE.

vanish *v.* DISAPPEAR, DISSOLVE, EVAPORATE, FADE, SINK, DIE, PERISH.

vanished: see LOST.

vanity: see PRIDE.

vanity case: see COMPACT.

vanquish: see BEAT; CONQUER.

vanquisher: see VICTOR.

vantage: see ADVANTAGE.

vapid: see DULL.

vapor *n.* FOG, STEAM, MIST, condensation, smog, haze, SMOKE.

vaporize: see DISAPPEAR; EVAPORATE.

vaporizer: see SPRAY.

variable *adj.* inconstant, shifting, CHANGEABLE, fluctuating, deviating, unsteady.

variableness: see CHANGE.

variance: see DIFFERENCE.

variation *n.* alteration, CHANGE, irregularity, modification, deviation, DEPARTURE.

varied: see ASSORTED.

variety *n.* diversification, diversity, DIFFERENCE, MIXTURE, ASSORTMENT, KIND, BRAND.

various *adj.* DIFFERENT, diverse, NUMEROUS, SEVERAL, MANY, DISSIMILAR, multifarious.

variously *adv.* differently, inconsistently, diversely, CHANGEABLY, severally, OTHERWISE.

varmint: see ANIMAL.

varnish *n.* shellac, STAIN, lacquer, glaze, sizing, GLOSS, FINISH.
  — *v.* shellac, lacquer, japan, enamel, surface, size.

vary *v.* CHANGE, ALTER, fluctuate, DIFFER, diverge, deviate, DEPART, modulate.

varying: see DIFFERENT.

vase: see PITCHER.

vast *adj.* IMMENSE, stupendous, enormous, EXTENSIVE, widespread, boundless, INFINITE. See also AMBITIOUS.

vastly: see EXCEEDINGLY; EXTREMELY.

vastness: see DEEP; INFINITY.

vault *n.* **1** *(the casket was placed in a vault)* crypt, TOMB, sepulcher, GRAVE; **2** *(place your valuables in a vault)* SAFE, coffer, strong box, depository. See also ARCH; HOP; JUMP; LEAP; SPRING.
  — *v.*: see CLEAR; JUMP; LEAP; PITCH.

vaulted: see ARCHED.

veer: see TURN.

vegetable: see HERB.

vegetation: see GRASS; GROWTH; PLANT.

vehemence: see FIRE; FURY; PASSION; STRENGTH.

vehement: see INTENSE; PASSIONATE; VIOLENT.

vehemently: see FORCIBLY.

vehicle *n.* conveyance, CARRIAGE, CAR, TRANSPORTATION, INSTRUMENT, AGENCY, MEDIUM, METHOD.

veil *n.* gauze, FILM, mask, CONCEALMENT, COVER, SHADE, SCREEN.
— *v.* CONCEAL, mask, cloak, DISGUISE, SCREEN, HIDE, SHADE.

veiled: see UNSEEN.

vein *n.* SEAM, LEDGE, CRACK, flaw, crevice, BREAK, breach, GROOVE, STREAK, LINE, WAY, MANNER, STYLE, MOOD, TYPE, ilk.

velocity: see SPEED.

velvet *adj.* SOFT, PLUSH, DELICATE, SMOOTH, FUZZY.

velvety: see SMOOTH; SOFT.

venal: see SELFISH.

vend: see MARKET; PEDDLE; SELL.

vender: see PEDDLER.

vending: see SALE.

veneer: see COATING; COVERING; DISGUISE.

veneration: see RESPECT.

vengeance *n.* REVENGE, retaliation, repayment, PUNISHMENT.

venison: see GAME.

venom: see POISON.

venomous: see POISONOUS.

vent: see OUTLET.

ventilate: see AIR.

ventilator: see FAN.

venture *v.* ATTEMPT, TRY, TEST, EXPERIMENT, GAMBLE, RISK, chance.
— *n.* UNDERTAKING, PROJECT, enterprise, CHANCE, GAMBLE, RISK, DANGER.

venturesome: see DARING.

venturous: see DARING.

veracious: see RELIABLE.

veracity: see SINCERITY; TRUTH.

veranda: see PORCH.

verbal *adj.* spoken, ORAL, said, stated, told, expressed, literal, verbatim, word-for-word.

verbatim: see EXACT; VERBAL.

verbose: see CHATTY; LONG-WINDED.

verdict *n.* pronouncement, DECISION, OPINION, JUDGMENT, DETERMINATION, finding, decree, SETTLEMENT.

verge: see BRIM; MARGIN; RIM.

verging: see MARGINAL.

verification *n.* PROOF, EVIDENCE, validation, CERTIFICATION, confirmation, affirmation, substantiation.

verify *v.* PROVE, validate, DOCUMENT, affirm, authenticate, CONFIRM, substantiate.

verily: see EVEN.

verity: see TRUTH.

vermilion: see RED.

vernacular: see SLANG.

versatile: see ADJUSTABLE.

verse *n.* **1** (*how many verses does the poem have?*) LINE, stanza, meter; **2** (*what biblical verse is that from?*) DIVISION, SECTION, PART, PASSAGE, TEXT, SENTENCE.

versed: see SKILLED.

version *n.* INTERPRETATION, rendition, SIDE, ACCOUNT, REPORT, TALE, STORY, take.

vertebrae: see BACKBONE; SPINE.

vertical *adj.* ERECT, UPRIGHT, perpendicular, STRAIGHT.

verve: see DASH.

very *adj.* SAME, IDENTICAL, TRUE, REAL, ACTUAL.
— *adv.* MUCH, GREATLY, EXTREMELY, hugely, EXCEEDINGLY, EXACTLY, ABSOLUTELY.

vessel *n.* **1** (*to sail on a vessel*) SHIP, BOAT, CRAFT; **2** (*a cooking vessel*) CONTAINER, receptacle, KETTLE, UTENSIL, POT, BOWL.

vest: see INVEST; POWER.

vestal: see PURE.

vestibule: see ENTRY; HALL.

vestige: see ANTIQUE; REMNANT.

veteran *n.* oldster, SENIOR, MASTER, dean, trooper, adept, EXPERT, SPECIALIST, AUTHORITY.
— *adj.* OLD, experienced, seasoned, PRACTICED, disciplined, blasé.

veterinarian: see DOCTOR.

veto *n.* PROHIBITION, refusal, denial, NO, nay, rejection.
— *v.* REFUSE, DENY, FORBID, PROHIBIT, REJECT, DISAPPROVE.

vex: see BORE; BOTHER; IRRITATE; PROVOKE; TORMENT.

vexation: see IRRITATION.

vexatious: see MISCHIEVOUS.

vexing: see BOTHERSOME.

via: see AROUND; PER; THROUGH.

viaduct: see BRIDGE; SPAN.

vibrant: see LIVELY.

vibrate *v.* QUIVER, MOVE, SHAKE, quake, waver, fluctuate, wobble.

vibration *n.* fluctuation, wavering, FLUTTER, quiver, oscillation, shake, tremble.

vice: see CRIME; EVIL; SIN; WRONG.

vicinity *n.* CLOSENESS, nearness, neighborhood, environs, SURROUNDINGS, proximity, AREA.

vicious *adj.* EVIL, WICKED, corrupt, FOUL, vile, CRUEL, SAVAGE.

viciousness: see WICKEDNESS.

victim *n.* PREY, sufferer, martyr, GAME, scapegoat, SACRIFICE.

victimize: see CHEAT; PERSECUTE.

victor *n.* winner, CHAMPION, CONQUEROR, vanquisher, MASTER.

victorious *adj.* triumphant, SUCCESSFUL, CHAMPION, winning, conquering.

victory *n.* TRIUMPH, SUCCESS, win, mastery, CONQUEST, OVERTHROW.

victuals: see FARE.

vie: see COMPETE; CONTEST; TANGLE.

view *n.* LOOK, panorama, vista, SURVEY, PROSPECT, SCENE, SPECTACLE.
  — *v.* LOOK, SEE, SCAN, EXPLORE, INSPECT, SURVEY, EXAMINE.

viewer: see SPECTATOR.

viewers: see AUDIENCE.

viewpoint: see ASPECT; CHARACTER; DIRECTION; OPINION; OUTLOOK; SIDE; SLANT; VISION.

vigil: see WATCH.

vigilance: see ALERTNESS; ATTENTION; CAUTION; EYE.

vigilant: see AWAKE; CAREFUL; CAUTIOUS; CONSCIOUS; JEALOUS; OBSERVANT; WATCHFUL.

vigor *n.* FORCE, POWER, STRENGTH, ENERGY, SPIRIT, ENTHUSIASM, INTENSITY.

vigorous *adj.* ENERGETIC, STRONG, ACTIVE, FORCEFUL, POWERFUL, INTENSE, spirited.

vigorously: see FORCIBLY; HARD.

vile: see DIRTY; FOUL; NASTY; SLIMY; VICIOUS; VILLAINOUS.

vileness: see DIRT; MEANNESS.

vilify: see ABUSE; INSULT; SHAME; SMEAR.

villa: see MANSION.

village *n.* TOWN, hamlet, municipality, SETTLEMENT.

villain *n.* SCOUNDREL, rogue, BRUTE, DEVIL, evildoer, malefactor, CRIMINAL, violator, cad, meanie.

villainous *adj.* base, vile, MEAN, WICKED, sinful, depraved, corrupt.

villainy: see WICKEDNESS.

vim: see ENERGY.

vinegar: see ACID.

violate *v.* BREAK, TRESPASS, INVADE, disobey, DEFY, disregard, ABUSE.

violation *n.* disregard, ABUSE, breaking, flouting, misbehavior, infraction, dishonor. See also ASSAULT.

violator: see VILLAIN.

violence *n.* RAGE, ANGER, FURY, FORCE, INTENSITY, PASSION, ferocity.

violent *adj.* FURIOUS, ANGRY, raging, vehement, PASSIONATE, ferocious.

viper: see SNAKE; WRETCH.

virgin *n.* MAID, maiden, miss, damsel, lass.
  — *adj.* chaste, PURE, MODEST, SPOTLESS, untouched, undisturbed, unused, NEW.

virginity *n.* purity, chastity, INNOCENCE, MODESTY, newness.

virile: see MALE; MASCULINE.

virtually: see PRACTICALLY.

virtue *n.* morality, HONOR, VALUE, MERIT, GOODNESS, righteousness, decency.

virtuosity: see SKILL.

virtuoso: see ARTIST.

virtuous *adj.* HONEST, UPRIGHT, righteous, HONORABLE, DECENT, ethical, chaste.

virus: see GERM; INFECTION; INSECT; POISON.

visa: see PASSPORT.

visage: see FACE; FRONT; MUG.

visibility *n.* VIEW, perceptibility, clearness, prominence, noticeability.

visible *adj.* observable, NOTICEABLE, APPARENT, OBVIOUS, EVIDENT, perceptive, revealed.

visibly *adv.* APPARENTLY, EVIDENTLY, obviously, noticeably, discernibly, perceivably, CLEARLY.

vision *n.* **1** *(twenty-twenty vision)* eyesight, SIGHT, perception, VIEW; **2** *(a vision of the world)* OBSERVATION, UNDERSTANDING, KNOWLEDGE, penetration, viewpoint, OUTLOOK. See also FORESIGHT.

visit *v.* CALL, SEE, STAY, STOP, ATTEND, FREQUENT. — *n.* CALL, STOP, INTERVIEW, APPOINTMENT, CONVERSATION.

visitant: see GUEST.

visitor *n.* GUEST, caller, COMPANY, sojourner, frequenter.

vista: see SIGHT; VIEW.

visual *adj.* optic, seen, perceptible, seeable, observable, CONSPICUOUS, NOTICEABLE.

visualize: see DREAM; IMAGINE.

vital *adj.* SIGNIFICANT, IMPORTANT, NECESSARY, ESSENTIAL, CRITICAL, BASIC, indispensable.

vitality *n.* animation, liveliness, ENERGY, SPIRIT, LIFE, VIGOR.

vittles: see NOURISHMENT.

vituperation: see ABUSE.

vivacious: see ALIVE; BRIGHT; CRISP.

vivacity: see LIFE.

vivid *adj.* DISTINCT, STRONG, BRIGHT, CLEAR, BRILLIANT, LIVELY, animated.

vividly: see SHARPLY.

vividness: see RELIEF.

vivisection: see ANATOMY.

vixen: see FOX.

vocable: see WORD.

vocabulary *n.* word list, DICTIONARY, wordbook, thesaurus, GLOSSARY, terminology, words, LANGUAGE.

vocal: see ORAL.

vocalist: see SINGER.

vocalize: see SING.

vocalized: see ORAL.

vocally: see ALOUD.

vocation: see BUSINESS; CAREER; MISSION; OCCUPATION; PROFESSION.

vocational: see EDUCATIONAL; PROFESSION.

vogue: see FASHION; POPULARITY; RAGE; STYLE.

voice *n.* **1** *(a shrill voice)* SPEECH, UTTERANCE, PRONUNCIATION, enunciation, DELIVERY; **2** *(a voice in politics)* say-so, CHOICE, VOTE, option, REPRESENTATION. — *v.*: see STATE.

voiced: see ORAL.

voiceless: see SOUNDLESS.

void: see CAVITY; EMPTY; VACANCY; VACANT; VACUUM; VAIN.

volatile: see EXPLOSIVE; MOBILE; TEMPERAMENTAL.

voluble: see TALKATIVE.

volume *n.* **1** *(the volume of a container)* CAPACITY, content, bulk, SIZE, dimension; **2** *(turn down the volume)* SOUND, LOUDNESS, INTENSITY.

voluminous: see HUGE.

voluntarily: see FREE; FREELY.

voluntary *adj.* FREE, WILLING, optional, INTENTIONAL, DELIBERATE, spontaneous.

volunteer *n.* enlistee, recruit, taker, CANDIDATE. — *v.* SIGN, ENLIST, OFFER, tender.

voluptuous: see LUXURIOUS.

vomit: see ERUPT.

voodoo: see MAGIC; RELIGION; SUPERSTITION.

vote *n.* ELECTION, BALLOT, POLL, referendum, DECISION, CHOICE. — *v.* ELECT, CHOOSE, SELECT, DECIDE, DETERMINE.

vouch: see GUARANTEE; PLEDGE; SWEAR; VOW.

voucher: see RECEIPT.

vouch for: see ASSURE; CERTIFY.

vouchsafe: see SWEAR.

vow *n.* PROMISE, assurance, OATH, PLEDGE, guaranty, affirmation. — *v.* PROMISE, ASSURE, SWEAR, PLEDGE, affirm, vouch, GUARANTEE.

voyage *n.* TRIP, JOURNEY, excursion, TOUR, cruise, SAIL, crossing. — *v.*: see SAIL.

voyager: see PASSENGER; SAILOR; TRAVELER.

vulgar *adj.* COARSE, CHEAP, COMMON, obscene, CRUDE, INDECENT, gross.

vulgarity: see COARSENESS.

vulgate: see SLANG.

W

wacky: see INSANE.

wad: see CASH.

wadding: see PAD; PLUG.

wade: see SWIM; TRUDGE.

wafer: see COOKIE; FLAKE; TABLET.

wag *v.* SWAY, SWING, FLAP, WAVE, FLUTTER, BOB, wobble.
— *n.*: see COMEDIAN.

wage *v.* DO, MAKE, PRACTICE, CONDUCT, PURSUE, FULFILL.

wage earner: see EMPLOYEE.

wager: see BET; CHANCE; GAMBLE; PAWN; RISK; STAKE.

wages *pl.n.* pay, SALARY, EARNINGS, INCOME, PAYMENT, compensation, RATE.

waggish: see MISCHIEVOUS.

wagon *n.* CART, CARRIAGE, CAR, coach, TRUCK, van, VEHICLE.

wail *v.* CRY, WEEP, SOB, MOAN, lament, MOURN.
— *n.* HOWL, SCREECH, CRY, lament, MOAN.

waist: see LAP; MIDDLE.

waistband: see BELT.

wait *v.* DELAY, tarry, dally, LINGER, PAUSE, procrastinate.
— *n.*: see DELAY.

waiter *n.* server, counterman, ATTENDANT, steward, valet, SERVANT. See also TRAY.

waiting *n.* tarrying, staying, delaying, EXPECTATION.

waiting room: see LOUNGE.

wait on: see ATTEND; SERVE.

waive: see YIELD.

wake *v.* AWAKEN, ARISE, ROUSE, AROUSE, STIR, STIMULATE, EXCITE.

wakeful *adj.* sleepless, RESTLESS, insomniac.

wakened: see AWAKE.

wake up: see AWAKEN.

walk *v.* promenade, step, STROLL, PACE, TREAD, amble, ramble, MARCH.
— *n.* PATH, ALLEY, way, PROMENADE, AVENUE.

walking: see TREAD.

walkout: see STRIKE.

walkway: see AISLE; GALLERY.

wall *n.* FENCE, HEDGE, BANK, BARRIER, BAR, obstruction, hurdle.
— *v.*: see FENCE.

wallet: see BILLFOLD.

wallop: see BELT; SLAM; SMASH.

wallpaper: see PAPER.

wan: see GREEN; PALE.

wand: see BATON; ROD.

wander *v.* ROAM, STRAY, ROVE, ramble, DRIFT, SHIFT, meander.

wanderer: see DRIFTER; LOAFER; PILGRIM; ROVER; TRAMP.

wandering: see RESTLESS; STRAY.

wane: see DECLINE.

want *v.* DESIRE, WISH, CRAVE, NEED, REQUIRE, hanker, FANCY.
— *n.*: see ABSENCE; FAMINE; LACK; NEED; POVERTY; WISH.

wanting *adj.* lacking, deficient, MISSING, inadequate, defective, ABSENT.
— *prep.*: see MINUS.

war *n.* hostilities, strife, fighting, COMBAT, BATTLE, WARFARE.

warble: see SING.

ward: see CLIENT.

warden *n.* custodian, KEEPER, overseer, GUARDIAN, superintendent, JAILER, GUARD.

ward off: see AVERT.

wardrobe *n.* apparel, CLOTHES, clothing, garments, ensemble, COSTUME, CLOSET.

warehouse *n.* storehouse, stockroom, depot, depository, SHED, magazine.

wares: see MERCHANDISE.

warfare *n.* WAR, fighting, hostilities, COMBAT, BATTLE, CONFLICT, CONTEST.

wariness: see CAUTION; PRECAUTION.

warlike: see AGGRESSIVE; HOSTILE; MILITARY.

warlock: see MAGICIAN.

warlord: see CHIEF.

warm *adj.* MILD, temperate, heated, SYMPATHETIC, fervent, EAGER, PASSIONATE.
— *v.* COOK, PREPARE, HEAT, TOAST, ROAST.

warm-hearted: see LOVABLE; OPEN-HEARTED; SYMPATHETIC.

warmth *n.* GLOW, zeal, fervor, ENTHUSIASM, cordiality, congeniality, friendliness.

warm-up: see THAW.

warn *v.* CAUTION, ALERT, ADVISE, apprise, ACQUAINT, SIGNAL, INFORM.

warning *n.* CAUTION, ADVICE, NOTICE, ALERT, SIGNAL, ALARM, premonition, ultimatum, monition.

warp *v.* TWIST, BEND, SPRING, distort, curve, TURN, contort.
— *n.*: see TWIST.

warped: see BENT.

warrant *n.* guaranty, PLEDGE, surety, VERIFICATION, CERTIFICATION, subpoena.
— *v.* JUSTIFY, CERTIFY, ASSURE, GUARANTEE, PERMIT, ALLOW, empower.

warranty *n.* AGREEMENT, stipulation, GUARANTY, PLEDGE, SECURITY.

warrior *n.* FIGHTER, SOLDIER, battler, HERO, combatant.

warships: see NAVY.

wart: see GROWTH.

wary: see CAREFUL; CAUTIOUS.

wash *v.* launder, CLEANSE, CLEAN, SCRUB, BATHE, RINSE, moisten.
— *n.* bathing, cleansing, LAUNDRY, scrubbing.

washbowl: see SINK.

washcloth: see CLOTH; RAG.

washing *n.* bathing, LAUNDRY, linen, immersion.

washout: see FAILURE.

washrag: see RAG.

washroom: see TOILET.

washtub: see SINK.

waste *v.* squander, EXHAUST, CONSUME, SPEND, deplete, dissipate, misuse.
— *n.* EXPENDITURE, EXHAUSTION, squandering, REFUSE, GARBAGE, RUBBISH, TRASH.

wasted: see WORN.

wasteful *adj.* squandering, extravagant, thriftless, immoderate, LIBERAL, CARELESS.

wasteland: see DESERT; WILDERNESS.

watch *v.* OBSERVE, MARK, REGARD, PROTECT, MIND, TEND, oversee.
— *n.* vigil, GUARD, OBSERVATION, lookout, ATTENTION, sentinel, PROTECTION. See also ALERT; CLOCK.

watchdog: see ESCORT; GUARDIAN.

watcher: see OBSERVER; WITNESS.

watchful *adj.* vigilant, ATTENTIVE, CAREFUL, prudent, prepared, ALERT, CAUTIOUS.

watchfulness: see ALERTNESS; CARE; CAUTION.

watchman: see GUARD; JANITOR; KEEPER; PROTECTOR.

watchtower: see TOWER.

watchword: see WORD.

water *v.* WET, drench, steep, SPRINKLE, irrigate, SPRAY, moisten.

watercourse: see RIVER.

waterfront: see BEACH.

waterless: see DRY.

waterproof: see DRY.

watershed: see BASIN.

waterside: see SHORE.

watertight: see DRY.

waterway: see CANAL; RIVER; STREAM.

watery: see FLUID; JUICY; WET.

wave *v.* undulate, SWAY, FLUTTER, ripple, SHAKE, CALL, SIGNAL, BECKON.
— *n.* undulation, RIPPLE, swell, roller, breaker, surge, whitecap.

waver: see FLAP; HESITATE; REEL; STAGGER; SWAY; TREMBLE; VIBRATE.

wavering: see HESITATION; VIBRATION.

wax: see CANDLE; GROW; LUBRICATE; SMOOTH.

way *n.* MANNER, CUSTOM, TRADITION, PRACTICE, USAGE, METHOD, MEANS. See also FOOTPATH; ROUTE; STREET; WALK.

wayfarer: see EXPLORER; PASSENGER; PILGRIM; TRAVELER.

weak *adj.* FEEBLE, sickly, puny, impotent, POWERLESS, HELPLESS, SHAKY, namby-pamby.

weaken *v.* enfeeble, undermine, SHAKE, LESSEN, FAIL, DECLINE, DROOP.

weakened: see BROKEN.

weakling: see COWARD.

weakly: see COWARDLY.

weak-minded: see FEEBLE-MINDED.

weakness *n.* feebleness, helplessness, impotence, fragility, frailty, deterioration.

wealth *n.* MONEY, RICHES, TREASURE, affluence, ABUNDANCE, possessions, assets, opulence.

wealthy *adj.* RICH, substantial, PROSPEROUS, moneyed, ABUNDANT, LUXURIOUS, well-to-do.

weapon *n.* munitions, ARMS, armament, PROTECTION.

weaponry: see ARMS; ARTILLERY.

wear *v.* **1** *(what will you wear to the beach?)* BEAR, carry, don, COVER, DRESS; **2** *(to wear from usage)* WASTE, fray, DECAY, FADE, SHRINK.
— *n.* deterioration, decay, DAMAGE, LOSS, impairment, diminution.

wearied: see WORN.

weariness *n.* tiredness, FATIGUE, EXHAUSTION, IMPATIENCE, DISCONTENT, lethargy.

wear out: see EXHAUST; TIRE; USE.

weary *adj.* TIRED, WEAK, fatigued, exhausted, WORN, bored.
— *v.*: see ANNOY; BORE; TIRE.

weather: see CLIMATE; RESIST; WITHSTAND.

weave *v.* LACE, braid, FOLD, intertwine, intermix, zigzag, crisscross.

web *n.* net, mesh, MAT, intermixture, interweaving.

webbing: see LACE.

wed: see COMBINE; MARRY.

wedded: see MARRIED.

wedding *n.* MARRIAGE, matrimony, wedlock.

wedge: see JAM; PLUG.

wedlock: see MARRIAGE; UNION; WEDDING.

wee: see LITTLE.

weed *v.* REMOVE, SEPARATE, segregate, RID, FREE, eradicate, ELIMINATE.
— *n.*: see POT.

weekly: see NEWSPAPER.

weep *v.* SOB, CRY, lament, bemoan, WAIL, blubber, BAWL.

weeping: see SOB; TEARFUL.

weigh *v.* SCALE, MEASURE, BALANCE, ponder, contemplate, deliberate, CONSIDER. See also LOAD.

weight *n.* heaviness, LOAD, CARGO, SIGNIFICANCE, IMPORTANCE, CONSEQUENCE, VALUE.

weightless: see LIGHT.

weighty: see HEAVY; HEFTY; HUSKY; INFLUENTIAL; PREGNANT.

weird: see CURIOUS; MAGICAL; MYSTERIOUS; ODD; SICK.

welcome *n.* greeting, SALUTATION, SALUTE, RECEPTION.
— *v.* GREET, SALUTE, RECEIVE, HAIL, EMBRACE.
— *adj.* AGREEABLE, PLEASANT, GRATEFUL, esteemed, appreciated, cherished.
— *interj.* hello, GREETINGS, salutations, hi.

welcoming: see HOSPITABLE; OPEN-HEARTED.

weld: see JOIN.

welfare *n.* BENEFIT, good, well-being, ADVANTAGE, HAPPINESS, PROSPERITY, COMFORT.

welkin: see SKY.

well *adv.* FINE, satisfactorily, safely, soundly, adequately, splendidly, THOROUGHLY.
— *n.* SOURCE, BEGINNING, START, derivation, origin, FOUNTAIN.
— *v.*: see ISSUE.

well-balanced: see LEVEL.

well-behaved: see OBEDIENT; ORDERLY.

well-being: see COMFORT; HAPPINESS; HEALTH; PROSPERITY; WELFARE.

well-bred: see CIVIL; GENTLE; MANNERLY.

well-built: see HUSKY; SHAPELY; STURDY.

well-conditioned: see SANE.

well-dressed: see SWELL.

well-formed: see HANDSOME; SHAPELY.

well-informed: see LEARNED.

well-kept: see NEAT.

well-known *adj.* FAMOUS, esteemed, renowned, appreciated, FAMILIAR, recognized, reputable.

well-liked: see POPULAR.

well-mannered: see CIVIL.

well-nigh: see ALMOST; NEARLY.

well-off: see FORTUNATE; PROSPEROUS; RICH.

well-organized: see NEAT.

well-proportioned: see SHAPELY.

well-to-do: see PROSPEROUS; RICH; WEALTHY.

welt: see BUMP.

welter: see CONFUSION.

wet *adj.* MOIST, DAMP, soaked, drenched, soggy, dripping, watery.

— v. moisten, dampen, SOAK, SPRINKLE, WATER, drench.

wetness *n.* dampness, MOISTURE, humidity, mistiness, fogginess.

wet nurse: see NURSE.

whack: see BANG; BLOW; CLUB; RAP; SMACK.

wharf *n.* pier, DOCK, landing, HARBOR.

what *pron.* SOMETHING, ANYTHING, EVERYTHING, which.

whatever *pron.* EVERYTHING, ANYTHING, WHAT.

whatsoever: see HOWEVER.

wheedle: see COAX; PERSUADE.

wheel *n.* **1** *(the wheels of a car)* disk, RIM, caster, hoop, RING, roller; **2** *(he's a big wheel)* CELEBRITY, EXECUTIVE.
— v.: see ROLL; ROTATE.

wheelbarrow: see CART.

wheeled: see MOBILE.

wheeze: see GASP; PANT.

when *adv.* whereas, SINCE, ALTHOUGH, CONSIDERING.

whence: see HOW.

whenever: see ONCE.

whensoever: see ONCE.

whereas: see ALTHOUGH; BECAUSE; SINCE; WHEN; WHILE.

whereby: see HOW.

wherever: see ANYWHERE.

wherewith: see HOW.

whet: see SHARPEN.

whether: see IF; SUPPOSING.

which: see WHAT.

whiff: see BREATH; PANT.

while *n.* SEASON, TIME, MEANTIME, INTERVAL, interim.
— adv. THOUGH, ALTHOUGH, whereas, whilst.

whilst: see WHILE.

whim: see IMPULSE; NOTION.

whimper: see MUMBLE; SOB; WHINE.

whimpering: see TEARFUL.

whimsical: see IMPULSIVE; ODD; QUAINT.

whine *v.* whimper, CRY, MOAN, COMPLAIN, GRUMBLE, MURMUR.

— n. COMPLAINT, grumbling, murmuring, droning, WAIL.

whip *n.* STRAP, SWITCH, LASH, cane, ROD, cat-o'-nine-tails.
— v. flog, BEAT, THRASH, LASH, SPANK.

whir: see RUSTLE.

whirl *v.* SPIN, gyrate, ROTATE, pivot, swirl, REEL, REVOLVE.
— n.: see ROLL; ROTATION.

whirlpool: see GULF.

whirlwind: see STORM; WIND.

whisk *v.* WHIP, MIX, SWEEP, BRUSH, RUSH, HASTEN, SPEED.
— n.: see BRUSH.

whisker: see BRISTLE.

whiskers: see BEARD; HAIR.

whiskey: see LIQUOR.

whisper *v.* MURMUR, HUM, MUTTER, MUMBLE.
— n. MURMUR, mumble, undertone, HINT, TRACE, disclosure, RUMOR.

whistle: see PIPE; SIGNAL.

white *adj.* silvery, milky, ivory, chalky, snowy, PALE, blanched, bleached, BLANK.
— n.: see CHALK.

whitecap: see WAVE.

whiten *v.* blanch, bleach, FROST, silver, pale.

whitewash: see COVER UP.

whitish: see PALE.

whittle: see CARVE; CHIP; TAPER.

whiz: see EXPERT.

whole *adj.* ALL, ENTIRE, TOTAL, COMPLETE, undamaged, intact, uncut.
— n. entirety, UNITY, totality, all, bulk, BODY, SUM, ensemble.

wholehearted: see ENTHUSIASTIC.

wholeness: see PERFECTION.

wholesaler: see MERCHANT.

wholesome: see FRESH; GOOD; HEALTHY; SANITARY.

wholesomeness: see SANITATION.

wholly: see ALL; ALTOGETHER; COMPLETELY; ENTIRELY; FULLY; PURELY.

whoop: see SHRIEK.

wicked *adj.* EVIL, VICIOUS, malevolent, immoral, depraved, SINFUL, unrighteous, satanic, unspeakable.

wickedness *n.* EVIL, ungodliness, impurity, sinfulness, viciousness, malevolence, shamefulness, villainy.

wicker: see BASKET.

wide *adj.* EXTENSIVE, BROAD, VAST, LARGE, expansive, AMPLE, widespread.

wide-awake: see ALERT; AWAKE.

widely: see ABROAD; FAR.

widen: see BROADEN; EXTEND.

widespread: see EXTENSIVE; GENERAL; UNIVERSAL; VAST; WIDE.

width *n.* breadth, EXTENT, expanse, SPAN, STRETCH, amplitude.

wield: see HANDLE; USE.

wife *n.* spouse, MATE, PARTNER, consort, missus, provider.

wifely: see BRIDAL.

wiggle: see SQUIRM.

wigwam: see TENT.

wild *adj.* untamed, uncivilized, uncultivated, uncontrolled, SAVAGE, FIERCE, ferocious. See also ABSURD.
— *n.* WILDERNESS, BUSH, DESERT, JUNGLE.

wilderness *n.* WILD, wilds, wasteland, woods, FOREST, JUNGLE, DESERT, emptiness, labyrinth.

wilds: see WILDERNESS.

will *n.* **1** *(to make a will)* testament, bequest, legacy; **2** *(to use will power)* self-control, DECISION, RESOLUTION, DETERMINATION, PURPOSE.
— *v.* **1** *(to will a million dollars)* leave, bequeath, GIVE; **2** *(to will it so)* DECIDE, RESOLVE, DETERMINE, INTEND, CHOOSE, WISH.

willful: see INTENTIONAL.

willfully: see DELIBERATELY.

willing *adj.* READY, EAGER, ENTHUSIASTIC, GAME, consenting, zealous, inclined, obliging.

willingly: see GLADLY; SOON.

willingness: see CONSENT.

willowy: see SLENDER.

wilt *v.* WITHER, DROOP, FADE, sag, WEAKEN.

wily: see FOXY; SLY; TRICKY.

wimper: see CRY.

win *v.* SUCCEED, TRIUMPH, ACQUIRE, secure, GAIN.
— *n.*: see CONQUEST; VICTORY.

wince: see SMART.

wind *n.* BREATH, GAS, DRAFT, BREEZE, zephyr, GUST, GALE, windstorm, whirlwind, hurricane, cyclone, typhoon, tornado, HINT, intimation.
— *v.* TURN, CRANK, ROLL, COIL, TWIST, TWINE, entwine, meander, WANDER.

winded: see BREATHLESS.

windless: see CALM.

windmill: see MILL.

window: see PANE.

windowpane: see GLASS.

windpipe: see PIPE.

windstorm: see STORM; WIND.

windy *adj.* drafty, BREEZY, gusty, blowy, blustery, squally. See also CHATTY.

wine: see REFRESHMENTS.

winery: see CELLAR.

wing: see ANNEX; ARM; BRANCH; FLANK; FLAP; FLY; PAVILION; UNIT.

winging: see FLIGHT.

wink *v.* BLINK, TWINKLE, SHINE, GLEAM, FLASH.
— *n.* blink, TWINKLE, FLASH, sparkle, GLEAM, INSTANT, SIGNAL, come-on.

winner: see CHAMPION; CONQUEROR; FIRST; LEADER; MASTER; VICTOR.

winning *adj.* charming, ATTRACTIVE, engaging. See also VICTORIOUS.

winnow: see PICK.

win over: see PERSUADE.

winsome: see SWEET.

wintry: see COLD; RAW.

wipe *v.* RUB, SMEAR, BRUSH, MOP, swab, SPONGE, CLEAN, DRY, REMOVE.

wiper: see HANDKERCHIEF; RAG; TOWEL.

wire: see CABLE; FIBER; GUY; LINE; THREAD.

wiring: see GROUND.

wiry: see ATHLETIC; LIMBER.

wisdom *n.* KNOWLEDGE, LEARNING, FORESIGHT, CARE, FORETHOUGHT, common sense, horse sense.

wise *adj.* knowing, shrewd, astute, prudent, SENSIBLE, judicious, discreet, far-sighted, perceptive, INTELLIGENT, BRIGHT, SMART, oracular, omniscient.

wiseacre: see COMEDIAN; WIT.

wish *v.* DESIRE, WANT, CRAVE, aspire, long for, bid, TELL.
— *n.* DESIRE, want, WILL, REQUEST, longing, yearning, craving, aspiration, AMBITION, COMMAND, ORDER.

wish for: see DESIRE.

wispy: see THIN.

wit *n.* **1** *(a joke by one of the local wits)* comic, humorist, punster, joker, wiseacre; **2** *(at one's wit's end)* WISDOM, INTELLIGENCE, SENSE, UNDERSTANDING, JUDGMENT, brains, MIND, INTELLECT, repartee.

witch *n.* sorceress, hag, shrew, crone.
— *v.* enchant, CHARM, captivate, BEWITCH.

witchcraft: see MAGIC; SUPERSTITION.

witchery: see SUPERSTITION.

with *prep.* THROUGH, BY, AMONG, attending, accompanying, BESIDE, PLUS, upon.

withdraw *v.* take back, RETRACT, REMOVE, RESERVE, RETIRE, RETREAT, secede, EXTRACT.

withdrawal: see EXIT; PARTING; RETREAT.

wither *v.* WILT, shrivel, parch, dry up, FADE, DECAY, blight, WASTE.

withhold *v.* RESERVE, RETAIN, keep back, hold back, restrain, refrain.

within *prep.* inside of, INSIDE, IN, INCLUDING, DURING.
— *adv.*: see IN; INDOORS; WITHIN.

without *prep.* out of, outside of, BEYOND, lacking, LESS, MINUS.

withstand *v.* RESIST, OPPOSE, hold out, DEFY, weather, ENDURE.

witless: see SENSELESS.

witlessness: see FOOLISHNESS.

witness *n.* eyewitness, SPECTATOR, OBSERVER, watcher, bystander, TESTIMONY, EVIDENCE.
— *v.* OBSERVE, WATCH, NOTICE, SEE, perceive, BEHOLD, TESTIFY, CERTIFY, SIGN, countersign.

witticism: see CRACK; JOKE.

witty: see CLEVER.

wizard *n.* MAGICIAN, sorcerer, miracle-worker, enchanter, MASTER, shark.

wizardry: see MAGIC.

wobble: see BOB; ROCK; STAGGER; VIBRATE; WAG.

woe *n.* GRIEF, MISERY, SORROW, SADNESS, DISTRESS, affliction, SUFFERING, PAIN, MISFORTUNE.

woeful: see SAD.

wolf: see DEVOUR.

woman *n.* LADY, FEMALE, WIFE, MATE, GIRL, MAID.

womanlike: see FEMALE.

womanly *adj.* FEMININE, ladylike, matronly, TENDERLY, GENTLE.

womb: see INSIDE.

wonder *v.* **1** *(we wonder at her intelligence)* marvel at, ADMIRE, idolize, gape; **2** *(we wonder if he is honest)* DOUBT, QUESTION, disbelieve, THINK, ponder, meditate.
— *n.* MIRACLE, MARVEL, AMAZEMENT, ASTONISHMENT, awe.

wonderful *adj.* MARVELOUS, astounding, AMAZING, astonishing, EXTRAORDINARY, SURPRISING, REMARKABLE, spectacular, SUPERB, FABULOUS.

wonderment: see ASTONISHMENT.

wondrous: see MARVELOUS; MIRACULOUS.

wonted: see USUAL.

woo: see COURT.

wood *n.* FOREST, GROVE, woodland, woods, LUMBER, TIMBER, hardwood, firewood, PLANK, BEAM.

wooden: see STIFF.

woodland: see GROVE; TIMBER; WOOD.

woodlands: see COUNTRY.

woods: see BUSH; FOREST; WILDERNESS; WOOD.

woodwork: see TRIM.

wooer: see LOVER.

woolly: see FUZZY.

woozy: see DIZZY.

word *n.* vocable, TERM, synonym, antonym, neologism, password, watchword, PLEDGE, affirmation, DECISION, PROMISE, UTTERANCE, REMARK, ORDER, COMMAND, SPEECH, saying, EXPRESSION, INFORMATION, NEWS.

wordbook: see DICTIONARY; VOCABULARY.

word finder: see DICTIONARY.

word-for-word: see VERBAL.

wordless: see SPEECHLESS.

word list: see DICTIONARY; VOCABULARY.

words: see CHARM; LANGUAGE; SPEECH; VOCABULARY.

wordy: see CHATTY; LONG-WINDED.

work *n.* LABOR, TOIL, drudgery, EMPLOYMENT, JOB, OCCUPATION, TASK, UNDERTAKING, ACCOMPLISHMENT, ACHIEVEMENT, PRODUCT, EFFORT, EXERTION.
— *v.* LABOR, TOIL, MAKE, FORM, SHAPE, fashion, PERFORM, PRODUCE, OPERATE, RUN, FUNCTION, GO, PREPARE, manipulate, ferment.

workability: see POSSIBILITY.

workable: see PRACTICAL.

workaday: see ORDINARY.

workbench: see BENCH.

worked: see BEATEN.

worker *n.* workingman, WORKMAN, LABORER, toiler, craftsman, operative, doer, PERFORMER.

workers: see LABOR.

working: see OPERATION.

workingman: see LABORER; WORKER; WORKMAN.

workman *n.* WORKER, workingman, craftsman, artisan, ARTIST, operative, mechanic.

workmanship: see ARCHITECTURE; HANDIWORK.

workroom: see STUDIO; STUDY.

works: see FACTORY; MECHANISM.

workshop: see SHOP; STUDIO.

world *n.* UNIVERSE, EARTH, GLOBE, NATURE, PEOPLE, CIVILIZATION, MANKIND, HUMANITY, SPHERE, domain, STATE, SYSTEM.

worldly *adj.* EARTHLY, materialistic, profane, irreligious, SELFISH, AMBITIOUS, PROUD. See also INTERNATIONAL.

world-wide: see INTERNATIONAL.

worm *n.* WRETCH, BUM, sneak.
— *v.* CRAWL, CREEP, wriggle, writhe, insinuate.

worn *adj.* fatigued, TIRED, wearied, worn out, impaired, wasted, SHABBY.

worn out: see BEAT; BUSHED; USED; WORN.

worried: see CONCERNED.

worrisome: see FUSSY.

worry *v.* TROUBLE, disquiet, BOTHER, STEW, FRET, FUSS, harass, TORMENT, agonize.
— *n.*: see BURDEN; CARE; CONCERN; TENSION.

worse: see BACKWARD.

worsen: see FAIL.

worship *v.* ADORE, IDOLIZE, RESPECT, HONOR, glorify, PRAISE, KNEEL, BOW.
— *n.* adoration, reverence, PRAISE, homage, ADMIRATION, DEVOTION, services, PRAYER, rites.

worshiper: see PILGRIM.

worst: see OUTWIT.

worth *n.* VALUE, EXCELLENCE, usefulness, MERIT, IMPORTANCE, ADVANTAGE, BENEFIT, WEALTH, RICHES, CHARACTER, integrity.

worthless *adj.* USELESS, valueless, VAIN, CHEAP, good-for-nothing, TRASHY, WRETCHED, worthless.

worthwhile: see WORTHY.

worthy *adj.* worthwhile, deserving, EXCELLENT, VALUABLE, PROFITABLE, advantageous, RESPECTABLE, HONORABLE, meritorious.

wound *n.* INJURY, hurt, CUT, BRUISE.
— *v.* INJURE, HURT, HARM, CUT, BRUISE, pain, WRONG, OFFEND, INSULT.
— *adj.* coiled, turned, rolled up.

wounded *adj.* injured, hurt, cut, bruised, ILL, offended, annoyed, pained.

wrangle: see BARGAIN; DISAGREE.

wrap *v.* enfold, ENVELOP, WIND, FOLD, ROLL.
— *n.*: see CLOAK; FUR.

wrapper: see CONTAINER; COVERING; ENVELOPE; FOLDER.

wrapping: see ENVELOPE.

wrap up: see FINISH.

wrath: see ANGER; FURY; IRRITATION; RAGE.

wrathful: see ANGRY.

wreath *n.* garland, bouquet, RING, curl, spiral, ringlet, BAND, CIRCLE.

wreathe: see TWIST.

wreck *v.* DESTROY, DAMAGE, bust, RUIN, DEMOLISH, SMASH, dismantle.
— *n.* wreckage, JUNK, RUIN, DESTRUCTION.

wreckage: see WRECK.

wrecker: see VANDAL.

wrench *v.* TWIST, SPRAIN, TURN, distort, JERK, TUG, PULL, pang, WRING.
  — *n.* TWIST, TURN, sprain, tug, PULL, JERK, STRAIN, pang, distortion.

wrest: see SQUEEZE.

wrestle *v.* STRUGGLE, grapple, tussle, STRIVE.

wretch *n.* SNAKE, viper, sneak, WORM, skunk.

wretched *adj.* MISERABLE, LOW, MEAN, PITIFUL, SORRY, pathetic, forlorn, inadequate, POOR, UNHAPPY, dejected.

wretchedness: see MISERY.

wriggle: see SQUIRM; TWIST; WORM.

wring *v.* SQUEEZE, TWIST, TURN, EXTRACT, PRY, throttle, CHOKE, CLASP, WRENCH.

wrinkle *n.* **1** *(a wrinkle in the tablecloth)* crease, FOLD, crinkle, pucker, ruffle; **2** *(a new wrinkle)* IMPROVEMENT, NOVELTY, IDEA.
  — *v.* crease, FOLD, crinkle, crumple, ruffle.

write *v.* COMPOSE, DRAFT, author, CORRESPOND, RECORD, typewrite, doodle, scrawl, scribble, PEN, PENCIL.

write out: see SPELL.

writer *n.* scribe, penman, CORRESPONDENT, AUTHOR, poet, novelist, playwright, essayist, COLUMNIST, EDITOR.

writhe: see SQUIRM; SUFFER; THRASH; TWIST; WORM.

writing *n.* COMPOSITION, CRAFT, ESSAY, THEME, ARTICLE, BOOK, manuscript, typescript, CORRESPONDENCE, longhand, handwriting, inscription.

writings: see TEXT.

wrong *adj.* incorrect, MISTAKEN, FALSE, inaccurate, erroneous, untruthful, inappropriate, amiss, unfit, UNSUITABLE, improper, UNJUST, CRIMINAL, ILLEGAL, injurious, BAD, perverse, immoral, sinful, NAUGHTY, WICKED, EVIL.
  — *adv.* incorrectly, mistakenly, falsely, inaccurately, erroneously, untruthfully, inappropriately, unjustly, improperly.
  — *n.* EVIL, SIN, CRIME, vice, WICKEDNESS, immorality, illegality, injustice, unfairness, INJURY, grievance, offense, tort, misdeed, blame, GUILT, falsity, error, incorrectness.
  — *v.* INJURE, HARM, HURT, ABUSE, DAMAGE, maltreat, oppress.

wrongdoer: see DELINQUENT.

wrongdoing: see CRIME; MISCHIEF; SIN.

wrong-headed: see STUBBORN.

XYZ

yank: see JERK; PLUCK; TUG.

yap: see BARK.

yard *n.* GROUND, LAWN, courtyard, quadrangle, ENCLOSURE.

yardstick: see RULER; STANDARD.

yarn *n.* STORY, TALE, anecdote, ACCOUNT, LIE.

year: see CALENDAR; CLASS.

yearlong: see ANNUAL.

yearly: see ANNUAL.

yearn *v.* long for, CRAVE, DESIRE.

yearning: see AMBITION; HUNGER; WISH.

years: see AGE.

yegg: see BURGLAR; THIEF.

yell *v.* cheer, SHOUT, CRY, holler, SCREAM, SCREECH.
  — *n.* SHOUT, CHEER, CRY, SCREAM, SCREECH.

yellow: see GOLDEN.

yelp: see BARK; HOWL.

yen: see DESIRE.

yep: see YES.

yes *adv.* OK, aye, yep, agreed, true, SURELY, undoubtedly, of course, INDEED, CERTAINLY.
  — *n.* OK, aye, CONSENT, assent, acceptance, affirmation, endorsement, NOD.

yes-man: see FOLLOWER.

yesterday: see PAST.

yesteryear: see PAST.

yet *adv.* NOW, BESIDES, FURTHER, hitherto, NEVERTHELESS, FINALLY, EVENTUALLY, STILL.
  — *conj.* notwithstanding, HOWEVER, BUT, STILL.

yield *v.* **1** *(to yield to oncoming traffic)* give way, give in, SUBMIT, concede, waive, GRANT, ADMIT, SURRENDER; **2** *(to yield six percent interest)* bring in, PRODUCE, PROVIDE, give off.
  n. PRODUCTION, HARVEST, PRODUCT, CROP.

yielding: see FLABBY; FLEXIBLE; OBEDIENT; SOFT; SPARING.

yoke *n.* **1** *(a yoke of oxen)* PAIR, TEAM, MATCH, COUPLE, SPAN, LINK, BOND, TIE; **2** *(an oppressive yoke)* RULE, dominion, domination.

— *v.*: see HARNESS; TEAM.

yore: see PAST.

young *adj.* YOUTHFUL, EARLY, newborn, VIGOROUS, FRESH, JUNIOR, juvenile, adolescent, GREEN, IMMATURE, inexperienced, UNRIPE.
pl.n. youngsters, YOUTH, OFFSPRING.

younger: see JUNIOR.

youngness: see YOUTH.

youngster *n.* YOUTH, CHILD, shaver, LAD, lassie, BOY, GIRL, KID, adolescent, teen-ager, fledgling, BEGINNER.

youngsters: see YOUNG.

youth *n.* youngness, PRIME, bloom, springtime, immaturity, adolescence, LAD, MAID.

youthful *adj.* YOUNG, FRESH, VIGOROUS, buoyant, CHILDLIKE, IMMATURE, inexperienced.

yowl: see HOWL.

zeal: see AMBITION; ENTHUSIASM; FIRE; LIFE; WARMTH.

zealous: see AMBITIOUS; ENTHUSIASTIC; WILLING.

zenith: see CROWN; PRIME; TOP.

zephyr: see BREEZE; WIND.

zero *n.* cipher, nought, NOTHING, LOW, BOTTOM, nonentity.

zest: see CHEERFULNESS; RELISH; SALT; SPICE.

zigzag: see STAGGER; WEAVE.

zigzagged: see JAGGED.

zinc: see METAL.

zip: see CHEERFULNESS.

zone *n.* BELT, BAND, DISTRICT, GIRDLE, STRIP, AREA, REGION, SPHERE, DIVISION, PATH, CLIMATE.
— *v.* ENCIRCLE, RESTRICT, DIVIDE, SPECIFY.

zoo: see GARDEN.

zoom: see SWOOP.